SECOND EDITION

Access Cookbook™

Ken Getz, Paul Litwin,
and Andy Baron

O'REILLY®

Beijing · Cambridge · Farnham · Köln · Paris · Sebastopol · Taipei · Tokyo

Access Cookbook™, Second Edition

by Ken Getz, Paul Litwin, and Andy Baron

Published by O'Reilly Media, Inc., 1005 Gravenstein Highway North, Sebastopol, CA 95472.

O'Reilly & Associates books may be purchased for educational, business, or sales promotional use. Online editions are also available for most titles (*safari.oreilly.com*). For more information, contact our corporate/institutional sales department: (800) 998-9938 or *corporate@oreilly.com*.

Editor:	John Osborn
Developmental Editor:	David Clark
Production Editor:	Reg Aubry
Cover Designer:	Ellie Volckhausen
Interior Designer:	David Futato

Printing History:

February 2002:	First Edition.
March 2004:	Second Edition.

 This book uses RepKover™, a durable and flexible lay-flat binding.

ISBN: 0-596-00678-0

[M]

Table of Contents

Preface

What This Book Is About

This is an idea book. It's a compendium of solutions and suggestions devoted to making your work with Microsoft Access more productive. If you're using Access and you aspire to create database applications that are more than wizard-created clones of every other database application, this is the book for you.

If, on the other hand, you're looking for a book that shows you how to create a form, or how to write your first Visual Basic for Applications (VBA) function, or how to use the Crosstab Query Wizard, this may *not* be the book you need. For those kinds of things, we recommend one of the many Access books geared toward the first-time user.

Promotes Creative Use of the Product

Rather than rehashing the manuals, *Access Cookbook* offers you solutions to problems you may have already encountered, have yet to encounter, or perhaps have never even considered. Some of the issues discussed in this book are in direct response to questions posted in the Microsoft Access newsgroups online (at *news:// msnews.microsoft.com*); others are problems we've encountered while developing our own applications. In any case, our goal is to show you how to push the edges of the product, making it do things you might not even have thought possible.

For example, you'll learn how to create a query that joins tables based on some condition besides equality, how to size a form's controls to match the form's size, how to store and retrieve the locations and sizes of forms from session to session, and how to create a page-range indicator on every report page. You'll see how to use some of the common Windows dialogs from your Access application, how to internationalize your messages, how to *really* control your printer, and how to store the username and date last edited for each row. There are tips for securing your database, filling list boxes a number of different ways, and optimizing your applications.

You'll find details on using Access in multiuser environments, creating transaction logs, adjusting database options depending on who's logged in, and programmatically keeping track of users and groups. There are instructions for using the Windows API to restrict mouse movement to a specific area of a form, exiting Windows under program control, and checking the status of and shutting down another Windows application. You'll see how, using COM and Automation, you can use Access together with other applications such as Word, Excel, PowerPoint, and Outlook.

If you've never tried data access pages (DAPs), you're in for a treat—this feature makes it simple for you to display and edit data using a web browser. You'll learn enough to really get you started with this exciting technology, and you'll learn solutions to common but tricky problems. You'll find tips and techniques for using Access and SQL Server together, taking advantage of Access Data Projects (ADPs). You'll learn how smart tags have been implemented in Access 2003, and how to create your own smart tags. And you'll also see how you how Access allows you to work with XML data. You'll explore how to work with SharePoint lists from within Access as well as how to use SharePoint and FrontPage to publish Access data on the Internet or an intranet. Finally, you'll discover how easy it is to interoperate with Microsoft .NET from Access, learning both how to call .NET programs and Web services from Access and how to work with Access data and reports from .NET programs.

You won't, however, find that this book pushes you into using new technology just because it's new. Many of the techniques in this book are "old chestnuts" that Access developers have used for years to solve common problems. Most of the VBA code that performs data manipulation chiefly uses the older technology, DAO, rather than the newer ADO, because DAO is still the most efficient way to work with Access data. When ADO provides a better approach to solving a particular problem, you'll learn how to use it for that purpose. For example, you'll learn how you can use an ADO recordset to retrieve a list of all the users logged on to your application— something that was never possible with DAO.

Uses the Tools at Hand

This book focuses on using the right tool for each problem. Some solutions here require no programming, while others require a little (or a lot) of VBA coding. Sometimes even plain VBA code isn't sufficient, and you'll need to use the Windows API or other available code libraries. In each case, we've tried to make the implementation of the technique as simple, yet generic, as possible.

We did, however, decide to focus the data access features of this book squarely on using the Jet database engine (instead of SQL Server). There are several reasons why we made this choice, but first and foremost is that most Access developers still prefer the convenience and simplicity of using Jet. The Jet database engine remains a cost-effective and capable solution for database applications used by small workgroups, which make up the vast majority of the Access user base. Most of the techniques described in this book, however, will work just as effectively with data from SQL Server or from other ODBC data sources, even if the example uses a Jet database. And if you are working with non-Access data sources, you'll find plenty of tips focused on helping you do so more efficiently.

Follows a Problem-Solution Format

The structure of this book is simple. The chapters are arranged by categories: queries, forms, reports, application design, printing, data manipulation, VBA, optimization, user interface, multiuser, Windows API, Automation, DAPs, and SQL Server applications. Each section consists of a single problem and its solution, followed by a discussion. Each solution contains a sample database (e.g., *01-01.MDB*) with complete construction details, indicating which modules you'll need to import, what controls you'll need to create, and what events you'll need to handle. In one case, Recipe 4-10, any MDB file used elsewhere in the chapter will do. To use certain Chapter 14 examples, you will need to be connected to either the Northwind or Pubs databases that ship with SQL Server. All the code, bitmaps, sample data, and necessary tools are included with the CD-ROM that accompanies this book. (CD content is available online at *http://examples.oreilly.com/accesscook*.)

Who This Book Is For

You don't have to be a VBA whiz to use this book. It's designed for all levels of readers: end users, power users, and developers.

In every case, we've made the steps needed to implement our solution as simple as possible. When VBA is involved, we've recommended which modules to import from the sample database and discussed the important features of the code within the text. You shouldn't have to retype any of the code unless you care to—in fact, you shouldn't retype the code, since we rarely include every single line of code here in the book. We've pointed out the important code here but left much of the support code on the CD-ROM (see *http://examples.oreilly.com/accesscook*). What's more, you don't actually have to understand the solutions to most of the problems covered in this book in order to make use of them. In each case, you'll find a sample database that demonstrates the technique and explicit instructions on how to implement the same technique in your own applications. Of course, you'll learn the most by digging into the samples to see how they work, and each solution includes comments to help you understand the underlying technology.

What You Need to Use This Book

To use this book, you'll need a computer capable of running Windows 98 (or later), Windows Me, Windows NT 4.0 SP5 (or later), Windows 2000, or Windows XP, and Microsoft Access 2003 or Microsoft Access 2002 (part of Office XP). You'll find, however, that most of the solutions work just as effectively with prior versions of Access, in case you are supporting mixed-user environments. (We've provided all the solutions for the first 14 chapters in Access 2000 format, so that you can open them in Access 2000, Access 2002, or Access 2003. Some of the code will only run in Access 2002 or later).

The final four chapters include features new to Access 2003, and the samples there are guaranteed not to run in Access 2000, although some may work in Access 2002. To demonstrate the topics in Chapter 12, Automation, you'll need to have copies of Microsoft Excel, Word, PowerPoint, and Outlook. These applications aren't strictly necessary, but having them installed on your system will allow you to try out the example databases. Chapter 14 uses tools that are part of SQL Server, which you may also want to have accessible, along with the Northwind and Pubs sample databases that ship with SQL Server. Some of the solutions in Chapter 15 require you to own a copy of FrontPage and have access to a SharePoint Web server. You'll need a copy of Visual Basic 6.0 to complete the custom smart tag DLL sample shown in Chapter 16. The solutions in Chapter 17 require the Microsoft .NET Framework 1.1 and Visual Studio .NET 2003. .NET Framework 1.1 is available as a free download through the Microsoft Developer Network (MSDN) (See http://msdn.microsoft.com/netframework/technologyinfo/howtoget/). A 60-day Trial Edition of Visual Studio .NET 2003 that includes a copy of SQL Server Developer Edition (MSDE) is also available (See http://msdn.microsoft.com/vstudio/productinfo/trial/default.aspx).

How This Book Is Organized

This book is organized into 18 chapters, each of which focuses on a particular Access programming topic.

Chapter 1, *Queries*

> This chapter covers the many types of queries and the power you have over the Access environment through the use of queries. From simple select queries through parameter, crosstab, totals, and Data Definition Language (DDL) queries, this chapter will show many different ways to use queries in your applications. Queries are the real heart of Access, and learning to use them intelligently will make your work in Access go much more smoothly.

Chapter 2, *Forms*

> Most database applications require some sort of user interface, and in Access, that user interface is almost always centered around forms. This chapter demonstrates some useful ways to make forms do your bidding, whether in terms of

controlling data or making forms do things you didn't think were possible. We demonstrate how to create multipaged forms and how to create an incremental search list box. We also show how to create your own pop-up forms, with a technique you can use in many situations. Forms can do much more than you might have imagined, and this chapter is a good place to look for some new ideas.

Chapter 3, *Reports*

It seems as though reports ought to be simple: just place some data on the design surface and "let her rip!" That's true for simple reports, but Access's report writer is incredibly flexible and allows a great deal of customization. In addition, the report writer is quite subtle in its use of properties and events. The topics in this chapter will advance your understanding of Access's report writer, from creating snaking column reports to printing alternating gray bars. Some of the solutions in the chapter will require programming, but many don't. If you need to create attractive reports (and everyone working with Access does, sooner or later), the topics in this chapter will make your work a lot easier.

Chapter 4, *Applications*

This chapter is a compendium of tips and suggestions for making your application development go more smoothly, more professionally, and more internationally. Rather than focusing on specific topics, this chapter brings up a number of issues that many developers run across as they ready their applications for distribution. How do you build a list of objects? How do you make sure all your objects' settings are similar? How do you translate text in your application? How do you use the common Windows dialogs? All these questions, and more, make up this group of tips for the application developer.

Chapter 5, *Printers*

Many developers need to gain tight control over printed output, but earlier versions of Access made this quite difficult. Starting with Access 2002, you'll find direct support for selecting a specific printer device, changing print layout settings, and more. This chapter introduces the Printer object and its properties, allowing you to perform tricks that were difficult, if not impossible, in earlier versions. (Although many of the chapter databases will work in Access 2000, this chapter's examples will not. Because the functionality presented here was new in Access 2002, the samples simply won't do anything useful in Access 2000.)

Chapter 6, *Data*

This chapter concentrates on working with data in ways that traditional database operations don't support. You'll learn how to filter your data, back it up, locate it on the filesystem, calculate a median, perform sound-alike searches, save housekeeping information, and more. Most examples in this chapter use some form of VBA, but they are clearly explained, and "testbed" applications are supplied to show you how each technique works.

Chapter 7, *VBA*

The solutions in this chapter cover some of the details of VBA that you might not find in the Access online help. We've included topics on several issues that plague many Access developers, from handling embedded quotes in strings and creating procedure stacks and code profilers, to programmatically filling list boxes, to working with objects and properties. We've included code to sort an array and solutions that combine several of the previous topics, such as filling a list box with a sorted list of filenames. If you're an intermediate VBA programmer, this chapter is a good place to expand your skills. If you're already an expert, this chapter can add some new tools to your toolbox.

Chapter 8, *Optimization*

Access is a big application, and when designing applications you have a number of choices to make, each of which can affect the application's performance. Unless you're creating only the most trivial of applications, you'll have to spend some time optimizing your applications. This chapter's topics work through several different areas of optimization—steps you can take to make your databases work as smoothly as possible. The topics range from optimizing queries, forms, and VBA, to testing the speed of various optimization techniques, to accelerating client/server applications. If you want your applications to run as quickly as possible, this chapter is a good place to look for tips.

Chapter 9, *User Interface*

This chapter presents a compendium of user interface tips and techniques. By implementing the ideas and techniques in this chapter, you'll be able to create a user interface that stands out and works well. You'll find some simple, but not obvious, techniques for controlling the Access environment, such as altering your global keyboard mappings as you move from one component of your application to another and creating forms that hide the menus and toolbars when they're active. The chapter shows how to create combo boxes that accept new entries and how to provide animated images on buttons. You'll also find useful tips on working with data on your forms, using an ActiveX control to improve your interface.

Chapter 10, *Multiuser Applications*

Few modern database applications run on standalone machines; most must be able to coordinate with multiple users. This chapter offers solutions to some of the common problems of networking and coordinating multiple simultaneous users. The most important issues are security and locking, and this chapter has examples that cover each. In addition, the topics in this chapter focus on replication, transaction logging, password control, and keeping users from holding locks on data. If you're working in a shared environment, you won't want to miss this chapter!

Chapter 11, *Windows APIs*

No matter how much you've avoided using the Windows API in Access applications, in this chapter you'll discover that it's really not a major hurdle. We'll present some interesting uses of the Windows API, with example forms and modules for each solution. In most cases, using these examples in your own applications takes little more work than importing a module or two and calling some functions. You'll learn how to restrict the mouse movement to a specific area on the screen, how to run another program from your VBA code, and how to wait until that program is done before continuing. We'll demonstrate a method for exiting Windows under program control and how to retrieve information about your Access installation and the current Windows environment. The possibilities are endless once you start diving into the Windows API, and this chapter is an excellent place to start.

Chapter 12, *Automation*

This chapter gives you examples of using Automation to interact with most of the Microsoft Office applications. One solution uses the statistical, analytical, and financial prowess of the Excel function libraries, directly from Access; another shows how to programmatically create an Excel chart. You'll learn how to retrieve document summary information for any selected Word document and how to perform mail merges using Access data. Other examples demonstrate how to use Access to control PowerPoint and how to add contacts in Outlook.

Chapter 13, *Data Access Pages*

Distributing Access applications normally means that your users have to install Access (or the Access runtime version, available as part of Microsoft Office XP Developer) on their local machines. What if users could run your applications over a corporate intranet, without requiring Access to be installed? That's the goal of DAPs. This chapter introduces some of the concepts you'll need to understand in order to take advantage of this feature, which was added in Access 2000 and significantly improved in Access 2002. You'll learn how to customize the navigation controls and how to use your own controls for navigation. You'll find tips on creating pages that allow users to update data and valuable techniques for managing your data connections, and you'll learn how to adjust the default settings for the different sections of new DAPs to give your applications a consistent look.

Chapter 14, *SQL Server*

This chapter shows you how to take advantage of the new data options available in Access Data Projects, which connect directly to a SQL Server database, and provides solutions that address traditional MDB databases linked to SQL Server data. You'll learn how to dynamically connect to SQL Server at runtime, whether you are using an ADP or an MDB, and you'll learn how to allow multiple users to share a single ADP. You'll see how to make the most of the Server Filter By Form feature in ADPs and how to pass parameters to stored procedures in both ADPs and MDBs. You'll also discover how you can use an ADP to connect to multiple SQL Server databases at once, even though the ADP seems to force you to select a single one.

Chapter 15, *Office Web and SharePoint*

As powerful as Data Access Pages are, they only represent one way to gain access to your Access data from a browser. This chapter introduces you to other Microsoft Office web technologies you can use to "webify" your Access databases. You'll learn how to use Microsoft FrontPage to create a web form that posts its data to an Access database. You'll also learn how to use the FrontPage Database Interface Wizard to create an ASP or ASP.NET front end to an Access database. You'll learn how to use Windows SharePoint Services along with FrontPage to create web pages that draw data from Access databases without writing any code. You will also learn how to use Access as a frontend for managing SharePoint lists.

Chapter 16, *Smart Tags*

Smart Tags were introduced in Office XP, but they weren't available in Access until now. This chapter shows you how to use the built-in smart tags in your applications, attaching them to form controls or to fields in a table. You'll learn to configure smart tags interactively or by writing code. You'll also learn how to extend smart tag functionality by creating your own custom smart tags.

Chapter 17, *.NET*

Microsoft .NET and Access live in two different programming worlds, but you can use a set of interoperability tools to bridge the two worlds. This chapter shows you how to take advantage of these tools to call a .NET component from an Access application. You'll also learn how to call a .NET web service from Access, and how to manipulate the .NET objects returned by some web services. You'll learn how to retrieve data from an Access database using ADO. NET. And you'll learn how to automate an Access report from a .NET application.

Chapter 18, *XML*

One of the strengths of Access is its ability to work with data from many disparate sources. XML has emerged as a dominant standard for exchanging data between applications, and Access now enables you to work with this data. In this chapter you'll learn how to import and export XML data and schema, and how you can use XSLT to reformat XML data. For example, you'll see how to use XML technologies to export a report to an HTML or ASP Web page, preserving the look and feel of the original Access report.

What We Left Out

To keep this book to a reasonable length, we have made some assumptions about your skills. First and foremost, we take it for granted that you are interested in using Microsoft Access and are willing to research the basics in other resources. This isn't a reference manual or a "getting started" book, so we assume you have access to that information elsewhere. We expect that you've dabbled in creating Access objects (tables, queries, forms, reports, and pages) and that you've at least considered working with VBA (Visual Basic for Applications, the programming language included with Access). We encourage you to look in other resources for answers to routine questions, such as "What does this Option Explicit statement do?" For example, see *Access Database Design & Programming*, Third Edition, by Steven Roman (O'Reilly) or *VB & VBA in a Nutshell* by Paul Lomax (O'Reilly)

To get you started, though, following are basic instructions for what you'll need in order to use the solutions in this book. For example, you'll encounter requests to "create a new event procedure." Rather than including specific steps for doing this in each case, we have gathered the most common techniques you'll need into this section. For each technique we've included a help topic name from the Access online help, so you can get more information. The procedures here are not the *only* way to get the desired results, but rather are single methods for achieving the required goals.

How Do I Set Control Properties?

In the steps for many of the solutions in this book, you'll be asked to assign properties to objects on forms or reports. This is a basic concept in creating any Access application, and you should thoroughly understand it. To assign properties to a control (or group of controls), follow these steps:

1. In design mode, select the control or group of controls. You can use any of the following methods (each of the items here refers to form controls but works just as well with reports):

   Single control

   Click on a single control. Access will mark it with up to eight sizing handles—one in each corner, and one in the middle of each side of the control, if possible.

   Multiple controls

   Click on a single control, then Shift+Click on each of the other controls you want to select. Access will mark each of them with sizing handles.

   Multiple controls

   Drag the mouse through the ruler (either horizontal or vertical). Access will select each of the controls in the path you dragged over. If partially selected controls don't become part of the selection and you'd like them to, open Tools → Options → Forms/Reports and look at the Selection Behavior option. It should be set to Partially Enclosed.

Multiple controls

If you need to select all but a few controls, select them all and then remove the ones you don't want. To do this, choose the Edit → Select All menu item. Then Shift+Click on the controls you don't want included.

2. Make sure the properties window is visible. If it's not, use View → Properties (or the corresponding toolbar button).

3. If you've selected a single control, all the properties will be available in the properties window. If you've selected multiple controls, only the intersection of the selected controls' properties will be available in the properties window. That is, only the properties all the selected controls have in common will appear in the list. As shown in Figure P-1. Select a property group and then assign the value you need to the selected property. Repeat this process for any other properties you'd like to set for the same control or group of controls.

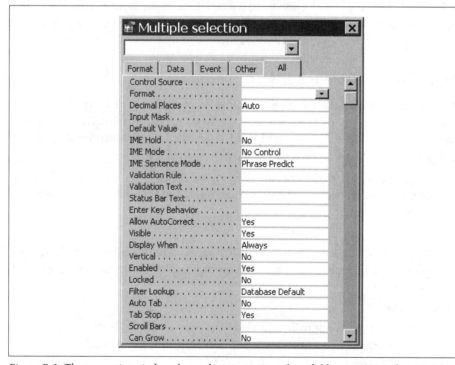

Figure P-1. The properties window shows the intersection of available properties when you've selected multiple controls

For more information, browse the various topics under *properties; setting* in Access online help.

How Do I Create a New Module?

VBA code is stored in containers called *modules*, each consisting of a single declarations section, perhaps followed by one or more procedures. There are two kinds of modules in Access: *global modules* and *class modules*. Global modules are the ones you see in the database window, once you choose the Modules tab. Class modules are stored with either a form or a report and never appear in the database window. (Actually, you can also create standalone class modules, which do appear in the database window. The use of these types of modules, which allow you to define the behavior for your own objects, is beyond the scope of this book.) There are various reasons to use one or the other of the two module types, but the most important consideration is the availability of procedures and variables. Procedures that exist in global modules can, for the most part, be called from any place in Access. Procedures that exist in a class module generally can be called only from that particular form or report and never from anywhere else in Access.

You'll never have to create a form or report module, because Access creates those kinds of modules for you when you create the objects to which they're attached. To create a global module, follow these steps:

1. From the Database Explorer, click on the Modules tab to select the collection of modules, then click on the New button (or just choose the Insert ‡ Module menu item).

2. When Access first creates the module, it places you in the declarations section. A discussion of all the possible items in the declarations section is beyond the scope of this Preface, but you should always take one particular step at this point: if you don't see Option Explicit at the top of the module, insert it yourself. Then use the Tools → Options menu from within the VBA editor to turn on the Require Variable Declaration option (see Figure P-2). With this option turned on, all new modules you create will automatically include the Option Explicit statement. If you don't insert this statement and Access encounters a reference to an unknown variable, Access will create the variable for you. With the Option Explicit statement, Access forces you to declare each variable before you use it.

   Although this may seem like an unnecessary burden for a beginner, it's not. It's an incredible time saver for all levels of users. With the Option Explicit statement in place, you can let Access check your code for misspellings. Without it, if you misspell a variable name, Access will just create a new one with the new name and go about its business.

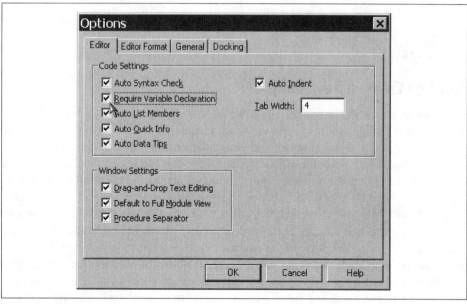

Figure P-2. Use the Tools → Options dialog from within VBA to turn on the Require Variable Declaration option

3. If you are asked to create a new function or subroutine, the simplest way to do so is to use Insert → Procedure. For example, if the solution instructs you to enter this new procedure:

```
Function SomeFunction(intX as Integer, varY as Variant)
```

you can use Insert → Procedure to help you create the function.

4. Click OK in the Add Procedure dialog, as shown in Figure P-3. Access will create the new procedure and place the cursor in it. For the example in Step 3, you must also supply some function parameters, so you'll need to move back up to the first line and enter intX as Integer, varY as Variant between the two parentheses.

How Do I Import an Object?

In this book's solutions, you'll often be asked to import an object from one of the sample databases. Follow these steps:

1. With your database open on the Access desktop, select the database window by pressing F11. (If you're in the VBA editor, first press Alt+F11 to get back to Access.)

2. Choose File → Get External Data → Import, or right-click on the database window and choose Import.

3. Find the database from which you want to import a module, and click Import.

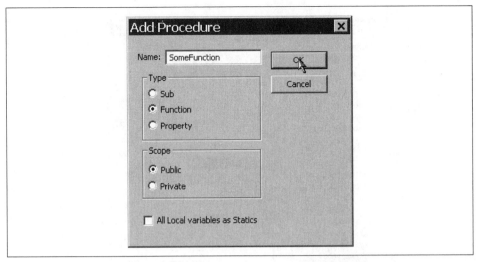

Figure P-3. The Add Procedure dialog helps you create a new function or subroutine

4. In the Import Objects dialog, select all of the objects you'd like to import, moving from object type to object type. When you've selected all the objects you want to import, click OK.

If a solution instructs you to import a module from one of the sample databases that you've already imported (for a different solution), you can ignore the instruction. Any modules with matching names in the sample database contain the exact same code, so you needn't import it again.

How Do I Create an Event Macro?

Programming in Access often depends on having macros or VBA procedures reacting to events that occur as you interact with forms. You'll find that most of the solutions in this book use VBA code rather than macros, because code provides better control and safety. But occasionally a macro is the right tool for the job. To create a macro that will react to a user event, follow these steps:

1. Select the appropriate object (report, form, or control) and make sure the properties window is displayed.

2. Choose the Event properties page on the properties window, or just scroll down the list until you find the event property you need.

3. Click on the ellipsis (...) button to the right of the event name, as shown in Figure P-4. This is the Build button; it appears next to properties window items that have associated builders. In this case, clicking the Build button displays the Choose Builder dialog, shown in Figure P-5. Choose the Macro Builder item to create a new macro. (If you don't often use macros, in the Tools → Options dialog, on the Forms/Reports page, you can choose to "Always use event procedures". The Build button will immediately take you to the Visual Basic Editor.)

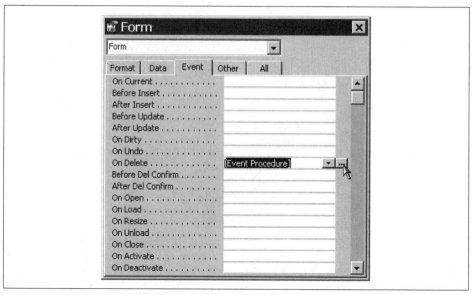

Figure P-4. Press the Build button to invoke the Choose Builder dialog

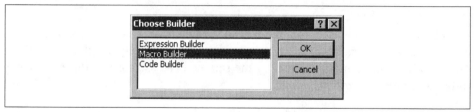

Figure P-5. The Choose Builder dialog: choose Macro Builder for macros and Code Builder for VBA

4. Give the macro a name, so Access can save it and place its name in the proper-ties window. You can always delete it later if you change your mind. Give your new macro the name suggested in the solution, and fill in the rows as directed. When you're done, save the macro and put it away.

5. Once you're done, you'll see the name of the macro in the properties window, as shown in Figure P-6. Whenever the event occurs (the Change event, in this case), Access will run the associated macro (mcrHandleChange).

6. If you want to call an existing macro from a given event property, click on the drop-down arrow next to the event name, rather than the Build button. Choose from the displayed list of available macros (including macros that exist as part of a macro group).

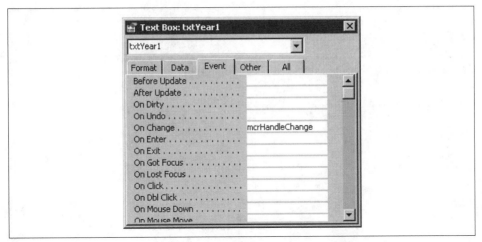

Figure P-6. The properties window with the selected macro assigned to the OnChange event property

 For more information on attaching macros to events, see *macros; creating* in Access online help.

How Do I Create an Event Procedure?

Programming in Access often depends on having VBA procedures react to events that occur as you interact with forms or reports. To create a VBA procedure that will react to a user event, follow these steps:

1. Select the appropriate object (report, form, or control) and make sure the properties window is displayed.

2. Choose the Event Properties page on the properties window, or just scroll down the list until you find the event property you need.

3. Select the property, then click the down arrow button next to the property. Select [Event Procedure] from the list of options.

4. Click the "..." button to the right of the event name, as shown in Figure P-7. This is the Build button, and it appears next to properties window items that have associated builders. In this case, clicking the Build button takes you to a stub for the event procedure you need to create.

```
Sub cmdClose_Click( )

End Sub
```

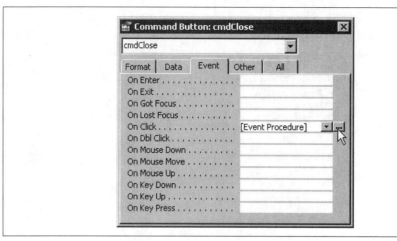

Figure P-7. Press the Build button to invoke the Choose Builder dialog

Property Names Versus Event Names

The naming of event properties, as opposed to the events themselves, is rather ambiguous in Access. The event properties, in general, have an "On" prefix, as in "OnClick" or "OnActivate." The events themselves, however, are named without the "On" prefix, as in "the Click event" or "the Activate event." We've tried to be consistent throughout the book, but there are some places where the context just doesn't indicate which is the correct usage. You'll need to be aware that with or without the "On" prefix, when the event occurs, it activates the procedure whose name is listed in the properties window for that event.

When you create a new event procedure, Access creates the subroutine name, fills in the parameters that it passes, and places the subroutine into the form or report's class module. The name of the procedure is always the name of the object, followed by an underscore and the name of the event. For example, had you created the Click event procedure for the cmdClose command button, you'd see a code skeleton like this:

Now follow these steps to complete the process:

1. If the solution asks you to enter code into the event procedure, enter it between the lines of code that Access has created for you. Usually, the code example in the solution will include the Sub and End Sub statements, so don't enter them again.

2. When you're done, close the module window and save the form. By saving the form or report, you also save the form's module.

How Do I Place Code in a Form or Report's Module?

When a solution asks you to place a procedure in a form or report's module that isn't directly called from an event, follow these simple steps:

1. With the form or report open in design mode, choose View → Code, press F7, or click on the Code button on the toolbar, as shown in Figure P-8.

Figure P-8. Click on the Code toolbar button to view a form or report's module

2. To create a new procedure, follow the steps in Section P.5.2, starting at Step 3.
3. Choose File → Save, close the module, then save the form, or just click on the Save icon on the toolbar.

How Do I Know What to Do with Code Examples?

In most cases, the solutions suggest that you import a module (or multiple modules) from the sample database for the particular solution, rather than typing in code yourself. In fact, code that isn't referenced as part of the discussion doesn't show up at all in the body of the solution. Therefore, you should count on importing modules as directed. Then follow the instructions in each solution to finish working with and studying the code.

If the solution tells you to place some code in a form's module, follow the steps in Section P.5.6. If you are instructed to place code in a global module, follow the steps in Section P.5.2. In most cases, you'll just import an existing module and won't type anything at all.

How Do I Use Data Access Objects (DAO) in New Databases?

By default, new databases that you create in Access 2000 and later assume that you'll want to use ActiveX Data Objects (ADO) rather than the older set of objects for accessing data, DAO. Many of the examples in this book take advantage of DAO, because it's simpler, more consistent with earlier programming techniques, and is in general just as efficient (or more efficient) than using ADO for programming against Access data (that is, data stored in an MDB or MDE file). Both ADO and DAO are simply ActiveX/COM components provided for you by Windows and Microsoft Office, and before you can use either, you must set a reference to the appropriate type library.

If you use the projects that come with this book, you'll find that the code already includes a reference to the necessary type library so that each example works. If you create your own projects that use the techniques you find here, you may need to set a reference to the DAO type library yourself. Follow these steps to set the reference:

1. Within the VBA code editor, select the Tools → References menu to display the References dialog box, shown in Figure P-9.

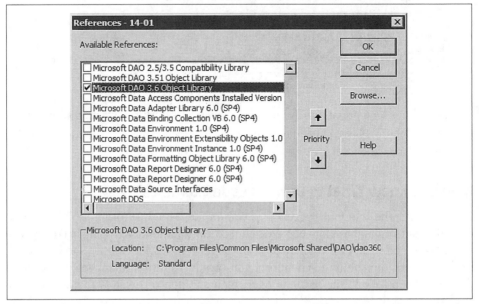

Figure P-9. Set a reference to the Microsoft DAO type library, which allows you to use DAO within applications in Access 2000 and later

2. Scroll down within the dialog box until you find the reference to Microsoft DAO, and select it.

3. Click OK to dismiss the dialog box.

You'll use this same technique to set a reference to any external component (including Word, Excel, PowerPoint, and Outlook, in Chapter 14), but you'll need to set a reference to DAO as shown here for many of the samples in other chapters.

 You don't need to explicitly set a reference to DAO within Access 97 or earlier versions. The change, in which the use of DAO became optional, happened in Access 2000.

Conventions Used in This Book

Throughout this book, we've used the following typographic conventions:

Constant width

    Constant width in body text indicates a language construct, such as the name of a stored procedure, a SQL statement, a VBA statement, an enumeration, an intrinsic or user-defined constant, a structure (i.e., a user-defined type), or an expression (e.g., `dblElapTime = Timer - dblStartTime`). Code fragments and code examples appear exclusively in constant-width text. In syntax statements and prototypes, text set in constant width indicates such language elements as the function or procedure name and any invariable elements required by the syntax.

Constant width italic

    Constant width italic is used in body text for variables and parameter names. In syntax statements or prototypes, constant width italic indicates replaceable parameters.

Italic

    Italicized words in the text indicate intrinsic or user-defined function and procedure names. URLs and email addresses are also italicized, as are many system elements, such as paths and filenames. Finally, italics are used the first time a new term appears.

 This icon indicates a tip, suggestion, or general note.

 This icon indicates a warning or caution.

Comments and Questions

Please address comments and questions concerning this book to the publisher:

O'Reilly & Associates, Inc.
1005 Gravenstein Highway North
Sebastopol, CA 95472
(800) 998-9938 (in the United States or Canada)
(707) 829-0515 (international/local)
(707) 829-0104 (fax)

There is a web page for this book, which lists errata, examples, or any additional information. You can access this page at:

http://www.oreilly.com/catalog/accesscook/

To comment or ask technical questions about this book, send email to:

bookquestions@oreilly.com

For more information about books, conferences, Resource Centers, and the O'Reilly Network, see the O'Reilly web site at:

http://www.oreilly.com

Acknowledgments

No book is written without some help from outside sources, and this one is no exception. In this case, we had special help: Mary Chipman did the bulk of the conversion work for the previous edition, making sure each topic worked in Access 2002, creating current screen captures, and rewriting code when necessary. We continued to rely on Mary's work for this edition. Needless to say, without Mary's help, this book would never have been completed.

In addition, we'd like to thank Helen Feddema, Mike Gunderloy, and Dan Haught for their contributions to the first edition of this book, some of which remain (though altered for Access 2002). This book also went through a second edition, for Access 95, but was never revised for Access 97 or Access 2000. We appreciate the support of John Osborn and the editorial team at O'Reilly and Associates (including our editor, David Clark) for having the faith in the book, and in Access, to allow us to revise and publish this edition. We would also like to thank those fervent readers who sent many, many emails asking about Access 97 and Access 2000 versions of the book, which were never published. You know who you are, and we hope this revision satisfies your requests!

Special thanks also go to those who contributed suggestions and read chapters in their early stages, including Joe Maki, Sue Hoegemeier, and Jim Newman.

We also wish to acknowledge all the hard-working people at Microsoft who've given us these great products. In particular, Bill Ramos, Tim Getsch, Christina Storm, and Rita Nikas were very helpful to us as we prepared this latest edition.

Jan Fransen did a terrific job creating the chapter covering data access pages—we're very grateful to Jan for this important contribution.

We'd like to thank Michael Kaplan, a technical editor on the Access 95 edition of this book, who reviewed every word and every byte on the CD for that edition with loving care. The success of this book will be, in part, due to Michael's diligence.

Finally, the authors would like to acknowledge the constant support of their families and loved ones, especially Peter, Suzanne, and Mary.

CHAPTER 1

Queries

Access queries—the six types that can be created on the easy-to-use query by example (QBE) grid, plus the three SQL-specific queries—give you a tremendous amount of power and flexibility in selecting, sorting, summarizing, modifying, and formatting the data stored in your tables before presenting it to the user on forms or printing it on reports. Access queries can be intimidating at first, but mastering queries will give you complete control over the appearance and functionality of your forms and reports. And Access queries are flexible—once you learn how to control them, you can use them in places where you might have written less efficient program code.

In this chapter you'll learn to create parameter queries, which allow you to control selected rows of a report at runtime rather than at design time. You'll use this same technique to control the available values in one combo box based on the choice in another. You'll study the ways to control the output of crosstab queries and will learn a handy technique for mailing labels that lets you group labels by residence to avoid sending duplicate mailings to family members. You'll learn to take advantage of update queries to alter the values in one table based on the values from another, and you'll learn a trick that can be used to filter a query based on the value of a Visual Basic for Applications (VBA) variable. In case you need to pull random sets of data from a data source, you'll see how to use a query to create a random set of rows. And you'll examine a query that uses a *Partition* function to perform an aging analysis.

You'll also find solutions dealing with more advanced uses of queries. You'll learn how to create a join that's based on a non-equality comparison, how to use union queries to horizontally splice together the data from two tables, and how to take advantage of union queries to add an extra choice to a combo box. You'll find out how to create self-join queries to model powerful recursive relationships, how to perform case-sensitive searches using a query, and how to use data definition language (DDL) queries to create or alter the structure of a table. You'll also examine a suggested method for storing query information in a table, which can be protected and made invisible in applications, giving you complete control over which queries are run and when. Finally, you'll learn a technique for creating recordsets in VBA code based on parameter queries.

Many of the examples in this chapter are based on a fictional music collection database that you could use to keep track of your favorite musicians and your album collection.

1.1 Specify Query Criteria at Runtime

Problem

When you design a query, you don't always know which subset of records you would like to see when you run the query. Instead of creating several queries with the same basic design but slightly different criteria, you'd like to be able to create one query that can be used to return the same fields, but a different set of records, each time it's run.

Solution

Use a parameter query with one or more replaceable parameters that it will request at runtime (when you run the query). This solution demonstrates how you can create and run parameter queries using the default parameter prompt.

Here are the steps to create a parameter query using default prompts:

1. Create any type of query in query design view.
2. Choose a field for which you wish to define a parameter. Create a parameter for that field by entering the prompt you would like to see when the query is executed surrounded by square brackets ([]) in the Criteria row for that field. For the example query qryAlbumsPrm1, you would create a parameter for the MusicType field by typing:

   [Type of Music?]

   in the Criteria row under MusicType.
3. Select Parameters from the Query menu to open the Query Parameters dialog, where you declare the parameter. For this example, enter:

   Type of Music?

   in the Parameter column of the Query Parameters dialog, and choose:

   Text

   from the data type combo box to tell Access that this is a text parameter. This step is optional in this query, but some queries require it (see Section 1.1.3), so make it a habit. Steps 2 and 3 are shown in Figure 1-1.
4. Save the query and run it. Access will prompt you to enter the type of music with a parameter dialog (see Figure 1-2).

qryAlbumsPrm1 : Select Query
tblArtists
*
ArtistID
ArtistName
MusicType
tblAlbums
ArtistID
MusicType
Title
LabelID
Year
tblLabels
*
LabelId
Field: MusicType | ArtistName | Year | Title
Table: tblAlbums | tblArtists | tblAlbums | tblAlb
Sort: | Ascending | Ascending
Show:
Criteria: [Type of music?]
or:
Query Parameters
Parameter | Data Type
Type of music? | Text
OK
Cancel

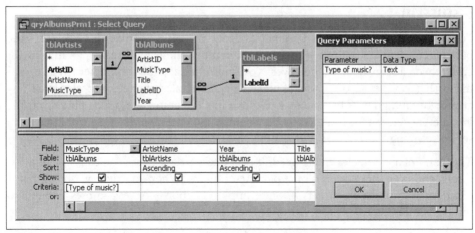

Figure 1-1. The qryAlbumsPrm1 parameter in design view

Enter Parameter Value
Type of music?
Alternative Rock
OK
Cancel

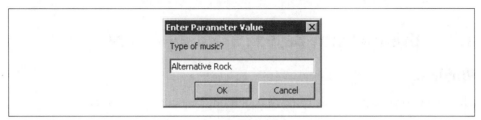

Figure 1-2. The Enter Parameter Value dialog for qryAlbumsPrm1

To see how this works using the sample database, open *01-01.MDB* and run the qryAlbumsPrm1 query. You will be prompted for the type of music. Enter a music type, such as rock, alternative rock, or jazz. The query will then execute, returning only the records of the specified music type. For example, if you enter "Alternative Rock" at the prompt, you'll see the datasheet shown in Figure 1-3.

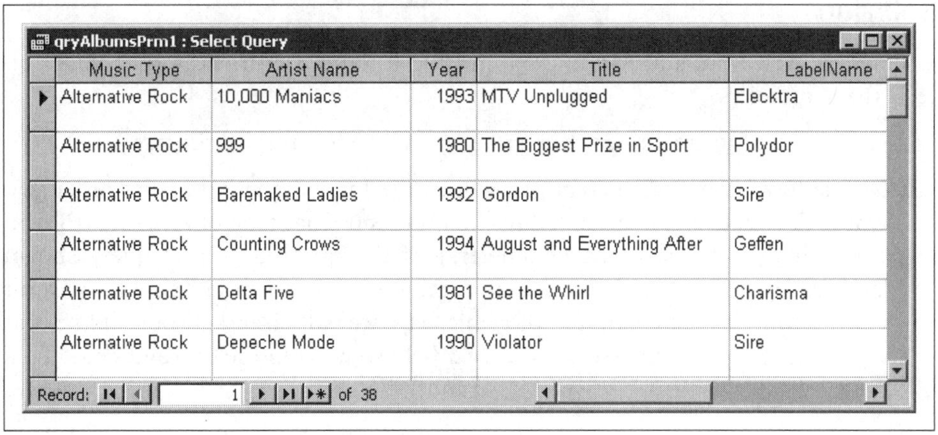

qryAlbumsPrm1 : Select Query
Music Type | Artist Name | Year | Title | LabelName
Alternative Rock | 10,000 Maniacs | 1993 | MTV Unplugged | Elecktra
Alternative Rock | 999 | 1980 | The Biggest Prize in Sport | Polydor
Alternative Rock | Barenaked Ladies | 1992 | Gordon | Sire
Alternative Rock | Counting Crows | 1994 | August and Everything After | Geffen
Alternative Rock | Delta Five | 1981 | See the Whirl | Charisma
Alternative Rock | Depeche Mode | 1990 | Violator | Sire
Record: 1 of 38

Figure 1-3. The datasheet for qryAlbumsPrm1

Discussion

For queries with simple text parameters, you can get away without declaring the parameter using the Query → Parameters command. If you create parameters for crosstab or action queries, however, you must declare the parameter. We recommend that you get in the habit of always declaring all parameters to eliminate any chance of ambiguity. The entries you make in the Parameters dialog end up in the Parameters clause that is added to the beginning of the query's SQL, which you can see by selecting View → SQL View.

The result of a parameter query needn't be a query's datasheet. You can base reports, forms, and even other queries on a parameter query. When you run the object that is based on the parameter query—for example, a report—Access knows enough to resolve the parameters prior to running the report.

You can use parameters in any type of query, including select, totals, crosstab, action, and union queries.

1.2   Using a Form-Based Parameter Query

Problem

The default type of parameter query is useful but has several drawbacks:

- You get one Enter Parameter Value dialog for each parameter. Since these are sequential, you can't return to a previous dialog to change an incorrect value.
- You can't select the value from a combo box or use a format or input mask, which makes it likely that the user will enter invalid data or data not found in the database.
- You can't write any VBA event procedures to run behind the Parameters dialog.

Solution

Use a form-based parameter query by creating a more user-friendly form that collects the parameters.

Here are the steps to create a parameter query using a form-based prompt:

1. Decide how many parameters you will define for the query, in what order you would like them to be presented to the user, and what type of form control you would like to use for each parameter. For the qryAlbumsPrm2 query shown later, in Figure 1-4, we defined three parameters, as shown in Table 1-1. (Don't worry about the last column in the table yet—we will discuss it soon.) Note that we included two parameters for the Year field so we could select rows based on a range of years, such as "between 1970 and 1975."

Table 1-1. Parameters for qryAlbumsPrm2

Query field	Data type	Control type	Parameter reference
MusicType	Text	Combo box	Forms!frmAlbumsPrm2!cboMusicType
Year	Integer	Text box	Forms!frmAlbumsPrm2!txtYear1
Year	Integer	Text box	Forms!frmAlbumsPrm2!txtYear2

2. Create an unbound form with controls that will be used to collect the query's parameters. For qryAlbumsPrm2, we created a form named frmAlbumsPrm2 with three controls that will be used to collect the parameters from Table 1-1. All three controls are unbound; that is, they have no entry for the ControlSource property. We named the text boxes txtYear1 and txtYear2. We also created a combo box called cboMusicType to allow the user to select the type of music from a list of music types. You can use the combo box control wizard to assist you in creating this control, or you can create it by hand. If you decide to create it by hand, select Table/Query for the RowSourceType property and tblMusic-Type for the RowSource (not the ControlSource). Leave all the other properties at their default settings.

3. Add one command button to the form that will be used to execute the query and another that will be used to close the form. For frmAlbumsPrm2, we created two buttons with the captions OK and Cancel. To accomplish this, you can use the command button wizard, which will write the VBA code for you. Here's what the code in the two event procedures looks like:

```
Private Sub cmdCancel_Click( )
    DoCmd.Close
End Sub

Private Sub cmdOK_Click( )
    DoCmd.OpenQuery "qryAlbumsPrm2", acViewNormal, acEdit
End Sub
```

4. Create the query. You will now create the parameters that reference the controls on the form created in Steps 2 through 4. You create form-based parameters a little differently than default parameters. Instead of creating a prompt surrounded by square brackets, you will enter references to the form control for each parameter. For qryAlbumsPrm2, create the parameters shown in Table 1-1. In the MusicType field, enter:

```
Forms![frmAlbumsPrm2]![cboMusicType]
```

Enter brackets only around each form and control reference, not around the entire parameter. For the Year field, enter:

```
Between Forms![frmAlbumsPrm2]![txtYear1] And Forms![frmAlbumsPrm2]![txtYear2]
```

5. Select Query → Parameters to declare the data types of the parameters. Use the same parameter names you used in the previous step. Choose the data types shown in Table 1-1.

6. Save the query and close it.

7. Open the parameter form in form view. Select or enter each of the parameters. Click on the OK button to execute the parameter query, returning only the rows selected using the parameter form.

To see how a form-based query works using the sample database, open the frmAlbumsPrm2 form in *01-02.MDB* (see Figure 1-4). This form collects three parameters for the parameter query qryAlbumsPrm2. Choose the type of music from the combo box and the range of years to include in the two text boxes. Click on the OK button to execute the parameter query using the parameters collected on the form.

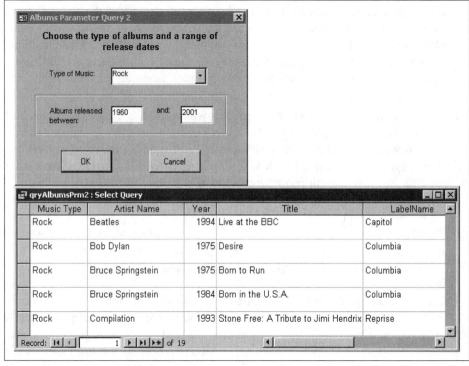

Figure 1-4. The form-based parameter query, qryAlbumsPrm2

Discussion

When you add a parameter to the criteria of a query, Access knows that it needs to resolve that parameter at runtime. You must either reference a control on a form or enter a prompt surrounded by square brackets to let Access know you wish to use a parameter. If you don't use the brackets, Access will interpret the entry as a text string.

When Access runs a query, it checks to see if there are any parameters it needs to resolve. It first attempts to obtain the value from the underlying tables. If it doesn't find it there, it looks for any other reference it can use, such as a form reference. Finally, if there is no form reference (or if you created a form-based parameter and the form is not open), Access prompts the user for the parameter. This means that you must open the form prior to running any parameter queries that contain references to forms.

 Parameter dialogs can sometimes be a symptom of an error in the design of one or more objects in your database. If you ever run a query, form, or report and are prompted for a parameter when you shouldn't be, you probably misspelled the name of a field or renamed a field in a table without changing the reference in the query. Access sometimes creates queries on its own to support subforms or sorting and grouping in reports. You may need to check the LinkChildFields or LinkMasterFields properties of a subform or the Sorting and Grouping dialog of a report to find the unrecognized term that is triggering the errant Enter Parameter Value dialog. Also, if you change a parameter in the query grid, remember to change it in the Parameters dialog too!

1.3 Limit the Items in One Combo Box Based on the Selected Item in Another

Problem

Sometimes in a form-based parameter query it would be nice to limit the values in one combo box based on the value selected in another combo box. For example, if a form has two combo boxes, one for the type of music and the other for artists, when you select the type of music in the first combo box, you'd like the list of artists in the second combo box to be limited to artists of the selected music type. But no matter which type of music you select, you always see all the artists in the second combo box. Is there any way to link the two combo boxes so you can filter the second combo box based on the selected item in the first?

Solution

When you place two combo boxes on a form, Access by default doesn't link them together. But you can link them by basing the second combo box on a parameter query whose criteria point to the value of the first combo box. This solution demonstrates how you can use a parameter query tied to one combo box on a form as the row source for a second combo box to limit the second combo box's drop-down list to items appropriate to the user's selection in the first combo box.

Follow these steps to create linked combo boxes:

1. Create a form bound to a table or query. Make it a continuous form by setting the DefaultView property of the form to Continuous Forms. This will be used as a subform, like fsubAlbumBrowse in the frmAlbumBrowse example.

2. Create a second form with two unbound combo boxes. In the frmAlbumBrowse example found in *01-03.MDB*, we named the combo boxes cboMusicType and cboArtistID. Drag the subform from the Access Forms object list in the database window onto the main form. We dragged the icon for fsubAlbumBrowse onto frmAlbumBrowse, underneath the combo boxes.

3. Set the LinkChildFields and LinkMasterFields properties of the subform control to keep the subform in sync with the main form. We entered ArtistID as the LinkChildFields and cboArtistID as the LinkMasterFields.

4. Create the query that will supply rows for the first combo box. The query that's the source of rows for cboMusicType is a simple one-column query based on tbl-MusicType and sorted alphabetically by MusicType.

5. Create the query that will supply rows to the second combo box. The query that provides rows for the cboArtistID combo box, qryFilteredArtists, contains three columns—ArtistID, ArtistName, and MusicType—and is sorted by ArtistName.

6. Create the parameter that links this query to the first combo box. For qryFilteredArtists, enter the following in the MusicType field:

   ```
   Forms![frmAlbumBrowse]![cboMusicType]
   ```

7. Select Query → Parameters to declare the data type of the parameter. Use the exact same parameter name you used in the previous step. For qryFilteredArtists, choose Text for the data type. This query is shown in Figure 1-5.

8. Adjust the properties of the two combo box controls so they now obtain their rows from the queries created in Steps 3 through 6. In the frmAlbumBrowse example, set the properties of the combo boxes as shown in Table 1-2.

9. When the value selected for the first combo box changes, you need two things to happen:

   • Blank out any value in the second combo box to avoid a mismatch.

   • Requery the second combo box so that only matching values will show. In the example, we want to see artists of only the selected music type.

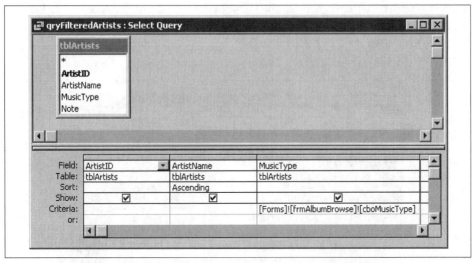

Figure 1-5. The qryFilteredArtists parameter query links the two combo boxes on frmAlbumBrowse

Table 1-2. Key properties for the combo boxes on frmAlbumBrowse2

Name	RowSourceType	RowSource	ColumnCount	ColumnWidth	BoundColumn
cboMusicType	Table/Query	qryMusicType	1	<blank>	1
cboArtistID	Table/Query	qryFilteredArtists	2	0 in; 2 in	1

You could use a macro to accomplish this, but adding a VBA procedure is just as easy. To make your code run automatically when the value in the first combo box, cboMusicType, changes, use that combo box's AfterUpdate property. Select [Event Procedure] on the properties sheet, and click the "..." button that appears to the right of the property. This brings up the VBA Editor, with the first and last lines of your event procedure already created. Enter an additional two lines of code, so that you end up with this:

```
Private Sub cboMusicType_AfterUpdate( )
    cboArtistID = Null
    cboArtistID.Requery
End Sub
```

To see a form-based query in which one drop-down combo box depends on the value selected in another, open and run frmAlbumBrowse from *01-03.MDB*. This form has been designed to allow you to select albums by music type and artist using combo boxes, with the selected records displayed in a subform. If you select a type of music using the first combo box, cboMusicType—for example, Alternative Rock—the list of artists in the second combo box, cboArtistID, is filtered to show only Alternative Rock musicians (see Figure 1-6). Once you pick an artist, the form displays all the albums by that artist.

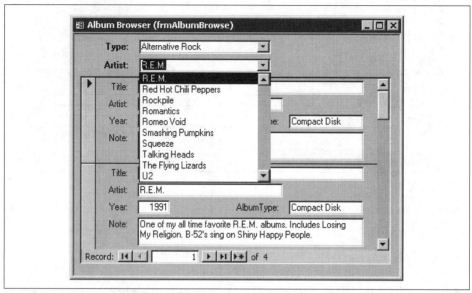

Figure 1-6. The choices in cboArtistID are filtered to show only Alternative Rock artists

Discussion

The parameter query (in this example, qryFilteredArtists) causes the second combo box's values to be dependent on the choice made in the first combo box. This works because the criteria for the MusicType field in qryFilteredArtists point directly to the value of the first combo box.

This works without any macro or VBA code until you change the value in the first combo box. To keep the two combo boxes synchronized, however, you must create an event procedure to force a requery of the second combo box's row source whenever the first combo box's value changes. Any value in the second combo box (cboArtistID) will probably become invalid if the first combo box (cboMusicType) changes, so it is also a good idea to blank out the second combo box when that happens. This is accomplished in the frmAlbumBrowse example by using two simple lines of VBA code placed in the AfterUpdate event procedure of the first combo box.

The subform in this example automatically updates when an artist is selected, because cboArtistID was entered as the LinkMasterFields (the property name is plural because you may need to use more than one field). The LinkMasterFields property can contain the names of one or more controls on the main form or fields in the record source of the main form. If you use more than one field, separate them with semicolons. The LinkChildFields property must contain only field names (not control names) from the record source of the subform.

The example shown here uses two unbound combo boxes and a subform. Your use of this technique for relating combo boxes, however, needn't depend on this specific style of form. You can also use this technique with bound combo boxes located in the detail section of a form. For example, you might use the frmSurvey form (also found in the *01-03.MDB* database) to record critiques of albums. It contains two linked combo boxes in the detail section: cboArtistID and cboAlbumID. When you select an artist using the first combo box, the second combo box is filtered to display only albums for that artist.

To create a form similar to frmSurvey, follow the steps described in this solution, placing the combo boxes in the detail section of the form instead of the header. Create an event procedure in the AfterUpdate event of the first combo box, cboArtistID, to blank out and requery the second combo box, cboAlbumID. Because the artist may be different on different records in the form, cboAlbumID also needs to be requeried as you navigate from record to record. You can accomplish this by requerying cboAlbumID in the Current event of the form:

```
Private Sub Form_Current( )
    cboAlbumID.Requery
End Sub
```

Using related combo boxes in the detail section of a continuous form can cause problems. Unbound combo boxes will show the same value on every row, and bound ones may mysteriously turn blank when they lose focus. This happens if a dependent combo box has a displayed column that isn't also its bound column. You can demonstrate this by changing the DefaultView property of frmSurvey from Single Form to Continuous Forms. You'll find that cboAlbumID appears blank on all rows that have a different artist than the one selected on the current row. That's because the bound column in cboAlbumID is not the displayed column (the bound AlbumID column has a column width of 0). Access can't display a value that's not in the current row source unless it's in the bound column.

See Also

To fill a combo box programmatically, see "Programmatically Add Items to a List or Combo Box" in Chapter 7. To optimize your combo box performance, see "Make Combo Boxes Load Faster" in Chapter 8.

1.4 Make Formatted Date Columns Sort Correctly in a Crosstab Query

Problem

If you have a crosstab query that uses the built-in *Format* function to convert dates into text for column headings, Access sorts them alphabetically (Apr, Aug, and so on) rather than chronologically. For example, open *01-04.MDB* and run the qryAlbumTypeByMonth1 crosstab query (see Figure 1-7). This query shows the cross-tabulation of the number of albums purchased by album type and the month the albums were purchased. The month columns are sorted alphabetically instead of chronologically.

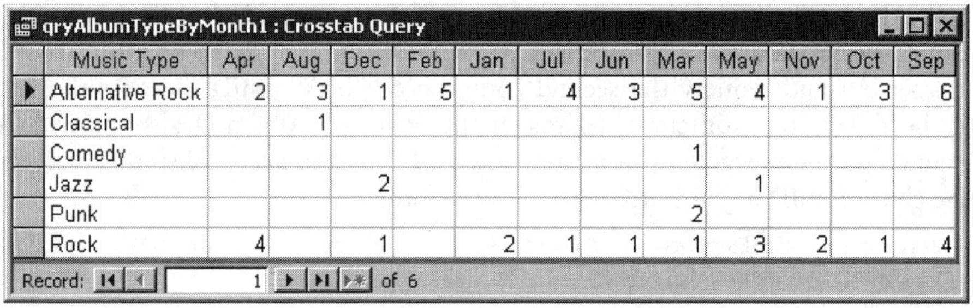

qryAlbumTypeByMonth1 : Crosstab Query												
Music Type	Apr	Aug	Dec	Feb	Jan	Jul	Jun	Mar	May	Nov	Oct	Sep
▶ Alternative Rock	2	3	1	5	1	4	3	5	4	1	3	6
Classical		1										
Comedy								1				
Jazz			2						1			
Punk								2				
Rock	4		1		2	1	1	1	3	2	1	4

Record: I◄ ◄ [1] ► ►I ►✳ of 6

Figure 1-7. The months in qryAlbumTypeByMonth1 sort alphabetically

When the purpose of using the month in a crosstab query is to examine chronological variation by month, this makes the crosstab query all but useless. Is there some way to tell Access to sort the columns by date rather than alphabetically?

Solution

The query properties sheet allows you to specify fixed column headings for a crosstab query. This solution illustrates how to use the ColumnHeadings property to specify column headings so that formatted dates sort chronologically.

Follow these steps to create a crosstab query with correctly sorted formatted-date columns:

1. Create a select query. Select Query → Crosstab to convert the query into a crosstab query.

2. Add the columns you want to the crosstab query. Use a calculation for the Column Heading field. This calculation should use the built-in *Format* function to convert a normal date into an alphabetic string for cross-tabulation purposes. This might be the day of week or the month of year—in the example shown in

Figure 1-7, we took the date field, DateAcquired, and formatted it as a three-letter month string. Add the remaining fields to qryAlbumTypeByMonth2, as shown in Table 1-3.

Table 1-3. Field settings for the qryAlbumTypeByMonth2 crosstab query

Field	Table	Total	Crosstab
AlbumType	tblAlbums	Group By	Row Heading
Month: Format([DateAcquired], "mmm")		Group By	Column Heading
Album ID	tblAlbums	Count	Value

All crosstab queries must have at least three fields: Row Heading, Column Heading, and Value.

3. Select View → Properties if the properties sheet is not already visible. Click on any part of the background of the upper-half of the query screen. This will select the properties for the query itself (as opposed to the Field or FieldList properties). Enter the values of the formatted date, in the order in which you want them to appear, into the ColumnHeadings property. For the qryAlbumTypeByMonth2 query, add three-letter strings for each month of the year (see Figure 1-8). Separate each entry with a comma.

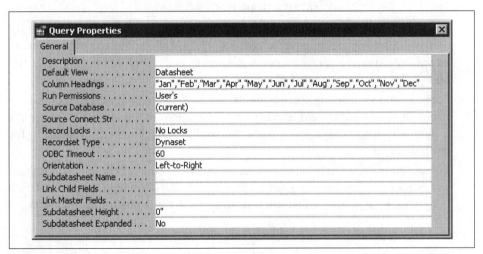

Figure 1-8. The query properties sheet for qryAlbumByMonth2

4. Save and run the query. The date columns should be ordered chronologically.

Now run qryAlbumTypeByMonth2, which you'll also find in *01-04.MDB*. In this query, the months are ordered chronologically (see Figure 1-9).

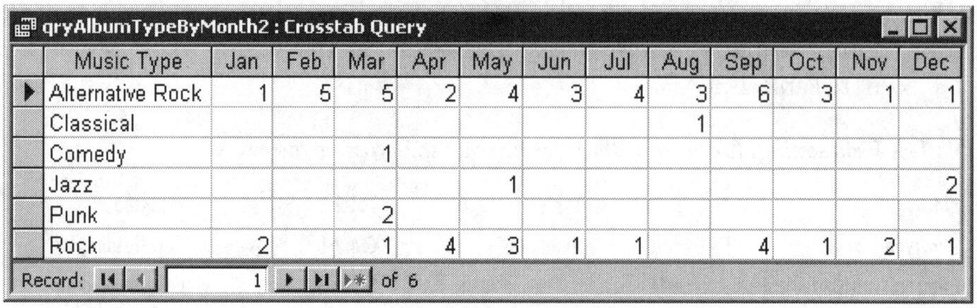

Music Type	Jan	Feb	Mar	Apr	May	Jun	Jul	Aug	Sep	Oct	Nov	Dec
▶ Alternative Rock	1	5	5	2	4	3	4	3	6	3	1	1
Classical								1				
Comedy			1									
Jazz						1						2
Punk			2									
Rock	2		1	4	3	1	1		4	1	2	1

Record: ◄ ◄ [1] ► ►► ►* of 6

Figure 1-9. The months in qryAlbumTypeByMonth2 sort chronologically

Discussion

When you convert a date/time field to a formatted date using the Format function, Access converts the date into a string. This means that the formatted date will sort alphabetically, like any other string. Access includes a special query property, ColumnHeadings, to make it easy to work around this unpleasant side effect of using the *Format* function.

You aren't limited to using fixed column headings with formatted date strings. This crosstab query property comes in handy for several other situations. For example, you might use the ColumnHeadings property to:

- Force a crosstab to always contain a column heading, even if no values exist for that column. For example, you could use the ColumnHeadings property to include all employee names in a crosstab report, even if one of the employees has no sales for the reporting period.

- Force a unique ordering for the columns of a crosstab query. For example, if your Column Heading field is made up of the names of regions, you can use the ColumnHeadings property to ensure that the home region always appears as the leftmost column.

- Eliminate a column value. If the ColumnHeadings property contains any values, any column headings in the result set that are not listed in the property will be left out of the crosstab query. You can also accomplish this by using query criteria.

When you use the ColumnHeadings property, you must spell the column heading values exactly as they appear in your data. If you misspell a column heading value, that value will not appear in the crosstab query. For example, if you use Format(datefield, "ddd") as the Column Heading field and create fixed column headings of Mon, Tue, Wed, Thr, Fri, Sat, and Sun, the Thr column will be completely blank because the *Format* function returns Thu (not Thr) for day of week.

You cannot set the ColumnHeadings property programmatically. Setting this property in the Access user interface causes an IN clause to be added to the SQL of the query, and the only way to accomplish this in code is to add or modify that IN clause yourself.

1.5 Group Mailing Labels by Address

Problem

You need to print mailing labels intended for the general public. If your mailing list contains multiple occurrences of the same last name at the same address, you want to print only one label (addressed to the entire family). Otherwise, you need to print one label for each person in the table.

Solution

To avoid sending duplicate mailings to multiple members of a family, you can use a totals query to group label data so that people with the same last name who live at the same address will make up only one row in the output query. In addition, if you count the number of occurrences of combinations of last name, address, and zip code, you can create the mailing-label text with different text for mailings to a family based on that count.

To create this grouping in your own data, follow these steps:

1. Create a new query (qryCountNames, in this example) based on your table. Turn this query into a totals query by choosing View → Totals or by clicking on the Sigma button on the toolbar. This query will group the data using one row for each unique combination of the grouping fields.

2. Add a column to the query grid for each column in your table on which you want to group rows. Our example uses [LastName], [Address], and [Zip]. For each column, set the Total field to Group By. If you want to specify column names, place those names, followed by a colon, before the field names, as shown in Figure 1-10.

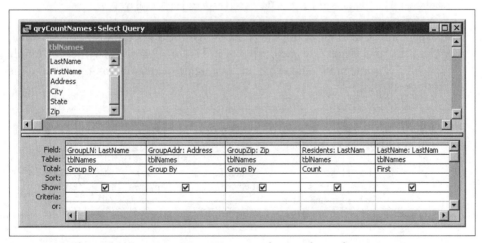

Figure 1-10. The grouping query, qryCountNames, with new column aliases

3. Add a column to the query grid in which Access will count the number of rows that it groups together to make a single row in the output. Choose any field that won't have null values (i.e., a required field), place it in the query grid, and set its Total row to Count. (This field is called [Residents] in this example.) This instructs Access to count the number of rows in the same grouping, as shown in Figure 1-10. You can also use the expression `Count(*)` instead of using a field.
4. Add any other fields that you want to show on your labels to the query grid. For each field, set the value in the Total row to First. For each column, add a specific title—if you don't, Access will change each title to FirstOf*<ColumnName>*. When you run this query, its output will look something like that shown in Figure 1-11. Note that there's only one row in the output for each unique grouping of last name, address, and zip code.

qryCountNames : Select Query

GroupLN	GroupAddr	GroupZip	Residents	LastName	FirstName	Address	City	State	Zip
Diller	4567 Planet Road	19284	2	Diller	Clark	4567 Planet Ro	Kansas	KS	19284
Diller	Luthor Towers	19000	1	Diller	Lex	Luthor Towers	Anytown	KS	19000
Jones	Luthor Towers	19000	1	Jones	Alexis	Luthor Towers	Anytown	KS	19000
Stevens	Kent Lane	87623	2	Stevens	Martha	Kent Lane	Smallvill	AK	87623

Record: 1 of 4

Figure 1-11. The output of the grouping query qryCountNames

5. To create the text for your labels, create a new query (qryLabels, in this example) based on the previous query (qryCountNames). You'll base the mailing label name on the field in which you counted rows ([Residents], in this example), along with the [FirstName] and [LastName] fields. Pull in whatever columns you want in your label, and add one more for the label name. In our example, the expression for this column ([LabelName]) is:

```
LabelName: Iif ([Residents] > 1, "The " & [LastName] & " Family",
 [FirstName] & " " & [LastName])
```

6. On the mailing label itself, use the [LabelName] field instead of the [FirstName] and [LastName] fields. This field (shown in Figure 1-12) shows either the family name or the single individual's first and last name, depending on the value in the [Residents] column.

qryLabels : Select Query

Residents	LabelName	Address	City	State	Zip
2	The Diller Family	4567 Planet Road	Kansas Cit	KS	19284
1	Lex Diller	Luthor Towers	Anytown	KS	19000
1	Alexis Jones	Luthor Towers	Anytown	KS	19000
2	The Stevens Family	Kent Lane	Smallville	AK	87623

Record: 1 of 4

Figure 1-12. The LabelName field showing the family name or the individual's name

To see how this works, open the tblNames table in *01-05.MDB*. The raw data appears as in Figure 1-13. Note that there are several examples of family members living at the same address, and we want to create only one label for each of these families. There's also an example of two people with different last names at the same address—we don't want to combine these names into one label. Open the rptLabels report (shown in Figure 1-14). This mailing label report groups the people with common last names and addresses onto single labels, using the family name instead of individual names.

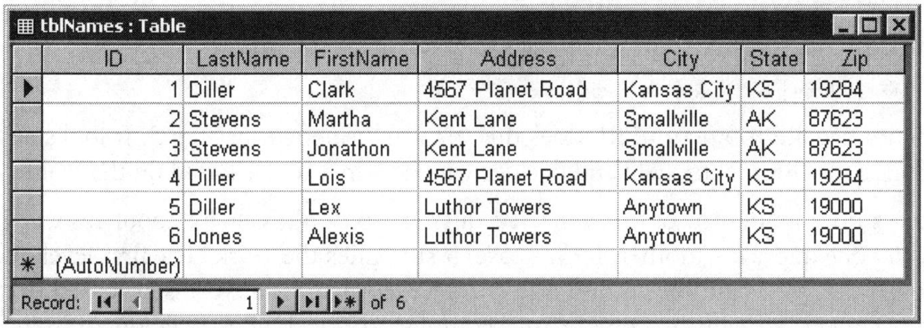

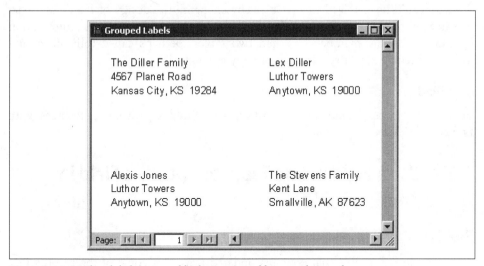

Figure 1-13. *Sample data from tblNames that includes multiple people per address*

Figure 1-14. *Mailing labels, grouped by last name, address, and zip code*

Discussion

By creating a totals query that groups on a combination of fields, you're instructing Access to output a single row for each group of rows that have identical values in those columns. Because you're grouping on last name and address (the zip code was thrown in to ensure that you wouldn't group two families with the same name at the same address in different cities), you should end up with one output row for each household. You included one column for counting (the [Residents] field, in our example), so Access will tell you how many rows collapsed down into the single output row. This way, the query can decide whether to print an individual's name or the family name on the label.

If the value in the counted field is greater than 1, the query builds an expression that includes just the family name:

```
"The " & [LastName] & " Family"
```

If the count is exactly 1, the query uses the first and last names:

```
[FirstName] & " " & [LastName]
```

The immediate If function, *IIf*, does this for you, as shown in Step 5. It looks at the value in the [Residents] field and decides which format to use based on that value.

Access does its best to optimize nested queries, so don't feel shy about resorting to basing one query on another. In this case, it simplifies the work. The first-level query groups the rows, and the second one creates the calculated expression based on the first. Though it might be possible to accomplish this task in a single query, splitting the tasks makes it easier to conceptualize.

We also could have solved this problem by changing the design of the database so that instead of having a single table, tblNames, with repeating address information for multiple family members, we had two tables, perhaps called tblFamilies and tblFamilyMembers, related in a one-to-many relationship.

See Also

To include quotes inside quoted strings, see "Build Up String References with Embedded Quotes" in Chapter 7.

1.6 Use a Field in One Table to Update a Field in Another Table

Problem

You've imported a table that contains updated prices for some of the records in a table in your database. The data in all the other fields in the existing table is still correct. Is there any way—short of using a complex VBA procedure—to update the price data in the existing table based on the updated prices from the imported table without overwriting any of the other fields in the existing table?

Solution

You probably already know that you can use an Update query to update the values of fields in a table, but did you know that you can use an Update query to update the values in one table with the values from another? This solution will show you how to do just that. If you can join the two tables on some common field or combination of fields, you can use an Update query to update a field in one table based on the values found in a second table.

Here are the steps to create an Update query that updates values across tables:

1. Create a standard Select query. Add the two tables to the query and join them on the common field or fields. In the sample database, we added the tblAlbums and tblAlbumsUpdated tables to the query. We will refer to tblAlbumsUpdated as the *source table* because it will supply the values to be used to update the other table; tblAlbums is the *target table* because it will be the target of the updates. Access has automatically joined the two tables on AlbumID. If the name of the common field is not the same, you will have to join the two tables by dragging the common field from one table to the other.

2. Select Query → Update to change the type of query to an update action query.

3. Drag the field to be updated in the target table to the query grid. In the Update To cell for the field that will be updated, specify the fully qualified name of the field in the source table that will be the source of the updated values. This field name should include the name of the table surrounded by square brackets, a period, and the name of the field surrounded by square brackets. For qryUpdateAlbumPrices, drag the PurchasePrice field from tblAlbums to the query grid. The field settings for PurchasePrice are shown in Table 1-4.

Table 1-4. Field settings for qryUpdateAlbumPrices

Field	Table	Update To	Criteria
PurchasePrice	tblAlbums	[tblAlbumsUpdated].[PurchasePrice]	Is Null

 Be careful when specifying the Update To value. If you misspell the source field name, you run the risk of changing the values to the misspelled string rather than to the values in the source field. If Access surrounds the Update To value with quotes or prompts you for an unexpected parameter when you attempt to execute the update query, it's likely that you made a spelling mistake.

4. Optionally specify criteria to limit the rows to be updated. In the qryUpdateAlbumPrices example, we used criteria to limit the updated rows to those with null (missing) prices (see Table 1-4). This prevents Access from overwriting any existing non-null values in tblAlbums.

5. Execute the query by selecting Query → Run or by clicking on the exclamation point icon.

 You can preview the selected records in an action query by choosing View → Datasheet or by clicking on the Datasheet icon. The query will not be run, but you'll be able to see which records would be updated had you run the query.

For an example of updating a field in a table based on the value of a field in another table, open the tblAlbums table found in the *01-06.MDB* database. Note that most of the purchase prices are null (see Figure 1-15). Open tblAlbumsUpdated, and you'll see that many of the purchase prices for the same albums have been entered (see Figure 1-16).

Album ID	Title	Date Purchased	Purchase Price
1	The Very Best of Elvis Costello and the A	2/25/1995	
2	Gish	12/15/1994	$0.00
3	August and Everything After	2/25/1995	
4	Little Pearls of Czech Classics	8/15/1991	$5.00
5	Paradiso	12/15/1992	$0.00
6	Mighty Like a Rose	5/16/1991	
7	With The Beatles	4/26/1994	
8	Whats Hits!?	6/7/1993	
9	The Unplugged Collection	9/5/1994	$0.00
10	Rock 'N' Roll	1/16/1985	
11	What I Like About You (and Other Roman	3/15/1990	
12	Gordon	9/5/1994	$0.00
13	Classics Volume 6	5/13/1989	
14	Spike	7/14/1990	
15	Outlandos D'Amour	5/13/1989	
16	Stone Free: A Tribute to Jimi Hendrix	9/5/1994	$0.00
17	Green	9/1/1990	
18	Last of the Independents	10/25/1994	
19	Live at the BBC	12/15/1995	$39.00
20	Dookie	9/5/1994	$0.00

Record: I◄ ◄ [1] ► ►I ►* of 65

Figure 1-15. Many of the purchase values in tblAlbums are null

Now run the qryUpdateAlbumPrices query found in the same database (see Figure 1-17). This action query will take the PurchasePrice values from tblAlbumsUpdated and copy it into the Purchase Price field in tblAlbums for each record where the two AlbumID fields match and the price value in tblAlbums is currently null. When the query is finished, open tblAlbums again—you should see that the

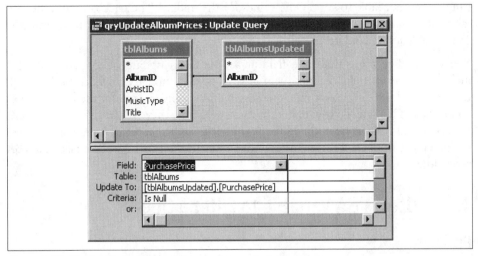

Figure 1-16. tblAlbumsUpdated contains updated purchase prices for several albums in tblAlbums

Purchase Price field in this table has been updated based on the values in tblAlbumsUpdated (see Figure 1-18).

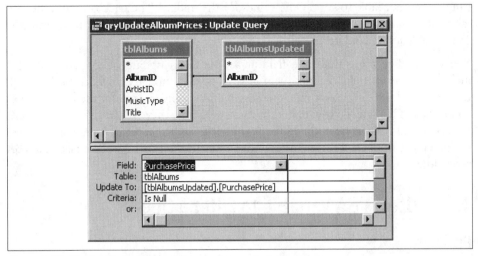

Figure 1-17. The qryUpdateAlbumPrices update query in design view

Album ID	Title	Date Purchased	Purchase Price
1	The Very Best of Elvis Costello and the A	2/25/1995	$9.99
2	Gish	12/15/1994	$0.00
3	August and Everything After	2/25/1995	$10.99
4	Little Pearls of Czech Classics	8/15/1991	$5.00
5	Paradiso	12/15/1992	$0.00
6	Mighty Like a Rose	5/16/1991	$12.99
7	With The Beatles	4/26/1994	$12.99
8	Whats Hits!?	6/7/1993	$11.99
9	The Unplugged Collection	9/5/1994	$0.00
10	Rock 'N' Roll	1/16/1985	$8.99
11	What I Like About You (and Other Romar	3/15/1990	$7.00
12	Gordon	9/5/1994	$0.00
13	Classics Volume 6	5/13/1989	$9.50
14	Spike	7/14/1990	$8.99
15	Outlandos D'Amour	5/13/1989	$9.99
16	Stone Free: A Tribute to Jimi Hendrix	9/5/1994	$0.00
17	Green	9/1/1990	$12.99
18	Last of the Independents	10/25/1994	$12.99
19	Live at the BBC	12/15/1995	$39.00
20	Dookie	9/5/1994	$0.00

Record: 1 of 65

Figure 1-18. The updated purchase prices for albums in tblAlbums

Discussion

You can use update queries in Access to update the values in a target table, and you can use another table to supply the values for the update. The trick is to join the two tables using a common field and to properly specify the name of the field from the source table in the Update To cell.

You can update more than one field at a time in an update query. You can also include additional fields in the query grid to further limit the rows to be updated. Drag these additional fields to the query grid and specify criteria for them. As long as you leave the Update To row blank for these columns, they will be used for their criteria only and will not be updated. Update queries are the most efficient way to make bulk changes to data; they are much more efficient than using a recordset in a VBA procedure.

1.7 Use a VBA Variable to Filter a Query

Problem

You'd like to be able to return rows in a query that have a test score greater than a specified value, which is stored in a VBA variable. When you try to use the variable in the query design grid, Access thinks it's a literal value. Is there some way to get queries to understand VBA variables?

Solution

To use a VBA variable in a query, you need to write a VBA function that returns the value of the variable as its return value and then reference the VBA function either as part of a calculation or in the criteria of a field. The only way to work with VBA in queries is to call a function. This solution shows you how to do that.

In the sample database *01-07.MDB* you'll find tblScores, a table of names and test scores. The goal of the sample is to allow you to specify a cutoff value and list everyone whose scores are greater than that value.

Open the frmScores form. This form allows you to choose between a randomly selected cutoff value and a user-specified cutoff value. If you choose the user-specified cutoff value, a text box is made visible to allow you to enter the cutoff value. When you click on the "Show the results" command button, an event procedure runs that saves the cutoff value—either the randomly chosen cutoff or the user-specified cutoff—to a private variable and then runs the qryScores query.

The qryScores query references the private variable using the *GetCutoff* function and then returns the rows in tblScores in which the score is greater than the cutoff value (see Figure 1-19).

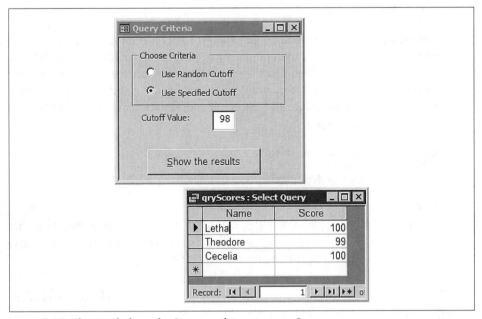

Figure 1-19. The sample form, frmScores, and its output, qryScores

Follow these steps to use a VBA variable in a query:

1. Create a select query, adding the tables and fields you wish to include in the query. The sample query, qryScores, is based on the tblScores table and contains two fields, Name and Score.

2. Create a VBA function or subroutine for which you wish to pass a variable to the query from Step 1. The sample database includes the frmScores form.

   The following event procedure is attached to the cmdRunQuery command button:

```
Private Sub cmdRunQuery_Click( )

    Dim intCutoff As Integer

    If Me.grpCriteria = 1 Then
        ' Use a random cutoff.
        ' You generate a random number between x and y
        ' by using the formula Int((y-x+1)*Rnd+x).
        ' This example generates a number between 0 and 100.
        Randomize
        intCutoff = Int(101 * Rnd)
        MsgBox "The random cutoff value is " & intCutoff, _
          vbOKOnly + vbInformation, "Random Cutoff"
        Me.txtCutOff = intCutoff
    End If
    SetCutoff Me.txtCutOff
    DoCmd.OpenQuery "qryScores"
End Sub
```

   Based on the user choice made using the grpCriteria option group, the procedure will either generate its own randomly chosen cutoff or grab the cutoff value from the txtCutoff text box. Once the value is generated, the event procedure calls the public subroutine *SetCutoff*, which stores the value in a private variable. The *SetCutoff* procedure and the variable declaration are shown here:

```
Private intCutoff As Integer

Public Sub SetCutoff(Value As Integer)
    ' Set the module variable to be
    ' the value passed in from externally.
    intCutoff = Value
End Sub
```

3. Reference the module-global variable *intCutOff* using a wrapper function that returns the value currently stored in the variable. For the sample query qryScores, enter the following criteria for the Score field:

```
>GetCutoff( )
```

   The design view for this query is shown in Figure 1-20. The code for the *GetCutoff* function is:

```
Public Function GetCutoff( )
    ' Return the value of the module variable.
```

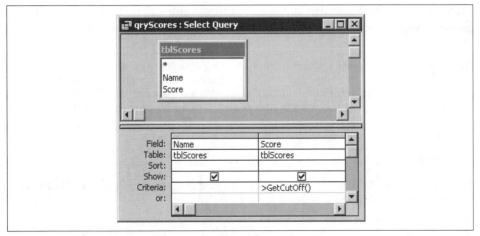

Figure 1-20. The sample query, qryScores, in design view

```
    GetCutoff = intCutoff
End Function
```

4. Execute the VBA procedure from Step 2. This causes the variable to be set, and the query then runs. When the query is executed, it references a function that returns the value stored in the VBA variable.

Discussion

A query cannot directly reference a VBA variable. It can, however, call a VBA function that returns the value stored in the VBA variable. To do this, you write a VBA wrapper function for each variable you wish to pass to a query. Because functions on form and report modules are normally local to that form or report (although you can make these functions public), you'll usually want to call a function stored in a global module—a module you can see in the database container.

In the example, we used a form to collect the values to pass to the VBA variable, *intCutoff*. Another way to solve this problem would be to use a parameter query that directly references the text box on frmScores. The example form frmScoresTextbox combined with qryScoresTextbox show this approach in action.

Using a form to feed the values to a query will not, however, always be so convenient. There will be times where you need to use a variable without a form. For example, you might use global variables to store settings that are read from an options table upon application startup. This options table might store, for example, the complete name of the user, her address, and other preferences. You may decide to store these values in a set of global variables to minimize the number of times you have to reread the values from the options table. In this case, these variables will not be stored on any form. As another example, you may need to base the query on some value obtained from another application using Automation. Even in those cases, however, you can always use a hidden form if you prefer that approach.

 You can use a variation on this technique to reference combo box columns in a query. The query grid won't recognize Forms!MyForm!MyCombo.Column(2), but you can use a function that grabs the value in the desired column and delivers it to your query.

See Also

For more information on declaring variables and creating modules, see "How Do I Create a New Module?" in the Preface.

1.8 Use a Query to Retrieve a Random Set of Rows

Problem

You need to be able to retrieve a random set of rows from a table or a query so you can identify a random sample for a research study. You can't find a way to make this happen in the normal query design grid. What's the trick to getting a random sample of a certain number of rows?

Solution

The solution to this problem is not quite as simple as it might first appear, because of the way Access attempts to optimize the use of function calls in queries. You can call a VBA function to generate a random value for each row, but to ensure that your function runs for each row, and not just once, you need to feed it a value from the row. Once you've generated the random numbers, you can sort by that random column and use a Top Values query to select a random group.

In *01-08.MDB*, open tblRandom. This table includes 50 rows of data. Your goal is to pull five randomly selected rows for this set of data. To do this, follow these steps:

1. Import the module basRandom from *01-08.MDB* or create your own, including this single function:

```
Public Function acbGetRandom(varFld As Variant)

    ' Though varFld isn't used, it's the only way to force the query
    ' to call this function for each and every row.

    Randomize
    acbGetRandom = Rnd
End Function
```

2. Create a new select query or use an existing one. Add any fields you're interested in.

3. Add an extra column, with the following expression replacing the reference to the State field with a single field in your query's underlying table or query (this query won't run correctly unless you pass one of your field names to the function):

```
acbGetRandom([State])
```

You can clear this field's Show checkbox, because there's not much point in viewing a continually changing random number as part of your query output. Set the Sort value for the newly calculated field to Ascending (see Figure 1-21).

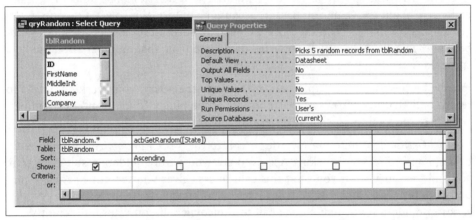

Figure 1-21. The sample query, qryRandom, set up to retrieve five random rows

4. Open the query's properties sheet (make sure the View → Properties menu item is checked, and click on the upper area of the query design surface so the properties sheet's titlebar says Query Properties). Fill in the number of rows you'd like to return in the TopValues property. Figure 1-21 shows the sample query, qryRandom, in design view with the property filled in.

5. Run the query. Your query grid should show you as many rows as you specified in the properties sheet. If you press Shift-F9, asking Access to requery the data, you will see a different set of rows. Repeating the process will return a different set of rows each time.

Discussion

The general concept behind this solution is simple: you add a new column to your query, fill it with a list of random numbers, sort on those random numbers, and retrieve the top *n* rows, where *n* is a number between 1 and the number of rows in your underlying data. There's only one complicating factor: to create the random number, you need to call a function for each row. Access tries to optimize such a function call and will call it only once for the entire set of data, unless the function call involves a field in the data. That is, if you replace the call to acbGetRandom (in Step 3) with a simpler call directly to Access's random number function (Rnd), you'll find that every value in every row will be exactly the same. Access's query engine thinks that the function has nothing to do with data in the query, so it calls the function only once. This makes the random number meaningless, as the whole point of using a random number is to generate a different one for each row.

The workaround, though, is simple: pass a field, any field, as a parameter to the function you call. That way, Access believes that the return value from the function is dependent on the data in each row and so calls the function once per row, passing to it the field you specify in the expression. The *acbGetRandom* function doesn't really care about the value you pass it, because its only goal is to get a random number and return that back to the query. Once you successfully place a random number in each row Access will sort the data based on that number, because you specified Ascending for the column's sorting.

Finally, by specifying the TopValues property for the query, you're asking Access to return only that many rows as the result set of the query. If you want a certain percentage of the total rows, change it by adding the % sign after the Top value.

The *acbGetRandom* function includes a call to the VBA *Randomize* subroutine. By calling *Randomize*, you're asking Access to give you a truly random result every time you call the function. If you omit this call, Access gives you the same series of random numbers each time you start it up and run this query. If you want a repeatable series of random rows, remove the call to *Randomize*. If you want a different set of rows each time you run the query, leave the *Randomize* statement where it is.

Because Access will pass a field value to the *acbGetRandom* function for each and every row of data in your data source, you'll want to optimize this function call as much as you can. If possible, use either a very short text field (zip code, for example) or, even better, an integer. You must pass some value, but you want it to be as small as possible to minimize the amount of information that must be moved around for each row of the data.

1.9   Create a Query That Will Show Aging of Receivables

Problem

Using a crosstab query, you need to age transactions, grouped by Account ID, into ranges of 1-30 days, 31-60 days, 61-90 days, and greater than 120 days. You know that you can group transactions by month using the standard query tools, but you can't find a way to group them by 30-day increments.

Solution

Access provides the seldom-used *Partition* function, which is perfect for this task. It allows you to take a range of values and partition it into even-sized chunks. By specifying a 30-day partition size, you can create a crosstab query that will give you the information you need.

To create a query in your own application, follow these steps:

1. Create a new query based on a table or query containing the appropriate account, date, and amount information.

2. Convert this query to a crosstab query by choosing the Query → Crosstab menu item or by clicking on the Crosstab button on the Query Design toolbar.

3. As when you create any crosstab query, specify at least three columns in the query grid: one for the column headings, one for the row headings, and one for the values that make up the crosstab. In this case, choose the account number (or account name, depending on your data) as the Row Heading and the amount (summed) as the Value. Figure 1-22 shows the sample query in design mode, and Figure 1-23 shows the sample data that will be used in this example.

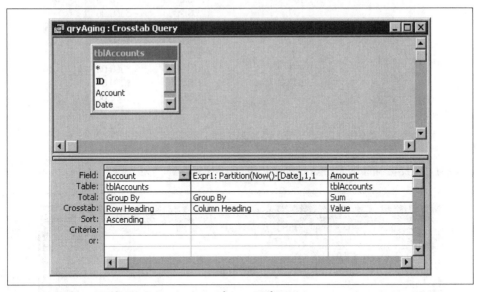

Figure 1-22. The sample query, qryAging, in design mode

4. For the column headings, group the dates in 30-day increments, using the built-in *Partition* function. For this specific example, use the following value:

```
Expr1:Partition(Now( )-[Date],1,120,30)
```

for the column's expression. This tells the query to break the information into groups based on the difference between today and the field named Date, starting with 1 day old, ending with 120 days old, and breaking every 30 days. Set the Total item to Group By and the Crosstab item to Column Heading.

5. When you execute the query, you will see output similar to that shown in Figure 1-24, which shows the aging data grouped in 30-day increments. You would usually create a report based on this query, but you can also use this raw output to get an overview of the aging of your receivables.

To see an example of a query that shows the aging of receivables, load the sample database, *01-09.MDB*. This database includes a simple table, tblAccounts (see Figure 1-23), containing sample data about accounts and their activity to be used in an aging query. The query qryAging, shown in Figure 1-24, shows the final outcome: a crosstab query including the aging information, grouped in 30-day increments. You may want to update this small table with dates that are closer to the date on which you are testing it.

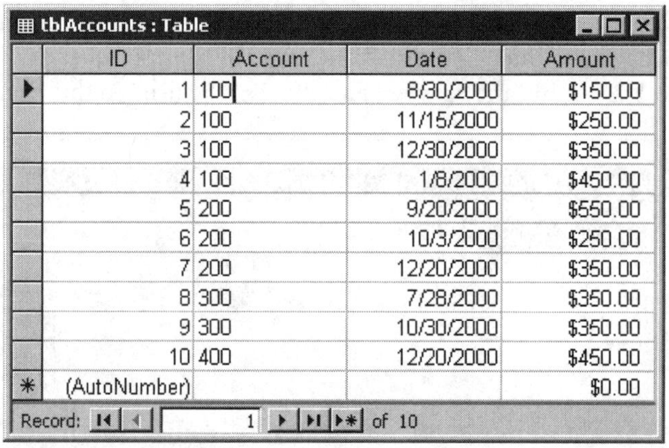

ID	Account	Date	Amount
1	100	8/30/2000	$150.00
2	100	11/15/2000	$250.00
3	100	12/30/2000	$350.00
4	100	1/8/2000	$450.00
5	200	9/20/2000	$550.00
6	200	10/3/2000	$250.00
7	200	12/20/2000	$350.00
8	300	7/28/2000	$350.00
9	300	10/30/2000	$350.00
10	400	12/20/2000	$450.00
*	(AutoNumber)		$0.00

Record: 1 of 10

Figure 1-23. tblAccounts contains sample data to be used in an aging query

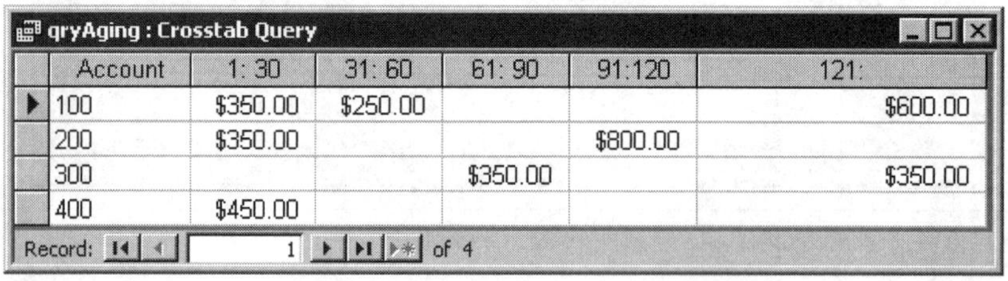

Account	1: 30	31: 60	61: 90	91:120	121:
100	$350.00	$250.00			$600.00
200	$350.00			$800.00	
300			$350.00		$350.00
400	$450.00				

Record: 1 of 4

Figure 1-24. qryAging shows the aging data grouped in 30-day increments

Discussion

Except for the use of the *Partition* function, this crosstab query is no different from any other. It summarizes rows of data, summing the amount column, grouped on a range of values in various columns. The only innovation is the use of the *Partition* function.

The *Partition* function returns a string indicating where a value occurs within a calculated series of ranges. That string (in the format *start*:*end*) becomes the column heading in your query and is based on the starting value, the ending value, and the range size. You tell Access each of these values when you call the *Partition* function. Table 1-5 shows the four parameters you'll use.

Table 1-5. Parameters for the Partition function

Argument	Description
number	Long integer to evaluate against specified ranges.
start	A long integer: the start of the specified ranges. Can't be less than 0.
stop	A long integer: the end of the specified ranges. Can't be less than the value specified in *start*.
interval	A long integer: the interval spanned by each range in the series from *start* to *stop*. Can't be less than 1.

For example, the following expression:

```
Partition(42, 1, 120, 30)
```

would return the value " 31: 60". This function call asks, "Where does the number 42 occur within the range of 1 to 120, broken into 30-day ranges?" Clearly, it falls in the 31- to 60-day range. That's what's indicated by the return value " 31: 60" from the previous example. In doing its calculation, Access formats the result for you, in the format you see in the column headings in Figure 1-25.

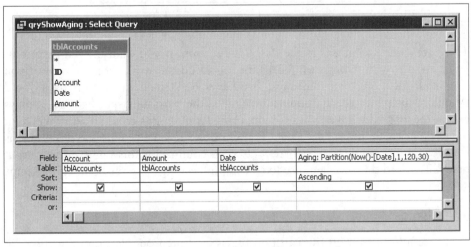

Figure 1-25. A simple select query, qryShowAging, using the Partition function

If a value falls outside the requested range, Access returns an open-ended result. For example, the previous case will return "121: " if the value is greater than 120 or " : 0" if the value is less than 1. Access always includes enough space in the two halves of the result string for the largest possible value. This way, the result strings will sort correctly.

To see the Partition function doing its work, open the query qryShowAging from *01-09.MDB* in design mode (see Figure 1-25). This simple select query will show the account number, the amount due, the date on which the transaction occurred, and the age range into which the transaction fits, using the Partition function to calculate the ranges. Figure 1-26 shows the same query in datasheet view, using the data as shown in Figure 1-23. The last column of the datasheet shows the output from the Partition function. When you group the rows on the values in this column, you end up with the crosstab query you created earlier in this section.

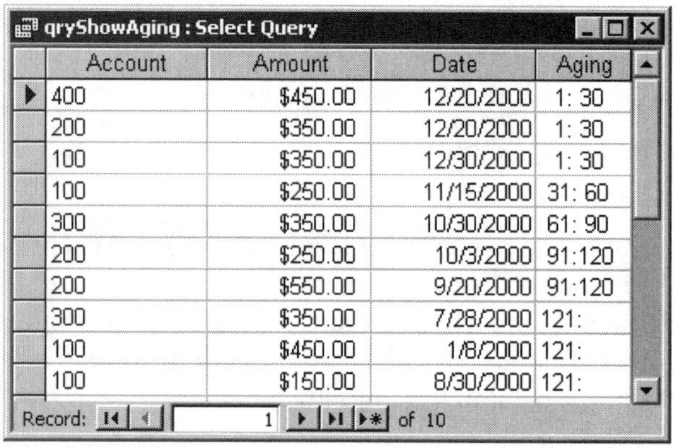
qryShowAging : Select Query

Account	Amount	Date	Aging
400	$450.00	12/20/2000	1: 30
200	$350.00	12/20/2000	1: 30
100	$350.00	12/30/2000	1: 30
100	$250.00	11/15/2000	31: 60
300	$350.00	10/30/2000	61: 90
200	$250.00	10/3/2000	91:120
200	$550.00	9/20/2000	91:120
300	$350.00	7/28/2000	121:
100	$450.00	1/8/2000	121:
100	$150.00	8/30/2000	121:

Record: 1 of 10

Figure 1-26. Rows returned by qryShowAging

There are some limitations to the *Partition* function. If you want uneven partitions, you'll need to write your own VBA function to do the work. For example, if you want your partitions to be 0-30 days, 31-60 days, 61-90 days, and 91-120 days, you'd be out of luck with the *Partition* function: all the partitions specified are 30 days except the first, which is 31. In addition, using *Partition* in a crosstab query will omit ranges for which no values exist. For example, if no account has transactions between 31 and 60 days ago, there will be no column for this range in the output query. To avoid this problem, use fixed column headings (see the Solution in Recipe 1.4).

See Also

For more information on the Partition function, search on "Partition Function" in Access' online help.

1.10 Create a Join That's Based on a Comparison Other than Equality

Problem

You need to join together two tables in a query on the Between operator. For example, you have a table of students and their grades, and a table of grade ranges and the matching letter grade. Though there are lots of ways to solve this problem with complex expressions and VBA, you know there must be a solution involving just queries. You need a way to join these two tables, finding matches when a value in the first table is between two values in the second table.

Solution

In Access, relationships between tables are normally based on equality, matching values in one table with those in another. Two tables in an Access query are normally joined in the upper half of the query design screen—the table pane—by dragging the join field from one table or query to the other. You can join tables this way for joins based on equality ("equijoins") that can be inner or outer in nature.

Sometimes, though, you need to join two tables on some other relationship. However, Access doesn't graphically support joins between tables that are based on an operator other than =. To perform these types of joins, you must specify the join in the criteria of the linking field.

From 01-10.MDB, open the tblGrades and tblLookup tables, both shown in Figure 1-27. The first table, tblGrades, includes a row for each student and the student's numeric grade. The lookup table, tblLookup, contains two columns for the ranges of numeric grades and a third for the corresponding letter grade.

Your goal is to create a query listing each student along with his letter grade. To accomplish this goal, follow these steps:

1. Create a new query including both the sample tables. Don't attempt to use the standard Access methods to create a join between the tables, because there's no mechanism for creating the kind of join you need.

2. Drag the fields you'd like to include in your query to the query grid. Make sure to include the field that will link the two tables together (Grade, from tblGrades, in this case).

3. In the Criteria cell for the linking field, enter the expression you'll use to link the two tables, using the following syntax for any fields in the second table:

   `TableName.FieldName`

   Because you have not related the two tables, Access needs the table name to know what you're referring to. In the sample, the expression is:

   `Between [tblLookup].[LowGrade] And [tblLookup].[HighGrade]`

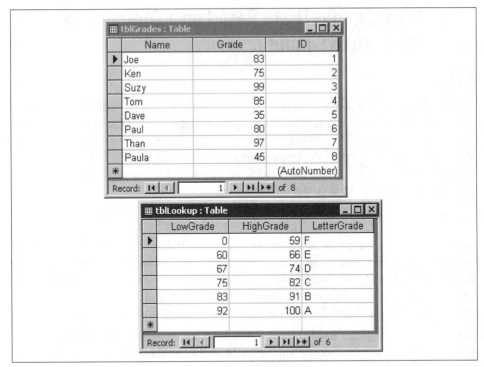

Figure 1-27. The two sample tables, tblGrades and tblLookup

Your finished query should resemble Figure 1-28.

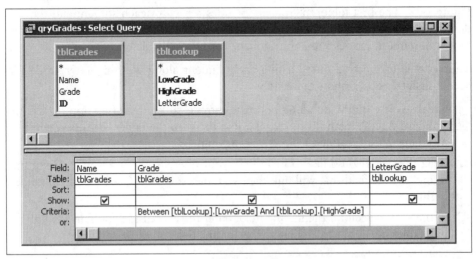

Figure 1-28. The sample query, qryGrades, in design mode

4. Run the query. The output should look something like Figure 1-29. For each numeric grade, you have related the data in tblGrades to the values in tblLookup, matching one row in tblLookup to each numeric grade.

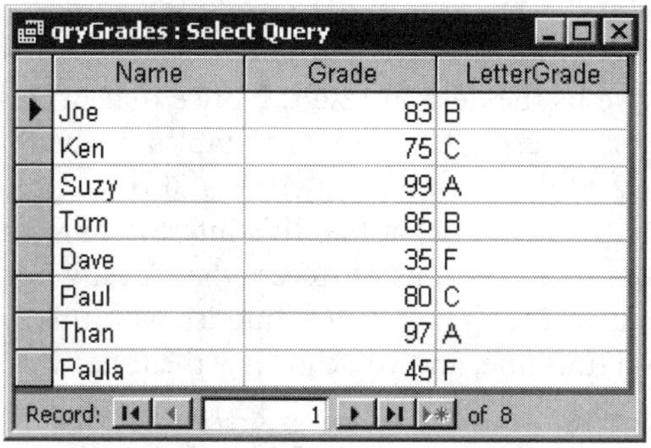

Name	Grade	LetterGrade
Joe	83	B
Ken	75	C
Suzy	99	A
Tom	85	B
Dave	35	F
Paul	80	C
Than	97	A
Paula	45	F

Figure 1-29. Data returned by qryGrades

Discussion

In a normal join relating two tables, Access takes each value in the lefthand table (imagine the two tables laid out in the query design, one on the left and one on the right), finds the first matching value in the related field in the righthand table, and creates a new row in the output set of rows containing information from the two joined rows. In this case, however, you want to match the two tables not on equality, but rather on "betweenness." Access doesn't graphically support this type of join in query design view, but you can get the same result by specifying that you want values for the linking field in the lefthand table only when they are between the two comparison values in the righthand table. As it builds the output set of rows, Access looks up each value of the linking field in the righthand table, searching for the first match. It joins the rows in the two tables based on the value from the lefthand table being between the two values in the righthand table.

All queries in Access are converted to SQL. If you select View → SQL or use the SQL icon on the toolbar, you can view the SQL for the qryGrades query. When you do, you'll see the following SQL:

```
SELECT tblGrades.Name, tblGrades.Grade,
tblLookup.LetterGrade
FROM tblGrades, tblLookup
WHERE (((tblGrades.Grade) Between [tblLookup].[LowGrade]
And [tblLookup].[HighGrade]));
```

The inequality join has been translated into the WHERE clause of Access SQL. If you're familiar with Access SQL, however, you may notice that the join information is not where Access normally places it. For example, if we had created a "normal" equijoin between these two tables, joining Grade from tblGrades to LowGrade in tblLookup, the SQL would look like this:

```
SELECT tblGrades.Name, tblGrades.Grade,
tblLookup.LetterGrade
FROM tblGrades INNER JOIN tblLookup
ON tblGrades.Grade = tblLookup.LowGrade;
```

This query will not give us the desired result. Notice that Access has placed the join information in the FROM clause. (The joining of tables in the FROM clause was introduced in the ANSI 92 SQL standard, but Access also supports joins in the WHERE clause, which is ANSI 89 SQL compatible.) It's interesting to note that you can run queries converted from older versions of Access that specify non-equijoins using the FROM clause syntax, but you can't create new queries with this syntax. qryScoresSQL in the sample database runs fine, and you can view the following syntax in SQL view:

```
SELECT DISTINCTROW tblGrades.Name, tblGrades.Grade, tblLookup.LetterGrade
FROM tblGrades INNER JOIN tblLookup ON tblGrades.Grade
BETWEEN tblLookup.LowGrade AND tblLookup.HighGrade
```

However, if you copy this SQL and paste it into the SQL View pane of a new query, you'll find that Access will report a syntax error and won't let you save it. So, if you need to create non-equijoins, just stick to using the WHERE clause to define them.

This technique isn't limited to the Between operator. You can use any comparison operator (Between, In, >, <, >=, <=, or <>) to perform a search in the second table, finding the first row that meets the required criterion. You can even link two tables using the *InStr* function (which indicates if and where one string occurs within another) to match words in a column of the first table with messages that contain that word in the second table.

As with any relationship between two tables, you'll get the best performance if the values in the matching fields in the righthand table are indexed. This won't always help (using *InStr*, for instance, there's really no way for an index to help Access find matches within a string), but in many cases it will. Consider indexing any fields used in the matching condition in either of the tables involved in your relationships, whether you build them yourself or use Access's primary key indexes.

 The recordset produced by a query containing a non-equijoin will be read-only.

1.11 Create a Query to Combine Data from Two Tables with Similar Structures

Problem

You have two tables of addresses, one for clients and one for leads. Generally you send different mailings to these two groups, but sometimes you need to send the same letter to both. You can always create a third table and append to it the data from each of the two tables, but there must be an easier way that doesn't involve the use of temporary tables. Is there a way to combine the data from these two tables into a single recordset, including only the U.S. addresses and sorted by zip code?

Solution

Access provides a special type of query that you can use to vertically splice together the data from two or more tables. The tables don't even need to have the same fields or fields of exactly the same data types. This is the union query, which can be constructed only by using the SQL View pane in the query designer.

The following steps show you how to construct a union query to combine data from two tables into a single recordset, limited to addresses in the U.S. and sorted by zip code:

1. Open *01-11.MDB*. Open the two tables (tblClients and tblLeads) and examine their structure and data.

2. Create a new select query. Click on Close when you are prompted to add a table.

3. Select Query → SQL Specific → Union. Access will present a blank SQL view.

4. If you'd like, open tblClients in design view so you can see the field names while typing. Then type in the first part of the query:

   ```
   SELECT Company, Address1, Address2, Address3, City, StateProvince, ZipPostalCode,
   Country
   FROM tblClients
   WHERE Country = "U.S.A."
   ```

   Yes, you must type it—there is no query by example equivalent to a union query. However, you could create this select query first using the query grid and then copy and paste the SQL into your new union query.

5. Type UNION, and then enter the matching fields from tblClients in the same order in which they were entered in Step 4:

   ```
   UNION SELECT LeadName, Address1, Address2, "", City, State, Zip, Country
   FROM tblLeads
   WHERE Country = "U.S.A."
   ```

6. To sort the query's output by zip code, add an ORDER BY statement using the name of the field as it appears in the first table:

ORDER BY ZipPostalCode;

The completed query is shown in Figure 1-30.

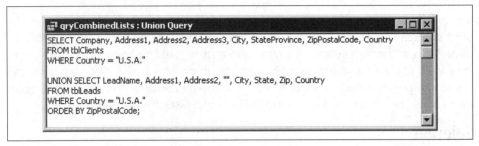

```
qryCombinedLists : Union Query

SELECT Company, Address1, Address2, Address3, City, StateProvince, ZipPostalCode, Country
FROM tblClients
WHERE Country = "U.S.A."

UNION SELECT LeadName, Address1, Address2, "", City, State, Zip, Country
FROM tblLeads
WHERE Country = "U.S.A."
ORDER BY ZipPostalCode;
```

Figure 1-30. The completed union query

7. Switch to datasheet view to see the output of the query, as shown in Figure 1-31. Notice that the Canadian addresses are excluded and that all the addresses are sorted by zip code.

ZipPostalCode	Company	Address1	Address2	Address3	City	StateProvince	Country
02077	Johnson Computer	114 East Main Stre			Scituate	MA	U.S.A.
02210	Coffee Bean Empo	One Orange Street			Boston	MA	U.S.A.
03580	Garnishes Inc.	100 West Second S			Franconia	NH	U.S.A.
05446-1672	Software Unlimited	25 Main Street			Colchester	VT	U.S.A.
07094	Jay's Conversions	Division of Data Cor			Secaucus	NJ	U.S.A.
11531	Applied Data Integr	102 Second Avenue	Suite 150		Garden City	NY	U.S.A.
12084	Minis & Micros	1 East Larner Aven			Guilderland	NY	U.S.A.
12484	New Age Computir	10 East Wilson Driv	Suite 20		Stone Ridge	NY	U.S.A.
12525	Ann's Kitchen	R.D. 2, Box 25			Saugerties	NY	U.S.A.
12558	Ed Smith Enterpris	12 Old Route 108			Fulton	NY	U.S.A.
15508	Xylox Corporation	25 Emery Drive	Suite 1000		Altoona	PA	U.S.A.
20092	Data Shapers, Inc.	14 Eye Street			Washington	DC	U.S.A.
20818-9988	Query Builders	P.O. Box 1000			Cabin John	MD	U.S.A.
29474	Systems Supply H	25 Route 129			Mount Pleasant	SC	U.S.A.
37744-4804	Industrial Repair Se	1000 Industrial Drive	Wing A		Greeneville	TN	U.S.A.
53595	Larry's Sofa Factor	R. D. 2, Box 50			Dodgeville	WI	U.S.A.
60778	Symbiotics Inc.	2000 Ashley Circle	Suite 2000		Ashford	IL	U.S.A.
80400	Pentacle Software	P.O. Box 1200			Denver	CO	U.S.A.
92714	Associated Specia	1000 Wilton Avenue			Gardena	CA	U.S.A.
94925	Code Cleaners	25 Ocean Boulevard			Corte Madera	CA	U.S.A.
95014-2132	Support Services	25 Rancho Bouleva			Santa Barbara	CA	U.S.A.
95119	David's Dry Goods	400 Via Rancho	Suite 240		San Jose	CA	U.S.A.
98035	Power Software	25 Eighth Avenue S	Suite 150	P.O. Box 1	Kent	WA	U.S.A.
98073-9717	Mabel's Old Fashic	1000 Garland Court			Redmond	WA	U.S.A.
98109	Astoria Manageme	150 Third Avenue N	Suite 150		Seattle	WA	U.S.A.

Record: |◄| ◄ | 1 | ► | ►I | ►* | of 25

Figure 1-31. Output of the union query

8. Save the new query with a name of your choice; in the sample database, it is called qryBothLists.

Discussion

The SQL UNION statement joins together the output of two or more SELECT statements into a single result set. The field names from the tables need not match, but they must be entered in the same order. If matching fields in the tables appear in different positions but have the same name, you must reorder them in the SELECT statements because Access uses the order of the fields—not their names—to determine which fields' data to combine together.

If a matching field is absent from one of the tables—as is the case for tblLeads, which lacks an Address3 field—you can include a constant. In the qryCombinedLists example, we used a zero-length string constant (""), but we could have used another constant, such as None or N/A.

You can also add a column called Type that contains either "Client" or "Lead," depending on which table it comes from, as shown in qryCombinedListswType in the sample database. Here's the SQL for that query:

```
SELECT Company, Address1, Address2, Address3, City, StateProvince, ZipPostalCode,
Country, "Client" AS Type
FROM tblClients
WHERE Country = "U.S.A."

UNION SELECT LeadName, Address1, Address2, "", City, State, Zip, Country,
"Lead" AS Type
FROM tblLeads
WHERE Country = "U.S.A."
ORDER BY ZipPostalCode;
```

While typing in the text of the union query, you may find it helpful to keep the source tables open in design view so you can be sure you are entering the field names correctly. Or you can just "cheat" and use the query designer to create SELECT statements that you copy and paste into your union query.

Some dialects of SQL require the SQL statement to end with a semicolon. Access does not, but it doesn't hurt to use the standard syntax, especially if you program in other databases too.

A union query is a snapshot of the data in the underlying tables, so it can't be updated.

To sort a union query, add one ORDER BY clause at the end of the last SELECT statement, referring to the sort fields using the field names from the first SELECT clause (as in the sample query). You can't sort each SELECT clause individually; you have to sort the whole union query. Any criteria should be included in WHERE clauses in the respective SELECT statements. You can't use one WHERE clause at the end of a union query to filter all the records.

A union query automatically screens out duplicate records (if any); if you want to include duplicates in the query's result set, use UNION ALL in place of the word UNION. This can also improve performance, since Access can skip the extra work of checking for duplicates.

1.12 Create a Combo Box That Allows a User to Select N/A

Problem

You'd like to be able to create a combo box that looks up items in a table and is limited to this list of items, but with the additional choice of <N/A>, which can be used to enter a null value for the field. You don't want your users to be able to enter any invalid entries, just <N/A> (or some other special code).

Solution

You can set the LimitToList property for the combo box to Yes to limit entries to those that your combo box provides and use a sorted union query to add an additional <N/A> row to the row source for the combo box. We suggest using <N/A> rather than simply N/A to force the entry to sort to the top of the combo box list. To make this work right, you'll need to make the combo box unbound and use a bit of VBA code to move values between the underlying table and the combo box.

To create a combo box with an <N/A> entry on a form of your own, follow these steps:

1. Create an unbound combo box that draws its records from a table. In the sample database, we created a combo box called cboArtistID on the form frmAlbums. To duplicate the combo box in the sample database, create a combo box with the properties shown in Table 1-6.

Table 1-6. Properties for the cboArtistID combo box

Property	Value
Name	cboArtistID
ControlSource	
RowSourceType	Table/Query
RowSource	
ColumnCount	2
ColumnHeads	No
ColumnWidths	0 in;2 in
BoundColumn	1

Table 1-6. Properties for the cboArtistID combo box (continued)

Property	Value
ListRows	8
ListWidth	2 in
LimitToList	Yes

The other properties for this control don't matter. We purposely left RowSource blank; you will fill this in after you create the union query. The ColumnWidths entries of "0 in;2 in" will make the first column, which will hold the ArtistID, hidden from the user. Only the second column, with the ArtistName (or <N/A>), will show.

2. Create a new query that will supply the values for the combo box control. Click on Close when you are prompted to add a table. Switch to SQL view by selecting Query → SQL Specific → Union. For the frmAlbums sample form, enter:

```
SELECT  ArtistID, ArtistName
FROM tblArtists

UNION

SELECT "<N/A>","<N/A>"
FROM tblArtists
ORDER BY ArtistName;
```

3. Save the query and close it. In this example, we saved the query as qryArtists.

4. Open the form again in design view, and select the name of the query you created in Steps 2 through 3 in the RowSource property of the combo box.

5. Select [Event Procedure] in the combo box AfterUpdate property, click the "..." button, and enter the following code:

```
Private Sub cboArtistID_AfterUpdate( )
    If cboArtistID = "<N/A>" Then
        ArtistID = Null
    Else
        ArtistID = cboArtistID
    End If
End Sub
```

6. Select [Event Procedure] in the form's OnCurrent property, click the "..." button, and enter the following code:

```
Private Sub Form_Current( )
    If IsNull(ArtistID) Then
        cboArtistID = "<N/A>"
    Else
        cboArtistID = ArtistID
    End If
End Sub
```

7. Run the form. You should now be able to select <N/A> from the list of values for the combo box. Null values will be entered in the ArtistID field in the table for those items, and as you scroll through the form they will show up as <N/A>.

To see how this works using the sample database, open the frmAlbums form in the 01-12.MDB database. You can use this form to edit or add new albums to tblAlbums. Add a new album that has no single artist. For example, enter a record for Woodstock, which is a compilation of multiple artists. When you pull down the Artist combo box you will see, at the top of the list, the choice <N/A> (see Figure 1-32). Select this item from the list and a null value will be entered into the underlying ArtistID long integer field.

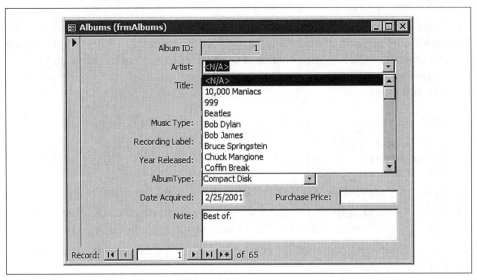

Figure 1-32. The Artist combo box with an <N/A> item

Discussion

The key to this solution is using a union query and an unbound combo box. You use a union query—which was discussed in the Solution in Recipe 1.11—to splice together the data from two tables. This union query is different from the usual variety because it combines the values in one table with values that you are providing in the query. This is accomplished by the union query's second SELECT statement, shown here:

```
UNION
SELECT "<N/A>","<N/A>"
FROM tblArtists
```

Notice that this SELECT statement selects two constants from a table. These constants aren't actually stored in the tblArtists table (or anywhere else, for that matter), but you need to refer to some existing table in the SELECT statement—we used tblArtists, since that table is already referenced in the query. This part of the query creates a single row that contains <N/A> in both the bound and displayed columns and combines it with the first half of the union query. Finally, the ORDER BY clause for the query tells Access to sort the entries by ArtistName, but because < comes before any letter in the alphabet, the <N/A> entry will sort to the top. If you run this query outside of the form, it will return a datasheet with a row made up of two constants and combined with the rows from tblArtists, as shown in Figure 1-33.

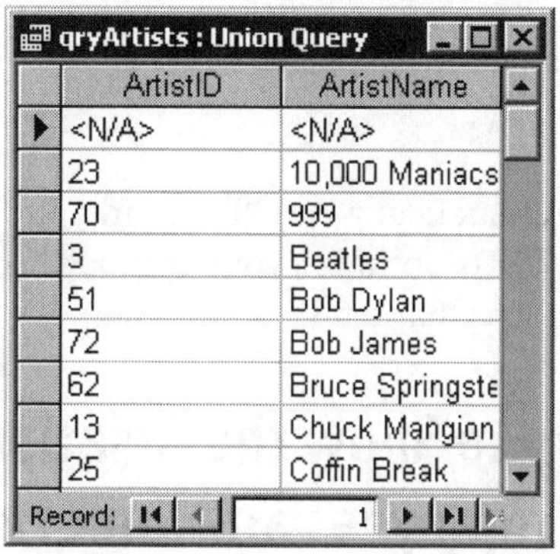

Figure 1-33. Datasheet returned by the union query

It is easy to see why <N/A> is entered in the displayed column (the second column)—that's the value you want the user to see. But why also place it in the first column? Actually, any value would work in the first column, as long as it doesn't match one of the actual values that might show up in that column. We used the same <N/A> value for simplicity. This first column is used by the VBA code only for setting and reading the value selected by the user. The VBA code in the Current event of the form takes care of selecting the correct row in the combo box when a record becomes current, and the code in the AfterUpdate event of the combo box enters the appropriate value into the ArtistID field when a selection is made.

You may wonder why we didn't use a combo box bound to the ArtistID field in the form. You might think that we could have used our union query to add a row with a null value in the first column and <N/A> in the displayed column. Unfortunately, this simple solution just won't work. When a combo box is set to null or even to "" it will always show a blank, even if there is a null (or "") value in a row in its bound column. The <N/A> value would not show up for records where the ArtistID was null—instead, the combo box would just be blank. To work around this column, we needed to use an unbound combo box and VBA code.

The combination of using the Current event of the form and the AfterUpdate event of a control is a common pattern when programming Access forms. Both events are needed to keep the user interface of a form in sync with data as the user edits the data and scrolls through the form. This pattern is often used with bound controls too—not just with unbound controls, as demonstrated in this example.

With simple text boxes, you can use the Format property of the text box to control how nulls are displayed. For example, a text box bound to a date field could have this Format setting:

Short Date;;;"<not scheduled>"

This will automatically display the specified message for null dates. The four optional parts of the Format setting respectively control positive, negative, zero, and null values. But this technique won't work for a combo box.

See Also

To fill a combo box programmatically, see "Programmatically Add Items to a List or Combo Box" in Chapter 7. To optimize your combo box performance, see "Make Combo Boxes Load Faster" in Chapter 8.

1.13   Use a Query to Show the Relationship Between Employees and Supervisors

Problem

You have a table that includes information on every employee in the company, including management. You'd like to be able to store information on who supervises each employee in this same table and then be able to create a query to show this hierarchical relationship.

Solution

You can display an employee-supervisor hierarchical relationship, also known as a *recursive relationship*, in Access with a select query that uses a self-join to join another copy of a table to itself. This solution shows how to create the table that will store the necessary recursive information and then how to create the self-join query to list each employee and his or her supervisor.

To create the employee table and a query that displays the recursive employee-supervisor relationship, follow these steps:

1. Create the employee table. This table should contain both an EmployeeID field and a SupervisorID field. These fields must have the same field size. In the sample database, tblEmployees contains the EmployeeID and SupervisorID fields. Because EmployeeID is an AutoNumber field with the FieldSize property set to Long Integer, SupervisorID must be a Number field with a FieldSize of Long Integer.

2. Enter data into the employee table, making sure that the SupervisorID field is equal to the EmployeeID field of that employee's immediate supervisor.

3. Create a new select query. Add two copies of the employee table. The second copy of the table will automatically have a "_1" appended to the end of the table name to differentiate it from the first one. Now join the two tables together by dragging the SupervisorID field from the first copy of the table (the one without the _1 suffix) to the EmployeeID field in the second copy of the table (the one with the _1 suffix).

4. Drag any fields you wish to include in the query to the query grid. The fields from the first copy of the table describe the employee; the fields from the second copy of the table describe the supervisor. Because the fields of the two tables have the same names—remember they're really two copies of the same table—you need to alias (rename) any fields from the second table to avoid confusion. For example, in the qryEmployeeSupervisors1 query, we included the following calculated field, named Supervisor, which displays the name of the employee's immediate supervisor:

```
Supervisor: [tblEmployees_1].[FirstName] & " " &
[tblEmployees_1].[LastName]
```

Notice that the fields that make up the supervisor name both come from the second copy of the employee table.

5. If you run the query at this point, you will get only employees with supervisors (see Figure 1-34). That's because this version of the query—named qryEmployeeSupervisors in the sample database—uses an inner join. To see all employees, even those without a supervisor (in our example this would include Shannon Dodd, the company's president), you must change the type of join between the two tables to a left outer join. Double-click on the join line you created in Step 3. At the Join Properties dialog, select choice #2 (see Figure 1-35).

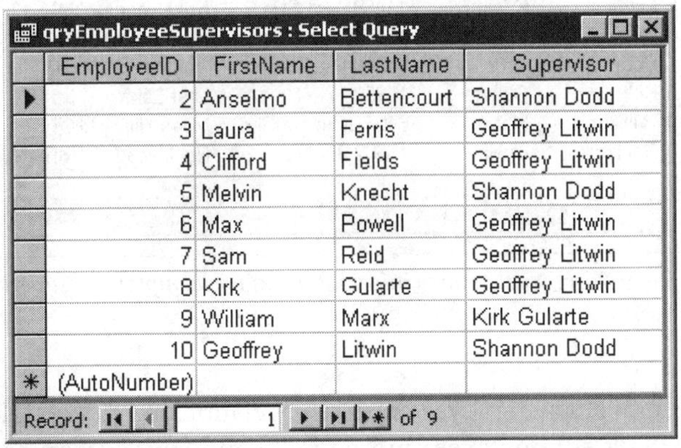

EmployeeID	FirstName	LastName	Supervisor
2	Anselmo	Bettencourt	Shannon Dodd
3	Laura	Ferris	Geoffrey Litwin
4	Clifford	Fields	Geoffrey Litwin
5	Melvin	Knecht	Shannon Dodd
6	Max	Powell	Geoffrey Litwin
7	Sam	Reid	Geoffrey Litwin
8	Kirk	Gularte	Geoffrey Litwin
9	William	Marx	Kirk Gularte
10	Geoffrey	Litwin	Shannon Dodd
(AutoNumber)			

Figure 1-34. This self-join query uses an inner join

6. Run the query, and the datasheet will display the employee-supervisor relationship.

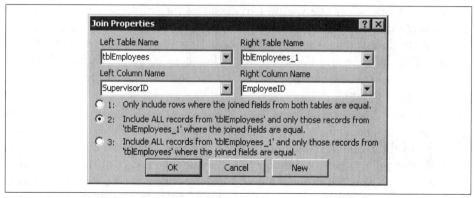

Figure 1-35. The Join Properties dialog allows you to create left or right outer joins

Now, open tblEmployees in *01-13.MDB*. This table, which is shown in Figure 1-36, contains a primary key, EmployeeID, and the usual name and address fields. In addition, it contains a field, SupervisorID, which stores the EmployeeID of the employee's immediate supervisor. Now run the query qryEmployeeSupervisors1. This query uses a self-join to display a recursive relationship between employee and supervisor; its datasheet lists each employee and his or her immediate supervisor (see Figure 1-37).

EmployeeID	FirstName	LastName	Address	City	State	SupervisorID
1	Shannon	Dodd	9283 Skyline Blvd.	Millers Falls	ID	
2	Anselmo	Bettencourt	2252 63rd Cir.	Indian Mound	AK	1
3	Laura	Ferris	13706 Pine Way	Lost Bridge	NH	10
4	Clifford	Fields	3504 Oak St.	Newport	VI	10
5	Melvin	Knecht	14958 43rd Blvd.	Rockwood	MN	1
6	Max	Powell	7927 Oceanside Ln.	Millers Falls	IL	10
7	Sam	Reid	2481 Luna Terr.	Oakview	SC	10
8	Kirk	Gularte	12350 57th St.	Lost Lake	NJ	10
9	William	Marx	6905 Johnson Blvd.	Moss Hill	CT	8
10	Geoffrey	Litwin	13602 93rd Ln.	Rockwood	MS	1

Figure 1-36. The SupervisorID field stores information on each employee's supervisor

Discussion

You can always model an employee-supervisor relationship as two tables in the database. Put all supervised employees in one table and supervisors in a second table. Then create a regular select query to list out all employees and their supervisors. This design, however, forces you to duplicate the structure of the employee table. It also means that you must pull data from two tables to create a list of all employees in the

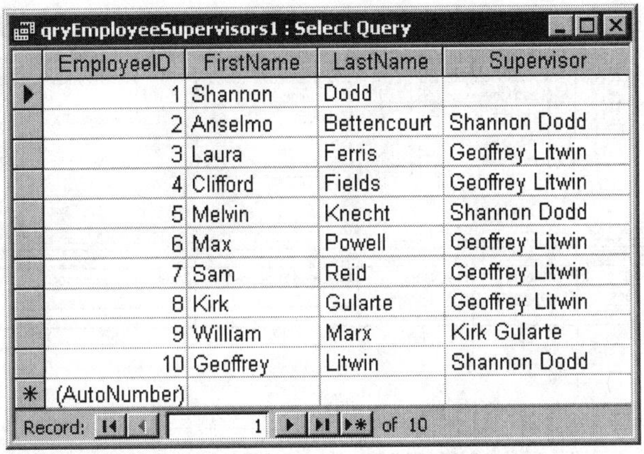

Figure 1-37. Output of qryEmployeeSupervisors1

company. Finally, this design makes it difficult to model a situation in which employee A supervises employee B, who supervises employee C.

A better solution is to store both the descriptive employee information and the information that defines the employee-supervisor hierarchy in one table. You can view the employee-supervisor relationship using a self-join query. You can create a self-join query by adding a table to the query twice and joining a field in the first copy of the table to a different field in the second copy of the table. The key to a self-join query lies in first having a table that is designed to store the information for the recursive relationship.

The sample query qryEmployeeSupervisors1 displays the employee-supervisor relationship to one level. That is, it shows each employee and his or her immediate supervisor. But you aren't limited to displaying one level of the hierarchy—the sample query qryEmployeeSupervisors3 displays three levels of the employee-supervisor relationship using four copies of tblEmployees and three left outer joins. The design of qryEmployeeSupervisors3 is shown in Figure 1-38; the output is shown in Figure 1-39.

You can use the Access Relationships dialog to enforce referential integrity for recursive relationships. Select Tools → Relationships to display the Relationships dialog and add two copies of the table with the recursive relationship. Join the two copies of the table together as if you were creating a self-join query. Choose to establish referential integrity, optionally checking the cascading updates and deletes checkboxes. Click on Create to create the new relationship. Now when you enter a value for SupervisorID, Access will prevent you from entering any reference to an EmployeeID that doesn't already exist.

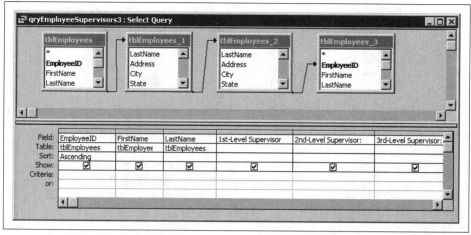

Figure 1-38. qryEmployeeSupervisors3 shows three levels of the employee-supervisor relationship

EmployeeID	FirstName	LastName	1st-Level Supervisor	2nd-Level Supervisor	3rd-Level Supervisor
1	Shannon	Dodd			
2	Anselmo	Bettencourt	Shannon Dodd		
3	Laura	Ferris	Geoffrey Litwin	Shannon Dodd	
4	Clifford	Fields	Geoffrey Litwin	Shannon Dodd	
5	Melvin	Knecht	Shannon Dodd		
6	Max	Powell	Geoffrey Litwin	Shannon Dodd	
7	Sam	Reid	Geoffrey Litwin	Shannon Dodd	
8	Kirk	Gularte	Geoffrey Litwin	Shannon Dodd	
9	William	Marx	Kirk Gularte	Geoffrey Litwin	Shannon Dodd
10	Geoffrey	Litwin	Shannon Dodd		

Record: 1 of 10

Figure 1-39. Output of qryEmployeeSupervisors3

Although the sample database uses an employee-supervisor relationship example, you can use the techniques discussed in this solution to model other types of hierarchical relationships. This will work, however, only if each "child" record has only one "parent." In this example, each employee has only one supervisor. For hierarchies in which one child can have many parents—such as parts and assemblies in a bill of materials database—a separate table is needed to contain the multiple records needed for each child, each one specifying a different parent.

1.14   Create a Query That Uses Case-Sensitive Criteria

Problem

You have a table of words, some of which appear multiple times. Each instance of these words is spelled using a different combination of upper- and lowercase. You'd like to create a query that finds exact matches using case-sensitive criteria, but no matter what you type into the criteria for the query, Access always returns all instances of the same word, disregarding each instance's case. Is there any way to create a query that can select records based on case-sensitive criteria?

Solution

Access normally performs case-insensitive string comparisons. You can use the Option Compare Binary statement in the declarations section of a module to force VBA to make string comparisons that are case-sensitive within the bounds of that module, but this affects only string comparisons made in a VBA module, not comparisons made by the Jet engine. Thus, even when you run the query from a VBA Option Compare Binary procedure, any comparisons made in the query are case-insensitive. The problem is that the Jet engine doesn't know how to make case-sensitive string comparisons using any of the standard query operators. Fortunately, you can create your own case-sensitive string-comparison function in an Option Compare Binary module and call this function from the query. This solution shows you how to create the VBA function and how to use it to perform case-sensitive searches.

To use this technique in your own database, follow these steps:

1. Import the basExactMatch module from 01-14.MDB into your database.

2. Create a query for which you wish to perform a case-sensitive search. Add all the desired fields in the query grid.

3. Create a computed field in the query grid that references the *acbExactMatch* function found in basExactMatch. For example, if you wish to compare the Word field with a user-entered parameter, create a field like that shown in Table 1-7.

Table 1-7. Settings for the acbExactMatch field

Attribute	Value
Field	acbExactMatch([Word], [Enter word])
Table	(Blank)
Sort	(Blank)
Show	(Unchecked)
Criteria	-1

You can also use a hard-coded string instead of a parameter. We used a parameter in the qryWordCS query, shown in design view in Figure 1-40.

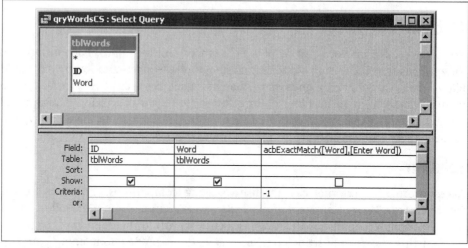

Figure 1-40. qryWordCS uses acbExactMatch to filter records using case-sensitive criteria

4. When you execute the query, it will return only exact, case-sensitive matches. If you run qryWordCS in the *01-14.MDB* database and enter "SwordFish" at the parameter prompt, you should get the datasheet shown in Figure 1-41.

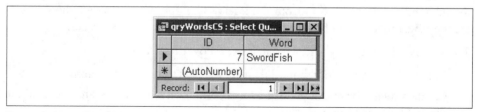

Figure 1-41. qryWordCS is case-sensitive, so it returns only one matching record

Now, open the tblWords table in *01-14.MDB* (see Figure 1-42). Notice that the word "swordfish" appears in four records, each spelled using a different combination of upper- and lowercase letters. Run the qryWordsCI parameter query and enter SwordFish at the prompt. When the query executes, it returns all four swordfish records, not the specific version you typed at the prompt. Now run the qryWordsCS query, entering the same string at the prompt. This time the query returns only one swordfish record, the one that's spelled exactly as you typed it.

Discussion

This solution uses a simple VBA function to perform a string comparison. Because this function resides in a module that contains the Option Compare Binary statement, any string comparisons made using procedures in this module are case-sensitive. The *acbExactMatch* function is simple:

Figure 1-42. tblWords contains four swordfish records with different capitalizations

```
Option Compare Binary
Public Function acbExactMatch(var1 As Variant, var2 As Variant) As Boolean
    acbExactMatch = (var1 = var2)
End Function
```

This function returns True only when the strings are spelled exactly the same way. The code compares the values in var1 and var2, and returns True if the values are equal, and False if they're not.

Another alternative, which provides slightly less flexibility, is to use the VBA *StrComp* function. This function can compare two strings on a binary basis (that is, it compares each character in the strings, taking case into account) and returns 0 if the two strings are exact matches. The syntax for calling *StrComp* in qryWordsCS looks like this:

```
StrComp([Word], [Enter Word], 0)
```

and the Criteria is 0 (not -1, as shown earlier).

1.15 Use a Query to Create a New Table Complete with Indexes

Problem

You know how to create a table from a make-table query, but when you create a table in this way it has no primary key or any other indexes. Furthermore, you can only create a new table with a structure based on that of an existing table. You'd like a way to create a table on the fly with the data types and field sizes you want and with appropriate indexes.

Solution

Access provides the data definition language (DDL) query, which is used to programmatically create or modify tables. It is one of the SQL-specific queries, which can be created only using SQL view. This solution shows you how to create and modify table definitions using DDL queries.

Follow these steps to create a table using a DDL query:

1. Design your table, preferably on paper, deciding which fields and indexes you wish to create. For example, before creating qryCreateClients, we came up with the design for tblClients shown in Table 1-8.

Table 1-8. Design for tblClients

FieldName	DataType	FieldSize	Index
ClientID	AutoNumber	Long Integer/Increment	Yes, primary key
FirstName	Text	30	Yes, part of ClientName index
LastName	Text	30	Yes, part of ClientName index
CompanyName	Text	60	Yes
Address	Text	80	No
City	Text	40	No
State	Text	2	No
ZipCode	Text	5	No

2. Create a new query. Click on Close at the Add Table dialog. Select Query → SQL Specific → Data Definition. This will place you in SQL view.

3. Enter a CREATE TABLE SQL statement. To create the sample table tblClients, enter the following SQL:

```
CREATE TABLE tblClients
(ClientID AutoIncrement CONSTRAINT PrimaryKey PRIMARY KEY,
FirstName TEXT (30),
LastName TEXT (30),
CompanyName TEXT (60) CONSTRAINT CompanyName UNIQUE,
Address TEXT (80),
City TEXT (40),
State TEXT (2),
ZipCode TEXT (5),
CONSTRAINT ClientName UNIQUE (LastName, FirstName) );
```

4. Save your query and run it by selecting Query → Run or clicking on the exclamation point icon on the toolbar. You should now see the newly created table in the database container.

To see how this works, open *01-15.MDB*. Note that there are no sample tables in this database. Open the sample DDL query, qryCreateClients (see Figure 1-43). Select Query → Run or click on the exclamation point icon on the toolbar to execute the DDL query. The tblClients table will be created, complete with a primary key and two other indexes.

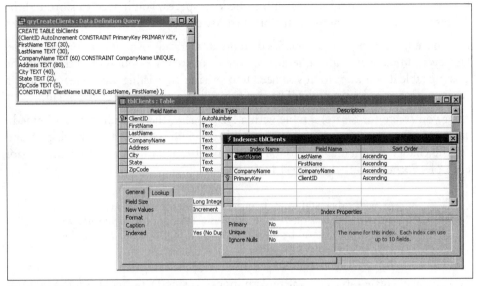

Figure 1-43. A sample DDL query and the table it creates

Discussion

When you run a DDL query, Access reads through the query's clauses and creates a table according to your specifications. This allows you to precisely control the structure of the table and its indexes.

A DDL query can contain only one data-definition statement. The five types of data-definition statements are:

CREATE TABLE
  Creates a table

ALTER TABLE
  Adds a new field or constraint to an existing table (a constraint creates an index on a field or group of fields)

DROP TABLE
  Deletes a table from a database

CREATE INDEX
  Creates an index for a field or group of fields

DROP INDEX
  Removes an index from a field or group of fields

Note that we specified the lengths of most of the text fields in the sample query to save space. If you don't specify a length for a text field in a DDL query, Access will assign it the maximum length of 255 characters, but that length won't necessarily affect the size of the database. The field length is just a maximum—the space is not used unless it is needed.

If you wish to create field names with embedded spaces, you'll need to surround the names with brackets; otherwise, the brackets are optional.

Like make-table queries, DDL queries do not automatically overwrite an existing table. However, unlike make-table queries, you aren't offered the option of overwriting the existing table if you want to. If you need to overwrite an existing table when running a DDL query, first execute another DDL query containing a DROP TABLE statement.

After you create (or delete) a table with a DDL query, the new table won't immediately appear in (or disappear from) the database window. To refresh the display and see the change you made, click on another object type in the database window (for example, Forms) and then on the Table tab again.

As with other SQL-specific queries, be careful not to switch a DDL query to another query type, such as a Select query. If you do, your SQL statement will be discarded, because SQL-specific queries don't have a design-view equivalent.

You can also create tables complete with indexes using Data Access Objects (DAO) or ADOX, using VBA code, and you can use DAO QueryDefs or ADO commands to execute your DDL statements in code.

New DDL syntax was added in Access 2000 (Jet 4.0), but few Access programmers ever used it because it didn't work in the SQL pane of the Access user interface. The only way to take advantage of the new syntax was by executing ADO commands. In Access 2002 and Access 2003, this syntax is supported inside of Access. For example, you can use ALTER TABLE ALTER COLUMN to change the data type of an existing field in a table. In the past, you had to drop the column and create a new one.

1.16   Save My Queries in a Table for Better Programmatic Access and Security

Problem

Your application uses a lot of queries, and you don't want these queries available or even visible to the users of your application. Also, you call your queries from VBA code. How can you hide the queries from users and make them easier to retrieve, modify, and execute?

Solution

You can create a query-management table that stores the SQL string of your queries in a memo field. Each query is named and includes a description. This technique allows you to store your queries in a table rather than in the Access collection of queries. You can also create a simple VBA function that you can use to quickly retrieve the SQL string of any of your saved queries.

Open and run frmSavedQueries from *01-16.MDB*. After a few moments of processing, the form shown in Figure 1-44 should appear. This form is based on the tblQueryDefs table, which stores a record for each query you save. To add a new query to the table, add a new record and enter the SQL statement in the SQL Text control. You may find it easier to copy the SQL from an existing query (see Step 2 for more details). Type in a name and description. Notice that creation and modification times are automatically updated.

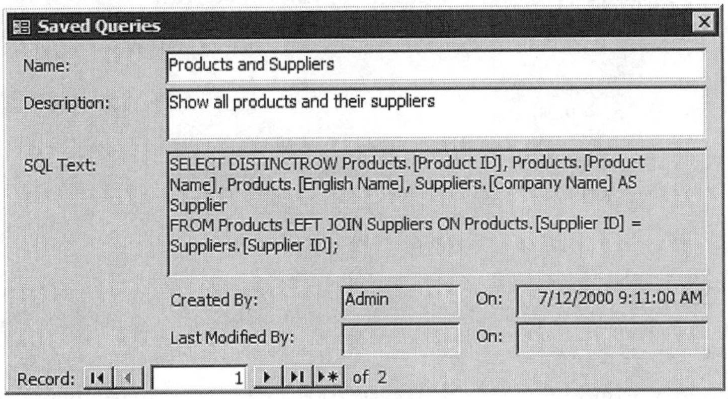

Figure 1-44. The saved queries form, frmSavedQueries

To use a saved query in your code, search the tblQueryDefs table for the name of a query and get the value from the SQLText field. To use this technique in your application, follow these steps:

1. Import the tblQueryDefs table, the frmSavedQueries form, and the basSavedQueries module from *01-16.MDB* into your database.

2. To add a query to the tblQueryDefs table using the frmSavedQueries form, design and test the query using the Access query designer. Then, from query design view, select View → SQL. When the query's SQL string is displayed, highlight it and copy it to the clipboard. Next, add a new record in the frmSavedQueries form and paste the SQL string into the SQLText text box. Type in a name and description.

3. To get the SQL string of a saved query, use the *acbGetSavedQuerySQL* function, located in the basSavedQueries module. The syntax for this function is:

```
strSQL = acbGetSavedQuerySQL("queryname")
```

where strSQL is the string variable in which you want to store the query's SQL string and queryname is the name of the saved query you want to retrieve.

Discussion

The core of this technique is a simple function that retrieves a value from the tblQueryDefs table. The function uses the Seek method to find the supplied value and, if it finds a match, returns the record's SQLText field value.

```
Public Function acbGetSavedQuerySQL(strName As String) As String

    ' Returns a SQL string from tblQueryDefs
    ' In  : strName - name of query to retrieve
    ' Out : SQL string

    Dim db As DAO.Database
    Dim rst As DAO.Recordset

    Set db = CurrentDb( )
    Set rst = db.OpenRecordset("tblQueryDefs")

    rst.Index = "PrimaryKey"
    rst.Seek "=", strName

    If Not rst.NoMatch Then
        acbGetSavedQuerySQL = rst!SQLText
    End If

    rst.Close
    Set rst = Nothing
    Set db = Nothing
End Function
```

(If you import this module into an Access 2000 or later database, make sure to use the Tools → References menu item to add a reference to the Microsoft DAO type library. The code uses DAO objects, and later versions of Access don't reference this library by default.) By extending this technique, you can create a replacement for saved queries in Access. Because you have full programmatic access to each query, you can load, modify, execute, and save queries at will without having to open QueryDef objects. Additionally, because you can store the queries table in a library database, you can completely remove a user's access to saved queries except through your code. One drawback of this technique is that you cannot base forms or reports on queries saved in tblQueryDefs without using some VBA code. However, this drawback is easily overcome by writing a function that retrieves a saved query's SQL string from tblQueryDefs and assigns the value to the form or report's RecordSource property before the form or report is run.

An obvious enhancement to this technique would be a conversion routine that reads each of your database's saved queries and converts them to records in the tblQueryDefs table. Once this conversion is complete, you can delete the queries from the database window.

Using saved queries gives you a slight performance advantage over saved SQL strings. The Jet database engine creates and saves a query plan the first time it runs a query after the design has been saved. With saved queries this plan can be reused, but with ad hoc queries a new plan must be generated each time. The time required to generate these plans, however, probably will not noticeably impact your performance. There are also ways to hide saved queries from users—you can give them names that start with "Usys" or set their Hidden property. You can also protect their design using Access security. Nevertheless, it is useful to understand that queries can be encapsulated in SQL strings, since you may find it helpful to be able to manage them yourself in a table rather than as Access objects.

1.17 Create a Recordset Based on a Parameter Query from VBA Code

Problem

You have a parameter query that is linked to a form by three parameters. When you open the form, enter the information into the form's controls to satisfy the parameters, and then run the query interactively, everything is fine. But when you open the form, satisfy the parameters, and create a recordset from VBA code based on the same query, you get an error message complaining that no parameters were supplied. This doesn't make sense, since you've already supplied the parameters on the form. Is there any way to create a recordset from VBA based on a parameter query?

Solution

When you run a parameter query from the user interface, Access can find the parameters if they have already been satisfied using a form and run the query. When you create a recordset from VBA, however, the Jet engine isn't able to locate the parameter references. Fortunately, you can help the Jet engine find the parameters by opening the QueryDef prior to creating the recordset and telling Jet where to look for the parameters.

Open the frmAlbumsPrm form found in *01-17.MDB*. This form, which is similar to a form used in the Solution in Recipe 1.1, is used to collect parameters for a query, qryAlbumsPrm. Select a music type from the combo box, enter a range of years in the text boxes, and click on OK. An event procedure attached to the cmdOK command button will run, making the form invisible but leaving it open. Now run qryAlbumsPrm from the database container. This query, which has three parameters linked to the now-hidden frmAlbumsPrm, will produce a datasheet limited to the records you specified on the form.

Now open the basCreateRst module from *01-17.MDB*. Select the function *CreatePrmRst1* from the Proc drop-down list. Its source code is shown here:

```
Public Sub CreatePrmRst1( )

    ' Example of creating a recordset based on a parameter query.
    ' This example fails!

    Dim db As DAO.Database
    Dim rst As DAO.Recordset

    Set db = CurrentDb( )

    ' Open the form to collect the parameters.
    DoCmd.OpenForm "frmAlbumsPrm", , , , , acDialog

    ' OK was pressed, so create the recordset.
    If IsFormOpen("frmAlbumsPrm") Then

        ' Attempt to create the recordset.
        Set rst = db.OpenRecordset("qryAlbumsPrm")

        rst.MoveLast

        MsgBox "Recordset created with " & rst.RecordCount & _
          " records.", vbOKOnly + vbInformation, "CreatePrmRst"

        rst.Close
    Else
        ' Cancel was pressed.
        MsgBox "Query canceled!", vbOKOnly + vbCritical, _
          "CreatePrmRst"
    End If

    DoCmd.Close acForm, "frmAlbumsPrm"
    Set rst = Nothing
    Set db = Nothing
End Sub
```

As you can see, this routine starts by opening the form in dialog mode to collect the three parameters. When the user satisfies the parameters and clicks OK, the form is hidden by an event procedure and control passes back to *CreatePrmRst1*. The procedure then attempts to create a recordset based on the parameter query and display a message box with the number of records found. To test this procedure, select View →
Debug Window and enter the following in the debug window:

```
Call CreatePrmRst1
```

The procedure will fail with error 3061—"Too few parameters. Expected 3"—at this line:

```
Set rst = db.OpenRecordset("qryAlbumsPrm")
```

Now select the function *CreatePrmRst2* from the Proc drop-down list. This subroutine is the same as *CreatePrmRst1*, except for some additional code that satisfies the query's parameters prior to creating the recordset. Run this version of the subroutine by entering the following in the debug window:

```
Call CreatePrmRst2
```

You should now see a dialog reporting the number of records in the recordset.

Discussion

The VBA code for the second version of the routine, *CreatePrmRst2*, is shown here:

```
Sub CreatePrmRst2( )

    ' Example of creating a recordset based on a parameter query.
    ' This example succeeds!

    Dim db As DAO.Database
    Dim qdf As DAO.QueryDef
    Dim rst As DAO.Recordset

    Set db = CurrentDb( )

    ' Open the form to collect the parameters.
    DoCmd.OpenForm "frmAlbumsPrm", , , , , acDialog

    ' OK was pressed, so create the recordset.
    If IsFormOpen("frmAlbumsPrm") Then

        ' Satisfy the three parameters before attempting to create a recordset.
        Set qdf = db.QueryDefs("qryAlbumsPrm")

        qdf("Forms!frmAlbumsPrm!cboMusicType") = Forms!frmAlbumsPrm!cboMusicType
        qdf("Forms!frmAlbumsPrm!txtYear1") = Forms!frmAlbumsPrm!txtYear1
        qdf("Forms!frmAlbumsPrm!txtYear2") = Forms!frmAlbumsPrm!txtYear2

        ' Attempt to create the recordset.
        Set rst = qdf.OpenRecordset( )

        rst.MoveLast

        MsgBox "Recordset created with " & rst.RecordCount & " records.", _
            vbOKOnly + vbInformation, "CreatePrmRst"

        qdf.Close
        rst.Close
    Else
        ' Cancel was pressed.
        MsgBox "Query cancelled!", vbOKOnly + vbCritical, "CreatePrmRst"
    End If

    DoCmd.Close acForm, "frmAlbumsPrm"
    Set qdf = Nothing
    Set rst = Nothing
    Set db = Nothing
End Sub
```

The main difference between the two procedures is the inclusion of the following lines of code prior to the line that creates the recordset:

```
Set qdf = db.QueryDefs("qryAlbumsPrm")

qdf("Forms!frmAlbumsPrm!cboMusicType") = Forms!frmAlbumsPrm!cboMusicType
qdf("Forms!frmAlbumsPrm!txtYear1") = Forms!frmAlbumsPrm!txtYear1
qdf("Forms!frmAlbumsPrm!txtYear2") = Forms!frmAlbumsPrm!txtYear2
```

The extra code opens the parameter QueryDef and then sets each of its parameters equal to its current value. You do this using the following syntax:

```
qdf("Parameter") = Parameter
```

Then the recordset is created based on the opened QueryDef:

```
Set rst = qdf.OpenRecordset( )
```

This time the recordset is created without a problem because you supplied the parameters prior to executing the OpenRecordset method.

You can also use this technique to satisfy parameters using VBA variables, instead of actually going to the form. For example, if you collected the parameters for qryAlbumPrm and stored them in three variables—*varMusicType*, *varYear1*, and *varYear2*—you could open the QueryDef and create the recordset using the following code:

```
Set qdf = db.QueryDefs("qryAlbumsPrm")

qdf("Forms!frmAlbumsPrm!cboMusicType") = varMusicType
qdf("Forms!frmAlbumsPrm!txtYear1") = varYear1
qdf("Forms!frmAlbumsPrm!txtYear2") = varYear2

Set rst = qdf.OpenRecordset( )
```

The advantage of using this approach instead of the one demonstrated in the Solution in Recipe 1.7, which uses a function to satisfy a parameter, is that this technique allows you to use the same parameter query and run it either interactively or from VBA code.

If you know that all your parameters are references to controls on forms, and if you do want to get the values from the forms, you can use a generic shortcut for filling in the parameter values. Thus, instead of hardcoding the parameter names, you could do this:

```
Dim prm as DAO.Parameter


For Each prm in qdf.Parameters
    prm.Value = Eval(prm.Name)
Next prm
```

If you feed a control reference to the Access *Eval* function, it will give you back the value contained in the control.

CHAPTER 2

Forms

As far as users of your applications are concerned, your forms *are* the application. The forms are the windows into the data that makes Access applications work. Access forms are incredibly flexible and can take on as many different personalities as there are Access developers. The tricks and techniques covered in this chapter are not as complex as ones you might find in other chapters of this book, but they will help form the foundation of your entire application. You'll want to use these tips to help give a consistent look to your forms and to help users find exactly which control currently has the focus. You'll also use them to control where users go on your forms by restricting their movement so they can't move to a new row until you allow them to and by giving your forms custom navigation controls. Your understanding of controls will grow as you learn to use option groups to collect and display non-numeric information and to control the display of multipage forms. You'll also learn how to resize the controls inside your forms to match the size of the form. You'll see how to combine controls to create new "hybrid" controls by linking a text box and a list box to form a combination that works like a permanently opened combo box, and you'll find out how to create your own pop-up forms, such as a replacement for Access's *InputBox* function. You'll learn how to save and restore program settings or application variables to the system registry and how to save and restore the size of your forms from one session to another. Finally, you'll learn how to control multiple instances of a form, allowing you to view multiple rows simultaneously.

2.1 Make Custom Templates for Forms and Reports

Problem

When you make a new blank form, the form properties and the properties of any control placed on it use the Access defaults. You've decided upon a standard look for your forms and reports that is significantly different from these defaults, and you spend too much time changing control properties on every new form you create to make them match your look. You'd like some way to change the standard default values.

Solution

Access allows you to specify a particular form or report to use as a template for new forms or reports that you create. This solution lists the steps you'll need to take to create your own template for form design. The technique is the same for form templates and report templates.

To see the advantages of using a template to define a new form's settings, load *02-01. MDB* and create a new form. Add controls of various types to the form. Notice that some of them look different from the normal Access defaults. To see where the properties are coming from, load the form named Normal from *02-01.MDB* in design mode. Each of the controls on this form will act as a template for any new controls on any forms you create in this database. In addition, any new form you create will inherit its own properties from this template form.

To create your own template form, follow these steps:

1. Create a new blank form.

2. Make any general changes you want in the form properties, such as changing the GridX and GridY properties to different settings—many users may prefer 24 24, the smallest grid that will show dots. To do this, first display the properties sheet: click on the gray in the upper-left corner of the form or select the Edit → Select Form menu item. If you don't want a record selector, navigation buttons, minimize or maximize buttons, a control box, and/or scrollbars on your form template, turn them off in the layout section of the form's properties sheet. In addition, you can choose to center the form automatically when it is opened by changing the AutoCenter property to Yes.

3. You may also wish to change the form's background color by changing the background color for the form's detail section (click on the detail section bar in form design to select the section). If you want your forms to have page headers/footers or form headers/footers, activate them by checking Format → Page Header/Footer or Form Header/Footer and set their colors as well.

4. Once you have finished setting up the form's general properties, repeat the process to change the default settings for each control you want to modify. There are two ways you can do this:

   • Click on the tool for that control in the toolbox and change the properties in the control's properties sheet. Note that when you do this, the properties sheet's titlebar says Default Label (or whatever control you have selected), as shown in Figure 2-1.

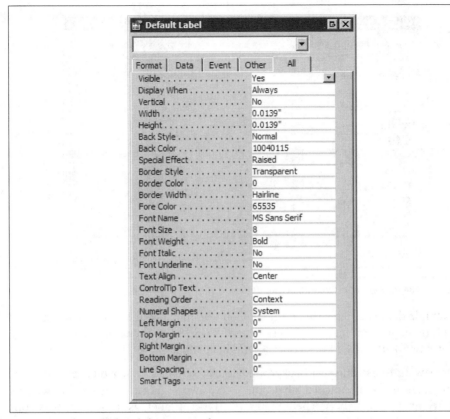

Figure 2-1. The Default Label properties sheet

- Change the controls directly on your form. Add to your form each control type you want to change, and set the properties visibly. Once you're done, select the Format → Set Control Defaults menu item, with all the controls selected.

5. Save your form with any name you like.

6. Finally, open the Tools → Options → Forms/Reports dialog, as shown in Figure 2-2. (The dialog box may appear differently in your version of Access.) Enter your form's name in the Form Template text box.

Discussion

Access normally uses a hidden form named Normal for its form template (and a report of the same name for its report template). If you don't specify your own default properties, all your new forms will use Access's built-in form, report, and control properties. If you create a form named Normal and set the default control and form properties for that form, Access will use that form as a template (that's how

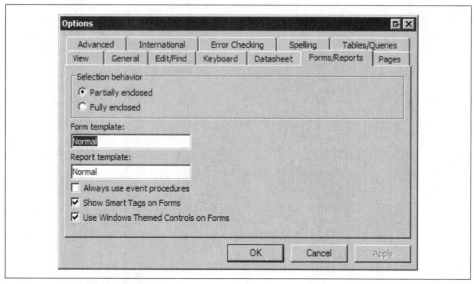

Figure 2-2. The Form/Report tab of the Options dialog

the example database has been configured). If you name your form something other than Normal, you can instruct Access to use that form as the template by changing the Form template value in the Tools → Options dialog.

You may want to use different background colors for labels attached to text boxes or combo boxes or for unattached labels, but Access won't let you save specific settings for different types of labels. There is just one type of label, as far as Access is concerned. The default label has one background color, and you must change it as needed depending on its attachment.

To make a report template, follow the same procedure as for a form template (you can omit controls that aren't useful on reports, such as combo boxes and command buttons).

A form or report template only supplies styles (such as color, presence of headers and/or footers, and grid granularity) to new forms; it doesn't supply the controls themselves. If you would like all your forms to contain standard controls at fixed locations, you'll need to make a copy of a standard form and work from that copy. If you copy the entire form, any code attached to the control's event procedures (in the form's module) will also be copied—that's not true if you use templates to create your new forms and reports.

The template form (or report) affects only *new* objects. If you create a form based on the template and then change the template, any previously created forms based on that template will not be affected.

You can maintain several form or report templates in your database. If you want a specific template for dialog forms and a different one for data-entry forms, keep them both in the database and change the option when you want to create a new form based on a specific template.

See Also

See "How Do I Set Control Properties?" in the Preface for more basic information on control properties.

2.2 Highlight the Current Field in Data-Entry Forms

Problem

The text cursor is too small in Access, and you can't always tell which text box on a form has the focus. You need some way to *really* highlight the current field.

Solution

There are many visual cues you can use to tell the user which text box contains the cursor. You can change the color of the text or the background, change the appearance of the text box, or change the appearance of the text box's label.

The simplest solution, which works quite well, is to change the BackColor and SpecialEffect properties of the active control. This solution uses some simple VBA code, which is attached to each control's Enter and Exit events, to do the work. Figure 2-3 shows the sample form, frmEffects, in use (with the City field currently selected).

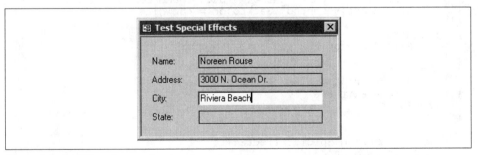

Figure 2-3. frmEffects in use, showing the active field

Open *02-02.MDB* and load frmEffects. As you move from field to field on the form, note that the special effect and the background color of each control change when you enter and again when you leave the control.

Follow these steps to create a form with this same sort of functionality:

1. Create a new module and name it basSpecialEffects. In the declaration section, create the following constants, which will represent the controls' SpecialEffect and BackColor property settings:

```
Option Compare Database
Option Explicit


Private Const conWhite = 16777215
Private Const conGray = -12632256
Private Const conIndent = 2
Private Const conFlat = 0
```

2. Create two functions named *SpecialEffectEnter* and *SpecialEffectExit* that will toggle the values of the BackColor and SpecialEffects properties for the text boxes. The completed module is shown in Figure 2-4.

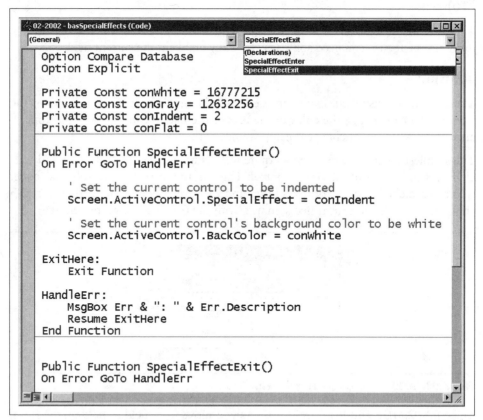

Figure 2-4. The completed basSpecialEffects module

Here are the code listings for the two functions:

```
Public Function SpecialEffectEnter( )
On Error GoTo HandleErr

    ' Set the current control to be indented.
    Screen.ActiveControl.SpecialEffect = conIndent

    ' Set the current control's background color to be white.
    Screen.ActiveControl.BackColor = conWhite

ExitHere:
    Exit Function

HandleErr:
    MsgBox Err & ": " & Err.Description
    Resume ExitHere
End Function

Public Function SpecialEffectExit( )
On Error GoTo HandleErr

    ' Set the current control to be flat.
    Screen.ActiveControl.SpecialEffect = conFlat

    ' Set the current control's background color to be gray.
    Screen.ActiveControl.BackColor = conGray

ExitHere:
    Exit Function

HandleErr:
    MsgBox Err & ": " & Err.Description
    Resume ExitHere
End Function
```

3. Create your input form, if you haven't already. In design mode, select all of the text boxes to which you'd like to attach this effect. (Shift-clicking with the mouse allows you to select multiple controls.) When you select a group of controls, you can set properties for all of them at once. Set the properties of this group of controls as shown in Table 2-1. Figure 2-5 shows the design surface with all the text boxes selected. (Note that once you select multiple controls, the properties sheet's title can no longer display the name of the selected control and it will only show "Multiple selection," as shown in Figure 2-5.)

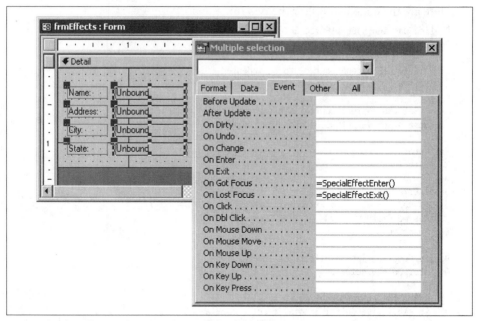

Figure 2-5. frmEffects in design mode, with all the text boxes selected

Table 2-1. Property settings for selected controls on frmEffects

Property	Value
BackColor	12632256
OnGotFocus	=SpecialEffectEnter( )
OnLostFocus	=SpecialEffectExit( )

4. Add the following code to the form's Load event procedure (see the Preface for information on creating event procedures):

```
Sub Form_Open (Cancel As Integer)
    Me.SetFocus
End Sub
```

Discussion

The *SpecialEffectEnter* and *SpecialEffectExit* functions do their work by reacting to the events that occur when you enter or leave a control on the form. Every time you enter one of the text boxes to which you've attached a function, Access executes that function. Therefore, whenever you enter one of these special text boxes, Access will cause the text box to appear sunken and will change its background color to white. When you leave the control (by tab or mouseclick), Access will set it back to being flat and will reset its background color to gray.

The pair of functions do their work for any control by using the built-in Screen. ActiveControl object. This object always provides a reference to the currently active control. Therefore, when you enter a control, the function acts on that particular control, setting the SpecialEffects and BackColor properties.

The only problem with this mechanism is that, when Access first opens a form, there *isn't* a current control. Attempting to refer to Screen.ActiveControl before the form is fully loaded results in an Access error. Because Access attempts to enter the first control on your form when it first opens the form and there isn't yet a current control, the code you've attached to that first text box's OnGotFocus event property will fail. To work around this problem, you need to use the code attached to the Open event, as shown in Step 4. This tiny bit of code forces Access to load the form completely before it attempts to enter the first text box on the form. You may find this technique useful in other applications you create that use Screen.ActiveControl.

The functions used in this solution could be extended to include many other changes to the controls as you enter and leave them. For example, you can change the font or its size, or the foreground color. You might wonder why this example calls functions directly from the Properties window, instead of using the standard mechanism for setting up event handlers. In this case, because multiple controls call the same procedures in reaction to the same events, it's simpler to set up the function calls directly from the Properties window. This isn't the only solution, but it's a quick and easy one, when you need to have multiple events of multiple controls call the same procedure.

See Also

See "How Do I Create a Module" in the Preface for information on creating a new module.

2.3   Restrict the User to a Single Row on a Form

Problem

When you press Tab or Shift-Tab, you can't keep Access from moving the cursor to the next or previous row of data if you happen to be on the first or last control in a form's tab order. The same thing happens when you press the PgUp or PgDn key. Often, however, you want the cursor to stay on the same row, and you want complete control over when the user moves to a different row. Is there some way to keep Access from moving the cursor to the next or previous row when these keys are pressed?

Solution

To gain complete control over row movement, you'll need to incorporate two different techniques. You can use your form's Cycle property to decide whether leaving the first or last control on the row moves you to a different row. If you want to ensure that PgUp and PgDn don't move the cursor to a different row, you'll need to write a bit of code that will trap these particular keystrokes in the KeyDown event for the form and disregard them. This solution uses both techniques to limit row movement.

Follow these steps to add this functionality to your own form:

1. Create your form. Set its Cycle property (on the Other properties page) to Current Record. This causes the Tab and Shift-Tab keys to work correctly.

2. Set the form's KeyPreview property (on the Event properties page) to Yes. This causes the form to intercept keystrokes before any controls on the form can react to them.

3. Enter the following code for the form's KeyDown event (see the Preface for information on creating event procedures).

```
Private Sub Form_KeyDown(KeyCode As Integer, Shift As Integer)
    Select Case KeyCode
        Case vbKeyPageUp, vbKeyPageDown
            KeyCode = 0
        Case Else
            ' Do nothing.
    End Select
End Sub
```

Figure 2-6 shows the form and its properties.

To see how this works, open and run frmRestricted from *02-03.MDB*. Press Tab to move from field to field. When you get to the final field on the form, press Tab once more, and your cursor will move back up to the first control, rather than moving on to the next row, as it normally would. The same thing occurs when you use Shift-Tab to move backward through the controls. When you reach the first control, the cursor will wrap around and go to the final control on the same row, rather than moving to the previous row. Try pressing the PgUp or PgDn keys: they're completely disregarded. The only way to move from row to row is to use the navigation buttons on the form. Try unchecking the Control Movement checkbox, and see how the default behavior differs.

Discussion

There are actually two techniques at work in this sample form. The first technique, using the form's Cycle property, forces the cursor to wrap around from bottom to top if moving forward through controls on the form, or from top to bottom if moving backward. You can set the property to All Records (the default), Current Record,

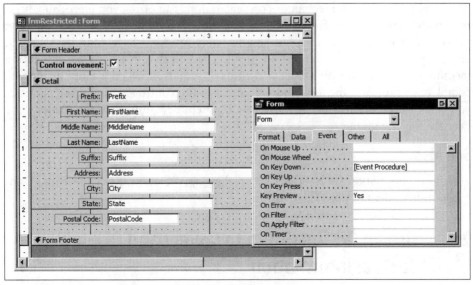

Figure 2-6. Use the KeyDown event to trap keystrokes and control form movement

or Current Page. This example uses the Current Record setting, which wraps around for each full record. The Solution in Recipe 2.5 uses the Current Page setting so that the cursor wraps around on the current page of a multipage form.

The second technique involves trapping keystrokes and convincing Access to disregard specific ones. A form's KeyDown event occurs every time you press any key, and Access informs the event procedure exactly which key was pressed by passing to it the *KeyCode* and *Shift* parameters; the former contains the keycode of the key pressed, and the latter is a flag that indicates whether or not the Shift key was depressed when the key designated by *KeyCode* was pressed. You want Access to ignore the keystroke if you press the PgUp or PgDn key. To make that happen, you can modify the value of the KeyCode parameter, setting it to 0. This tells Access that you want the keystroke to be ignored. Step 3 includes the code that performs this transformation. (Think what fun you could have intercepting each keystroke and converting it to something else behind the scenes, just to amuse your users!)

The sample form uses the following code, in reaction to the check box's AfterUpdate event, to control how the form reacts to keystrokes:

```
Private Sub chkMovement_AfterUpdate( )
    If Me.chkMovement Then
        Me.Cycle = acbcCycleCurrentPage
        Me.OnKeyDown = "[Event Procedure]"
    Else
        Me.Cycle = acbcCycleAllRecords
        Me.OnKeyDown = vbNullString
    End If
    Me.Prefix.SetFocus
End Sub
```

If you're going to use the techniques presented in this solution, you'll probably want to provide some method of navigating through the rows on your form. You could use the built-in navigation buttons, but you probably wouldn't have gone to this much effort if you didn't want a bit more control. The Solution in Recipe 2.6 provides a method you can use for placing your own navigation buttons on a form, giving you complete control over the look and placement of the controls. Using those controls, you can ensure that users can't move to a different row until they've satisfied your needs in the current one.

See Also

For more information on handling keystrokes, see "Classify Keypresses in a Language-Independent Manner" in Chapter 11.

2.4   Use an Option Group to Collect and Display Textual Information

Problem

Option groups are great for collecting and displaying numeric values, but sometimes you need to use an option group bound to a column of values that isn't numeric. For instance, in each row you have a field that contains just one of four different alphabetic codes. You want some way to let the user choose from those four codes on a form.

Solution

When you want a control on a form bound to a column in a table that contains a few alphabetic items, you usually can use a list or combo box to display and collect the information. Sometimes, though, you want to be able to use an option group, where you can have option buttons or even toggle buttons containing pictures. But option groups, as Access implements them, can be bound only to numeric columns.

The solution is to use an unbound option group. Rather than moving the data directly from the form to the underlying data, you'll make a pit stop along the way.

Open and run frmOptionExample in *02-04.MDB*. This form, shown in Figure 2-7, pulls in two columns from the underlying table, tblShipments. Each row contains a Contents field and a Shipper field. The Shipper field can be just one of four values: UPS, Fed Ex, US Mail, or Airborne. The form displays the Contents field in a text box and the Shipper field in an option group. It also shows another text-box control: the pit stop mentioned earlier. This (normally hidden) text box is the bound control, not the option group.

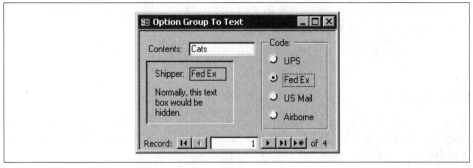

Figure 2-7. Example form using an option group to store character data

To create a minimal sample form that works with the same data, follow these steps:

1. In *02-04.MDB*, create a new form. Choose tblShipments for the form's Record-Source property.

2. Create controls on your new form, as shown in Table 2-2. Make sure that you've created the option group before you attempt to place any option buttons inside it. The option group should turn dark when you attempt to place an option button in it.

Table 2-2. Control properties for the new sample form

Control type	Property	Value
Option group	Name	grpCode
Option button (UPS)	Name	optUPS
	OptionValue	1
Option button (Fed Ex)	Name	optFedEx
	OptionValue	2
Option button (US Mail)	Name	optUSMail
	OptionValue	3
Option button (Airborne)	Name	optAirborne
	OptionValue	4
Text box	Name	txtShipper
	ControlSource	Shipper

3. Create the following event procedure in the form's OnCurrent event:

```
Private Sub Form_Current( )
    Me.grpCode = Switch( _
    Me.txtShipper = "UPS", 1, _
    Me.txtShipper = "Fed Ex", 2, _
    Me.txtShipper = "US Mail", 3, _
    Me.txtShipper = "Airborne", 4)
End Sub
```

4. Create the following procedure in the option group's AfterUpdate event:

```
Private Sub grpCode_AfterUpdate( )
    Me.txtShipper = Choose( _
    Me.grpCode, "UPS", "Fed Ex", "US Mail", "Airborne")
End Sub
```

Discussion

Using just two simple event procedures, you've managed to make the sample form store the data as required. The example works because of two distinct events and two distinct VBA functions that you call from those events.

The form's Current event occurs every time you move from one row to another in the underlying data. In this case, you'll need to convert the data from its raw form (as the shipper's code text strings) into a format that the option group on the form can display for each row as you move to that row.

The option group's AfterUpdate event occurs whenever you change its value. For this control, choosing any of the option buttons within it will trigger the event. Use this event to place a new value into the text box on the form, which is directly bound to the correct column in the underlying data.

When you want to convert the raw data into an integer representation (so the option group can display the value), use the *Switch* function. Its syntax is:

```
returnValue = Switch(expr1, value1 [,expr2, value2][, expr3, value3]...)
```

Access will evaluate *each* of the expressions but will return the value corresponding to the first one that returns a True value. In this example, the *Switch* function assigns the value of this expression:

```
Switch([txtShipper] = "UPS", 1, [txtShipper] = "Fed Ex", 2, _
    [txtShipper] = "US Mail", 3, [txtShipper] = "Airborne", 4, Null, Null)
```

to the option group. If the value in [txtShipper] is "UPS," the option group gets the value 1. If [txtShipper] is "Fed Ex," the option group is 2, and so on. The final pair (the two Null values) ensures that if the value of [txtShipper] is Null, the option group will be Null too. Access calls this function from the form's Current event, so that every time you move from row to row, Access assigns the appropriate value to the option group based on what it finds in the bound text box.

To convert a choice made in the option group into its appropriate text value to be stored in the table, use the *Choose* function. Its syntax is:

```
returnValue = Choose(index, value1 [, value2][, value3]...)
```

Based on the value in *index*, the function will return the matching value from its list of values. In our example, the code assigns the value of this expression:

```
Choose([grpCode], "UPS", "Fed Ex", "US Mail", "Airborne")
```

to the bound text box once you've made a selection in the option group. If you choose item 1 from the option group, it'll assign "UPS" to the text box. If you choose option 2, it'll assign "Fed Ex," and so on.

You can use the two events (After Update and Current) and the two functions described here to handle your conversions from integers (option group values) to text (as stored in the table), but you should be aware of a few limitations that apply to the *Switch* and *Choose* functions:

- Both functions support only a limited number of options. *Switch* can support up to seven pairs of expressions/values. *Choose* can support up to 13 expressions. If you need more than that, you'll need to convert your event handlers to VBA. Of course, you should avoid putting more than seven items in an option group anyway.

- Both functions evaluate *all* of the expressions they contain before they return a value. This can lead to serious errors unless you plan ahead. The following expression details the worst possible case:

```
returnVal = Choose(index, MsgBox("Item1"), MsgBox("Item2"), MsgBox("Item3"), _
 MsgBox("Item4"), MsgBox("Item5"), MsgBox("Item6"), MsgBox("Item7"), _
 MsgBox("Item8"), MsgBox("Item9"), MsgBox("Item10"), MsgBox("Item11"), _
 MsgBox("Item12"), MsgBox("Item13"))
```

You might assume that this expression would display the message box corresponding only to the value of *index*, but in fact it will always display 13 message boxes, no matter what the value of *index* is. Because *Switch* and *Choose* both evaluate all of their internal expressions before they return a value, they both execute any and all functions that exist as parameters. This can lead to unexpected results as Access runs each and every function used as a parameter to *Switch* or *Choose*.

In most cases, you'd be better off using a list or combo box with a separate lookup table, allowing your users to choose from a fixed list. If you have a small number of fixed values and you need to store those values in your table (as opposed to an *index* value from a small lookup table), the technique presented here should work fine.

To use the techniques outlined here in your own applications, you'll need to modify the screen display and the code. Once you've done that, you should be able to use an option group to gather text information.

2.5 Display Multiple Pages of Information on One Form

Problem

You have a large number of fields that you need to display on a form. If you place them all on the form at once, it looks too complicated. You need some way to group them by category and display only the ones that correspond to each category as the user works through all the groups.

Solution

Access 97 introduced the native Tab control, which is useful for organizing information into multiple pages. Simply organize your fields into categories, creating one page on the Tab control for each category.

Load *02-05.MDB* and open frmMain. This sample form (shown in Figure 2-8) contains a Tab control. By clicking on a tab, you cause one of the four possible pages of the form to be displayed in the Tab control section.

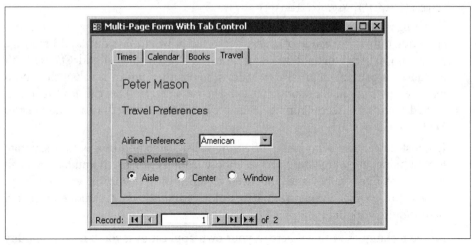

Figure 2-8. The sample form, frmMain

To create your own version of a multipage form, follow these steps:

1. Create the table and/or query on which you want to base your form (tblSample in *02-05.MDB*). Make sure your data includes a primary key (ID in tblSample).

2. Open your form (frmMain in *02-05.MDB*) in design view. Insert a Tab control on the form.

3. Set at least the properties shown in Table 2-3 for the form itself.

Table 2-3. Form property values for the main form, frmMain

Property	Value
RecordSource	tblSample (or the name of your table or query)
AllowAdditions	No
ViewsAllowed	Form
RecordSelectors	No

4. Right-click on the Tab control to add two more tabs, so that there are a total of four. Figure 2-9 shows the Tab control with the right-click menu options. Note the other Tab control options that are also available from the right-click menu. Give each tab one of the following captions: Times, Calendar, Books, and Travel.

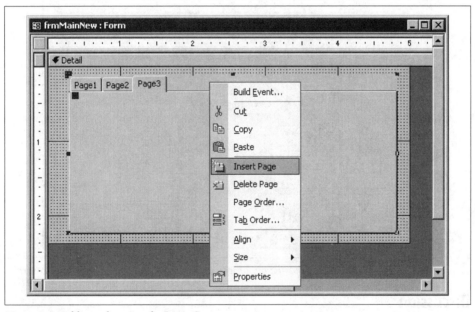

Figure 2-9. Adding tabs using the Insert Page pop-up menu option

5. Add controls to each tab on the Tab control. Note that as you select each tab, the background turns dark. This will cause the controls dropped on that page to appear only on that page.

6. To create a control that appears on all of the pages, drag the control from the Field List to the form, not the Tab control. If you then drag it from the form to the Tab control, none of the tabs will be selected. This will cause the control to appear on all of the pages. The Name text box will be visible on every page of the Tab control.

7. Set the Cycle property of the form to Current Page, so that you won't move from record to record by tabbing around the form. (See The Solution in Recipe 2.3 for more information on the Cycle property.) To move from page to page on the Tab control, press Ctrl-Tab. Ctrl-Shift-Tab will move you backward from page to page on the Tab control.

8. Use the View → Tab Order dialog to set the tab order for the controls on your form. To set the tab order inside of the Tab controls, right-click on the page of the Tab control where you want to set the tab order, and choose Tab Order. This will load the dialog shown in Figure 2-10, where you can change the tab order for the individual controls on that tab page.

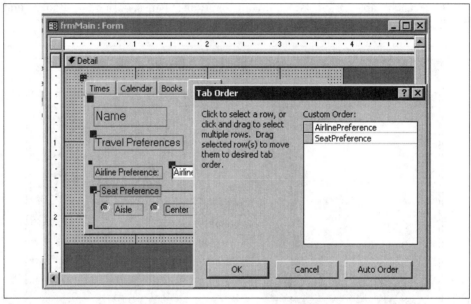

Figure 2-10. The Tab Order dialog sets the tab order for the controls on a page in the Tab control

Discussion

There are three other methods that you can use to create multipage forms, but each of these methods requires more work than using the Tab control:

- You can create a continuous form with page breaks in between the pages. If you open the form in dialog view, the user will be prevented from maximizing the form. You can write code utilizing the GoToPage method of the form to navigate from page to page.

- You can use multiple subforms, placing each of the subforms on the main form and setting all but one of them to be invisible. In the AfterUpdate event of the option group, you can make the current subform invisible and the new one visible. This method can be cumbersome because working with long multipage forms can be awkward. This method also consumes more system resources than the method shown in this solution.

- You can create one subform control and, in reaction to pressing buttons in the option group, change the SourceObject property of the subform control. This is a very "neat" solution, because there's only one subform on the main form (as opposed to four in the previous alternative). The drawback here is that changing the SourceObject property is quite slow.

2.6 Provide Record Navigation Buttons on a Form

Problem

You'd like to provide some mechanism for allowing users to move from row to row on a form, but you think the navigation buttons Access provides are too small and unattractive. Also, you can't control when the user can or can't move to another row.

Solution

Access provides navigation buttons for you to use on forms, allowing you to move easily from row to row. However, you can neither move nor resize these buttons, and you can't change anything about their appearance.

You can create your own buttons, place them on a form, and have each button use the GoToRecord macro action. Unfortunately, this has two drawbacks:

- If you attempt to move to the previous or next row and you're already at the end of the recordset, the macro will fail. The GoToRecord macro action just isn't smart enough to work in this case.

- Your buttons will always be available, giving no indication of when you can use them.

To avoid errors, you *must* use VBA. This solution demonstrates the steps you can take to add the appropriate code to your application so that navigation buttons will move you safely from row to row and shows how to disable the navigation buttons when they are unavailable. The form frmNav in *02-06.MDB* (see Figure 2-11) works this way. You can load it and give it a try before attempting to build your own. Use the navigation buttons to move from row to row (there are only a few rows in the table so far). Note that, as you move around in the table, the appropriate buttons become enabled and disabled. Also try using the PgUp and PgDn keys. You'll see that the appropriate buttons still become disabled as necessary. Try entering a row number into the text box in the navigation controls; when you leave the text box, you will move to the selected row number.

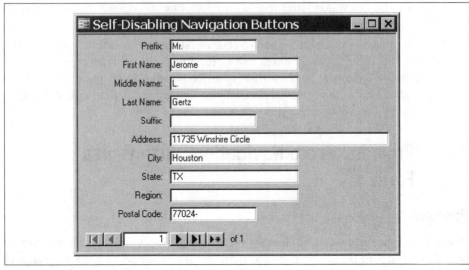

Figure 2-11. The frmNav form

Follow these steps to include this functionality in your own applications:

1. Set your form's properties as shown in Table 2-4, removing the form's scrollbars and built-in navigation buttons. (Because this method works only for scrolling through rows of data, your form must also have its RecordSource property set so that the form displays rows of data.)

Table 2-4. Property settings for forms to remove the built-in navigation buttons

Property	Value
ScrollBars	Neither
NavigationButtons	No

2. Copy the buttons from frmNav, or create your own five buttons on your form. Do not use the Access Button Wizard to create your buttons, because it will add inappropriate code to the buttons; you want to be able to supply the code yourself. If you create your own buttons, you can add pictures from Access's selection of pictures. Click on the Build button to the right of the Picture property on the properties sheet for each button. Also, create a text box named txtCurrentRow to display the current row number and a label named lblTotalRows to display the total number of rows. (In these solutions, the exact names of the controls you create usually don't matter. In this one, however, the names do matter; make sure your names match ours exactly.)

3. Set the Name property for each of the command buttons, based on the following list (the code you'll use later depends on these particular names):

cmdFirst

cmdPrev

cmdNew

cmdNext

cmdLast

4. Add the following code to cmdFirst's Click event (for information on adding code to a form event, see the Preface):

```
Private Sub cmdFirst_Click( )
    acbMoveFirst Me
End Sub
```

5. Add the following code to cmdPrev's Click event:

```
Private Sub cmdPrev_Click ( )
    acbMovePrevious Me
End Sub
```

6. Add the following code to cmdNew's Click event:

```
Private Sub cmdNew_Click ( )
    acbMoveNew Me
End Sub
```

7. Add the following code to cmdNext's Click event:

```
Private Sub cmdNext_Click( )
    acbMoveNext Me
End Sub
```

8. Add the following code to cmdLast's Click event:

```
Private Sub cmdLast_Click ( )
    acbMoveLast Me
End Sub
```

9. Add the following code to your form's Current event:

```
Private Sub Form_Current ( )
    acbHandleCurrent Me
End Sub
```

10. Add the following code to your form's KeyPress event:

```
Private Sub Form_KeyPress(KeyAscii As Integer)
    acbHandleKeys Me
End Sub
```

11. Set the form's KeyPreview property to True.

12. Add the following code to txtCurrentRow's AfterUpdate event:

```
Private Sub txtCurrentRow_AfterUpdate( )
    acbMove Me, Me.txtCurrentRow
End Sub
```

13. Import the basMovement module from *02-06.MDB* into your own application. (You'll need to verify that you've also set a reference to Microsoft DAO, using the Tools → References menu item from within the VBA editor. This code uses the DAO library, and later versions of Access don't add this reference by default.)

Discussion

This solution actually has three parts. The first part deals with the record navigation (Steps 1 through 8), the second part handles disabling the unavailable buttons (Steps 9 through 11), and the third part controls the direct movement to a specific row (Step 12).

For each of the five buttons, you've attached code that will call a common procedure whenever you press the button, thus reacting to the Click event. For each button, the subroutine you call calls a procedure that handles all the motion. Clicking on the first button calls this code:

```
Public Sub acbMoveFirst(frm As Form)
    HandleMovement frm, acFirst
End Sub
```

which calls the *HandleMovement* procedure:

```
Private Sub HandleMovement(frm As Form, intWhere As Integer)
    ' It's quite possible that this will fail.
    ' Knowing that, just disregard any errors.
    On Error Resume Next
    DoCmd.GoToRecord , , intWhere
    On Error GoTo 0
End Sub
```

Every subroutine that calls *HandleMovement* passes to it a reference to a form and an Access constant that indicates to what row it wants to move (acFirst, acPrevious, acNewRec, etc.). *HandleMovement* disables error handling, so Access won't complain if you try to move beyond the edges of the recordset. *HandleMovement* then uses the GoToRecord macro action to go to the requested row.

The second, and most complex, part of this solution handles enabling/disabling the buttons, depending on the current row. In Step 9, you attached a subroutine call to the form's Current event. This tells Access that every time you attempt to move from one row to another, Access should call this procedure before it displays the new row of data. This procedure, then, can do the work of deciding where in the recordset the current row is and, based on that information, can disable or enable each of the five navigation buttons. It also fills in the current row number and updates the display of the total number of rows.

A discussion of the full *acbHandleCurrent* code is beyond the scope of this solution (you can find the fully commented code in basMovement). As part of its work, however, the code must determine whether the current row is the "new" row. The new row is the one you get to if you press the PgDn key until you're on the last row of data and then press the key once more (if your data set allows you to add rows). Access's NewRecord property tells you if you're on the new row. (See the Solution in Recipe 6.2 for more information on using this property.)

To enable cmdNew once you've entered some data on the new row, the form's Key-Press event calls *acbHandleKeys*, as shown here. This code checks each keystroke, and if cmdNew isn't enabled and the form is dirty, the code enables cmdNew.

```
Public Sub acbHandleKeys(frm As Form)

    Dim fEnabled As Boolean
    fEnabled = frm.cmdNew.Enabled
    If Not fEnabled And frm.Dirty Then
        frm.cmdNew.Enabled = True
    End If
End Sub
```

To match the functionality of the standard Access navigation controls, the sample form reacts to the AfterUpdate event of the txtCurrentRow text box by moving to the row you've specified. The event procedure calls the *acbMove* subroutine, which does all the work. This procedure, shown later, does the following:

1. Retrieves a pointer to the form's recordset, using the recordset retrieved with the form's RecordsetClone property.
2. Moves to the first row (rst.MoveFirst) and then moves the specified number of rows from there (rst.Move).
3. Makes the form display the same row that's current in the recordset.

By equating the form's bookmark (a binary value, indicating the current row, whose exact contents are of no interest) and the recordset's bookmark, you make the form display the row that is current in the underlying recordset. If there is no current row (that is, if you've asked to go beyond the final row of data), an error occurs, and the code moves you directly to the new row on the form.

The source code for *acbMove* is:

```
Public Sub acbMove(frm As Form, ByVal lngRow As Long)

    ' Move to a specified row.
    On Error GoTo HandleErr
    Dim rst As DAO.Recordset

    ' Get a pointer to the form's recordset.
    Set rst = frm.RecordsetClone

    ' Move to the first row, and then hop to
    ' the selected row, using the Move method.
    rst.MoveFirst
    If lngRow > 0 Then
        rst.Move lngRow - 1
    End If
    ' Finally, make the form show the
    ' same row as the underlying recordset.
    frm.Bookmark = rst.Bookmark
    rst.Close
    Set rst = Nothing
```

```
ExitHere:
    Exit Sub

HandleErr:
    ' If an error occurs, it's most likely that
    ' you requested to move to the row past the
    ' last row, the New row, and there's no bookmark
    ' there.  If that's the error, just move
    ' to the New row programmatically.
    Select Case Err
        Case acbcErrNoCurrentRow
            DoCmd.GoToRecord , , acNewRec
            Resume Next
        Case Else
            MsgBox Error & " (" & Err & ")"
            Resume ExitHere
    End Select
End Sub
```

The code provided in basMovement makes it easy for you to move this functionality from one application to another just by hooking the correct form and control events. You can get similar results by creating your own toolbar and using the record navigation buttons that Access provides. A toolbar you create will control whatever form happens to be the current form. Figure 2-12 shows a form/toolbar combination in action. You'll need to decide for yourself which technique you like best. The toolbar approach is simpler, but it is difficult to move toolbars from one database to another, and they do clutter up the work area. You also have little programmatic control over the toolbars.

The sample form updates the display of the total number of rows in lblTotalRows every time you move from row to row. When you first open the form, Access may not yet know how many rows will be in the recordset, and the value returned in the recordset's RecordCount property may be inaccurate. You can move to the last row when you first open the form, forcing Access to find out how many rows there will be, but this can be slow if your form's recordset contains a large number of rows. Access continues to calculate as you use the form, and eventually it will supply the correct value in the RecordCount property of the form's recordset. The compromise is that the total number of rows may be incorrect until you use the form for a few seconds. If this bothers you, you can add to the form's Open event code that works like this:

```
Dim rst As DAO.Recordset

Set rst = Me.RecordsetClone
rst.MoveLast
```

For small recordsets, this will be fast but also unnecessary, because the Record-Count property will already be accurate. For large recordsets, this might take a few seconds to calculate and will make opening your form seem slower.

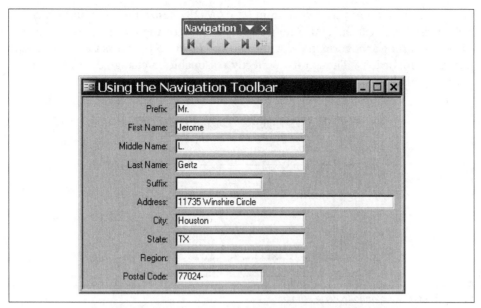

Figure 2-12. A record navigation toolbar can replace navigation buttons on the form

See Also

For more information on using DAO in Access databases, see "How Do I Use Data Access Objects (DAO) in New Databases?" in the Preface.

2.7 Size a Form's Controls to Match the Form's Size

Problem

Windows users have become accustomed to resizing forms on their screens. A professional-looking application will proportionally resize the controls on a form when you stretch or shrink that form. You'd like to be able to resize your forms while the application is running and have the controls on the form react appropriately. For example, the Database Explorer window's list box expands when you expand the window. How can you do this on your own forms?

Solution

Because Access can notify your application when the user resizes a form, you can attach code to the Resize form event and react to the change in size. Access also triggers this event when it first draws the form, so you can place your controls correctly then, too. Base your calculations on the form's InsideWidth and InsideHeight properties.

Load and run the form frmExpando in *02-07.MDB*. Resize the form and watch the size of the large text box. Also notice the positions of the two command buttons. Figure 2-13 shows the form in design mode, and Figure 2-14 shows the form sized to different proportions. Though it's perfectly reasonable to change the size of all the controls, this form does not. It uses three different techniques:

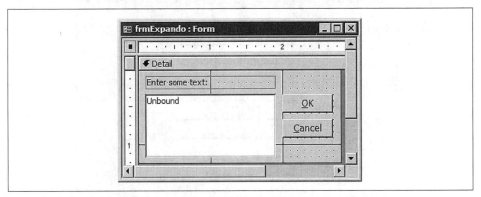

Figure 2-13. frmExpando in design mode

Do nothing
> The label above the text box doesn't change at all as you resize the form.

Change position only
> The two command buttons move with the right edge of the form, but they don't change size.

Change size
> The large text box changes its size to match the size of the form.

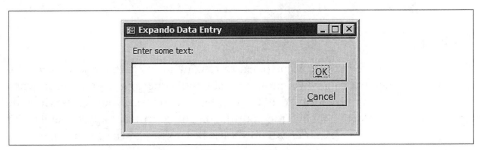

Figure 2-14. frmExpando at runtime, with different proportions

The code that does the work in this case is specific to the particular form. Follow the steps below to create a form similar to frmExpando. Once you've gone through these steps, you should be able to expand on the concepts (pun intended) and create your own self-sizing forms.

1. Create a new form and create controls and properties as shown in Table 2-5.

Table 2-5. Controls and their properties for frmExpando

Control type	Property	Value
Label	Name	lblSample
	Left	0.1 in
	Top	0.0833 in
	Width	1.7917 in
	Height	0.1667 in
	Caption	Enter some text
Text box	Name	txtEntry
	Left	0.1 in
	Top	0.3333 in
	Width	1.8 in
	Height	0.8333 in
Command button (OK)	Name	cmdOK
	Caption	&OK
	Left	2 in.
	Top	0.3333 in
	Width	0.6979 in
	Height	0.25 in
Command button (Cancel)	Name	cmdCancel
	Caption	&Cancel
	Left	2 in.
	Top	0.6667 in
	Width	0.6979 in
	Height	0.25 in

2. Place the following code in the form's Resize event procedure. You can copy this code from frmExpando's.

```
Private Sub Form_Resize( )
    Dim intHeight As Integer
    Dim intWidth As Integer
    Dim ctl As Control
    Static fInHere As Integer

    Const acbcMinHeight = 2000
    Const acbcMinWidth = 4000

    ' Optimize a bit. If you're already executing the code in here,
    ' just get out. This can happen if you're in here because of an
    ' auto-resize (if you try and size the form too small).
    If fInHere Then GoTo ExitHere
    fInHere = True

    On Error GoTo HandleErr
```

```
' Get the current screen coordinates.
intHeight = Me.InsideHeight
intWidth = Me.InsideWidth

' Make sure the width and height aren't too small. If they are,
' resize the form accordingly. This could force Access to call
' this sub again, so use fInHere to avoid that extra overhead.
If intWidth < acbcMinWidth Then
    DoCmd.MoveSize , , acbcMinWidth
    intWidth = Me.InsideWidth
End If
If intHeight < acbcMinHeight Then
    DoCmd.MoveSize , , , acbcMinHeight
    intHeight = Me.InsideHeight
End If

' Set the detail section's height to be the same as the form's.
' Change this if you want to include header and footer sections.
Me.Section(0).Height = intHeight

' Align all the other controls, based on the left margin of the text box.
Set ctl = Me.txtEntry
With ctl
    ' Make the left and bottom margins equal.
    .Height = intHeight - (.Left + .Top)
    ' The new width is the width of the form, minus the width of the
    ' buttons, minus 3 times the gap (the left margin). Two gaps are
    ' for the buttons, and one more is for the left margin itself.
    .Width = intWidth - Me.cmdOK.Width - (3 * .Left)
End With
' Set the positions of the two buttons.
With Me.cmdOK
    .Left = intWidth - .Width - ctl.Left
End With
With Me.cmdCancel
    .Left = intWidth - .Width - ctl.Left
End With

ExitHere:
    Exit Sub

HandleErr:
    fInHere = False
    Resume ExitHere
End Sub
```

Discussion

The code used in this solution reacts to the Resize events that occur when you resize a form in run mode (and when you open the form). The code retrieves the form's current size (its InsideWidth and InsideHeight properties) and resizes the controls accordingly.

This example starts out by checking a flag, fInHere, and causes the subroutine to exit if the variable's value is True. It's possible that the procedure itself might cause another Resize event (if you've sized the form smaller than the preset minimum size); this flag ensures that the routine doesn't do more work than it needs to do.

Using the Static Keyword

The fInHere flag was declared with the Static keyword. This keyword indicates that Access will maintain the value of the variable between calls to the function. You could accomplish the same effect by making fInHere global, but making the variable static makes it exist as long as the form is loaded, maintains its value from one call to another, and is local to the current procedure. The variable performs its task (as a sentry) without possible intervention from any other procedure.

The code next retrieves the current form size and stores the values into local variables. By placing these values into variables, Access eliminates the need to retrieve the values of the properties every time you need to use them. This speeds up the operation, because retrieving property values is expensive in terms of operating speed.

```
' Get the current screen coordinates.
intHeight = Me.InsideHeight
intWidth = Me.InsideWidth
```

Once it has retrieved the sizes, the procedure verifies that the form hasn't been sized too small by the user. If it has been, it forces the form to be at least as large as the preset values of acbcMinWidth and acbcMinHeight:

```
If intWidth < acbcMinWidth Then
    DoCmd.MoveSize , , acbcMinWidth
    intWidth = Me.InsideWidth
End If
If intHeight < acbcMinHeight Then
    DoCmd.MoveSize , , , acbcMinHeight
    intHeight = Me.InsideHeight
End If
```

Finally, the procedure sets the sizes and locations of each of the controls based on the new width and height of the form. First, it sets the height of the form's detail section, Section(0), so that there will be room for all of the controls at the new height. It then sets the width and height of the text box and sets the left coordinates of the command buttons. This preserves their sizes but resets their positions:

```
Set ctl = Me.txtEntry
With ctl
    .Height = intHeight - (.Left + .Top)
    .Width = intWidth - Me.cmdOK.Width - (3 * .Left)
```

```
End With
' Set the positions of the two buttons.
With Me.cmdOK
    .Left = intWidth - .Width - ctl.Left
End With
With Me.cmdCancel
    .Left = intWidth - .Width - ctl.Left
End With
```

The values used as offsets in this example were all arbitrarily chosen. They work for this particular example, but you'll need to vary them for your own forms. Remember, also, that this example was quite simple. You'll be doing many more calculations if you want to resize a multicolumn list box, for example. In any case, the concepts are the same: resize each of the controls based on the current size of the form. The tricky part is finding some "reference" on which you can base your sizing decisions; in this example, we used the offset of the expanding text box from the left edge of the form.

2.8   Make a Simple "Searching" List Box

Problem

You'd like to create a text box/list box combination like the one in Windows Help. As you type in the text box portion of the control, you want the list box to scroll to match whatever's been typed so far. You know you could use a combo box for this, but the combo box keeps closing up. You want something that's permanently open.

Solution

Entering a portion of the value they're looking for and seeing the matches displayed as users type is an excellent way to find specific values in a list. You get the best of both worlds: the functionality of a combo box and the "permanently open" look of a list box.

The key to implementing this functionality is the text box's Change event. Every time the text in the text box changes, the code you'll use will automatically find the matching value in the associated list box. You'll be able to call a function that will handle all the work for you. In addition, because searching through indexed tables is so much faster than walking through dynasets (the results of running a query or a SQL expression), this solution offers two solutions to this problem: one for list boxes that are bound to tables and another for list boxes that are bound to queries or SQL expressions. Figure 2-15 shows frmSearchFind in action.

The methods you'll find in this solution apply only to bound list boxes.

To test out the functionality, open the database *02-08.MDB* and then open either frmSearchFind or frmSearchSeek. As you type in the text box, you'll see the associ-

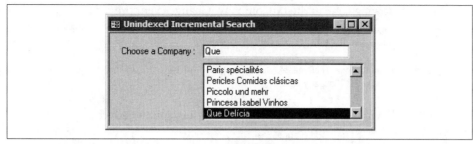

Figure 2-15. Using Incremental Search on frmSearchFind

ated list box scroll to match what you've typed. If you backspace to delete some characters, the list box will still match the characters that remain in the text box. When you leave the text box or click on an item in the list box, you'll see the full text of the chosen item in the text box. The functionality is the same no matter which form you use. frmSearchSeek will look up items faster, though, because it's guaranteed to use an index to do its work.

Follow these steps to build a form like frmSearchFind, which will use a query or SQL expression as the row source for the list box:

1. In your own database, create a new form that contains at least a text box and a list box. For the sake of this example, name the text box txtCompany and the list box lstCompany.

2. Set properties, as shown in Table 2-6.

Table 2-6. Controls and properties for search project form

Control type	Property	Setting
Text box	Name	txtCompany
	OnExit	[Event Procedure]
	OnChange	[Event Procedure]
List box	Name	lstCompany
	AfterUpdate	[Event Procedure]
	RowSource	qryCustomers
	ColumnCount	2
	ColumnWidths	0
	BoundColumn	2

3. Import the table Customers and the query qryCustomers from *02-08.MDB*.

4. Put the following code in the lstCompany_AfterUpdate event procedure:

```
Private Sub lstCompany_AfterUpdate( )
    acbUpdateSearch Me.txtCompany, Me.lstCompany
End Sub
```

5. Put the following code in the txtCompany_Change event procedure:

```
Private Sub txtCompany_Change( )
    Dim varRetval As Variant

    varRetval = acbDoSearchDynaset(Me.txtCompany, _
        Me.lstCompany, "Company Name")
End Sub
```

6. Put the following code in the txtCompany_Exit event procedure:

```
Private Sub txtCompany_Exit(Cancel As Integer)
    acbUpdateSearch Me.txtCompany, Me.lstCompany
End Sub
```

7. Import the module basSearch from *02-08.MDB*. This module contains the code that does all the work.

Every time you change the value in txtCompany, Access triggers txtCompany's Change event. The code attached to that event calls down into the common function, *acbDoSearchDynaset*. In general, the syntax for calling *acbDoSearchDynaset* is:

```
varRetval = acbDoSearchDynaset(textbox, listbox, "Field to search")
```

where *textbox* is a reference to the text box in which you're typing, *listbox* is the list box in which you're searching, and "*Field to search*" is the field in the list box's underlying record source through which you're going to search.

The function *acbDoSearchDynaset* creates a dynaset-type Recordset object, searches through it for the current value of the text box, then sets the value of the list box to match the value the code found in the underlying record source. Its source code is:

```
Public Function acbDoSearchDynaset(ctlText As Control, _
    ctlList As Control, strBoundField As String) As Variant

        ' Search through a bound list box, given text to find from
        ' a text box. Move the list box to the appropriate row.
        ' The list box can have either a table or a dynaset (a query
        ' or a SQL statement) as its row source.
        ' In:
        '       ctlText: A reference to the text box you're typing into
        '       ctlList: A reference to the list box you're looking up in
        '       strBoundField: The name of the field in the underlying
        '           table in which you're looking for values
        ' Out:
        '       Return value: Either 0 (no error) or an error variant
        '           containing the error number

        Dim rst As DAO.Recordset
        Dim varRetval As Variant
        Dim db As DAO.Database

        On Error GoTo HandleErr

        Set db = CurrentDb( )
```

```
    Set rst = db.OpenRecordset(ctlList.RowSource, dbOpenDynaset)
    ' Use the .Text property, because you haven't left the control
    ' yet. Its value (or its .Value property) isn't set until you
    ' leave the control.
    rst.FindFirst "[" & strBoundField & "] >= " & acbcQuote & _
                  ctlText.Text & acbcQuote
    If Not rst.NoMatch Then
        ctlList = rst(strBoundField)
    End If
    varRetval = acbcErrNoError

ExitHere:
    acbDoSearchDynaset = varRetval
    On Error Resume Next
    rst.Close
    Set rst = Nothing
    Exit Function

HandleErr:
    varRetval = CVErr(Err)
    Resume ExitHere
End Function
```

The example in this solution is also set up so that if you leave the text box, it pulls in the currently selected item from the list box. That means that you can use Tab to leave the text box, and the code will place the value that matches as much as you've typed so far in the text box.

Discussion

Notice that the list box's ColumnCount property is 2 and the ColumnWidths property is 0 in this example. This occurs because the query used, qryCustomers, contains two columns, with the first column hidden in the list box. Because you're searching for the second column, that must be the bound column.

This example, as shown so far, uses a query as the data source for the list box. This method can really slow things down for large data sets, since it's not guaranteed that it will be able to use an index. If possible you should base your list box directly on a table instead, especially if your data set is much larger than a few hundred rows. In that case, you can use the Seek method, which is generally much faster than the FindFirst method used in this example. On the other hand, because it works with only a single table as its data source, it's a lot more limiting.

To use the Seek method, you'll need to change a few properties. To test it out, make a copy of frmSearchFind and call the new form frmSearchSeek. Change the RowSource property of your list box to be Customers, rather than qryCustomers. In addition, change the function that txtCompany calls from its Change event procedure to the following:

```
Private Sub txtCompany_Change ( )
    Dim varRetval As Variant
```

```
    varRetval = acbDoSearchTable(Me.txtCompany, _
    Me.lstCompany, "Company Name", "Company Name")
```

```
End Sub
```

In this case, you'll be calling the *acbDoSearchTable* function, which searches through an indexed table instead of through an unindexed dynaset. In general, you'll call *acbDoSearchTable* with the following syntax:

```
    intRetval = acbDoSearchTable(textBox, listBox, "BoundField", "IndexName")
```

where *textbox* is a reference to the text box in which you're typing, *listbox* is the list box in which you're searching, "*BoundField*" is the field in the list box's underlying record source through which you're going to search, and "*IndexName*" is the name of the index you're going to use. (Usually it'll just be "PrimaryKey," but in this example use "Company Name". This table is indexed both on the Customer ID field (the primary key) and the Company Name field; you're using the Company Name index.)

The code for *acbDoSearchTable* is almost identical to that for *acbDoSearchDynaset*, except that the table search uses the Seek method to search through an indexed recordset instead of the FindFirst method. Because it can use the index, it should be able to find matches much more rapidly than *acbDoSearchDynaset*.

 Because *acbDoSearchTable* requires that the list box's record source be a table, it will trap for that error and return a nonzero value as an error variant if you try to use it with some other data source. In addition, the function will not work correctly if you mismatch the bound field and the index. That is, the bound field must be the only field in the selected index).

The code for *acbDoSearchDynaset*, *acbDoSearchTable*, and *acbUpdateSearch* is in the module basSearch. If you want to use this functionality in other applications, import that module into your application and follow the steps outlined earlier to set the properties for your text and list boxes. In addition, if you import the sample code into a database created in Access 2000 or later, make sure you use the Tools → References menu item from within VBA to add a reference to the Microsoft DAO type library. By default, Access applications created in those versions don't include a reference to DAO, and the sample code in this demonstration requires this reference in order to do its work.

2.9   Create a Replacement for Access's InputBox

Problem

You'd like to be able to use Access's *InputBox* function in your applications, but it's so *ugly*! There doesn't appear to be any way to modify the way it looks, so you'd like to replace it with a standardized input form of your own. You'd also like to be able to call into your help file with a Help button on the input box.

Solution

The dialog you see when you run Access's *InputBox* function is just a form, like any other form, except that it's built into Access. You can create your own form, open it as a dialog form, and have it look any way you like. This solution demonstrates a technique you can use in many situations: creating a pop-up form that waits for input and, once it's done, allows the caller to retrieve the information gathered on the form. In this case, you'll call the *acbInputBox* function instead of *InputBox*, but the results will be the same.

Load and run frmTestInputBox from *02-09.MDB*. This sample form gathers information and then calls the *acbInputBox* function to display the replacement input form. Once you're done with the input form, choose OK (to return the text you've entered) or Cancel (to discard it). The sample form will pop up a message box with the text you entered. Figure 2-16 shows the two forms at work.

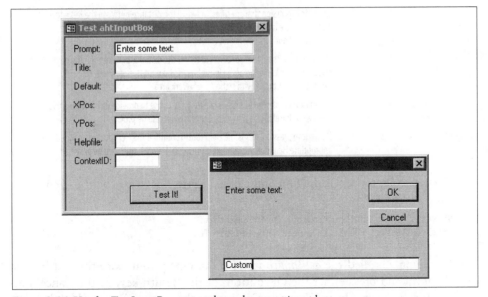

Figure 2-16. Use frmTestInputBox to test the replacement input box

Follow these steps to include this functionality in your own applications:

1. Import frmInputBox from *02-09.MDB* into your database. Modify its appearance any way you like: change its size, colors, fonts, or any other layout properties. Because the form includes a module that handles its setup, you'll want to use the form we've supplied rather than creating your own.

2. Import the module basInputBox from *02-09.MDB*. If you modified the form's name in Step 1, you'll need to modify the code in basInputBox, making the `acbcInputForm` constant match the actual name of the form.

3. To use the new input box, call the *acbInputBox* function that's in basInputBox. It requires one parameter and accepts a number of optional parameters, as shown in Table 2-7. These parameters exactly match the parameters used by Access's own *InputBox* function. The general syntax for *acbInputBox* is:

```
varRetval = acbInputBox(Prompt[, Title][, Default][, Xpos][, Ypos] _
[, Helpfile, Context])
```

Table 2-7. Parameters for acbInputBox

Argument	Optional?	Description
Prompt	No	String expression to be displayed as the prompt in the input box.
Title	Yes	String expression for the caption of the input box. If you omit this parameter, the caption will be empty.
Default	Yes	String expression displayed in the text box when the input box first pops up. If you omit this parameter, the text box will be empty.
XPos	Yes	Numeric expression that specifies, in twips, the distance between the left edge of the screen and the left edge of the input box. If you omit this parameter, the input box will be centered horizontally within the Access work area.
YPos	Yes	Numeric expression that specifies, in twips, the distance between the top edge of the screen and the top edge of the input box. If you omit this parameter, the input box will be centered vertically within the Access work area.
Helpfile	Yes	String expression that identifies the Help file to use to provide context-sensitive Help for the dialog. If Helpfile is provided, Context must also be provided.
Context	Yes	Numeric expression that is the Help context number the Help author assigned to the appropriate Help topic. If Context is provided, Helpfile must also be provided.

For example, to match the function call in Figure 2-16, you could use code like this:

```
varRetval = acbInputBox(Prompt:="Enter some text:", _
Title:="This is the title", Default:="Default Text", _
HelpFile:="msaccess.hlp", ContextID:=101)
```

4. Once you've called the *acbInputBox* function, type a value into the text box on the form and press either the OK button (or the Return key) or the Cancel button (or the Escape key). Choosing OK returns the text you've typed, and choosing Cancel returns `Null`.

Discussion

This solution presents several useful techniques: how to use optional parameters, how to pop up a form and wait for a user response before returning a value back to the caller, how to initialize a pop-up form with values before presenting it to the user, and how to access online help programmatically.

Using optional parameters

Access allows you to declare and pass optional parameters to procedures that you create. That way, you can decide not to pass certain parameters and to use built-in defaults instead. For the *acbInputBox* function, only one parameter is required: the prompt. You can leave off all the rest, and the function will assign logical defaults for you. Here are a few comments on using optional parameters in your own procedures:

- Once you use the Optional keyword in your procedure's declaration, all the subsequent parameters must also be optional.

- Optional parameters can either be variants, or any specific data type.

- If a Variant parameter is optional, use the *IsMissing* function in your code to determine whether the caller supplied a value for the parameter. If an optional parameter includes a specific type, specify the default value in the formal declaration of the method. See the VBA documentation for more information on this technique.

The code in *acbInputBox* either checks to see if the caller passed in a value for the optional parameters using the IsMissing function, or simply passes along the values supplied by the caller:

```
Public Function acbInputBox(Prompt As Variant, _
  Optional Title As Variant, Optional Default As Variant, _
  Optional XPos As Variant, Optional YPos As Variant, _
  Optional HelpFile As Variant, Optional Context As Variant)

    ' This parameter is not optional.
    varPrompt = Prompt

    ' Use a blank title if the caller didn't supply one.
    varTitle = IIf(IsMissing(Title), " ", Title)

    ' Put text into the text box to start with.
    varDefault = Default

    ' Specify the screen coordinates, in twips.
    varXPos = XPos
    varYPos = YPos

    ' Specify the help file and context ID.
    varHelpFile = HelpFile
    varContext = Context
    ' See the next section for the rest of the function.
```

Creating pop-up forms

You want to be able to call a function (*acbInputBox*) that will gather information and then pop up a form. That form will retain the focus until you are done with it, and then the function will return back to you the information it gathered on that form. The key to this process is in using acDialog as the *WindowMode* argument when opening the form. That way, the code processing in the original function waits, and the form doesn't relinquish the focus until you've either hidden it (which is what pressing the OK button does) or closed it (which is what pressing the Cancel button does). Once back in the original function, it can check to see if the form is still loaded (indicating that you pressed the OK button) and, if so, retrieve the information it needs directly from the form and then close the pop-up form. Here's the code from *acbInputBox* that does all that work:

```
' Open the form in dialog mode.  The code will
' stop processing, and wait for you to either close
' the form, or hide it.
DoCmd.OpenForm acbcInputForm, WindowMode:=acDialog

' If you get here and the form is open, you pressed
' the OK button. That means you want to handle the
' text in the textbox, which you can get as the
' Response property of the form.
If IsFormOpen(acbcInputForm) Then
    acbInputBox = Forms(acbcInputForm).Response
    DoCmd.Close acForm, acbcInputForm
Else
    acbInputBox = Null
End If
```

How do you know if the form is still open? This code uses the *IsFormOpen* function, as follows:

```
Private Function IsFormOpen(strName As String) As Boolean
    ' Is the requested form open?
    IsFormOpen = (SysCmd(acSysCmdGetObjectState, acForm, strName) <> 0)
End Function
```

IsFormOpen relies on the Access *SysCmd* function, which, among other things, can tell you the current state of any object. In this case, if there is any state for the object (that is, if *SysCmd* returns anything besides 0), the form must be open.

Finally, to retrieve the return value from the pop-up form, you can use a user-defined property of the form. In this case, we set up Response to be a property of the form that returns the value that you typed into the text box on the form. You could, of course, retrieve that value directly, but this means that the caller has to have information about the controls on the pop-up form. This way, by exposing a defined interface between the caller and the form, it doesn't matter how you rename or change controls on the form; as long as the form continues to provide the Response property, your code will still work.

To provide the read-only Response property, frmInputBox's module includes the following Property Get procedure:

```
Property Get Response( )
    ' Create a user-defined property, Response. This property
    ' returns the value from the text box on the form.
    Response = Me.txtResponse
```

```
End Property
```

This procedure allows outsiders to retrieve what appear to be properties of the form itself. With this Property Get procedure in place, you can use syntax like this to retrieve the property:

```
acbInputBox = Forms(acbcInputForm).Response
```

VBA supports Property Let, Get, and Set procedures. See the VBA online help for more information.

Initializing pop-up forms

You've handled the input parameters and opened the dialog form. How do you tell that form what those parameters were? Just as forms can expose properties, modules can expose public variables that other modules and forms can view and modify. In this case, *acbInputBox* placed the appropriate parameters into various module public variables (*varPrompt*, *varDefault*, *varXPos*, etc.). Code attached to the pop-up form's Open event retrieves the values of those public variables and uses them to initialize itself. As shown in the following code, these variables can be accessed as properties of the module (basInputBox.varDefault, for example). Here is the Form_Open event procedure:

```
Private Sub Form_Open(Cancel As Integer)
    On Error GoTo HandleErr

    Me.txtResponse = basInputBox.varDefault
    Me.Caption = basInputBox.varTitle
    Me.lblPrompt.Caption = basInputBox.varPrompt
    If Not IsNull(basInputBox.varHelpFile) And _
     Not IsNull(basInputBox.varContext) Then
        Me.cmdHelp.Visible = True
        ' Set things up for the Help button.
        mvarContext = basInputBox.varContext
        mvarHelpFile = basInputBox.varHelpFile
    Else
        Me.cmdHelp.Visible = False
    End If
    If Not IsNull(basInputBox.varXPos) Then
        DoCmd.MoveSize basInputBox.varXPos
    End If
    If Not IsNull(basInputBox.varYPos) Then
        DoCmd.MoveSize , basInputBox.varYPos
    End If

ExitHere:
    Exit Sub

HandleErr:
    ' Disregard errors.
    Resume Next
End Sub
```

Programmatically accessing online help

If you specify a help file and a context ID when you call *acbInputBox*, the code will enable a Help button on the form. When you click on that button, Access will load the help file, opened to the appropriate page. How did that all happen? The code attached to the Help button's Click event, shown here, calls the *WinHelp* API function, giving it a help file name, an action (acbcHELP_CONTEXT, indicating that the code wants to supply a context ID and have that page visible when the file opens), and the context ID you supplied. The following is the code that enables this functionality:

```
Const acbcHELP_CONTEXT = &H1&

Private Declare Function WinHelp _
  Lib "user32" Alias "WinHelpA" _
  (ByVal Hwnd As Long, ByVal lpHelpFile As String, _
  ByVal wCommand As Long, ByVal dwData As Any) As Long
Private Sub cmdHelp_Click()
    WinHelp Me.hWnd, mvarHelpFile, acbcHELP_CONTEXT, CLng(mvarContext)
End Sub
```

Every page of a Windows help file can be accessed via the unique context ID that's assigned to it when you build the help file. Unfortunately, this is of use only if you've built the help file yourself or have a list of the context IDs for the various pages. No such list is available for the Access help file; even if it was, you cannot distribute the Access help file with your own applications. If you provide your own help file with your Access application, however, this technique makes it easy to have a help topic available at the click of a button.

Miscellaneous comments

The techniques presented here are not limited to this particular solution. You can use them any time you need to provide a modal dialog that gathers information and then returns that information once you're done with it. Once you've mastered the concepts in the "Creating pop-up forms" section, you will have a technique you can use over and over (for example, to provide a pop-up calendar form or a password input form).

The method we chose for initializing the pop-up form (using module public variables) is not the only method we could have used. Another popular method is to pass information to the form in its OpenArgs property: adding an *OpenArgs* parameter to the Open Form action allows you to pass information directly to the opening form. In this case, because there were many pieces of information to pass over (and the OpenArgs property is limited to a single string value), we would have had to write treacherous code to parse the string out to retrieve the values. Using the technique we chose, it's just a matter of reading the values from the module where they were declared. Though this may seem a little messy, it's a lot simpler in the long run.

See Also

To learn more about the IsMissing VBA function, search for "IsMissing" in the Access online help. See "Pass a Variable Number of Parameters to a Procedure" in Chapter 7 to learn another technique for handling parameters. See "Create a Generic, Reusable Status Meter" in Chapter 9 for another example of creating a reusable form. For more examples that call API functions, see Chapter 11.

2.10   Store the Sizes and Locations of Forms

Problem

Your application uses a number of forms that you can move around the screen. You'd like to store the last location away somewhere so that the forms will appear in the same location the next time you start the application.

Solution

Some Windows applications are "smart" and can save the locations of their windows when they exit. Your application can do this, too, using the system registry. You can store settings when you close a form and read them back the next time you open it.

Open and run the form frmSavePos in *02-10.MDB*. Move it around the screen, and perhaps resize it. When you close the form, code attached to the Close event will save its coordinates in the system registry database. When you reopen the form, if the form can find the saved values in the registry, it will reload the last set of coordinates and will size and position itself accordingly.

To use this technique with your own forms, follow these steps:

1. Import the module basSaveSize from *02-10.MDB* into your own application. This module contains the functions necessary to save and restore a form's size and location in the registry.

2. Add the following code to your form's Load event procedure. This will restore the form's size and location when you load the form:

```
Private Sub Form_Load ()
    acbRestoreSize Me
End Sub
```

3. Add the following code to your form's Unload event procedure. This will save the size and location when you close the form:

```
Private Sub Form_Unload (Cancel As Integer)
    acbSaveSize Me
End Sub
```

Discussion

Most of the work involved in saving and restoring the form size and location happens in the imported module, basSaveSize. The two event procedures, called from the form's Load and Unload events, simply call procedures in the imported module, passing a reference to the current form.

This solution relies heavily on two built-in functions: *SaveSetting* and *GetSetting*. These two functions store and retrieve values from the registry database that's a part of Windows 9x, Windows ME, Windows NT, and Windows 2000. The sample code uses *SaveSetting* to save each of the four coordinates for a form and *GetSetting* to retrieve the same information.

SaveSetting and *GetSetting* make it easy to get and put values in the registry, but they're very limited. They work only with the path HKEY_CURRENT_USER\Software\VB and VBA Program Settings (see Figure 2-17), and they create a new key for each value you save (rather than storing multiple values in one key). If you're interested, investigate their coverage in online help, along with their companion functions, *DeleteSetting* and *GetAllSettings*.

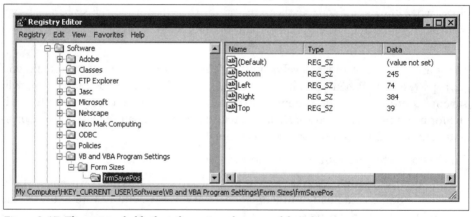

Figure 2-17. The registry holds the information about saved form locations

The procedures in basSaveSize also hinge on two Windows API functions. *GetWindowRect*, aliased as *acb_apiGetWindowRect*, gets the coordinates of a screen window. *MoveWindow*, aliased as *acb_apiMoveWindow*, moves and sizes a window on screen.

The *GetRelativeCoords* subroutine in basSaveSize retrieves the coordinates of a given form. Because the *MoveWindow* function requires a position relative to that of the window's parent to move a window, *GetRelativeCoords* must find the coordinates of both the requested window and its parent window. It calls the Windows API function *GetParent*, aliased as *acb_apiGetParent*, to find the parent and retrieves the coordinates of both. It fills in a user-defined structure with the relative coordinates.

Why Use MoveWindow Rather than MoveSize?

You might wonder why you shouldn't use the Access built-in *MoveSize* macro action: it requires that you select a form first, and this causes the form to display at the time you call the MoveSize action. This looks ugly on screen and makes the procedure less generic. In addition, it requires some work to convert from screen coordinates (pixels), which *GetWindowRect* uses, to twips, which *MoveSize* uses. To avoid all these issues, the sample project uses the Windows API method, MoveWindow, instead.

```
' Store rectangle coordinates.
Type acbTypeRect
    lngX1 As Long
    lngY1 As Long
    lngX2 As Long
    lngY2 As Long
End Type

' Windows 95/98/NT4/2000 puts a 2-pixel
' border around the MDI client area, which
' doesn't get taken into account automatically.
' If you're using NT 3.51, you're on your own.
Private Const adhcBorderWidthX = 2
Private Const adhcBorderWidthY = 2

Private Sub GetRelativeCoords(frm As Form, rct As acbTypeRect)

    ' Fill in rct with the coordinates of the window.
    Dim hwndParent As Long
    Dim rctParent As acbTypeRect

    ' Find the position of the window in question, in
    ' relation to its parent window (the Access desktop, most
    ' likely, unless the form is modal).
    hwndParent = acb_apiGetParent(frm.Hwnd)

    ' Get the coordinates of the current window and its parent.
    acb_apiGetWindowRect frm.Hwnd, rct
    ' If the form is a popup window, its parent won't
    ' be the Access main window.  If so, don't
    ' bother subtracting off the coordinates of the
    ' main Access window.
    If hwndParent <> Application.hWndAccessApp Then
        acb_apiGetWindowRect hwndParent, rctParent

        ' Subtract off the left and top parent coordinates, since you
        ' need coordinates relative to the parent for the
        ' acb_apiMoveWindow( ) function call.
        rct.lngX1 = (rct.lngX1 - rctParent.lngX1 - adhcBorderWidthX)
        rct.lngY1 = (rct.lngY1 - rctParent.lngY1 - adhcBorderWidthY)
        rct.lngX2 = (rct.lngX2 - rctParent.lngX1 - adhcBorderWidthX)
```

```
        rct.lngY2 = (rct.lngY2 - rctParent.lngY1 - adhcBorderWidthY)
    End If
End Sub
```

The *acbSaveSize* procedure first retrieves the current coordinates for the requested form and then saves those values to the registry. Figure 2-17 shows the registry after saving the settings for the sample form. The function creates a key named Form Sizes in the registry, with a subkey for each form whose coordinates you save. Within each subkey, the procedure creates a separate value entry for each of the four coordinates. The source code related to the *acbSaveSize* procedure is:

```
Private Const acbcRegTag = "Form Sizes"
Private Const acbcRegLeft = "Left"
Private Const acbcRegRight = "Right"
Private Const acbcRegTop = "Top"
Private Const acbcRegBottom = "Bottom"
Public Sub acbSaveSize(frm As Form)
    Dim rct As acbTypeRect

    GetRelativeCoords frm, rct
    With rct
        SaveSetting acbcRegTag, frm.Name, acbcRegLeft, .lngX1
        SaveSetting acbcRegTag, frm.Name, acbcRegRight, .lngX2
        SaveSetting acbcRegTag, frm.Name, acbcRegTop, .lngY1
        SaveSetting acbcRegTag, frm.Name, acbcRegBottom, .lngY2
    End With
End Sub
```

When it comes time to retrieve the saved coordinates, the *acbRestoreSize* procedure retrieves the four coordinates from the registry and then, if the width and the height of the new form would be greater than 0, resizes the form. Its source code is:

```
Public Sub acbRestoreSize(frm As Form)
    Dim rct As acbTypeRect
    Dim lngWidth As Long
    Dim lngHeight As Long

    rct.lngX1 = GetSetting(acbcRegTag, frm.Name, acbcRegLeft, 0)
    rct.lngX2 = GetSetting(acbcRegTag, frm.Name, acbcRegRight, 0)
    rct.lngY1 = GetSetting(acbcRegTag, frm.Name, acbcRegTop, 0)
    rct.lngY2 = GetSetting(acbcRegTag, frm.Name, acbcRegBottom, 0)

    lngWidth = rct.lngX2 - rct.lngX1
    lngHeight = rct.lngY2 - rct.lngY1

    ' No sense even trying if both aren't greater than 0.
    If (lngWidth > 0) And (lngHeight > 0) Then
        ' You would think the MoveSize action would work here, but that
        ' requires actually SELECTING the window first.  That seemed like
        ' too much work, when this procedure will move/size ANY window.
        ' Also, MoveSize must DISPLAY the window before it can move it.
        ' It looked quite ugly.
        acb_apiMoveWindow frm.Hwnd, _
```

```
        rct.lngX1, rct.lngY1, lngWidth, lngHeight, True
    End If
End Sub
```

You may want to store properties other than the size and location of the form—for instance, the current record number for a bound form, or which control was last selected. In any case, the example in *02-10.MDB* stores information in such a way that you can store as many properties as you would like by adding to the group describing each form in the registry.

See Also

For more examples using the Windows API, see Chapter 11.

2.11   Open Multiple Instances of a Form

Problem

In an application, you have a form showing information about a customer. You would like to be able to open another copy of the form so you could move to a different row, compare values, perhaps copy from one row to another, or just look at more than one customer's record at once. As far as you can tell, you can have only one open copy of a form at a time.

Solution

In older versions of Access, you were limited to having only a single copy of a form open at any time. Starting with Access 95, you can open multiple instances of a form, under complete program control. There's no user interface for this functionality, however, so you must write code to make it happen. This solution demonstrates how to create, handle, and delete multiple instances of a form using the New keyword and user-defined collections.

Follow these steps to convert your own forms to allow for multiple instances:

1. Add two buttons to your form, with captions like Create New Instance (named cmdViewAnother in the example) and Delete All Extra Instances (named cmd-CloseAll in the example).

2. Add the following code to the Click event procedure of the Create New Instance button:

```
Private Sub cmdViewAnother_Click()
    Call acbAddForm
End Sub
```

3. Add the following code to the Click event procedure of the Delete All Extra Instances button:

```
Private Sub cmdCloseAll_Click()
    Call acbRemoveAllForms
End Sub
```

4. Add the following code to the Close event procedure for the form:

```
Private Sub Form_Close()
    Call acbRemoveForm(Me)
End Sub
```

5. Import the module basMultiInstance from *02-11.MDB*.

To see this functionality in action, load and run frmCustomers from *02-11.MDB*. Once it's open, click View Another Customer. This will create a new instance of the original form, with its own set of properties and current row. You can create as many new forms as you like and move from row to row on any or all of them. When you're done, click Close All Extra Copies, which will run code to delete all the extra forms. Figure 2-18 shows the original form, along with three extras.

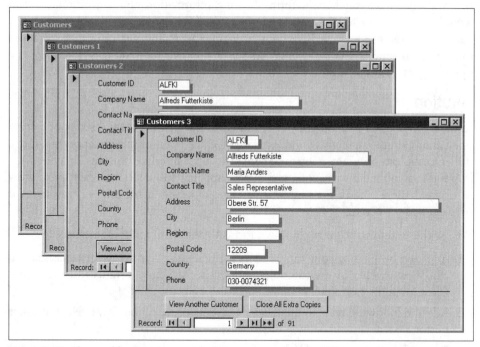

Figure 2-18. Clones of frmCustomers with their own current rows

Discussion

Working with multiple instances of forms requires three skills: creating the new forms, storing their references, and deleting them. All three topics center around user-defined collections. These collections allow you to add and delete items at will, based on either their position in the collection or a string value that uniquely identifies each element. This example uses each form's hWnd property (its window handle) to identify the form in the collection.

In Access, each form stored in the database can be viewed as its own "class" of form: it's an object that you can replicate in memory, using the New keyword. The following statement will create a new instance of the form named frmCustomers:

```
Set frm = New Form_frmCustomers
```

Form_frmCustomers is the object type, and its name originates from its type (Form) concatenated with the actual class name (frmCustomers). Once you've executed this line of code, frm refers to a new, invisible form. You can set its properties, if you like, or make it visible with the following statement:

```
frm.Visible = True
```

If you want to refer to your new form later, you'll need to store a reference to it somewhere. In the example code, we used a user-defined collection. When you create a new instance of the form, the code adds that form reference to the collection so you can find the form, under program control, when you need to refer to it again.

Life Span of a Form

The variables that refer to the newly created forms must have a life span longer than that of the procedure that created the forms. In this case, the form references are stored in a module-level collection, so their lifetime is the same as the database itself. When you create a new instance of a form, if the variable referring to that form goes out of scope, Access destroys the new form instance. Because you'll want your forms to hang around longer than that, make sure your form variables have a static, module, or global scope.

In this example, the *acbAddForm* subroutine creates and stores the new form references. As it creates a new form (when requested to do so by that button click on frmCustomers), it adds the form reference to the collection of forms. A collection's Add method allows you to add the item and optionally store a unique string value describing the value at the same time. In this case, the code stores the form's hWnd property, converted to a string, as its unique identifier. The code also increments a variable that keeps track of the number of instances and places the new form at a convenient location before making it visible. This is the *acbAddForm* subroutine:

```
Private colForms As New Collection
Private mintForm As Integer

Const acbcOffsetHoriz = 75
```

```
Const acbcOffsetVert = 375

Public Sub acbAddForm()
    Dim frm As Form

    Set frm = New Form_frmCustomers

    ' You have to convert the key to a string, so tack a "" onto
    ' the hWnd (which uniquely identifies each form instance)
    ' to convert it to a string.
    colForms.Add Item:=frm, Key:=frm.Hwnd & ""

    ' Build up the caption for each new instance.
    mintForm = mintForm + 1
    frm.Caption = frm.Caption & " " & mintForm

    ' The numbers used here are arbitrary and are really useful
    ' only for this simple example.
    frm.SetFocus
    DoCmd.MoveSize mintForm * acbcOffsetHoriz, mintForm * acbcOffsetVert
    ' Finally, set this form to be visible.
    frm.Visible = True
End Sub

Sub acbRemoveForm(frm As Form)
    ' All the forms call this from their Close events. Since
    ' the main form isn't in the collection at all, it'll cause
    ' an error. Just disregard that.
    On Error Resume Next
    colForms.Remove frm.Hwnd & ""
    Err.Clear
End Sub
```

Eventually you'll want to close down all the extra instances of your form. This is quite simple: once you delete the form reference, Access will close the form for you. Therefore, in reaction to the Close All Instances button you created on your form, Access runs this subroutine:

```
Public Sub acbRemoveAllForms()
    Dim varForm As Variant

    ' Reset the static variables.
    mintForm = 0
    For Each varForm In colForms
        colForms.Remove 1
    Next varForm
End Sub
```

This subroutine first resets the total number of instances back to 0, then walks through the collection of form instances one at a time, removing the first item each time. Because Access renumbers the collection each time you remove an item, this is the simplest way to remove all the items.

To keep things neat, we instructed you to attach to the form's Close event code that removes the specific form from the collection of forms when you close that form. Though this example doesn't need that functionality, you may find that in other situations you do need your collection to reflect accurately the forms that are currently loaded (if you want to list all the open forms, for example). There is one wrinkle here, however: when you ask the application to close all extra instances, Access closes each form, one by one. This, in turn, triggers the Close event for each of those forms. The Close event calls code attached to that event that attempts to remove the form from the collection of forms, but that form has already been removed from the collection. Therefore, the *acbRemoveForm* subroutine, shown here, disables error handling; attempting to remove an already removed form won't trigger an error.

```
Public Sub acbRemoveForm(frm As Form)
    ' All the forms call this from their Close events. Since
    ' the main form isn't in the collection at all, it'll cause
    ' an error. Just disregard that.
    On Error Resume Next
    colForms.Remove frm.hWnd & ""
    Err.Clear
End Sub
```

Extra instances of forms aren't really treated exactly the same as their originals. For example, all the copies of a form share the same name as the original, so if you attempt to use the syntax:

```
Forms!frmCustomers
```

or:

```
Forms("frmCustomers")
```

to refer to an instance of a form, you'll be able to access only the original form. Access does add each instance to the Forms collection, but you can access them only by their ordinal positions in the collection. If you loop through the Forms collection to close all open forms, the code will close the instances, too.

Form instances have their own properties and their own current rows, but any changes you make to a form instance are not saved. That is, all instances of a form other than the original are read-only. That's not to say that the data on the form is read-only—it's the *design* of the form instance that's read-only.

You'll find multiple instances of forms to be a useful addition to your programming arsenal. They allow users to view multiple rows with their forms in Form View (the proverbial "have their cake and eat it, too" situation), and from there to copy/cut/paste data from one row to another. Your responsibility as the developer is to carefully manage the creation, storage, and deletion of these forms, because the Access user interface provides no help.

CHAPTER 3

Reports

You may devote days, weeks, or even months of work to designing tables and queries and writing the macros and code to put an application together, but along with your application's forms, its reports *are* the application. Because of this, you'll want make them as clear and attractive as possible.

The first solution in this chapter shows you how to do something that should be (and is) easy: printing a report with line numbers. Next, you'll learn how to print the value of query parameters on a report based on a parameter query and how to create an attractive multiple-column report.

The next group of solutions will teach you how to use Visual Basic for Applications (VBA) code and macros to print a message on a report only if certain conditions are met, how to create telephone-book-style page-range indicators, how to print a bar graph on a report using rectangle controls, and how to calculate page totals.

Next, you'll employ more challenging VBA code to work around the limitations of the CanGrow/CanShrink properties and prevent blank rows on reports by combining an entire address into a single expression for a mailing-label report. You'll see how to suppress printing a report if there are no records to print. Using an event procedure run from the report's Format event, you'll learn how to print one set of headers and footers on odd pages and another (mirror-image) set on even pages. Then you will learn how to use the Line method to draw lines or rectangles on a report—in this case, to make a line the same height as a variable-height text box. Next, you'll learn how to alternate gray bars on every other row of the report.

The final three solutions in this chapter show you how to tie a report's recordset to the filtered recordset of a form, how to prevent your report from breaking at an inappropriate place (such as right after a group header), and finally, in the most complex solution in this chapter, how to modify a report's grouping and sorting fields on the fly.

3.1   Create a Report with Line Numbers

Problem

You have a legal report that has a list of items in the detail section. You're required to sequentially number each item in the list. You thought about using an AutoNumber field, but this won't work because you want the number to reset itself for each group and you often want to print the items in a different order from how you entered them. Is there an easy way to create on the fly report line numbers that pertain only to the data printed on the report?

Solution

Yes, there is an easy way to do this that makes use of an underused property of a text box, RunningSum. This solution shows you how to add line numbers to your report by creating an unbound text box based on a simple calculation and adjusting the RunningSum property of this control.

To create line numbers on your own reports, follow these steps:

1. Create a new report or open an existing report in design mode. Add an unbound text box control to the detail section with the following ControlSource setting:

   =1

2. For the sample report, we named the control txtLineNumber.

3. Change the RunningSum property for the control from the default of No to either Over Group or Over All. We chose Over Group for the sample report (see Figure 3-1).

4. Save the report and preview it to confirm that it now includes sequential line numbers.

To see an example of this solution, open *03-01.MDB*. Run the rptEvidenceByCase report in preview view (see Figure 3-2). This report prints out a list of all evidence items, grouped by CaseId. Notice the line number field on the left side of the report, which resets to zero at the start of each group.

Discussion

Setting the ControlSource of the line number control to =1 tells Access to print a constant of 1 for all records. This is what would happen if you didn't also adjust the RunningSum property of the control.

Setting the RunningSum property to Over Group or Over All tells Access to print the value of the first record as it would normally (in this case, to print 1) but, for the second record, to take the value of the first record and add it to the value of the second record, printing the cumulative total instead of the value it would normally print (in this case, 2). For the third record, Access adds the value of the second record (which

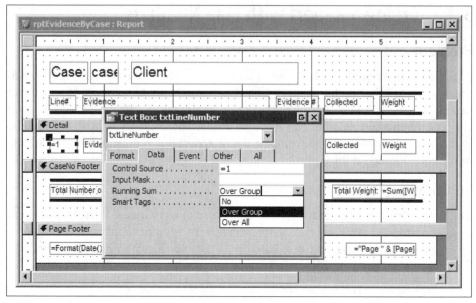

Figure 3-1. The RunningSum property can be set to No, Over Group, or Over All

is really a sum of the first and second records' values) to the value of the third record (in this case, 3). This accumulation of values continues until the end of the report (if you set RunningSum to Over All) or until the beginning of the next group (if you set RunningSum to Over Group).

You can use RunningSum to accumulate nonconstant values, too. For example, if you want a running total of the weight of evidence items in the rptEvidenceByCase report for each record, you can add a second Weight text box control to the right of the existing Weight control, making the second control identical to the first but this time setting RunningSum to Over Group. You'll also find the RunningSum property useful for financial reports for which you'd like to include a cumulative year-to-date column.

3.2   Print the Value of a Parameter on a Report

Problem

You've created a report based on a parameter query that prompts the user for one or more parameters when the query is run. The report works just fine, but you'd like to be able to document somewhere on the report what parameter values were entered by the user. That way you'll know, for example, which years' records are included in the report. Is there any way to do this with Access?

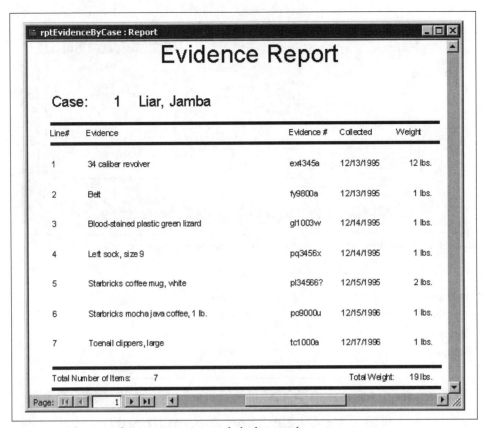

Figure 3-2. The rptEvidenceByCase report includes line numbers

Solution

You can print the values of query parameters on a report by referring to the parameters as if they were fields in the underlying query. This solution shows you how to create controls on a report that document the user-entered runtime parameters.

Load the *03-02.MDB* database and open the qryAlbumsPrm query in design mode to verify that this query has three parameters (Figure 3-3). Now open the rptAlbumsPrm in preview view. Because this report is based on qryAlbumsPrm, you will be prompted for the three parameters.

Enter your values at the parameter prompt. If you enter the parameter values from Table 3-1, you should see a report that looks similar to the one shown in Figure 3-4.

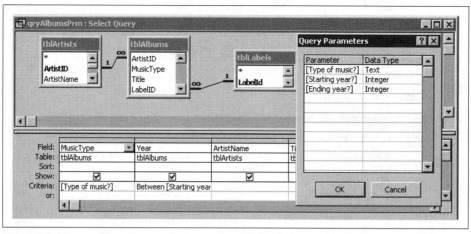

Figure 3-3. The qryAlbumsPrm parameter query includes three parameters

Table 3-1. Parameters and sample values for qryAlbumsPrm

Parameter	Sample value
Type of music?	Rock
Starting year?	1960
Ending year?	1979

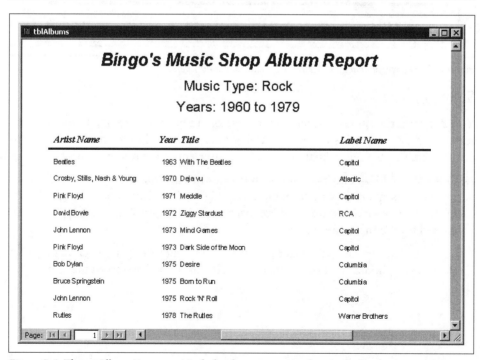

Figure 3-4. The rptAlbumsPrm report includes the parameter values in the header

Notice that the selected parameters are included in the page header of the report. Run the report again, entering different parameters, and verify that the new parameters are correctly printed on the report.

Follow these steps to print the values of query parameters on your own report:

1. Create a query with one or more parameters. If you aren't sure how to do this, read the Solution in Recipe 1.1. Don't forget to declare your parameters using the Query → Parameters command (see Figure 3-3). In the sample database, we created a parameter query named qryAlbumsPrm with three parameters.

2. Create a report based on the parameter query from Step 1. In the page header of the report (or any other section you'd like), create text boxes that reference the parameters as if they were fields in the underlying query. Surround each parameter reference with square brackets. We used two text boxes in the rptAlbumsPrm sample report, as summarized in Table 3-2.

Table 3-2. These two text boxes reference three parameters from the underlying query

Text box name	Control source
txtMusic	="Music Type: " & [Type of music?]
txtYears	="Years: " & [Starting year?] & " to " & [Ending year?]

 These parameter fields will not be listed in either the field list window or the drop-down list of fields in a control's ControlSource property.

Discussion

During report design, you are free to reference any "unknown" you'd like as long as you put brackets around it. (If you don't put brackets around it and it's not a field in the underlying record source, Access thinks you entered a string constant and forgot to surround it with quotes, so it puts the quotes in for you.) When you run the report, Access tries to locate the unknown references. If it locates a query parameter or form control that satisfies the reference, it copies the value into the control and continues running the report. If it can't locate the unknown reference, however, it puts up a parameter dialog, requesting help in locating that unknown piece of data.

 If you run a report and get a parameter dialog when you didn't expect one, it's likely that you misspelled either a field name or a reference to a query's parameter.

You can also create parameters directly on reports that are independent of query parameters. For example, you might use this type of "report parameter" if you create a report that requires a person's name and signature at the bottom of a page when you know that the name will vary every time you run the report (and cannot be obtained from the report's record source). Simply add a text box that references the new parameter—for example, [Enter signature name:]. Access will prompt you for this report parameter when you run the report, just as if you had defined the parameter in the report's underlying query.

3.3   Create a Report with Multiple Columns

Problem

You want to print a two-column, phone-book-style report with large initial capital letters to set off each alphabetical grouping. There is no Report Wizard for creating such a report, and you don't see a Column property to set up the number of columns you want. How can you make a multiple-column report in Access?

Solution

There is a way to format a report for multiple columns, but it's not where you might look for it, on a report's properties sheet or the report design menu. Instead, you'll find it on the Columns tab of the Page Setup dialog. This solution guides you through setting up a multiple-column, phone-book-style report that includes a large drop cap for each letter of the alphabet.

Follow these steps to create your own multiple-column report:

1. Open in design view the report you want to format for multiple columns, and select File → Page Setup. The Page Setup dialog appears. Click on the Columns tab of the Page Setup dialog (see Figure 3-5).

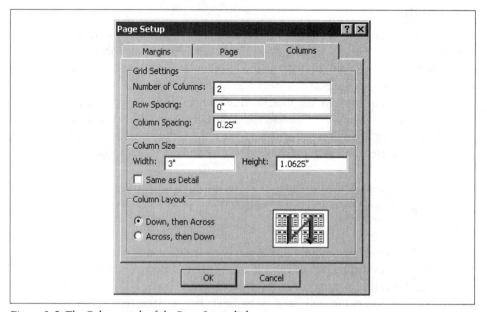

Figure 3-5. The Columns tab of the Page Setup dialog

2. Enter the appropriate settings for your report. You'll find a brief description of these settings and the settings used for the sample report in Table 3-3. Click OK when you're done.

Table 3-3. The Page Setup dialog Layout settings

Setting	Purpose	Sample
Number of Columns	Number of columns.	2
Row Spacing	Extra space, in inches, between rows.	0
Column Spacing	Extra space, in inches, between columns.	0.25"
Column Size: Width	Width of each column.	3"
Column Size: Height	Height of each column.	1.0625"
Same as Detail	When you check this, Access will copy the width and height of the report's detail section into the Width and Height controls.	Unchecked
Layout Column	Select "Down, then Across" for snaking columns or "Across, then Down" for mailing-label-style columns.	Down, then Across

3. Leave the report and page headers and footers as they are (if your report has these sections); they will still print across the entire report width.

4. To keep each name, phone number, and address from breaking inappropriately, set the detail section's KeepTogether property to Yes.

5. Preview the report; it should now display in two columns.

Follow these additional steps to create the first letter grouping shown in Figure 3-7:

1. Select View → Sorting and Grouping to display the Sorting and Grouping window. Add the grouping field (in rptPhoneBook, we grouped on Company) twice to the Sorting and Grouping grid. Adjust the settings of each grouping field as shown in Table 3-4 for the sample report.

Table 3-4. Sorting and Grouping settings for rptPhoneBook

Setting	First Company field	Second Company field
Field/Expression	Company	Company
Sort Order	Ascending	Ascending
Group Header	Yes	No
Group Footer	No	No
Group On	Prefix Characters	Each Value
Group Interval	1	1
Keep Together	No	No

2. Add a text box to the header section of the grouping field. In the rptPhoneBook report, we used the property settings in Table 3-5. The completed rptPhone-Book report is shown in design view, with the Sorting and Grouping and properties sheets visible, in Figure 3-6.

Table 3-5. Property settings for rptPhoneBook

Property	Setting
Name	txtFirstLetter
ControlSource	=Left([Company],1)
Width	0.4375″
Height	0.4375″
BackColor	12632256 (grey)
ForeColor	0 (black)
FontName	Arial
FontSize	24
FontWeight	Bold

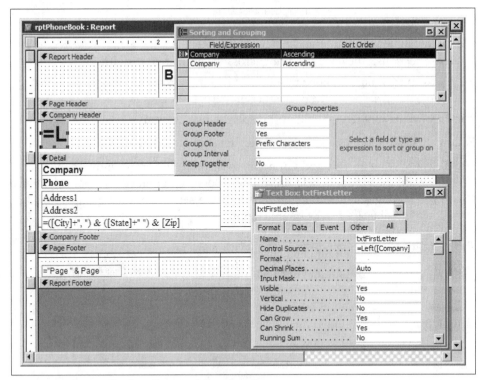

Figure 3-6. The completed rptPhoneBook report in design view

3. Save the report. Switch to print preview mode to preview how it will look when you print it.

Now, load *03-03.MDB*. The tblCompanyAddresses table contains a list of businesses and their addresses and phone numbers. Open rptPhoneBook in preview view. This report prints the data in two snaking (newspaper-style) columns (see Figure 3-7).

Business Phone Book

Ackerman Recreation Corporation
(206) 951-1720

867 Butternut Way
Pittsburgh, PA 83904

Ackerman, Limited
(908) 472-3491

10110 59th Lane
Suite 392
Adamsville, AK 97238

AVANCO Specialties, Ltd.
(402) 814-6571

12532 36th Blvd.
Lost Lake, AR 09999

CheckMaster Limited, Incorporated
(908) 919-1779

6315 37th Street
Building 132, Room 456
Miners Cut, MY 89533

City Alternatives, Inc.
(631) 104-9549

2412 21st Lane
Rice Lake, CT 23444

Dolphin Software, Incorporated
(957) 288-3852

3832 67th Lane
Suite 511
Wallace, MI 65544

Figure 3-7. The two-column rptPhoneBook report

Discussion

When you create a report, Access assumes you want only one column unless you specify otherwise. If you want more than one column, you must adjust the layout properties of the page using the Columns tab of the Page Setup dialog. The key settings are Number of Columns, Column Spacing (the extra margin between columns), Width (the width of each column), and Column Layout (whether Access first prints an entire column or an entire row). If you want to produce snaking-column (newspaper-style) reports, select "Down, then Across" for Column Layout; for mailing-label-type reports, choose "Across, then Down". For most purposes, you can ignore the other settings.

You will usually create groups in reports that break on the value of a field itself. For example, grouping on Company will trigger a new group for each new unique value of the Company field. Access, however, includes two group properties that allow you to alter the frequency of groupings: GroupOn and GroupInterval. Depending on the data type of the grouping field (see Table 3-6), you can use GroupOn to group on some subset of characters (Text), a range of numbers (Number, Currency), or a period of time (Date/Time). Using the GroupInterval property, you can adjust the grouping further—for example, you could break on the first two characters of a name, every $10, or every two months.

Table 3-6. GroupOn property choices

Data type of field	GroupOn choices
Text	Each Value (default)Prefix Characters
Number, Currency	Each Value (default)Interval
Date/Time	Each Value (default)YearQtrMonthWeekDayHourMinute

When you use the GroupOn property to group on anything other than Each Value, you must realize that the records within the groupings will not be sorted. This means that in most cases you'll also need to include a second sorted copy of the field with GroupOn set to Each Value. This is what we did in the rptPhoneBook example.

Sorting or Grouping?

When you add a field or expression to the Sorting and Grouping window, you may wonder what determines whether a field is a group or merely a sort. No single property determines this—rather, a field becomes a group field if you set either GroupHeader or GroupFooter (or both) to Yes. You can convert an existing group field to a sort field by setting both of these properties to No.

There are several section, report, and group properties that you can adjust to control whether a group is kept together on the same column or page and whether a new column or page is started before or after a group.

See Also

See the Solution in Recipe 3.14 for more details on controlling page and column breaks.

3.4   Print a Message on a Report if Certain Conditions Are Met

Problem

On a letter that you mail to all the customers on a mailing list, you want to print a message on only some customers' letters (depending on, for example, the customer's zip code, credit status, or past orders). How do you make a text box print only when certain conditions are met?

Solution

You can create an event procedure that's called from the Format event of a report section to make a single control—or an entire section—visible or invisible depending on a condition you specify. This solution shows you how to create a simple event procedure that checks each report record for a certain condition and then prints a message only if that condition is met.

Follow these steps to add an event procedure to your report that prints a message only for certain rows:

1. Create a new report or open an existing report in design view. Add to the page header section any controls that you wish to show for only selected records. In the rptMailingByZipWithCondition sample, we included three labels and a rectangle control in the page header section.

2. While the cursor is still located in the page header section, select View → Properties to view the section's properties sheet (if it's not already open).

3. Create a new event procedure for the section's Format event. (If you're unsure of how to do this, see the Section P.5.5 in the the preface of this book.)

4. Add to the Format event procedure an If...Then statement with the following basic structure:

```
If (some condition) Then
    Me.Section(acPageHeader).Visible = True
Else
    Me.Section(acPageHeader).Visible = False
End If
```

For example, in rptMailingByZipWithCondition, we added an event procedure that tests if the first two characters of the Zip Code field are equal to 98. The complete event procedure is shown here:

```
Private Sub PageHeader0_Format(Cancel As Integer, _
  FormatCount As Integer)

    ' Set the visibility of the page header section,
    ' depending on whether or not the current
    ' zip code starts with "98".

    If Left(Me.ZipPostalCode, 2) = "98" Then
        Me.Section(acPageHeader).Visible = True
    Else
        Me.Section(acPageHeader).Visible = False
    End If
End Sub
```

5. Save the report and preview it to see if the event procedure is working properly.

Load the rptMailingByZip report from *03-04.MDB*. This sample report, which is bound to the tblCompanyAddresses table, is used to print a letter to customers who are sorted by zip code. It includes a message in the page header that announces the company's booth in an upcoming conference. The message prints for all customers, even those outside the Seattle area. Now load rptMailingByZipWithCondition to see an example of a report that selectively prints a message. Notice that this version of the report prints the message only for customers whose zip codes begin with 98 (see Figure 3-8 and Figure 3-9).

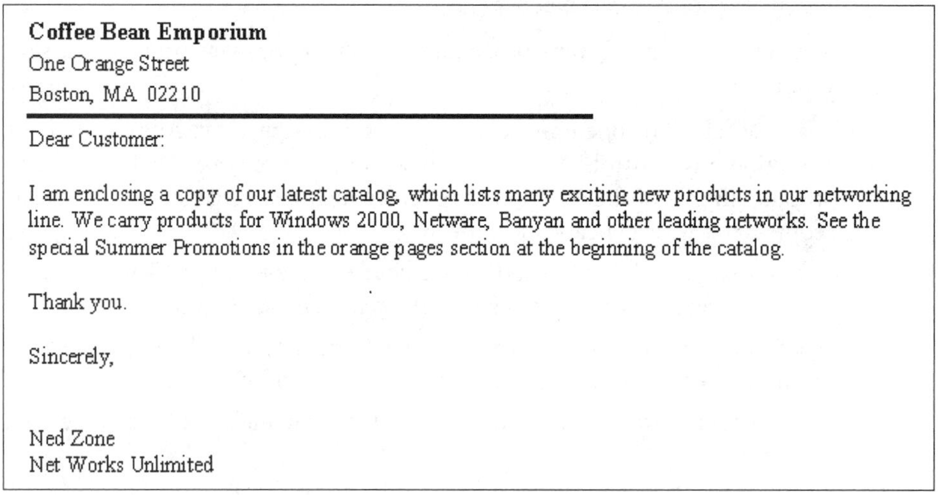

Coffee Bean Emporium
One Orange Street
Boston, MA 02210

Dear Customer:

I am enclosing a copy of our latest catalog, which lists many exciting new products in our networking line. We carry products for Windows 2000, Netware, Banyan and other leading networks. See the special Summer Promotions in the orange pages section at the beginning of the catalog.

Thank you.

Sincerely,

Ned Zone
Net Works Unlimited

Figure 3-8. An address whose zip code does not start with 98, with no message

Discussion

The event procedure uses the report's Section property and the section's Visible property to make an entire section visible or invisible when the report is formatted. Whether the section is visible depends on its meeting the condition in the If...Then expression. In our example, only zip codes starting with 98 meet this condition, so the message about the Seattle Expo will print only on pages for customers located in or near Seattle.

Table 3-7 lists the values and constants you can use in expressions to refer to the various sections on a form or report. Group levels 3 through 10 (reports only) continue the numbering scheme shown here, but have no corresponding VBA constants.

Visit our booth at the Seattle Expo this September!

Power Software
200 Eighth Avenue S.
Kent, WA 98035

Dear Customer:

I am enclosing a copy of our latest catalog, which lists many exciting new products in our networking line. We carry products for Windows 2000, Netware, Banyan and other leading networks. See the special Summer Promotions in the orange pages section at the beginning of the catalog.

Thank you.

Sincerely,

Ned Zone
Net Works Unlimited

Figure 3-9. An address whose zip code starts with 98, with the message

Table 3-7. Values used to identify form and report sections in expressions

Setting	VBA constant	Description
0	acDetail	Detail section
1	acHeader	Form or report header section
2	acFooter	Form or report footer section
3	acPageHeader	Form or report page header section
4	acPageFooter	Form or report page footer section
5	acGroupLevel1Header	Group level 1 header section (reports only)
6	acGroupLevel1Footer	Group level 1 footer section (reports only)
7	acGroupLevel2Header	Group level 2 header section (reports only)
8	acGroupLevel2Footer	Group level 2 footer section (reports only)

In the code, you'll find expressions like the following:

```
Me.ZipPostalCode
```

and

```
Me.Section(acPageHeader)
```

In these expressions, the built-in object named Me always refers to the form in which the code is running. (It's actually slightly more complex than this—"Me" actually refers to the class containing the code, not the form, but that's a topic best left for a more advanced book.) Whenever you see code that contains "Me." you can be assured that the code is referring to an object on the form, or a field provided by the form's data source. You may also find code that uses "Me!" syntax. For all intents and purposes, this is equivalent to the "Me." syntax, and you should simply treat the two syntaxes the same. At this time, the "Me." syntax is preferred because it provides a very slight performance edge. In addition, the "Me." is almost always optional—you'll see cases in this book in which the code simply doesn't include this prefix when referring to controls and fields provided by a form.

In the sample report, which prints one record per page, four controls need to be turned on or off together: the label with the message, two labels with Wingdings pointing-hand graphics, and a rectangle surrounding the other controls. Placing all of these controls in one section and making the section as a whole visible or invisible is more efficient than making each control visible or invisible. Often, however, you'll need to print a message on a report that contains multiple records per page. For example, you might print the word "Outstanding" alongside a sales report when a salesperson has had more than $1 million in sales for a year. In this case, you'll have to use code that works with the Visible property of individual controls, such as that shown here:

```
If Me.Sales >= 1000000 Then
    Me.txtOutstanding.Visible = True
Else
    Me.txtOutstanding.Visible = False
End If
```

If you look at rptMailingByZip or rptMailingByZipWithCondition in design view, you may notice an odd expression as the ControlSource property for the txtCityStateZip control in both reports:

```
=([City]+", ") & ([StateProvince]+"  ") & [ZipPostalCode]
```

Note that we have used both the + and & concatenation operators in this expression. These two operators have a subtle difference: When you use + and one of the concatenated strings is Null, the whole expression becomes Null; when you use &, the null part of the expression is ignored. The effect caused by the + operator is termed *null propagation*, which you can short-circuit by surrounding that part of the expression in parentheses. The net effect of all this is that in the previous expression, if City is Null, City *and* the comma and space following it will drop out of the expression. Likewise, if StateProvince is Null, it *and* the two spaces to which it is concatenated will drop out of the expression. Selective use of the + concatenation operator is both easier to read and more efficient than using one or more *IIf* functions.

You may find it useful to collapse an `If...Then` statement down into a single expression. For example, the code in the sample report can be collapsed down to the following single statement:

```
Me.Section(acPageHeader).Visible = (Left(Me.ZipPostalCode, 2) = "98")
```

The second code example could be collapsed into this single statement:

```
Me.txtOutStanding.Visible = (Me.Sales >= 1000000)
```

It's up to you to decide which syntax you'd like to use. Some developers like the full `If...Then` statement. Others like the compactness of the single expression.

3.5   Create a Page-Range Indicator on Each Page

Problem

You're creating a report that contains a large number of items. To make it easier to see the range of items on each page, you'd like to create a page-range indicator. This would show the first and last items on the page, as in a telephone book. Is there a way to do this?

Solution

The answer to your question is a qualified yes. You can create such a page-range indicator, but placing it anywhere but in the page footer is difficult. Although you can place it in the page header, the method to do so is quite complex and is the subject of a topic in the Microsoft Access Solutions database (*SOLUTIONS.MDB*), which shipped with Access 95 and Access 97. You can also download an Access 2000 version of this very useful sample database, called *Solutions9.mdb*. Search for that name at *http://msdn.microsoft.com* to find the download.

Because Access prints documents from top to bottom, by the time you know the last item on the page it's too late to print it at the top of the page. The Solutions database workaround involves forcing the report to format itself twice, capturing the page ranges for all the pages during the first pass and storing the values in an array. When it makes the second pass, you supply the values from the array. That solution requires VBA and is cumbersome. The solution we present here focuses on a simpler method, placing the information you need in the page footer. If you can live with that placement, this solution is straightforward.

To create a page-range indicator on your own reports, follow these steps:

1. Create a new report or open an existing one in design view. Make sure that the report includes page header and footer sections (if it doesn't, choose Format → Page Header/Footer to add them). In the page header section, add a text box and

set its properties, as shown in Table 3-8. This text box will hold the first row's value when you print the page.

Table 3-8. Property values for the hidden text box in the report's page header

Property	Value
Name	txtFirstItem
Visible	No

2. Add a text box in the report's page footer section. None of its properties are important to this technique except one, its ControlSource property. Set the text box's ControlSource property to be the expression:

```
=[txtFirstItem] & " -- " & [ProductName]
```

replacing the [Product Name] reference with the name of the field you'd like to track in the page-range indicator. This must match the field name you used in Step 1.

3. Set the OnFormat event property for the report's page header section to be the following event procedure:

```
Private Sub PageHeader0_Format(Cancel As Integer, FormatCount As Integer)
    Me.txtFirstItem = Me.ProductName
End Sub
```

This tells Access to run the code every time it formats the page header (once per page). Figure 3-10 shows the report and the properties sheet as they will look after you've assigned the property.

4. Save and run your report. You should see the page-range indicator as in the sample report, rptPageRange.

To view an example of this solution, load the rptPageRange report from *03-05.MDB* in preview view (see Figure 3-11). You'll see, at the bottom of each page, a listing of the items printed on that page.

Discussion

The technique presented in this solution is based on the fact that when Access prints the page header (or the report header or a group header), it gives you access to the row of data it's about to print. The same goes for footers, in reverse—there you have access to the row of data that's just been printed.

When you call the event procedure from the Format event of the page header, you place the data from the page's first row into the hidden text box, txtFirstItem. The data in that text box doesn't change until you again format the page. When Access gets to the bottom of the page and attempts to print the page footer, it calculates the value of the text box you've placed there. That text box retrieves the value you previously stored in txtFirstItem and combines it with the data from the last row that printed on the page to create the page-range indicator.

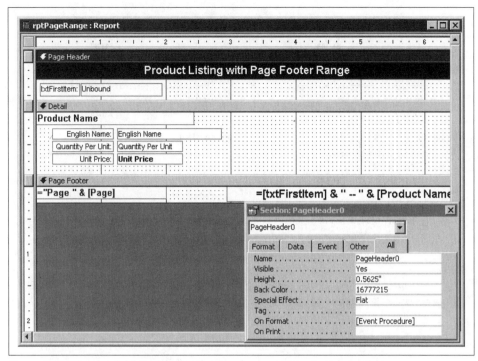

Figure 3-10. The sample report, rptPageRange, after setting the OnFormat event property

Though simple, this method does have a few limitations:

- The page-range indicator must go in the page footer. If you attempt to place it in the page header, the data it prints will always be off by a page in one direction or the other, depending on how you're viewing the report.

- For this method to work, you must include the page header section on every page. (The PageHeader property for the report must be set to All Pages.) Because you must fill in the hidden text box once for each page, the only place you can do that is in the page header.

 It's interesting to note that within an expression you place within the Properties window, you must surround field names and control references with brackets ([ ]). Within VBA code, the brackets are optional, and you generally don't need to use them unless the field or control name isn't a valid VBA identifier (if it includes spaces in its name, for example).

English Name:	Tibetan Barley Beer		English Name:	Green Chartreuse (Liqueur)
Quantity Per Unit:	24 - 12 oz bottles		Quantity Per Unit:	750 cc per bottle
Unit Price:	**$19.00**		Unit Price:	**$18.00**

Chef Anton's Cajun Seasoning

English Name:	Chef Anton's Cajun Seasoning
Quantity Per Unit:	48 - 6 oz jars
Unit Price:	**$22.00**

Chef Anton's Gumbo Mix

English Name:	Chef Anton's Gumbo Mix
Quantity Per Unit:	36 boxes
Unit Price:	**$21.35**

Chocolade

English Name:	Dutch Chocolate
Quantity Per Unit:	10 pkgs.
Unit Price:	**$12.75**

Côte de Blaye

English Name:	Côte de Blaye (Red Bordeaux wi
Quantity Per Unit:	12 - 75 cl bottles
Unit Price:	**$263.50**

Escargots de Bourgogne

English Name:	Escargots from Burgundy
Quantity Per Unit:	24 pieces
Unit Price:	**$13.25**

Filo Mix

English Name:	Mix for Greek Filo Dough
Quantity Per Unit:	16 - 2 kg boxes
Unit Price:	**$7.00**

Fløtemysost

English Name:	Fløtemys Cream Cheese
Quantity Per Unit:	10 - 500 g pkgs.
Unit Price:	**$21.50**

Geitost

English Name:	Goat Cheese
Quantity Per Unit:	500 g
Unit Price:	**$2.50**

Page 1   **Alice Mutton -- Geitost**

Figure 3-11. rptPageRange includes a page-range indicator in the page footer

3.6 Create a Simple Bar Graph on a Report

Problem

You need to create a simple bar graph on a report. Microsoft Graph or the Office Web Components would probably work, but you're hoping for a simpler native Access solution. You need a bar for each row showing the relative score for each student. Can't you do this with the standard Access controls?

Solution

You can place a rectangle control in the detail section of your report and set its width during the Format event that occurs as Access lays out each row of data. This solution shows how you can create a simple bar graph, setting the width of the rectangle control to be based on a numeric value in your data.

Open and run the report rptGraph in *03-06.MDB* (see Figure 3-12). This report shows a list of students and their scores, along with a bar whose width represents the value of the score.

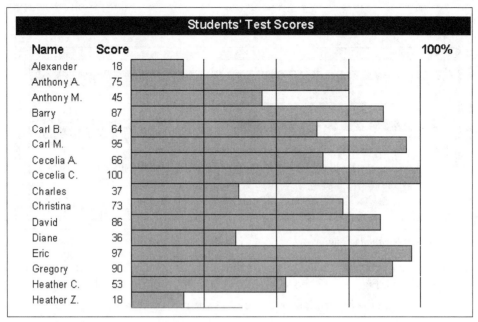

Figure 3-12. The sample report, rptGraph

To create a bar graph like this one in your own applications, follow these steps:

1. Create your report, including the text data you'd like to show for each row. The sample report shows the Name and Score fields from tblScores, using controls named txtName and txtScore.

2. Add a rectangle control from the report toolbox and place it next to the data in the detail section. In the sample report, the rectangle's control name is rctBar. The control's width isn't important, because you'll be adjusting that programmatically (the example report sets the width of the rectangle to be the maximum width for the report, four inches). For appearance purposes, you'll probably want to set its height to be the same as the height of the text boxes you've already placed on the report. Figure 3-13 shows the report in design view.

3. If you want, you can place vertical lines at regular intervals along the maximum length of the bar. In the sample report, the vertical lines are placed at the 25%, 50%, and 75% locations. You can place these lines wherever you like; if they're the same height as the detail section, they'll appear as continuous lines on the printed report. If you've used group headers and/or footers in your report, you'll need to place the vertical lines in those sections as well to make them appear continuous.

4. To set the width of the rectangle for each row, create the following event procedure in the OnFormat event property of the report's detail section:

```
Private Sub Detail1_Format(Cancel As Integer, FormatCount As Integer)
    Me.rctBar.Width = (Me.txtScore / 100) * (1440 * 4)
End Sub
```

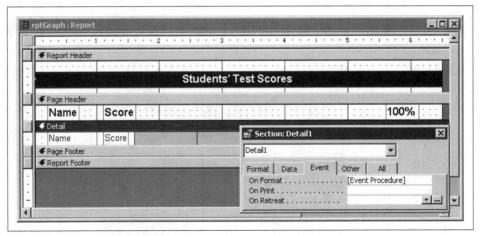

Figure 3-13. rptGraph in design view

This event procedure tells Access to run your new macro each time it formats a row of data. Figure 3-13 shows the properties sheet for the detail section.

5. Save and run the report. It should look like the report shown in Figure 3-12.

Discussion

As Access lays out the report and prepares to print it, it formats each row of data for presentation. As it does this, it runs the VBA code attached to the OnFormat event property. In this case, for each row of data, you've told Access to set the width of the rectangle control based on the value in a numeric field. When it prints that row, the rectangle has a width proportional to the value in that numeric field.

In the sample report, the maximum width of the rectangle is four inches. If a student has a score of 100%, you want the printed bar to be 4 inches wide. Therefore, the expression:

```
Me.txtScore/100 * 4
```

evaluates to the number of inches wide that you'd like the bar to be. To set the width of the bar from the Format event, however, you'll need to specify the width in twips, not inches, because that's what Access expects. There are 20 twips in a point and 72 points in an inch, so there are 1,440 twips in an inch. To convert the number of inches to twips, multiply the calculated value by 1,440. The final expression in the sample report is:

```
(Me.txtScore/100) * (1440 * 4)
```

This expression will evaluate to be the width of the bar in twips, which is exactly what you need. If your report needs a scaling factor other than 100 or a maximum width other than 4, you'll need to adjust the expression accordingly.

Though the method presented in this solution will work only for the simplest of cases, when it does work it does a great job. It's quick, it's simple, and it produces nice output. To achieve the effect you want, experiment with different shadings, border colors, and gaps between the rows.

3.7   Create a Page Total

Problem

Access allows you to create a group total in the group footer on a report or a report total on the report footer, but you can't find a way to create a page total in the page footer. You understand that this problem doesn't come up too often, but for your report you could really use this element. Is there a way to sum up values over a single page?

Solution

It's true that Access allows aggregate calculations only in group or report footers. You can, however, easily create page totals using two simple macros. This solution demonstrates this technique and shows how to add this capability to any of your own reports.

To create page totals for your own reports, follow these steps:

1. Create your report, and sort and group the data as desired. In the report's page footer section, include a text box named txtPageTotal.

2. Create the following event procedure in the Format event of the page header and report header sections:

```
Private Sub PageHeader0_Format(Cancel As Integer, FormatCount As Integer)
    Me.txtPageTotal = 0
End Sub

Private Sub ReportHeader0_Format(Cancel As Integer, FormatCount As Integer)
    Me.txtPageTotal = 0
End Sub
```

3. Create an additional event procedure in the OnPrint event for the detail section:

```
Private Sub Detail1_Print(Cancel As Integer, PrintCount As Integer)
    Me.txtPageTotal = Me.txtPageTotal + Me.Freight
End Sub
```

4. Save your report. When you run it, you will see the total of the field you set in the OnPrint event procedure.

Now load rptPageTotals from *03-07.MDB* in preview view (see Figure 3-14). This report is used to track orders and their freight costs. The items are grouped by month, and each group has a total in the group footer. At the bottom of each page, you'll see the total for all items on the current page.

Figure 3-15 shows the sample report in design view.

Ordered: August 1992			
Ana Trujillo Emparedados y	Avda. de la Constitución 2222	México D.F.	$1.61
			$1.61
Ordered: September 1992			
Bólido Comidas preparadas	C / Araquil, 67	Madrid	$77.92
Bon app'	12, rue des Bouchers	Marseille	$10.19
Bon app'	12, rue des Bouchers	Marseille	$166.31
			$254.42
		Page Total:	$898.42

Figure 3-14. Page 2 of the rptPageTotals report with page totals

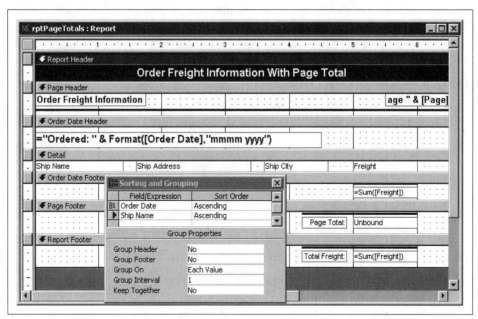

Figure 3-15. rptPageTotals in design view

Discussion

Access makes it simple to sum values in group or report footers: use the *Sum* function in the ControlSource property for a text box. For example, to sum the freight costs in either a group footer or a report footer, you could use an expression like this:

```
=Sum([Freight])
```

and Access would perform the sum over the range included in the footer section (for either the group or the entire report). To create a page total, however, you must dig a bit deeper into the way Access prints reports.

The report-printing engine in Access works as a forward-marching machine: the engine formats and then prints each section in turn, such that each section is handled in the order in which it appears on the page. The report-printing engine deals first with the report header, then any page header, then any group header, then each row of the detail section, and so on. At each point, Access allows you to "hook" into various events, doing work alongside its work.

The two events described in this solution are the Format event and the Print event. Normally, you'll attach a VBA procedure to the Format event of a section if you want to affect the section's layout on the page. You'll use the Print event to make calculations based on the data as you know it's going to print. When Access calls your macro or VBA code from the Print event, you are guaranteed that the current row is going to be printed. You can't assume this from the Format event, because Access calls the code attached to the Format event before it decides whether or not the current row will fit on the current page. From either event, you have access to the current row of data that's about to be printed, and you can use that as part of your event procedure.

In this case, calculating a page total requires two steps: you must reset the page total for each page (and before you start printing the report), and you must accumulate the value in each row as you print the row.

The accumulation part is simple: every time you print a row, the procedure attached to the detail section's Print event adds the value in the current row's Freight field (or whatever field you're tracking on your own report) to the current value in txtPageTotal. When Access needs to print the page footer, that value is filled in and ready to print. The event procedure should be written on the Print event, not the Format event, to ensure that you never add a value to the page footer unless you're sure the row will be printed on the current page. Calling the code from the Print event guarantees this.

You can reset the page total so it starts from zero from the Format event of the page header section. Because this is the first section that will print on every page, resetting the total in the page header should work. You *could* use the Print event here, but because you're guaranteed that the page header section will fit on its page, you might as well do the work as early as possible. The problem here arises from the fact that, in some reports, you may tell Access to print the page header only on pages where there isn't a report header (see the report's PageHeader property). If you do this, Access won't format the page header on the first page, and it therefore won't call the necessary code. To make up for this, the example report (rptPageTotals in *03-07. MDB*) also calls the code from the report header's Format event. Because this event occurs only when Access prints the first page, there's no redundancy here. You may not need to reset the page total from the report header, but it can't hurt.

Be wary of performing any calculations during a section's Format event. Because you aren't guaranteed that the section will actually print on the current page, you could be calculating based on a value that won't be a part of the page. Making this mistake in the sample report, for example, would be a major error. Because this report is set up so that Access will print a group only if the entire group can fit on a page, it might format a number of rows, then decide that the whole group can't fit. Each time it attempts to format a row, it will call the code attached to the Format event, which will add the value to the total. To avoid this problem, perform calculations from a section's Print event only. Use the Format event to change the layout of a section—for example, to make a specific control visible or invisible, depending on the data you find in the current row (see the Solution in Recipe 3.4 for an example of this usage).

3.8 Avoid Unwanted Blank Rows on Mailing Labels

Problem

When you print mailing labels, especially when you use a small font size and place the address text boxes close together, you sometimes get unwanted blank rows in the addresses when the labels print. You also can't seem to use lines or graphics on your labels without causing blank rows. How can you get your labels to print correctly—without blank rows—in these situations?

Solution

The CanGrow and CanShrink text box properties for reports allow text boxes to grow or shrink vertically as needed. These properties normally work well, but sometimes overlapping text boxes or graphics can interfere with text boxes' ability to shrink or grow. This solution shows how you can avoid these problems by combining the output of several fields into a single expression and using that expression as the row source of a single text box.

Open the tblCompanyAddresses table from *03-08.MDB* in datasheet view. You can see that this table contains typical address data, with three address fields (Address1, Address2, and PO Box). Some of the sample records have blanks in at least one of these address fields.

Close the table and open the rptLabels report in preview mode. This is a typical mailing-label report, as might have been produced by the Mailing Label Report Wizard. Notice that there are no blank rows in the addresses. Now open the rptLabelsWithImageBroken report in preview view (see Figure 3-16). We added to the left side of each label an Image control that causes unwanted blank lines. Finally, open the rptLabelsWithImageFixed report in preview view (see Figure 3-17). Notice that this version of the report doesn't have any unwanted blank lines, even though the same image appears on the left side of each label.

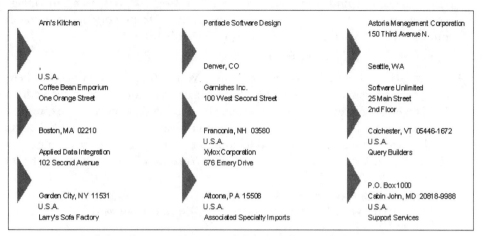

Figure 3-16. rptLabelsWithImageBroken prints labels with unwanted blank rows

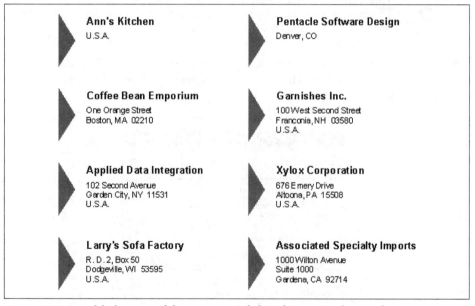

Figure 3-17. A modified version of the report, rptLabelsWithImageFixed, prints fine

Follow these steps to create a mailing-label report, complete with a graphic on each label but without any unwanted blank lines:

1. Create a new mailing-label report. The easiest way to do this is to use the Mailing Label Report Wizard. The rptLabels sample report was created using this wizard. Its record source is tblCompanyAddresses.

2. Add a line, unbound object frame, or Image control to the label. In the sample database, rptLabelsWithImageBroken includes an Image control containing a gray triangle (a Paintbrush image) to the left of the addresses. Here, the Image control prevents the text boxes' CanShrink property from working, resulting in numerous blank rows in the addresses (see Figure 3-16).

3. Import the basCrLf module from *03-08.MDB* into your database.

4. Delete the multiple address-line controls (five in rptLabelsWithImageBroken) and replace them with a single text box that concatenates each of the address lines together. For each text box that may be missing data, create an expression to wrap the field in the *acbMakeLine* function (discussed in Section 3.8.3). The final control-source expression should look something like the control source for the txtWholeAddress control in rptLabelsWithImageFixed, which is shown here:

```
=acbMakeLine([Address1]) & acbMakeLine([Address2]) & acbMakeLine([POBox]) &
acbMakeLine(([City]+", ") & ([StateProvince]+" ") & [ZipPostalCode]) &
acbMakeLine([Country])
```

 Press Shift+F2 when your cursor is in the text box's ControlSource property (or any other property) to open up the Zoom box, which lets you see the whole expression as you work with it.

5. Save the report and run it to make sure it produces the desired output (like that shown in Figure 3-17). The completed report is shown in design view in Figure 3-18.

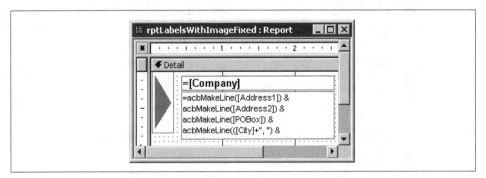

Figure 3-18. rptLabelsWithImageFixed in design view

Discussion

When you combine several address fields into a single expression and use that expression as the row source of a single text box, you have only one text box to grow or shrink as needed. The elimination of multiple text boxes prevents problems with CanShrink/CanGrow that occur when a text box that needs to shrink is placed on the same row as a text box or other control (such as an Image control) that can't shrink.

We used the *acbMakeLine* function to check for nulls in a text field and return a null value for the line if the *varValue* argument is `Null`; otherwise, *acbMakeLine* adds carriage-return and line-feed characters after the field. Thus, a new line is created only if the address line is non-null, giving us essentially the same effect as using the CanShrink property. The *acbMakeLine* function is shown here:

```
Public Function acbMakeLine(varValue as Variant)
    If IsNull(varValue) Then
        acbMakeLine = Null
    Else
        acbMakeLine = varValue & vbCrLf
    End If
End Function
```

acbMakeLine uses the built-in `vbCrLf` constant, which is equivalent to typing `Chr$(13) & Chr$(10)`.

If you use a concatenated expression for an address, you can accommodate more fields on a label than you could if you placed each address text box on a separate line. This method works fine as long as you know that each address will be missing at least one row of address data. If your labels have room for only four lines of data, for example, you could put five lines of data into a concatenated expression if you know that no address will use all five lines.

Unlike specialized label-printing programs, Access does not lock the report size to the label's dimensions to prevent you from accidentally changing the sizes of labels after you have created them with the Mailing Label Report Wizard. It is very easy to accidentally nudge the right edge or bottom edge of a mailing-label report (by moving a control, for example) so that the report contents overprint the labels.

We could have used a series of *IIf* functions here instead of using the *acbMakeLine* function, but using *acbMakeLine* is simpler and less confusing.

Another approach would be to take further advantage of the fact that the + operator propagates nulls—a feature we're already using to avoid printing commas after blank cities or extra spaces after blank states. For example, the following expression will eliminate extra lines, because everything inside a set of parentheses that includes a null value will be converted to `Null`:

```
([Address1]+Chr$(13)+Chr(10)) & ([Address2]+Chr$(13)+Chr(10)) _
 & ([POBox]+Chr$(13)+Chr(10)) & (([City]+", ") & ([StateProvince]+"  ") _
 & [ZipPostalCode] +Chr$(13)+Chr(10)) & ([Country])
```

 When you first create a mailing-label report, write down its width and detail section height so that you can quickly recover from any accidental resizing of the report, which could result in label text printing outside of the label's boundaries.

3.9 Suppress Printing a Report if There Are No Records to Print

Problem

You have a report that prints records you select from a criteria form. Sometimes there aren't any records that match the criteria and the report opens with *#Error* in the detail section, which is unattractive and confusing. Is there any way you can prevent the report from printing when it has no records to print?

Solution

Access includes an event, OnNoData, that fires when no records are present in the report's underlying recordset. This solution shows you how to use this new event to suppress printing of the report when no records match the specified criteria.

To create a report that suppresses printing when there are no records, follow these steps:

1. Create a new report or open an existing report in design view.

2. Create an event procedure attached to the report's OnNoData property. (If you're unsure of how to do this, see Section P.5.5 in the the preface of this book.) Enter the following VBA code in the event procedure:

```
Private Sub Report_NoData(Cancel As Integer)
    MsgBox "Sorry, no records match these criteria!", _
       vbExclamation, "No Records to Print"
    Cancel = True
End Sub
```

3. Save and run the report. If you enter criteria that do not match any records, you will get a message box telling you that no records meet the criteria (like the one shown in Figure 3-21).

The following example demonstrates this solution. Load the *03-09.MDB* database. Open the frmCriteria1 pop-up criteria form. This form allows you to enter criteria for the rptSelect1 report (see Figure 3-19).

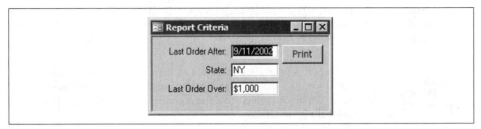

Figure 3-19. The frmCriteria1 pop-up criteria form with default values

When you press the traffic-light button, a simple event procedure will execute that opens the report in print preview mode. The rptSelect1 report is based on the qryCriteria1 parameter query, which derives its parameter values from the controls on the frmCriteria1 form. If you accept the default values, the parameter query will return a recordset with no records. This will produce the report shown in Figure 3-20.

Figure 3-20. rptCriteria1 prints a page of errors when no records are selected

Now open the frmcriteria2 pop-up criteria form. This form is identical to the first, except that the event procedure attached to its command button runs the rptSelect2 report instead. If you accept the default values, the rptSelect2 report will attempt to run, again with no records. But this version of the report has an event procedure attached to its OnNoData event that suppresses printing and instead displays the message box shown in Figure 3-21.

Figure 3-21. rptCriteria2 displays this message and cancels printing when there are no records

Discussion

The OnNoData event is triggered whenever a report attempts to print with no records. If you attach an event procedure to the OnNoData event, your code will run whenever the report prints without any records. While the *MsgBox* statement informs the user what has happened, the key line of code is:

```
Cancel = True
```

This line tells Access to cancel printing of the report (by setting the passed *Cancel* argument to True).

If you use VBA code to open a report that has no data and allow the report's OnNo-Data event to cancel the report, you will get an error in the code that attempted to open the report. So, in this solution, you'll find error-handling code in the button-click event that opens the report in frmCriteria2. When an error occurs, the code checks whether it's the expected error, which has a number of 2501. If so, it ignores the error. Here's the code behind the cmdPrint button:

```
Private Sub cmdPrint_Click()

    On Error GoTo HandleErr

    Me.Visible = False
    DoCmd.OpenReport "rptSelect2", acPreview

ExitHere:
    DoCmd.Close acForm, Me.Name
    Exit Sub

HandleErr:
    Select Case Err.Number
        Case 2501
            ' The OpenReport action was canceled.
            ' There were no rows. So do nothing.
        Case Else
            MsgBox Err.Number & ": " & Err.Description
    End Select
    Resume ExitHere

End Sub
```

The report header contains controls to display the selection criteria, which are picked up from the criteria form, using expressions like this one:

```
=[Forms]![frmCriteria1]![txtLastOrderAfter]
```

The form disappears from view when the report opens in print preview mode because the event procedure attached to the traffic-light button sets the form's Visible property to False before opening the report. Making the form invisible (rather than closing it) ensures that the selection criteria are still available for the report's data source.

See Also

For more information on printing query criteria on reports, see the Solution in Recipe 3.2.

3.10 Print Different Headers or Footers on Odd and Even Pages

Problem

Some of your reports are printed double-sided, and you would like to have mirror-image headers and footers on odd and even pages. How do you do this in Access?

Solution

This technique makes use of two sets of header and footer controls, one for odd pages and one for even pages. An event procedure run from the section's Format event uses the Page property and the Mod operator to determine whether the page is odd or even and makes the appropriate controls visible or invisible.

The following steps show you how to create your own report that prints different headers and footers on odd and even pages:

1. Open the report you want to print double-sided (or even single-sided, with different odd and even headers and footers).

2. Make a copy of the header control, and place one of the copies of the control on the left of the header and the other on the right. Make the lefthand control left-aligned (to print on even-numbered pages) and the righthand control right-aligned (to print on odd-numbered pages).

3. Create an event procedure attached to the OnFormat property of the report's page header section. In the event procedure, enter code similar to the following:

```
Private Sub PageHeader_Format(Cancel As Integer, FormatCount As Integer)
    On Error GoTo PageHeader_FormatError

    Dim fIsEven As Boolean

    fIsEven = acbIsEven(Me.Page)

    Me.lblTitleLeft.Visible = Not fIsEven
    Me.lblTitleRight.Visible = fIsEven

End Sub
```

You'll need to replace the controls in the event procedure with the names of your controls.

4. Make copies of the footer controls as well, and make a similar event procedure for the footer's OnFormat event property, referencing its left and right controls. In the event procedure, enter code similar to the following:

```
Private Sub PageFooter_Format(Cancel As Integer, FormatCount As Integer)

    Dim fIsEven As Boolean

    fIsEven = acbIsEven(Me.Page)

    Me.txtPageLeft.Visible = Not fIsEven
    Me.txtPageRight.Visible = fIsEven
    Me.txtPrintedOnLeft.Visible = fIsEven
    Me.txtPrintedOnRight.Visible = Not fIsEven

End Sub
```

Again, you'll need to replace the controls in the event procedure with the names of your controls.

5. Without closing the module, add the following function to the form's module:

```
Private Function acbIsEven(ByVal intValue As Integer) As Boolean
    ' Return True if intValue is even, False otherwise.
    acbIsEven = ((intValue Mod 2) = 0)
End Function
```

6. Save and execute the report to confirm that it performs as desired. The completed report is shown in design view in Figure 3-22.

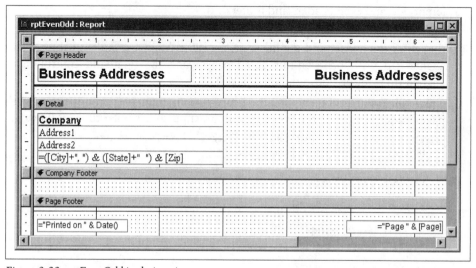

Figure 3-22. rptEvenOdd in design view

To see the sample report, load *03-10.MDB*. Open rptEvenOdd in print preview mode; you should get a report that has one header and footer for odd pages (see Figure 3-23) and a different header and footer for even pages (see Figure 3-24).

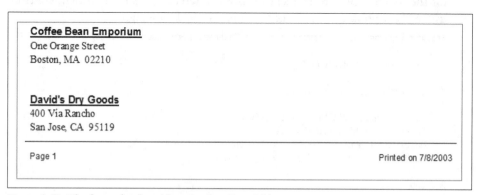

Figure 3-23. The footer for the odd pages of rptEvenOdd

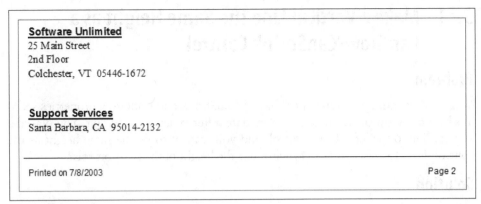

Software Unlimited
25 Main Street
2nd Floor
Colchester, VT 05446-1672

Support Services
Santa Barbara, CA 95014-2132

Printed on 7/8/2003   Page 2

Figure 3-24. The footer for the even pages of rptEvenOdd

Discussion

The two event procedures call the *acbIsEven* function to determine whether the current page is even or odd, passing the current page number to the function. The current page number is determined by referencing the Page property of the report (Me. Page). *acbIsEven* uses the Mod operator, which returns the remainder when the page number is divided by 2, yielding 0 for even pages or 1 for odd pages. The following statement:

```
acbIsEven = ((intValue Mod 2) = 0)
```

returns True to the calling procedure if the page Mod 2 is 0 (i.e., if the page is even); otherwise, it returns False.

If you set fIsEven to the return value of *acbIsEven*, you can then set the visibility of the rest of the controls based on its value.

You can't see them in Figure 3-22, but there are four text boxes in the footer section of the example report. On the left side of the footer, the txtPagePrintedOnLeft control has been placed on top of the txtPageLeft control. On the right side of the footer, the txtPageRight control has been placed on top of the txtPrintedOnRight control. This works because only one set of controls (txtPagePrintedOnLeft and txtPageRight, or txtPageOnRight and txtPageLeft) are visible at the same time.

As an alternative to using two controls in the header of the report, you could use just one control that is as wide as the report and alternately set its TextAlign property to Left or Right based on the return value of *acbIsEven*. (You can't do this in the footer because of the need for two sets of controls with different alignments.)

3.11   Make a Vertical Line the Same Height as a CanGrow/CanShrink Control

Problem

You have a control on a report that has its CanShrink and CanGrow properties set to Yes so it can grow or shrink to accommodate different amounts of text. You placed a vertical line to the left of the control, and you want it to be the same height as the control. Is there a way you can synchronize the height of the two controls?

Solution

If you place a line on a report using the Line tool, it will always be the same size. To make a line change its height to match the height of another control (or group of controls), you need to use the Line method in a procedure attached to the Print event of a report section. This solution uses the Line method to make a line whose height varies to accommodate the changing height of a text box that displays a memo field.

Follow these steps to add to your own report a vertical line that shrinks or grows to match one or more CanShrink/CanGrow controls in a section:

1. Create a report or open an existing report in design view. Don't use the Line control to create a vertical line in the report. If you've already created such a line, remove it now.

2. Create an event procedure for the Print event of the group footer section (or the section on your report where you'd like the line to appear). (For more information on creating event procedures, see this book's Preface.) In the event procedure, add code similar to this:

```
Private Sub GroupFooter0_Print(Cancel As Integer, PrintCount As Integer)

    Dim sngLineTop As Single
    Dim sngLineLeft As Single
    Dim sngLineWidth As Single
    Dim sngLineHeight As Single

    Const acbcSMTwips = 1
    Const acbcDSSolid = 0

    Me.ScaleMode = acbcSMTwips
    Me.DrawStyle = acbcDSSolid

    ' Set the coordinates for the line.
    sngLineTop = Me.lblConditions.Top
    sngLineLeft = 0
    sngLineWidth = 100
    With Me.txtConditions
        sngLineHeight = .Top + .Height
    End With
```

```
' Draw the line.
Me.Line (sngLineLeft, sngLineTop)-Step(sngLineWidth, sngLineHeight), , BF

End Sub
```

Replace the references to lblConditions and txtConditions with the names of the controls in your own report.

3. Save and preview the report to verify that the line alongside the CanShrink/Can-Grow controls changes, as in Figure 3-27. The completed sample report is shown in design view in Figure 3-25.

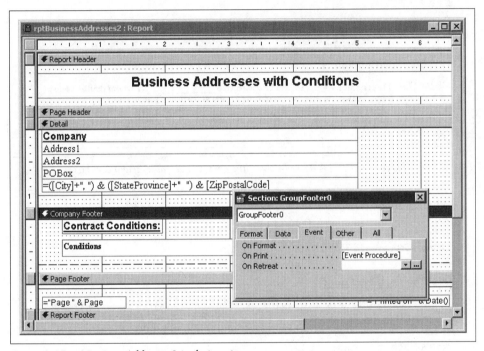

Figure 3-25. rptBusinessAddresses2 in design view

To see an example of this solution, load *03-11.MDB*. Open rptBusinessAddresses1 in preview view (Figure 3-26). This report lists business addresses and contract conditions. Notice that the line in the company footer section is of fixed height and does not vary to match the height of this section.

Now open rptBusinessAddresses2 in preview view (Figure 3-27). This version of the report contains a line whose height matches the height of the company footer section.

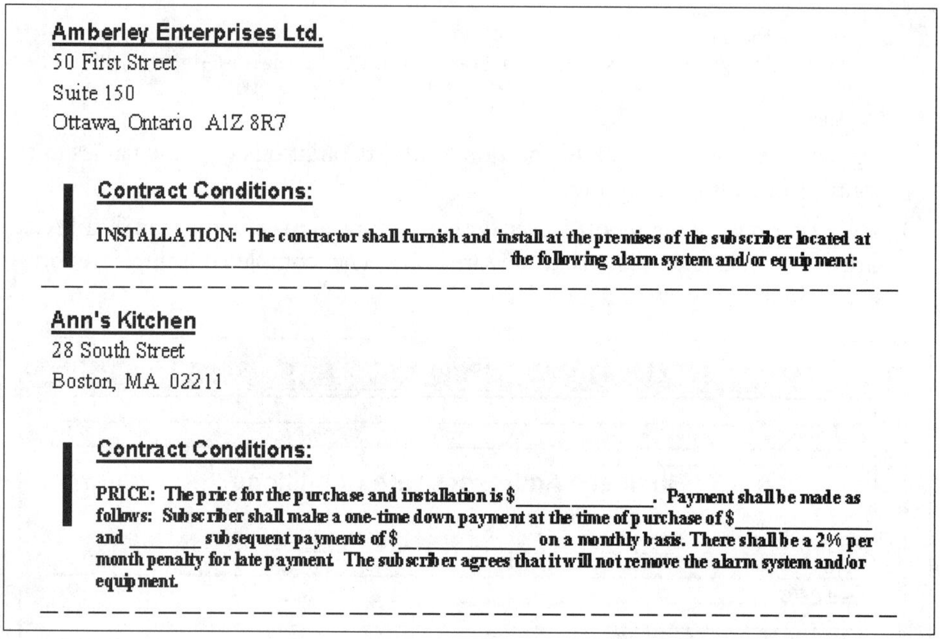

Amberley Enterprises Ltd.
50 First Street
Suite 150
Ottawa, Ontario A1Z 8R7

Contract Conditions:

INSTALLATION: The contractor shall furnish and install at the premises of the subscriber located at
_____ the following alarm system and/or equipment:

Ann's Kitchen
28 South Street
Boston, MA 02211

Contract Conditions:

PRICE: The price for the purchase and installation is $_____. Payment shall be made as
follows: Subscriber shall make a one-time down payment at the time of purchase of $_____
and _____ subsequent payments of $_____ on a monthly basis. There shall be a 2% per
month penalty for late payment. The subscriber agrees that it will not remove the alarm system and/or
equipment.

Figure 3-26. This report contains a fixed-height line next to a variable-height text box

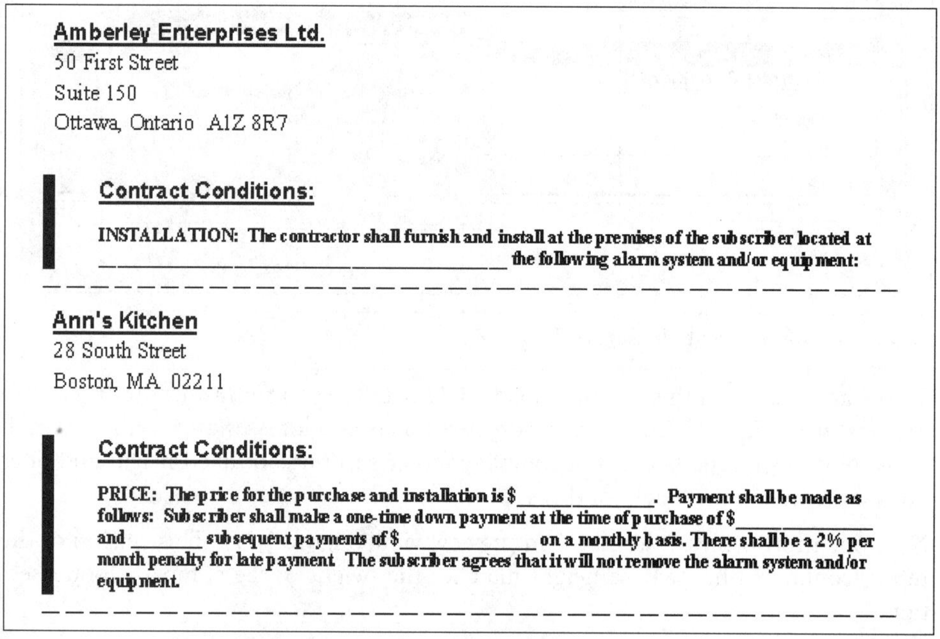

Amberley Enterprises Ltd.
50 First Street
Suite 150
Ottawa, Ontario A1Z 8R7

Contract Conditions:

INSTALLATION: The contractor shall furnish and install at the premises of the subscriber located at
_____ the following alarm system and/or equipment:

Ann's Kitchen
28 South Street
Boston, MA 02211

Contract Conditions:

PRICE: The price for the purchase and installation is $_____. Payment shall be made as
follows: Subscriber shall make a one-time down payment at the time of purchase of $_____
and _____ subsequent payments of $_____ on a monthly basis. There shall be a 2% per
month penalty for late payment. The subscriber agrees that it will not remove the alarm system and/or
equipment.

Figure 3-27. A report with a programmatically created variable-length line

Discussion

The event procedure uses the Line method to create a line that starts at the top of the lblConditions label and extends to the bottom of the txtConditions text box, growing and shrinking in proportion to the text box. You can use the Line method to draw lines or rectangles on reports using the coordinates you specify (sngLineHeight through sngLineWidth in the sample procedure). The event procedure sets the sngLineTop argument to the top of the lblConditions label, sngLineLeft to 0, sngLineWidth to 100, and sngLineHeight to the bottom of the txtConditions text box. Because Access does not provide a VBA Bottom property for controls, this value is calculated by adding the text box's Height property to its Top property, using the following piece of code (which makes use of the VBA With...End With construct):

```
With Me.txtConditions
    sngLineHeight = .Top + .Height
End With
```

The line itself (actually, a rectangle) is drawn by the following line of code:

```
Me.Line (sngLineLeft, sngLineTop)-Step(sngLineWidth, sngLineHeight), , BF
```

where the variables in the first set of parentheses define the upper-left corner of the rectangle and those in the second set of parentheses define its width and height. The reserved word Step allows you to use height and width values for the rectangle instead of specifying the lower-right corner. The last argument, BF, indicates that the line will be a rectangle (B) instead of a line and that it will be filled with the same color as its border (F).

The ScaleMode property specifies the unit of measurement. Because Access uses twips as its measurement unit, this property is generally set to twips, as in the acbcSMTwips constant in the sample code. The available settings are listed in Table 3-9.

Table 3-9. Available ScaleMode property settings

Setting	Description
0	Custom values for ScaleHeight, ScaleWidth, ScaleLeft, and ScaleTop
1	Twip (default)
2	Point
3	Pixel
4	Character
5	Inch
6	Millimeter
7	Centimeter

The DrawStyle property specifies the line type; it is set to Solid in the sample code using the `acbcDSSolid` constant. The available settings are listed in Table 3-10.

Table 3-10. Available DrawStyle property settings

Setting	Description
0	Solid (default)
1	Dash
2	Dot
3	Dash-dot
4	Dash-dot-dot
5	Invisible
6	Inside solid

3.12   Alternate Gray Bars on My Reports

Problem

You have some reports on which you'd like to print alternate rows with gray bars in the background. Printing these bars makes the reports easier to read, especially when there's lots of data or the report is very wide. Is there a way to create these bars in Access?

Solution

There are a number of ways to print alternate rows with gray and white backgrounds. The simplest method is to alternate the background color of the detail section for each new record. This solution shows you how to use this method to achieve the desired effect on your reports.

To create your own reports with alternating gray bars in the detail section, follow these steps:

1. Create your report. Because this method will fill the entire detail section with gray shading, the effect will work best if your detail section is one line high. (It will work with taller detail sections, but it won't look as good.)

2. Make sure that every control in the detail section has its BackStyle property set to Transparent. You can quickly change this property for all the controls in the section by marquee-selecting all the controls and then changing the BackStyle property in the properties sheet, which will now have the title Multiple Selection (see Figure 3-28).

3. Edit the report's module (click on the Code button on the Report Design toolbar or choose the View → Code menu option) and enter the following lines of code in the module's declarations area:

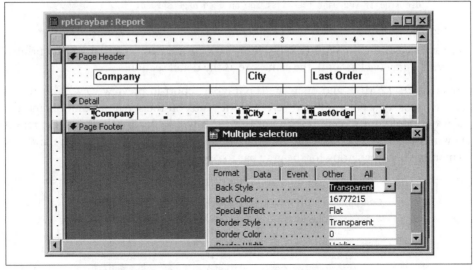

Figure 3-28. Changing all the controls' BackStyle properties in one operation

```
' Shade this row or not?
Dim blnShade As Boolean
```

4. Create an event procedure attached to the OnPrint event property of your report's detail section and add the code that follows. This code must be attached to the OnPrint event property because the Line method for reports will not work when called during the Format event.

```
Private Sub Detail1_Print(Cancel As Integer, PrintCount As Integer)

    ' If all three color components are the same value,
    ' the result will be some shade of gray (ranging
    ' all the way from black (0, 0, 0) to white (255, 255, 255)
    Dim lngGray As Long
    lngGray = RGB(221, 221, 221)

    If blnShade Then
        Me.Detail1.BackColor = lngGray
    Else
        Me.Detail1.BackColor = vbWhite
    End If

    ' Alternate the value of blnShade
    blnShade = Not blnShade
End Sub
```

5. If it matters whether the first row on a page is shaded, create an event procedure attached to the OnPrint property of the report's page header. Replace the False value with True if you want the first row on each page to be shaded.

```
Sub PageHeader0_Print (Cancel As Integer, PrintCount As Integer)
    ' Make sure the first row on the page isn't shaded.
```

```
        ' Use True if you want the first row on each page shaded.
        blnShade = False
    End Sub
```

6. Save and print the report. Every other row in the detail section will be printed with a gray background, the same size as the detail section.

Now load *03-12.MDB* and open the rptGrayBar report in preview view. This report may not look very good on your screen (it depends on the screen resolution and the color depth of your screen driver), but printed it will look something like the report shown in Figure 3-29. (The exact output will depend on your printer; you may need to modify the color setting for the gray bar to optimize it.)

Company	City	Last Order
Amberley Enterprises Ltd.	Ottawa	1/12/1992
Ann's Kitchen	Boston	2/25/1993
Applied Data Integration	Garden City	6/15/1994
Associated Specialty Imports	Gardena	8/22/1993
Astoria Management Corporation	Seattle	2/4/1993
Coffee Bean Emporium	Boston	9/19/1993
David's Dry Goods	San Jose	5/17/1994
Garnishes Inc.	Franconia	5/22/1994
Holography Inc.	Beaconsfield	4/7/1993
Larry's Sofa Factory	Dodgeville	7/22/1993
Mabel's Old Fashioned Soda Fountain	Redmond	7/1/1994
Pentacle Software Design	Denver	7/14/1993
Power Software	Kent	2/2/1993
Query Builders	Cabin John	4/3/1994
Software Unlimited	Colchester	4/14/1994
Support Services	Santa Barbara	8/15/1993
Xylox Corporation	Altoona	8/2/1992

Figure 3-29. A report with gray bars on alternate rows

Discussion

The code shown in Step 4 relies on a module-level variable, *blnShade*, that alternates between True and False. If you followed the instructions for Step 5, you set the value of *blnShade* to a particular value every time you print the page header (before any rows are printed on that page). From then on, every time Access prints the detail section, it decides what to do based on the value in *blnShade*. What's more, every time it prints the detail section, it alternates the value of *blnShade* using this line of code:

```
    blnShade = Not blnShade
```

That is, if *blnShade* was False, now it will be True, and vice versa.

Once the code has decided whether to shade the section, it sets the background color to the color value of gray or white, based on the value of *blnShade*, using the following If...Then...Else statement:

```
If blnShade Then
    Me.Detail1.BackColor = acbcColorGray
Else
    Me.Detail1.BackColor = vbWhite
End If
```

We used the built-in VBA constant for white, but there is no constant for gray, so we defined a value corresponding to the color gray earlier in the procedure, using the built-in VBA function, RGB. An easy way to determine the numeric values for colors is by selecting a section or a control in design view and using the color palette to set the desired color. Then you can read the color value off of the properties sheet. Another option is to use vbGreen, which looks good when previewing the report and also results in a pleasing gray color when printed on a black-and-white printer.

3.13   Print Only Records Matching a Form's Filter

Problem

You have a form that you use to view and edit your collection of record and CD albums. On the form, you've placed a command button that you use to print the records contained in the form's recordset. This works fine, but you'd like to enhance the functionality of the form so that when you filter records on the form and then print the report, only the filtered records will print. Is there any way to do this in Access?

Solution

Access includes properties (Filter and FilterOn) of forms and reports that you can use to manipulate form and report filters programmatically. This solution shows you how to use these properties to print on a report only those records filtered by a form.

Load *03-13.MDB* and open the frmAlbums form. When you press the Print Records button, you should see the preview of a report, rptAlbums, which includes all 65 records from qryAlbums. Close the report and go back to frmAlbums, which should still be open. Now create a filter of the form's records using one of the Filter toolbar buttons or the Records → Filter command. For example, you might create a filter by using the Filter by Form facility (see Figure 3-30).

When you finish creating the filter, apply it. You should see a filtered subset of the records (Figure 3-31).

Now press the Print Records button. You should see a preview of the same report, rptAlbums, this time filtered to match the records you filtered using frmAlbums. If you print the filtered report, you should see a report similar to the one shown in Figure 3-32.

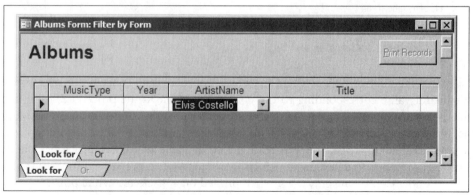

Figure 3-30. Filter by Form is used to filter records on frmAlbums

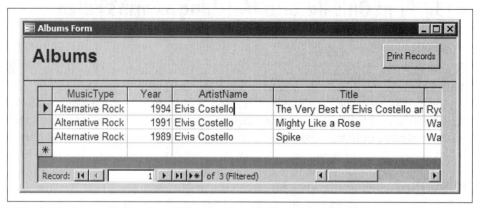

Figure 3-31. The records have been filtered, resulting in three records

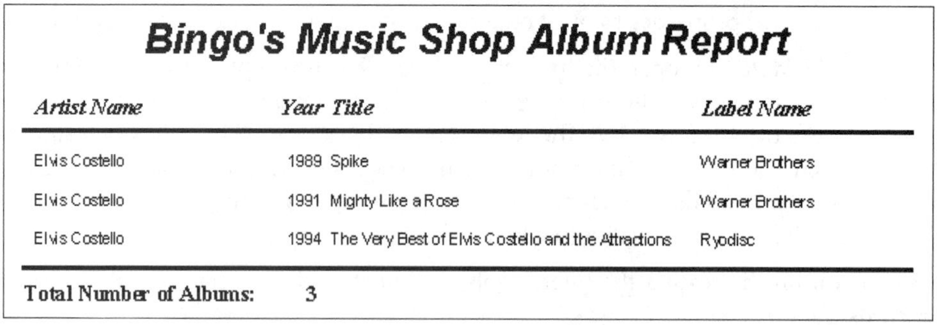

Bingo's Music Shop Album Report

Artist Name	Year Title	Label Name
Elvis Costello	1989 Spike	Warner Brothers
Elvis Costello	1991 Mighty Like a Rose	Warner Brothers
Elvis Costello	1994 The Very Best of Elvis Costello and the Attractions	Ryodisc

Total Number of Albums: 3

Figure 3-32. The report includes only those records from the filtered form

To create your own report that synchronizes its records with those of a form's, follow these steps:

1. Create a new form or edit an existing one. The sample form, frmAlbums, is an unbound main form with an embedded subform bound to the qryAlbums query, but you can use any style of form you like.

2. Create a new report or edit an existing one that's based on the same record source as the form (or, if you are using an embedded subform, that's based on the same record source as the subform) from Step 1. Save the report and give it a name. The sample report is named rptAlbums.

3. Switch back to the form. Add to the form a command button with an event procedure that uses the DoCmd.OpenReport method to open the report from Step 2 in preview view. (For more information on creating event procedures, see the Preface.) The code for the cmdPrint button on frmAlbums is shown here:

```
Private Sub cmdPrint_Click()
    DoCmd.OpenReport "rptAlbums", View:=acPreview
End Sub
```

Change "rptAlbums" to the name of the report created in Step 2. Save the form and close it.

4. Switch back to the report and create an event procedure attached to the report's Open event. Add code similar to that shown here for rptAlbums:

```
Private Sub Report_Open(Cancel As Integer)

    Dim frmFilter As Form

    Const acbcFilterFrm = "frmAlbums"
    Const acbcFilterSubFrmCtl = "subAlbums"

    ' Is the the report's filtering form open?
    If SysCmd(acSysCmdGetObjectState, acForm, acbcFilterFrm) <> 0 Then

        Set frmFilter = Forms(acbcFilterFrm)

        ' Is the form currently filtered?
        If frmFilter.FilterOn Then
            ' Set the report's filter to the subform's filter.
            Me.Filter = frmFilter(acbcFilterSubFrmCtl).Form.Filter
            ' If the filter form didn't include a subform, use this
            ' (simpler) syntax instead:
            ' Me.Filter = frmFilter.Filter
            Me.FilterOn = True
            Me.Caption = Me.Caption & " (filtered)"
        End If

    End If

End Sub
```

5. Change the value of the acbcFilterFrm constant to the name of the form and the acbcFilterSubFrmCtl constant to the name of the subform control created in Step 1. If your form *doesn't* include an embedded subform, either delete "(acbcFilter-SubFrmCtl).Form" from the 11th line of code or completely delete this line of code and the two comment lines that follow and uncomment (remove the leading single quote from) the following line of code:

```
' Me.Filter = frmFilter.Filter
```

You should also delete the following line of code if you aren't using a subform (although leaving it in won't hurt):

```
Const acbcFilterSubFrmCtl = "subAlbums"
```

6. If you wish to display the filter value on the report whenever the report is based on a filtered subset of records, add a text box control to the page footer (or any other section you prefer) and name this control txtFilter. Next, add the following code to an event procedure attached to the section's Format event:

```
Private Sub ReportFooter_Format(Cancel As Integer, FormatCount As Integer)

    ' If this report is filtered, make the txtFilter control visible
    ' and set its value to the Filter property of the report.
    If Me.FilterOn Then
        Me.txtFilter = Me.Filter
        Me.txtFilter.Visible = True
    Else
        Me.txtFilter.Visible = False
    End If
End Sub
```

7. Save the report and close it. You can test the report by opening the filtering form, choosing various filters, and then pressing the Print Records button on the form.

Discussion

This solution works by setting the report's Filter property to the value of the form's Filter property. The form's and report's Filter properties contain the last filter created for the object. Because the last filter hangs around even after you've turned it off (by using the Records → Remove Filter/Sort command or the equivalent toolbar button), the code in Step 4 first checks the status of the FilterOn property. This property is set to True when a filter is active and False when there is no filter or when the existing filter isn't currently active.

At the beginning of the report's Open event procedure, the code checks to see if the form associated with this report is open, using the following code:

```
If SysCmd(acSysCmdGetObjectState, acForm, acbcFilterFrm) <> 0 Then
```

SysCmd is a function that handles a number of different chores including the following:

- Displaying a progress meter or text in the status bar.
- Returning status information about Access (such as the Access directory, whether the runtime or retail product is running, and so on).
- Returning the state of a database object to indicate whether it is open, is a new object, or has been changed but not saved.

You indicate to Access which flavor of *SysCmd* you want by passing it an enumerated value as the first parameter. (See the online help topic for the SysCmd function for more information on the possible parameter values.) The code in the Open event procedure passes *SysCmd* the acSysCmdGetObjectState constant, which tells *SysCmd* that you would like information on the open status of the frmAlbums form. *SysCmd* obliges by returning one of the values listed in Table 3-11 (the value 3 is skipped so that any combination of values added together will result in a unique number). In this case, you care only if the *SysCmd* return value is nonzero.

Table 3-11. The SysCmd object state return values

SysCmd return value	Access constant	Meaning
0	None	The object either doesn't exist or is closed.
1	acObjStateOpen	The object is open, but not new or dirty.
2	acObjStateDirty	The object is in an unsaved state.
4	acObjStateNew	The object is new and in an unsaved state.

The next stretch of code does all the work:

```
Set frmFilter = Forms(acbcFilterFrm)

' Is the form currently filtered?
If frmFilter.FilterOn Then
    ' Set the report's filter to the subform's filter.
    Me.Filter = frmFilter(acbcFilterSubFrmCtl).Form.Filter
    ' If the filter form didn't include a subform, use this
    ' (simpler) syntax instead:
    ' Me.Filter = frmFilter.Filter
    Me.FilterOn = True
    Me.Caption = Me.Caption & " (filtered)"
End If
```

If the form is currently filtered (i.e., if frmFilter.FilterOn is set to True, which in VBA is the same as just saying frmFilterOn), the report's filter is set to the form's filter. Because the subform control on the form is actually being filtered, we set the report's filter equal to the subform's filter.

Notice that we used "frmFilter(acbcFilterSubFrmCtl).Form.Filter" rather than "frm-Filter(acbcFilterSubFrmCtl).Filter". This odd-looking syntax tells Access that you want the Filter property of the subform that the subform control contains, not the Filter property of the subform control itself (which doesn't have such a property).

If no subform is used on the form, you can simplify the statement to this:

```
Me.Filter = frmFilter.Filter
```

Next, the code sets the report's FilterOn property to True, which causes the report to be filtered using the previously set Filter property. Finally, the code changes the caption of the report so that "(filtered)" appears in the titlebar when you preview the report. This last statement is optional—it provides a nice added touch.

The optional code in Step 5—which we added to the page footer's Format event in the sample report—documents the filter by displaying it in a text box on the report. The syntax of the filter is the same as that of a SQL Where clause (without the WHERE keyword).

You may also wish to set the report's OrderBy property to the form's OrderBy property. If you do this, you must also check the status of the OrderByOn property, which is analogous to the FilterOn property. The syntax of the OrderBy property is similar to that of the SQL Order By clause (without the ORDER BY keyword).

3.14 Keep a Report from Breaking at an Inappropriate Place

Problem

On some of your reports, you use the Keep Together property to keep a whole group together or to ensure that a group header won't print without at least one detail item. When detail items are long, you may not want to keep an entire detail item together; however, you do want to have a reasonable number of lines under the header so that the header won't be the last line on the report page. How do you make a report start a new page instead of printing the group header with just a single detail line at the bottom of a page?

Solution

You can use an event procedure called from a report's Format event to evaluate the length of a report page before it actually prints and take an action (in this case, activating a page break control) only if certain criteria are met. This technique uses the *acbConditionalBreak* function and a page break control. This solution demonstrates how to use *acbConditionalBreak* to force a page break if there is not enough room to print at least one line of text from the detail section under a group header.

Open *03-14.MDB* and print the report rptBadBreaks. This typical business-address report, which has its detail section's KeepTogether property set to Yes, occasionally prints a page with the Category group header as the last line of the page, as shown in Figure 3-33.

Now print the rptConditionalBreaks report. Notice that it has avoided the bad break by moving the New World Communications record to the top of page 3 (see Figure 3-34).

Follow these steps to avoid bad breaks in your own reports:

1. Import the basConditionalPageBreak module from *03-14.MDB* into your database.

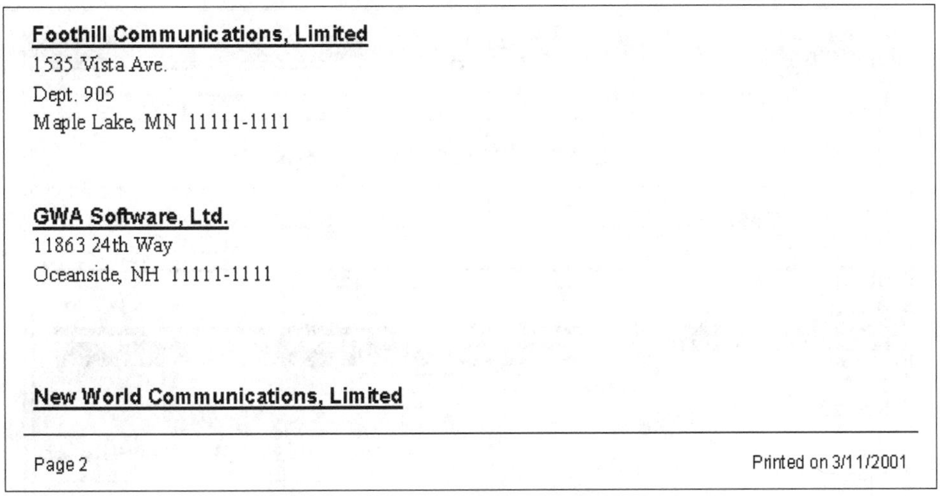

Foothill Communications, Limited
1535 Vista Ave.
Dept. 905
Maple Lake, MN 11111-1111

GWA Software, Ltd.
11863 24th Way
Oceanside, NH 11111-1111

New World Communications, Limited

Printed on 3/11/2001

Figure 3-33. Page 2 of rptBadBreaks shows an inappropriate break for New World Communications

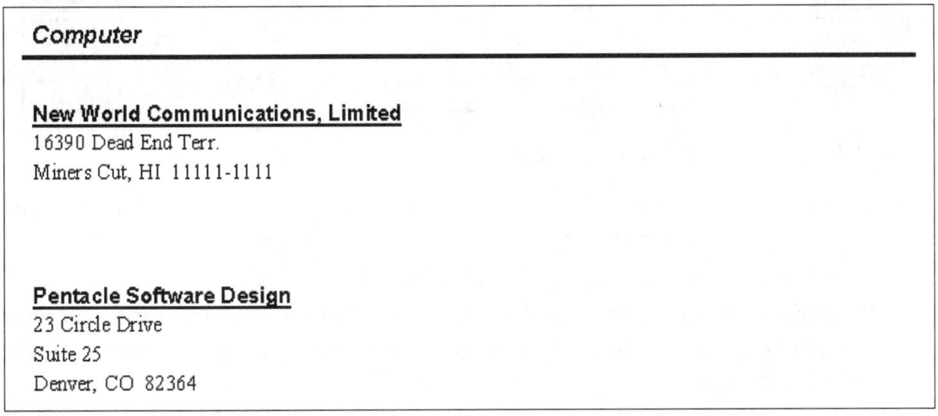

Computer

New World Communications, Limited
16390 Dead End Terr.
Miners Cut, HI 11111-1111

Pentacle Software Design
23 Circle Drive
Suite 25
Denver, CO 82364

Figure 3-34. rptConditionalBreaks moves New World Communications to the top of page 3

2. Create a new report or open an existing one in design view. Select the group header you want to keep together with some text. Insert a page break control above any other controls in this group section (you may need to move some controls down a bit). You can see the page break control above the txtCompany text box in the company header section of the sample report, rptConditionalBreaks, in design view in Figure 3-35.

3. If it's not already open, open the group header properties sheet (View → Properties) and set Force New Page to None and Keep Together to Yes (this ensures that the group section itself won't be broken up).

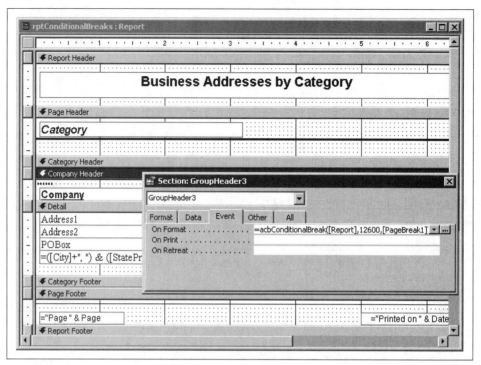

Figure 3-35. rptConditionalBreaks in design view

4. Enter the following expression in the OnFormat property (substituting the name of your page break control for "PageBreak1" if it is different):

```
=acbConditionalBreak ([Report], 12600, [PageBreak1])
```

We used 12,600 in the previous function call to indicate that we want a break at 8.75 inches (8.75 × 1,440 = 12,600). Adjust this argument as necessary until the report breaks appropriately (see Section 3.14.3).

5. Set the detail section's Keep Together property to No to allow it to break.

6. Save and print the report, which should look like the sample report shown in Figure 3-35.

Discussion

The *acbConditionalBreak* function forces a page break if the section will print at or below the specified location on the page. This function takes three arguments: a report object variable, the point at which to force a new page in twips, and an object variable pointing to the page break control that you wish to make visible if the section's location is at or below the specified position.

Here is the *acbConditionalBreak* function:

```
Function acbConditionalBreak(rpt As Report, intBreak As Integer, ctl As Control)

    ctl.Visible = (rpt.Top >= intBreak)

End Function
```

Access evaluates the expression to the right of the equals sign ((rpt.Top >= intBreak)) as either True or False and then assigns that value to the expression to the left of the equals sign. Thus, the code makes the page break control visible or invisible, depending on whether the current page top value has gone beyond the value in *intBreak*. When the control is made visible, a page break is forced before the section is printed.

You may need to experiment with different numbers for the *intBreak* argument until you get it working right for your report. Start by measuring the amount of vertical space needed to print a group header, together with the minimum number of detail lines you want to print with it. Add to this amount the height of the page footer. If you are measuring in inches, multiply this sum by 1,440 to convert it to twips; if you are measuring in centimeters, multiply the sum by 567. Subtract the resulting amount from the total height of the page in twips (15,840 = 1,440 × 11 for a standard letter-sized sheet in portrait orientation). This will give you a starting point; adjust as necessary until the report starts a new page unless there is enough room to print the number of lines you want under a group heading.

You can determine the amount of blank space to leave between the bottom of the last address on a page and the footer by changing the twips value in the *acbConditionalBreak* function. The current value allows a generous amount; to save space, you can reduce the twips argument by a few hundred twips.

Several report properties affect how a page (or column in a multiple-column report) breaks. For many reports, you may be able to use some combination of these properties instead of the technique used in this solution. The properties are listed in Table 3-12.

Table 3-12. Properties that affect where a page or column breaks

Property set	Property name	Effect
Report	GrpKeepTogether	Controls whether groups in a report that have their KeepTogether property set to Whole Group or With First Detail will be kept together by page or by column.
Group	KeepTogether	When set to Whole Group or With First Detail, Access attempts to keep all of the sections of a group (header, footer, and detail) on the same page (or column).
Section	KeepTogether	When set to Whole Group or With First Detail, Access attempts to keep the whole section on the same page (or column).
	ForceNewPage	Tells Access to force a new page never, before, after, or before *and* after the section.

Property set	Property name	Effect
	NewRow or NewCol	Similar to ForceNewPage, except this property tells Access to force a new row or column never, before, after, or before *and* after the section. If you select "Across, then Down" in the Column Layout option in the Layout tab of the Page Setup dialog, a new row is started; if you select "Down, then Across", a new column is started.
	RepeatSection	When set to Yes, Access will repeat this section at the top of the next page (or column) when the group spans more than one page (or column).

3.15   Customize a Report's Grouping and Sorting at Runtime

Problem

You have a report that has several different grouping and sorting fields that you need to rearrange every time you run the report. To do this, you've created five or six different versions of the same report, changing only the order of the fields and which fields are sorted or grouped. This is a maintenance nightmare, especially when you want to change some aspect of the report, which means having to change all the variants of this same report. Is there any easier way to do this in Access?

Solution

You can manipulate most aspects of a report's design using VBA code. This solution shows you how to programmatically open a report in design mode and manipulate several properties of controls and groups. Using this technique and a driving form, you can create a single report that can be customized using different sorting and grouping fields every time it is run.

Load *03-15.MDB* and open frm_rptCompaniesSetup, which is shown in Figure 3-36.

Select a grouping field and zero, one, two, or three other fields for the report (any or all of which can be sorted). When you're done, press the Preview or Print button and a report matching the chosen sorting/grouping fields will be previewed or printed for you. A sample report using the settings from Figure 3-36 is shown in Figure 3-37.

To create a customizable report of your own, follow these steps:

1. Identify the table or query on which the report will be based. In our example, the report is based on the tblCompanies table. Decide which of the fields in this table or query you wish to allow to be selected, grouped, or sorted. In the sample database, we decided to use all of the fields from tblCompanies.

2. Create a table with one field, ReportFieldName, with a data type of Text. Make this field the primary key of the table. Save the table—in the example, we named

Companies Report Setup
Companies Report Setup
Fields
Sorting options
Grouping Field:
Company
No sort
Ascending
Descending
1st Detail Field:
City
No sort
Ascending
Descending
2nd Detail Field:
OfficeId
No sort
Ascending
Descending
3rd Detail Field:
FirstOrder
No sort
Ascending
Descending
Preview
Print

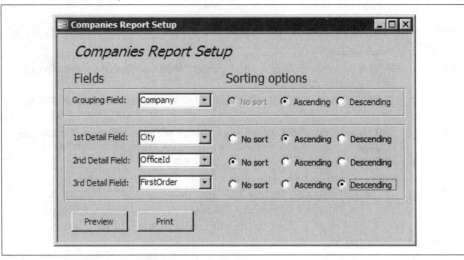

Figure 3-36. The frm_rptCompaniesSetup form is used to set up the rptCompanies report

Companies Report
Company
City
OfficeId
FirstOrder
Amberley Enterprises Ltd.
Ottawa
5
12/13/1993 5:31:52 PM
Amberley Enterprises Ltd.
Ottawa
2
10/8/1993 2:05:28 PM
Amberley Enterprises Ltd.
Ottawa
4
2/16/1993 6:24:13 PM
Amberley Enterprises Ltd.
Ottawa
3
2/14/1993 1:45:26 AM

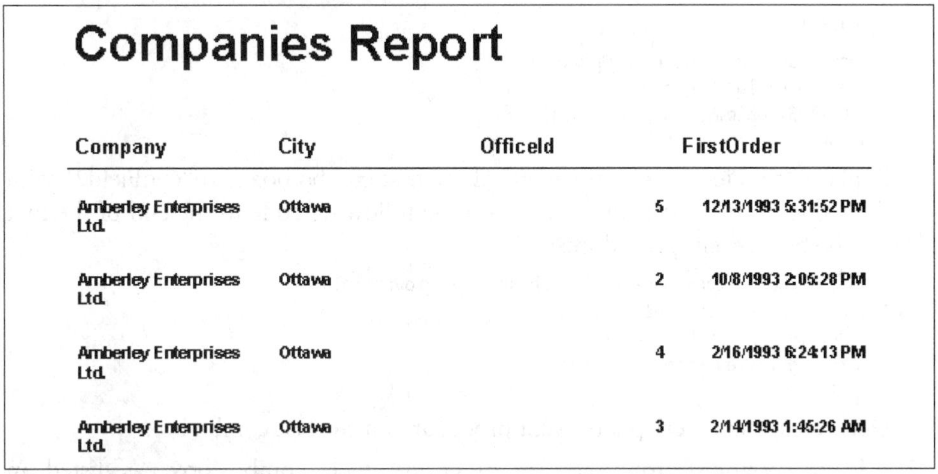

Figure 3-37. The rptCompanies report is customized every time it is run

it zstbl_rptCompaniesFields—and switch to datasheet view, adding a record for each field identified in Step 1.

3. Create a new unbound form. Add one unbound combo box for each field you want to be able to customize at runtime. For example, in the frm_rptCompanies-Setup form, we allow for one grouping field and up to three sorting fields (see Figure 3-36). The names of the combo box fields and their RowSource properties are listed in Table 3-13. All other properties are set to the default values.

Table 3-13. Combo box field settings on the sample form

Name	RowSource
cboField0	zstbl_rptCompaniesFields
cboField1	SELECT ReportFieldName FROM zstbl_rptCompaniesFields WHERE ReportFieldName <> Forms!frm_rpt-CompaniesSetup!cboField0;
cboField2	SELECT ReportFieldName FROM zstbl_rptCompaniesFields WHERE ReportFieldName <> Forms!frm_rpt-CompaniesSetup!cboField0 And ReportFieldName <> Forms!frm_rptCompaniesSetup!cboField1
cboField3	SELECT ReportFieldName FROM zstbl_rptCompaniesFields; WHERE ReportFieldName <> Forms!frm_rpt-CompaniesSetup!cboField0 And ReportFieldName <> Forms!frm_rptCompaniesSetup!cboField1 And ReportFieldName <> Forms!frm_rptCompaniesSetup!cboField2;

Change "zstbl_rptCompaniesFields" to the name of the table from Step 2. Change "frm_rptCompaniesSetup" to the name of your form. Create additional combo boxes as needed, following the pattern of Name and RowSource properties from Table 3-13.

4. For all but the last combo box created in Step 3, create an event procedure attached to the AfterUpdate event of the control containing code similar to the following:

```
Private Sub cboField1_AfterUpdate()
    Me.cboField2.Requery
    Call FixUpCombos(Me.cboField1)
End Sub
```

Replace "cboField1" with the name of the first combo box and "cboField2" with the name of the next combo box. Add the following code to the end of the first combo box's event procedure:

```
' Enable the buttons once you've chosen the group field.
If Not IsNull(Me.cboField0) Then
    Me.cmdPrint.Enabled = True
    Me.cmdPreview.Enabled = True
End If
```

Don't create an AfterUpdate event procedure for the last combo box.

5. Add one option group control alongside each combo box, as listed in Table 3-14. If you have more than four fields, add additional option groups, following the same naming pattern and assigning default values of 1 to each additional option group.

Table 3-14. Option groups for the sample form

Name	Default value
grpSort0	0
grpSort1	1
grpSort2	1
grpsort3	1

For each option group, add three option buttons, as listed in Table 3-15. The names of the option buttons don't matter.

Table 3-15. Option buttons

Label	Option value
No sort	1
Ascending	0
Descending	-1

6. Add a command button named cmdPreview with the caption "Preview" to the form. Attach the following code to its AfterUpdate event:

```
Private Sub cmdPreview_Click()
    Call HandlePrinting(acbcReport, acPreview)
End Sub
```

7. Add a command button named cmdPrint with the caption "Print" to the form. Attach the following code to its AfterUpdate event:

```
Private Sub cmdPrint_Click()
    Call HandlePrinting(acbcReport, acNormal)
End Sub
```

8. Edit the form's module (click on the Code button on the Report Design toolbar or choose the View → Code menu option) and enter the following lines of code in the module's declarations section:

```
Const acbcReport As String = "rptCompanies"
Const acbcTemp As String = "rptTemp"

Const acbcNoSort = 1
Const acbcMaxGroupFields = 1
Const acbcMaxSortFields = 3
```

9. With the form's module still open, add the following two procedures to the module (or copy them into your form's module from the sample database):

```
Private Sub FixUpCombos(ctlCalling As Control)

    Dim intIndex As Integer
    Dim intI As Integer

    ' Grab the last character of the calling
    ' control's name and convert to an integer
    intIndex = CInt(Right(ctlCalling.Name, 1))

    ' Enable the next control if and only if the
    ' value of the calling control is non-null
    If intIndex < acbcMaxSortFields Then
        With Me("cboField" & intIndex + 1)
            .Value = Null
            .Enabled = (Not IsNull(ctlCalling))
        End With
```

```
            Me("grpSort" & intIndex + 1).Enabled = (Not IsNull(ctlCalling))
        End If


        ' Disable all controls after the next one
        If intIndex < acbcMaxSortFields - 1 Then
            For intI = intIndex + 2 To acbcMaxSortFields
                With Me("cboField" & intI)
                    .Value = Null
                    .Enabled = False
                End With
                With Me("grpSort" & intI)
                    .Value = acbcNoSort
                    .Enabled = False
                End With
            Next intI
        End If
End Sub


Public Sub HandlePrinting(strReport As String, ByVal intPrintOption As Integer)

    Dim intI As Integer
    Dim intFieldCnt As Integer
    Dim avarFields(0 To acbcMaxSortFields) As Variant
    Dim aintSorts(0 To acbcMaxSortFields) As Integer
    Dim rpt As Report
    Dim varGroupLevel As Variant


    On Error GoTo HandleErr

    DoCmd.Hourglass True

    ' Count up the non-null grouping/sorting fields
    ' and the sort property fields and store them in
    ' two arrays
    intFieldCnt = -1
    For intI = 0 To acbcMaxSortFields
        If Not IsNull(Me("cboField" & intI)) Then
            intFieldCnt = intFieldCnt + 1
            avarFields(intFieldCnt) = Me("cboField" & intI)
            aintSorts(intFieldCnt) = Me("grpSort" & intI)
        End If
    Next intI

    ' Delete old temp copy of report
    On Error Resume Next
    DoCmd.DeleteObject acReport, acbcTemp
    On Error GoTo HandleErr
    DoCmd.CopyObject , acbcTemp, acReport, strReport

    ' Turn off screen updating and open the report in
    ' design mode where it will be manipulated
    Application.Echo False
    DoCmd.OpenReport acbcTemp, View:=acDesign
```

```
    ' Set up a report object to point to the report
    Set rpt = Reports(acbcTemp)

    ' Always have a single grouping field.
    ' First set the properties of the group
    rpt.GroupLevel(0).ControlSource = avarFields(0)
    rpt.GroupLevel(0).SortOrder = aintSorts(0)
    ' Set the first label and text box to match
    ' the grouping properties
    rpt("txtField0").ControlSource = avarFields(0)
    rpt("lblField0").Caption = avarFields(0)

    ' Already used GroupLevel(0) for the grouping field,
    ' so now work through the remaining fields
    For intI = 1 To intFieldCnt
        ' Set the text box to be visible
        ' and bind to the chosen field
        With rpt("txtField" & intI)
            .Visible = True
            .ControlSource = avarFields(intI)
        End With

        ' Set the label to be visible with its caption
        ' equal to the name of the field
        With rpt("lblField" & intI)
            .Visible = True
            .Caption = avarFields(intI)
        End With

        ' Now create each sorting field group
        If aintSorts(intI) <> acbcNoSort Then
            varGroupLevel = CreateGroupLevel(rpt.Name, _
              avarFields(intI), False, False)
            rpt.GroupLevel(varGroupLevel).SortOrder = aintSorts(intI)
        End If
    Next intI

    ' Make any unneeded fields invisible
    For intI = intFieldCnt + 1 To acbcMaxSortFields
        rpt("txtField" & intI).Visible = False
        rpt("lblField" & intI).Visible = False
    Next intI

    ' Save changes to the new report, then open the temporary report:
    DoCmd.Save acReport, acbcTemp
    DoCmd.OpenReport acbcTemp, View:=intPrintOption

ExitHere:
    DoCmd.Hourglass False
    Application.Echo True
    Exit Sub

HandleErr:
    Resume ExitHere
End Sub
```

Save the form. The complete frm_rptCompaniesSetup sample form is shown, in design view, in Figure 3-38. Close the form.

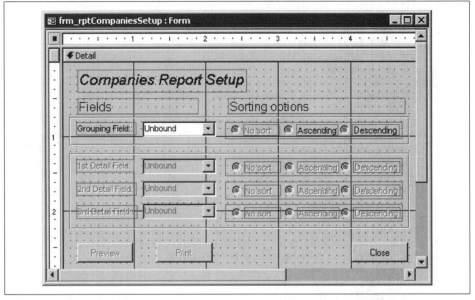

Figure 3-38. The sample form in design view

10. Create a new report. Add one sorting/grouping field to the report. The actual field you choose doesn't matter because the code behind frm_rptCompanies-Setup will change the field name. What is important is that you set the Group-Header and GroupFooter properties to Yes (which makes it a grouping field). Don't add any additional sorting fields.

11. Add a label control for each combo box field from frm_rptCompaniesSetup to the group header section of the report. Make all the labels the same size and give them names in the following style: lblField0, lblField1, and so on.

12. Add an unbound text box control for each combo box field from frm_rptCompaniesSetup to the detail section of the report. These fields should line up under the labels added in Step 13, should all be the same dimensions, and should have names like txtField0, txtField1, and so on.

13. Add any page and report headers and footers. Save the report and close it. The completed sample report is shown in Figure 3-39 in design view.

Discussion

The zstbl_rptCompaniesFields table holds the names of all the possible fields in the report. This table supplies the row source for the combo boxes on the driving form.

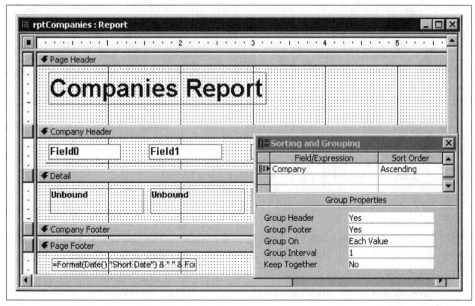

Figure 3-39. The rptCompanies report in design view

Each record in this table corresponds to one field that may be selected, sorted, or grouped. In the sample database, we used all five fields from tblCompanies.

Most of the work in this solution is done by the *driving form*. This form (frm_rpt-CompaniesSetup, in the sample database) drives the report-customization process. For the person running the report to be able to customize it, you must provide some user interface (UI) mechanism for picking and choosing fields. The combo boxes and option groups provide this mechanism.

Many of the solution steps (Steps 3 through 5 and the *FixUpCombos* subroutine in Step 9) are used to make the UI for the driving form as easy to use and as foolproof as possible. For example, we created RowSource properties (listed in Table 3-15) that make it difficult for the user to select the same grouping/sorting field twice by refining the combo box list for each field that eliminates any fields already chosen from the list.

The RowSource properties make it difficult to select the same field twice, but the code in the *FixUpCombos* procedure makes doing so next to impossible. When the form first opens, all of the controls except the first combo box and the first option group are disabled. After you have selected a field from a combo box, the code enables the next combo box/option group while keeping controls that come after that combo box/option group disabled. This takes care of forward movement. However, the user can always back up and change a combo box field out of order—hence, in addition to disabling the controls, the code also nulls out any values that may have been entered into subsequent combo boxes.

When the cmdPrint or cmdPreview buttons are pressed, the *HandlePrinting* subroutine is called. This subroutine takes all the data entered on the form, opens the report in design mode, and customizes it prior to printing the form to the screen or printer.

HandlePrinting begins by counting up the non-null combo box controls on the form and storing their values and the values of the associated option groups into two arrays:

```
intFieldCnt = -1
For intI = 0 To acbcMaxSortFields
    If Not IsNull(Me("cboField" & intI)) Then
        intFieldCnt = intFieldCnt + 1
        avarFields(intFieldCnt) = Me("cboField" & intI)
        aintSorts(intFieldCnt) = Me("grpSort" & intI)
    End If
Next intI
```

Next, the code opens the report in design view (after suspending most, but not all, screen updating) and adjusts the properties of the first field, which makes up the one and only grouping field:

```
' Always have a single grouping field. First set the properties
' of the group.
rpt.GroupLevel(0).ControlSource = avarFields(0)
rpt.GroupLevel(0).SortOrder = aintSorts(0)
' Set the first label and text box to match the grouping properties.
rpt("txtField0").ControlSource = avarFields(0)
rpt("lblField0").Caption = avarFields(0)
```

The next stretch of code iterates through the remaining fields, which are all sorting (or nonsorting detail) fields. First, the unbound text box controls are made visible and their control sources are set to the names of the fields selected from the form. Next, the labels are made visible and their captions are set to match the text boxes. The *CreateGroupLevel* function is then called to create any and all sorting fields based on the selection from the option groups on the form. (The last two parameters of this function tell Access whether you want a header or a footer. Because this code is creating sorting fields only, both of these parameters are set to False.) This chunk of *HandlePrinting* is shown here:

```
For intI = 1 To intFieldCnt
    ' Set the text box to be visible and bind it to the chosen field.
    With rpt("txtField" & intI)
        .Visible = True
        .ControlSource = avarFields(intI)
    End With

    ' Set the label to be visible with its caption equal to
    ' the name of the field.
    With rpt("lblField" & intI)
        .Visible = True
        .Caption = avarFields(intI)
    End With
```

```
        ' Now create each sorting field group.
        If aintSorts(intI) <> acbcNoSort Then
            varGroupLevel = CreateGroupLevel(rpt.Name, _
              avarFields(intI), False, False)
            rpt.GroupLevel(varGroupLevel).SortOrder = aintSorts(intI)
        End If
    Next intI
```

Next, any unneeded fields are made invisible:

```
For intI = intFieldCnt + 1 To acbcMaxSortFields
    rpt("txtField" & intI).Visible = False
    rpt("lblField" & intI).Visible = False
Next intI
```

The code creates a temporary copy of the report, earlier in the procedure:

```
On Error Resume Next
DoCmd.DeleteObject acReport, acbcTemp
On Error GoTo HandleErr
DoCmd.CopyObject , acbcTemp, acReport, strReport
```

This is necessary because the code makes design-time changes to the report. Making a copy eliminates the chance that the user will save the modified report over the original, which could mess things up the next time the report is run. The code completes its work by saving the new report and opening the report in the requested mode:

```
' Save changes to the new report, then open the temporary report:
DoCmd.Save acReport, acbcTemp
DoCmd.OpenReport acbcTemp, View:=intPrintOption
```

Making a temporary copy of the report eliminates the possibility of the original report being left in a state that makes it unusable the next time the report is run. This is important because there is no programmatic way to remove sort fields—you can't make a report that has been saved with two sort fields into a report with one sort field. If the user is allowed to save a modified version of the report, this is exactly what might happen. Therefore, we made the decision to use a temporary copy of the report (but only after trying numerous other workarounds).

The sample report and accompanying code assume that you want only one grouping field. We did this to simplify the example, but you could extend it by including code to make additional grouping fields (just like the code that now makes the sorting fields). If you do this, you'll have to deal with creating controls and placing them in the headers of the groups. You can create controls using the *CreateReportControl* function, which is described in the Access online help.

Any technique that relies on programmatically making changes to a report (or a form) while it's open in design view won't work in an Access MDE or ADE, where design changes aren't permitted. In those cases, however, you can use a modified version of this solution. In a report's Open event, you can't add new grouping and sorting levels, but you can change the control sources of existing ones. So, as long as you have enough grouping and sorting levels in the saved report, you can modify them at runtime rather than at design time with code like this:

```
rpt.GroupLevel(0).ControlSource = avarFields(0)
```

If necessary, you can create "dummy" grouping levels in your report, using a control source like =1, to make it possible to avoid having to open the report in design view.

CHAPTER 4

Applications

This chapter is a compendium of tips and suggestions for making your application development go more smoothly and your applications look more professional. You'll learn how to convert queries into embedded SQL strings providing data for forms or reports. You'll learn how to build an object inventory so you can document your applications better, how to ensure that properties for objects that should match up actually do, and how to disable screen output more effectively than the methods Access provides internally can. You'll find tips on discerning the current language version of Access and modifying text in error messages and on forms and reports to accommodate the current language. You'll see how to set and restore the Access caption and how to set startup options for your application. You'll also see how to use the Windows File Open/Save dialogs and how to clear out test data before shipping your application. The final topic explains how to implement user-level Access security.

 Some of the topics in this chapter take advantage of the Microsoft Data Access Objects (DAO) library. By default, when you create a new application in Access 2000 or later, Access doesn't include a reference to this library. Although each of the samples for this chapter includes this reference, if you create a new application and import modules from the samples, your code won't work. In order to be able to use imported code that uses DAO objects, you'll need to select Tools → References... to display the References dialog box, and select the Microsoft DAO library.

4.1 Convert Queries into Embedded SQL Statements

Problem

Access's Query Builder makes it easy to create SQL statements as row sources for combo boxes or as record sources for forms and reports. You'd prefer to use SQL statements for row and record sources because they reduce the number of unnecessary objects in your databases. Is there an easy way to make these conversions? What's the trade-off of using embedded SQL statements instead of query objects to provide your data?

Solution

There is no automatic conversion utility to transform queries into SQL statements, but you can use the View SQL button on the Query Design toolbar to display a query's SQL statement, copy it to the Windows clipboard, and then paste it into the RecordSource or RowSource property of a form or combo box.

Open *04-01.MDB* and look at the form frmCompanyInfoQuery. This form has a simple query as its record source; the combo box in its header also has a query as its row source. Neither of these queries is needed elsewhere, so they are prime candidates for conversion into SQL statements.

Take the following steps to convert a query, using the form's record source query as an example. These steps have already been taken for the form frmCompanyInfoSQL, both for the form's RecordSource property and for the combo box's RowSource property.

1. Open the form whose record source you want to convert to a single SQL statement in design view, and make sure that the properties sheet is open (Figure 4-1).

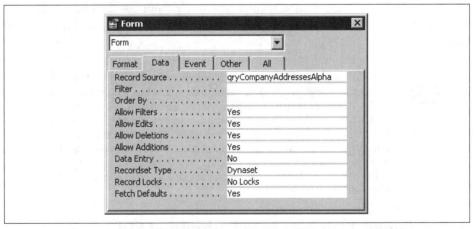

Figure 4-1. A form's properties sheet, with a query as its RecordSource property

2. Click on the Build button (...) next to the RecordSource property to open the Query Builder for the record source query.

3. With the Query Builder open, click on the View SQL button on the toolbar or select View → SQL.

4. The SQL window opens, displaying the query as a SQL statement, as shown in Figure 4-2.

Figure 4-2. The SQL window for a simple query

5. Highlight the entire SQL statement and press Ctrl-C or select Edit → Copy to copy it to the clipboard.

6. Close the SQL window.

7. Highlight the query name in the RecordSource properties sheet and press Ctrl-V or select Edit → Paste to replace the query name with the SQL statement. Figure 4-3 shows the form's RecordSource property with the SQL statement in place.

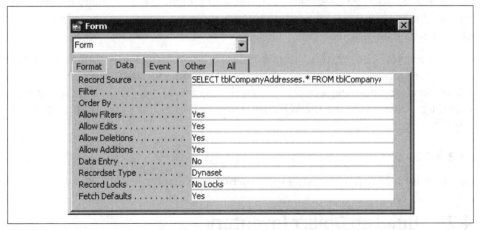

Figure 4-3. A form's properties sheet with a SQL statement as its RecordSource property

8. Delete the original RecordSource query from the database container.

Discussion

Most Access queries can be converted back and forth between the graphical representation shown in the Query Builder window and the SQL representation of the query. The SQL window makes it easy to extract a query's SQL statement and use it directly as a record source or row source or in VBA code. Because all queries in Access can be represented as SQL statements, you have a choice—you can base a form or report on a query, or you can supply the SQL string directly in the properties sheet.

Converting row source queries into SQL statements lets you eliminate many trivial queries that have no purpose other than filling forms or combo boxes. If you have a SQL statement as a record or row source, you can open the Query Builder window to view or modify it, which makes it easy to use SQL statements in place of queries. Access always saves your SQL statements as hidden queries in the background, anyway, so you still get the slight performance benefit of having the execution plan for the query saved rather than recalculated each time the query runs.

We should mention a few caveats. First, if you use the same complex query as a row source for several different database objects, especially if you anticipate changing the query, it may be best to leave the query as a query object rather than converting it into a SQL statement. If you use one query as a record source for several forms or reports, when you change the query all the forms or reports that use it will pick up the changes. Also, there are some query properties that apply only to saved queries, such as the RunPermissions property. If you need to use these properties in a secured database, you must leave the queries as query objects.

In some cases, you may need to convert a SQL statement into a query (for example, if you need to use it as a record source for several forms or reports). In that case, simply reverse the steps given earlier: open the SQL statement in the Query Builder window and then save it as a named query, which you can use as a record source for other database objects.

In addition, you can use the Query Builder to help create a row source or control source from scratch. Simply click on the Build button and build a SQL statement as though you were building a query. Rather than saving a query object in the database container, Access will save the SQL string you've created into the appropriate property.

See Also

For more information on working with queries, see Chapter 1.

4.2   Build an Object Inventory

Problem

To document your application, you'd like to be able to create a list of all the objects in your databases, including their owners, date of creation, and date of last update. You're sure you can do it manually, but is there a better way to create a table containing all this information?

Solution

Access's Data Access Objects (DAO) can give you the information you need. By programmatically working your way through each of Access's container collections, you can add a row to an inventory table for each object in your application, storing information about that object. You should be able to use the techniques for this operation to write your own code for enumerating other collections in Access. There are a few tricks along the way, which this solution discusses, but in general this is a straightforward project.

To create an object inventory for your applications, take only two steps:

1. Import the form zsfrmInventory from *04-02.MDB* into your own application.

2. Load and run the form. As it opens, it builds the object inventory, saving the data in zstblInventory. If you want to rebuild the inventory once the form's up, click the Rebuild Object Inventory button. This recreates the inventory table and fills it with information about all the objects in your database. Figure 4-4 shows the form once it's been run on a sample database.

Container	Name	Creation Date	Last Updated
Forms	zsfrmInventory	01/22/01 (8:20 pm)	01/22/01 (8:20 pm)
Tables	MSysAccessObjects	03/08/01 (9:48 pm)	03/08/01 (9:48 pm)
Tables	MSysACEs	01/22/01 (8:19 pm)	01/22/01 (8:19 pm)
Tables	MSysObjects	01/22/01 (8:19 pm)	01/22/01 (8:19 pm)
Tables	MSysQueries	01/22/01 (8:19 pm)	01/22/01 (8:19 pm)
Tables	MSysRelationships	01/22/01 (8:19 pm)	01/22/01 (8:19 pm)
Tables	zstblInventory	03/11/01 (7:59 pm)	03/11/01 (7:59 pm)

Figure 4-4. The inventory-creating form once it's done its work on a sample database

 This example form includes the Access system tables, which you may never have encountered. These tables are part of every Access database and are not cause for alarm. You can view them in the Database Explorer by choosing the Tools → Options menu and turning on the Show System Objects option.

Discussion

How this solution works is a lot more interesting than the final product. The object inventory itself can be useful, but the steps involved in creating the inventory may be more useful to you in the long run. All the code examples used in this section come from the form module attached to zsfrmInventory (in *04-02.MDB*).

When the form loads, or when you click the Rebuild Object Inventory button on zsfrmInventory, you execute the following code. (The "zs" prefix, by the way, reminds you that zsfrmInventory is a "system" form, used only by your application.

The z forces this form to sort to the bottom of the database container so you won't get it confused with your "real" forms.)

```
Private Sub RebuildInventory( )
    On Error GoTo HandleErr
    DoCmd.Hourglass True

    Me.lstInventory.RowSource = ""
    Call CreateInventory
    Me.lstInventory.RowSource = "SELECT ID, Container, Name, " & _
      "Format([DateCreated],'mm/dd/yy (h:nn am/pm)') AS [Creation Date], " & _
      "Format([lastUpdated],'mm/dd/yy (h:nn am/pm)') AS [Last Updated], " & _
      "Owner FROM zstblInventory ORDER BY Container, Name;"

ExitHere:
    DoCmd.Hourglass False
    Exit Sub

HandleErr:
    Resume ExitHere
End Sub
```

This code turns on the hourglass cursor and sets the main list box's RowSource property to Null. (It must do this because it's about to call the *CreateInventory* procedure, which attempts to delete the table holding the data. If the list box were still bound to that table, the code couldn't delete the table—it would be locked!) It then calls the *CreateInventory* subroutine. This procedure fills zstblInventory with the object inventory, and it can take a few seconds to run. When it's done, the code resets the list box's RowSource property, resets the cursor, and exits.

Documenting all the containers

The *CreateInventory* subroutine first creates the zstblInventory table. If *CreateTable* succeeds, *CreateInventory* then calls the *AddInventory* procedure for each of the useful Access containers (Tables, Relationships, Forms, Reports, Scripts, and Modules) that represent user objects. (Tables and queries are lumped together in one container. As you'll see, it will take a bit of extra effort to distinguish them.) Because each of the *AddInventory* procedure calls writes to the status bar, *CreateInventory* clears out the status bar once it's done, using the Access *SysCmd* function. The following code fragment shows the *CreateInventory* subroutine:

```
Private Sub CreateInventory( )
    If (CreateTable( )) Then
        ' These routines use the status line,
        ' so clear it once everyone's done.
        Call AddInventory("Tables")
        Call AddInventory("Forms")
        Call AddInventory("Reports")
        Call AddInventory("Scripts")
        Call AddInventory("Modules")
        Call AddInventory("Relationships")
```

```
        ' Clear out the status bar.
        Call SysCmd(acSysCmdClearStatus)
    Else
        MsgBox "Unable to create zstblInventory."
    End If
End Sub
```

Creating the inventory table

The *CreateTable* function prepares the zstblInventory table to hold the current database's inventory. The code in *CreateTable* first attempts to delete zstblInventory (using the Drop Table SQL statement). If the table exists, the code will succeed. If it doesn't exist, the code will trigger a runtime error, but the error-handling code will allow the procedure to continue anyway. *CreateTable* then recreates the table from scratch by using a data definition language (DDL) query to create the table. (See the Solution in Recipe 1.15 for more information on DDL queries.) *CreateTable* returns True if it succeeds or False if it fails. The following is the complete source code for the *CreateTable* function:

```
Private Function CreateTable( ) As Boolean
    ' Return True on success, False otherwise.
    Dim qdf As DAO.QueryDef
    Dim db As DAO.Database
    Dim strSQL As String

    On Error GoTo HandleErr
    Set db = CurrentDb( )

    db.Execute "DROP TABLE zstblInventory"

    ' Create zstblInventory.
    strSQL = "CREATE TABLE zstblInventory (Name Text (255), " & _
     "Container Text (50), DateCreated DateTime, " & _
     "LastUpdated DateTime, Owner Text (50), " & _
     "ID AutoIncrement Constraint PrimaryKey PRIMARY KEY)"
    db.Execute strSQL

    ' If you got here, you succeeded!
    db.TableDefs.Refresh
    CreateTable = True

ExitHere:
    Exit Function

HandleErr:
    Select Case Err
        Case 3376, 3011 ' Table or Object not found
            Resume Next
        Case Else
            CreateTable = False
    End Select
    Resume ExitHere
End Function
```

Documenting each container

The *AddInventory* subroutine is the heart of the inventory-creating operation. In Access, each database maintains a group of container objects, each of which contains a number of documents. These documents are the saved objects of the container's type, such as tables, relationships, forms, reports, scripts (macros), or modules. *AddInventory* looks at each document in each container, adds a new row to zstblInventory for each document, and copies the information contained in the document into the new row of the table. (All the code examples in this section come from *AddInventory* in zsfrmInventory's module.)

The first step *AddInventory* performs is to set up the necessary DAO object variables:

```
Set db = CurrentDb
Set con = db.Containers(strContainer)
Set rst = db.OpenRecordset("zstblInventory")
```

The code then loops through each document in the given container, gathering information about the documents:

```
For Each doc In con.Documents
...
Next doc
```

For each document in the Tables container, the code must first determine whether the given document is a table or query. To do this, it calls the *IsTable* function, which attempts to retrieve a reference to the requested object from the database's TableDefs collection. If this doesn't trigger a runtime error, that table must exist. Because attempting to retrieve a query's name from the TableDefs collection will certainly fail, you can use *IsTable* to determine if an element of the Tables container (which contains both tables and queries) is a table. The *isTable* function appears as follows:

```
Private Function IsTable(ByVal strName As String) As Boolean
    Dim db As DAO.Database
    Dim tdf As DAO.TableDef

    On Error Resume Next

    Set db = CurrentDb( )

    ' See the following note for information on why this
    ' is commented out.
    ' db.Tabledefs.Refresh

    Set tdf = db.TableDefs(strName)
    IsTable = (Err.Number = 0)
    Err.Clear
End Function
```

Normally, before retrieving information about any Access persistent object collection (TableDefs, QueryDefs, etc.), you must refresh the collection. Because Access doesn't keep these collections up to date unless necessary, it's possible that a table recently added by a user in the user interface might not yet have been added to the TableDefs collection. In this case, you'll be calling *IsTable* repeatedly. To speed the operation of zsfrmInventory, the *IsTable* function used here does not use the Refresh method each time it's called; it counts on the caller to have refreshed the collection. In almost any other use than this one, you'd want to uncomment the call to the Refresh method in the previous code example and allow the code to refresh the collection before checking for the existence of a particular table.

This code fragment fills a string variable, *strType*, with the type of the current document. The type is one of Tables, Relationships, Queries, Forms, Reports, Scripts, or Modules.

```
If strContainer = "Tables" Then
    If IsTable(doc.Name) Then
        strType = "Tables"
    Else
        strType = "Queries"
    End If
Else
    strType = strContainer
End If
```

The value of *strType* will be written to zstblInventory along with the document information.

Caching Object References

Note that the previous code sample uses an object variable, *doc*, to refer to the current document. The For Each...Next statement sets up this reference for you. This construct loops through every item in a collection, assigning a reference to each object as it loops. We could have use a simple For...Next loop, but that solution would have been less efficient.

Because later code will refer to this particular document a number of times, it's more efficient to set up this direct reference than to ask Access to parse the general reference, con.Documents(intI), each time it needs to refer to the document. In general, any time you need to refer to an object more than once, you can make your code run a little better by setting an object variable to refer to that object. This will save Access from having to look up the object repeatedly.

Once *AddInventory* has determined the correct value for *strType*, it can add the information to zstblInventory. *AddInventory* retrieves the various properties of the document referred to by *doc* and copies them to the current row in zstblInventory, referred to by *rst*. Once it's done, it uses the recordset's Update method to commit the new row. This process is illustrated in the following code fragment from the *Add-Inventory* procedure:

```
rst.AddNew
    rst("Container") = strType
    rst("Owner") = doc.Owner
    rst("Name") = doc.Name
    rst("DateCreated") = doc.DateCreated
    rst("LastUpdated") = doc.LastUpdated
rst.Update
```

Avoiding errors

The list box on zsfrmInventory has the following expression as its RowSource property:

```
SELECT ID, Container, Name,
 Format([DateCreated],"mm/dd/yy (h:nn am/pm)") AS [Creation Date],
 Format([lastUpdated],"mm/dd/yy (h:nn am/pm)") AS [Last Updated],
 Owner FROM zstblInventory ORDER BY Container, Name;"
```

There are two issues to consider here. First, the SQL string used as the RowSource pulls data from zstblInventory. It's quite possible, though, that when you load the form, zstblInventory doesn't exist. To avoid this problem, we saved the form with the list box's RowSource set to a null value. When the form loads, it doesn't attempt to retrieve the data until the code has had time to create the table, as you can see in the *RebuildInventory* procedure shown earlier.

The second thing to bear in mind is that Access doesn't always keep the collections completely up-to-date: you may find deleted objects in the collections. (These deleted objects have names starting with "~TMPCLP".) You probably won't want to include these objects in the inventory, so the code that loops through the collections specifically excludes objects with names that start with "~TMPCLP". To determine which objects are deleted, the code calls the *IsTemp* function, as shown in the following code fragment:

```
For Each doc In con.Documents
    If Not IsTemp(doc.Name) Then
        ...
    End If
Next doc

Private Function IsTemp(ByVal strName As String)
    IsTemp = Left(strName, 7) = "~TMPCLP"
End Function
```

Comments

If you want to remove system objects from your inventory, you'll need to check each object and, if it's a system object, skip it in the display. You can use an object's Attributes property to see if it's a system object. See Access's online help for more information.

You might wonder why this application uses the Access containers to retrieve information about tables and queries, since this requires more effort than if the code had just used the TableDefs and QueryDefs collections. It makes sense to use the containers because the TableDefs/QueryDefs collections don't contain information about the owners of the objects, one of the items of information this application is attempting to track.

You can also use the collections provided by Access, such as AllForms, AllReports, AllTables, which can be useful for gathering information on your objects. But these too lack ownership information, which is part of the Jet database engine's security system and therefore must be accessed using the Jet Containers and Documents collections. The AllForms and AllReports collections do contain additional useful information, however, including an IsLoaded property for each of the AccessObjects in the collections.

See Also

For more information on using DAO in Access databases, see "How Do I Use Data Access Objects (DAO) in New Databases?" in the Preface.

4.3   Verify That Objects Use Consistent Settings

Problem

You've finished your application and you're ready to deliver it, but you notice that your use of color, fonts, alignment, and other layout properties isn't consistent across all your forms or reports. You know you can manually check the values of all the properties of all the controls on your forms and reports, but there's got to be a faster way. Is there some method you can use to compare similar properties for all the objects in your application?

Solution

Access doesn't provide a "cross-section" of your properties, which is really what you need—some way to look at properties not listed by item, but by property name, across all objects. Building on the technology introduced in the Solution in Recipe 4. 2, this solution creates a group of tables containing information about all the properties on any forms or reports you select. Once it builds those tables, it constructs a query that will allow you, using the Quick Sort menu items, to view all the property settings for various objects, sorted any way you'd like. Once you've sorted the output by property name, for example, you'll quickly be able to see which objects have incorrect settings for that particular property.

The *04-03.MDB* sample database includes a single form, zsfrmVerifySettings. Figure 4-5 shows the form after it has done its cataloging in *Northwind.MDB*, ready to present property information on three different forms. Figure 4-6 shows the output data, sorted by property name, showing that several controls have different background colors.

To use zsfrmVerifySettings to catalog properties in your own applications, follow these steps:

1. Import zsfrmVerifySettings from *04-03.MDB* into your own database.

2. Load zsfrmVerifySettings in form view. As it loads, it will build the object property inventory, creating tables and queries as necessary.

3. Once the form has presented the list of forms and reports, click on the items you want documented. Click again on an item to remove it from the list of selected items. In Figure 4-5, for example, three items are to be documented. You can also use the Select All, Select All Forms, and Select All Reports buttons to select groups of items.

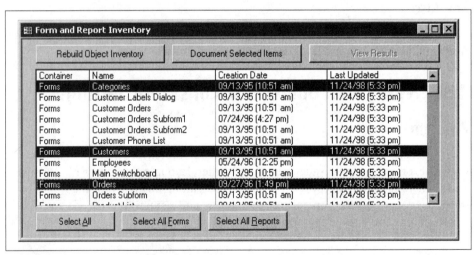

Figure 4-5. zsfrmVerifySettings is ready to catalog all controls on three selected forms

4. When you've selected all the forms or reports you'd like to manipulate, click the Document Selected Items button. This will work its way through the list of selected items and document all the properties of each control on each of those items.

5. When the documentation process is finished (it may take some time to work through all the items you've selected), click the View Results button. This will

open zsqryProperties, which is shown in Figure 4-6. It lists all the properties of all the objects and the sections and controls on those objects.

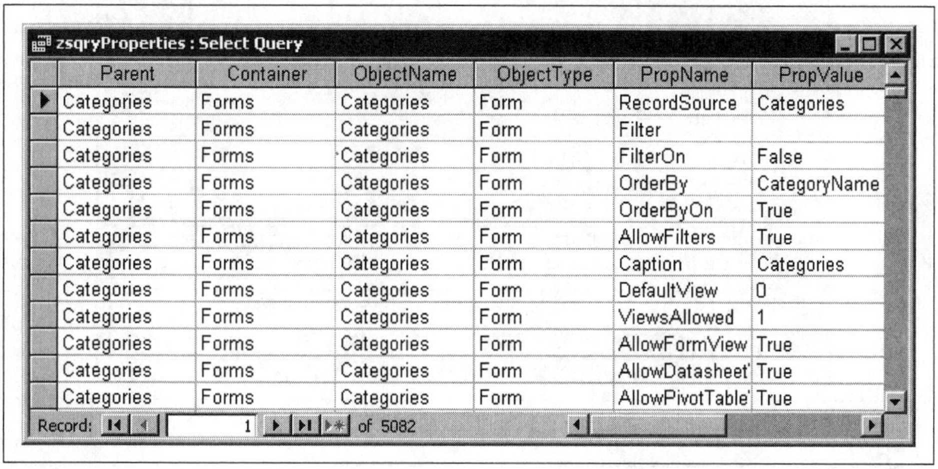

Parent	Container	ObjectName	ObjectType	PropName	PropValue
Categories	Forms	Categories	Form	RecordSource	Categories
Categories	Forms	Categories	Form	Filter	
Categories	Forms	Categories	Form	FilterOn	False
Categories	Forms	Categories	Form	OrderBy	CategoryName
Categories	Forms	Categories	Form	OrderByOn	True
Categories	Forms	Categories	Form	AllowFilters	True
Categories	Forms	Categories	Form	Caption	Categories
Categories	Forms	Categories	Form	DefaultView	0
Categories	Forms	Categories	Form	ViewsAllowed	1
Categories	Forms	Categories	Form	AllowFormView	True
Categories	Forms	Categories	Form	AllowDatasheet	True
Categories	Forms	Categories	Form	AllowPivotTable	True

Record: ◄◄ ◄ 1 ► ►◄ ►* of 5082

Figure 4-6. zsqryProperties allows you to sort by any categories to view your property settings

6. Use the toolbar buttons to control sorting and filtering so that you can view only the properties you want for the objects in which you're interested.

For example, you might want to ensure that all command buttons on all your forms have their ControlTipText properties set. To do that, follow these steps (assuming you've followed the previous steps):

1. Open zsfrmVerifySettings and select all the forms in your application from the list of objects.

2. Click on the Document Selected Items button. Go out for lunch while it does its work.

3. Once it's finished, click on the View Results button, which brings up zsqryProperties, showing one row for each property of each object you selected. For a large set of forms or reports, this query could return tens of thousands of rows.

4. Choose Records → Filter → Advanced Filter/Sort and build a filter that sorts on Parent and limits the output to rows with "ControlTipText" in the PropName field and "Command Button" in the ObjectType field. Figure 4-7 shows this filter.

5. Apply the filter by clicking on the funnel button on the toolbar or by right-clicking on the filter design area and choosing Apply Filter/Sort. You will see only the rows for the command buttons' ControlTipText properties. Look for the rows in which there's no value in the PropValue column. Those are the buttons that don't yet have a value set. Figure 4-8 shows the output of the sample query. It's quite clear which buttons don't yet have their ControlTipText properties set.

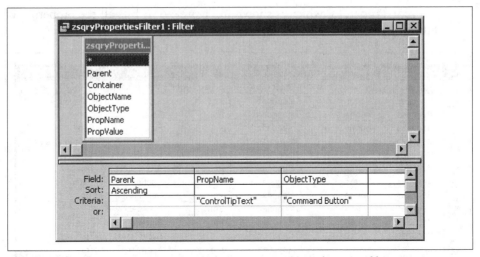

Figure 4-7. This filter limits rows to the ControlTipText property of command buttons

Parent	Container	ObjectName	ObjectType	PropName	PropValue
Customer Labels [	Forms	Print	Command button	ControlTipText	
Customer Labels [	Forms	Cancel	Command button	ControlTipText	
Customer Labels [	Forms	Preview	Command button	ControlTipText	
Employees	Forms	RemovePicture	Command button	ControlTipText	
Employees	Forms	AddPicture	Command button	ControlTipText	
Main Switchboard	Forms	Categories	Command button	ControlTipText	Open the Categories form.
Main Switchboard	Forms	Products	Command button	ControlTipText	Open the Products form.
Main Switchboard	Forms	Suppliers	Command button	ControlTipText	Open the Suppliers form.

Record: 1 of 37 (Filtered)

Figure 4-8. The result query shows which buttons don't have their ControlTipText properties set

Discussion

To build the list of forms and reports, zsfrmVerifySettings borrows code from the example in the Solution in Recipe 4.2. Instead of looping through all the collections, however, it works only with the Forms and Reports collections. Otherwise, the mechanics of creating the list of objects are the same as in the Solution in Recipe 4.2; investigate that topic if you'd like more information on building the object inventory.

Creating the temporary tables and query

The Solution in Recipe 4.2 created a single table, zstblInventory, to hold the list of objects. In this case, however, you need three tables (zstblInventory for main objects, zstblSubObjects for objects on those forms or reports, and zstblProperties for property information). You also need a query (zsqryProperties) to join the three tables and display the output. The *CreateTables* function, shown here, uses DDL queries to create each of the necessary tables (see the Solution in Recipe 1.15 for more information on DDL queries) and DAO to create the query (see Chapter 6 for more information on using DAO):

```
Private Function CreateTables( ) As Boolean

    ' Return True on success, False otherwise.

    Dim db As DAO.Database
    Dim qdf As DAO.QueryDef
    Dim strSQL As String

    On Error GoTo HandleErr

    Set db = CurrentDb

    db.Execute "DROP TABLE zstblInventory"
    db.Execute "DROP TABLE zstblSubObjects"
    db.Execute "DROP TABLE zstblProperties"

    ' Create zstblInventory.
    strSQL = "CREATE TABLE zstblInventory (Name Text (255), " & _
      "Container Text (50), DateCreated DateTime, " & _
      "LastUpdated DateTime, Owner Text (50), " & _
      "ID AutoIncrement Constraint PrimaryKey PRIMARY KEY)"
    db.Execute strSQL

    ' Create zstblSubObjects.
    strSQL = "CREATE TABLE zstblSubObjects (ParentID Long, " & _
      "ObjectName Text (50), ObjectType Text (50), " & _
      "ObjectID AutoIncrement Constraint PrimaryKey PRIMARY KEY)"
    db.Execute strSQL

    ' Create zstblProperties.
    strSQL = "CREATE TABLE zstblProperties (ObjectID Long, " & _
      "PropName Text (50), PropType Short, " & "PropValue Text (255), " & _
      "PropertyID AutoIncrement Constraint PrimaryKey PRIMARY KEY)"
    db.Execute strSQL

    ' Create zsqryProperties.
    strSQL = "SELECT zstblInventory.Name AS Parent, " & _
      "zstblInventory.Container, zstblSubObjects.ObjectName, " & _
      "zstblSubObjects.ObjectType, zstblProperties.PropName, " & _
      "zstblProperties.PropValue FROM zstblInventory " & _
      "INNER JOIN (zstblSubObjects INNER JOIN zstblProperties " & _
      "ON zstblSubObjects.ObjectID = zstblProperties.ObjectID) " & _
      "ON zstblInventory.ID = zstblSubObjects.ParentID;"

    db.CreateQueryDef ("zsqryProperties")
    Set qdf = db.QueryDefs("zsqryProperties")
    qdf.SQL = strSQL

    ' If you got here, you succeeded!
    CurrentDb.TableDefs.Refresh
    CreateTables = True
```

```
ExitHere:
    Exit Function

HandleErr:
    Select Case Err
        Case acbErrTableNotFound, acbErrObjectNotFound, _
            acbErrAlreadyExists
                Resume Next
        Case Else
            CreateTables = False
    End Select
    Resume ExitHere
End Function
```

Getting ready to document items

When you click on the Document Selected Items button, the form walks through the list of selected items and then documents the object. The code in cmdDocumentSelected_Click does the work: it looks through the ItemsSelected collection of the list box and, for each selected item, calls either *DocumentForm* or *DocumentReport*, depending on the value in the second column of the list box. Each of those procedures requires the ID of the parent object (the form or report in question) and the name of the object. The source code for the cmdDocumentSelected_Click event procedure is:

```
Private Sub cmdDocumentSelected_Click( )

    ' In the list box:
    ' ParentID == Column(0)
    ' Container == Column(1)
    ' Name == Column(2)

    Static fInHere As Boolean
    Dim varItem As Variant
    Dim strName As String
    Dim lngParentID As Long

    On Error GoTo HandleErr
    ' Don't allow recursive entry. If this routine is doing
    ' its thing, don't allow more button clicks to get you
    ' in again, until the first pass has finished its work.
    If fInHere Then Exit Sub
    fInHere = True

    With Me.lstInventory
        For Each varItem In .ItemsSelected
            strName = .Column(2, varItem)
            lngParentID = .Column(0, varItem)
            Select Case .Column(1, varItem)
                ' This will handle only forms and reports.
                Case "Forms"
```

```
                Call DocumentForm(strName, lngParentID)
            Case "Reports"
                Call DocumentReport(strName, lngParentID)
        End Select
      Next varItem
    End With

    Call SysCmd(acSysCmdClearStatus)
    Me.cmdViewResults.Enabled = True

ExitHere:
      fInHere = False
    Exit Sub

HandleErr:
    MsgBox Err.Number & ": " & Err.Description, , "DocumentSelected"
    Resume ExitHere
End Sub
```

Visiting all the objects

The *DocumentForm* and *DocumentReport* procedures do the same things, though in slightly different ways. They both document the properties of the main object itself, followed by the properties of each of the sections (forms can have up to 5 sections, reports up to 25). Finally, both procedures walk through the collection of controls on the main object, documenting all the properties of each control. The following code shows *DocumentForm*, but *DocumentReport* is almost identical:

```
Private Sub DocumentForm( _
  ByVal strName As String, ByVal lngParentID As Long)
    ' You must first open the form in design mode, and then
    ' retrieve the information. With forms, you can open the
    ' form in hidden mode, at least.

    Dim db As Database
    Dim rstObj As DAO.Recordset
    Dim rstProps As DAO.Recordset
    Dim lngObjectID As Long
    Dim frm As Form
    Dim ctl As Control
    Dim intI As Integer
    Dim obj As Object

    On Error GoTo HandleErr
    Call SysCmd(acSysCmdSetStatus, "Getting information on form " & _
      strName & ".")

    Set db = CurrentDb( )
    ' No need to open the form if it's THIS form.
    If strName <> Me.Name Then
        DoCmd.OpenForm strName, View:=acDesign, WindowMode:=acHidden
    End If
    Set rstObj = db.OpenRecordset("zstblSubObjects", _
```

```
            dbOpenTable, dbAppendOnly)
        Set rstProps = db.OpenRecordset("zstblProperties", _
            dbOpenTable, dbAppendOnly)

        ' Handle the form properties first.
        Set frm = Forms(strName)
        AddProps rstObj, rstProps, frm, "Form", lngParentID

        ' Handle the five possible form sections.
        For intI = 0 To 4
            Set obj = frm.Section(intI)
            AddProps rstObj, rstProps, obj, "Section", lngParentID
Form_Next_Section:
        Next intI

        ' Handle all the controls.
        For Each ctl In frm.Controls
            AddProps rstObj, rstProps, ctl, GetControlType(ctl), lngParentID
        Next ctl

        ' Don't close the form that's running all this.
        If Me.Name <> strName Then
            DoCmd.Close acForm, strName
        End If

ExitHere:
    Exit Sub

HandleErr:
    Select Case Err
        Case acbErrInvalidSection
            Resume Form_Next_Section
        Case Else
            MsgBox Err & ": " & Err.Description, , "DocumentForm"
    End Select
    Resume ExitHere
End Sub
```

The procedure starts by opening the requested object in design mode so it can get the information it needs. It cannot open the objects in normal view mode, because that would run the objects' event procedures, which might have unpleasant side effects.

Starting with Access 2002, you can specify a *WindowMode* when you use DoCmd. OpenReport. This allows you to hide a report when you open it, which is nice when you are opening it in design view.

As shown in our example, if the code tries to open the current form, it simply skips the open step. (This means, of course, that your documentation on the current form will be different than that of other forms: it's already open in form view, and the rest will be opened in design view.) Skipping the current form isn't an issue if you're documenting reports. When it's complete, *DocumentForm/Report* also closes the object (as long as it wasn't the current form). This is shown in the following code fragment from the *DocumentForm* procedure:

```
' No need to open the form if it's THIS form.
If strName <> Me.Name Then
    DoCmd.OpenForm strName, View:=acDesign, WindowMode:=acHidden
End If
.
. ' All the real work happens here...
.
' Don't close the form that's running all this.
If Me.Name <> strName Then
    DoCmd.Close acForm, strName
End If
```

DocumentForm next opens two recordsets, to which it adds rows as it documents your objects. These are specified as append-only recordsets in order to speed up the processing. The relevant code is:

```
Set rstObj = db.OpenRecordset("zstblSubObjects", _
  dbOpenTable, dbAppendOnly)
Set rstProps = db.OpenRecordset("zstblProperties", _
  dbOpenTable, dbAppendOnly)
```

Next, the procedure documents all the properties of the main object itself. As it will do when documenting all the objects, it calls the *AddProps* procedure. *AddProps* expects to receive references to the two recordsets, a reference to the object to be documented, the text to appear in the list box for the object's type, and the ID value for the main, parent object. The code fragment that calls *AddProps* appears as follows:

```
' Handle the form properties first.
Set frm = Forms(strName)
AddProps rstObj, rstProps, frm, "Form", lngParentID
```

The procedure then documents the properties of the sections. For forms, there can be at most five sections (detail, form header/footer, page header/footer). For reports, there can be up to 25: the same 5 as for forms, plus a header and footer for up to 10 report grouping sections. Note that any section may or may not exist. Therefore, the code traps for this error and jumps on to the next numbered section if the current one doesn't exist. The portion of the code that documents section properties is:

```
    ' Handle the five possible form sections.
    For intI = 0 To 4
        Set obj = frm.Section(intI)
        AddProps rstObj, rstProps, obj, "Section", lngParentID
Form_Next_Section:
    Next intI
```

Finally, *DocumentForm/Report* visits each of the controls on the form or report, calling *AddProps* with information about each control:

```
' Handle all the controls.
For Each ctl In frm.Controls
    AddProps rstObj, rstProps, ctl, GetControlType(ctl), lngParentID
Next ctl
```

Recording property information

The *AddProps* procedure, shown here, does the work of recording information about the selected object into zstblSubObject and about all its properties into zstblProperties. Note the large error-handling section; several properties of forms, reports, sections, and controls are not available in design mode, and attempting to retrieve those property values triggers various error messages.

```
Private Sub AddProps(rstObj As DAO.Recordset, _
    rstProps As DAO.Recordset, obj As Object, _
    ByVal strType As String, ByVal lngParentID As Long)

    Dim lngObjectID As Long
    Dim prp As Property

    On Error GoTo HandleErr

    rstObj.AddNew
        rstObj("ParentID") = lngParentID
        rstObj("ObjectName") = obj.Name
        rstObj("ObjectType") = strType
        ' Get the new ID
        lngObjectID = rstObj("ObjectID")
    rstObj.Update
    For Each prp In obj.Properties
        rstProps.AddNew
            rstProps("ObjectID") = lngObjectID
            rstProps("PropName") = prp.Name
            rstProps("PropType") = prp.Type
            ' Store the first 255 bytes of the
            ' property value, converted to text.
            rstProps("PropValue") = Left(prp.Value & "", 255)
        rstProps.Update
    Next prp

ExitHere:
    Exit Sub

HandleErr:
    Select Case Err.Number
        ' Some property values just aren't available in the design view.
        Case acbErrInvalidView, acbErrNotInThisView, _
          acbErrCantRetrieveProp, acbErrCantGetProp
            Resume Next
        Case Else
```

```
            MsgBox Err.Number & ": " & Err.Description, , "AddProps"
        End Select
        Resume ExitHere
    End Sub
```

To add a row about the object to zstblSubObjects, *AddProps* uses the AddNew method of the recordset and then fills in the appropriate fields. Just like on an Access form, when you add a new row to a recordset, Access fills in any autonumber values as soon as you begin editing the row. Here, we grab that new ObjectID value and store it in the variable *lngObjectID*, for use later as the object ID in the related properties table:

```
    rstObj.AddNew
        rstObj("ParentID") = lngParentID
        rstObj("ObjectName") = obj.Name
        rstObj("ObjectType") = strType
        ' Get the new ID
        lngObjectID = rstObj("ObjectID")
    rstObj.Update
```

Next, *AddProps* loops through all the properties in the object's Properties collection, adding a row for each to zstblProperties. Note that because tables don't support Variant fields, we've set the PropValue field to be a 255-character text field; the code converts the property value to text and truncates it to no more than 255 characters. Few properties require more text than that, but some, such as the row sources of combo boxes, could. You might want to use a memo field for these properties instead. Memo fields are somewhat less efficient, but they are more efficient starting with Jet 4.0 (Access 2000 or later) than they were in previous versions.

```
    For Each prp In obj.Properties
        rstProps.AddNew
            rstProps("ObjectID") = lngObjectID
            rstProps("PropName") = prp.Name
            rstProps("PropType") = prp.Type
            ' Store the first 255 bytes of the
            ' property value, converted to text.
            rstProps("PropValue") = Left(prp.Value & "", 255)
        rstProps.Update
    Next prp
```

 The rest of the code in zsfrmVerifySettings's module deals with selecting items in the list box. You're welcome to peruse that code, but it's not crucial to understanding the object/property inventory.

Comments

If you're interested in working with multiselect list boxes in your applications, take the time to work through the code that manipulates the list box in this example. The code uses the Selected property of the list box, setting various rows to be selected or not by setting the value of the property. It also makes heavy use of the Column property, allowing random access to any item stored in the list box.

More than for most of the solutions in this book, effective use of the techniques covered here requires some of your own imagination. Not only are the techniques for providing the object and property inventory interesting, but the output itself can be useful as well. Since we developed this example, we've used it in several applications to verify that all the controls used the same fonts, that all the command buttons had their ControlTipText properties set, and that all the detail sections used the same background color. You should strive for design consistency in your applications, and this tool can help you achieve it.

See Also

For more information on using DAO in Access databases, see "How Do I Use Data Access Objects (DAO) in New Databases?" in the Preface.

4.4   Hide Access Screen Activity

Problem

You can use a form's Painting property to disable updates to that form, but some activities still seem to show through or cause flashing on the screen. Is there any way to hide screen activity?

Solution

Sometimes you need more control over screen repainting than you get with either Form.Painting. You may also need to investigate the Application.Echo method. By passing this method a True or a False value, you can indicate whether you want to display updating within the main Access window. You can also optionally pass the method a second parameter—a string indicating text to be displayed within the status bar while screen updating is disabled.

Load and run frmLockScreen (Figure 4-9) from *04-04.MDB*. This sample form simply opens three reports in design mode and then closes them. The form includes a checkbox that allows you to run the test with screen updates enabled or disabled. Try it both ways; you should see a clear difference between the two ways of running the test. With the checkbox set, the underlying code disables screen updates, so you shouldn't see the reports' icons pop up. Without the checkbox set, you will see the reports open and minimize, in design view.

To use Application.Echo to disable screen updates in your own applications, follow these steps:

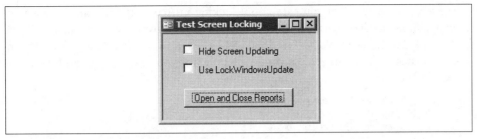

Figure 4-9. The sample form, frmLockScreen, ready to run its tests

1. Import the module basLockScreen from *04-04.MDB*. This module includes the simple code that's required in order to disable updates to the Access main window.

2. When you want to disable screen updates, call the *acbShowUpdates* subroutine, passing it a False value. To reenable screen updates, call the subroutine again, passing it a True value. In other words, your code that uses *acbShowUpdates* should take the following form:

```
Call acbShowUpdates(False)
' Do your work in here...
Call acbShowUpdates(True)
```

Discussion

The Application.Echo method is simple to use, but many developers miss it, allowing their applications to appear somewhat dizzying as objects appear and disappear from the screen. The acbShowUpdates method really doesn't do much besides what a direct call to Application.Echo does:

```
Sub acbShowUpdates(blnShow As Boolean)
    If blnShow Then
        Application.Echo True
    Else
        Application.Echo False
    End If
End Sub
```

As a matter of fact, the reason this procedure exists at all is because the techniques used in this topic work great in Access 2002 and later, but may not work correctly in earlier versions—it may be that if you're running Access 2000 or earlier, using Application.Echo to turn off screen updating while opening a report in design view may not hide screen updates. In that case, you may want to try an alternate technique, calling the parallel *acbShowUpdatesAPI* method.

The *acbShowUpdatesAPI* subroutine (in basLockScreen) does its work by calling the Windows API function *LockWindowUpdate*. This function takes as its only parameter a window handle. If that handle is nonzero, Windows simply stops updating the contents of that window on screen. If the handle is 0, Windows reenables screen updates to the locked window.

Because the only window you care about locking in Access is the main Access window itself, the *acbShowUpdatesAPI* routine shields you from any of the details. If you pass it a False value, it blocks window updates. If you pass it a True value, it reenables updates. It finds the Access window handle for you, if necessary, and then calls *LockWindowUpdate*. Its source code is simple:

```
Sub acbShowUpdatesAPI (blnShow As Integer)
    If blnShow Then
        acb_apiLockWindowUpdate 0
    Else
        acb_apiLockWindowUpdate Application.hWndAccessApp
    End If
End Sub
```

 In Access 2.0, finding the window handle (the unique integer that identifies every window) for the main Access window was difficult. It required a good deal of work with multiple Windows API functions. In later versions, the Application object exposes the hWndAccessApp property, which returns the window handle of the main Access window.

You may find, depending on the version of Access you're using, that this method of disabling screen updates isn't perfect. Because Access has no idea that you've turned them off, Access itself occasionally turns on screen updates. For example, depending on how you open forms and reports in design mode, completely hiding the properties sheet may be difficult. In the sample application, *04-04.MDB*, the reports' properties sheet isn't showing. If you open one of the reports, open the properties sheet, and then save the report, no combination of Application.Echo and calls to *LockWindowUpdate* will completely remove that properties sheet from the screen when you open the report in design view.

Hiding reports in design view

In older versions of Access, you had to resort to hacks to hide reports in design view. Fortunately, that is no longer necessary in Access 2002 and later, because Microsoft has finally supplied a WindowMode parameter that can be used to hide a report when you open it, even if it's opened in design view. Also, many of the printer settings that made it necessary to open reports in design view are no longer necessary starting in Access 2002 because of the Printer object (see Chapter 5 for several examples).

If you are working in Access 97, you can take advantage of an undocumented but effective technique for hiding the hard-to-hide properties windows of reports that are open in design view. Be warned, however, that this method is totally undocumented, is unsupported by Microsoft, and doesn't work in Access 2000 or later.

The Application object in Access supports the GetOption and SetOption methods, which allow you to get and set global options. Most of these options are documented (see the online help topics for GetOption/SetOption), while a few items are not documented but do useful work. One such option allows you to retrieve and set the coordinates for the form or report properties sheet (in versions of Access prior to Access 2000) and to set whether or not you want the properties sheet to be visible when you open a form or report in design view.

To retrieve the information about the report properties sheet in Access 97 or 95, use a call like this:

```
strInfo = Application.GetOption("_26")
```

This will retrieve a string containing information on the report properties sheet's location and whether or not to display it when you open a report in design view. The string will be in this format:

```
open?;left;top;width;height;
```

For example, it might look like this:

```
1;510;433;835;683;
```

indicating that the properties sheet will be visible when you load a report and that when it does show up it will be at 510, 433 with a width of 835 and a height of 683.

To make sure that your application doesn't show the properties sheet while it does its work, you can retrieve this property, set the first character to 0, and then save it. The code might look like this:

```
Dim strInfo As String
strInfo = Application.GetOption("_26")
strInfo = "0" & Mid(strInfo, 2)
Application.SetOption "_26", strInfo
```

The only way this will have any influence is if you call this code before you've loaded any reports in design mode. Access looks at this information only once, when it loads the properties sheet for the first time. Once it has loaded the properties sheet, it doesn't look at these values again. Every time you leave design mode Access stores information about the properties sheet, so if you're going to try to set these values for the next time you start Access, make sure you do it when there's no report open in design mode. Otherwise, Access will override your settings when it saves them itself.

To use this technique for forms, use option "_24" instead. It's not nearly as useful with forms as it is with reports, however, because in older versions of Access you can open hidden forms but not hidden reports.

As an example of an error handler that resets screen updates, the code executed by frmLockScreen handles errors by using the normal exit route from the routine:

```
Private Sub cmdOpenReports_Click()
    Dim intI As Integer
    Dim intSuccess As Integer
```

Never Turn off the Screen Without an Error Handler!

Though this same advice goes for using Application.Echo or Form.Painting, it's especially true for using *LockWindowUpdate*. Any time you turn off the screen display, you absolutely must include an error handler in your routine that will immediately reenable screen updates if an error occurs. Sooner or later, a runtime error *will* occur, and your code must react to this and clean up. Users tend to do unpleasant things, such as rebooting their computers, when their screens stop dead (that's what would happen if an error occurred while you had screen updates turned off). This can be detrimental to their data and to your application, so never consider turning off the screen unless you also include an error handler to turn it back on.

```
    On Error GoTo HandleErr

    If Me.chkHideUpdates Then
        If Me.chkUseAPI Then
            Call acbShowUpdatesAPI(False)
        Else
            Call acbShowUpdates(False)
        End If
    End If
    For intI = 1 To 3
        Call acbOpenReport("rptReport" & intI, acDesign)
    Next intI
    For intI = 1 To 3
        DoCmd.Close acReport, "rptReport" & intI
    Next intI

ExitHere:
    If Me.chkHideUpdates Then
        If Me.chkUseAPI Then
            Call acbShowUpdatesAPI(True)
        Else
            Call acbShowUpdates(True)
        End If
    End If
    Exit Sub

HandleErr:
    MsgBox Err.Number & ": " & Err.Description
    Resume ExitHere
End Sub
```

If an error occurs while this subroutine is active, the code will jump to the HandleErr label and from there will resume at the ExitHere label. The code will re-enable screen updates and then exit the routine. Your own code may not look exactly like this, but you must handle errors so that the screen never remains locked up when an error occurs.

See Also

For more information on working with the Windows API, see Chapter 11.

4.5   Find out What Language Version of Access Is Installed

Problem

You distribute your applications in several countries, and your users have different internationalized versions of Access installed. You'd like your applications to be able to make decisions based on the installed version of Access. How can you find out which language version of Access is currently running?

Solution

In older versions of Access, you had to use an API call to get this information. However, starting with Access 2000, it is possible to retrieve language information using the Microsoft Office Object Library. This solution demonstrates how you can gather the language information you need.

Load and run the form frmLanguage in *04-05.MDB*. As it loads, it calls the necessary functions to determine the currently running language version of Access. Figure 4-10 shows the form after it's been loaded into a retail U.S. English version of Access.

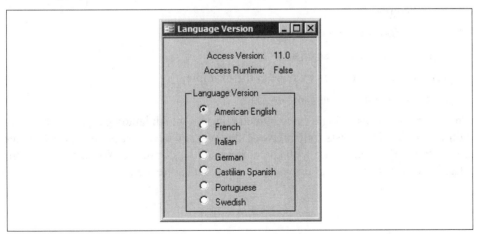

Figure 4-10. frmLanguage indicates the language version of Access that's running

To include this functionality in your own applications, follow these steps:

1. Import the module basFileLanguage from *04-05.MDB* into your own application. This module includes constants representing the seven most commonly used languages and their related intrinsic constants and values.

2. Declare a long integer variable, *lngLanguage*. When your application starts up, make a call to *acbAccessLanguage*, which will return a number representing the current running language version of Access. You can assign this return value to the *lngLanguage* variable, as follows:

```
lngLanguage = acbAccessLanguage( )
```

You can then pass that variable to procedures in your application that make decisions based on the current language version of Access.

In the example application, the language ID is stored in an option group, which will work only if you are supporting a known, limited set of languages. The example also includes code that detects the version of Access in use and whether it is a runtime version.

Discussion

Retrieving language information requires setting a reference to the Microsoft Office Object Library. You can then refer to the Application object's LanguageSettings property to retrieve the language being used. Each language has its own LanguageID property, which is an integer value. These language IDs are represented by enumerated constants. When you set a reference to the Microsoft Office Object Library, you can see a complete list of constants by examining the msoLanguageID enumeration, as shown in Figure 4-11.

The call to *acbAccessLanguage* requires a simple variable:

```
lngRetval = acb_apiGetLanguage( )
```

Or you can use a control, as we have in the example:

```
Me.grpLanguage = acbAccessLanguage( )
```

The function returns a single value, which tells you which language version the function found. Table 4-1 lists only a few of the Windows languages and the ID values associated with them, along with the corresponding constants. You can see a complete list by using the Object Browser, as shown in Figure 4-11.

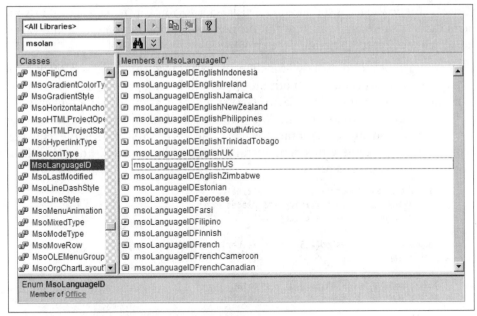

Figure 4-11. Each language value has a corresponding constant

Table 4-1. Windows languages and ID values

Language	Constant	ID
American English	msoLanguageIDEnglishUS	1033
French	msoLanguageIDFrench	1036
German	msoLanguageIDGerman	1031
Italian	msoLanguageIDItalian	1040
Russian	msoLanguageIDRussian	1049
Spanish	msoLanguageIDSpanish	1034
Portuguese	msoLanguageIDPortuguese	2070
Swedish	msoLanguageIDSwedish	1053
Zulu	msoLanguageIDZulu	1077

The simple function in basFileLanguage, *acbAccessLanguage*, returns only the national language ID number (from Table 4-1) for the installed version of Access:

```
Function acbAccessLanguage( ) As Long
    acbAccessLanguage = _
    Application.LanguageSettings.LanguageID(msoLanguageIDUI)
End Function
```

Once you know the ID for the national language, you can make choices in your application. For example, as shown in the next two solutions, you can modify labels on forms and reports and modify the error messages that you display.

The example form also uses two functions from basAccessInfo in *04-05.MDB*, *acb-GetVersion* and *acbIsRuntime*. Both are quite simple, comprising only calls to the built-in *SysCmd* function. The first, *acbGetVersion*, returns the version number of the currently running copy of Access. The second, *acbIsRuntime*, returns True if your application is running in the runtime version of Access or False if it's in the retail version. You may find these functions useful if your application needs to react differently to different environments.

```
Public Function acbGetVersion( ) As String
    ' Retrieve the Access version for places
    ' that can't use symbolic constants.

    acbGetVersion = SysCmd(acSysCmdAccessVer)
End Function

Public Function acbIsRuntime( ) As Boolean
    ' Use SysCmd( ) to gather the information.

    acbIsRuntime = SysCmd(acSysCmdRuntime)
End Function
```

4.6   Internationalize Text in Your Applications

Problem

You'd like to be able to pop up translated error messages in your applications, based on the currently running language version of Access. You'd also like other text on your forms and reports to adjust automatically based on the current language version. You know there are a number of ways to do this, but you can't decide which is best. How should you store and retrieve messages in multiple languages?

Solution

The translated version of Access handles its own error messages (in the German version, for example, the Access error messages appear in German). But you do need to translate your own messages if you want your application to run smoothly in other languages. Though there are several methods of handling text, the most generic solution uses a table of messages, which you can look up by ID number.

Load and run the form frmTestMessage from *04-06.MDB*. This form, shown in Figure 4-12, allows you to choose from three different languages (English, French, and Spanish) in an option group. As you choose each language, code attached to the option group's AfterUpdate event changes accordingly the captions for labels on the form and the status-bar text for text boxes. To try a sample error message in the chosen language, click the Test Message button.

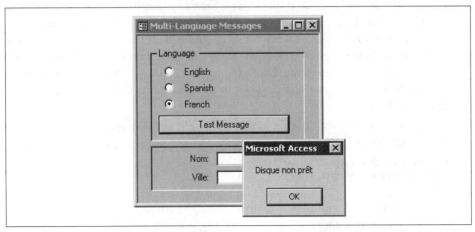

Figure 4-12. The sample form, frmTestMessage, showing the French test error message

In each case, the messages are coming from the table tblMessages. This table includes a column for the message identifier (the primary key) and one column for each of the languages your application supports. Figure 4-13 shows the table, filled in for the sample application.

	MsgNum	English	Spanish	French
▶	1	The disk drive is not ready	El disco no está listo	Disque non prêt
	2	Name:	Nombre:	Nom:
	3	City:	Ciudad:	Ville:
	4	Enter your name	Tecle su nombre	Tapez votre nom
	5	Enter the address	Tecle su ciudad	Tapez votre ville
✳	(AutoNumber)			

Figure 4-13. The message table, tblMessages, filled in for the sample application 04-06.MDB

To include similar functionality in your own applications, follow these steps:

1. From *04-06.MDB*, import the modules basFileLanguage (which includes the procedures from the Solution in Recipe 4.5 for obtaining the current language version of Access) and basGetMessages (which looks up particular messages in tblMessages).

2. From *04-06.MDB*, import the table tblMessages. This is the table you'll use to hold your messages. Delete the existing rows, if you like. Also, you can modify the structure and add more languages if necessary.

3. Add the necessary rows to tblMessages, filling in each column with the translated text, as shown in Figure 4-13.

4. On any form for which you'd like to have language-sensitive captions and status-bar text, place the message ID (the MsgNum column from tblMessages) in the Tag property for the control whose text you'd like to change. For labels, the code you'll call is set up to change the Caption property; for text boxes, the code is set up to change the StatusBarText property. (If you want to include other control types, you can modify the code in the subroutine *GetInfo*, as described in Section 4.6.3.)

5. To set the captions for labels and the status-bar text for text boxes when your form loads, place the following code in the Open event procedure for your form:

```
Private Sub grpLanguage_AfterUpdate( )
    acbSetText Me, Me.grpLanguage
End Sub
```

The *acbSetText* subroutine walks through all the controls on your form, searching for ones with a numeric value in the Tag property. For any such controls, it looks up the appropriate message and assigns it to the Caption or StatusBarText property.

Discussion

The technique presented in this solution includes two basic pieces of functionality: retrieving the correct messages from the table of messages and replacing all the required property values on your form or report. Together, these two operations accomplish the goals of changing labels and status bar text and providing translated error messages.

The *acbGetMessage* function retrieves the messages you need from tblMessages. You pass to it, as parameters, a long integer specifying the message number you want and an integer specifying the correct language.

```
Public Function acbGetMessage( _
    ByVal lngMessage As Long, _
    ByVal lngLanguage As Long) As Variant

        ' Retrieve a message from tblMessages, given a message
        ' ID and a language.


    Dim db As DAO.Database
    Dim rst As DAO.Recordset
    Dim varLanguage As Variant
    Dim varResult As Variant

    On Error GoTo HandleErr

    varResult = Null
    Set db = CurrentDb( )
    Set rst = db.OpenRecordset("tblMessages", dbOpenTable)
```

```
        With rst
            If Not .EOF Then
                ' Set the index, which is the message number
                .Index = "PrimaryKey"
                .Seek "=", lngMessage
                If .NoMatch Then
                    ' You could raise an error here,
                    '  but we're just returning a null value.
                    varResult = Null
                Else
                    varLanguage = GetLanguageName(lngLanguage)
                    If Not IsNull(varLanguage) Then
                        varResult = rst(varLanguage)
                    Else
                        varResult = Null
                    End If
                End If
            End If
        End With
ExitHere:
    If Not rst Is Nothing Then
        rst.Close
        Set rst = Nothing
    End If
    acbGetMessage = varResult
    Exit Function

HandleErr:
    varResult = Null
    MsgBox Err.Number & ": " & Err.Description, , "acbGetMessage"
    Resume ExitHere
End Function
```

This function starts by creating a table-type recordset based on tblMessages:

```
Set rst = db.OpenRecordset(acbcMsgTable, dbOpenTable)
```

If there are any rows in tblMessages, the function looks for the row you've requested. If it doesn't find a match, you must have requested a message number that's not in the table, so the function returns Null:

```
With rst
    If Not .EOF Then
        ' Set the index, which is the message number.
        .Index = "PrimaryKey"
        .Seek "=", lngMessage
        If .NoMatch Then
            varResult = Null
```

If it does find a match, it converts the language number into the table's column name for the language (using the *GetLanguageName* function). If it finds a language name, it retrieves the appropriate message from tblMessages:

```
        Else
            varLanguage = GetLanguageName(intLanguage)
            If Not IsNull(varLanguage) Then
```

```
            varResult = rst(varLanguage)
        Else
            varResult = Null
        End If
    End If
End With
```

If any error occurs along the way, *acbGetMessage* returns Null. If things work out, it returns the message it found in tblMessages.

You can call *acbGetMessage* directly (e.g., to fill the text for a message box or to build up a more complex error string). In addition, the *acbSetText* subroutine—which does the work of replacing text when you load a form or report—calls *acbGetMessage* multiple times, once for each message.

The *acbSetText* procedure takes two parameters: an object containing a reference to the form or report, and the language ID. The procedure walks through all the controls on the requested form or report, calling the *GetInfo* function for each. The complete text of the *acbSetText* procedure is:

```
Public Sub acbSetText(obj As Object, ByVal lngLanguage As Long)

    ' Set text for labels (caption) and text boxes (status-bar
    ' text) on the specified report or form.

    Dim ctl As Control

    For Each ctl In obj.Controls
        Call GetInfo(ctl, lngLanguage)
    Next ctl
End Sub
```

The *GetInfo* subroutine does the actual work; this is the procedure you'll need to change if you want to handle more than just labels' Caption properties and text boxes' StatusBarText properties. It checks the Tag property and, if it's numeric, looks up the associated text string in the appropriate language. Once it has the string, it checks the control type and places the string in the correct property for the given control type. The complete source code for the *GetInfo* subroutine is:

```
Private Sub GetInfo(ctl As Control, lngLanguage As Long)
    ' Given a control and a language, look up the label
    ' or status-bar text for it.

    Dim varCaption As Variant

    With ctl
        If IsNumeric(.Tag) Then
            varCaption = acbGetMessage(.Tag, lngLanguage)
            If Not IsNull(varCaption) Then
                Select Case .ControlType
                    Case acLabel
                        .Caption = varCaption
```

```
                    Case acTextBox
                        .StatusBarText = varCaption
                End Select
            End If
        End If
    End With
End Sub
```

If you want to support more languages than just the three used in this example, you'll need to modify the structure of tblMessages (adding a new column for each new language) and modify the *GetLanguageName* procedure in the basGetMessage module. As it is now, *GetLanguageName* looks like this:

```
Private Function GetLanguageName( _
    ByVal lngLanguage As Long) As Variant
    ' Make sure to set a reference to the Office Library.
    ' Given a language identifier, get the column name in
    ' tblMessages that corresponds to it. This function
    ' expects, for lngLanguage:
    '    msoLanguageIDEnglishUS (1033),
    '    msoLanguageIDSpanish (1034), or
    '    msoLanguageIDFrench (1036).

    Dim varLang As Variant

    Select Case lngLanguage
        Case msoLanguageIDEnglishUS
            varLang = "English"
        Case msoLanguageIDFrench
            varLang = "French"
        Case msoLanguageIDSpanish
            varLang = "Spanish"
    End Select
    GetLanguageName = varLang
End Function
```

Add more cases to the Select Case statement, matching the new columns in your messages table. The constants come from the Office Library, a reference to which you must add to your project. An alternative approach is to use the language IDs themselves as the column headings—that way you won't need the extra step of translating the IDs to names. You could also redesign the solution to use three columns—MsgNum, LanguageID, and ErrorMessage—which would make adding a language a matter of adding records rather than modifying code.

The sample form contains only a few controls. Attempting to modify the properties of several hundred controls would noticeably increase load time for a form. For forms that contain many controls, you might be better off creating one version of the form per language and distributing translated versions of your application. Alternatively, you could preload the form invisibly when your application starts up so that it appears instantly when made visible.

Another problem you should consider when attempting to modify captions on the fly is that many non-English languages take more space to present the same information. You'll find that some languages require twice as much space (or more) for a given text string. This may mean that dynamic translation isn't feasible, due to real-estate problems. Again, the best solution is to plan the translated versions carefully and prepare a different set of forms and reports for each language, or to leave enough space for the most verbose language you need to support. You could also include width values for each language and adjust the controls as needed, but this would get complicated because you would also need to adjust their positions and perhaps even the size of the form. A comprehensive solution would require you to store many property values for each control and for each form and report.

Message boxes don't present such a problem, of course, because Access automatically resizes them to fit the data you send to them. The same goes for ControlTip-Text. Call the *acbGetMessage* function to provide the text for any message box you wish to fill, as in this example:

```
Call MsgBox(acbGetText(intLanguage, 1), vbExclamation, acbGetText(intLanguage, 2))
```

You can use this technique to alter any messages within your application at runtime. For example, if you want to provide different levels of help for different users, you can keep all your messages in a table and retrieve the correct help messages depending on who the current user is. In this case, rather than looking up language names, you'd be looking up user or group names.

4.7   Change and Reset the Access Caption Bar

Problem

You'd like to be able to change the caption of the main Access window as part of your application. Of course, you need to be able to reset it back to its original value when you're done. You've found the AppTitle property in Access, but you just can't get it to work. Is there some simple way to retrieve and set the Access caption, as you can with any of the windows within Access?

Solution

This is one situation where it's simpler to use the Windows API than it is to use the built-in functionality. Although Access does support a property of the current database, AppTitle, that you can use to set and retrieve the Access titlebar, it's clumsy to use because AppTitle is a user-defined property. If the property doesn't yet exist in a database, you must create it. With the Windows API, retrieving and setting the Access caption both require just a few predictable steps, and neither process is terribly difficult. This solution demonstrates the steps to set and retrieve the Access caption with the Windows API. The AppTitle property is discussed in Section 4.7.3.

To try changing the Access caption, load and run frmSetTitleBarCaptionAPI from *04-07.MDB*. The form displays the current Access caption. By filling in a new value in the New Access Caption text box and pressing the Set New Caption button, you can change the caption on the main Access window. Figure 4-14 shows the form once it's already done its work. Press the Reset Caption button when you're done to reset the Access caption.

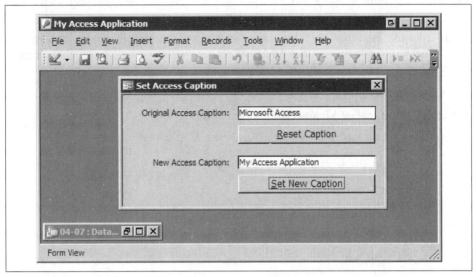

Figure 4-14. frmSetTitleBarCaptionAPI after it has set the new Access caption

To include this functionality in your own applications, follow these steps:

1. Import the module basCaption (which supplies the necessary Windows API declarations and the interface routines) from *04-07.MDB*.

2. To retrieve the current Access caption, call the *acbGetAccessCaption* function. For example:

    ```
    strOldCaption = acbGetAccessCaption( )
    ```

3. To set a new Access caption, call the *acbSetAccessCaption* subroutine, passing to it a string that holds your new caption, as follows (by appending an empty string to the contents of the text box, you guarantee that the value you pass to acbSetAccessCaption is indeed a string, even if the text box's content is empty):

    ```
    Call acbSetAccessCaption(Me.txtOldCaption & "")
    ```

4. To set the caption of any window given its window handle, call the *SetWindowText* API directly:

    ```
    Call SetWindowText(hWnd, "Your New Caption")
    ```

Discussion

To retrieve the Access window caption, call the *acbGetAccessCaption* function, which passes the Access window handle (Application.hWndAccessApp) to the more generalized *acbGetWindowCaption* function, which does its work in the following three steps:

1. It uses the built-in *Space* function to size a string buffer large enough to hold all the characters.

2. It calls the Windows API function *GetWindowText* to fill the buffer with the actual window caption. *GetWindowText* returns the number of characters it filled in.

3. It uses the built-in *Left* function to remove extra characters.

The code for the *acbGetWindowCaption* function is as follows:

```
Private Function acbGetWindowCaption(ByVal hWnd As Long) As Variant

    ' Get any window's caption, given its hWnd.

    Dim intLen As Integer
    Dim strBuffer As String

    Const acbcMaxLen = 255

    If hWnd <> 0 Then
        strBuffer = Space(acbcMaxLen)
        intLen = GetWindowText(hWnd, strBuffer, acbcMaxLen)
        acbGetWindowCaption = Left(strBuffer, intLen)
    End If
End Function
```

To set the Access caption, call the *acbSetAccessCaption* subroutine, passing to it the new caption you'd like to use. This procedure is much simpler than the previous one: it passes the Access window handle and the caption to the *SetWindowText* API procedure. The code for the *acbSetAccessCaption* subroutine is as follows:

```
Public Sub acbSetAccessCaption(ByVal strCaption As String)

    ' Set the Access caption to be the value in strCaption.
    Call SetWindowText(Application.hWndAccessApp, strCaption)
End Sub
```

Access does provide a built-in mechanism for setting the caption to be used while a specific database is loaded: the Tools → Startup dialog, shown in Figure 4-15. Using this dialog, you can set many of the startup options you'll need to deliver any application: the startup form, titlebar, icon, shortcut menu bar, and global menu bar. You can control other Access behavior as well, such as displaying the database window at startup, displaying the status bar, using built-in toolbars, or allowing toolbar changes.

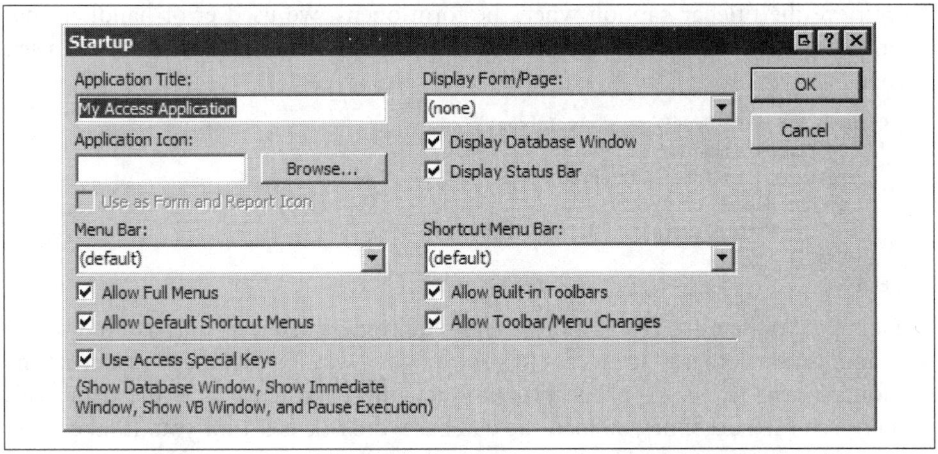

Figure 4-15. Use the Tools → Startup dialog to set application startup options

The AppTitle property allows you to set the database's titlebar, and the AppIcon property allows you to set an icon for the application. Both are usually set using the Startup dialog, but you can also modify them programmatically, as long as you remember that they're not built-in properties of the database. You must first create the properties and append them to the collection of properties; then you'll be able to use them.

The example database includes a form called frmSetTitleBarCaptionProperty that uses the AppTitle database property, creating the property on the fly if necessary. Here's the code that sets a new titlebar caption:

```
Private Sub cmdNewCaption_Click( )
    Dim prp As DAO.Property
    On Error GoTo HandleErr
    CurrentDb.Properties("AppTitle") = Me.txtNewCaption & ""

ExitHere:
    Application.RefreshTitleBar
    Exit Sub

HandleErr:
    Select Case Err.Number
        Case 3270 'Property not found
            Set prp = CurrentDb.CreateProperty( _
            "AppTitle", dbText, Me.txtNewCaption)
            CurrentDb.Properties.Append prp
        Case Else
            MsgBox _
            Err.Number & ": " & Err.Description, , "cmdNewCaption"
    End Select
    Resume ExitHere
End Sub
```

To retrieve the titlebar caption when the form opens, we used error handling that assumes the caption is "Microsoft Access" if the AppTitle property hasn't been used to change it:

```
Private Sub Form_Open(Cancel As Integer)
    On Error Resume Next
    Me.txtOldCaption = CurrentDb.Properties("AppTitle")
    If Err.Number <> 0 Then
        Me.txtOldCaption = "Microsoft Access"
    End If
End Sub
```

What are the trade-offs? The Windows API requires less code, runs faster, and works with applications other than Access (if you can get a window handle, you can set the caption). However, the AppTitle property actually persistently sets the database's property, so the next time you load the database, the title is set for you. It takes a bit more work to use the non-API Access method, but it does allow you to preserve the setting for your next session.

One final note: the Windows API allows you to set the caption to be an empty string. You cannot set the Access AppTitle property to be an empty string; Access will reject it. If you want to remove the text from the titlebar altogether, use the API method.

Create Your Own Splash Screen

The Tools → Startup menu does not provide a method by which you can supply your own startup bitmap image. If you want to supply your own bitmap splash screen to use rather than Access's built-in image, you can place a bitmap (*.bmp) file in the same directory as your application with the same name as your application. When you double-click on your MDB file to start it, or create a shortcut that starts it, Access will find your bitmap and use it as your startup splash screen. If you want no splash screen at all, simply create a single-pixel bitmap (use a light color for that single pixel). It will be so small that no one will notice it as Access opens.

4.8   Use the Windows File Open/Save Common Dialogs

Problem

You need to allow users to choose filenames for opening and saving files. You know that Windows supports a common way to get these names. How can you use this mechanism from within Access?

Solution

Not only can you use the common File Open/Save dialogs, but you even have three ways to do it:

- You can use the ActiveX control, *COMMDLG.OCX*, that ships with the some versions of the developer version of Office, and with Visual Basic.
- In Access 2002 and later, you can use the FileDialog object.
- You can call the Windows API directly.

If you don't have the developer version of Office, or Visual Basic, the first suggestion won't help. In addition, distribution of applications that use the common dialog ActiveX can get complex, because of ActiveX versioning issues. The FileDialog object added in Access 2002 makes it easier to select files, but it's not available in earlier versions. Therefore, this solution shows how to call the Windows API directly and lists all the options you have when using these common dialogs.

Open and run the form frmTestOpenSave from *04-08.MDB*. This sample form allows you to set various flags (described later in this solution) and to see the results. You can try both the File Save and File Open common dialogs. Try changing some of the settings and see what happens. Figure 4-16 shows the File Open dialog—with the Read Only checkbox hidden and allowing for multiple selections—displayed in explorer mode (as opposed to the older Program Manager look, which is what Windows will use if you specify the multiselect option by itself).

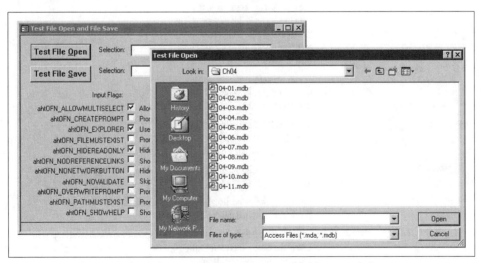

Figure 4-16. The sample form, frmTestOpenSave, showing the File Open dialog in use

To use this functionality within your own applications, follow these steps:

1. Import the module basCommonFile from *04-08.MDB* into your own application. This module provides the type and API function declarations you'll need and the wrapper functions that make it easy for you to use the common dialogs.

2. To use the File Open or File Save dialogs, call the *acbCommonFileOpenSave* function, passing to it information indicating what you want it to do. Table 4-2 lists the options available when you call the function. None of the parameters is required; the table lists the default values the function will use if you leave off each of the parameters. As a simple example, the following function call will ask for the name of the file to which you'd like to save, suggesting *FOO.TXT* and returning the full path of the file you choose:

```
varFileName = acbCommonFileOpenSave(FileName:="FOO.TXT", OpenFile:=False)
```

Table 4-2. Parameters for the acbCommonFileOpenSave function (all optional)

Parameter name	Description	Default value
Flags	A combination of zero or more flags from Table 4-1 that control the operation of the dialog. Combine them using the OR operator.	0
InitialDir	The initial directory that the dialog should use.	""
Filter	A string listing the available file filters. Use *acbAddFilter*, as shown in the examples, to build this parameter. The format of this item is important, so make sure to use the function rather than just setting the value by hand.	""
FilterIndex	The number of the filter item to use when the dialog first opens. The first filter is numbered 1.	1
DefaultExt	A default file extension to be appended to the filename if the user doesn't supply one. Don't include a period.	""
FileName	The filename to use when the dialog is first displayed.	""
DialogTitle	The title for the dialog. Usually, you won't specify this parameter.	Open/Save As
hWnd	The window handle for the parent window of the dialog. This value controls where the dialog will be placed.	Application.hWndAccessApp
OpenFile	Whether it's the Open or Save dialog. (True = Open, False = Save).	True

Because the *acbCommonFileOpenSave* function accepts so many optional parameters, and you'll generally want to set only a few of them, you may find VBA's support for named parameters useful. That is, rather than depending on the exact order of the parameters you send to *acbCommonFileOpenSave*, use the name of the parameter, a : =, and then the value, as we've done in this example. This will make your code easier to read and far less error-prone.

3. If you also want to specify filter choices that show up in the "Files of type:" combo box on the dialog, call the *acbAddFilterItem* function. This function accepts three parameters: the string of filters to which you want to add items; the description for your filter ("Databases (*.mdb, *.mda)", for example); and the actual filter file specifications, delimited with a semicolon ("*.mda;*.mda", to match the previous example). The function returns the new filter string. You can call *acbAddFilterItem* as many times as you need to build up your list of filters. For example, the following example (similar to the example in basCommonFile) sets up four filter expressions. You can call TestIt from the debug window in Access to test the filters:

```
Function TestIt( )
    Dim strFilter As String

    strFilter = acbAddFilterItem(strFilter, "Access Files (*.mda, *.mdb)", _
      "*.MDA;*.MDB")
    strFilter = acbAddFilterItem(strFilter, "dBASE Files (*.dbf)", "*.DBF")
    strFilter = acbAddFilterItem(strFilter, "Text Files (*.txt)", "*.TXT")
    strFilter = acbAddFilterItem(strFilter, "All Files (*.*)", "*.*")

    MsgBox "You selected: " & acbCommonFileOpenSave(InitialDir:="C:\", _
      Filter:=strFilter, FilterIndex:=3, DialogTitle:="Hello! Open Me.")
End Function
```

4. You may want to specify some of the available options for controlling the common dialogs, as shown in frmTestOpenSave. You can specify any of the options shown there, and more, when you call the function. To specify your selected options, choose values from the items in Table 4-2, combine them together with the OR operator, and send this value to the *acbCommonFileOpenSave* function as the *Flags* argument. For example, the following statement will build up a *Flags* value that tells Windows to hide the Read Only checkbox and the Network button, and that the output path must already exist:

```
lngFlags = acbOFN_HIDEREADONLY Or acbOFN_NONETWORKBUTTON Or _
    acbOFN_PATHMUSTEXIST
```

Discussion

When you call *acbCommonFileOpenSave*, you're actually calling the *GetOpenFileName* or *GetSaveFileName* Windows API functions. The *acbCommonFileOpenSave* function takes only the parameters you send it, replacing missing ones with the default values shown in Table 4-2, and fills in a user-defined data structure that both API functions expect to receive. The API functions actually do the work, and *acbCommonFileOpenSave* returns to you the chosen filename. Although you may find it interesting to dig into the details of calling the API functions directly, that's beyond the scope of this solution. The wrapper function, *acbCommonFileOpenSave*, handles a large majority of the cases in which you'll need to use common File Open/Save dialogs.

Table 4-3 lists all the values you can use in the *Flags* parameter of the call to *acbCommonFileOpenSave*. You can skip the parameter altogether, or you can use one or more of these values, combined with the OR operator. For example, to hide the Read Only checkbox and allow multiple files to be selected, use this code:

```
lngFlags = acbOFN_HIDEREADONLY Or acbOFN_ALLOWMULTISELECT
```

Table 4-3. Values to be combined in acbCommonFileOpenSave's Flags parameter

Constant name	On input	On output
acbOFN_ALLOWMULTISELECT	Allows you to select more than one file-name (File Open only). Unless you also select the acbOFN_EXPLORER flag, you'll get an old-style dialog box.	The strFile member will contain the chosen path, followed by all the files within that path that were chosen, separated with spaces, as in C:\ ResultFolder File1.TXT File2.TXT.
acbOFN_CREATEPROMPT	Prompts you if the selected file doesn't exist, allowing you to go on or make a different choice.	
acbOFN_EXPLORER	Creates an Open or Save As dialog that uses user-interface features similar to the Windows Explorer. If you've specified the acbOFN_ALLOWMULTISELECT flag, you'll generally also want to include this flag.	
acbOFN_EXTENSIONDIFFERENT		Set if the chosen filename has a different extension than that supplied in the *DefaultExt* parameter.
acbOFN_FILEMUSTEXIST	Forces you to supply only existing file-names.	
acbOFN_HIDEREADONLY	Hides the Read Only checkbox.	
acbOFN_LONGNAMES	Causes the Open or Save As dialog to display long filenames. If this flag is not specified, the dialog displays filenames in 8.3 format. This value is ignored if acbOFN_EXPLORER is set.	
acbOFN_NOCHANGEDIR		Restores the current directory to its original value if the user changed the directory while searching for files.

Table 4-3. Values to be combined in acbCommonFileOpenSave's Flags parameter (continued)

Constant name	On input	On output
acbOFN_NODEREFERENCELINKS		Returns the path and filename of the selected shortcut (.LNK) file. If you don't use this flag, the dialog returns the path and filename of the file referenced by the shortcut.
acbOFN_NOLONGNAMES	Specifies that long filenames are not displayed in the File Name list box. This value is ignored if acbOFN_EXPLORER is set.	
acbOFN_NONETWORKBUTTON	Hides the Network button.	
acbOFN_NOREADONLYRETURN		Specifies that the returned file does not have the Read Only checkbox checked and is not in a write-protected directory.
acbOFN_NOTESTFILECREATE	Normally, COMMDLG.DLL tests to make sure that you'll be able to create the file when you choose a filename for saving. If set, it doesn't test, providing no protection against common disk errors.	
acbOFN_NOVALIDATE	Disables filename validation. Normally, Windows checks the chosen filename to make sure it's a valid name.	
acbOFN_OVERWRITEPROMPT	Issues a warning if you select an existing file for a File Save As operation.	
acbOFN_PATHMUSTEXIST	Forces you to supply only valid pathnames.	
acbOFN_READONLY	Forces the Read Only checkbox to be checked.	Set if the user checked the Read Only checkbox.
acbOFN_SHAREAWARE	Ignores sharing violations. Because Access code cannot handle the errors that occur when sharing violations occur in this code, you should not set this flag.	
acbOFN_SHOWHELP	Shows a Help button on the dialog. Though this option works, the button will not, so its use in Access is limited.	

Not all of the flags make sense for both File Open and File Save operations, of course. Your best bet is to experiment with the flags, either in your own code or using the sample form frmTestOpenSave from *04-08.MDB*.

Some of the flags are useful only on return from the function call. For example, if you select the Read Only checkbox on the common dialog, Windows passes that fact back to you in the *Flags* parameter. To retrieve that information from your call to *acbCommonFileOpenSave*, pass the Flags argument in a variable, not directly as a literal value. Because *acbCommonFileOpenSave* accepts the *Flags* argument by reference, it can return the value to your calling procedure after you've selected a filename. To check if a particular flag value was set during the call to *acbCommonFileOpenSave*, use the AND operator with the return value, as in this example fragment (see the Solution in Recipe 11.1 for more information on using the AND and OR operators):

```
Dim lngFlags As Long
Dim varFileName As Variant

lngFlags = 0
varFileName = antCommonFileOpenSave(Flags:=lngFlags)
If lngFlags AND acbOFN_READONLY <> 0 Then
    ' The user checked the Read Only checkbox.
End if
```

If you pass a variable to *acbCommonFileOpenSave* containing the *Flags* information (rather than not sending the parameter, or sending a literal value), the function will return to the caller information about what happened while the dialog was in use. Several of the flags listed in Table 4-3 provide information on output. That is, you can check the state of the *Flags* variable, and if it contains the flags from Table 4-3, you know that the tested condition was true. For example, to open a file and then check to see if the selected file is to be opened read-only, you could use code like this:

```
Dim lngFlags As Long
Dim varRetval As Variant

varRetval = acbCommonFileOpenSave(Flags:=lngFlags)
If Not IsNull(varRetval) Then
    If lngFlags AND acbOFN_READONLY Then
        MsgBox "You opened the file read-only!"
    End If
End If
```

As you can see in this example, you can use the AND operator to see if *Flags* contains the specific flag in which you're interested.

The file filter (the *Filter* parameter to *acbCommonFileOpenSave*) has a unique format: it consists of pairs of strings. Each item is terminated with vbNullChar (Chr$(0)). The first item in the pair supplies the text portion, which appears in the combo box in the lower-left corner of the dialog. The second item supplies the file specifications that Windows uses to filter the list of files. Though it doesn't matter what you use in the first item, by convention, most applications use something like this:

```
Oogly Files (*.oog)
```

listing the file description. The conventional file specification looks something like this:

```
*.oog
```

To simplify building these filter strings, use the *acbAddFilter* function from basCommonFile. See Step 3 for an example.

If you select the *acbOFN_AllowMultiSelect* flag, the result value may contain a null-delimited list of files, starting with the folder containing the files. For example, if you navigated to C:\AccessCookbook, and selected 04-04.mdb and 04-06.mdb, the return value from acbCommonFileOpenSave would contain the following text (we've used the vertical pipe symbol here to represent Chr(0) within the text):

```
C:\AccessCookbook|04-04.mdb|04-06.mdb
```

The sample form replaces the Chr(0) with a space character for you:

```
Private Sub cmdFileOpen_Click( )
    Dim varResult As Variant
    varResult = FileOpenSave(True)

    Me.txtFileOpen = Replace(varResult, vbNullChar, " ")
End Sub
```

If you allow multiple file selection, it's up to you to parse the various the file path and names yourself.

Take the time to study all the parameters in Table 4-2 and all the options in Table 4-3. There's not room here to go into detail for each one, so your best bet is to try out all of them. You can play with frmTestOpenSave to test the effects of some of the flag values. See what happens when you place a value into one of them, and then experiment from there.

Although you have no direct control over the placement of the common dialogs when they pop up, the choice of the parent window can affect the location. If you pass 0, Application.hWndAccessApp, or a normal form's hWnd property for the *hWnd* argument to *acbCommonFileOpenSave* (or just don't send a value, so it uses the default value), the dialog will appear in the upper-left corner of the Access MDI client window. If, on the other hand, you pass it the hWnd property of a pop-up form, Windows will place the dialog in the upper-left corner of that pop-up form *even if the form is not visible*. Therefore, for complete control over the placement of the dialog, create a form, set its PopUp property to True, and use that form to place the dialog.

Finally, remember that these dialogs don't actually *do* anything—they just supply you with the names of files. It's up to your application code to open or save the requested files.

See Also

For more information on working with the Windows API, see Chapter 11.

4.9 Clean Test Data out of a Database When You're Ready to Ship It

Problem

You're finished designing and building a database; it's ready to ship to your client. Before they can use it, you need to remove the artificial data you've entered, without destroying permanent lookup tables. Is there a simple way to do this without running into referential-integrity problems?

Solution

One solution is to open every data table in datasheet view, select all the records, press the Delete key, and confirm the deletion. However, there are three problems with this simple method:

- You have to open tables in a particular order (i.e., tables on the many side of a many-to-one relationship before their related one-side tables).

- You have to remember which tables contain test data and which ones contain production data.

- The task is tedious and repetitive.

Instead of clearing out your test data by hand, you can write a general-purpose routine that uses a table of tables and a simple SQL statement to remove only the test data, in the correct order.

Open *04-09.MDB* and view the tables in the database container. Open the tblFood table and try to delete some records. You'll get a referential-integrity error, because there are related records in txrefFoodRestaurant. Figure 4-17 shows the relationships set up for the sample database. Now open frmDemo and click on the Clear button to remove all the test data from the database without any manual intervention.

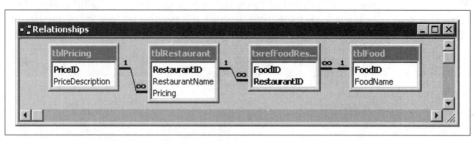

Figure 4-17. Relationships in the sample database

To implement this technique in your own database, follow these steps:

1. Import the table zstblDeleteOrder (structure only, without data) into your own database, or create a new table with the fields shown in Table 4-4.

Table 4-4. Structure of zstblDeleteOrder

Field name	Data type	Field size	Properties
Order	Number	Integer	PrimaryKey
TableName	Text		

2. Import the module zsbasMaintain into your database, or create a new module with the single function shown here:

```
Public Function acbClearData( ) As Boolean
    ' Remove all data from tables specified in zstblDeleteOrder.
    ' Data is removed in the order specified to avoid
    ' referential-integrity violations.

    On Error GoTo HandleErr

    Dim db As DAO.Database
    Dim rst As DAO.Recordset

    Set db = CurrentDb( )
    Set rst = db.OpenRecordset("zstblDeleteOrder", dbOpenSnapshot)

    Do Until rst.EOF
        db.Execute "DELETE * FROM " & rst("TableName")
        rst.MoveNext
    Loop

    rst.Close
    Set rst = Nothing
    acbClearData = True

ExitHere:
    Exit Function

HandleErr:
    acbClearData = False
    MsgBox "Error " & Err & ": " & Err.Description, , "acbClearData( )"
    Resume ExitHere
End Function
```

3. Open zstblDeleteOrder in datasheet view and add one record for each table you want to clear out before shipping. These tables must be listed in the order in which you want them cleared. Assign each table a unique order number, with the lowest number belonging to the first table to be cleared. Tables on the many side of a one-to-many relationship should be listed before tables on the one side of the relationship. Tables that you don't want to clear (including zstblDeleteOrder) should not be entered at all. Figure 4-18 shows the sample version of zstblDeleteOrder.

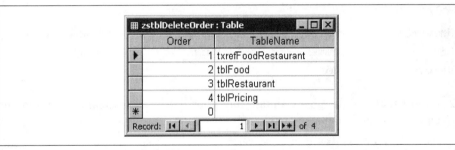

Figure 4-18. Sample zstblDeleteOrder

4. If you'd like a form to control the deletion process, create a new, blank form. Place one command button on the form and modify the command button's Click event handler to call acbClearData:

```
Private Sub cmdClear_Click( )
    Call acbClearData
End Sub
```

Discussion

The *acbClearData* function automates the task of selecting the order of your tables and then deleting the data table by table. You select the order when you build the zstblDeleteOrder table. The function works by opening a snapshot of this table and looping through the snapshot one line at a time. The line in the function that does the actual work is:

```
db.Execute "DELETE * FROM " & rst("TableName")
```

This line concatenates the table name found in rstTables, using SQL keywords to form a complete SQL statement. For example, if you specify tblFood as one of the tables to delete, Access builds the following SQL statement:

```
DELETE * FROM tblFood;
```

This is the SQL equivalent of a delete query that selects all rows from the table and deletes them. The db.Execute statement turns this query over to the Jet engine for execution.

The sample database has a second button, Restock, on the demo form. This button runs a procedure that in turn runs four append queries to take backup copies of the data and return them to the main data tables. This lets you test the function in the sample database more than once.

When you use this technique in your own database, be sure to compact the database before you distribute it to your users. To do this, select Tools → Database Utilities → Compact and Repair Database. There are two reasons to compact your database at this point:

- Until you compact, the Access file won't shrink at all. When you delete data from tables, Access marks the data pages as empty, but it doesn't give them back to your hard drive as free space. This occurs only when you compact the database.

- When you compact a database, Access resets the next counter values for all incrementing autonumber fields. If you remove all the data from a table with an autonumber in it and compact the database, the next record added will have an autonumber value of 1.

See Also

For more information on using DAO in Access databases, see "How Do I Use Data Access Objects (DAO) in New Databases?" in the Preface.

4.10   Secure Your Access Database

Problem

You've created an Access database that you'd like to secure. The database contains some sensitive data to which you wish to limit access. You'd like to be able to create different classes of users, so that some users have no access to this data, others can read the data but can't change it, and still others can modify the data. How can you accomplish this?

Solution

The Microsoft Jet database engine, which Access uses to store and retrieve its objects and data, employs a workgroup-based security model that allows you to secure your Access databases, assigning permissions to users and groups. Access supports two mechanisms for securing your database: the database password feature and user-level security. The database password feature is an all-or-nothing proposition—users who know the password aren't restricted in any way once they're in the database. If you want to assign varying permissions to different users, you'll need user-level security. User-level security is fairly complex—it doesn't work if you leave out a step. It consists of creating a new workgroup file (which holds user, group, and password information) and then using this new workgroup file to secure the database. There is a Security Wizard built into Access that will help you secure your database, but you can also manually perform the process, which will help you understand what's happening.

User-level security relies on a special database, called a *workgroup file*, to store users, the groups to which they belong, and their passwords. When you install Access, you are automatically hooked up to a default workgroup file called *System.mdw*. To secure your database, you will need to create your own unique workgroup file.

Every Access workgroup file includes two built-in groups: the Users group, which contains every user; and the Admins group, the members of which automatically get permission to administer security. There is also one built-in user, Admin. The Admin user starts out in the Admins group, but don't let the name Admin confuse you. You can remove Admin from the Admins group and take away all its administrative privileges, as long as some other user is left in Admins to act as the administrator. The Admin user has the same identity in every Access workgroup file, so any privileges that you give Admin will be available to anyone.

Securing a database involves adding a new member to the Admins group, removing the Admin user from that group, removing permissions from the Admin user and from the Users group, and assigning permissions to the custom groups that you define. The steps that follow show you how to implement user-level security in your Access database:

1. Create a new, unique workgroup file. In Access 2002 and later, this capability is built into the product, but in older versions you must run a separate utility called the Workgroup Administrator (Wrkgadm.exe). Write down the Name, Organization, and Workgroup ID strings that will be requested when you create your new workgroup file, and store them in a safe place. These strings will be encrypted to form the unique identity of your new workgroup file—if the original ever becomes lost or corrupted, it can be reconstructed as long as you input the identical strings. Each database "knows" the workgroup file it was secured with by this unique token (the Workgroup ID, or WID) and will not recognize a workgroup file that has a different WID. This means that you'll be permanently locked out of your database if you lose these strings. Also, upgrading a secured Access database to a newer version of Access is almost impossible if you don't have this information, because the recommended upgrade path is to recreate the workgroup file in the new version of Access and then upgrade the secured database. Figure 4-19 shows the Workgroup Administrator dialog with the new workgroup information. You can try this solution with any of the MDB files used in this chapter, such as 04-09.MDB.

2. The Workgroup Administrator automatically switches you to the new workgroup file, so you can simply close when you're finished. The Workgroup Administrator will create the necessary entries in the registry, making the new workgroup file the default. Start Access and load your database.

3. You will be logged on as a user named Admin. Use the Security menu options to set a password for the Admin user. This causes Access to prompt for a logon name and password the next time you try to open a database using this workgroup file.

4. Create a new user, which is the account you will use to secure the database. Add this new user to the Admins group, to make it the administrator. None of the

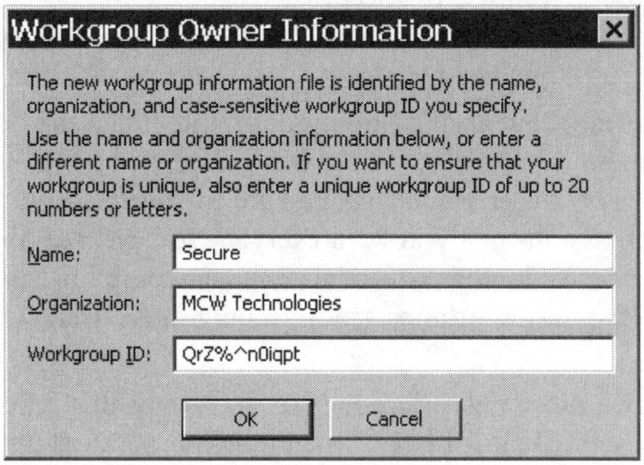

Figure 4-19. The Workgroup Administrator dialog

user accounts has any built-in capabilities. You also need to write down the strings used for the Name and Personal Identifier (PID). Part of recreating a workgroup file is recreating the key accounts stored in it. The PID is not a password—it is encrypted along with the name string to create a System Identifier, or SID. The SID is the token used when assigning permissions and when distinguishing users from each other. The name alone isn't secure, although Access won't let you have duplicate names in the same workgroup file.

5. Quit Access entirely and restart, logging on as the new user account that you created in Step 4. Don't type anything in the Password dialog—you haven't set one for this account yet.

6. Remove the Admin user from the Admins group so that Admin is a member of only the Users group. Every user is automatically added to the Users group, which is similar to Everyone in Windows. You can't delete any of the built-in users or groups (Admin, Admins, and Users), but you can move users in and out of various groups. Access requires that there always be one member of the Admins group (that would be you). Later you'll create additional groups, assigning permissions to the groups for various database objects. Users then inherit permissions from their group membership. You'll probably want to remove all permissions from the Users group, since permissions granted to Users are granted to all.

7. At this point you'll want to secure the database. You can either run the Security Wizard or manually secure it. If you manually secure it, you'll create a new database (this is how you transfer ownership of the database) and then import all of the objects. Next, remove all permissions for the Users group and the Admin user. The Admins group has full permissions by default—only the Admins group can work with users and groups and has irrevocable administrative permissions

on the database. If you use the Security Wizard, it will also remove all permissions from the Admin user and the Users group and encrypt the new database (you can do this manually if you choose).

8. You need to create your own custom groups and assign the desired level of permissions to these groups. Every user is required to be a member of the Users group (otherwise, a user would not be able to start Access), so grant to Users only those permissions that you want everyone to have. Members of the Admins group have irrevocable power to administer database objects, so make sure to limit membership in the Admins group to only those users who are administrators.

9. Create your own users and assign them to the groups that reflect the level of permissions you want them to have. Do not assign permissions directly to users, because that is extremely difficult to administer; users inherit permissions from the groups of which they are members, and keeping track of the permissions assigned to a group is much easier than keeping track of the separate permissions of individuals. If a user is a member of multiple groups, that user will have all the permissions granted to any of those groups plus any permissions assigned specifically to the user (this is known as the "least-restrictive" rule). There is no way to deny permissions to a user if that user is a member of a group that has been granted those permissions. If you need to create specific permissions for only a single user, create a group for that user and assign the permissions to the group; then add the user to the group. The reason for this becomes clear when you consider that the user may leave unexpectedly, and you may have to set up permissions for the replacement on short notice.

10. Test security by logging on as users with varying levels of permissions. Try to do things that a user at that level shouldn't be able to do. The only way you'll be able to see if your database security is working is to bang on it and try to break it.

Discussion

The Microsoft Jet database engine, which Access uses to store and retrieve its objects and data, employs a workgroup-based security model. Every time the Jet database engine runs, it looks for a workgroup file, which holds information about the users and groups of users who can open databases during that session. The default workgroup file, *System.mdw*, is identical across all installations of Access. That's why it's important not to skip the first step of creating a new workgroup file.

The workgroup file contains the names and security IDs of all the groups and users in that workgroup, including passwords. Each workgroup file contains built-in groups (Admins and Users) and a generic user account (Admin). You can't delete any of the built-in accounts, but you can add your own group and user accounts.

The built-in accounts each have their own characteristics and properties:

- The built-in Admins group is always present, and its users have administration rights that cannot be revoked. You can remove rights from the Admins group through the menus or through code, but any member of Admins can assign them right back. Access ensures that there is always at least one member in the Admins group to administer the database. The Admins group is the only built-in account that has any special properties.

- The default user account, Admin, is a member of the Admins group in an unsecured database and is the only user account present in the default *System.mdw* workgroup file. It has no special properties of its own; all of its power is inherited through membership in the Admins group.

- The Users group is a generic group to which all users belong. You can create users in code and not add them to the Users group, but they won't be able to start Access—internal tables and system objects are mapped to the permissions of the Users group. Other than the fact that all users must belong to the Users group, it has no special properties.

Permissions to various Access objects can be assigned directly to users (explicit permissions) or to groups. Users inherit permissions from the groups to which they belong (implicit permissions). It's always a good idea from an administrative point of view to assign permissions only to groups, and not to users, which could become endlessly complicated.

Access employs the least-restrictive rule: users have the sum total of their explicit and implicit permissions. In other words, if a user belongs to a group that has full permissions and you make that user a member of a group that has restricted permissions, the user will still have full permissions because he is a member of the unrestricted group.

User and group information, including passwords, is saved in the workgroup file, or *System.mda/mdw*, which validates user logons at startup. Permissions to individual objects are saved in the database itself. You can give the groups and users within a workgroup various levels of permission to view, modify, create, and delete the objects and data in a database. For example, the users of a particular group might be permitted to read only certain tables in a database and not others, or you could permit a group to use certain forms but not to modify the design of those forms.

Most Access database applications consist of a frontend with linked tables against a backend database. You need to secure both the frontend and the backend using the same workgroup file.

Access user-level security works best when securing data—if you want to secure your code, the best solution is to compile your application as an MDE. This prevents anyone from viewing or altering the design of forms, reports, or module code. It also prevents users from creating new Access objects, but it has no effect on data objects (tables and queries). You'll need to save a backup copy of the original *.mdb* file if you want to make alterations later—there's no way to decompile an MDE to recover the source code and source objects.

Also bear in mind that security in an Access database is mainly good for deterrence only. In any situation in which the physical files are exposed, it is impossible to guard against determined hackers. An additional weakness is that the network share where the Access *.mdb* and *.mdw* files are located also needs to have read, write, and delete permissions, which means you can't prevent users from deleting or copying the *.mdb* and *.mdw* files. The only alternative is to create an n-tier application where the middle-tier objects alone have access to the physical files. However, this means that you need to write the application "unbound," since the users will no longer be directly connected to the database. When you get to that point, you'll probably be considering SQL Server or another database platform that is capable of scaling to support more users and larger volumes of data.

CHAPTER 5

Printers

Printing output is a major component of any database product, and Access gives you a great deal of control over the "look" of your forms and reports. Programmatic control over the printer itself, however, has always been somewhat complex in Access. Windows provides rich and intricate support for output devices, and Access attempts to shield you from most of that intricacy. Sometimes, however, you do need to take control of your output devices; for example, you may need to change a particular device or a setting pertaining to a particular device. Historically, Access made this possible but not easy. However, starting with Access 2002, you can use the Printers collection with a Printer object that makes it relatively easy to accomplish the most common printing tasks. The sections in this chapter describe the details of handling your output devices using these new objects.

This chapter focuses on the Printers collection and the associated Printer object. We'll cover the properties of these objects in detail and show examples of their use. You'll be able to retrieve a list of all the installed printers and make a choice from that list, setting the new default Access printer. You'll learn how to modify margin settings in forms and reports, thereby avoiding the use of Access's File → Page Setup dialog in your applications. You'll get help on changing printer options, such as the number of copies to print, the page orientation, and the printer resolution. Then you'll learn how to programmatically print the first page of a document from one paper tray and the rest of the pages from a different paper tray. This allows you to print the first page on letterhead paper and the rest on normal paper.

Finally, you'll find out how to determine which device has been selected to print a report and whether it's the default device. If it is, you can change the destination from your application, provide users with a choice of output devices, and print the object to a particular device. You'll also find a development tool that will run through all your reports and let you know which aren't set up to print to the default printer. By ensuring that all your reports print to the default printer, you will be able to send them to any output device simply by changing what Access thinks is the default printer.

5.1 Retrieve a List of All the Installed Output Devices

Problem

You'd like to be able to present your users with a list of all the installed printers. Is there some way to fill a list box with the printer names?

Solution

Access makes it easy to fill a list or combo box with all the available printers. You can iterate through the members of the Application.Printers collection, retrieving the DeviceName and Port of each printer.

To create a list of installed printers, follow these steps:

1. Add a list box to a form. Set the Name property of the list box to lstPrinters.

2. Place the following code in the form's Load event procedure (see the Preface for more information on creating event procedures):

```
Private Sub Form_Load( )
    Dim prt As Printer

    lstPrinters.RowSourceType = "Value List"
    For Each prt In Application.Printers
```

```
        lstPrinters.AddItem prt.DeviceName & " on " & prt.Port
    Next prt
End Sub
```

To see an example of an application that lists a system's installed printers, load and run the form frmPrinterList from *05-01.MDB*. Figure 5-1 shows the form displaying the installed printers on a test machine. Section 5.1.3 describes in detail the techniques used in building the list in Figure 5-1.

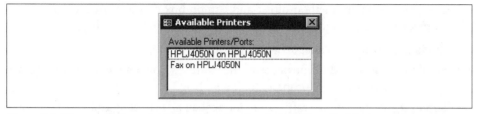

Figure 5-1. The sample form, frmPrinterList, showing the list of installed devices

Discussion

Access 2002 added several new objects that make working with printers and printing easier than these activities have been in the past. First, Access provides a Printers collection as a property of its Application object. This collection provides one Printer object corresponding to each output device installed on your computer. Each Printer object provides many properties, including DeviceName and Port, as used in this example.

Once you declare an object As Printer, you can iterate through the Printers collection, working with properties of each printer, like this:

```
Dim prt As Printer

For Each prt In Application.Printers
    Debug.Print prt.DeviceName & " on " & prt.Port
Next prt
```

The Printer object provides a long list of available properties, each of which is discussed at some point in this chapter. The properties can be divided into three basic categories: printer name information (the DeviceName, Port, and DriverName properties); device capability information (e.g., the ColorMode, Copies, Duplex, Orientation, and PaperSize properties); and print layout information (e.g., the BottomMargin, ItemLayout, and RowSpacing properties). Later topics will discuss these groups of properties and will list and describe each property and its possible values. This example uses the DeviceName and Port properties, indicating the printer name and its associated output port.

There are several uses of the term "Printer" in Access. Access itself provides the Application.Printer object, which keeps track of the application's default printer. You can also declare and use a Printer object, which represents one entry in the application's Printers collection. Finally, each form and report in Access 2002 and later provides its own Printer object, which represents all the printer-related properties of the individual form or report. Later topics discuss how you can use each of these objects.

Adding items to a list box

The example form, frmPrinterList, adds information about each printer to a list box, using the new AddItem method of list and combo box controls. Access has historically provided three techniques for getting data into a list or combo box:

- Binding the control to a table or query's output
- Providing a delimited list of values in the control's RowSource property (and setting the RowSourceType property to "Value List")
- Supplying an intricately crafted function (called a "list-filling callback function") that Access calls to retrieve data filling the list

None of these methods was perfect. The first option required you to have a table from which to retrieve the data. The second option limited your data source to a small number of characters (the size of the property has been increased a great deal starting in Access 2002, however). The third technique required advanced programming skills. None of the techniques made it easy to work with individual items in the lists.

Starting with Access 2002 this is all simpler. Modeled after the similar controls in Visual Basic, Access's list and combo boxes now support adding and removing individual items without needing to use any of the older techniques. Now you can add and remove items individually, as shown here. You can specify a location within the list where you'd like to add an item, like this:

```
' Add the new items at the top of the list.
lstPrinters.AddItem prt.DeviceName & " on " & prt.Port, 0
```

You can also add items to the end of the list by simply not specifying the location for the new item. To remove items from the list, call the RemoveItem method, specifying the index (starting at 0) of the item you'd like to remove.

If you want to add items to a list or combo box, you must set the RowSourceType property of the control to "Value List" before you start. Although you could set that property while laying out your form, we like to set these "make or break" properties as forms load. If you set one of these properties incorrectly, the form won't load—setting the property in code ensures that the form will load correctly. This is a matter of style, but it never hurts to make sure important properties are set properly in code.

See Also

For more information on working with list and combo boxes, see "Programmatically Add Items to a List or Combo Box" in Chapter 7.

5.2   Set and Retrieve the Name of the Default Output Device

Problem

Windows allows you to install a number of printer drivers, but one of them must always be denoted as the default printer. Although Windows provides its own concept of its default printer, Access maintains its own, independent default printer. You'd like to be able to control which printer Access thinks is the default printer, perhaps even choosing from a list of all the installed printers. Is there a way to do this from within Access?

Solution

Windows maintains its own list of available printers and stores information about the default printer. When Access starts up, it automatically uses Windows's default printer as its own default printer. Access's Application object provides a Printer property. Setting this property to refer to an item within the Printers collection allows you to control the default printer for all Access objects.

 In Access, you always have the choice of printing an object to the default printer or to a specific printer. None of the techniques shown in this chapter that allow you to change the output destination will work if you set up your reports to print to a specific printer. In addition, printing to a specific printer will almost always lead to trouble if you distribute your applications to end users who may or may not have the same printer available. We suggest that, if possible, you set your reports so that they all print to the default printer.

To create a combo box in your own application that allows the user to choose a new default printer, follow these steps:

1. Add a combo box to your form and name it cboPrinters.

2. Add the following procedure to your form's module:

```
Private Sub FillPrinterList(ctl As Control)
    ' Fill the provided control (ctl) with a list of printers. This
    ' will cause a runtime error if ctl isn't a list or combo box.
    Dim prt As Printer
```

```
        ctl.RowSourceType = "Value List"
        For Each prt In Application.Printers
            ctl.AddItem prt.DeviceName
        Next prt
End Sub
```

3. Modify the form's Open event procedure, so that it looks like this:

```
Private Sub Form_Load
    Call FillPrinterList(Me.cboPrinters)
    ' Select the default printer, in the combo box.
    ' This may fail, so simply disregard errors.
    On Error Resume Next
    Me.cboPrinters = Application.Printer.DeviceName
End Sub
```

4. Modify the AfterUpdate event procedure of cboPrinters, so that it looks like this:

```
Private Sub cboPrinters_AfterUpdate( )
    Dim lngIndex As Long
    lngIndex = Me.cboPrinters.ListIndex
    Set Application.Printer = Application.Printers(lngIndex)
End Sub
```

To see a sample application that allows you to select the default printer, load and run the form frmDefaultPrinterList from *05-02.MDB*. This form, shown in Figure 5-2, includes a combo box from which you can select a new default printer for Access. When you first load the form, the combo box should already have the current default output device selected. If you make a choice, the code attached to the AfterUpdate event for the combo box will change the printer that Access uses for its default. This change will affect any printing you do from within Access, if the printed object has been set up to print to the default printer.

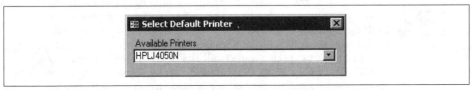

Figure 5-2. frmDefaultPrinterList allows you to choose a new Access default printer

Discussion

You saw the code in the *FillPrinterList* procedure in the previous section. This time it's separated out into its own procedure, so it will be easier for you to use in future projects. The form's Load event procedure fills the combo box with its list of printers and then attempts to set the value of the combo box to match the name of the currently selected default printer, using this code:

```
Me.cboPrinters = Application.Printer.DeviceName
```

After you select an item from the list of printers in the combo box, the AfterUpdate event procedure for that control sets the application's default printer to the printer you just selected, using this code:

```
Set Application.Printer = Application.Printers(lngIndex)
```

Access uses the default output device for printing, unless you specify otherwise in Access's File → Page Setup dialog. The Solution in Recipe 5.7 will combine methods from this section and others to show you how to send a report to the printer you choose at runtime. The methods shown there allow you to direct a report to the printer one day and to the fax modem the next.

If you change Access's default printer and then determine that you'd like to put it back to its original value, you can. Simply set the Application.Printer value to the built-in value Nothing, and Access will revert to its original default printer:

```
Set Application.Printer = Nothing
```

Although setting the value to Nothing instead of to a specific printer seems odd, Access understands the special value and simply reverts to the original default printer it found in Windows when it started the current session.

Although you could use the Windows API to change Windows's understanding of its own default printer, there's really no need to do that from within Access. Access maintains its own default printer (assuming the default printer from Windows when it first starts a session), and you can easily manipulate that value using the techniques shown here.

5.3   Programmatically Change Margin and Column Settings for Reports

Problem

You'd like to give your applications' users some control over report layout, especially in designating column and margin settings. You could just let them loose in report design mode, but you'd like to maintain a little control over their actions. Is there some way to modify these layout settings from VBA?

Solution

Starting with Access 2002, each form and report object includes a Printer property. Retrieving this property gets you an object with many properties, several of which deal with margin and column settings for reports.

You can use properties of a report's Printer object to retrieve and set layout properties. You'll find properties representing the left, top, bottom, and right margins; the number of columns; and the size, spacing, and item order of the columns. In addition, the Printer object contains the Data Only option in the File → Page Setup dialog. This solution demonstrates how to use the print layout properties provided by the Printer object.

Load and run the form frmPrintSettings from *05-03.MDB*. Figure 5-3 shows the form (which emulates Access's File → Page Setup dialog) after the report Report1 has been selected from the list of reports. Choose a report from the drop-down list, and the form will load that report in preview mode. You can change the settings for the selected report by typing new values into the text boxes. To save the changes to the selected report, click on Save Settings. You'll see those changes in the preview window.

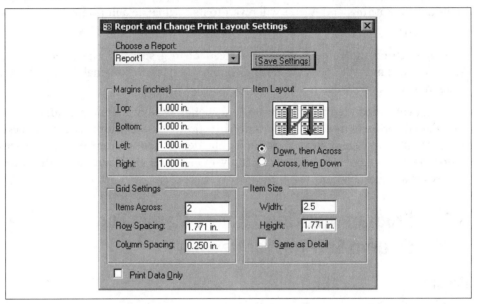

Figure 5-3. *frmPrintSettings provides the same functionality as the Access File → Page Setup dialog*

Some of the items on the form are available only if you've specified more than one column for the Items Across value, so you'll want to use a number greater than 1 in that field. (Because this example opens the report in preview mode, changes you make aren't saved with the report. If you want to permanently save the report with the new settings, you'll need to modify the code so that the report opens in design view; changes you make will then be saved with the report when you close and save it.) The following sections explain both how to use the sample form from *05-03. MDB* and how to work with these properties and your own objects.

To use the sample form in your own applications, follow these steps:

1. Import the form frmPrintSettings into your application. This form allows you to choose from the existing reports in your database.

2. Once you've chosen the report (which the form will open in preview mode), you can alter print layout settings. Once you're done, you can print the report.

Discussion

The sample form for this topic does very little work—it simply copies values from the Printer property of the selected report to controls on the form, converting from twips (1/1,440 inch) to inches for display purposes. When you click Save Settings, the code writes the settings back to the appropriate properties of the report's Printer property.

Access's Printer object provides a number of properties dealing with print layout. Table 5-1 describes the subset of Printer object properties used in this example form.

Table 5-1. Printer object properties associated with print layout

Property	Comments
LeftMargin	Distance between the left edge of the paper and the object to be printed (in twips)
TopMargin	Distance between the top edge of the paper and the object to be printed (in twips)
RightMargin	Distance between the right edge of the paper and the object to be printed (in twips)
BottomMargin	Distance between the bottom edge of the paper and the object to be printed (in twips)
DataOnly	If True (-1), Access prints just data, not labels, control borders, gridlines, and display graphics; if False (0), Access prints all elements
ColumnSpacing	Distance between detail section columns (if ItemsAcross > 1), in twips
DefaultSize	If True (-1), Access uses the width and height of the design-mode detail section when printing; if False (0), Access uses the values specified in the ItemSizeWidth and ItemSizeHeight properties
ItemLayout	acPRHorizontalColumnLayout (Across, then Down), or acPRVerticalColumnLayout (Down, then Across) for multiple-columned reports
ItemSizeWidth	Width of the detail section; if the DefaultSize property is False and the ItemsAcross property is greater than 1, the width of each column (in twips)
ItemSizeHeight	Height of the detail section (read-only)
ItemsAcross	Integer that specifies the number of columns across the page for multiple-columned reports
RowSpacing	Vertical distance between detail sections (in twips)

After you select a report on the sample form, the combo box's AfterUpdate event procedure calls the following code, which opens the report in preview mode, then copies the report's properties to the controls on the form:

```
strReport = Me.cboReportList
DoCmd.OpenReport strReport, View:=acViewPreview
With Reports(strReport).Printer
```

```
      Me.txtLeft = ToInches(.LeftMargin)
      Me.txtRight = ToInches(.RightMargin)
      Me.txtTop = ToInches(.TopMargin)
      Me.txtBottom = ToInches(.BottomMargin)
      Me.chkDataOnly = .DataOnly
      Me.txtXFormSize = ToInches(.ItemSizeWidth)
      Me.txtYFormSize = ToInches(.ItemSizeHeight)
      Me.txtCxColumns = .ItemsAcross
      Me.txtYFormSpacing = ToInches(.ItemSizeHeight)
      Me.chkfDefaultSize = .DefaultSize
      Me.txtXFormSpacing = ToInches(.ColumnSpacing)
      Me.grpRadItemOrder = .ItemLayout
   End With
```

Don't forget that all the measurements in the Printer object are stored in twips. The *ToInches* function simply divides its parameter value by 1,440 and adds the text "in." to its output value. The corresponding *FromInches* function does the opposite—it strips off extra text and multiplies its parameter value by 1,440 to convert back to twips. Why 1,440? A twip is defined as 1/20 of a point. There are 72 points per inch and 20 twips per point; therefore, $72 \times 20 = 1,440$ twips per inch.

When you click Save Settings, the command button's Click event procedure copies data back to the properties of the report, like this:

```
Dim strChosen As String
Dim rpt As Report

strChosen = Me.cboReportList
With Reports(strChosen).Printer
   .LeftMargin = FromInches(Me.txtLeft)
   .RightMargin = FromInches(Me.txtRight)
   .TopMargin = FromInches(Me.txtTop)
   .BottomMargin = FromInches(Me.txtBottom)
   .DataOnly = Me.chkDataOnly
   .DefaultSize = Me.chkDefaultSize
   If Not .DefaultSize Then
      .ItemSizeWidth = FromInches(Me.txtXFormSize)
      .ItemSizeHeight = FromInches(Me.txtYFormSize)
   End If
   .ItemsAcross = Val(Me.txtCxColumns)
   .RowSpacing = FromInches(Me.txtYFormSpacing)

      .ColumnSpacing = FromInches(Me.txtXFormSpacing)
   .ItemLayout = Me.grpRadItemOrder
End With
```

The combo box containing the list of reports uses a common but undocumented technique. The Access system tables (check Tools → Options → View → System Objects to see the system tables in the database container) contain information about the current database. One table in particular, MSysObjects, contains a row for each object in the database. To fill the combo box with a list of reports, you can use this SQL expression:

```
SELECT Name FROM MSysObjects WHERE Type = -32764 ORDER BY Name;
```

The Name column includes the name for each object, and the Type column contains -32764 for reports (or -32768 for forms). Microsoft suggests using DAO or ADO instead of querying against the system tables to retrieve lists of items; however, our method is much faster and much simpler for filling lists. This method has worked in every version of Access so far; we can only assume it will continue to do so.

The Printer object provides one more bit of unexpected behavior: unless you've set the DefaultSize property to False, you cannot set the ItemSizeWidth or ItemSizeHeight properties—you'll trigger a runtime error if you try. The sample code determines the value in the DefaultSize property and attempts to change the other two properties only if doing so won't cause an error.

5.4   Programmatically Change Printer Options

Problem

You've tried using *SendKeys* to change printing options in the File → Setup Page dialog, but this really isn't satisfactory. Sometimes it works and sometimes it doesn't, depending on the circumstances and the printer driver that's loaded. Is there some way to modify printer options without using *SendKeys*?

Solution

Windows makes many of the printer driver settings available to applications, including the number of copies, page orientation, and page size. Starting with Access 2002, it's easy to retrieve and modify these values, using the Printer property of forms and reports. This solution focuses on the print settings features of the Printer object and demonstrates how to read and write values in the Printer object.

To be able to modify printer settings for reports or forms in your own applications, follow these steps:

1. Open the report in either preview or design view. (If you want to make your changes persistent, open the report in design view. If you want to apply changes for just this particular instance, open it in preview mode.)

2. Modify some of the properties of the Printer object provided by your form or report. For example, the sample form works with a small subset of the available printer-specific properties, using code like this:

```
DoCmd.OpenReport strReport, View:=acViewPreview
With Reports(strReport).Printer
    Me.txtCopies = .Copies
    Me.grpOrientation = .Orientation
    Me.grpPaperSize = .PaperSize
End With
```

3. When you're done working with the properties, write them back to the report's Printer object, using code like this (from the sample form):

```
strReport = Me.cboReportList
With Reports(strReport).Printer
    .Copies = Me.txtCopies
    .Orientation = Me.grpOrientation
    .PaperSize = Me.grpPaperSize
End With
```

For an example, load and run the form frmPrintSettings in *05-04.MDB*. Figure 5-4 shows the sample form in action. This form allows you to choose a report from a combo box. Once you've made your choice, the form loads the report in preview mode and retrieves the number of copies, page size, and page orientation from the report's Printer property. You can change any of these values; once you click Save Settings, the form will write the values back to the report's Printer property and the changes will display immediately in the preview window.

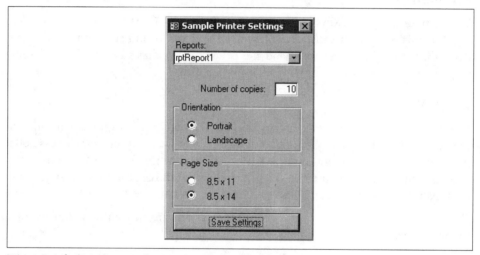

Figure 5-4. frmPrintSettings shows print information for rptReport1

Discussion

Each form and report has a Printer property that holds a reference to a Printer object for that form or report. By setting the properties of a form/report's Printer object, you can control how the form/report will print. Table 5-2 lists the object's properties, along with their possible values. None of these properties is read-only. Table 5-3 shows a list of all the defined paper sizes. You can use one of these constants in the PaperSize property to set a new paper size. Table 5-4 shows possible values for the PaperBin property of the Printer object.

Table 5-2. Properties of the Printer object

Field name	Contains	Data type	Values
Orientation	Paper orientation	`AcPrintOrientation`	`acPRORLandscape` or `acPRORPortrait`
PaperSize	Size of the physical page to print on	`AcPrintPaperSize`	A value from Table 5-3 (depending on which paper sizes the printer supports)
Copies	If the printing device supports multiple copies, the number of copies to be printed	`Long`	
PaperBin	Default bin from which paper is to be fed	`AcPrintPaperBin`	A value from Table 5-4
PrintQuality	Printer resolution	`AcPrintObjQuality`	`acPRPQDraft`, `acPRPQHigh`, `acPRPQLow`, or `acPRPQMedium`
ColorMode	Color usage, if the printer supports color printing	`AcPrintColor`	`acPRCMColor` or `acPRCMMonochrome`
Duplex	Duplex usage, if the printer supports duplex printing	`AcPrintDuplex`	`acPRDPHorizontal`, `acPRDPSimplex`, or `acPRDPVertical`

Table 5-3. Constants and descriptions for the PaperSize property

Constant	Value	Description
acPRPS10X14	16	10 × 14 in
acPRPS11X17	17	11 × 17 in
acPRPSA3	8	A3 (297 × 420 mm)
acPRPSA4	9	A4 (210 × 297 mm)
acPRPSA4SMALL	10	A4 Small (210 × 297 mm)
acPRPSA5	11	A5 (148 × 210 mm)
acPRPSB4	12	B4 (250 × 354 mm)
acPRPSB5	13	B5 (182 × 257 mm)
acPRPSCSHEET	24	C size sheet (17 × 22 in)
acPRPSDSHEET	25	D size sheet (22 × 34 in)
acPRPSEnv10	20	Envelope #10 (4.125 × 9.5 in)
acPRPSEnv11	21	Envelope #11 (4.5 × 10.375 in)
acPRPSEnv12	22	Envelope #12 (4.25 × 11 in)
acPRPSEnv14	23	Envelope #14 (5 × 11.5 in)
acPRPSEnv9	19	Envelope #9 (3.875 × 8.875 in)
acPRPSEnvB4	33	Envelope B4 (250 × 353 mm)
acPRPSEnvB5	34	Envelope B5 (176 × 250 mm

Table 5-3. Constants and descriptions for the PaperSize property (continued)

Constant	Value	Description
acPRPSEnvB6	35	Envelope B6 (176 × 125 mm)
acPRPSEnvC3	29	Envelope C3 (324 × 458 mm)
acPRPSEnvC4	30	Envelope C4 (229 × 324 mm)
acPRPSEnvC5	28	Envelope C5 (162 × 229 mm)
acPRPSEnvC6	31	Envelope C6 (114 × 162 mm)
acPRPSEnvC65	32	Envelope C65 (114 × 229 mm)
acPRPSEnvDL	27	Envelope DL (110 × 220 mm)
acPRPSEnvItaly	36	Envelope (110 × 230 mm)
acPRPSEnvMonarch	37	Envelope Monarch (3.875 × 7.5 in)
acPRPSEnvPersonal	38	6-3/4 Envelope (3.625 × 6.5 in)
acPRPSESheet	26	E size sheet (34 × 44 in)
acPRPSExecutive	7	Executive (7.25 × 10.5 in)
acPRPSFanfoldLglGerman	41	German Legal Fanfold (8.5 × 13 in)
acPRPSFanfoldStdGerman	40	German Std Fanfold (8.5 × 12 in)
acPRPSFanfoldUS	39	US Std Fanfold (14.875 × 11 in)
acPRPSFolio	14	Folio (8.5 × 13 in)
acPRPSLedger	4	Ledger (17 × 11 in)
acPRPSLegal	5	Legal (8.5 × 14 in)
acPRPSLetter	1	Letter (8.5 × 11 in)
acPRPSLetterSmall	2	Letter Small (8.5 × 11 in)
acPRPSNote	18	Note (8.5 × 11 in)
acPRPSQuarto	15	Quarto (215 × 275 mm)
acPRPSStatement	6	Statement (5.5 × 8.5 in)
acPRPSTabloid	3	Tabloid (11 × 17 in)
acPRPSUser	256	User-defined

Table 5-4. Constants and descriptions for the PaperBin property

Constant	Value	Description
acPRBNAuto	7	Automatic bin
acPRBNCassette	14	Cassette bin
acPRBNEnvelope	5	Envelope bin
acPRBNEnvManual	6	Envelope manual bin
acPRBNLargeCapacity	11	Large-capacity bin
acPRBNLargeFmt	10	Large-format bin
acPRBNLower	2	Lower bin
acPRBNManual	4	Manual bin
acPRBNMiddle	3	Middle bin

Constant	Value	Description
acPRBNSmallFmt	9	Small-format bin
acPRBNTractor	8	Tractor bin
acPRBNUpper	1	Upper bin
acPRBNFormSource	15	Form source

The sample form opens reports in preview mode and allows you to modify and view printer-specific properties, then print the report. If you want to modify the design properties for a report, you'll need to open it in design view, modifying the call to the DoCmd.OpenReport method in the code, like this:

```
DoCmd.OpenReport strReport, View:=acViewPreview
```

When you're done, save the report using code like this:

```
DoCmd.Close acReport, "YourReportName", acSaveYes
```

Although Access makes it easy to work with printer settings, the Printer object is missing some important features. For example, although you can select acPRPSUser for the PaperSize property, you cannot define your own sizes (making this option effectively useless).

5.5 Programmatically Control the Paper Source

Problem

You'd like to be able to print the first page of your reports from a paper tray containing letterhead paper and then print the rest on normal paper stock. Is there some way in Access to switch paper trays programmatically from within your application?

Solution

The paper source is one of the properties of the Printer object associated with a report (see the Solution in Recipe 5.4 for a description of the Printer object) that you can programmatically control. Given the information in the Solution in Recipe 5.4, it's relatively easy to change the paper source for a report so that the first page prints from one paper bin and the rest prints from another.

Load and run frmPaperSource in *05-05.MDB* (Figure 5-5).

1. With frmPaperSource loaded, choose a report. The report will load, minimized, in preview mode.

2. Choose a paper bin for the first page and a bin for the rest of the pages. Note that the lists of paper bins contain all the possible paper sources; your printer may not support all of the options listed in the combo boxes. You'll need to find the bins that work correctly with your printer driver.

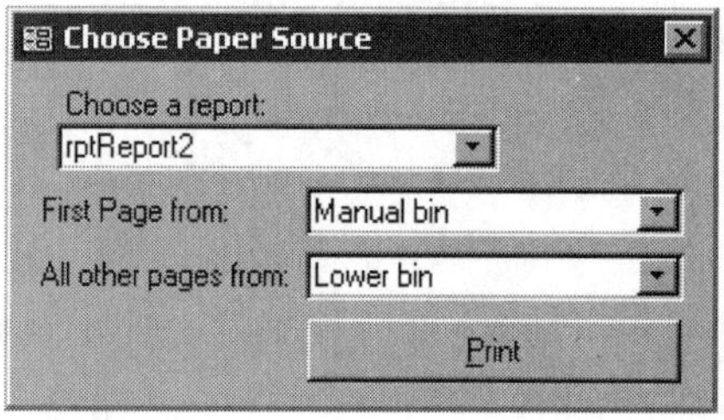

Figure 5-5. frmPaperSource allows you to print from different paper sources

3. Click the Print button. Access should print the first page of the report from the bin chosen for the first page and the rest from the bin chosen for the other pages.

To use this technique in your own applications, you'll need to add code that supports printing the first page, then the rest of the pages, as the result of some action (such as clicking a command button). In reaction to this event, call the *PrintPages* procedure, shown here:

```
Private Sub PrintPages(strReport As String, _
    FirstPagePaperBin As AcPrintPaperBin, _
    AllPagesPaperBin As AcPrintPaperBin)

    Dim rpt As Report

    On Error GoTo HandleErrors

    DoCmd.OpenReport strReport, acViewPreview, WindowMode:=acIcon
    Set rpt = Reports(strReport)
    rpt.Printer.PaperBin = FirstPagePaperBin

    ' Unfortunately, you have to select the report in order to print it.
    ' Who wrote the PrintOut method this way, anyway?
    DoCmd.SelectObject acReport, strReport
    DoCmd.PrintOut acPages, 1, 1

    ' Define the paper source.
    rpt.Printer.PaperBin = AllPagesPaperBin

    ' Print all the rest of the pages (up to 32000).
    DoCmd.PrintOut acPages, 2, 32000

ExitHere:
    DoCmd.Close acReport, strReport, acSaveNo
    Exit Sub

HandleErrors:
    MsgBox "Error: " & Err.Description & " (" & Err.Number & ")"
    Resume ExitHere
End Sub
```

In the sample form, this code is called from the Click event of the Print button, like this:

```
Private Sub cmdPrint_Click( )
    Call PrintPages(Me.cboReportList, Me.cboFirstPage, Me.cboAllOther)
End Sub
```

Discussion

As you saw in the Solution in Recipe 5.4, you can use a form or report's Printer property to change its paper source. Printing one page of a report from one bin and the rest from another is easy. First, open the report in preview mode and get a reference to the open report:

```
DoCmd.OpenReport strReport, acViewPreview, WindowMode:=acIcon
Set rpt = Reports(strReport)
```

Then set the PaperBin property of the report's Printer object, select the report, and print the first page, like this:

```
rpt.Printer.PaperBin = FirstPagePaperBin
DoCmd.SelectObject acReport, strReport
DoCmd.PrintOut acPages, 1, 1
```

Set the PaperBin property for the rest of the pages, and print them (the report is already selected, so you don't need to select it again):

```
rpt.Printer.PaperBin = AllPagesPaperBin
' Print all the rest of the pages (up to 32000).
DoCmd.PrintOut acPages, 2, 32000
```

The PrintOut method's implementation is somewhat unfortunate. It's the only way you can control the specific pages you want printed, yet it requires you to select the object to be printed before printing it. This combination of requirements means that you must first open the report in preview or design view and set its properties, then select and print it. You cannot select a hidden report (Access will unhide it before selecting it), so your best bet is to open it with the *WindowMode* parameter of the DoCmd.OpenReport method set to acIcon. That way, the report is minimized. If this behavior truly bothers you, you can use Application.Echo to turn off screen display before you open the report and then turn it back on when you're done. In addition, if you specify the first page to be printed, you must also specify the last page. Therefore, even if you don't know how many pages your report contains, you must specify an upper bound (32,000, in our example) when you print. Hopefully, your report won't contain more than 32,000 pages. If it does, bump up that number.

If you're going to provide this functionality in an application to be distributed to users who have printers on which it hasn't been tested, you'll need to make it clear that some of the bins listed in the combo boxes may not work with their printers. It may require some experimentation on their part to determine which settings are correct.

5.6 Retrieve Information About a Report or Form's Selected Printer

Problem

Access's File → Page Setup dialog allows you to specify either the default printer or a specific printer for each printable object. You'd like to be able to find out, programmatically, which printer has been selected for an object and whether the object is set to print to the default printer. How can you retrieve that information?

Solution

In addition to the properties you've seen so far, the Printer object keeps track of the three pieces of information that Windows must know about an output device: the device name (for example, "HP LaserJet 4"), the driver name ("WINSPOOL"), and the output port ("LPT1:"). Access also keeps track of whether the report has been set to print to the default printer or to a specific printer, in the UseDefaultPrinter property of the report. You'll use these properties to determine the information you need.

Load and run the form frmSelectedPrinters in *05-06.MDB*. Figure 5-6 shows the form after rptReport3 is selected and the report's output device, driver, and port are filled in on the form. Because this report was set up to print to the default printer, the "Printing to Default Printer" checkbox is selected.

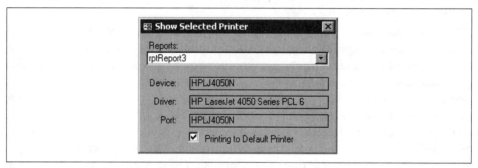

Figure 5-6. frmSelectedPrinters, after selecting rptReport3

The sample form uses this code to do its work:

```
Private Sub cboReportList_AfterUpdate( )

    Dim strReport As String
    Dim rpt As Report

    On Error GoTo HandleErrors

    strReport = Me.cboReportList
    DoCmd.OpenReport strReport, View:=acViewPreview, WindowMode:=acHidden
    With Reports(strReport)
```

```
                With .Printer
                    Me.txtDevice = .DeviceName
                    Me.txtDriver = .DriverName
                    Me.txtPort = .Port
                End With
                Me.chkDefault = .UseDefaultPrinter
            End With
        ExitHere:
            DoCmd.Close acReport, strReport
            Exit Sub

        HandleErrors:
            MsgBox "Error: " & Error & " (" & Err & ")"
            Resume ExitHere
        End Sub
```

To retrieve printer information about forms or reports in your own applications, follow these steps:

1. Open the selected report in either preview or design view:

```
DoCmd.OpenReport strReport, View:=acViewPreview, WindowMode:=acHidden
```

2. Use the DeviceName, DriverName, and Port properties of the report's Printer property to retrieve information about the report's output location:

```
With Reports(strReport)
    With .Printer
        Me.txtDevice = .DeviceName
        Me.txtDriver = .DriverName
        Me.txtPort = .Port
        ' Code removed.
    End With
End With
```

3. Check the report's UseDefaultPrinter property to determine if the report has been set to print to the default printer:

```
With Reports(strReport)
    ' Code removed.
    Me.chkDefault = .UseDefaultPrinter
End With
```

The UseDefaultPrinter property hangs off of the report itself, while the rest of the properties discussed in this chapter are members of the Printer object returned by the report's Printer property. You may look for the UseDefaultPrinter property in the wrong place—remember, it's a property of the report.

The UseDefaultPrinter property becomes more important, as you'll see in the next section, when you want to change the output device at runtime. Because of the way the Printer object was designed, you cannot change the output device from the Open event of the report—you must change it from outside the report. The easiest way to do this is to change Access's default printer, then print the report, then put Access's default printer back to what it was. You can accomplish this only if the report has been set to print to Access's default printer. You can look at the UseDefaultPrinter property to determine if that's how the report was set up. (You cannot, however, change a report's UseDefaultPrinter property if it's open in preview or print mode—you can change it only when you've opened the report in design view.)

5.7   Choose an Output Device at Runtime

Problem

You'd like to be able to select an output device while your application is running without popping up the File → Page Setup dialog. Is there a way to present a list of available printers and have the chosen report print to the chosen device? For example, you want to print your reports to the printer sometimes and sometimes to the fax machine.

Solution

Though this topic sounds complex, its solution is really just a combination of other solutions in this chapter. The Solution in Recipe 5.2 shows how to retrieve a list of available print devices and retrieve and set the default device. The Solution in Recipe 5.6 shows how to determine if a given report or form is configured to print to the default printer. Given those two techniques, this solution shows you how to set a new output device, print the Access object (using the new default device), and then restore the original default device.

Starting with Access 2002, you'll find two ways in which you can change the output device: you can either change Access's default printer, then print your report to the new default printer; or you can simply change the report's selected output device. The first solution is easier and generally works better. The second requires an extra step (selecting the report on screen) but gives you more flexibility.

Load and run frmDefaultPrinterList from *05-07.MDB*. Figure 5-7 shows the form in use, with the report rptReport3 selected and ready to print. Because rptReport3 has been configured to print to the default printer (you can open the File → Page Setup dialog to confirm this), the "Print to Default Printer" checkbox on the sample form is checked. You can choose a different output device from the combo box on the bottom of this form (of course, this will be interesting only if you happen to have more than one output device installed). If you choose a different output device (a fax driver, for example), the sample form will send the selected report to that output device.

The sample form also includes a checkbox ("Change Default Printer") that is available only if your selected report has been set up to print to the default printer. If so, you can elect to either change the default printer or select a new printer for the report. If the report has been designed so that it prints to a specific printer, you won't have the option of changing the default Access printer.

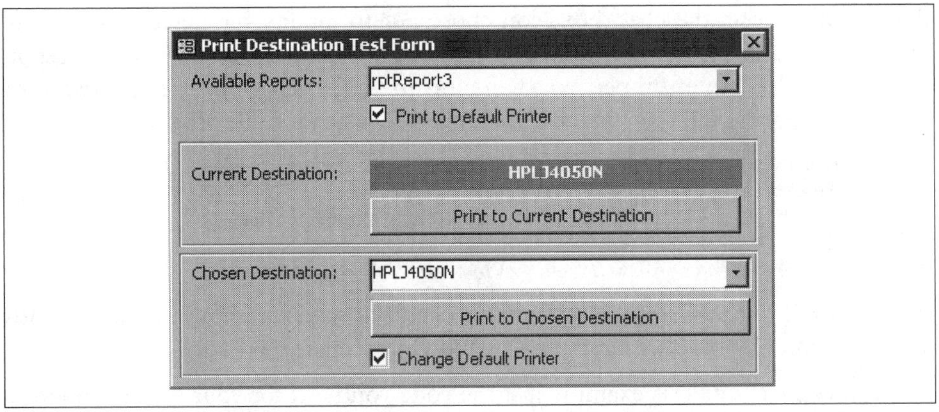

Figure 5-7. frmDefaultPrinterList, ready to choose a new output device

Discussion

Previous topics have discussed all but one of the issues demonstrated in this demo. The only outstanding issue is the code for printing the report (setting the new printer, printing the report to the new printer, and then resetting the original device).

When you click "Print to Chosen Destination" on the sample form, you execute the following code in the form's module:

```
Private Sub cmdChosen_Click( )
    On Error Resume Next

    Dim strRptName As String
    strRptName = cboObjects.Value

    If chkChangeDefaultPrinter.Value Then
        Set Application.Printer = Application.Printers(cboDestination.ListIndex)
        DoCmd.OpenReport strRptName, View:=acViewNormal
        Set Application.Printer = Nothing
    Else
        DoCmd.OpenReport strRptName, View:=acPreview, WindowMode:=acHidden
        With Reports(strRptName)
            Set .Printer = Application.Printers(cboDestination.ListIndex)
        End With
        DoCmd.OpenReport strRptName, View:=acViewNormal
    End If
End Sub
```

This code takes two different paths, depending on the value of the "Change Default Printer" checkbox. If it's selected, the code sets the default printer to the printer you selected in the combo box on the form, then prints the report. Finally, it sets the Application.Printer property to Nothing, resetting it back to its original value:

```
Set Application.Printer = Application.Printers(cboDestination.ListIndex)
DoCmd.OpenReport strRptName, View:=acViewNormal
Set Application.Printer = Nothing
```

If you didn't select the checkbox, you chose not to modify the default printer but instead to modify the report's internal printer. In this case, the code opens the report hidden, sets the Printer property of the report to be the report you've selected, then opens the report again, this time in normal view (causing it to be printed):

```
DoCmd.OpenReport strRptName, View:=acPreview, WindowMode:=acHidden
With Reports(strRptName)
    Set .Printer = Application.Printers(cboDestination.ListIndex)
End With
DoCmd.OpenReport strRptName, View:=acViewNormal
```

If you click "Print to Current Destination", the form sends the report to its currently selected printer by simply calling the DoCmd.OpenReport method.

You can extract from this example just the code you need for your own situation. If you want to modify the default Access printer, use the first code fragment. If you want to change the report's printer (leaving the Access printer intact), use the second fragment.

You can make many changes to this sample application. You might, for example, want to supply the report name without providing a combo box for it on the form. In that case, you would use a form like the sample form in the Solution in Recipe 5.2, showing only the list of output devices. You would modify the procedure described in this section to take the report name from a variable instead of from the form's combo box.

It's unfortunate that you cannot modify the output device from within the report's Open event. If that was possible, you could avoid opening the report first in preview or design view, setting its Printer property, and then printing the report. For the most part, you'll be better off simply changing Access's default printer.

5.8 Find Which Reports Are Not Set to Print to the Default Printer

Problem

You are about to distribute your application to other Access users. You want to ensure that all your reports are set to print to the default printer so that they will work with the users' installations of Windows. How do you create a list of all your reports and show whether or not they have been saved with the default printer setting?

Solution

Building on the code examples in this chapter, you can investigate the UseDefault-Printer property of each report to determine if it has the default printer selected. This solution uses this property, along with some simple ActiveX Data Objects (ADO) code, to get a list of reports in your database, to check the default printer setting, and to save the results to a table. This table feeds a report that you can print, rptReport-Printers. Once you have this list, you can set the output device for each report that has been set to print to a specific printer rather than to the Windows default printer.

Open and run frmShowReports from *05-08.MDB*. Figure 5-8 shows the form once it's done all its calculations. It will show the name of every report in your database, along with the default printer setting for each.

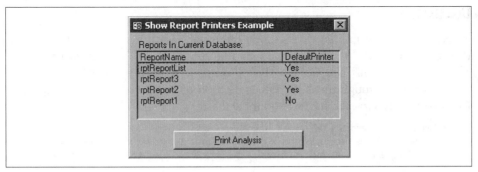

Figure 5-8. The frmShowReports example form

You can obtain a printout of this information by pressing the Print Analysis button, which prints the rptReportPrinters report (Figure 5-9).

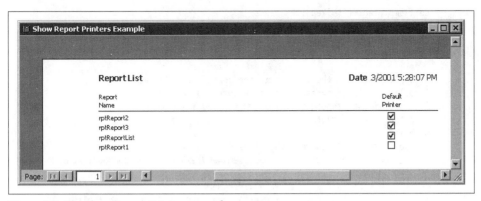

Figure 5-9. The Show Report Printers example report

To use this form in your own applications, follow these steps:

1. Import the objects listed in Table 5-5 from *05-08.MDB*.

Table 5-5. Objects to import from 05-08.MDB, allowing the creation of output status report

Object type	Object name
Table	tblReportPrinters
Form	frmShowReports
Report	rptReportPrinters

2. Once you've imported the objects, open the form frmShowReports to create the list of reports in your application, along with their output status.

Discussion

To see how this technique works, open the frmShowReports form in design view, then open the form's module window and locate the Form_Load event procedure. This subroutine calls the *GetReports* subroutine, which does most of the actual work. Iterating through the AllReports collection of the CurrentProject object gives *GetReports* access to each report in your database:

```
Private Sub GetReports( )
    ' Get a list of reports from the current database and write the name,
    ' along with the default printer status, to the output table.

    Dim rst As ADODB.Recordset
    Dim doc As AccessObject

    On Error GoTo HandleErrors

    Call EmptyTable("tblReportPrinters")
    Set rst = New ADODB.Recordset
    rst.Open "tblReportPrinters", CurrentProject.Connection, _
     adOpenDynamic, adLockOptimistic

    ' Loop through all the reports in the container's documents
    ' collection, opening each report in turn and checking
    ' to see if that report is formatted to send its output
    ' to the default printer.
    With rst
        For Each doc In CurrentProject.AllReports
            DoCmd.OpenReport doc.Name, View:=acViewDesign, WindowMode:=acHidden
            .AddNew
                .Fields("ReportName") = doc.Name
                .Fields("DefaultPrinter") = Reports(doc.Name).UseDefaultPrinter
            .Update
            DoCmd.Close acReport, doc.Name
        Next doc
    End With
```

```
ExitHere:
    On Error Resume Next
    rst.Close
    Exit Sub

HandleErrors:
    Resume ExitHere
End Sub
```

This code needs to empty the tblReportPrinters table. It uses the following procedure to clear the data from the table:

```
Private Sub EmptyTable(strTable As String)

    ' Remove all the rows from the table whose name is in strTable.
    With DoCmd
        .SetWarnings False
        .RunSQL "DELETE * FROM " & strTable
        .SetWarnings True
    End With
End Sub
```

This procedure uses a simple SQL DELETE statement to delete all the rows from the table, first turning off Access's warnings and then turning them back on once it's done.

GetReports uses ADO to write information about each report into the tblReport-Printers table. See Chapter 6 for more information on working with data programmatically.

CHAPTER 6

Data

The point of a database program is to manage data. Although Access provides most of the tools you'll need, there are many tasks for which you have to roll your own solution. This chapter concentrates on working with data in ways that traditional database operations don't support. You'll learn how to search for records phonetically, back up your database objects, perform lightning-fast finds on linked tables, save housekeeping information, and more. All the examples in this chapter use some form of Visual Basic for Applications (VBA) code, but don't worry—they are all clearly explained, and "testbed" applications are supplied to show you how each technique works. We present more tips for working with data in Chapter 14, focusing on techniques you can use when your data is stored in SQL Server, rather than in an Access Jet database (an *.MDB* or *.MDE* file).

 Many of the examples in this chapter take advantage of the DAO type library, rather than the default ADO library used by Access 2002 and Access 2003. Even though it's less "modern," DAO provides greater functionality, and generally better performance. In addition, using DAO makes it possible for these demonstrations to work in earlier versions of Access. If you want to try these techniques in your own applications, make sure you add the DAO reference to your project using the Tools → References menu item from within VBA—it won't be added by default.

6.1 Save with Each Record the Name of the Last Person Who Edited It and the Date and Time

Problem

Your application is used in a multiuser environment with users regularly adding and editing records. Access keeps track of when an object was created and last modified. However, it does not track this information at the record level. With each record, you want to log who created the record, who last edited the record, and the date and time associated with each of these actions. Is this possible?

Solution

Access has no built-in feature that records who edited a record and when the edit was made, but it's fairly easy to create your own. You'll need to add four fields to each of your tables to hold this information. You'll also need to create two simple procedures and attach them to the BeforeInsert and BeforeUpdate events of your forms.

To add this functionality to your applications, follow these steps:

1. Modify your table to include four new fields, as shown in Table 6-1.

Table 6-1. New fields for tblCustomer

Field name	Field type	Default value
DateCreated	Date/Time	=Now( )
UserCreated	Text (20)	
DateModified	Date/Time	=Now( )
UserModified	Text (20)	

2. Open your form in design view. Add new text box controls, as shown in Table 6-2. You can place these controls anywhere on the form; they needn't be visible. In the example form, we placed these controls along the bottom of the form (see Figure 6-2).

Table 6-2. New controls for frmCustomer1

Control name	Control source
txtDateCreated	DateCreated
txtUserCreated	UserCreated
txtDateModified	DateModified
txtUserModified	UserModified

3. Set the Enabled property of these controls to No and the Locked property to Yes. This prevents users from modifying the values that will be computed automatically. You may also wish to set the TabStop property of these controls to No to remove these fields from the normal tab sequence of the form.

4. Create the following event procedure in the form's BeforeInsert event, which uses the *CurrentUser* function to insert the user's name. You don't need to insert the date because it has already been supplied as a default value in the tblCustomers table:

```
Private Sub Form_BeforeInsert(Cancel As Integer)
    Me.UserCreated = CurrentUser( )
End Sub
```

5. Create the following event procedure in the form's BeforeUpdate event. This time you must insert both the username and the date and time:

```
Private Sub Form_BeforeUpdate(Cancel As Integer)
    Me.DateModified = Now( )
    Me.UserModified = CurrentUser( )
End Sub
```

6. The event procedures should show up in the form's properties sheet, as shown in Figure 6-1. Save and close the form. Open the form and run it to test your new code.

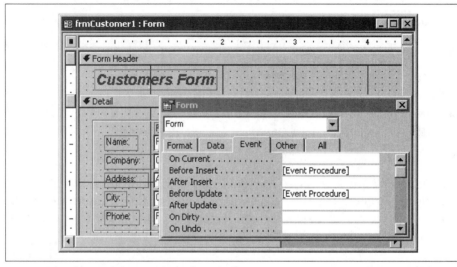

Figure 6-1. Referencing the event procedures for frmCustomer1

To see an example, load the frmCustomer1 form from *06-01.MDB*. This form, shown in Figure 6-2, allows you to enter and edit data in the tblCustomer table. Make a change to an existing record, and the DateModified and UserModified fields will be updated with the current date and time and username. Add a new record, and the DateCreated and UserCreated fields will be updated.

Discussion

To keep track of the username and the date and time a record is created and updated, you must do two things:

- Create additional fields in the table to hold the information.
- Create the application code to ensure that these fields are properly updated when a record is added or modified.

We added four fields to tblCustomer: two fields to hold the username and date/time the record was created, and another two fields to hold the username and date/time

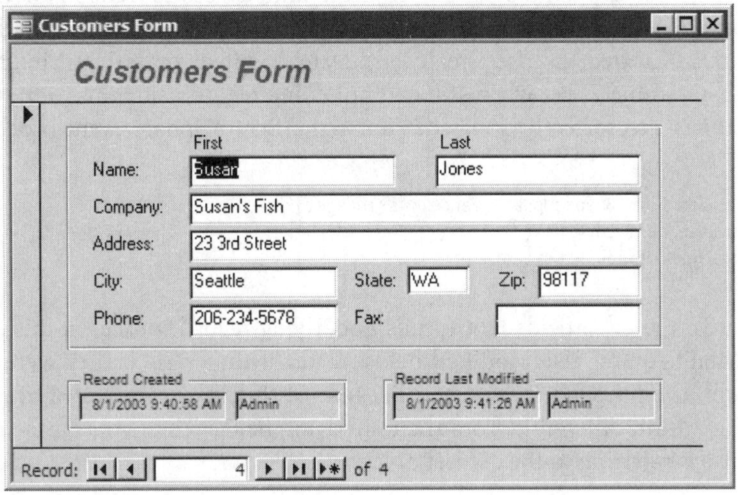

Figure 6-2. The frmCustomer1 form

the record was last modified. You don't have to create all four fields, only the fields for which you wish to log information.

We also created event procedures to update these columns whenever a record is inserted or updated. The *Now* function supplies the date and time; if you'd prefer to record only the date of the change without a time, you can use the *Date* function instead. The built-in *CurrentUser* function saves the name of the current user.

Access doesn't support the specification of calculated fields at the table level, so all of the logic presented in this solution occurs at the form level. This means that you must recreate this logic for every form that updates the data in this table. It also means that if you add new records or update existing records outside of a form—perhaps by using an update query or by importing records from another database—the fields in Table 6-1 will not all be automatically updated.

You can ensure that one of the fields, DateCreated, is correctly updated for every record by adding the following expression to its DefaultValue property:

```
=Now( )
```

Unfortunately, you can't use the DefaultValue property for either of the updated fields, because DefaultValue is evaluated only when the record is initially created. You can't use this property to update the UserCreated field, either, because Default-Value cannot call built-in or user-defined functions (except for the special *Now* and *Date* functions).

You may have noticed that placing the four controls from Table 6-2 on the form takes up a considerable amount of screen space. Fortunately, you don't need controls to make this technique work, because Access lets you refer to a form's record-source fields directly. In the sample database you'll find a second version of the form, frmCustomer2, that demonstrates this variation of the technique. Notice that there are no txtDateCreated, txtUserCreated, txtDateModified, or txtUserModified controls on frmCustomer2, yet when you enter or edit a record using this form, the fields in tblCustomer are correctly updated. Here's the BeforeUpdate event procedure for this form:

```
Private Sub Form_BeforeUpdate(Cancel As Integer)
    Me.DateModified = Now( )
    Me.UserModified = CurrentUser( )
End Sub
```

Access lets you refer to fields in a form's underlying record source (in this example, the DateModified and UserModified fields in tblCustomer) as if they were controls on the form, even though they're not. Because of this, it's a good idea to name the controls on a form differently from the underlying fields. Then you can be sure that you are always referring to the correct object.

Another consideration is that the *CurrentUser* function is useful only if you have implemented user-level security on your database. In an unsecured Access database it will always return "Admin", which is not very informative. In that case, you can use Windows API calls to retrieve either the computer name or the network login (or both) of the current user, instead of the Access security account. In the sample application, frmCustomer3 calls *acbNetworkUserName* when a record is inserted or edited. Here are the API declaration and the function, which you can find in basNetworkID:

```
Private Declare Function GetUserName Lib "advapi32.dll" Alias _
    "GetUserNameA" (ByVal lpBuffer As String, nSize As Long) As Long

Function acbNetworkUserName( ) As String
' Returns the network login name.
Dim lngLen As Long, lngX As Long
Dim strUserName As String
    strUserName = String$(254, 0)
    lngLen = 255
    lngX = GetUserName(strUserName, lngLen)
    If lngX <> 0 Then
        acbNetworkUserName = Left$(strUserName, lngLen - 1)
    Else
        acbNetworkUserName = ""
    End If
End Function
```

The basNetworkID module also includes the following API call, which you can use to obtain the name of the current user's computer:

```
Private Declare Function GetComputerName _
  Lib "kernel32" Alias "GetComputerNameA" _
  (ByVal lpBuffer As String, nSize As Long) As Long
```

```
Private Const acbcMaxComputerName = 15

Public Function acbComputerName( ) As String
    ' Retrieve the name of the computer.
    Dim strBuffer As String
    Dim lngLen As Long

    strBuffer = Space(acbcMaxComputerName + 1)
    lngLen = Len(strBuffer)
    If CBool(GetComputerName(strBuffer, lngLen)) Then
        acbComputerName = Left$(strBuffer, lngLen)
    Else
        acbComputerName = ""
    End If
End Function
```

Another option is to create your own public function called *CurrentUser* that returns the network name. That way, you won't need to change any of the code that calls *CurrentUser* in your forms. Access will use your function rather than the built-in one, and if you do implement Access security, all you need to do is rename or remove the custom *CurrentUser* function to have the form code start retrieving Access security names using the built-in *CurrentUser* function.

See Also

For more information on using DAO in Access databases, see "How Do I Use Data Access Objects (DAO) in New Databases?" in the Preface.

6.2   Determine if You're on a New Record in a Form

Problem

Often, you need to do different things depending on whether the current row is the "new" row on a form. For example, you might want to display a certain message box only when adding records. How can you do this?

Solution

You can use a form's NewRecord property to determine if you are on a new record by checking its value from an event procedure attached to the OnCurrent event property or some other event property of the form.

Follow these steps to implement this functionality in your own forms:

1. Create a new form or modify the design of an existing form.

2. Create an event procedure for the form's Current event. In that event procedure, create an If...Then statement that will branch based on the value of the form's NewRecord property. The code of the event procedure should look like this:

```
Private Sub Form_Current( )
    If Me.NewRecord Then
        ' Do something for a new record.
    Else
        ' Do something for an existing record.
    End If
End Sub
```

3. You may wish to alter some visual cue on the form to indicate whether you are on a new record. For example, you might change the text of a label, the text of the form's titlebar, or the picture of an image control. In the sample form, we changed the picture of an image control in the form's header, imgFlag, by copying the picture from one of two hidden image controls that are also located on the form. The final Current event procedure looks like this:

```
Private Sub Form_Current( )

    ' Determine if this is a new record and change the bitmap
    ' of the imgFlag control to give the user visual feedback.

    ' See the Solution in Recipe 9.7 for an explanation of using the
    ' PictureData property.

    If Me.NewRecord Then
        Me.imgFlag.PictureData = Me.imgFlagNew.PictureData
    Else
        Me.imgFlag.PictureData = Me.imgFlagEdit.PictureData
    End If
End Sub
```

4. Create any additional code that reacts to the NewRecord property. In the sample form, we decided to remind the user to log in the new record when saving it. Thus, we created the following event procedure attached to the form's BeforeUpdate event:

```
Private Sub Form_BeforeUpdate(Cancel As Integer)

    Dim strMsg As String

    If Me.NewRecord Then
        strMsg = "You just added a new record " & _
        "(# " & Me.ContactID & ")" & vbCrLf & _
        "Please don't forget to log it in!"
        Beep
        MsgBox strMsg, vbOKOnly + vbInformation, "New Record Added"
    End If

End Sub
```

To see an example, load and open frmContacts from *06-02.MDB*. Notice that the picture in the upper-left corner of the form changes to indicate whether you are editing an existing record (Figure 6-3) or adding a new record (Figure 6-4). In addition, when you save a newly added record, a message box is displayed that reminds you to log the new record (Figure 6-4). The message box does not appear when you save changes to an existing record.

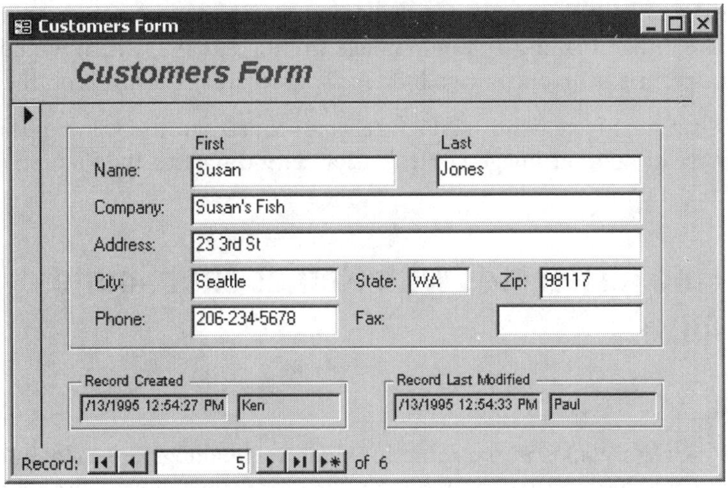

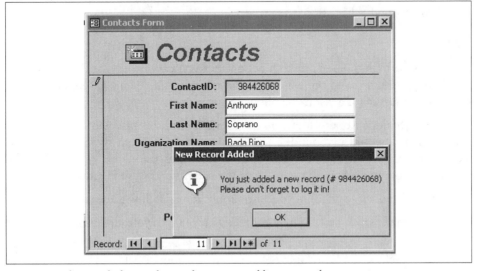

Figure 6-3. The sample form indicates that you are editing an existing record

Figure 6-4. The sample form indicates that you are adding a record

Discussion

The NewRecord property is simple: its value is True when adding a new record and False otherwise. This property is True from the moment the pending new record becomes current until the moment the record is saved. NewRecord is reset to False right after the BeforeUpdate event; it is False during both the AfterUpdate and After-Insert events.

The image control used to display the add/edit icon uses a trick to change its picture quickly. Rather than loading a bitmap image from a disk file, which would be slow, it copies the picture from one of two hidden "source" image controls on the form.

To do this, set the image control's PictureData property to the value of the Picture-Data property of another image control. Chapter 9 discusses the PictureData property in more detail.

6.3   Find All Records with Names That Sound Alike

Problem

You enter people's names into a table in which misspellings are a common occurrence. You would like a way to search for a person's record disregarding slight differences in spelling. You've tried using the Like operator with the first letter of the person's last name, but that produces too many names. Is there any way to search for records that sound alike?

Solution

Access has no built-in sound-alike function, but you can create one that employs a standard algorithm called the Russell Soundex algorithm. Using this algorithm, it's fairly easy to search for a last name phonetically.

Run the qrySoundex query found in *06-03.MDB*. Enter a last name in the query parameter dialog, and qrySoundex will return all records from tblStaff that sound like the name you entered. For example, if you enter the name "Jahnsin" at the parameter prompt, qrySoundex will return the records shown in Figure 6-5.

To perform Soundex searches in your own applications, follow these steps:

1. Import the basSoundex module from *06-03.MDB* into your database.
2. Create a query based on a table that contains a field that holds people's last names. Include the LastName field and any additional fields you wish to see in the output of the query.

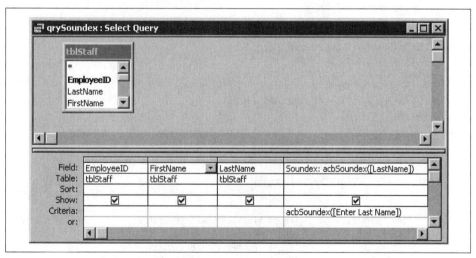

EmployeeID	FirstName	LastName	Soundex	Title	BirthDate	HireDate
2	Andrew	Jonsen	J525	Vice President, Sales	19-Feb-42	15-Jul-87
11	Phil	Johnson	J525	Temp	05-Mar-49	13-Jun-93
13	Andrew	Jonsen	J525	Vice President, Sales	19-Feb-42	15-Jul-87
22	Phil	Johnson	J525	Temp	05-Mar-49	13-Jun-93
149	Nelda	Jamison	J525	Temp		
304	Janice	Johnson	J525	Temp		

Figure 6-5. The records returned by searching for "Jahnsin"

3. Create a calculated field that calculates the Soundex code for the LastName field using the *acbSoundex* function. In qrySoundex, we used the following calculation to create a new field called Soundex:

```
Soundex: acbSoundex([LastName])
```

4. Enter criteria for the calculated field that compare that field against the Soundex code of a user-entered parameter. Use the *acbSoundex* function to obtain the Soundex code of the parameter. We used the following criteria in qrySoundex:

```
acbSoundex([Enter Last Name])
```

This qrySoundex query is shown in Figure 6-6.

Figure 6-6. The qrySoundex query in design view

5. Declare the parameter to be of type Text using the Query → Parameters dialog.
6. Save and run the query.

Discussion

You can find the *acbSoundex* function in basSoundex in *06-03.MDB*. This function takes a last name and returns a four-digit Soundex code for the name. If you look at the fourth column in Figure 6-5, you can see that the Soundex code for all rows is the same. In this case—for names sounding like "Jahnsin"—the code is "J525". Soundex codes always begin with the first letter of the name followed by three digits ranging between 0 and 6 that represent the remaining significant consonants in the name.

The *acbSoundex* function is shown here:

```
Public Function acbSoundex( _
  ByVal varSurName As Variant) As Variant

    ' Purpose:
    '     Takes a surname string and returns a 4-digit
    '     code representing the Russell Soundex code.
    ' In:
    '     varSurName: A surname (last name) as a variant
    ' Out:
    '     Return value: A 4-digit Soundex code as a variant

    Const acbcSoundexLength = 4

    On Error GoTo HandleErr

    Dim intLength As Integer
    Dim intCharCount As Integer
    Dim intSdxCount As Integer
    Dim intSeparator As Integer
    Dim intSdxCode As Integer
    Dim intPrvCode As Integer
    Dim strChar As String * 1
    Dim strSdx As String * acbcSoundexLength
    Dim strName As String

    ' We add vbNullString to take care of a passed Null
    strName = varSurName & vbNullString
    intLength = Len(strName)
    strSdx = String(acbcSoundexLength, "0")

    If intLength > 0 Then
        intSeparator = 0      'Keeps track of vowel separators
        intPrvCode = 0        'The code of the previous char
        intCharCount = 0      'Counts number of input chars
        intSdxCount = 0       'Counts number of output chars

        'Loop until the soundex code is of acbcSoundexLength
        'or we have run out of characters in the surname
        Do Until (intSdxCount >= acbcSoundexLength Or intCharCount >= intLength)
            intCharCount = intCharCount + 1
            strChar = Mid$(strName, intCharCount, 1)
```

```
            'Calculate the code for the current character
            Select Case strChar
                Case "B", "F", "P", "V"
                    intSdxCode = 1
                Case "C", "G", "J", "K", "Q", "S", "X", "Z"
                    intSdxCode = 2
                Case "D", "T"
                    intSdxCode = 3
                Case "L"
                    intSdxCode = 4
                Case "M", "N"
                    intSdxCode = 5
                Case "R"
                    intSdxCode = 6
                Case "A", "E", "I", "O", "U", "Y"
                    intSdxCode = -1
                Case Else
                    intSdxCode = -2
            End Select

            'Special case the first character
            If intCharCount = 1 Then
                Mid$(strSdx, 1, 1) = UCase(strChar)
                intSdxCount = intSdxCount + 1
                intPrvCode = intSdxCode
                intSeparator = 0

            'If a significant constant and not a repeat
            'without a separator then code this character
            ElseIf intSdxCode > 0 And _
              (intSdxCode <> intPrvCode Or intSeparator = 1) Then
                Mid$(strSdx, intSdxCount + 1, 1) = intSdxCode
                intSdxCount = intSdxCount + 1
                intPrvCode = intSdxCode
                intSeparator = 0

            'If a vowel, this character is not coded,
            'but it will act as a separator
            ElseIf intSdxCode = -1 Then
                intSeparator = 1
            End If
        Loop
        acbSoundex = strSdx
    Else
        acbSoundex = Null
    End If

ExitHere:
    Err.Clear
    Exit Function

HandleErr:
    Select Case Err.Number
    Case Else
```

```
            MsgBox Err.Number & ": " & Err.Description, _
                vbOKOnly + vbCritical, "acbSoundex"
        End Select
        Resume ExitHere
    End Function
```

The *acbSoundex* function is based on the Russell Soundex standard algorithm. Soundex is the most commonly used sound-alike algorithm in the U.S. It works by discarding the most unreliable parts of a name, while retaining much of the name's discriminating power. It works best when used with the English versions of names of people of European descent. Its discriminating power is reduced when it is used with very short or very long names or names with a high percentage of vowels. Other sound-alike algorithms may work better in these situations.

The Soundex algorithm was created to work with people's last names. It appears to work reasonably well with people's first names also, but not for names of businesses. Soundex does not work well for business names primarily because these names tend to be longer than people's names, and Soundex encodes only the first four significant characters. We've found that extending the number of encoded characters to eight works better for business names, although this is a nonstandard implementation of the algorithm. You can easily extend the number of encoded characters by changing the acbcSoundexLength constant found at the beginning of *acbSoundex*. If you decide to do this, however, we suggest you rename the function to something like *acbSoundex8* to distinguish it from the standard function.

Soundex will not work satisfactorily with data other than names.

6.4   Find the Median Value for a Field

Problem

You need to calculate the median for a numeric field. Access provides the *DAvg* function to calculate the mean value for a numeric field, but you can't find the equivalent function for calculating medians.

Solution

Access doesn't provide a built-in *DMedian* function, but you can make one using VBA code. This solution demonstrates a median function that you can use in your own applications.

Load the frmMedian form from *06-04.MDB*. Choose the name of a table and a field in that table using the combo boxes on the form. After you choose a field, the median value will be calculated and displayed in a text box using the *acbDMedian* function found in basMedian (see Figure 6-7). An error message will be displayed if you have chosen a field with a nonnumeric data type; the string "(Null)" will be displayed if the median value happens to be Null.

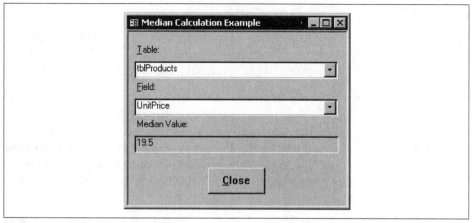

Figure 6-7. The frmMedian form

Follow these steps to use *acbDMedian* in your own applications:

1. Import the basMedian module from *06-04.MDB* into your database.
2. Call the *acbDMedian* function using syntax similar to that of the built-in *DAvg* function. The calling syntax is summarized in Table 6-3.

Table 6-3. The acbDMedian parameters

Parameter	Description	Example
Field	Name of field for which to calculate median	"UnitPrice"
Domain	Name of a table or query	"Products"
Criteria	Optional WHERE clause to limit the rows considered	"CategoryID = 1"

Make sure each parameter is delimited with quotes. The third parameter is optional. For example, you might enter the following statement at the debug window:

```
? acbDMedian("UnitPrice", "tblProducts", "SupplierID = 1")
```

The function would return a median value of 18 (assuming you are using the data in the *06-04.MDB* sample database).

3. The return value from the function is the median value.

> This example uses the DAO type library, and you'll need to include the reference to the most current version of DAO in your own applications in order to take advantage of this code. Use the Tools → References menu to add the necessary reference to use this code in your own database.

Discussion

The *acbDMedian* function in basMedian in *06-04.MDB* is patterned to look and act like the built-in *DAvg* domain function. The algorithm used to calculate the median, however, is more complicated than what you would use to calculate the mean. The median of a field is calculated using the following algorithm:

- Sort the dataset on the field.
- Find the middle row of the dataset and return the value of the field. If there is an odd number of rows, this will be the value in a single row. If there is an even number of rows, there is no middle row, so the function finds the mean of the values in the two rows straddling the middle. You could modify the function to pick an existing value instead.

After declaring a few variables, the *acbDMedian* function creates a recordset based on the three parameters passed to the function (*strField*, *strDomain*, and *varCriteria*), as shown in the following source code:

```
Public Function acbDMedian( _
 ByVal strField As String, ByVal strDomain As String, _
 Optional ByVal strCriteria As String) As Variant

    ' Purpose:
    '     To calculate the median value
    '     for a field in a table or query.
    ' In:
    '     strField: The field
    '     strDomain: The table or query
    '     strCriteria: An optional WHERE clause to
    '                  apply to the table or query
    ' Out:
    '     Return value: The median, if successful;
    '                   otherwise, an error value

    Dim db As DAO.Database
    Dim rstDomain As DAO.Recordset
    Dim strSQL As String
    Dim varMedian As Variant
    Dim intFieldType As Integer
    Dim intRecords As Integer

    Const acbcErrAppTypeError = 3169

    On Error GoTo HandleErr

    Set db = CurrentDb( )

    ' Initialize the return value.
    varMedian = Null

    ' Build a SQL string for the recordset.
    strSQL = "SELECT " & strField
```

```
strSQL = strSQL & " FROM " & strDomain

' Use a WHERE clause only if one is passed in.
If Len(strCriteria) > 0 Then
    strSQL = strSQL & " WHERE " & strCriteria
End If

strSQL = strSQL & " ORDER BY " & strField

Set rstDomain = db.OpenRecordset(strSQL, dbOpenSnapshot)

' Check the data type of the median field.
intFieldType = rstDomain.Fields(strField).Type
Select Case intFieldType
Case dbByte, dbInteger, dbLong, dbCurrency, dbSingle, dbDouble, dbDate
    ' Numeric field.
    If Not rstDomain.EOF Then
        rstDomain.MoveLast
        intRecords = rstDomain.RecordCount
        ' Start from the first record.
        rstDomain.MoveFirst

        If (intRecords Mod 2) = 0 Then
            ' Even number of records. No middle record, so move
            ' to the record right before the middle.
            rstDomain.Move ((intRecords \ 2) - 1)
            varMedian = rstDomain.Fields(strField)
            ' Now move to the next record, the one right after
            ' the middle.
            rstDomain.MoveNext
            ' Average the two values.
            varMedian = (varMedian + rstDomain.Fields(strField)) / 2
            ' Make sure you return a date, even when averaging
            ' two dates.
            If intFieldType = dbDate And Not IsNull(varMedian) Then
                varMedian = CDate(varMedian)
            End If
        Else
            ' Odd number of records. Move to the middle record
            ' and return its value.
            rstDomain.Move ((intRecords \ 2))
            varMedian = rstDomain.Fields(strField)
        End If
    Else
        ' No records; return Null.
        varMedian = Null
    End If
Case Else
    ' Nonnumeric field; raise an app error.
    Err.Raise acbcErrAppTypeError
End Select

acbDMedian = varMedian
```

```
ExitHere:
    On Error Resume Next
    rstDomain.Close
    Set rstDomain = Nothing
    Exit Function

HandleErr:
    ' Return an error value.
    acbDMedian = CVErr(Err)
    Resume ExitHere
End Function
```

The process of building the SQL string that defines the recordset is straightforward, except for the construction of the optional WHERE clause. Because *strCriteria* was defined as an optional parameter (using the Optional keyword), *acbDMedian* checks if a value was passed by checking that the string has a length greater than zero.

Once *acbDMedian* builds the SQL string, it creates a recordset based on that SQL string.

Next, *acbDMedian* checks the data type of the field: it will calculate the median only for numeric and date/time fields. If any other data type has been passed to *acbDMedian*, the function forces an error by using the Raise method of the Err object and then uses the special *CVErr* function in its error handler to send the error state back to the calling procedure:

```
' Check the data type of the median field.
intFieldType = rstDomain.Fields(strField).Type
Select Case intFieldType
    Case dbByte, dbInteger, dbLong, dbCurrency, dbSingle, dbDouble, dbDate
' ... more code follows ...
    Case Else
        ' Nonnumeric field; raise an app error.
        Err.Raise acbcErrAppTypeError
End Select

' ... more code follows ...

ExitHere:
    On Error Resume Next
    rstDomain.Close
    Set rstDomain = Nothing
    Exit Function

HandleErr:
    ' Return an error value.
    acbDMedian = CVErr(Err)
    Resume ExitHere
End Function
```

If the field is numeric, the *acbDMedian* function checks to see if there are any rows in the recordset using the following If...Then statement, returning Null if there are no rows:

```
' Numeric field.
If Not rstDomain.EOF Then
    ' ... more code follows ...
Else
    ' No records; return Null.
    varMedian = Null
End If
```

If there are rows, the function moves to the end of the recordset to get a count of the total number of records. This is necessary because the RecordCount property returns only the number of rows that have been visited. The code is:

```
rstDomain.MoveLast
intRecords = rstDomain.RecordCount
```

If the number of records is even, *acbDMedian* moves to the record just before the middle using the Move method, which allows you to move an arbitrary number of records from the current record. The number of records to move forward is calculated using the following formula:

```
intRecords \ 2 - 1
```

This tells Access to divide the total number of records by 2 and then subtract 1 from the result (because you are starting from the first record). For example, if you are on the first of 500 records, you would move (500 \ 2 - 1) = (250 - 1) = 249 records forward, which would bring you to the 250th record. Once the function has moved that many records, it's a simple matter to grab the value of the 250th and 251st records and divide the result by 2. This part of the function is shown here:

```
' Start from the first record.
rstDomain.MoveFirst

If (intRecords Mod 2) = 0 Then
    ' Even number of records. No middle record, so move
    ' to the record right before the middle.
    rstDomain.Move ((intRecords \ 2) - 1)
    varMedian = rstDomain.Fields(strField)
    ' Now move to the next record, the one right after
    ' the middle.
    rstDomain.MoveNext
    ' Average the two values.
    varMedian = (varMedian + rstDomain.Fields(strField)) / 2
```

Because *acbDMedian* supports dates, the function needs to make sure that a date value is returned when taking the average of two dates. The following code handles this:

```
' Make sure you return a date, even when
' averaging two dates.
If intFieldType = dbDate And Not IsNull(varMedian) Then
    varMedian = CDate(varMedian)
End If
```

The code for an even number of rows is much simpler:

```
Else
    ' Odd number of records. Move to the middle record
    ' and return its value.
    rstDomain.Move ((intRecords \ 2))
    varMedian = rstDomain.Fields(strField)
End If
```

Finally, *acbDMedian* returns the median value to the calling procedure:

```
acbDMedian = varMedian
```

The median, like the average (or arithmetic mean), is known statistically as a measure of central tendency. In other words, both measures estimate the middle of a set of data. The mean represents the mathematical average value; the median represents the middle-most value. For many datasets, these two measures are the same or very close to each other. Sometimes, however, depending on how the data is distributed, the mean and median will report widely varying values. In these cases, many people favor the median as a better "average" than the mean.

Calculating the median requires sorting the dataset, so it can be rather slow on large datasets. Calculating the mean, however, doesn't require a sort, so it will always be faster to calculate the mean.

 Microsoft Excel includes a *Median* function that you can call from Access using OLE Automation. Chapter 12 shows you how to do this. Because using OLE Automation with Excel requires starting a copy of Excel to do the calculation, you'll almost always find it simpler and faster to use the all-Access solution presented here.

6.5 Quickly Find a Record in a Linked Table

Problem

You like to use the ultra-fast Seek method to search for data in indexed fields in your table-type recordsets, but the Seek method won't work with linked tables because you can only open dynaset-type DAO recordsets against linked tables. You can use the Find methods to search for data in these types of recordsets, but Find is much slower at finding data than Seek. Is there any way to use the Seek method on linked tables?

Solution

The Seek method works only on table-type recordsets, so you can't perform seeks on linked tables. However, there's no reason why you can't open the source database that contains the linked table and perform the seek operation there. This solution shows you how to do this.

To use the Seek method on external tables, follow these steps:

1. Use the OpenDatabase method to open the source database that contains the linked table. For example, in the event procedure attached to the cmdSeek command button on the sample form, frmSeekExternal, you'll find the following code:

```
Set wrk = DBEngine.Workspaces(0)

' Directly open the external database. It will be opened
' nonexclusively, read-write, and with type = Access.
Set dbExternal = _
    wrk.OpenDatabase(acbGetLinkPath("tblCustomer"),, False, False, "")
```

2. Create a table-type recordset based on the source table. If you renamed the table when you linked to it, make sure you use the name used in the source database. The sample form uses this code:

```
' Create a table-type recordset based on the external table.
Set rstCustomer = dbExternal.OpenRecordset("tblCustomer", dbOpenTable)
```

3. Set an index and perform the seek operation, as in this code behind the sample form:

```
' This index consists of last and first names.
rstCustomer.Index = "FullName"

' Perform the seek and then check if the record was found.
rstCustomer.Seek "=", ctlLName.Value, ctlFName.Value
```

4. Any time you perform a seek or a find, you must next check to see if the operation was successful. You do this using the NoMatch property of the recordset. For example, on the sample form, you'll find the following code:

```
strMsg = "The record for " & ctlFName & ctlLName & " was"
If Not rstCustomer.NoMatch Then
    strMsg = strMsg & " found!" & vbCrLf & vbCrLf
    strMsg = strMsg & "Customer# = " & rstCustomer![Customer#]
    MsgBox strMsg, vbOKOnly + vbInformation, "External Seek"
Else
    strMsg = strMsg & " not found!"
    MsgBox strMsg, vbOKOnly + vbCritical, "External Seek"
End If
```

5. Close the recordset and the external database. The sample form uses this code:

```
rstCustomer.Close
dbExternal.Close
```

To see an example, copy the *06-05.MDB* and *06-05Ext.MDB* databases to a folder on your hard drive. The *06-05.MDB* database is linked to the tblCustomers table in *06-05Ext.MDB*. Code in frmRelink, the startup form in *06-05.MDB*, takes care of relinking to the tblCustomer table in *06-05Ext.MDB* (we explain this technique later in this chapter). Open the frmSeekExternal form from *06-05.MDB*. Enter a first and last name for which to search (you may find it helpful to browse through tblCustomer first) and press the Use Seek command button (see Figure 6-8). Even though this table does not exist in the *06-05.MDB* database, the row will be retrieved using the fast Seek method.

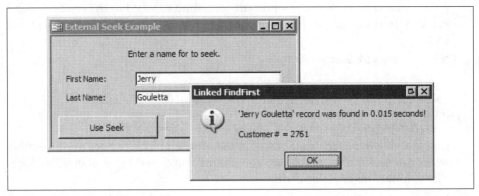

Figure 6-8. The frmSeekExternal form

Discussion

The key to this technique is using the OpenDatabase method on the workspace object to open the external database directly where the linked table physically resides. The OpenDatabase method takes four parameters, which are detailed in Table 6-4.

Table 6-4. The OpenDatabase method's parameters

Parameter	Description	frmSeekExternal example
dbname	The name of the database, including the path	acbGetLinkPath("tblCustomer")
exclusive	True to open the database exclusively	False
read-only	True to open the database in read-only mode	False
source	The Connect string for opening the database	"" indicates an Access database

Here's the code that opens the database in the sample form:

```
Set dbExternal = _
    wrk.OpenDatabase(acbGetLinkPath("tblCustomer"), False, False, "")
```

The function call, acbGetLinkPath("tblCustomer"), retrieves the path and filename of the linked database containing tblCustomer by parsing the Connect property of the linked table.

The code for *acbGetLinkPath* is shown here:

```
Function acbGetLinkPath(strTableName As String) As String
    On Error GoTo HandleErr
    Dim strConnect As String
```

```
    strConnect = CurrentDb.TableDefs(strTableName).Connect
    ' The path and filename are after ";DATABASE=".
    acbGetLinkPath = _
        Mid$(strConnect, InStr(strConnect, ";") + 10)

ExitHere:
    Exit Function
HandleErr:
    Select Case Err.Number
        Case Else
            MsgBox Err.Number & ": " & Err.Description, , "acbGetLinkPath"
    End Select
    Resume ExitHere

End Function
```

The logic behind this function is simple. The Connect property of a linked Access table always begins with ;DATABASE= and then contains the path to the linked database file. The *Mid$* function allows you to start in the middle of a string and retrieve the remaining characters (or, optionally, just a specified number of those characters). We used the *Instr* function to find the semicolon, rather than assuming it is the first character of the Connect string, because other kinds of linked tables will identify the type of link before the semicolon. For example, the Connect property of a table linked to an Excel spreadsheet will begin with Excel;DATABASE=.

You won't notice much difference between the Seek and FindFirst or FindNext methods with small tables, but with tables containing many thousands of records, the difference in speed can be significant. Because there is overhead involved with attaching to an external database, the FindFirst method will sometimes even be faster on very small tables. Another option for large amounts of data that offers better performance than FindFirst or Seek is a parameterized query or a custom SQL statement to retrieve just the single record that you need. Seeks are most useful when you need to jump around in a table, finding many different records that don't share any criteria.

Our example uses an API call to time how long it takes to perform seeks and finds, but you won't notice a significant difference on the small sample data. This method of timing database activity is explained in Chapter 7.

You are not limited to using the Seek method on Access databases. It works with indexed, nonnative ISAM databases also, and the tables needn't be linked to the current database.

You can't perform a seek on text, spreadsheet, or ODBC data sources.

6.6 Get a Complete List of Field Properties from a Table or Query

Problem

You want to get a list of fields in a table or query and their properties. The ListFields method is fine for certain situations, but it returns only a few of the fields' properties. Microsoft has also made it clear that this method will not exist in future releases of Access. How can you create a replacement for ListFields that supplies all the available field information?

Solution

In Access 1.x, the ListFields method was the only supported way to return a list of fields and their properties. Its usefulness is limited because it returns only a few field properties and always returns a snapshot. Using the more flexible Data Access Objects (DAO) hierarchy, however, you can get all the properties of field objects and create a replacement for the outdated ListFields method that returns all of a field's properties (or as many as you'd like), placing the results in a readily accessible table.

Open and run the frmListFields form from *06-06.MDB* (see Figure 6-9). Choose Tables, Queries, or Both, and whether you wish to include system objects. Select an object from the Object combo box. After a moment, the form will display a list of fields and their properties in the Fields list box. Scroll left and right to see additional properties and up and down to see additional fields.

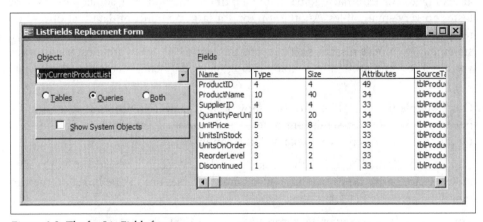

Figure 6-9. The frmListFields form

To use this technique in your applications, follow these steps:

1. Import the basListFields module into your database.
2. Call the *acbListFields* subroutine, using the following syntax:

```
Call acbListFields (strName, blnTable, strOutputTable)
```

The parameters are summarized in Table 6-5.

Table 6-5. The acbListFields subroutine's parameters

Parameter	Example	Description
strName	"Customers"	The name of the table or query
blnTable	True	True if strName is a table, False if it is a query
strOutputTable	"tmpOutputFields"	The name of the table that will hold the list of field properties

3. The subroutine creates a table with the name specified by *strOutputTable* and fills it with one record for every field in the specified table or query. The table is similar in structure to the snapshot returned by the ListFields method, except that it has new fields to hold the values of additional field properties. Table 6-6 lists the structure of the resulting table. Note that the first seven fields are identical to those returned by the Access Version 1 ListFields method. The remaining fields are additional information supplied only by *acbListFields*.

Table 6-6. The acbListFields output table structure

Field name	Data type	Description
Name	String	The name of the field.
Type	Integer	The data type of the field as represented by an integer. Search Access help under ListFields to decode this value.
Size	Integer	The size of the field.
Attributes	Long Integer	The field's attributes. Search Access help under Attributes to decode this value.
SourceTable	String	The name of the field's underlying table. If the table is an attached table, this field will contain the name of the table as it exists in the source database.
SourceField	String	The name of the field.
CollatingOrder	Integer	The collating order of the table. Search Access help under CollatingOrder to decode this value.
AllowZeroLength	Integer	True if zero-length strings are allowed in the field; False otherwise.
DataUpdateable	Integer	True if the field is updateable; False otherwise.
DefaultValue	Text	The field's default value.
OrdinalPosition	Integer	The field's position in the table, starting at 0.
Required	Integer	True if the field requires an entry; False otherwise.
ValidationRule	String	The field's ValidationRule property.
ValidationText	String	The field's ValidationText property.
Caption	String	The field's Caption property.
ColumnHidden	Integer	True if the field is hidden in datasheet view; False otherwise.

Table 6-6. The acbListFields output table structure (continued)

Field name	Data type	Description
ColumnOrder	Integer	The order in which the field appears in datasheet view.
ColumnWidth	Integer	The width of the field as it appears in datasheet view.
DecimalPlaces	Integer	The field's number of decimal places.
Description	Text	The field's description.
Format	Text	The field's format string.
InputMask	Text	The field's input mask string.

Discussion

The *acbListFields* subroutine uses a table-driven approach to populate the list fields output table with the properties of the fields in the input table or query. Here's the basic algorithm for *acbListFields*:

1. Call *acbMakeListTable* to create the output table. This routine either creates a new table or, if one already exists, deletes all of its rows. If it needs to create the output table, it uses a create table query. The names of the fields in the output table are the same as the properties that *acbListFields* will place there.

2. Open a recordset based on the table created in Step 1.

3. Count the fields in the input table/query.

4. For each field in the input table/query, add a new row in the output table and iterate through the fields in the output table, retrieving the properties for the input table/query field with the same name as the output table fields and adding them in turn to the new row in the output table.

The *acbListFields* subroutine is shown here:

```
Public Sub acbListFields( _
  strName As String, blnTable As Boolean, _
  strOutputTable As String)
    ' Purpose:
    '     Saves a list of the most common field properties
    '     of a table or query to a table.

    Dim db As DAO.Database
    Dim rst As DAO.Recordset
    Dim tdf As DAO.TableDef
    Dim qdf As DAO.QueryDef
    Dim fld As DAO.Field
    Dim intFieldCount As Integer
    Dim intI As Integer
    Dim intJ As Integer
    Dim strOutputField As String

    On Error GoTo HandleErr
```

```
    Call acbMakeListTable(strOutputTable)

    Set db = CurrentDb( )
    Set rst = db.OpenRecordset(strOutputTable)

    ' If the input object is a table, use a TableDef.
    ' Otherwise, use a QueryDef.
    If blnTable Then
        Set tdf = db.TableDefs(strName)
        intFieldCount = tdf.Fields.Count
    Else
        Set qdf = db.QueryDefs(strName)
        intFieldCount = qdf.Fields.Count
    End If

      ' Iterate through the fields in the TableDef
      ' or QueryDef.
     For intI = 0 To intFieldCount - 1
        ' Create a new record for each field.
        rst.AddNew
        If blnTable Then
           Set fld = tdf.Fields(intI)
        Else
           Set fld = qdf.Fields(intI)
        End If
        ' Iterate through the fields in rst. The names of these fields
        ' are exactly the same as the names of the properties we wish
        ' to store in them, so we take advantage of this fact.
        For intJ = 0 To rst.Fields.Count - 1
           strOutputField = rst.Fields(intJ).Name
           rst.Fields(strOutputField) = _
            fld.Properties(strOutputField)
        Next intJ
        rst.Update
      Next intI

ExitHere:
    Set rst = Nothing
    Set qdf = Nothing
    Exit Sub

HandleErr:
    Select Case Err.Number
        Case 3270        ' Property not found.
           ' Skip the property if it can't be found.
           Resume Next
        Case Else
           MsgBox Err.Number & ": " & Err.Description, , "acbListFields"
    End Select
    Resume ExitHere
End Sub
```

Once *acbListFields* has completed its work, you can open the output table and use it any way you'd like. The sample frmListFields form displays the output table using a list box control.

This technique is easy to implement and offers more functionality than the built-in ListFields method. Many more (although not all of the possible) field properties are retrieved, and because *acbListFields* returns a table instead of a snapshot, you have added flexibility.

acbListFields doesn't decide which properties to write to the output table. Instead, it drives the process using the names of the fields in the output table. If you wish to collect a different set of properties, all you need to do is modify the code in *acbMakeListFields* and delete the output table (which will be recreated the next time you run *acbListFields*).

There is useful sample code behind the frmListFields form. Look at the *GetTables* function for an example of how to get a list of tables and queries and at the *FillTables* function for an example of a list-filling function (see the Solutions in Recipe 6.8 and Recipe 7.8 for more details on list-filling functions).

 In your own applications, you may want to hide the output table in the database container. You can do this either by prefixing its name with "USys" or by checking the Hidden setting in the table's properties.

See Also

For more information on working with properties, see "Handle Object Properties, In General" in Chapter 7.

6.7   Create and Use Flexible AutoNumber Fields

Problem

You use AutoNumber fields in your tables to ensure that you have unique values for your key fields, but a key based on an auto-incrementing Long Integer AutoNumber field doesn't sort your tables in a useful order. Also, auto-incrementing AutoNumber fields always start at 1, and you want your AutoNumber values to start at another number. How can you create a replacement for Access's AutoNumber fields that gets around these limitations?

Solution

Access makes it easy to add unique value key fields to a table using the AutoNumber data type (referred to as the Counter data type prior to Access 95). AutoNumbers are automatically maintained by Access and ensure a unique value for each record. Auto-incrementing AutoNumber fields always start at 1, with 1 added for each new record. If your only concern is changing the starting number, you can do that by using an append query to insert a record with a specific value in the AutoNumber field. The next record added will automatically be assigned that value plus 1. However, you may have other good reasons for wanting to create a replacement for the built-in AutoNumbers. This solution shows how to create your own flexible AutoNumber fields that are multiuser-ready. You can also combine these custom AutoNumber values with other fields in the table to make your data sort more intuitively.

Open and run the frmFlexAutoNum form from *06-07.MDB*. Add a new record. Type in some data, and be sure to put a value in the LastName field. Save the new record by pressing Shift-Enter. When you save the record, a new auto-incremented value will be placed into the ContactID field (see Figure 6-10).

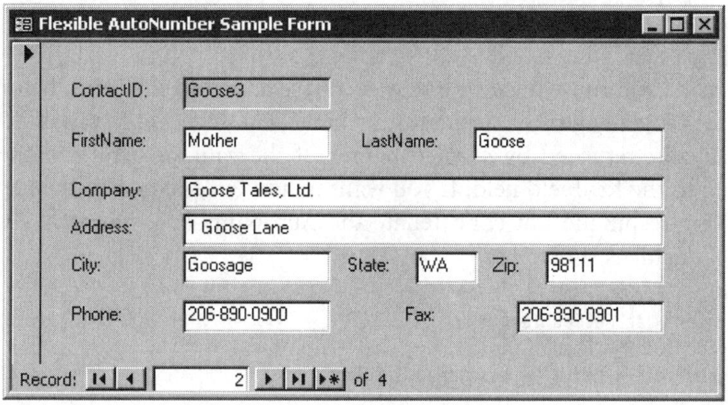

Figure 6-10. The frmFlexAutoNum sample form

You can add this functionality to your own applications by following these steps:

1. Import the tblFlexAutoNum table and the basFlexAutoNum module into your database.

2. Prepare your table by adding a new field to become the key value. If you want to store a numeric AutoNumber value, set the field's type to Number, Long Integer. If you want to add more information for sorting, set the new field's type to Text and set its length long enough to accommodate the numbers returned by the flexible AutoNumber routine plus the number of characters you want to concatenate to the field.

3. Open the tblFlexAutoNum table and edit the CounterValue field to start at the desired value.

4. Open the data-entry form for your application in design view. In the form's BeforeUpdate event procedure, add code that calls the *acbGetCounter* function,

writing the returned value to your key field. The following code shows a Before-Update event procedure that includes a call to the *abcGetCounter* function:

```
Private Sub Form_BeforeUpdate(Cancel As Integer)
    ' Try to get a unique counter and write it
    ' to the Contact ID field.

    Dim lngCounter As Long

    If IsNull(Me.txtContactID) Then
        lngCounter = acbGetCounter( )
        ' If no counter is available...
        If lngCounter < 1 Then
            ' cancel the Update event.
            Cancel = True
        Else
            ' Write the key field.
            Me.txtContactID = Left(Me.txtLastName, 5) & lngCounter
        End If
    End If
End Sub
```

This code will run whenever a new record is added to the form, before the new record is actually written to the form's table. The *lngCounter* variable is assigned to the value returned by *acbGetCounter*. If the value is greater than zero, it is written to the KeyField field. If you want to add information to the key field, use the same technique but concatenate the AutoNumber value with a value from another field, as shown here:

```
Dim lngCounter As Long
lngCounter = acbGetCounter( )
If lngCounter > 0 Then
    Me.KeyField = Left$(Me.LastName,5) & lngCounter
End If
```

If you are basing your key value on another field, your code should ensure that a value exists in that field before attempting to use it. The best way to ensure this is to set the Required property of the field to Yes.

Discussion

The heart of this technique is the *acbGetCounter* function. This function tries to open the tblFlexAutoNum table exclusively and, if it succeeds, gets the value in the CounterValue field and increments the stored value by some fixed number. The retrieved value is then returned to the calling procedure. *acbGetCounter* is shown here:

```
Public Function acbGetCounter( ) As Long
    ' Get a value from the counters table and
    ' increment it

    Dim db As DAO.Database
    Dim rst As DAO.Recordset
```

```
Dim blnLocked As Boolean
Dim intRetries As Integer
Dim lngTime As Long
Dim lngCnt As Long
Dim lngCOunter As Long

' Set number of retries
Const conMaxRetries = 5
Const conMinDelay = 1
Const conMaxDelay = 10

On Error GoTo HandleErr

Set db = CurrentDb( )
blnLocked = False

Do While True
    For intRetries = 0 To conMaxRetries
        On Error Resume Next
        Set rst = db.OpenRecordset("tblFlexAutoNum", _
         dbOpenTable, dbDenyWrite + dbDenyRead)
        If Err.Number = 0 Then
            blnLocked = True
            Exit For
        Else
            lngTime = intRetries ^ 2 * _
             Int((conMaxDelay - conMinDelay + 1) * Rnd + conMinDelay)
            For lngCnt = 1 To lngTime
                DoEvents
            Next lngCnt
        End If
    Next intRetries
    On Error GoTo HandleErr

    If Not blnLocked Then
        If MsgBox("Could not get a counter: Try again?", _
         vbQuestion + vbYesNo) = vbYes Then
            intRetries = 0
        Else
            Exit Do
        End If
    Else
        Exit Do
    End If
Loop

If blnLocked Then
    lngCOunter = rst("CounterValue")
    acbGetCounter = lngCOunter
    rst.Edit
        rst("CounterValue") = lngCOunter + 1
    rst.Update
    rst.Close
Else
```

```
        acbGetCounter = -1
    End If
    Set rst = Nothing
    Set db = Nothing

ExitHere:
    Exit Function

HandleErr:
    MsgBox Err.Number & ": " & Err.Description, , "acbGetCounter"
    Resume ExitHere
End Function
```

After declaring several variables, *acbGetCounter* attempts to open a Recordset object on the tblFlexAutoNum table. By specifying the dbDenyRead and dbDenyWrite constants as the *Options* argument to the OpenRecordset method, it attempts to lock the table exclusively, preventing other users from reading or writing to the table. You can use the dbDenyRead and dbDenyWrite options only with table-type recordsets, so if the table is in an external database you'll need to open the recordset using OpenDatabase, as shown earlier in this chapter.

The function attempts to obtain a lock on the acbcAutoNumTable by using a common multiuser coding construct: a retry loop. The retry loop from *acbGetCounter* is shown here:

```
For intRetries = 0 To conMaxRetries
    On Error Resume Next
    Set rst = db.OpenRecordset("tblFlexAutoNum", _
     dbOpenTable, dbDenyWrite + dbDenyRead)
    If Err.Number = 0 Then
        blnLocked = True
        Exit For
    Else
        lngTime = intRetries ^ 2 * _
         Int((conMaxDelay - conMinDelay + 1) * Rnd + conMinDelay)
        For lngCnt = 1 To lngTime
            DoEvents
        Next lngCnt
    End If
Next intRetries
```

Note what happens if the lock is not immediately obtained. The procedure calculates a long number based on the number of retries, the acbcMaxDelay and acbcMinDelay constants that were set at the beginning of the function, and a random number. This calculated number, lngTime, is then used to waste time using a For... Next loop that simply counts from 1 to lngTime. We placed a DoEvents statement inside the loop so that Access will process any screen activity during this dead time.

The retry loop and the time-wasting code force the function to pause briefly before attempting to obtain the lock again. Because this function is meant to work in a multiuser situation, it's important that retries are not repeatedly attempted without waiting for the lock to be released. *acbGetCounter* includes a random component to lngTime that gets larger with each retry to separate out multiple users who might be trying to obtain the lock at the same time.

If the function cannot lock the table after the number of retries specified by the acbcMaxRetries constant, it displays a message box allowing the user to retry or cancel. If the user chooses to cancel, a value of -1 is returned; if the user chooses to retry, the whole retry loop is restarted. If the lock succeeds, the value of the AutoNumber field is saved and the AutoNumber field is incremented by the value of the acbcAutoNumInc constant.

The tblFlexAutoNum table provides AutoNumber values for one table only. You may wish to extend this technique so that there is some provision for recording multiple AutoNumber values in tblFlexAutoNum. Alternately, you could create a separate AutoNumber table for each flexible AutoNumber value you need in your application. You can hide these tables in the database container either by prefixing the table names with "USys" or by checking the Hidden setting in the tables' properties sheets.

The example form concatenates the first five letters from the LastName field with the AutoNumber value. Although this convention can be helpful in sorting, it can also have a negative side effect: the AutoNumber field will have to be changed when the LastName field is changed. We included this functionality simply as an example of the kind of flexibility you have with this technique. In general, it's not good practice to combine multiple pieces of information in one field.

If you want to create AutoNumber values in two different copies of a database that could then be merged together at a later time, you could use a site-specific alphanumeric prefix to your AutoNumber field. Since each copy of the database would use a different site prefix, you wouldn't have duplicate values. However, you could also accomplish this goal by using a composite primary key comprised of two fields—the AutoNumber and the site ID.

Unlike Access AutoNumbers, the custom AutoNumbers in this solution are retrieved only when the record is about to be saved, in the BeforeUpdate event. If a user starts editing a new record and then cancels, no AutoNumber will be "wasted" on the canceled record. This technique therefore is useful in situations in which you need your numbers to be consecutive, such as for invoice or purchase-order numbers.

6.8 Back Up Selected Objects to Another Database

Problem

You use a standard backup program to save your databases, but this works only at the database level. This is fine for archival purposes, but you often want to back up individual objects. How can you get Access to display a list of objects and allow you to save selected ones to an output database you specify?

Solution

This solution shows how to create a form that selectively saves Access objects to another database. It works by using a multiselect list box and the CopyObject action.

Open frmBackup from *06-08.MDB* (Figure 6-11). You can use this form to back up selected objects from the current database to another database. Select one or more objects from the list box, using the Shift or Ctrl keys to extend the selection. When you are finished selecting objects and have specified a backup database (a default database name is created for you), press the Backup button. The backup process will begin, copying objects from the current database to the backup database.

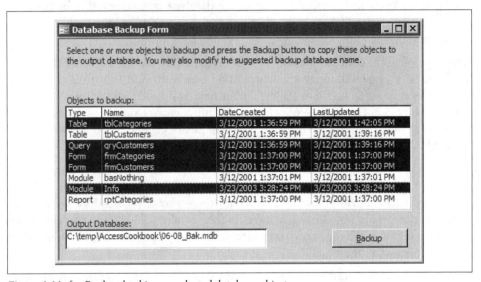

Figure 6-11. frmBackup backing up selected database objects

To add this functionality to your own database, follow these steps:

1. Import frmBackup from *06-08.MDB* to your database.
2. Call the backup procedure from anywhere in your application by opening the frmBackup form. For example, you might place a command button on your main switchboard form with the following event procedure attached to the button's Click event:

```
DoCmd.OpenForm "frmBackup"
```

Discussion

To see how it works, open frmBackup in design view. The form consists of a list box, two text boxes (one of which is initially hidden), and other controls. The list box control displays the list of objects. One text box is used to gather the name of the backup database; the other is used to display the progress of the backup operation. All of the VBA code that makes frmBackup work is stored in the form's module.

The MultiSelect property

The key control on the form is the lboObjects list box. We have taken advantage of the list box's MultiSelect property to allow the user to select more than one item in the list box. This property can be set to None, Simple, or Extended (see Figure 6-12). If you set MultiSelect to None, which is the default setting, only one item may be selected. If you choose Simple, you can select multiple items, and an item will be selected whenever you click on it and will remain selected until you click on it again. If you choose Extended, the list box will behave like most of Windows's built-in list box controls—you select multiple items by holding down the Shift or Ctrl keys while clicking on items.

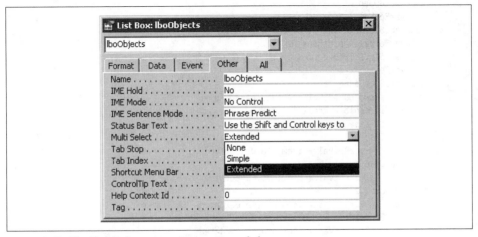

Figure 6-12. The MultiSelect property set to Extended

Filling the lboObjects list box

Unlike most list boxes, which derive their lists of values from either a fixed list of items or the rows from a table or query, lboObjects uses a list-filling callback function to fill the list box with the names of the database container objects. List-filling functions are described in detail in the Solution in Recipe 7.5. We use a list-filling function here because the list of database container objects is not stored in a user-accessible table. (Actually, you can fill a list box with a list of database container objects using a query based on the undocumented MSysObjects system table, but this practice is not supported by Microsoft and therefore is not recommended.) The list-filling function for lboObjects, *FillObjectList*, is shown here:

```
Private Function FillObjectList(ctl As Control, varID As Variant, _
    varRow As Variant, varCol As Variant, varCode As Variant) As Variant
```

```
' List filling function for lboObjects.
' Fills the list box with a list of
' the database container objects.

Dim varRetVal As Variant
Static sintRows As Integer
Dim itemInfo As Info

varRetVal = Null

Select Case varCode
Case acLBInitialize
    ' Fill mcolInfo with a list of
    ' database container objects
    Set mcolInfo = New Collection
    sintRows = FillObjCollection()
    varRetVal = True
Case acLBOpen
    varRetVal = Timer
Case acLBGetRowCount
    varRetVal = sintRows
Case acLBGetColumnCount
    varRetVal = 4
Case acLBGetValue
    ' varRow and varCol are zero-based so add 1
    Set itemInfo = mcolInfo(varRow + 1)
    Select Case varCol
        Case 0
            varRetVal = itemInfo.ObjectType
        Case 1
            varRetVal = itemInfo.ObjectName
        Case 2
            varRetVal = itemInfo.DateCreated
        Case 3
            varRetVal = itemInfo.LastUpdated
    End Select
Case acLBEnd
    Set mcolInfo = New Collection
End Select

FillObjectList = varRetVal

End Function
```

FillObjectList looks like most typical list-filling functions (see the Solution in Recipe
7.5 for more details). Most of the work is done during the initialization step, when
the *FillObjCollection* function is called to fill a module-level collection with the list of
database container objects:

```
Public Function FillObjCollection() As Integer

    ' Populates mcolInfo array with database container objects.

    Dim db As DAO.Database
```

```
Dim con As DAO.Container
Dim doc As DAO.Document
Dim tdf As DAO.TableDef
Dim qdf As DAO.QueryDef
Dim strObjType As String
Dim intObjCount As Integer
Dim intItem As Integer
Dim fReturn As Boolean

On Error Resume Next

Set db = CurrentDb()

' Setup the first row of field names
Call SaveToCollection("Type", "Name", "DateCreated", _
 "LastUpdated")

' Special case TableDefs
db.TableDefs.Refresh
For Each tdf In db.TableDefs
    ' Only include non-system tables
    If Not (tdf.Attributes And dbSystemObject) <> 0 Then
        Call SaveToCollection("Table", tdf.Name, tdf.DateCreated, _
        tdf.LastUpdated)
    End If
Next tdf

' Special case QueryDefs
db.QueryDefs.Refresh
For Each qdf In db.QueryDefs
    Call SaveToCollection("Query", qdf.Name, qdf.DateCreated, _
    qdf.LastUpdated)
Next qdf

' Iterate through remaining containers of interest
' and then each document within the container
For Each con In db.Containers
    Select Case con.Name
    Case "Scripts"
        strObjType = "Macro"
    Case "Forms"
        strObjType = "Form"
    Case "Modules"
        strObjType = "Module"
    Case "Reports"
        strObjType = "Report"
    Case Else
        strObjType = ""
    End Select

    ' If this isn't one of the important containers, don't
    ' bother listing documents.
    If strObjType <> "" Then
        con.Documents.Refresh
```

```
        For Each doc In con.Documents
            ' You can't backup the current form, since it's open.
            If Not (doc.Name = Me.Name And con.Name = "Forms") Then
                fReturn = SaveToCollection(strObjType, doc.Name, doc.DateCreated,

_
                        doc.LastUpdated)
            End If
        Next doc
    End If

    Next con
    FillObjCollection = mcolInfo.Count
End Function
```

The purpose of *FillObjCollection* is to fill a Collection object with a list of the names of each database container object, the type of each object, the date and time each object was created, and the date and time each object was last modified. Each item within this collection is an instance of the Info class, defined in the sample database. (Although the use of user-defined classes is beyond the scope of this book, you can investigate the Info class and see that it's quite simple. It behaves just like any other object available as part of Access or VBA—the only difference is that it's defined within your project.) In order to gather the necessary information, the code must work through all the available objects. This is accomplished by "walking" the Containers collection of the current database and working with the objects in each of the containers. There are eight different containers in the Containers collection, which are summarized in Table 6-7.

Table 6-7. The Containers collection

Container	Contains these documents	Backup documents?
Databases	General information about the database	No
Forms	Saved forms	Yes
Modules	Saved modules	Yes
Relationships	Enforced relationships	No
Reports	Saved reports	Yes
Scripts	Saved macros	Yes
SysRel	Unenforced relationships	No
Tables	Saved tables and queries	Yes

Because you are interested in backing up only the objects that appear in the Access database container, the function should ignore any containers in Table 6-7 for which "Backup documents" is No.

FillObjArray places the list box headings in the first item of the array:

```
' Set up the first row of field names
Call SaveToCollection("Type", "Name", "DateCreated", _
  "LastUpdated")
```

We want the information in this first row to become the headings of the list box, so we set the ColumnHeads property of the list box to Yes. This setting tells Access to freeze the first row of the list box so that it doesn't scroll with the other rows. In addition, you cannot select this special row.

The function needs to walk the collections storing away the information that will appear in the list box. This *should* be relatively simple, but there is one complicating factor: the Tables container includes both tables and queries, mixed together in unsorted order. Fortunately, there's an alternate method for getting separate lists of tables and queries in the database. Instead of using the Tables container, *FillObjCollection* walks the TableDefs and QueryDefs collections to extract the necessary information:

```
' Special case TableDefs
db.TableDefs.Refresh
For Each tdf In db.TableDefs
    ' Only include non-system tables
    If Not (tdf.Attributes And dbSystemObject) <> 0 Then
        Call SaveToCollection("Table", tdf.Name, tdf.DateCreated, _
        tdf.LastUpdated)
    End If
Next tdf

' Special case QueryDefs
db.QueryDefs.Refresh
For Each qdf In db.QueryDefs
    Call SaveToCollection("Query", qdf.Name, qdf.DateCreated, _
      qdf.LastUpdated)
Next qdf
```

The TableDefs collection requires an additional test to exclude the normally hidden system tables from the list.

With the tables and queries taken care of, the function can now walk the remaining container collections for macros, forms, modules, and reports:

```
' Iterate through remaining containers of interest
' and then each document within the container
For Each con In db.Containers
    Select Case con.Name
    Case "Scripts"
        strObjType = "Macro"
    Case "Forms"
        strObjType = "Form"
    Case "Modules"
        strObjType = "Module"
    Case "Reports"
        strObjType = "Report"
    Case Else
        strObjType = ""
    End Select
```

```
                ' If this isn't one of the important containers, don't
                ' bother listing documents.
                If strObjType <> "" Then
                    con.Documents.Refresh
                    For Each doc In con.Documents
                        ' You can't backup the current form, since it's open.
                        If Not (doc.Name = Me.Name And con.Name = "Forms") Then
                            fReturn = SaveToCollection(strObjType,
                                        doc.Name, _ doc.DateCreated,
                                        doc.LastUpdated)
                        End If
                    Next doc
                End If

        Next con
```

The *SaveToCollection* subroutine called by *FillObjArray* is shown here:

```
Private Function SaveToCollection(ByVal strType As String, ByVal strName As String, _
ByVal strDateCreated As String, ByVal strLastUpdated As String) As Boolean

    ' Skip deleted objects
    Dim itemInfo As Info
    Set itemInfo = New Info

    If Left$(strName, 1) <> "~" Then
        itemInfo.ObjectType = strType
        itemInfo.ObjectName = strName
        itemInfo.DateCreated = strDateCreated
        itemInfo.LastUpdated = strLastUpdated
        mcolInfo.Add itemInfo
        SaveToCollection = True
    Else
        SaveToCollection = False
    End If

End Function
```

Access doesn't immediately remove database container objects that you have
deleted. Instead, it renames each deleted object to a name that begins with "~TMP-
CLP". In addition, when you use SQL statements for row sources or record sources,
Access creates hidden queries with names that also start with a tilde character ("~").
We don't want these objects to appear in the list of objects to back up, so we
included code here to exclude them explicitly from the list box.

The backup process

Once you have selected one or more database objects in the lboObjects list box, you
initiate the backup process by clicking on the cmdBackup command button. The
event procedure attached to this button calls the *MakeBackup* subroutine. This routine begins by checking to see if the backup database exists. If it does, you are

warned that it will be overwritten before proceeding. Next, *MakeBackup* creates the output database using the following code:

```
Set dbOutput = DBEngine.Workspaces(0). _
 CreateDatabase(strOutputDatabase, dbLangGeneral)

dbOutput.Close
```

The output database is immediately closed, because the backup process doesn't require it to be open. *MakeBackup* then iterates through the selected objects and calls *ExportObject*, passing it the name of the output database and the name and type of the object to be backed up:

```
intObjCnt = 0
ctlProgress = "Backing up objects..."

For Each varItem In ctlObjects.ItemsSelected
    intObjCnt = intObjCnt + 1
    strType = ctlObjects.Column(0, varItem)
    strName = ctlObjects.Column(1, varItem)
    ctlProgress = "Backing up " & strName & "..."
    DoEvents
    Call ExportObject(strOutputDatabase, strType, strName)
Next varItem
```

The *ExportObject* subroutine backs up each object using the CopyObject action. *ExportObject* is shown here:

```
Private Sub ExportObject(strOutputDatabase As String, _
 strType As String, strName As String)

    Dim intType As Integer

    Select Case strType
        Case "Table"
            intType = acTable
        Case "Query"
            intType = acQuery
        Case "Form"
            intType = acForm
        Case "Report"
            intType = acReport
        Case "Macro"
            intType = acMacro
        Case "Module"
            intType = acModule
    End Select

    ' If export fails, let the user know.
    On Error Resume Next
```

```
    DoCmd.CopyObject strOutputDatabase, strName, intType, strName
    If Err.Number <> 0 Then
        Beep
        MsgBox "Unable to backup " & strType & ": " & strName, _
        vbOKOnly + vbCritical, "ExportObject"
    End If

End Sub
```

Comments

This technique uses the CopyObject action instead of the more traditional Transfer-Database action. CopyObject, which was added in Access 2.0, provides you with the same functionality as TransferDatabase, but because it supports only Access objects it requires fewer arguments. The CopyObject action also allows you to specify a new name for the object in the destination database. This is useful if you want give the copy a name that's different from that of the source object.

CHAPTER 7

VBA

Most applications that are distributed to users include at least some Visual Basic for Applications (VBA) code. Because VBA provides the only mechanism for performing certain tasks (for example, using variables, building SQL strings on the fly, handling errors, and using the Windows API), most developers eventually must delve into its intricacies. The sections in this chapter cover some of the details of VBA that you might not find in the Access manuals. First you'll find a complete explanation of embedding strings inside other strings, allowing you to build SQL strings and other expressions that require embedded values. Two solutions are devoted to creating a procedure stack, which allows you to keep track of the current procedure at all times. The second of the two also creates a profiling log file, which helps you document where and for how long your code wandered. Next you'll learn about the DoEvents statement, which gives Windows time to handle its own chores while your code is running. A group of four solutions covers the details of creating list-filling functions, passing arrays as parameters, sorting arrays, and filling a list box with the results of a directory search. The final two solutions cover some details of working with Data Access Objects (DAO): how to set and retrieve object properties, whether the properties are built-in, and how to tell whether an object exists in your application.

7.1   Build Up String References with Embedded Quotes

Problem

You want to create criteria for text and data fields, but no matter what syntax you try you seem to get errors or incorrect results. What are you doing wrong?

Solution

You'll face this problem in any place in Access where you're required to provide a string expression that contains other strings—for example, in using the domain functions (*DLookup*, *DMax*, *DMin*, etc.), in building a SQL expression on the fly, or in using the Find methods (FindFirst, FindNext, FindPrevious, and FindLast) on a recordset. Because all strings must be surrounded with quotes, and you can't embed quotes inside a quoted string, you can quickly find yourself in trouble. Many programmers agonize over these constructs, but the situation needn't be that difficult. This section explains the problem and shows you a generic solution.

To see an example of building expressions on the fly, load and run frmQuoteTest from *07-01.MDB*. This form, shown in Figure 7-1, allows you to specify criteria. Once you press the Search button, the code attached to the button will build the SQL expression shown in the text box and will set the RowSource property for the list box at the bottom of the form accordingly.

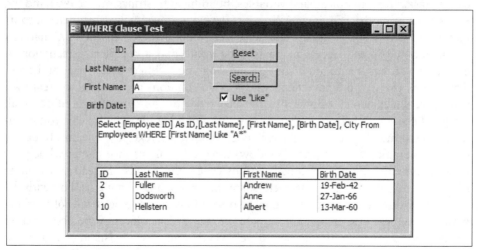

Figure 7-1. The test form, frmQuoteTest, with a subset of the data selected

To try all the features of the form, follow these three steps:

1. In the First Name text box, enter A. When you press Return, the form builds the appropriate SQL string and filters the list box. Note in the SQL string that the value you entered is surrounded by quotes. (This is the state in which Figure 7-1 was captured.)

2. In the Birth Date text box, enter 3/13/60. Again, the form should filter the data (down to a single row). Note that the SQL expression must have "#" signs around the date value you entered.

3. Press the Reset button to delete all the data from the four text boxes. That will again fill the list box with all the rows. Enter the value 8 in the ID text box, and

then press Return. Note that the SQL string this time has no delimiter around the value that you entered.

Discussion

The point of that exercise was to alert you to the fact that different data types require specific delimiters when they become part of an expression. For example, to use *DLookup* to find the row in which the [LastName] field was Smith, you'd need an expression like this:

```
[LastName] = "Smith"
```

Leaving off those quotes would confuse Access, because it would be looking for some variable named "Smith".

Date values don't require quotes. Instead, they require # delimiters. To find the row in which the [BirthDate] field is May 16, 1956, you'd need an expression like this:

```
[BirthDate] = #5/16/56#
```

If you left off the delimiters, Access would think you were trying to numerically divide 5 by 16, and then by 56.

Numeric values require no delimiters. If you were searching for the row in which the ID value was 8, you could use this expression:

```
[ID] = 8
```

and Access would know exactly what you meant.

Many situations in Access require that you create strings that supply search criteria. Because the Jet database engine has no knowledge of VBA or its variables, you must supply the actual values before you apply any search criteria or perform lookups. That is, you must create a string expression that contains the *value* of any variable involved, not the variable name.

Any of the three examples in this section could have been used as search criteria, and string values would need to have been surrounded by quotes. The next few paragraphs cover the steps you need to take in creating these search criteria strings.

To build expressions that involve variables, you must supply any required delimiters. For numeric expressions, there is no required delimiter. If the variable named *intID* contains the value 8, you could use this expression to create the search string you need:

```
"[ID] = " & intID
```

As part of a SQL string, or as a parameter to *DLookup*, this string is unambiguous in its directions to Access.

To create a search criterion that includes a date variable, you'll need to include the # delimiters. For example, if you have a variant variable named *varDate* that contains the date May 22, 1959, and you want to end up with this expression:

```
"[BirthDate] = #5/22/59#"
```

you have to insert the delimiters yourself. The solution might look like this:

```
"[BirthDate] = #" & varDate & "#"
```

The complex case occurs when you must include strings. For those cases, you'll need to build a string expression that contains a string itself, surrounded by quotes, with the whole expression also surrounded by quotes. The rules for working with strings in Access are as follows:

- An expression that's delimited with quotes can't itself contain quotes.
- Two quotes ("") inside a string are seen by Access as a single quote.
- You can use apostrophes (') as string delimiters.
- An expression that's delimited with apostrophes can't itself contain apostrophes.
- You can use the value of Chr$(34) (34 is the ANSI value for the quote character) inside a string expression to represent the quote character.

Given these rules, you can create a number of solutions to the same problem. For example, if the variable *strLastName* contains "Smith", and you want to create a WHERE clause that will search for that name, you will end up with this expression:

```
"[LastName] = "Smith""
```

However, that expression isn't allowed because it includes internal quotes. An acceptable solution would be the following:

```
"[LastName] = ""Smith"""
```

The problem here is that the literal value "Smith" is still in the expression. You're trying to replace that value with the name of the variable, *strLastName*. You might try this expression:

```
"[LastName] = ""strLastName"""
```

but that will search for a row with the last name of "strLastName". You probably won't find a match.

One solution, then, is to break up that expression into three separate pieces—the portion before the variable, the variable, and the portion after the variable (the final quote):

```
"[LastName] = """ & strLastName & """"
```

Although that may look confusing, it's correct. The first portion:

```
"[LastName] = """
```

is simply a string containing the name of the field, an equals sign, and two quotes. The rule is that two quotes inside a string are treated as one. The same logic works for the portion of the expression after the variable (""""). That's a string containing two quotes, which Access sees as one quote. Although this solution works, it's a bit confusing.

To make things simpler, you can just use apostrophes inside the string:

```
"[LastName] = '" & strLastName & "'"
```

This is somewhat less confusing, but there's a serious drawback: if the name itself contains an apostrophe ("O'Connor", for example), you'll be in trouble. Access doesn't allow you to nest apostrophes inside apostrophe delimiters, either. This solution works only when you're assured that the data in the variable can never itself include an apostrophe.

The simplest solution is to use Chr$(34) to embed the quotes. An expression such as the following would do the trick:

```
"[LastName] = " & Chr$(34) & strLastName & Chr$(34)
```

If you don't believe this works, go to the Immediate window in VBA and type this:

```
? Chr$(34)
```

Access will return to you by typing the value of Chr$(34)–a quote character.

To make this solution a little simpler, you could create a string variable at the beginning of your procedure and assign to it the value of Chr$(34):

```
Dim strQuote As String
Dim strLookup As String

strQuote = Chr$(34)
strLookup = "[LastName] = " & strQuote & strLastName & strQuote
```

This actually makes the code almost readable!

Finally, if you grow weary of defining that variable in every procedure you write, you might consider using a constant instead. You might be tempted to try this:

```
Const QUOTE = Chr$(34)
```

Unfortunately, Access won't allow you to create a constant whose value is an expression. If you want to use a constant, your answer is to rely on the "two-quote" rule:

```
Const QUOTE = """"
```

Although this expression's use is not immediately clear, it works just fine. The constant is two quotes (which Access will see as a single quote) inside a quoted string. Using this constant, the previous expression becomes:

```
strLookup = "[LastName] = " & QUOTE & strLastName & QUOTE
```

To encapsulate all these rules, you might want to use the *acbFixUp* function in the basFixUpValue module in *07-01.MDB*. This function takes as a parameter a variant value and surrounds it with the appropriate delimiters. Its source code is:

```
Function acbFixUp(ByVal varValue As Variant) As Variant

    ' Add the appropriate delimiters, depending on the data type.
    ' Put quotes around text, #s around dates, and nothing
    ' around numeric values.
    ' If you're using equality in your expression, you should
    ' use Basic's BuildCriteria function instead of calling
```

```
    ' this function.

    Const QUOTE = """"

    Select Case VarType(varValue)
        Case vbInteger, vbSingle, vbDouble, vbLong, vbCurrency
            acbFixUp = CStr(varValue)
        Case vbString
            acbFixUp = QUOTE & varValue & QUOTE
        Case vbDate
            acbFixUp = "#" & varValue & "#"
        Case Else
            acbFixUp = Null
    End Select
End Function
```

Once you've included this function in your own application, you can call it, rather than formatting the data yourself. The sample code in frmQuoteTest uses this function. For example, here's how to build the expression from the previous example:

```
"[LastName] = " & FixUp(strLastName)
```

abcFixUp will do the work of figuring out the data type and surrounding the data with the necessary delimiters.

> Access also provides a useful function, *BuildCriteria*, that will accept a field name, a data type, and a field value and will create an expression of this sort:
>
> ```
> FieldName = "FieldValue"
> ```
>
> with the appropriate delimiters, depending on the data type. We've used this in our example in the case where you uncheck the Use Like checkbox. It won't help if you want an expression that uses wildcards, but if you're looking for an exact match, it does most of the work of inserting the correct delimiters for you. To study the example, look at the *BuildWhere* function in frmQuoteTest's module.

7.2   Create a Global Procedure Stack

Problem

When you're writing an application, you often need to know the name of the current procedure from within your code. For example, if an error occurs, you'd like to be able to have a generic function handle the error and display the name of the procedure in which the error occurred (and all the procedures that have been called on the way to get there). VBA doesn't include a way to retrieve this information. How can you accomplish this?

Solution

By maintaining a list of active procedures, adding the current name to the list on the way into the procedure and removing it on the way out, you can always keep track of the current procedure and the procedure calls that got you there. There are many other uses for this functionality (see the next solution, for example), but one simple use is to retrieve the name of the current procedure in a global error-handling procedure.

The kind of data structure you'll need for maintaining your list is called a *stack*. As you enter a new procedure, you "push" its name onto the top of the stack. When you leave the procedure, you "pop" the name off the stack. Figure 7-2 shows a graphical representation of a procedure stack in action. The arrows indicate the direction in which the stack grows and shrinks as you add and remove items.

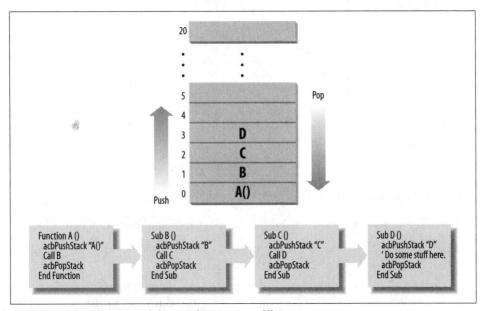

Figure 7-2. The call stack and the sample routines to fill it

To see the procedure stack in action, load *07-02.MDB*. Open the module basTest-Stack in design mode. Open the Immediate window (choose View ‡ Immediate Window). In the Immediate window, type:

```
? A( )
```

to execute the function named A. Figure 7-2 shows A and the procedures it calls. At each step, the current procedure pushes its name onto the procedure stack and then calls some other procedure. Once the calling procedure regains control, it pops its name off of the stack. In addition, each procedure prints the name of the current procedure (using the *acbCurrentProc* function, discussed later in this solution) to the Immediate window. Once all execution has finished, you should see in the Immediate window output like that shown in Figure 7-3.

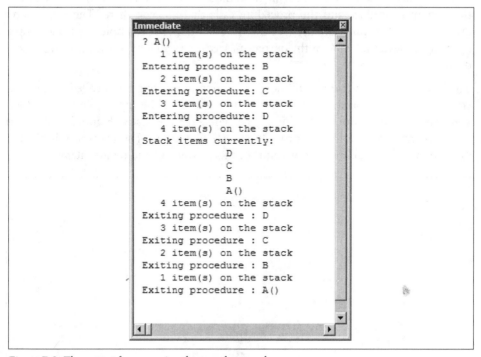

Figure 7-3. The output from running the sample procedure

Follow these steps to incorporate this functionality into your own applications:

1. Import the module basStack into your application. This includes the procedures that initialize and maintain the procedure stack.

2. Insert a call to the *acbInitStack* subroutine into code that's executed when your application starts up. Consider adding this procedure call to the code in your main form's Load event procedure. You'll want to call *acbInitStack* any time you restart your program during development, so you probably don't want to call it from the Autoexec macro, which is executed only when you first load the database. To call *acbInitStack*, either place its name alone on a line of code, like this:

```
acbInitStack
```

or use the Call construct, as follows:

```
Call acbInitStack
```

3. For each procedure in your application, place a call to *acbPushStack* as the first statement. This procedure will place the value it's passed on the top of the stack. As the single argument for each call, pass the name of the current procedure.

Our example places a pair of parentheses after function names and nothing after subroutine names, as a matter of style. As the last line in each procedure add a call to *acbPopStack*, which will remove the current name from the top of the stack.

4. You can retrieve the name of the currently executing procedure at any time by calling the *acbCurrentProc* function. This function looks at the top of the stack and returns the string it finds there. You can use this as part of an error handler or, as in the next solution, to help track procedure performance.

Discussion

The module you imported from *07-02.MDB*, basStack, includes code for maintaining the procedure stack and a module-local variable that is the stack itself. There are just six entry points (nonprivate procedures) in the module. Table 7-1 lists those procedures. Since all the code for the stack is encapsulated in that one module, you never really have to know how it all works. However, it's quite simple.

Table 7-1. The six entry points into basStack

Procedure name	Purpose	Parameters
acbInitStack	Initialize the stack.	
acbPushStack	Add an item to the stack.	A string to push
acbPopStack	Remove an item from the stack.	
acbCurrentProc	Retrieve the name of the current procedure.	
acbGetStack	Retrieve a specific item from the stack.	The item number to retrieve
acbGetStackItems	Retrieve the number of items on the stack.	

basStack includes two module-level variables: *mastrStack*, the array of strings that is the stack itself; and *mintStackTop*, an integer that holds the array slot into which the next stack item will be placed. When you begin your work with the stack, *mintStackTop* must be 0, so the first item will go in the slot numbered 0. The *acbInitStack* procedure does nothing other than initialize *mintStackTop*:

```
Public Sub acbInitStack( )
    ' Resets the stack top to 0.
    mintStackTop = 0
End Sub
```

You can add an item to the stack at any time by calling *acbPushStack*. Pass to this subroutine the item you want pushed. To push the item, the code places the item in the array at the location stored in *mintStackTop* and then increments the value of *mintStackTop*. Its code is:

```
Public Sub acbPushStack(strToPush As String)
```

```
        ' Push a string onto the call stack.
        ' If the stack is full, display an error.
        ' Otherwise, add the new item to the call stack.

        ' Handle the error case first.
        If mintStackTop > acbcMaxStack Then
            MsgBox acbcMsgStackOverflow
        Else
            ' Store away the string.
            mastrStack(mintStackTop) = strToPush

            ' Set mintStackTop to point to the NEXT
            ' item to be filled.
            mintStackTop = mintStackTop + 1
        End If
    End Sub
```

The only problem that might occur is that the stack might be full. The constant acbcMaxStack is originally set to 20, which should be enough levels. (Remember that *mintStackTop* goes up one only when a procedure calls another procedure. If you have 20 levels of procedure calling, you might consider rethinking your application, instead of worrying about procedure stacks!) If the stack is full, *acbPushStack* will pop up an alert and will not add the item to the stack.

When leaving a procedure, you'll want to remove an item from the stack. To do so, call the *acbPopStack* procedure:

```
    Public Sub acbPopStack( )

        ' Pop a string from the call stack.
        ' If the stack is empty, display an error.
        ' Otherwise, set the current item to be the
        ' next one to be filled in. If you're logging,
        ' send the information out to the log file.

        ' Handle the error case first.
        If mintStackTop = 0 Then
            MsgBox acbcMsgStackUnderflow
        Else
            ' Because you're removing an item, not adding one,
            ' set the stack top back to the previous row. Next time
            ' you add an item, it'll go right here.
            mintStackTop = mintStackTop - 1
        End If
    End Sub
```

Just as in *acbPushStack*, this code first checks to make sure that the stack integrity hasn't been violated; you can't remove an item from the stack if there's nothing to remove! If you try, *acbPopStack* will pop up an alert and exit. If the stack is intact, the procedure will decrement the value of *mintStackTop*. Decrementing that value sets up the next call to *acbPushStack* so that it will place the new value where the old one used to be.

To retrieve the value at the top of the stack without pushing or popping anything, call the *acbCurrentProc* function:

```
Public Function acbCurrentProc( ) As String
    ' Since mintStackTop always points to the next item to
    ' be filled in, retrieve the item from mintStackTop - 1.
    If mintStackTop > 0 Then
        acbCurrentProc = mastrStack(mintStackTop - 1)
    Else
        acbCurrentProc = ""
    End If
End Function
```

This function retrieves the value most recently placed on the stack (at the location one less than *mintStackTop*, because *mintStackTop* always points to the next location to be filled). You can't look at *mastrStack* yourself, because it's local to basStack— and that's the way it *ought* to be. Since the details of how the stack works are kept private, you can replace basStack, using a different architecture for the stack data structure, and the rest of your code won't have to change at all.

To retrieve more information about what's in the stack, you can call *acbGetStack-Items*, to find out how many items there are in the stack, and *acbGetStack*, which retrieves a specific item from the stack. For example, write code like this to dump out the entire stack (see subroutine *D*, which does just this, in the basTestStack module):

```
Debug.Print "Stack items currently:"
For intI = 0 To acbGetStackItems( ) - 1
    Debug.Print , acbGetStack(intI)
Next intI
```

The *acbGetStackItems* function is simple: it returns the value of *mintStackTop*, because that value always contains the number of items in the stack:

```
Public Function acbGetStackItems( ) As Integer
    ' Retrieve the number of items in the stack.
    acbGetStackItems = mintStackTop
End Function
```

The *acbGetStack* function is a little more complex. It accepts an item number (requesting item 0 returns the item at the top of the stack) and calculates the position of the item to retrieve. Its source code is:

```
Public Function acbGetStack(mintItem As Integer) As String
    ' Retrieve the item that's mintItems from the top of the
    ' stack. That is,
    ' ? acbGetStack(0)
    ' would return the same value as acbCurrentProc.
    ' ? acbGetStack(3) would return the third value from the top.
    If mintStackTop >= mintItem Then
        acbGetStack = mastrStack(mintStackTop - mintItem - 1)
    Else
        acbGetStack = ""
    End If
End Function
```

For the procedure stack to work, you have to place calls to *acbPushStack* and *acb-PopStack* on entry and exit from every procedure call. Good coding practice supports the concept of only one exit point from each procedure, but even the best programmer sometimes breaks this rule. To use the call stack, however, you must catch every exit point with a call to *acbPopStack*. Keep this in mind as you retrofit old code to use this mechanism and when you devise new code to use it. You can always code for a single exit point, and you will find code maintenance much easier if you do.

7.3   Create an Execution Time Profiler

Problem

You'd like to optimize your VBA code, but it's almost impossible to tell how long Access is spending inside any one routine and it's difficult to track which procedures are called by your code most often. You'd like some way to track which routines are called, in what order, and how much time each takes to run. Can you do this?

Solution

As outlined in the Solution in Recipe 7.2, you can create a code profiler using a stack data structure to keep track of the execution order and timing of the procedures in your application. Though the code involved is a bit more advanced than that in the Solution in Recipe 7.2, it's not terribly difficult to create the profiler. Using it is simple, as all the work is wrapped up in a single module.

Steps

Open the database *07-03.MDB* and load the module basTestProfiler in design mode. In the Immediate window, type:

```
? A( )
```

to run the test procedures. Figure 7-4 shows the profile stack and the code in *A*. As you can see, *A* calls *B*, which calls *C*, which calls *D*, which waits 100 ms and then returns to *C*. *C* waits 100 ms and then calls *D* again. Once *D* returns, *C* returns to *B*, which waits 100 ms and then calls *C* again. This pattern repeats until the code gets back to *A*, where it finally quits. The timings in the profile stack in Figure 7-4 are actual timings from one run of the sample.

As the code is set up now, the profiler writes to a text file named *C:\LOGFILE.TXT*. You can read this file in any text editor. For a sample run of function A, the file contained this text:

```
*******************************
Procedure Profiling
8/13/2003 3:29:11 PM
```

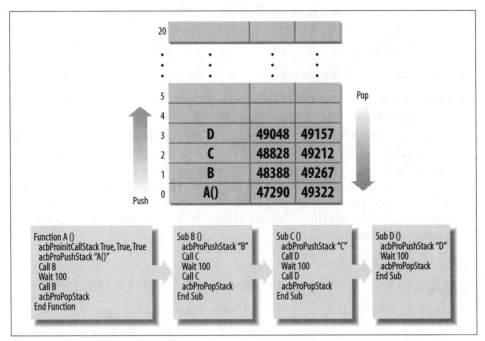

Figure 7-4. The profile stack and the sample routines used to fill it

```
********************************
+ Entering procedure: A( )
   + Entering procedure: B
      + Entering procedure: C
         + Entering procedure: D
         - Exiting procedure : D          101 msecs.
         + Entering procedure: D
         - Exiting procedure : D          100 msecs.
      - Exiting procedure : C             301 msecs.
      + Entering procedure: C
         + Entering procedure: D
         - Exiting procedure : D          100 msecs.
         + Entering procedure: D
         - Exiting procedure : D          100 msecs.
      - Exiting procedure : C             300 msecs.
   - Exiting procedure : B                701 msecs.
   + Entering procedure: B
      + Entering procedure: C
         + Entering procedure: D
         - Exiting procedure : D          100 msecs.
         + Entering procedure: D
         - Exiting procedure : D          100 msecs.
      - Exiting procedure : C             300 msecs.
      + Entering procedure: C
         + Entering procedure: D
         - Exiting procedure : D          100 msecs.
         + Entering procedure: D
```

```
          - Exiting procedure : D                    101 msecs.
        - Exiting procedure : C                      301 msecs.
      - Exiting procedure : B                        701 msecs.
    - Exiting procedure : A( )                      1513 msecs.
```

To incorporate this sort of profiling into your own applications, follow these steps:

1. Import the module basProfiler into your application. This module includes all the procedures needed to initialize and use the profile stack.

2. Insert a call to *acbProInitCallStack* into code that's executed when your application starts up. In the Solution in Recipe 7.2, you might have gotten by without calling the initialization routine. In this situation, however, you must call *acbProInitCallStack* each time you want to profile your code, or the profile stack will not work correctly. To call *acbProInitCallStack*, you must pass it three parameters, all of which are logical values (True or False). Table 7-2 lists the question answered by each of the parameters.

Table 7-2. Parameters for acbProInitCallStack

Parameter name	Usage
blnDisplay	Display message box if an error occurs?
blnLog	Write to a log file or just track items in an array in memory?
blnTimeStamp	If writing to the log file, also write out time values?

The procedure initializes some global variables and, if you're writing to a log file, writes a log header to the file. A typical call to *acbProInitCallStack* might look like this:

```
acbProInitCallStack False, True, True
```

3. For each procedure in your application, place a call to *acbProPushStack* as the first statement. This procedure places the value it's passed on the top of the stack, along with the current time. As the single argument for each call, pass the name of the current procedure. Our example places a pair of parentheses after function names and nothing after subroutine names, as a matter of style. As the last line in each procedure, add a call to *acbProPopStack*, which will remove the current name from the top of the stack and record the current time.

4. You can retrieve the name of the currently executing procedure at any time by calling the *acbProCurrentProc* function. This function looks at the top of the stack and returns the string it finds there.

5. To review the outcome of your logging, view the file *LOGFILE.TXT* (in your Access directory) in any text editor. If you followed the previous steps carefully, you should see matching entry and exit points for every routine. Nested levels are indented in the printout, and entry and exit points are marked differently (entry points with a "+" and exit points with a "-").

Discussion

The module you imported from *07-03.MDB*, basProfiler, includes all the code that maintains the profiler. There are five public entry points to the module, as shown in Table 7-3.

Table 7-3. The five entry points into basProfiler

Procedure name	Purpose	Parameters
acbProInitStack	Initialize the profile stack.	
acbProPushStack	Add an item to the profile stack.	A string to push
acbProPopStack	Remove an item from the profile stack.	
acbProCurrentProc	Retrieve the name of the current procedure.	
acbProLogString	Add any string to the log file.	A string to log

In general, the profiler works almost exactly like the simpler procedure stack shown in the Solution in Recipe 7.2. As a matter of fact, the code for this solution was written first and was then stripped down for use in the simpler example. This example includes the code necessary to write to the file on disk as well as to gather timing information. The next few paragraphs outline the major differences and how they work.

Whereas the Solution in Recipe 7.2 used a simple array of strings to hold the stack information, the profiler also needs to store starting and ending times for each routine. To create the stack, it uses an array of a user-defined type, acbStack, which is defined as follows:

```
Type acbStack
    strItem As String
    lngStart As Long
    lngEnd As Long
End Type
Dim maStack(0 To acbcMaxStack) As acbStack
```

Access provides the *Timer* function, which returns the number of seconds since midnight, but this resolution won't give you enough information for measuring the duration of procedures in VBA. Another option is Windows's t function, which returns the number of milliseconds since you started Windows. *TimeGetTime* resets itself to every 48 days, whereas *Timer* resets once every day—if you need to time a lengthy operation, *timeGetTime* provides a mechanism for measuring time spans longer than a single day (and makes it possible to measure time spans that cross midnight). Of course, if you're timing an operation that takes more than a day, you're probably not going to care about millisecond accuracy, but that's what you get! The code in basProfiler calls *timeGetTime* to retrieve the current "time" whenever you push or pop a value and stores it in the stack array. You can call *timeGetTime* in any application, once you include this declaration in a global module:

```
Public Declare Function timeGetTime _
  Lib "Kernel32" ( ) As Long
```

The code in basTestProfiler also uses *timeGetTime* in the *Wait* subroutine. This procedure does nothing but wait for the requested number of milliseconds, calling DoEvents inside the loop and giving Windows time to do its work:

```
Public Sub Wait (intWait As Integer)
   Dim lngStart As Long
   lngStart = timeGetTime( )
   Do While timeGetTime( ) < lngStart + intWait
      DoEvents
   Loop
End Sub
```

The code in basProfiler opens and closes the output file each time it needs to write a piece of information. This slows down your application, but it ensures that if your machine crashes for some reason, your log file will always be current. Although you'll never directly call this routine, if you've never used Access to write directly to a text file you may find it interesting to see how it does its work.

The *acbProWriteToLog* procedure first checks to see if an error has ever occurred in the logging mechanism (that is, if mfLogErrorOccurred has been set to True). If so, it doesn't try to write anything to the file, because something may be wrong with the disk. If not, it gets a free file handle, opens the log file for appending, writes the item to the file, and then closes it. The following is the source code for the *acbProWrite-ToLog* routine:

```
Private Sub acbProWriteToLog (strItem As String)
    Dim intFile As Integer

    On Error GoTo HandleErr

    ' If an error has EVER occurred in this session,
    ' just get out of here.
    If mfLogErrorOccurred Then Exit Sub

    intFile = FreeFile
    Open acbcLogFile For Append As intFile
    Print #intFile, strItem
    Close #intFile

ExitHere:
    Exit Sub

HandleErr:
    mfLogErrorOccurred = True
    MsgBox Err & ": " & Err.Description, , "Writing to Log"
    Resume ExitHere
End Sub
```

As in the Solution in Recipe 7.2, you'll find that for the procedure stack profiler mechanism to be of any value, you must be conscientious about the placement of your calls to *acbProPushStack* and *acbProPopStack*. If you have multiple exit points from routines, this is a good time to try to consolidate them. If you can't, you'll need to make sure that you've placed a call to *acbProPopStack* before every exit point in each procedure.

If you attempt to decipher the log file, you'll notice that the elapsed time for each procedure must also include any procedures it happens to call, as in the example of *A* calling *B*, which calls *C*, which calls *D*. The elapsed time for function *A* was 1,702 ms. That's the time that elapsed between the calls to *acbProPushStack* and *acbPro-PopStack* in function *A*, including the time it took to run all the calls to *B*, *C*, and *D*. This isn't necessarily a problem, nor is it wrong, but you should be aware that there's no way to "stop the clock" while in subordinate procedures.

The code for the profiler includes another public entry point, *acbProLogString*. The profiler doesn't actually call this procedure, but your own code can. Pass it a single string, and the profile will send that string to the log file for you. For example, the following code will append "This is a test" to the log file:

```
acbProLogString "This is a test"
```

7.4 Multitask Your VBA Code

Problem

If your VBA code includes a loop that runs for more than just a second or two, Access seems to come to a halt. You can't move the windows on the screen, and mouse-clicks inside Access are disregarded until your code has finished running. Why is this happening? Is there something you can do to relinquish some control?

Solution

You may have noticed that it's possible to tie up Access with a simple bit of VBA code. Though 32-bit Windows is multithreaded, this helps only if the applications running under it are also multithreaded. It appears that the executing VBA code ties up Access's processing, so the multithreaded nature of Windows doesn't help. If your code contains loops that run for a while, you should make a conscious effort to give Windows time to catch up and do its own work. VBA includes the DoEvents statement, which effectively yields time to Windows so that Access can perform whatever other tasks it must. Effective use of DoEvents can make the difference between an Access application that hogs Access's ability to multitask and one that allows Access to run smoothly while your VBA code is executing.

To see the problem in action, load and run the form frmDoEvents (in *07-04.MDB*). Figure 7-5 shows the form in use. The form includes three command buttons, each of which causes the label with the caption "Watch Me Grow!" to change its width from 500 to 3500 twips (in Figure 7-5, you can see only a portion of the label), in a loop like this:

```
Me.lblGrow1.Width = 500
For intI = 0 To 3000
    Me.lblGrow1.Width = Me.lblGrow1.Width + 1
    ' Without this call to Repaint, you'll
    ' never see any changes on the screen.
    Me.Repaint
Next intI
```

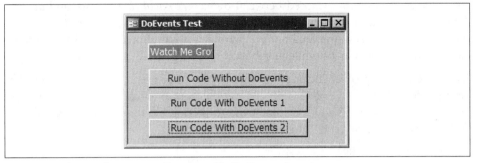

Figure 7-5. The sample DoEvents Test form, frmDoEvents, in action

To test the effects of DoEvents, try these steps:

1. Press the "Run Code Without DoEvents" button. The code attached to this button will change the width of the label inside a loop without yielding time to Access. While the code is running, try to click on another button on the form or to move or size the active window. You will find that any of these tasks is impossible while the label is expanding. Once the label has finished growing, Access will display any actions you attempted to make during the process.

2. Try the same loop with DoEvents inserted. Click the second button, labeled "Run Code With DoEvents 1". This time, as the code executes, you will be able to move or size the active window. In addition, you can click on any of the form's buttons while the code is running. The next step tests this capability.

3. While the label is growing, click on the "Run Code With DoEvents 1" button many times in quick succession. Every time you click the button, Access starts up another instance of the Click event procedure, and each instance continues to make the label grow. This is called recursion, in which multiple calls are made into the same routine, each starting before the last instance has completed. Each time you call the Click event, you use a bit of Access's stack space (a memory area set aside for each procedure's entry information and local variables). It's possible that, with many invocations, you will use up that memory. Using versions of Access later than Access 95, we've never made this happen. Using

Access 2, it was easy to do. The next step offers a solution to this recursion problem.

4. Click the third button, labeled "Run Code with DoEvents 2". While the label is expanding, try clicking on the button again. You'll see that this time your clicks won't have any effect. The code attached to this button checks to see if it's already running and, if so, exits the code. This method solves the problem of recursive calls to DoEvents.

Discussion

The code attached to the first button does its work without any concern for Windows or other running applications. When you press it, it executes this code:

```
Private Sub cmdNoDoevents_Click()
    Dim intI As Integer

    Me.lblGrow1.Width = 500
    For intI = 0 To 3000
        Me.lblGrow1.Width = Me.lblGrow1.Width + 1
        ' Without this call to Repaint, you'll
        ' never see any changes on the screen.
        Me.Repaint
    Next intI
End Sub
```

Because the code never gives Windows time to "catch up," you must include the call to Me.Repaint to make sure the form repaints itself after each change. To see how this works, comment out that line and press the first button again. You'll see that the screen won't repaint until the entire operation is done.

The code attached to the second button does the same work, but it calls DoEvents within the loop. With that statement added, you no longer need the call to Me. Repaint, because DoEvents allows Windows to take care of the pending repaints. It also allows you to use the mouse and other applications while this loop is running. The code attached to the second button looks like this:

```
Private Sub TestDoEvents()
    Dim intI As Integer

    Me.lblGrow1.Width = 500
    For intI = 0 To 3000
        Me.lblGrow1.Width = Me.lblGrow1.Width + 1
        DoEvents
    Next intI
End Sub

Private Sub cmdDoEvents1_Click()
    TestDoEvents
End Sub
```

The problem with this code, as mentioned in Step 2, is that nothing keeps you from initiating it again while it's running; if you press the same button while the code is in the middle of the loop, Access will start up the same procedure again. Every time Access starts running a VBA routine, it stores information about the routine and its local variables in a reserved area of memory, called its "stack". The size of this area is fixed and limits the number of procedures that can run concurrently. If you press that button over and over again in quick succession, it's possible that you'll overrun Access's stack space.

It's doubtful that you'll ever be able to reproduce this problem with this tiny example. Though the stack space was limited to 40 KB in Access 2, it was increased to a much larger size in Access 95 and later versions. You'd have to press that button very fast for a very long time to fill up that much stack space. However, in more complex situations, if you were passing a large amount of data to a procedure in its parameter list, this could still be a problem.

The third button on the form demonstrates the solution to this problem. It ensures that its code isn't already running before it starts the loop. If it's already in progress, the code just exits. The code attached to the third button looks like this:

```
Private Sub cmdDoEvents2_Click( )
    Static blnInHere As Boolean

    If blnInHere Then Exit Sub
    blnInHere = True
    TestDoEvents
    blnInHere = False
End Sub
```

It uses a static variable, *blnInHere*, to keep track of whether the routine is already running. If *blnInHere* is currently True, it exits. If not, it sets the variable to True and then calls cmdDoEvents1_Click (the previous code fragment). Once cmdDoEvents1_Click returns, cmdDoEvents2_Click sets *blnInHere* back to False, clearing the way for another invocation.

DoEvents is one of the most misunderstood elements of VBA. No matter what programmers would *like* DoEvents to do, under versions of Access later than Access 95 it does nothing more than yield time to Access so it can process all the messages in its message queue. It has no effect on the Access database engine itself and can't be used to slow things down or help timing issues (other than those involving Windows messages). When used in VBA code, DoEvents releases control to the operating environment, which doesn't return control until it has processed the events in its queue and handled all the keys in the SendKeys queue. Access will ignore DoEvents in:

- A user-defined procedure that calculates a field in a query, form, or report
- A user-defined procedure that creates a list to fill a combo or list box

As you can see from the second button on the sample form, recursively calling DoEvents can lead to trouble. You should take steps, as in the example of the third button, to make sure that this won't occur in your applications.

7.5 Programmatically Add Items to a List or Combo Box

Problem

Getting items into a list or combo box from a data source is elementary in Access. Sometimes, though, you need to put things into a list box that you don't have stored in a table. In Visual Basic and other implementations of VBA-hosted environments, and in Access 2002 and later, this is simple: you just use the AddItem method. But Access list boxes in versions prior to 2002 don't support this method. How can you add to a list box items that aren't stored in a table?

Solution

Access list boxes (and combo boxes) in versions prior to Access 2002 didn't support the AddItem method that Visual Basic programmers are used to using. To make it easy for you to get bound data into list and combo boxes, the Access developers originally didn't supply a simple technique for loading unbound data. To get around this limitation, there are two methods you can use to place data into an Access list or combo box: you can programmatically build the RowSource string yourself, or you can call a list-filling callback function. Providing the RowSource string is easy, but it works in only the simplest of situations. A callback function, though, will work in any situation. This solution demonstrates both methods. In addition, this solution demonstrates using the AddItem method of ListBox and ComboBox controls, added in Access 2002.

One important question, of course, is why you would ever need either of the more complex techniques for filling your list or combo box. You can always pull data from a table, query, or SQL expression directly into the control, so why bother with all this work? The answer is simple. Sometimes you don't know ahead of time what data you're going to need, and the data's not stored in a table. Or perhaps you need to load the contents of an array into the control and you don't need to store the data permanently. Prior to Access 2002, you had no choice but to either create a list-filling callback function, or modify the RowSource property of the control yourself. Starting in Access 2002, you can also use the AddItem method to solve many list filling requirements.

The following sections walk you through using all three of the techniques for modifying the contents of a list or combo box while your application is running. The first example modifies the value of the RowSource property, given that the RowSource-Type property is set to Value List. The second example covers list-filling callback functions. The final example shows how to use the AddItem method of the control.

Filling a list box by calling the AddItem method

1. Open the form frmAddItem in *07-05.MDB*.
2. Change the contents of the list box by choosing either Days or Months from the option group on the left. Try both settings and change the number of columns to get a feel for how this method works. Figure 7-6 shows the form set to display month names in three columns.

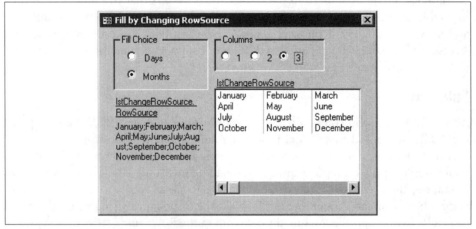

Figure 7-6. The sample form, frmRowSource, displaying months in three columns

Filling a list box by modifying the RowSource property

1. Open the form frmRowSource in *07-05.MDB*.
2. Change the contents of the list box by choosing either Days or Months from the option group on the left. Try both settings and change the number of columns, to get a feel for how this method works. Figure 7-6 shows the form set to display month names in three columns.

Filling a list box by creating a list-filling callback function

1. Open the form frmListFill in *07-05.MDB*.
2. Select a weekday from the first list box. The second list box will show you the date of that day this week, plus the next three instances of that weekday. Figure 7-7 shows the form with Wednesday, March 14, 2001, selected.
3. To use this method, set the control's RowSourceType property to the name of a function (without an equals sign or parentheses). Functions called this way must

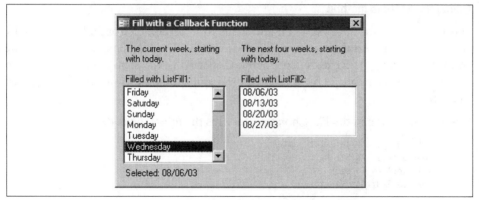

Figure 7-7. Using list-filling callback functions to fill the lists on frmListFill

meet strict requirements, as discussed in the next section. Figure 7-8 shows the properties sheet for the list box on frmListFill, showing the RowSourceType property with the name of the list-filling function.

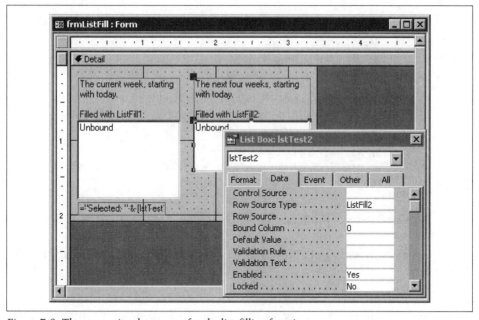

Figure 7-8. The properties sheet entry for the list-filling function

Discussion

This section explains the two methods for programmatically filling list and combo boxes. The text refers only to filling list boxes, but the same techniques apply to combo boxes. You may find it useful to open up the form module for each form as it's discussed here.

Calling the AddItem method

Starting with Access 2002, you can add items to a ListBox or ComboBox control by simply calling the AddItem method of the control. (You can remove items from the control by calling its RemoveItem method, specifying the item number or text to remove.) This technique is by far the simplest and should be your first choice, given the option.

Selecting an option in the Fill Choice group runs the following code:

```
Private Sub grpChoice_AfterUpdate( )
    Dim strList As String
    Dim intI As Integer
    Dim varStart As Variant

    lstAddItem.RowSourceType = "Value List"

    ' Clear out the list.
    lstAddItem.RowSource = vbNullString
    lstAddItem.ColumnCount = 1
    grpColumns = 1

    Select Case Me.grpChoice
        Case 1  ' Days
            ' Get last Sunday's date.
            varStart = Now - WeekDay(Now)
            ' Loop through all the week days.
            For intI = 1 To 7
                lstAddItem.AddItem Format(varStart + intI, "dddd")
            Next intI

        Case 2  ' Months
            For intI = 1 To 12
                lstAddItem.AddItem Format(DateSerial(2004, intI, 1), "mmmm")
            Next intI
    End Select

    Me.txtFillString = lstAddItem.RowSource
End Sub
```

This code starts by setting the RowSourceType property of the control to the text, "Value List":

```
lstAddItem.RowSourceType = "Value List"
```

This step is crucial: unless you've set the RowSourceType property correctly, either at design time or in your code, you won't be able to call the AddItem or RemoveItem methods.

Next, the code clears and resets the list's formatting:

```
lstAddItem.RowSource = vbNullString
lstAddItem.ColumnCount = 1
grpColumns = 1
```

Then, depending on the choice you've made, the code adds days of the week or months of the year to the ListBox control:

```
Select Case Me.grpChoice
    Case 1  ' Days
        ' Get last Sunday's date.
        varStart = Now - WeekDay(Now)
        ' Loop through all the week days.
        For intI = 1 To 7
            lstAddItem.AddItem Format(varStart + intI, "dddd")
        Next intI

    Case 2  ' Months
        For intI = 1 To 12
            lstAddItem.AddItem Format(DateSerial(2004, intI, 1), "mmmm")
        Next intI
End Select
```

In order to verify that, under the covers, the code is simply manipulating the Row-Source property for you, the example ends by displaying the RowSource property in a TextBox control on the form:

```
Me.txtFillString = lstAddItem.RowSource
```

 Beware that even though it appears that you're actually adding items to the control, what you're really doing is modifying the RowSource property of the control. As such, you're limited by the same restrictions as if you were setting the property manually (see the next section). Specifically, you're limited to the allowed size of the RowSource property, which was 2048 characters in Access 2002 (the size may be larger in your version of Access).

Modifying the RowSource property

If you're using Access 2002 or later, you won't want to use this technique. On the other hand, for earlier versions of Access, this can be a simple way to create unbound lists. If you set a list box's RowSourceType property to Value List, you can supply a list of items, separated with semicolons, that will fill the list. By placing this list in the control's RowSource property, you tell Access to display the items one by one in each row and column that it needs to fill. Because you're placing data directly into the properties sheet, you're limited by the amount of space available in the properties sheet (this value varies depending on the version of Access).

You can modify the RowSource property of a list box at any time by placing into it a semicolon-delimited list of values. The ColumnCount property plays a part, in that Access fills the rows first and then the columns. You can see this for yourself if you modify the ColumnCount property on the sample form (frmRowSource).

The sample form creates a list of either the days in a week or the months in a year, based on the value and option group on the form. The code that performs the work looks like this:

```
Select Case Me.grpChoice
    Case 1  ' Days
        ' Get last Sunday's date.
        varStart = Now - WeekDay(Now)
        ' Loop through all the days of the week.
        For intI = 1 To 7
            strList = strList & ";" & Format(varStart + intI, "dddd")
        Next intI

    Case 2   ' Months
        For intI = 1 To 12
            strList = strList & ";" & Format(DateSerial(2004, intI, 1), "mmmm")
        Next intI
End Select

' Get rid of the extra "; " at the beginning.
strList = Mid(strList, 2)
Me.txtFillString = strList
```

Depending on the choice in grpChoice, you'll end up with either a string of days like this:

```
Sunday; Monday; Tuesday; Wednesday; Thursday; Friday; Saturday; Sunday
```

or a string of months like this:

```
January; February; March; April; May; June; July; August; September; October; _
November; December
```

Once you've built up the string, make sure that the RowSourceType property is set correctly and then insert the new RowSource string:

```
lstChangeRowSource.RowSourceType = "Value List"
lstChangeRowSource.RowSource = strList
```

If you intend to use this method, modifying the RowSource property, make sure you understand its main limitation: because it writes the string containing all the values for the control into the control's properties sheet, it's limited by the number of characters the properties sheet can hold.

If you're using a version of Access prior to Access 2002, you can use at most 2,048 characters in the RowSource property. If you need more data than that, you'll need to use a different method. If you're using Access 2002 or later you shouldn't have a problem, because the size has been greatly expanded. On the other hand, in those versions, you're better off using the AddItem method instead.

Creating a list-filling callback function

This technique, which involves creating a special function that provides the information Access needs to fill your list box, is not well documented in the Access help. Filling a list using a callback function provides a great deal of flexibility, and it's not difficult. This technique provides the greatest flexibility, and isn't limited by the size of the RowSource property.

The concept is quite simple: you provide Access with a function that, when requested, returns information about the control you're attempting to fill. Access "asks you questions" about the number of rows, the number of columns, the width of the columns, the column formatting, and the actual data itself. Your function must react to these requests and provide the information so that Access can fill the control with data. This is the only situation in Access where you provide a function that you never need to call. Access calls your function as it needs information in order to fill the control. The sample form frmFillList uses two of these functions to fill its two list boxes.

To communicate with Access, your function must accept five specific parameters. Table 7-4 lists those parameters and explains the purpose of each. (The parameter names are arbitrary and are provided here as examples only. The order of the parameters, however, is not arbitrary; they must appear in the order listed in Table 7-4.)

Table 7-4. The required parameters for all list-filling functions

Argument	Data type	Description
ctl	Control	A reference to the control being filled.
varId	Variant	A unique value that identifies the control that's being filled (you assign this value in your code). Although you could use this value to let you use the same function for multiple controls, this is most often not worth the extraordinary trouble it causes.
lngRow	Long	The row currently being filled (zero-based).
lngCol	Long	The column currently being filled (zero-based).
intCode	Integer	A code that indicates the kind of information that Access is requesting.

Access uses the final parameter, *intCode*, to let you know what information it's currently requesting. Access places a particular value in that variable, and it's up to your code to react to that request and supply the necessary information as the return value of your function. Table 7-5 lists the possible values of *intCode*, the meaning of each, and the value your function must return to Access in response to each.

Table 7-5. The values of intCode, their meanings, and their return values

Constant	Meaning	Return value
acLBInitialize	Initialize the data.	Nonzero if the function will be able to fill the list; Null or 0 otherwise

Table 7-5. The values of intCode, their meanings, and their return values (continued)

Constant	Meaning	Return value
acLBOpen	Open the control.	Nonzero unique ID if the function will be able to fill the list; Null or 0 otherwise
acLBGetRowCount	Get the number of rows.	Number of rows in the list; -1 if unknown (see the text for information)
acLBGetColumnCount	Get the number of columns.	Number of columns in the list (cannot be 0)
acLBGetColumnWidth	Get the column widths.	Width (in twips) of the column specified in the *lngCol* argument (zero-based); specify -1 to use the default width
acLBGetValue	Get a value to display.	Value to be displayed in the row and column specified by the *lngRow* and *lngCol* arguments
acLBGetFormat	Get the column formats.	Format string to be used by the column specified in *lngCol*
acLBClose	Not used.	
acLBEnd	End (when the form is closed).	Nothing

You'll find that almost all of your list-filling functions will be structured the same way. Therefore, you may find it useful to always start with the *ListFillSkeleton* function, which is set up to receive all the correct parameters and includes a Select Case statement to handle each of the useful values of *intCode*. All you need to do is change its name and make it return some real values. The *ListFillSkeleton* function is as follows:

```
Function ListFillSkeleton (ctl As Control, _
  varId As Variant, lngRow As Long, lngCol As Long, _
  intCode As Integer) As Variant

    Dim varRetval As Variant

    Select Case intCode
      Case acLBInitialize
        ' Could you initialize?
        varRetval = True

      Case acLBOpen
        ' What's the unique identifier?
        varRetval = Timer

      Case acLBGetRowCount
        ' How many rows are there to be?

      Case acLBGetColumnCount
        ' How many columns are there to be?
```

```
    Case acLBGetValue
        ' What's the value in each row/column to be?

    Case acLBGetColumnWidth
        ' How many twips wide should each column be?
        ' (optional)

    Case acLBGetFormat
        ' What's the format for each column to be?
        ' (optional)

    Case acLBEnd
        ' Just clean up, if necessary (optional, unless you use
        ' an array whose memory you want to release).

    End Select
    ListFillSkeleton = varRetval
End Function
```

For example, the following function from frmListFill, *ListFill1*, fills in the first list box on the form. This function fills in a two-column list box, with the second column hidden (its width is set to 0 twips). Each time Access calls the function with acLBGetValue in *intCode*, the function calculates a new value for the date and returns it as the return value. The source code for *ListFill1* is:

```
Private Function ListFill1(ctl As Control, varId As Variant, _
   lngRow As Long,  lngCol As Long, intCode As Integer)

    Select Case intCode
        Case acLBInitialize
            ' Could you initialize?
            ListFill1 = True

        Case acLBOpen
            ' What's the unique identifier?
            ListFill1 = Timer

        Case acLBGetRowCount
            ' How many rows are there to be?
            ListFill1 = 7

        Case acLBGetColumnCount
            ' How many columns are there to be?

            ' The first column will hold the day of the week.
            ' The second, hidden column will hold the actual date.
            ListFill1 = 2

        Case acLBGetColumnWidth
            ' How many twips wide should each column be?

            ' Set the width of the second column to 0.
```

```
      ' Remember, they're zero-based.
      If lngCol = 1 Then ListFill1 = 0

  Case acLBGetFormat
    ' What's the format for each column to be?

    ' Set the format for the first column so
    ' that it displays the day of the week.
    If lngCol = 0 Then
       ListFill1 = "dddd"
    Else
       ListFill1 = "mm/dd/yy"
    End If

  Case acLBGetValue
    ' What's the value for each row in each column to be?

    ' No matter which column you're in, return
    ' the date lngRow days from now.
    ListFill1 = Now + lngRow

  Case acLBEnd
    ' Just clean up, if necessary.

   End Select
End Function
```

The next example, which fills the second list box on the sample form, fills an array of values in the initialization step (acLBInitialize) and returns items from the array when requested. This function, *ListFill2*, displays the next four instances of a particular day of the week. That is, if you choose Monday in the first list box, this function will fill the second list box with the date of the Monday in the current week, along with the dates of the next three Mondays. The source code for *ListFill2* is:

```
Private Function ListFill2( _
  ctl As Control, varId As Variant, lngRow As Long, _
  lngCol As Long, intCode As Integer)

Const MAXDATES = 4

    Static varStartDate As Variant
    Static adtmDates(0 To MAXDATES) As Date
    Dim intI As Integer
    Dim varRetval As Variant

    Select Case intCode
       Case acLBInitialize
          ' Could you initialize?

          ' Do the initialization.  This is code
          ' you only want to execute once.
          varStartDate = Me.lstTest1
          If Not IsNull(varStartDate) Then
```

```
            For intI = 0 To MAXDATES - 1
                adtmDates(intI) = DateAdd("d", 7 * intI, varStartDate)
            Next intI
            varRetval = True
        Else
            varRetval = False
        End If

    Case acLBOpen
        ' What's the unique identifier?
        varRetval = Timer

    Case acLBGetRowCount
        ' How many rows are there to be?
        varRetval = MAXDATES

    Case acLBGetFormat
        ' What's the format for each column to be?
        varRetval = "mm/dd/yy"

    Case acLBGetValue
        ' What's the value for each row in each column to be?
        varRetval = adtmDates(lngRow)

    Case acLBEnd
        ' Just clean up, if necessary.
        Erase adtmDates
    End Select
    ListFill2 = varRetval
End Function
```

Note that the array this function fills, adtmDates, is declared as a static variable. Declaring it this way makes it persistent: its value remains available between calls to the function. Because the code fills the array in the acLBInitialize case but doesn't use it until the multiple calls in the acLBGetValue case, adtmDates must "hang around" between calls to the function. If you fill an array with data for your control, it's imperative that you declare the array as static.

You should also consider the fact that Access calls the acLBInitialize case only once, but it calls the acLBGetValue case at least once for every data item to be displayed. In this tiny example, that barely makes a difference. If you're doing considerable work to calculate values for display, however, you should put all the time-consuming work in the acLBInitialize case and have the acLBGetValue case do as little as possible. This optimization can make a big difference if you have a large number of values to calculate and display.

There are three more things you should note about this second list box example:

- In the acLBEnd case, the function clears out the memory used by the array. In this small example, this hardly matters. If you are filling a large array with data, you'd want to make sure that the data is released at this point. For dynamic arrays (where you specify the size at runtime), Erase releases all the memory. For fixed-size arrays, Erase empties out all the elements.

- This example didn't include code for all the possible cases of *intCode*. If you don't need a specific case, don't bother coding for it. There was no need to set the column widths here, so there's no code handling acLBGetColumnWidth.

- At the time of this writing, there's a small error in the way Access handles these callback functions. Although it correctly calls the acLBInitialize case only once when you open a form that requires a control to be filled with the function, if you later change the RowSourceType in code, Access will call the acLBInitialize case twice. This doesn't come up often, but you should be aware that there are circumstances under which Access will erroneously call this section of your code more times than you intended. To solve this problem, you can use a static or global variable as a flag to keep track of the fact that the initialization has been done and opt not to execute the code after the first pass through.

In the list-filling callback function method, when Access requests the number of rows in the control (i.e., when it passes acLBGetRowCount in *intCode*), you'll usually be able to return an accurate value. Sometimes, however, you won't know the number of rows or won't be able to get the information easily. For example, if you're filling the list box with the results of a query that returns a large number of rows, you won't want to perform the MoveLast method you'd need to find out how many rows the query returned—MoveLast requires Access to walk through all the rows returned from the query and would make the load time for the list box too long. Instead, respond to acLBGetRowCount with a -1. This tells Access that you'll tell it later how many rows there are. Then, in response to the acLBGetValue case, return data until you've reached the end. Once you return Null in response to the acLBGetValue case, Access understands that there's no more data.

This method has its pitfalls, too. Although it allows you to load the list box with data almost immediately, the vertical scrollbar won't be able to operate correctly until you've scrolled down to the end. If you can tolerate this side effect, returning -1 in response to acLBGetRowCount will significantly speed the loading of massive amounts of data into list and combo box controls.

To provide values for the acLBGetColumnWidth case, you can specify a different width for each column based on the *lngCol* parameter. To convert from inches to twips, multiply the value by 1,440. For example, to specify a 1/2-inch column, return 0.5 × 1,440.

You might wonder when you would use any of these techniques. In Access 2002 or later, your best bet is to use the AddItem method whenever possible. Under the covers, this method executes the same sort of code as if you were to modify the Row-Source property value yourself. (You don't really need to ever modify the RowSource property manually, in Access 2002 or later—calling the AddItem and RemoveItem methods does the same sort of thing for you.) Remember, however, that the Row-Source property value is limited in size. For large lists of values, perhaps with many columns, you may run out of space before you run out of data. In that case, you'll be required to use the list-filling callback function technique. If you're using Access 2000 or an earlier version, you'll need to use the list-filling callback technique for complex lists, or to create the RowSource property value in code yourself for simpler lists.

7.6   Pass a Variable Number of Parameters to a Procedure

Problem

You need a procedure that will work on a list of items, and you don't know ahead of time how many there will be. You know that VBA will allow you to use optional parameters, but this requires you to know exactly how many items you might ever need to pass, and in your case, it's impossible to predict that value. How can you accomplish this?

Solution

You have two choices in solving this problem: you can pass an array as a parameter, or you can pass a comma-delimited list, which Access will convert into an array for you. An array (an ordered list of items) must contain a single data type. By using the variant data type, though, you can pass a list of varying types into your procedure. This solution demonstrates both these techniques.

From *07-06.MDB*, load the module basArrays in design mode and do the following:

1. Open the Immediate window (press Ctrl+G or choose the View → Immediate Window menu item). In these steps, you will run code from the Immediate window.

2. If you need a procedure that will take a list of words and convert each to upper-case, you can use the *UCaseArray* procedure. To test it, type the following in the Immediate window:

   TestUCase 5

   You can replace the 5 in the command line with any value between 1 and 26. The procedure will create as many strings as you request, place them into an array, and then call *UCaseArray*. This procedure will convert all the strings in the array to uppercase. The test procedure will display the original version, followed by the altered version of the array. As you can see, no matter how many items you specify for the *UCaseArray* procedure to work on, it'll convert them all to uppercase. Figure 7-9 shows this procedure in use.

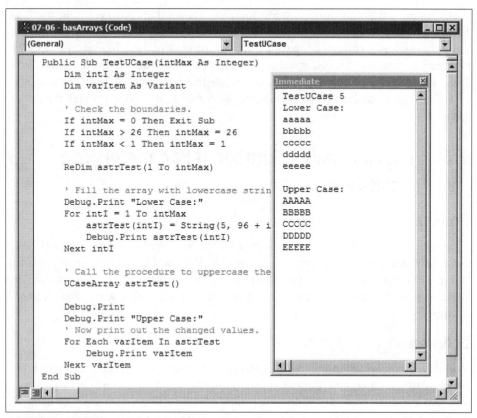

```
07-06 - basArrays (Code)                                    _ □ X

(General)                      ▼   TestUCase                      ▼

    Public Sub TestUCase(intMax As Integer)
        Dim intI As Integer
        Dim varItem As Variant              Immediate              ☒

        ' Check the boundaries.                 TestUCase 5
        If intMax = 0 Then Exit Sub             Lower Case:
        If intMax > 26 Then intMax = 26         aaaaa
        If intMax < 1 Then intMax = 1           bbbbb
                                                ccccc
        ReDim astrTest(1 To intMax)             ddddd
                                                eeeee
        ' Fill the array with lowercase strin
        Debug.Print "Lower Case:"               Upper Case:
        For intI = 1 To intMax                  AAAAA
            astrTest(intI) = String(5, 96 + i   BBBBB
            Debug.Print astrTest(intI)          CCCCC
        Next intI                               DDDDD
                                                EEEEE
        ' Call the procedure to uppercase the
        UCaseArray astrTest()

        Debug.Print
        Debug.Print "Upper Case:"
        ' Now print out the changed values.
        For Each varItem In astrTest
            Debug.Print varItem
        Next varItem
    End Sub
```

Figure 7-9. TestUCase with five strings converted

3. Say you need a procedure that can accept any number of numeric arguments and perform some operation on them. The sample procedure *SumThemUp* accepts an array of integers, calculates their sum, and returns the total. To try it, type:

    TestSum 15

in the Immediate window (you can use any number between 1 and 20). The sample routine, *TestSum*, will generate an array full of random integers between 1 and 9 and will send the array to *SumThemUp* for processing. Figure 7-10 shows *TestSum* working with 15 values.

4. You may need to write a function that can accept a list of values instead of an array. The ParamArray declaration modifier allows you to do this. Try the *Min-Value* function in basArrays: pass to it a comma-delimited list of values, and the function will return the minimum numeric value from the list you entered. For example:

    varMin = MinValue(0, -10, 15)

will return -10, which is the minimum of the three values you passed it.

```
07-06 - basArrays (Code)

(General)                              TestSum

   Public Sub TestSum(Optional intMax As Integer = 10)

       Dim intI As Integer
       Dim varItem As Variant

       ' Check the boundaries.
       If intMax = 0 Then Exit Sub
       If intMax > 20 Then intMax = 20
       If intMax < 1 Then intMax = 1

       ' Since your dimensioning to a variable size, you
       ' must use ReDim.
       ReDim aintValues(1 To intMax) As Integer

       ' Can't SET values with For...Each if
       ' using variant array.
       For intI = 1 To intMax
           aintValues(intI) = Int(9 * Rnd + 1)
       Next intI

       Debug.Print "The values are: ";
       For Each varItem In aintValues()
           Debug.Print varItem;
       Next varItem
       Debug.Print

       Debug.Print "The sum is: " & SumThemUp(aintValues())
   End Sub
```

```
Immediate
   TestSum 5
   The values are:   3   3   8   8   6
   The sum is: 28
```

Figure 7-10. TestSum summing 15 values

Both *UCaseArray* and *SumThemUp* accept a variant as a parameter. This variant variable can hold either a single value or an array of values. From the calling end, you can pass either a variant or an actual array of values. To send an array as a parameter, you must add the trailing ( ) characters, indicating to Access that the variable represents an array. Therefore, to pass the array named aintValues to *SumThemUp*, call the function like this, making sure to include the ( ) in the array name:

```
varSum = SumThemUp(aintValues( ))
```

To receive a parameter that is an array, the procedure declaration can include the parentheses:

```
Public Function SumThemUp (aintValues( ) As Integer) As Variant
```

in which case you can pass only an array. You can also declare it like this:

```
Public Function SumThemUp (varValues As Variant) As Variant
```

in which case you can pass it either a single variant value or an array of values.

Once the procedure has received the array, it needs a way to loop through all the elements of the array. Access provides two methods for walking the array: looping through the items either with a `For...Next` loop (by index number), or with a `For Each...Next` loop (without using the index). *UCaseArray* uses the first method to loop through all the members of its array, and *SumThemUp* uses the second.

To loop through the elements of an array by number, you must know the bounds of the array; i.e., the lowest and highest element numbers. Access provides two functions, *LBound* and *UBound*, to retrieve the lowest and highest element numbers. *UCaseArray* includes code like this:

```
For intI = LBound(varValues) To UBound(varValues)
    varValues(intI) = UCase(varValues(intI))
Next intI
```

This code loops through all the elements in the array, no matter what the starting and ending items are. In Basic, you can declare an array with any positive integer as its start and end points. For example, in this expression:

```
Dim avarArray(13 To 97) as Integer
```

you'd need to loop from 13 to 97 to access each element of the array. The *LBound* and *UBound* functions make it possible for generic routines to loop through all the elements of an array, even though they don't know ahead of time how many elements there will be.

The *UCaseArray* procedure is quite simple: once it determines that the input value is actually an array (using the *IsArray* function), it loops through all the elements of the passed-in array, converting each to uppercase. The array is passed by reference, using the ByRef keyword, which means that the modified array is returned to the calling procedure. The code for *UCaseArray* is:

```
Public Sub UCaseArray(ByRef varValues As Variant)

    ' Convert the entire passed-in array to uppercase.
    Dim intI As Integer

    If IsArray(varValues) Then
       For intI = LBound(varValues) To UBound(varValues)
          varValues(intI) = UCase(varValues(intI))
       Next intI
    Else
       varValues = UCase(varValues)
    End If
End Sub
```

The *SumThemUp* function is no more complex. It uses the `For Each...Next` syntax to walk through all the elements of the array, maintaining a running sum as it loops. In this case, the variant variable *varItem* takes on the value of each element of the array as it loops through the items, and adds its value to *varSum*. The source code for *SumThemUp* is:

```
Public Function SumThemUp(varValues As Variant) As Variant

    ' Find the sum of the values passed in.
```

```
      Dim varItem As Variant
      Dim varSum As Variant

      varSum = 0
      If IsArray(varValues) Then
         For Each varItem In varValues
            varSum = varSum + varItem
         Next varItem
      Else
         varSum = varValues
      End If
      SumThemUp = varSum
   End Function
```

Passing a list that Access converts to an array for you is no more difficult. To use this technique, you must declare your procedure's formal parameters so that the list of values is the last parameter the procedure expects to receive. Use the ParamArray keyword to indicate that you want to treat an incoming list as an array, and declare your array parameter as an array of variants:

```
   Public Function MinValue(ParamArray varValues( ) As Variant) As Variant
```

Once inside the procedure, you can treat the array parameter like any other array. That is, you can either loop from *LBound* to *UBound* for the array, or use a For Each. ..Next loop to visit each element.

Discussion

To use this method effectively, be aware that unless told otherwise, Access always creates arrays with the first element numbered 0. Some programmers insist on starting all arrays with 1 and so use the Option Base 1 statement in their modules' Declarations areas. Others are happy with 0 as their starting point, and some leave the option base setting at 0 (its default) but disregard the element numbered 0. You must never assume anything about the lower or upper bounds on arrays, or sooner or later generic routines won't work. If you're writing code that will be called by other programmers, you need to be aware of these variations on the normal usage.

If you decide to use the For Each...Next syntax to access all of the elements of an array, both the variable you use to loop through the elements and the array itself must be variants. In addition, note that you cannot set the values of items in an array using the For Each...Next syntax; it only allows you to retrieve the values from the array. If you want to loop through an array to set its values, you must use the standard For...Next syntax, using a numeric value as the loop counter.

In Access 2000 and later, you can use an array as the return value for a function. Thus, you could rewrite the *UCaseArray* procedure as follows:

```
   Public Function UCaseArrayFunc(ByVal varValues As Variant) As String( )
      ' Convert the entire passed in array to upper case.
      Dim intI As Integer
      Dim astrWorking( ) As String
```

```
        If IsArray(varValues) Then
            ReDim astrWorking(LBound(varValues) To UBound(varValues))
            For intI = LBound(varValues) To UBound(varValues)
                astrWorking(intI) = CStr(UCase(varValues(intI)))
            Next intI
            UCaseArrayFunc = astrWorking
        End If
    End Function
```

The advantage of this technique is that the function returns a second array and the original array, varValues, is not modified. Unlike the first example, *UCaseArray*, the array is passed ByVal, which means that *UCaseArrayFunc* works with a copy of the original array. Any modifications occurring in *UCaseArrayFunc* will affect only this copy, leaving the original array in the calling procedure unchanged.

7.7   Sort an Array in VBA

Problem

Although it's a database product, Access doesn't include a way to sort an array. You need to present sorted arrays in an application, and you can't find a reasonable way to sort them without first saving them to a table. You know you've seen array-sorting methods in other languages. Can you write a sorting routine that executes quickly?

Solution

It's true that Access doesn't provide a built-in sorting mechanism for arrays. Entire volumes in libraries are devoted to the study of various sorting and searching algorithms, but it's not necessary to dig too deep for array-sorting methods for Access. Because you'll probably place any large data sets into a table, most arrays in Access aren't very large. Therefore, almost any sort will do. This solution uses a variant of the standard quicksort algorithm. (For more information on various sorting and searching algorithms, consult your computer library. This is a *big* topic!)

To try the sorting mechanism, load the module named basSortDemo in *07-07.MDB*. From the Immediate window, type:

```
    TestSort 6
```

where the 6 can be any integer between 1 and 20, indicating the number of random integers between 1 and 99 that you want the routine to sort. The sample routine, *TestSort*, will create the array of integers and send it off to *VisSortArray*, a special version of the sorting routine *acbSortArray* that shows what it's doing as it works. Figure 7-11 shows the output from a sample session.

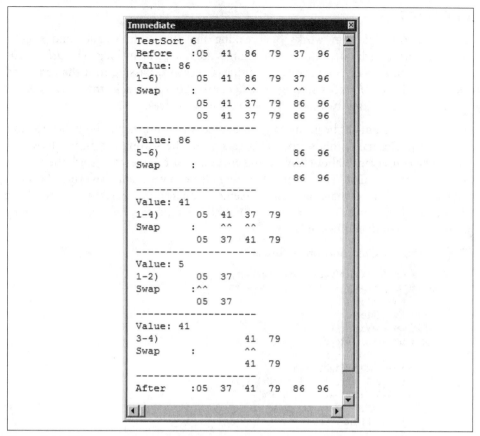

```
Immediate                                        [x]
TestSort 6
Before   :05   41   86   79   37   96
Value: 86
1-6)        05   41   86   79   37   96
Swap     :            ^^        ^^
            05   41   37   79   86   96
            05   41   37   79   86   96
--------------------
Value: 86
5-6)                            86   96
Swap     :                      ^^
                                86   96

--------------------
Value: 41
1-4)        05   41   37   79
Swap     :       ^^   ^^
            05   37   41   79
--------------------
Value: 5
1-2)        05   37
Swap     :^^
            05   37
--------------------
Value: 41
3-4)                  41   79
Swap     :            ^^
                      41   79
--------------------
After    :05   37   41   79   86   96
```

Figure 7-11. The output from a sample run of TestSort

To use this sorting code in your own applications, follow these steps:

1. Import the module named basSortArray into your application.

2. Create the array you'd like to sort. This must be an array of variants, but those variants can hold any datatype; this solution uses an array of Integers and the Solution in Recipe 7.8 uses an array of Strings.

3. Call *acbSortArray*, passing to it the name of the array you'd like to sort. For example, to sort an array named avarStates, use the following call:

```
acbSortArray avarStates( )
```

After the call to *acbSortArray*, your array will be sorted. Remember that *acbSortArray* is sorting your array in place: once it's sorted, there's no going back! If you don't want to sort your only copy of the array, make a duplicate first.

Discussion

The quicksort algorithm works by breaking the array into smaller and smaller chunks, sorting each one, until all the chunks are one element long. The *acbSortArray* procedure calls the main sorting routine, *QuickSort*, passing to it the array and the start and end points for sorting. The *QuickSort* routine breaks the array into two chunks, then calls itself twice to sort each of the two halves.

At this point, you might be grumbling about recursive routines and how they use lots of memory. Normally, that's true. This version of the sorting algorithm, however, tries to be conservative about how it uses memory. At each level, it sorts the smaller of the two chunks first. This means that it will have fewer recursive levels: the small chunk will end up containing a single element much more quickly than the large chunk. By always working with the smallest chunk first, this method avoids calling itself more often than it has to.

The code for the *QuickSort* procedure is:

```
Private Sub QuickSort(varArray As Variant, _
 intLeft As Integer, intRight As Integer)
    Dim i As Integer
    Dim j As Integer
    Dim varTestVal As Variant
    Dim intMid As Integer

    If intLeft < intRight Then
        intMid = (intLeft + intRight) \ 2
        varTestVal = varArray(intMid)
        i = intLeft
        j = intRight
        Do
            Do While varArray(i) < varTestVal
                i = i + 1
            Loop
            Do While varArray(j) > varTestVal
                j = j - 1
            Loop
            If i <= j Then
                SwapElements varArray( ), i, j
                i = i + 1
                j = j - 1
            End If
        Loop Until i > j
        ' To optimize the sort, always sort the
        ' smallest segment first.
        If j <= intMid Then
            QuickSort varArray( ), intLeft, j
            QuickSort varArray( ), i, intRight
        Else
            QuickSort varArray( ), i, intRight
            QuickSort varArray( ), intLeft, j
```

```
        End If
    End If
End Sub
```

The following are the basic steps of the *QuickSort* procedure. These steps use *intLeft* to refer to the beginning sort item and *intRight* for the ending item:

1. If *intLeft* isn't less than *intRight*, the sort is done.

2. The sort takes the value in the middle of the subset of the array that's being sorted as the "comparison" value. Its value will be the dividing factor for the two chunks. There are different schools of thought on how to choose the dividing item. This version of the sort uses the item that's physically in the middle of the chosen list of items:

```
intMid = (intLeft + intRight) \ 2
varTestVal = varArray(intMid)
```

3. The sort starts from the left, walking along the array until it finds an item that isn't less than the dividing value. This search is guaranteed to stop at the dividing value, which certainly isn't less than itself:

```
Do While varArray(i) < varTestVal
    i = i + 1
Loop
```

4. The sort starts from the right, walking backward through the array until it finds an item that isn't greater than the dividing value. This search is guaranteed to stop at the dividing value, which certainly isn't more than itself:

```
Do While varArray(j) > varTestVal
    j = j - 1
Loop
```

5. If the position from Step 3 is less than or equal to the position found in Step 4, the sort swaps the elements at the two positions, then increments the pointer for Step 3 and decrements the pointer for Step 4:

```
If i <= j Then
    SwapElements varArray( ), i, j
    i = i + 1
    j = j - 1
End If
```

6. The sort repeats Steps 3 through 5 until the pointer from Step 3 is greater than the pointer from Step 4 (i > j). At this point, every item to the left of the dividing element is less than or equal to it, and everything to the right is greater than or equal to it.

7. Choosing the smaller partition first, the sort repeats all these steps on each of the subsets to either side of the dividing value, until Step 1 indicates that it's done:

```
If j <= intMid Then
    QuickSort varArray( ), intLeft, j
    QuickSort varArray( ), i, intRight
Else
```

```
      QuickSort varArray( ), i, intRight
      QuickSort varArray( ), intLeft, j
   End If
```

There are probably sort algorithms that are simpler than the quicksort algorithm, but for arrays that aren't already sorted, quicksort's speed is hard to beat. (For presorted arrays, it doesn't do as well as some other sorts. But most arrays don't come to the *QuickSort* subroutine in order.) As it is, the *QuickSort* subroutine is capable of handling only single-column arrays. If you need to sort multicolumn arrays, you'll need to either modify the code to handle those cases or move the data into a table and let Access do the sorting for you.

See Also

See the next solution for an example of using *QuickSort*.

7.8 Fill a List Box with a List of Files

Problem

You need to present your users with a sorted list of files with a specific filename extension in a particular directory. You found the *Dir* function, but you can't find a way to get this information into a list box. Is there a way to do this?

Solution

This problem provides the perfect opportunity to use the past three solutions. It involves creating a list-filling callback function, passing arrays as parameters, and sorting an array. In addition, you'll fill that array with a list of files matching a particular criterion, using the *Dir* function.

Load the form frmTestFillDirList from *07-08.MDB*. Enter a file specification into the text box (for example, *c:*.exe*). Once you leave the text box (by pressing either Tab or Return), the code attached to the AfterUpdate event will force the list box to requery. When that happens, the list box will fill in with the matching filenames. Figure 7-12 shows the results of a search for *c:*.*.*

To include this functionality in your own applications, follow these steps:

1. On a form, create a text box and a list box, with properties set as shown in Table 7-6.

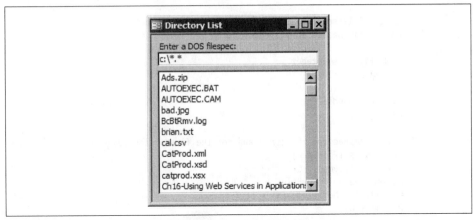

Figure 7-12. frmTestFillDirList, searching for *.* in the C:\ folder

Table 7-6. Property settings for the controls on the directory list form

Control	Property	Setting
Text box	Name	txtFileSpec
	AfterUpdate	[Event Procedure]
List box	Name	lstDirList
	RowSourceType	FillList
	AfterUpdate	[Event Procedure]

2. Enter the following code in the text box's AfterUpdate event procedure. (See the Preface for more information on creating event procedures.) This code forces the list box to requery itself when you enter a value in the text box, and then move to some other control:

```
Sub txtFileSpec_AfterUpdate ( )
   Me.lstDirList.Requery
End Sub
```

3. Enter the following code in the list box's AfterUpdate event. This is sample code that pops up a message box indicating which file you chose:

```
Sub lstDirList_AfterUpdate ( )
   MsgBox "You chose: " & Me.lstDirList.Value
End Sub
```

4. Enter the following code into a global module so that it can be called from any form. Though this code would work fine in a form's module, it's general enough that it will serve you best as part of a global module that can be copied from one database to another. This is the function that fills the array of files:

```
Public Function FillDirList(ByVal strFileSpec As String, _
   astrFiles( ) As String) As Integer
```

```
' Given the file specification in strFileSpec, fill in the
' dynamic array passed in avarFiles().

Dim intNumFiles As Integer
Dim strTemp As String

On Error GoTo HandleErr
intNumFiles = 0

' Set the filespec for the dir() and get the first filename.
strTemp = Dir(strFileSpec)
Do While Len(strTemp) > 0
    intNumFiles = intNumFiles + 1
    astrFiles(intNumFiles - 1) = strTemp
    strTemp = Dir
Loop

ExitHere:
    If intNumFiles > 0 Then
        ReDim Preserve astrFiles(intNumFiles - 1)
        acbSortArray astrFiles()
    End If
    FillDirList = intNumFiles
    Exit Function

HandleErr:
    Select Case Err.Number
        Case 9
            ' The array needs to be resized
            ' Just add room for 100 more files.
            ReDim Preserve astrFiles(intNumFiles + 100)
            Resume
        Case Else
            FillDirList = intNumFiles
            Resume ExitHere
    End Select
End Function
```

 Rather than resizing the array for each matching file name, the Fill-DirList function traps the error that occurs when the array is full, and resizes it 100 slots at a time. Using the Redim Preserve statement is quite expensive in VBA, and you should consider looking for ways to call it as seldom as possible. In this example, the code resizes the array to the correct size once it's done filling in all the file names.

5. Import basSortArray from *07-08.MDB*. This is the same sorting code that we used in the Solution in Recipe 7.7.

Discussion

The list box in this example uses a list-filling callback function, *FillList*, to supply its data. (See the Solution in Recipe 7.5 for information on callback functions.) Here's the code:

```
Private Function FillList(ctl As Control, _
 varID As Variant, lngRow As Long, lngCol As Long, _
 intCode As Integer)
    Static astrFiles() As String
    Static intFileCount As Integer

    Select Case intCode
        Case acLBInitialize
            If Not IsNull(Me.txtFileSpec) Then
                intFileCount = FillDirList(Me.txtFileSpec, astrFiles())
            End If
            FillList = True

        Case acLBOpen
            FillList = Timer

        Case acLBGetRowCount
            FillList = intFileCount

        Case acLBGetValue
            FillList = astrFiles(lngRow)

        Case acLBEnd
            Erase astrFiles
    End Select
End Function
```

In *FillList*'s acLBInitialize case, it calls the *FillDirList* function to fill in the astrFiles array, based on the value in the txtFileSpec text box. *FillDirList* fills in the array, calling *acbSortArray* along the way to sort the list of files, and returns the number of files it found. Given that completed array, *FillList* can return the value from the array that it needs when requested in the acLBGetValue case. It uses the return value from *FillDirList*, the number of files found, in response to the acLBGetRowCount case.

There's also an interesting situation you should note in the *FillList* and *FillDirList* routines. *FillList* declares a dynamic array, astrFiles, but doesn't give a size because it doesn't yet know the number of files that will be found. *FillList* passes the array off to *FillDirList*, which adds filenames to the array based on the file specification until it doesn't find any more matches. *FillDirList* returns the number of matching filenames, but it also has the side effect of having set the array's size and filled it in. Here's the code that does the work. This code fragment uses the ReDim Preserve keywords to resize the array every time it finds a matching filename:

```
' Set the filespec for the dir() and get the first filename.
strTemp = Dir(strFileSpec)
```

```
    Do While Len(strTemp) > 0
        intNumFiles = intNumFiles + 1
        astrFiles(intNumFiles - 1) = strTemp
        strTemp = Dir
    Loop
```

FillDirList uses the *Dir* function to create the list of files. This function is unusual in that you call it multiple times. The first time you call it, you send it the file specification you're trying to match, and *Dir* returns the first matching filename. If it returns a nonempty value, you continue to call it, with no parameters, until it *does* return an empty value. Each time you call *Dir*, it returns the next matching filename.

Once *FillDirList* has finished retrieving the list of filenames, it sorts the names in the array. Its return value is the number of files it found. The following code shows how this works:

```
    If intNumFiles > 0 Then
        ReDim Preserve astrFiles(intNumFiles - 1)
        acbSortArray astrFiles()
    End If
    FillDirList = intNumFiles
```

Note that when Access calls the list-filling callback function, values for the *lngRow* and *lngCol* parameters are always zero-based. Therefore, when you use arrays within callback functions, you should always consider using zero-based arrays to hold the data you'll display in the control. If you don't, you'll always be dealing with "off by one" errors. Using a zero-based array will mean that the row values (sent to your code in *lngRow*) will match your array indices.

7.9   Handle Object Properties, in General

Problem

You don't understand how to get and set property values in Access. It seems as if there are different kinds of properties, and what works for one object and property doesn't work for another. Is there some way to settle this once and for all?

Solution

There really are two kinds of properties for objects in Access. Built-in properties are those that always exist for an object, and user-defined properties are properties that you or Access creates for an object when requested. The syntax for referring to each type is different, but this solution provides a method that works for either type. This solution uses the user-defined Description property as an example, but the techniques will work just as well for any other property. The interesting part of this solution is that the Description property is not a built-in property, and attempting to set or retrieve this property using the standard *object.property* syntax will fail.

This solution provides a sample form, which is useful only for demonstrating the technique. The real power of the solution comes from the module, basHandleProperties, which provides procedures you can use to set and get any kind of property. To try out the sample form shown in Figure 7-13, load and run frmTestProperties from 07-09.MDB. Choose a table from the list of tables, and notice the Description property shown in the text box below the list. If you choose a field from the list of fields, you'll also see the description for that field in the text box below the list. You can enter new text into the two text boxes, and the code attached to the AfterUpdate event of either text box will write the text back to the Description property of the selected table or field.

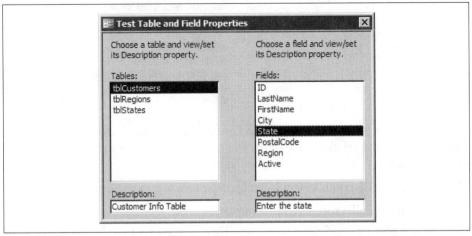

Figure 7-13. frmTestProperties lets you set and get the Description property of any table or field

The sample form uses two functions from basHandleProperties, as shown in Table 7-7. These functions allow you to get or set any property of any object, as long as the object either already supports the property you're working with or allows you to create new properties to add the property if it doesn't already exist.

Table 7-7. Using the acbGetProperty and acbSetProperty functions

Function name	Usage	Parameters	Returns
acbGetProperty	Retrieve the value of the specified property of the specified object.	obj As Object: a reference to any existing object. strProperty As String: the name of the property to retrieve.	The value of the requested property, or Null if that property or object doesn't exist.

Function name	Usage	Parameters	Returns
acbSetProperty	Set the value of the specified property of the specified object.	obj As Object: a reference to any existing object. strProperty As String: the name of the property to set. varValue As Variant: the value of the property; varPropType As Variant (optional): the data type of the new property (if the code has to create it). One of dbBoolean, dbByte, dbInteger, dbLong, dbCurrency, dbSingle, dbDouble, dbDate, dbText, dbLongBinary, dbMemo, or dbGUID. If you skip this, Access will use dbText.	The old value of the property, if it existed, or Null otherwise.

The only objects to which you can add properties are databases, tables, queries, fields, indexes, and relations. Attempts to add a new property to any other kind of object will fail.

To use these new functions in your own applications, follow these steps:

1. Import basHandleProperties into your application.

2. To set a property, call *acbSetProperty*. This function returns the old value of the property. For example:

```
Dim db As DAO.Database
Dim varOldDescription As Variant

Set db = CurrentDb( )
varOldDescription = acbSetProperty(db, "Description", "Sample Database")
If Not IsNull(varOldDescription) Then
    MsgBox "The old Description was: " & varOldDescription
End If
```

3. To get the value of a property, call *acbGetProperty*. For example:

```
Dim db As DAO.Database
Dim varDescription As Variant

Set db = CurrentDb( )
varDescription = acbGetProperty(db, "Description")
If Not IsNull(varDescription) Then
    MsgBox "The database description is: " & varDescription
End If
```

Discussion

Access provides two types of properties: built-in and user-defined. Built-in properties always exist and are part of the definition of the object. For example, the Name and Type properties are crucial for the existence of most objects. These are built-in properties. On the other hand, the Jet engine allows you to create new properties and add them to the Properties collection for all the objects it supports, including TableDefs, QueryDefs, Indexes, Fields, Relations, and Containers. These are user-defined properties.

In addition, Access itself, as a client of the Jet engine, creates several properties for you. For example, when you right-click on an object in the Database Explorer and choose Properties from the floating menu, Access allows you to specify the Description for the object. That Description property doesn't exist until you request that Access create it, using that dialog or in your own VBA code. The same goes for the Caption, ValidationRule, and DefaultValue properties of fields: those properties don't exist until you request that Access create them for you.

If you attempt to retrieve or set the value of a property that doesn't yet exist, Access will trigger a runtime error. Your code must be ready to deal with this problem. In addition, you may be used to working with built-in properties, to which you can refer using the simple *object.property* syntax. This syntax works only for built-in properties. For user-defined (and Access-created user-defined) properties, you must refer to the property using an explicit reference to the Properties collection that contains it. For example, to set the Format property of the City field within tblCustomers, you'll need an expression like this (and this expression will fail with a runtime error if the Format property hasn't yet been set):

```
CurrentDb.TableDefs("tblCustomers"). _
  Fields("City").Properties("Format") = ">"
```

Because you can always refer to any property using an explicit reference to the Properties collection, you can simplify your code, and ensure that all property references work, by using the same syntax for built-in and user-defined properties. For example, field objects support the AllowZeroLength property as a built-in property. Therefore, this reference will work:

```
CurrentDb.TableDefs("tblCustomers"). _
  Fields("City").AllowZeroLength = False
```

If you want to refer to the same property with an explicit reference, you can use this syntax:

```
CurrentDb.TableDefs("tblCustomers"). _
  Fields("City").Properties("AllowZeroLength") = False
```

This ability to refer to built-in and user-defined properties using the same syntax is the secret of the code presented in this solution.

To create a new property, you must follow these three steps:

1. Create a new property object, using the *CreateProperty* method of an existing object.

2. Set the properties of this new property, including its name, type, and default value (you can merge this step with the previous step by supplying the information when you call *CreateProperty*).

3. Append the new property to the Properties collection of the host object. For example, to add a Description property to the current database, you might write code like this:

```
Dim db As DAO.Database
Dim prp As Property

Set db = CurrentDb( )

' Step 1
Set prp = db.CreateProperty( )

' Step 2
prp.Name = "Description"
prp.Type = dbText
prp.Value = "Sample Database"

' Step 3
db.Properties.Append prp
```

To combine Steps 1 and 2, you could set the properties of the new property at the time you create it:

```
' Steps 1 and 2
Set prp = db.CreateProperty("Description", dbText, "Sample Database")

' Step 3
db.Properties.Append prp
```

Once you've followed these steps, you should be able to retrieve the database's Description property with a statement like this (note that you *must* use the explicit reference to the Properties collection in this case, because Description is a user-defined property):

```
Debug.Print CurrentDb.Properties!Description
```

To relieve you from worrying about the differences between user-defined and built-in properties and whether or not a property already exists for a given object, we've provided the *acbGetProperty* and *acbSetProperty* functions.

The *acbGetProperty* function is the simpler of the two: it attempts to retrieve the requested property. *acbGetProperty* may fail for two reasons: the object itself doesn't exist, or the property you've tried to retrieve doesn't exist (errors acbcErrNotInCollection and acbcErrPropertyNotFound, respectively). If either of these errors occurs, the function returns Null. If any other error occurs, the function alerts you with a message box before returning Null. If no error occurs, the function returns the value of the requested property. For an example of calling *acbGetProperty*, see Section 7.9.2 and *07-09.MDB*.

The source code for *acbGetProperty* is:

```
Public Function acbGetProperty(obj As Object, _
 strProperty As String) As Variant
    ' Retrieve property for an object.
    ' Return the value if found, or Null if not.

    On Error GoTo HandleErr

    acbGetProperty = obj.Properties(strProperty)

ExitHere:
    Exit Function

HandleErr:
    Select Case Err.Number
        Case 3265, 3270     ' Not in collection, not found.
            ' Do nothing!
        Case Else
            MsgBox Err.Number & ": " & Err.Description, , "acbGetProperty"
    End Select
    acbGetProperty = Null
    Resume ExitHere
End Function
```

The *acbSetProperty* function is more interesting. It attempts to set the value of the property you pass to it. This function has several interesting characteristics:

- If you ask it to set a property that doesn't currently exist, it attempts to create that property and then sets its value.

- The data type is declared optional, using the DataTypeEnum enumerated type, with dbText as the default value. If you don't tell it what the data type of the new property is to be (i.e., if you leave that parameter blank), the code will use the dbText type by default.

- The function returns the old value of the property, if there was one, so you can store it away and perhaps reset it once you're done with your application.

- To make sure the code will work with either user-defined or built-in properties, the code uses an explicit reference to the Properties collection.

- To tell if it needs to try to create the property, the function traps the acbcErrPropertyNotFound error condition (error 3270); if that error occurs, it uses the *CreateProperty* method to try to create the necessary property.

- If you try to assign an invalid property value, Access triggers the acbcErrDataTypeConversion error condition (error 3421). In that case, there's not much *acbSetProperty* can do besides alerting you to that fact and returning Null.

The source code for *acbSetProperty* is:

```
Public Function acbSetProperty( _
obj As Object, strProperty As String, varValue As Variant, _
Optional propType As DataTypeEnum = dbText)

    ' Set the value of a property.
    On Error GoTo HandleErr

    Dim varOldValue As Variant

    ' This'll fail if the property doesn't exist.
    varOldValue = obj.Properties(strProperty)
    obj.Properties(strProperty) = varValue
    acbSetProperty = varOldValue

ExitHere:
    Exit Function

HandleErr:
    Select Case Err.Number
        Case 3270        ' Property not found
            ' If the property wasn't there, try to create it.
            If acbCreateProperty(obj, strProperty, varValue, propType) Then
                Resume Next
            End If
        Case 3421        ' Data type conversion error
            MsgBox "Invalid data type!", vbExclamation, "acbSetProperty"
        Case Else
            MsgBox Err.Number & ": " & Err.Description, , "acbSetProperty"
    End Select
    acbSetProperty = Null
    Resume ExitHere
End Function
```

Only objects that are maintained by the Jet engine allow you to create new properties. That is, you can add properties to the Properties collections of Database, Table-Def, QueryDef, Index, Field, Relation, and Container objects. You won't be able to add new properties to any object that Access controls, such as forms, reports, and controls. If you attempt to use *acbSetProperty* to set a user-defined property for an invalid object, the function will return Null. You can, however, use *acbSetProperty* and *acbGetProperty* with any Access object, as long as you confine yourself to built-in properties for those objects that don't support user-defined properties. For example, this code fragment will work as long as frmTestProperties is currently open:

```
If IsNull(acbSetProperty(Forms("frmTestProperties"), "Caption", _
    "Test Properties")) Then
    MsgBox "Unable to set the property!"
End If
```

User-defined properties are persistent from session to session. That is, they are saved in the TableDef along with the built-in and Access-defined properties. You can, however, delete a user-defined property using the Delete method on the property's parent collection. For example, you could delete the user-defined property defined earlier using the following statement:

```
CurrentDb.TableDefs("tblSuppliers").Fields("Address"). _
    Properties.Delete "SpecialHandling"
```

7.10 Detect Whether an Object Exists

Problem

You create and delete objects as your application runs. At some point, you need to be able to tell whether an object exists and make decisions based on that fact. But you can't find a function in Access that will tell you if a specific object already exists. Are you missing something? This ought to be a basic part of the product!

Solution

You haven't missed anything: Access really doesn't supply a simple method of determining if a specific object already exists. On the other hand, this is really quite simple, as long as you understand two important concepts: Access's support for DAO Container objects, and the ways you can use error handling to retrieve information. This solution uses these two subjects to provide a function you can call to check for the existence of any object.

Load and run frmTestExist from *07-10.MDB*. This form, shown in Figure 7-14, lets you specify an object name and its type and then tells you whether that object exists. Certainly, you wouldn't use this form as-is in any application—its purpose is to demonstrate the *acbDoesObjExist* function in basExists (*07-10.MDB*). To make your exploration of frmTestExist easier, Table 7-8 lists the objects that exist in *07-10. MDB*. Try entering names that do and don't exist, and get the types right and wrong, to convince yourself that the *acbDoesObjExist* function does its job correctly.

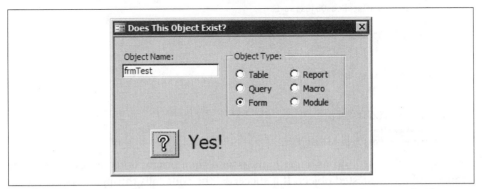

Figure 7-14. frmTestExist lets you check for the existence of any object in the current database

Table 7-8. The sample objects in 07-10.MDB

Object name	Object type
tblTest	Table
qryTest	Query
frmTest	Form
frmTestExist	Form
basExists	Module

Follow these steps to use *acbDoesObjExist* in your own applications:

1. Import the module basExists from *07-10.MDB*. This module contains the *acb-DoesObjExist* function.

2. To check for the existence of any object, call *acbDoesObjExist*, passing to it the name of the object to check for and a value from the AcObjectType enumeration indicating the object's type. The type parameter must be chosen from the values acTable, acQuery, acForm, acReport, acMacro, or acModule. For example, to check for the existence of a table named "Customers", call *acbDoesObjExist* like this:

```
If acbDoesObjExist("Customers", acTable) Then
    ' You know the table exists.
Else
    MsgBox "The table 'Customers' doesn't exist!"
End If
```

Discussion

The *acbDoesObjExist* function, shown in full here, checks for the existence of an object by attempting to retrieve that object's Name property. Because every object that exists exposes a Name property, this action can't fail unless the object doesn't exist. In skeleton format, the code works like this:

```
    Dim strName As String
    On Error Goto acbDoesObjExist_Err

    strName = obj.Name
    acbDoesObjExist = True

acbDoesObjectExist_Exit:
    Exit Function

acbDoesObjectExist_Err:
    acbDoesObjExist = False
    Resume acbDoesObjectExist_Exit
```

That is, the code sets up an error handler and then attempts to retrieve the Name property of the requested object. If it succeeds, the code falls through, sets the return value to True, and returns. If it triggers an error, the procedure can be assured that the object doesn't exist, and it will return False.

The only other issue is how to convert a string containing the name of the object and an integer containing its type to a real object reference. This is where the Jet engine's Container objects come in handy. The Container collections, supplied by Access so the Jet engine can support security for all the Access objects, contain collections of Document objects (one for each saved object in your database). The Containers collection contains collections named Tables, Forms, Reports, Scripts (that's *macros* for us users!), and Modules. Except for tables and queries, the code checks in those collections of documents, looking for the document whose name you've supplied. For tables and queries, it's simpler to use the TableDefs and QueryDefs collections directly. Access lumps tables and queries together in the Tables container, but keeps them separate in the TableDefs and QueryDefs collections. If the code looked in the Tables container, it would have to take an extra step to distinguish tables from queries; that step isn't necessary if it uses the collections instead.

The code for *acbDoesObjExist* is as follows:

```
Public Function acbDoesObjExist( _
 strObj As String, objectType As AcObjectType)
    Dim db As DAO.Database
    Dim strCon As String
    Dim strName As String

    On Error GoTo HandleErr

    Set db = CurrentDb()
    Select Case objectType
        Case acTable
            strName = db.TableDefs(strObj).Name
        Case acQuery
            strName = db.QueryDefs(strObj).Name
        Case acForm, acReport, acMacro, acModule
            Select Case objectType
                Case acForm
                    strCon = "Forms"
                Case acReport
                    strCon = "Reports"
                Case acMacro
                    strCon = "Scripts"
                Case acModule
                    strCon = "Modules"
            End Select
            strName = db.Containers(strCon).Documents(strObj).Name
    End Select
    acbDoesObjExist = True

ExitHere:
    Exit Function
```

```
HandleErr:
    acbDoesObjExist = False
    Resume ExitHere
End Function
```

Note that in the Select Case statement, the code first checks to see if you're asking about a table or a query. If so, it looks in the appropriate collection:

```
Select Case objectType
    Case acTable
        strName = db.TableDefs(strObj).Name
    Case acQuery
        strName = db.QueryDefs(strObj).Name
    .
    .
    .
End Select
```

If not, it assigns to *strCon* the name of the container it will need and then attempts to retrieve the Name property of the particular document within the selected container:

```
Case acForm, acReport, acMacro, acModule
    Select Case objectType
        Case acForm
            strCon = "Forms"
        Case acReport
            strCon = "Reports"
        Case acMacro
            strCon = "Scripts"
        Case acModule
            strCon = "Modules"
    End Select
    strName = db.Containers(strCon).Documents(strObj).Name
```

See Also

If you haven't done much investigation of DAO in Access, you may find it useful to study the appropriate chapters in the Building Applications manual that ships with Access. Though complete coverage of DAO is beyond the scope of this book, there are several examples using DAO in other chapters, especially Chapter 4 and Chapter 6. In addition, *DAO Object Model: The Definitive Reference*, by Helen Feddema (O'Reilly), provides complete documentation of the DAO object model.

CHAPTER 8

Optimization

One unavoidable fact of application design is that your application never runs as fast as you'd like it to. Unless you and your users are equipped with the latest and most powerful workstations with huge amounts of memory, performance will be less than ideal. Still, there are many techniques you can use to optimize your application, few of which are easily found in the Access documentation. Although your Access application may never run like that lean and mean dBASE II application you created 15 years ago, you certainly can make it run at an acceptable speed.

This chapter covers several optimizations that enable you to load forms faster, add and change data faster, and speed up your Visual Basic for Applications (VBA) code, for example. It also covers the optimization of queries, as well as multiuser and client/server optimization techniques. In addition, this chapter describes testing techniques that will help you gauge the speed gains of your optimizations.

Several of the examples in this chapter take advantage of the DAO type library, rather than the default ADO library used by Access 2002 and Access 2003. Even though it's less "modern," DAO provides greater functionality, and generally better performance. In addition, using DAO makes it possible for these demonstrations to work in earlier versions of Access. If you want to try these techniques in your own applications, make sure you add the DAO reference to your project using the Tools → References menu item from within VBA—it won't be added by default.

8.1   Accelerate the Load Time of Forms

Problem

The first time you open a form in your application, it seems to take forever to load. Is there any way to accelerate this?

Solution

You can radically improve the time it takes to load a form for the first time by preloading your forms when the database is initially opened. You can also decrease the load time for subsequent loadings by hiding instead of closing forms. This solution shows you how to improve form load time using these techniques.

Load the *08-01.MDB* database. Note the time it takes for the switchboard form to appear (see Figure 8-1). Make sure that the "Preload and keep loaded forms" checkbox is unchecked; if it's checked, uncheck it, close the database, and start over. Now press one of the command buttons, such as the Orders button, and note how long it takes Access to initially load the form. Close the form.

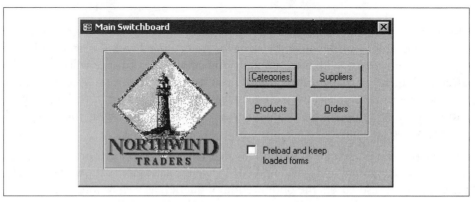

Figure 8-1. The 08-01.MDB switchboard form

Now check the "Preload and keep loaded forms" checkbox on the switchboard form and close the database. Reload the database and again note the time it takes for the switchboard form to appear. Load the Orders form, again recording the form load time.

You'll see that the switchboard form now takes longer to appear but that the subsequent form load time is significantly shorter. That's because checking the "Preload and keep loaded forms" checkbox and reloading the database flips an internal switch that causes the application to preload its forms (in a hidden state) as the switchboard form is loaded by Access. This lengthens the time it takes for the switchboard form to appear initially. However, because the Orders form is now preloaded, it takes less time for it to appear when you press the Orders command button.

 A switchboard form (or menu form) is an unbound form used for application navigation. Switchboard forms are usually made up of labels and command buttons with an optional picture.

Follow these steps to set up your application to preload its forms:

1. Create a table for storing the names of the forms you wish to preload. This table (zstblPreloadForms in the sample database) should have a single field, FormName, with a datatype of Text. Switch to datasheet view (see Figure 8-2) and add a row for each form in your application that you wish to preload.

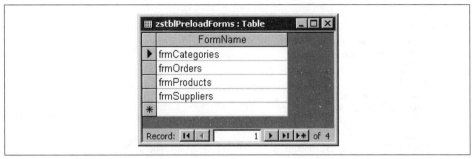

Figure 8-2. Store the list of preloaded forms in the zstblPreloadForms table

2. Create a switchboard form or edit your existing one.

3. Set the form's AutoCenter property to Yes.

4. Add the following code to the declarations section at the top of the form's module (replacing the values with the actual names for your table and splash form, if you've used different names):

```
Private Const acbPreloadTable = "zstblPreloadForms"
Private Const acbSplashForm = "frmSplash"
```

5. Create a new event procedure for the form's Open event. (If you're unsure of how to do this, see "How Do I Create an Event Procedure?" in the Preface of this book.)

6. Add the following code to the event procedure:

```
Private Sub Form_Open(Cancel As Integer)

    ' Preload forms.

    Dim db As DAO.Database
    Dim rst As DAO.Recordset
    Dim varFormName As Variant

    On Error GoTo HandleErr

    DoCmd.OpenForm acbSplashForm

    Set db = CurrentDb( )

    ' Preload the forms listed in zstblPreloadForms.
    Set rst = db.OpenRecordset(acbPreloadTable, dbOpenSnapshot)
```

```
        Do While Not rst.EOF
            varFormName = rst("FormName")
            If Not IsNull(varFormName) Then
                DoCmd.OpenForm FormName:=varFormName, _
                WindowMode:=acHidden, OpenArgs:="StayLoaded"
            End If
            rst.MoveNext
        Loop

    ExitHere:
        DoCmd.Close acForm, acbSplashForm
        If Not rst Is Nothing Then
            rst.Close
        End If
        Set rst = Nothing
        Exit Sub

    HandleErr:
        MsgBox "Error " & Err.Number & ": " & Err.Description, , "Form Open"
        Resume ExitHere
    End Sub
```

You can also copy this code from the frmSwitchboard1 form (*not* the frmSwitch-board form) in *08-01.MDB*. (The frmSwitchboard1 version of the form always preloads forms, thus eliminating all the code associated with the "Preload and keep loaded forms" checkbox.)

7. Create an event procedure for the switchboard form's Close event. Add this code to the event procedure:

```
Private Sub Form_Close( )

    ' Unload preloaded forms

    Dim db As DAO.Database
    Dim rst As DAO.Recordset
    Dim varFormName As Variant

    On Error GoTo HandleErr

    Set db = CurrentDb( )

    ' Unload the forms listed in zstblPreloadForms
    Set rst = db.OpenRecordset(acbPreloadTable, dbOpenSnapshot)

    Do Until rst.EOF
        varFormName = rst("FormName")
        If Not IsNull(varFormName) Then
            DoCmd.Close acForm, varFormName
        End If
        rst.MoveNext
    Loop

ExitHere:
    If Not rst Is Nothing Then
```

```
            rst.Close
        End If
        Set rst = Nothing
        Exit Sub

    HandleErr:
        MsgBox "Error " & Err.Number & ": " & Err.Description, , "Form Open"
        Resume ExitHere
    End Sub
```

8. Create the following functions in a global module (or import the basStayLoaded module from *08-01.MDB*):

```
Public Function acbOpenForm(strFormName As String, _
  fStayLoaded As Boolean) As Boolean

    ' Open specified form and pass it the
    ' StayLoaded argument.

    On Error GoTo acbOpenFormErr

    If fStayLoaded Then
        DoCmd.OpenForm strFormName, OpenArgs:="StayLoaded"
    Else
        DoCmd.OpenForm strFormName
    End If

acbOpenFormExit:
    Exit Function

acbOpenFormErr:
    MsgBox "Error " & Err.Number & ": " & Err.Description, _
      vbOKOnly + vbCritical, "acbOpenForm"
    Resume acbOpenFormExit
End Function

Public Function acbCloseForm(frmToClose As Form)

    ' If StayLoaded is True, hide the form instead of closing it.

    On Error GoTo acbCloseFormErr

    If InStr(frmToClose.OpenArgs, "StayLoaded") > 0 Then
        frmToClose.Visible = False
    Else
        DoCmd.Close acForm, frmToClose.Name
    End If

acbCloseFormExit:
    Exit Function

acbCloseFormErr:
    MsgBox "Error " & Err.Number & ": " & Err.Description, _
      vbOKOnly + vbCritical, "acbCloseForm"
    Resume acbCloseFormExit
End Function
```

9. Throughout your application, when you create code that opens a form and you wish to load that form only once, call the *acbOpenForm* function from Step 8. If you wish to open a form from code, you can use this syntax:

```
Call acbOpenForm("formname", True)
```

You can also call the function directly from an event property. In this case, enter the following in the event property:

```
=acbOpenForm("formname", True)
```

For those forms that you don't wish to keep loaded, change the second parameter of *acbOpenForm* to False.

10. For each form you are preloading or loading with the *acbOpenForm* function, add a command button with the caption "Close". Enter the following in the event property for the button's Click event:

```
=acbCloseForm(Form)
```

Don't place any quotes around the Form argument.

11. Make a copy of the form created in Step 2 and name it frmSplash. This is what's known as a "splash form." Open frmSplash in design view and remove all the command button controls. Also remove all the code behind the form for this copy. In the area where the command buttons used to be, add a label control that contains an initialization message. For example, the label on frmSplash has the attributes shown in Table 8-1. frmSplash is shown in form view in Figure 8-3.

Table 8-1. Properties of frmSplash's lblMessage control

Property	Value
Name	lblMessage
Caption	Initializing...
BackStyle	Transparent
BorderStyle	Transparent
FontName	Arial
FontSize	14
TextAlign	Center

12. Open the switchboard form created in Step 2. Open the form's module and add the following constants to the declarations section of the module:

```
Const acbcPreloadTable = "zstblPreloadForms"
Const acbcSplashForm = "frmSplash"
```

Change "zstblPreloadForms" to the name of your table from Step 1. Change "frmSplash" to the name of your form from Step 11.

13. Select Tools → Startup to open the database Startup dialog (see Figure 8-4). Select the switchboard form from Step 2 in the Display Form/Page field.

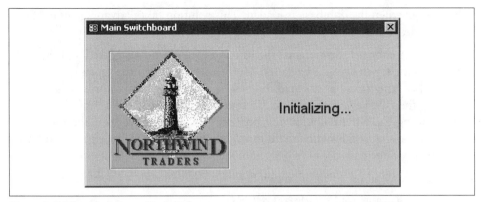

Figure 8-3. The splash form, frmSplash

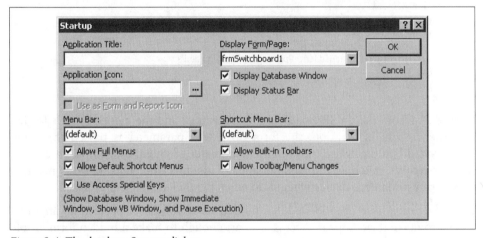

Figure 8-4. The database Startup dialog

14. Close the database and reload it to test your startup procedure and switchboard form.

Discussion

Access forms are stored as binary data in hidden system tables in your database. When you load a form, Access reads data from the system tables to recreate and display that form. This takes time. The solution described here improves the application load time of forms by preloading them when the database is first loaded. This means that the initial application load time will be slower, but users are more tolerant of a long application load time because it is a one-time commitment. As with most performance optimizations, the benefits of this technique are especially noticeable on slow machines.

Prior to Access 95, you had to use an AutoExec macro to initiate some action upon database startup; in recent versionsyou can use the Startup dialog to specify a form to be opened when the database is loaded. This solution takes advantage of the Startup properties, but you also could have used an AutoExec macro.

When the switchboard form opens, the form's Open event is triggered and the code attached to the Open event is executed. Unfortunately, when the Open event procedure is called, the form has not had time to paint itself, so users normally see nothing during the Open event procedure. To remedy this, we created a "splash" form to display during the potentially lengthy process. You don't have to make the splash form the same size as the switchboard form, but in this case, we made the two forms very similar in appearance.

The code to preload the forms is shown here:

```
Set rst = db.OpenRecordset(acbcPreloadTable)

Do While Not rst.EOF
    varFormName = rst("FormName")
    If Not IsNull(varFormName) Then
        DoCmd.OpenForm FormName:=varFormName, _
        WindowMode:=acHidden, OpenArgs:="StayLoaded"
    End If
    rst.MoveNext
Loop
```

Each record from the zstblPreloadForms table is read and the named form is loaded in hidden mode. In addition, the form's *OpenArgs* parameter is passed the string "StayLoaded". You can use the *OpenArgs* parameter of OpenForm to pass a custom string to a form, much as you pass parameters to a function. This *OpenArgs* parameter will be used later to decide what to do when the preloaded form is closed.

Once the forms have been loaded in a hidden state, you don't need to do anything special to make them appear. Access is smart enough to make a hidden form visible when you attempt to load it, which makes working with invisible forms easy. However, we include wrapper functions for opening and closing your application's forms in case you want some forms to be treated differently. For example, you may not wish to preload and keep all your forms loaded, because they will take up memory.

Like the Form_Open event procedure attached to the switchboard form, the *acbOpenForm* function passes the string "StayLoaded" to a form via its *OpenArgs* argument when you pass True as the function's second parameter. Closing the application form is then handled by *acbCloseForm*, which is called by the Click event of each form's Close button. This function determines whether to close or hide the form by checking its OpenArgs property, which was passed to the form when it was opened:

```
If InStr(frmToClose.OpenArgs, "StayLoaded") > 0 Then
    frmToClose.Visible = False
Else
    DoCmd.Close acForm, frmToClose.Name
End If
```

For forms that you do not wish to preload, don't add them to zstblPreloadForms. For forms that you wish to close normally when the Close button is pressed, open them using the following syntax:

```
=acbOpenForm("formname", False)
```

If you have enough memory, you may wish to preload all forms and not close them until the application exits. In some situations, however, you may wish to be more selective. By using the preload technique and the *acbOpenForm* and *acbCloseForm* functions throughout your application, you can easily change your mind or customize form preloading and form hiding for different requirements.

We did not remove from each sample form the Close button and control box provided by the system. This means that you can use one of these alternate mechanisms to bypass the application-defined Close button (and the *acbCloseForm* function) and close the form instead of hiding it. Thus, you may wish to set the CloseButton and ControlBox properties of your forms to No to prevent the use of these mechanisms.

You may wish to make zstblPreloadForms a hidden table. You can adjust the hidden property of an object by selecting View → Properties.

Benchmarking 101

Benchmarking different scenarios is a painstaking process. Because Windows includes a hard disk cache and because Access itself caches data, it's difficult to get fair and accurate timings. Because of caching, the order in which you time things does matter. Avoid jumping to conclusions without repeating the readings several times in different orders. Also, there is no reliable programmatic way to measure the time a form takes to load. Although you can set timers at each of the form's events, Access does some things internally after the last loading event has fired. You will find that the only accurate way to test a form's loading time is to manually test and average the form load using a stopwatch.

8.2   Make Slow Forms Run Faster

Problem

You are not happy with the speed at which your forms load and display. How can you change your forms so they will load and display faster?

Solution

Access gives you a lot of flexibility to develop dynamite-looking forms. Unfortunately, Access also makes it easy to create forms that run painfully slowly. The Solution in Recipe 8.1 explained how you can speed up the loading time of all forms by preloading them. This solution discusses how to track down and fix various performance bottlenecks, thus improving form execution performance. We also discuss the use and misuse of graphic elements and combo and list box controls.

You should consider several potential issues when analyzing your forms for performance. We discuss here two common performance bottlenecks: controls involving graphic or memo field data, and combo and list box controls.

Graphic and memo controls

Load the *08-02a.MDB* database. Open the frmCategoriesOriginal form (see Figure 8-5). This form, although attractive, loads slowly and has a noticeable delay on slower machines when moving from record to record. Now open frmCategoriesStep3, which is the final version of the form after various optimizations have been applied to it (see Figure 8-6). Its load and execution times should be noticeably faster.

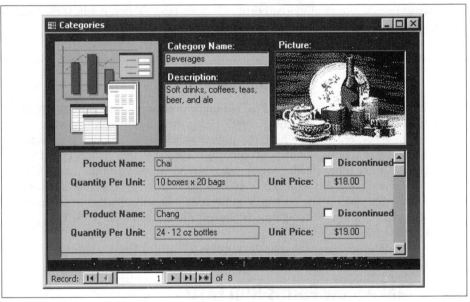

Figure 8-5. The original form, frmCategoriesOriginal, is slow

Follow these steps to improve the performance of forms that include unbound graphic controls or bound controls that hold OLE or memo fields:

1. Open the problem form in design view. If you have any unbound object frame controls (also know as unbound OLE controls) that are used to store fixed graphic images, change them to image controls by right-clicking on the object and selecting Change To Image (see Figure 8-7). The frmCategoriesStep1 form in the *08-02a.MDB* sample database is identical to frmCategoriesOriginal except

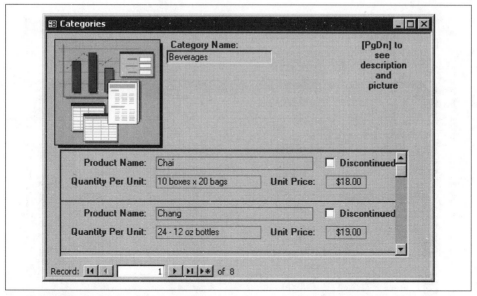

Figure 8-6. The final form, frmCategoriesStep3, is faster

that ctlLogo has been converted from an unbound object frame control to an image control.

2. If you created a watermark for the form, consider removing it. To do this, select the word "bitmap" in the form's Picture property, press the Del key, and answer Yes to the confirming dialog. The frmCategoriesStep2 form in *08-02a.MDB* is identical to frmCategoriesStep1, except that we deleted the watermark.

3. If your form contains any bound controls that hold either OLE or memo fields, consider moving the controls to a second page of the form. In the final version of the Categories form, named frmCategoriesStep3 (Figure 8-6), we moved the ctlDescription and ctlPicture controls to a second page.

Combo and list box controls

Load the *08-02b.MDB* database. Open the frmSurveySlow form. This form contains a combo box control, cboPersonId, that has as its row source a SQL Select statement that pulls in 15,000 rows from the tblPeople table. Load time for the form is slow because Access has to run the query that supplies the 15,000 rows to cboPersonId. Tab to the cboPersonId control and type "th" to search for the name "Thompson, Adrian" (see Figure 8-8).

Note the long delay before the "th" list of records appears. Now open the frmSurveyFast form (see Figure 8-9); its load time is significantly faster. Press the ">" command button to open the frmPersonPopup form. Type "th" in the first field and press Tab.

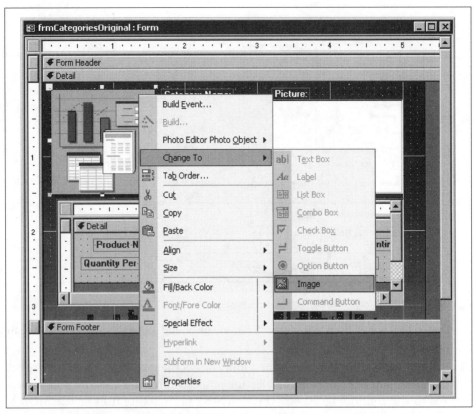

Figure 8-7. Changing an unbound object frame control to an image control

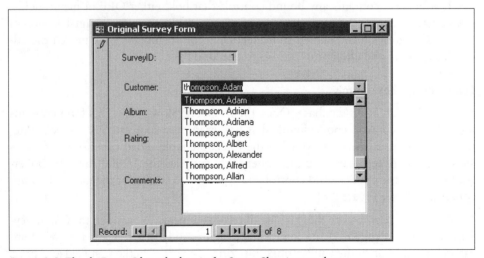

Figure 8-8. The cboPersonId combo box in frmSurveySlow is very slow

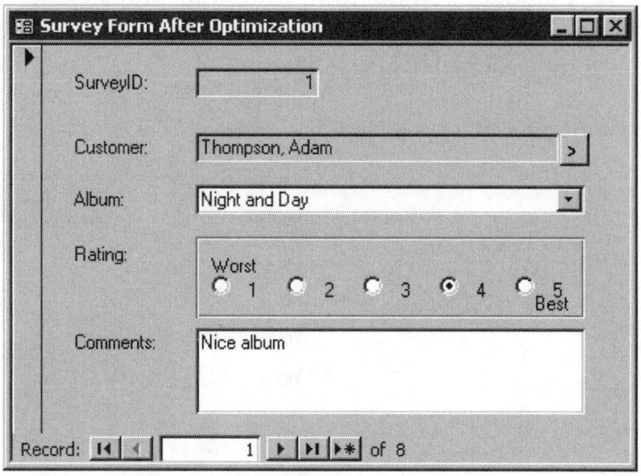

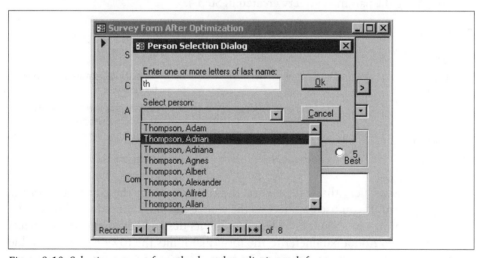

Figure 8-9. In frmSurveyFast, the combo box is replaced with a text box and command button

After a short delay, you'll be able to select "Thompson, Adrian" from the drop-down list as shown in Figure 8-10. Press the OK button, which will drop the chosen name back into the txtPersonName text box on frmSurveyFast.

Figure 8-10. Selecting a name from the drop-down list is much faster

Follow these steps to improve the speed of forms containing combo or list boxes that must display a lot of information:

1. Make a copy of the problem form and open the copy in design view. Select the slow combo or list box control. Right-click on the control and select Change To → Text Box.

2. Create a new unbound pop-up form with the property settings shown in Table 8-2. Leave the remaining property settings at their defaults. In the sample database, this form is named frmPersonPopup.

Table 8-2. Property settings for the pop-up form

Property	Setting
ScrollBars	Neither
RecordSelectors	No
NavigationButtons	No
AutoResize	Yes
AutoCenter	Yes
PopUp	Yes
Modal	Yes
MinMaxButtons	None

3. Create four unbound controls on this form: a text box, a combo box, and two command buttons. In the sample database, we created the controls shown in Table 8-3. The text box will be used to limit the number of items in the combo box, using the parameter query created in Step 4.

Table 8-3. The controls on frmPersonPopup

Control type	Control name	Notes
Text box	txtChar	Limits the values in the row source of the combo box
Combo box	cboPersonId	Uses the parameter query created in Step 4 as its row source
Command button	cmdOK	Hides form
Command button	cmdCancel	Closes form

4. Create a new query that will serve as the row source for the combo box of the pop-up form. If you used a query as the source for the combo or list box on the original form, you should be able to modify its design. Add the necessary fields to the query. Add a parameter to the form that limits the rows based on a value typed into the text box on the pop-up form. Choose any sort fields. In the sample database, we created the qryPersonComboBox query with the fields shown in Table 8-4. Save and close the query.

Table 8-4. The fields in qryPersonComboBox

Query field	Sort	Criteria
PersonId	(None)	(None)
FullName: [LastName] & ", " & [FirstName]	(None)	(None)

Table 8-4. The fields in qryPersonComboBox (continued)

Query field	Sort	Criteria
LastName	Ascending	Like [Forms]![frmPersonPopup2]![txt-Char] & "*"
FirstName	Ascending	(None)

5. Reopen the pop-up form created in Steps 2 and 3. Set the Enabled property of the combo box to No. Set the RowSource property to point to the query created in Step 4. In the sample database, we set the properties of the cboPersonId combo box to the values in Table 8-5.

Table 8-5. Property settings for cboPersonId

Property	Setting
Enabled	No
RowSourceType	Table/Query
RowSource	(Blank)
ColumnCount	2
ColumnHeads	No
ColumnWidths	0";2.5"
BoundColumn	1
ListRows	8
ListWidth	2.5"

6. Create a new event procedure for the text box's Change event. (If you're unsure of how to do this, see "How Do I Create an Event Procedure?" in the Preface of this book.) Add the following code to the event procedure:

```
Private Sub txtChar_Change( )

    If Not IsNull(Me.txtChar.Text) Then
        Me.cboPersonID.Enabled = True
    Else
        Me.cboPersonID.Enabled = False
    End If

End Sub
```

Change txtChar to the name of your text box and cboPersonId to the name of your combo box.

7. Create a new event procedure for the text box's AfterUpdate event and add the following code to it:

```
Private Sub txtChar_AfterUpdate( )

    Dim ctlPersonId As ComboBox
    Dim ctlChar As TextBox
```

```
Set ctlPersonId = Me.cboPersonID
Set ctlChar = Me.txtChar

If Not IsNull(ctlChar) Then
    ctlPersonId.RowSource = "qryPersonComboBox"
    ctlPersonId.SetFocus
    ctlPersonId.Dropdown
End If

End Sub
```

Change txtChar to the name of your text box, and cboPersonId to the name of your combo box. Change qryPersonComboBox to the name of the query you created in Step 4.

8. Create the following new event procedure for the OK command button's Click event:

```
Private Sub cmdOK_Click( )
    Me.Visible = False
End Sub
```

9. Create the following new event procedure for the Cancel command button's Click event:

```
Private Sub cmdCancel_Click( )
    DoCmd.Close acForm, Me.Name
End Sub
```

10. Save the pop-up form and close it.

11. Reopen the form from Step 1 in design view. Add a button called cmdPopup to the right of the text box. Add the following event procedure to cmdPopup's Click event:

```
Private Sub cmdPopup_Click( )

    Const acbcPopup = "frmPersonPopup"

    ' Open up pop-up form in dialog mode.
    DoCmd.OpenForm acbcPopup, WindowMode:=acDialog

    ' Check if form is still loaded.
    ' If yes, then OK button was used to close pop-up.
    If SysCmd(acSysCmdGetObjectState, acForm, acbcPopup) <> 0 Then
        Me.PersonID = Forms(acbcPopup)!cboPersonID
        DoCmd.Close acForm, acbcPopup
    End If

End Sub
```

Change frmPersonPopup to match the name of the pop-up form. Change PersonId and cboPersonId to the names of the appropriate controls.

Discussion

When you have a form that loads and executes slowly, you need to analyze the form and weigh the advantages and disadvantages of using graphic features. After a careful analysis of the frmCategoriesOriginal form in the *08-02a.MDB* database, we made several changes.

First, we changed the unbound object frame control to an image control. The OLE-based object frame control can be used to hold graphic images, sound, and other OLE-based data such as Excel spreadsheets or Word documents. But if you need to display only an unbound bitmap, you're better off using the more resource-conservative image control.

Second, we removed the form watermark, as this feature slows down form execution slightly. The improvement in performance depends on the color-depth of the removed image and the speed of your machine.

Finally, we created a second page and moved the text box bound to the memo field and the bound object frame bound to the OLE field to this second page. These field types (memo and OLE) are stored separately from the rest of the fields in a record and thus require additional disk reads to display. Fortunately, Access does not fetch these potentially large fields from the database unless they are visible on the screen. By placing them on the second page, you can quickly navigate from row to row without having to fetch the memo or OLE data. When you need to view the data in the fields, you can easily flip to the second page of the form.

The frmSurveySlow form in *08-02b.MDB* contains a combo box, cboPersonId, bound to a 15,000-row table. This makes form load and combo box list navigation slow. Combo and list box controls are excellent for allowing users to choose from a list of values and work well with a small number of list rows. However, they perform poorly when the size of the list exceeds a few thousand rows, even with very fast hardware.

We were able to improve the load time of the survey form significantly by limiting the rows in the person combo box. This was done using a pop-up form containing the same combo box control, but linked to a text box control that filtered the combo box's rows via a parameter query. Using a little VBA code, we disabled the combo box control until at least one character was entered into the text box. In this way, we reduced a 15,000-row combo box to, on average, 577 rows (15000 / 26), and that's when only the minimum number of characters (one) is typed into the text box. You could increase performance by waiting for at least two or even three characters, rather than filling the list after the user has typed only one letter.

Besides reducing the number of rows in the row source for cboPersonId, two other improvements were made to boost combo box performance. On the original frmSurveySlow form, a SQL statement was used as the row source for the combo box; the cboPersonId combo box on the pop-up form uses a saved query instead. Saved queries are always faster than SQL statements because the query optimizer optimizes the query when it is saved instead of when it is run.

In addition, the SQL statement for frmSurveySlow's combo box includes the following ORDER BY clause:

```
ORDER BY [LastName] & ", " & [FirstName]
```

In contrast, the SQL statement for the qryPersonComboBox query used as the row source for frmPersonPopup uses the following ORDER BY clause:

```
ORDER BY tblPeople.LastName, tblPeople.FirstName
```

Although these two ORDER BY clauses look similar, the first one sorts on an expression, whereas the second sorts on two indexed fields. It's always faster to sort on individual fields rather than expressions.

There are several other things to consider when looking for ways to speed up your forms. You may wish to try some or all of the following suggestions:

- Preload and keep loaded forms (see the Solution in Recipe 8.1).
- Ensure that fields used to sort or filter rows are indexed in the underlying tables (see the Solution in Recipe 8.4 for more on indexing and its effect on query performance).
- Use referential integrity throughout your database. Besides the obvious improvements to the quality of your data when you create enforced relationships, Access creates hidden foreign key indexes that improve the performance of queries, forms, and reports based on the joined tables.
- Create simpler forms with less color, fewer graphics, and fewer fonts.
- Limit the number of records in the form's recordset (see the Solution in Recipe 8.6).
- Watch out for Tab controls with many pages and subforms on each page. Loading all those subforms will slow the opening of your form. One alternative is to load the subforms on a Tab control page only when that page is selected. You can do this by using the Change event of the Tab control to check the Value of the control—this tells you the PageIndex of the selected page. You can set the SourceControl property of your subforms only when the page they appear on is selected; you can't set it in design view.

8.3   Make Combo Boxes Load Faster

Problem

Sometimes you need to use combo boxes that list many items. It takes the user a long time to scroll to the bottom of the list, because the list loads only a few rows at a time. Is there any way to get the list to load all at once?

Solution

There is a very simple VBA technique that forces the rows of a combo or list box to load all at once when you open the form. All you have to do is force the code behind the form to calculate the number of items in the list.

Load frmComboFast in *08-03.MDB*. Click the down arrow of the top combo box and scroll to the bottom of the list. Access loads only part of the list each time you scroll, so it takes many attempts to get to the last items on the list. Now do the same with the second combo box. This time, you can scroll immediately to the last item on the list.

Discussion

The Load event procedure in frmComboFast forces the second combo box to load the entire list, by calling the ListCount property of the control:

```
Private Sub Form_Load( )
  Dim lngCount As Long
  lngCount = cboFast.ListCount
End Sub
```

To use this code on your form, simply change the name of the control from cboFast to the name of your combo or list box. You can handle multiple controls by reusing the *lngCount* variable to retrieve the ListCount property value for each combo or list box that you want to load.

The form in this example loads a bit slower than it would if you didn't use this technique, because load time is sacrificed in order to improve the performance of the second combo box. If you need to use combo boxes that have very long lists, this is a price that your users probably will be quite willing to pay.

8.4   Use Jet Engine Optimizations to Speed Up Queries

Problem

You've heard that the Jet database engine includes optimizations you can use to improve the performance of your queries. How do you create queries that use take advantage of these optimizations?

Solution

The Jet engine (the database engine built into Access) can execute certain types of queries dramatically faster that others, depending on how you construct the queries. This solution explains how this technology works and how you can take advantage of it. It also introduces a technique for timing the execution of queries.

Load the *08-04.MDB* database. Open the qryOr1 query in design view. This query, which is shown in Figure 8-11, contains criteria on two fields, Menu# and Quantity. It returns all records from tblOrderDetailsNoIndexes where Quantity = 13 or where Menu# = 25. If you switch to SQL view, you'll see the following Where clause:

```
WHERE (((tblOrderDetailsNoIndexes.[Quantity])=13)) OR (((tblOrderDetailsNoIndexes.
[Menu#])=25))
```

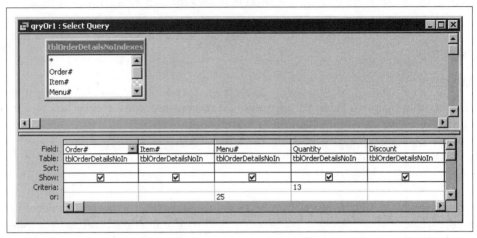

Figure 8-11. The qryOr1 returns rows where Quantity = 13 or Menu# = 25

Close the query and open the tblOrderDetailsNoIndexes table to confirm that this table has no indexes. The qryOr2 and qryOr3 queries are identical to qryOr1, but they are based on different tables. qryOr2 is based on tblOrderDetailsPartialIndexed, which contains an index on the Menu# field, and qryOr3 is based on tblOrderDetailsFullyIndexed, which contains indexes for both Menu# and Quantity.

Run the three queries in turn. You should notice that qryOr3 is much faster than qryOr1 or qryOr2, which are of similar speed. To get more accurate timings, open the frmQueryTimer form in form view and create a new test comparing the three queries, as shown in Figure 8-12. Press the Run Test button to begin executing each query the number of times specified in the Number of Reps text box. When the test is complete, press the Results button to view a Totals query datasheet that summarizes the results of the test (see Figure 8-13). When we ran this particular test on a 650-MHz Pentium III machine with 448 MB of memory, qryOr3 was 3.67 times faster than qryOr2 and almost 60 times faster than qryOr1! On a slower machine, the results would be even more dramatic.

Follow these steps to take advantage of query optimization in your own queries:

1. Index all table fields that are referenced in the criteria of your queries.

2. Create queries with either:

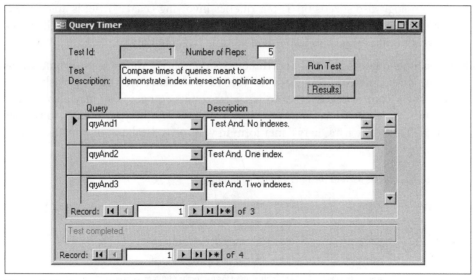

Figure 8-12. A test comparing three queries

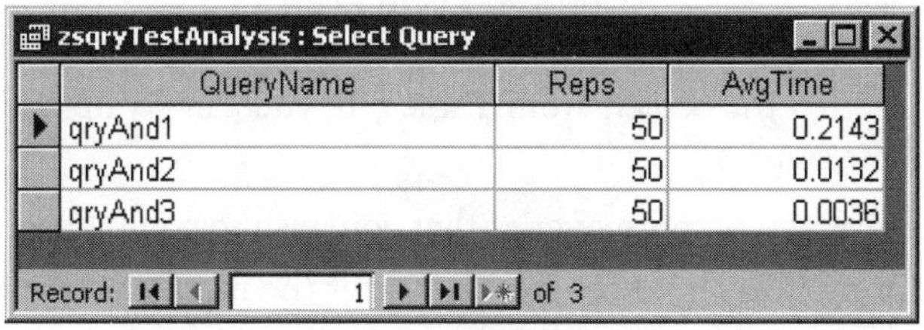

QueryName	Reps	AvgTime
qryAnd1	50	0.2143
qryAnd2	50	0.0132
qryAnd3	50	0.0036

Figure 8-13. The qryOr3 query is 60 times faster than qryOr1

- Two or more criteria on indexed fields in the same underlying table connected with the And operator

- Two or more criteria on indexed fields in the same underlying table connected with the Or operator

In addition, special query optimizations will be used whenever you create Totals queries that make use of the Count(*) expression and have either no criteria or criteria on indexed fields only.

Discussion

The Jet database engine can combine two or more indexes mathematically and thus execute a query using multiple indexes. The net result is faster execution when faced with this kind of query. This technology was originally created by the FoxBASE developers and is used by both Jet and SQL Server.

This technology also speeds up Totals queries involving Count(*). Jet is able to execute this type of query without reading any rows of data; instead, it counts the index rows, which is almost always faster than reading pages of data records.

In the sample database, you'll find three tests comparing the various optimizations using the three different versions of the tblOrderDetails table. You may wish to run these tests on your own computer to see what results you get. You may also wish to import the query timer form into your own database to time your queries in various scenarios. To use the frmQueryTimer form in your own database, import the objects from Table 8-6.

Table 8-6. The objects used in the query timer technique

Object type	Object	Description
Table	zstblTests	One row for each test in frmQueryTimer
Table	zstblQueries	One row for each query compared in a test
Table	zstblTimes	One row for each time recorded in a test
Query	zsqryTestAnalysis	Totals query used to analyze the results of a test
Form	frmQueryTimer	The query timer form
Form	fsubQueries	Subform used in frmQueryTimer

Once you've imported the objects from Table 8-6, you can set up and execute a new test following these steps:

1. Create and save two or more queries that you wish to compare.
2. Open frmQueryTimer in form view and enter the number of times to repeat the test in the Number of Reps text box.
3. Enter a description for the test in the Test Description text box.
4. Add a record to the subform for each query you wish to compare for the test. Use the Query combo box control to select the queries created in Step 1.
5. Click on the Run Test button to run the test. When it's done, the status text box will contain the message "Test completed." Click on the Results button to view a Totals query comparing the average execution times of the queries.

The frmQueryTimer form executes each query repeatedly using a For...Next statement that calls the *acbTimeQuery* function, which is shown here:

```
Public Function acbTimeQuery(ByVal strQry As String, _
    datStart As Date, lngRecs As Long) As Variant

    Dim db As DAO.DATABASE
    Dim qdf As DAO.QueryDef
    Dim rst As DAO.Recordset
    Dim lngStart As Long
    Dim lngEnd As Long
```

```
    Set db = CurrentDb( )
    Set qdf = db.QueryDefs(strQry)

    lngStart = acb_apiGetTickCount( )
    datStart = Now( )

    Set rst = qdf.OpenRecordset(dbOpenSnapshot)

    If Not rst.EOF Then
        rst.MoveLast
        lngRecs = rst.RecordCount
    Else
        lngRecs = 0
    End If

    lngEnd = acb_apiGetTickCount( )

    acbTimeQuery = lngEnd - lngStart
End Function
```

There are two interesting aspects to this function. First, it makes use of the *GetTick-Count* Windows API function to get more accurate measures of time than VBA's built-in *Timer* function can provide. Second, it executes the query by creating a snapshot recordset, not a dynaset-type recordset. This forces the query to execute completely rather than returning just the first page of records.

Query optimization can't work if you don't create indexes. In general, it's a good idea to create an index for every field used in:

- Query criteria
- Query sorts
- Ad-hoc joins (when enforced relationships have not been created)

 Don't create indexes on fields that are part of referential integrity relationships; Access already has indexes to enforce these relationships. Also be aware that Access has a limit of 32 indexes per table. And finally, don't go overboard indexing every field in every table of your database: indexes can slow down operations that modify data.

8.5 Accelerate VBA Code

Problem

You've optimized your forms and queries, but now you need to look at the entire application. Your application contains a lot of VBA code. What optimizations can you perform to make it run faster?

Solution

This solution demonstrates seven specific programmatic techniques you can apply to accelerate your code. The improvement can range from modest increases to increases of several orders of magnitude in performance.

To see the optimizations in action, open and run frmShowOptimizations from *08-05.MDB*, shown in Figure 8-14. Click the Run Tests button, and the tests will run one by one, displaying the results in milliseconds. The tests compare two different methods of using VBA to achieve a result.

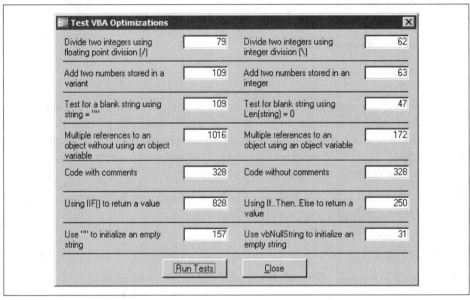

Figure 8-14. The frmShowOptimizations form

Follow these steps to apply the optimizations suggested by these tests to your applications:

1. When dividing integers, use integer division. A majority of the division operations performed by your application are probably done on integer values. Many developers use the slash (/) operator to divide two numbers, but this operator is optimized for floating-point division. If you're dividing integers, you should use the backslash (\) integer division operator instead. With \, Access works at the integer level instead of the floating-point level, so computation is faster. (Of course, this is useful only if you're assigning the results of the division operation to an integer. If you care about the fractional portion of the division, you'll need to use floating-point math and the / operator after all.) For example, instead of:

```
intX = intY / intZ
```

use:

```
intX = intY \ intZ
```

2. Use specific data types instead of variants. Variants offer convenience at the expense of performance. Every time you refer to a variant, Access needs to perform type conversion to ensure the data is in the correct format. By using the data type that matches your variable, you eliminate the need for this type conversion, and your code runs faster. In addition, a variant variable is twice as large as an integer (on a 32-bit operating system) and thus takes longer to manipulate.

3. Test for blank strings using the *Len* function. You probably have code that tests for blank strings by comparing them to an empty string (""). However, because Access stores the length of the string as the first byte in the string, testing for a length of zero using the *Len* function is always faster. Instead of:

```
If strTemp = "" Then
    MsgBox "The string is blank"
End If
```

use:

```
If Len(strTemp) = 0 Then
    MsgBox "The string is blank"
End If
```

4. If you refer to an object more than once in a section of code, assign it to an object variable. Every time you reference an object, Access has to perform some work to figure out which object you are referring to. This adds overhead to your code each time the object is referenced. But if you assign the object to an object variable, Access "finds" the object once and caches the reference in memory. So after the first reference, you can refer to the object through the object variable and your code will run faster. For example, instead of this code:

```
Dim strTmp As String
Dim lngCount As Long

For lngCount = 0 To acbcMaxIterations / 2
    strTmp = DBEngine.Workspaces(0).Groups(0).Name
Next lngCount
```

use:

```
Dim grp As DAO.Group
Dim strTmp As String
Dim lngCount As Long

Set grp = DBEngine.Workspaces(0).Groups(0)

For lngCount = 0 To acbcMaxIterations / 2
    strTmp = grp.Name
Next lngCount
```

We created two variations of this test. First, we changed the function to refer to a control on an open form instead of a DAO group. The cached reference version of the code was 2.8 times faster—significantly improved, but not of the same magnitude as the DAO group comparison. Second, we compared using an object variable against using the VBA With...End With construct (without an object reference). With...End With was slower than using an object variable, but still much faster than using neither an object variable nor With...End With.

5. Don't worry about comments. In VBA the use of comments exacts no measurable performance penalty, so there's no excuse for omitting them!

6. Use If...Then...Else instead of the *IIf* function. By replacing *IIf* statements with the equivalent If...Then...Else statement, your code will run faster. For example, instead of:

```
MsgBox IIf(intX = 1, "One", "Not One")
```

use:

```
If intX = 1 Then
    MsgBox "One"
Else
    MsgBox "Not One"
End If
```

7. When initializing a string so that it's empty, don't use a literal value (""). Instead, use the built-in vbNullString constant. You'll get better performance, as the test demonstrates.

Discussion

Many optimizations that apply to other languages can also apply to VBA. For example, checking for blank strings using the *Len* function is a common optimization in other languages. Don't be afraid to try new techniques. The small performance improvements you get from optimizing VBA code can add up if you are running code in a repetitive loop, and many small improvements may result in a noticeable overall difference in your application.

Optimization techniques for programming languages are a vital part of your toolbox. But don't sacrifice other vital elements for the sake of speed. First, make sure your code works correctly before you optimize. Second, write your code so that it's easily understood; it can be very difficult to optimize code you don't understand. Finally, don't break working code when optimizing it. By optimizing code that works correctly (albeit slowly), you may introduce bugs. Follow the three rules of optimization:

- Make it right before you make it faster.
- Make it clear before you make it faster.
- Keep it right as you make it faster.

You may find that there are no easy optimizations for a particular piece of code. No matter what you do, it just won't run fast enough. A favorite saying in software design is "Don't diddle code to make it faster; find a better algorithm." Often you need to step back from a piece of slow code. Maybe there is a better overall approach or a better algorithm you can employ. A good way to get over a hurdle such as this is to ask other programmers how they handle the same situation. Overall, you will find that code optimizations have a much smaller impact on your application's performance than optimizations to your data access; for example, adding one extra index can have a greater impact than hours and hours of time spent optimizing VBA.

 As they say in the auto commercials, "Your mileage may vary." Don't assume anything is faster until you've proven it yourself on the machine that will run your application!

8.6   Test the Comparative Benefits of Various Optimization Techniques

Problem

Now that you've tried the optimization techniques in this chapter, you'd like to test some additional optimization ideas. How can you test various VBA optimization techniques in a standardized fashion?

Solution

By using a Windows API call, some simple math, and a wrapper function, you can easily compare the performance of two optimization techniques with relatively high accuracy. This solution shows you how to create a form to compare the performance of two functions. It runs the functions and then displays how long each took to execute.

Open and run frmTestOptimize from *08-06.MDB*. The form shown in Figure 8-15 allows you to enter the names of two functions and test their performance relative to each other. The *08-06.MDB* database contains two sample functions that show the relative performance of integer division and floating-point division. (This optimization was discussed in the Solution in Recipe 8.4.) To run the test, enter:

```
FloatDivision( )
```

into the Function 1 text box, and enter:

```
IntegerDivision( )
```

into the Function 2 text box. Press the Test button. The form will run each function, show the time taken by each function, and tell you which function is faster and by how much.

To use frmTestOptimize to test your own functions, follow these steps:

1. Import frmTestOptimize from *08-06.MDB* into your database. This form is completely self-contained and requires no other objects.

2. Open frmTestOptimize in form view and enter the name of the two functions you wish to test along with any required parameters. Type the entries in the

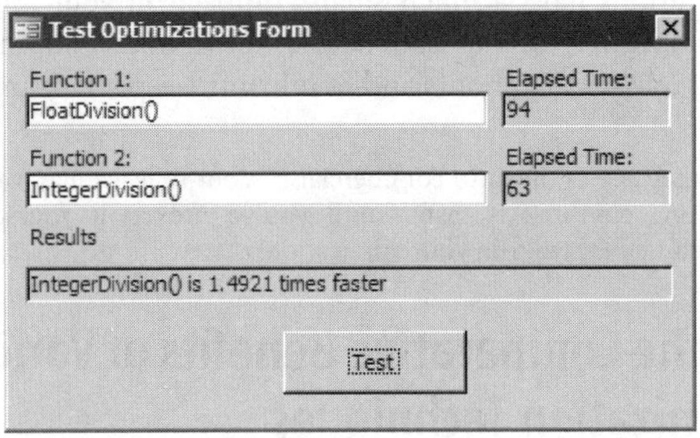

Figure 8-15. The Test Optimizations form

Function 1 and Function 2 text boxes exactly as if you were calling the functions in your VBA code, but omit the assignment operator and assignment object. For example, for a function that is called in your VBA code like this:

```
intReturned = MyTestFunction ("MyTable")
```

type the following into the frmTestOptimize text box:

```
MyTestFunction ("MyTable")
```

Discussion

There are two key aspects to this technique. First, we used the Windows API *Get-TickCount* function. *GetTickCount* returns the number of milliseconds elapsed since Windows was started. This number is useful when employed to compare two points in time. You may wonder if you can use the Timer function built into Access instead, or even the Now function; however, both of these return time values that are accurate only to within about one tenth of a second, even though they can show numbers that appear to have greater precision. You will lose a great deal of accuracy with these functions. Because *GetTickCount* returns time measurements in milliseconds, it is more accurate than VBA's *Timer* or *Now* functions.

Second, this optimization test technique makes use of the *Eval* function, which is one of the least understood yet most powerful functions in Access. You can use *Eval* to execute a function that is named in a variable or some other expression. If you have programmed in a lower-level language such as C or Pascal, you probably miss Basic's absence of pointers to functions. You can use the *Eval* function to simulate this by passing a function name as a parameter to *Eval*. This technique calls *Eval* for both functions you type into the form.

When you are testing optimization techniques, watch out for a couple of things that can yield false results:

• Both Access and Windows use caching algorithms to reduce disk writes. Any tests that access objects from the database must take this into account. For example, if you are testing an optimization on form load time, your results can be erroneous if you perform the comparison of the two methods one after the other. The first time you load the form, Access caches it in memory if possible; the second time, the form invariably loads faster because Access is retrieving it from memory rather than disk. This can skew your test results. There are several ways to get around the effects of caching; probably the simplest is to repeat all tests, reversing the order the second time you perform the test.

• Windows is a multitasking operating system. Because of this, your test results may be further skewed by the fact that Windows may be performing some other operation in the background while one of your tests is running—for example, a word-processing document may be automatically saved in the background in the middle of your test. The best way to minimize this factor is to ensure that no other Windows programs are running when you perform your tests. It is always a good idea to run the test several times and average the results.

8.7   Accelerate Multiuser Applications

Problem

You have a single-user application that you just converted to run on a network to be shared by multiple users. Your once-responsive application is now sluggish. How can you improve the performance of multiuser applications?

Solution

Moving a single-user application to a shared environment can make that application slower for at least three reasons. First, to read or write data from the database, the data must now travel across relatively slow network wires. This is almost always slower than reading and writing data directly to a local hard disk drive. Second, every time a record is written to disk, Access must spend time obtaining, releasing, and managing locks to make sure that two users do not write to a page of records at the same time. Third, if multiple users are trying to access the same records in the database, they must wait their turns before gaining access to the records. Because of these factors, you need to make an extra effort to optimize multiuser applications to bring their speed to an acceptable level. This solution discusses one way to improve performance by limiting the number of records in your form's recordsets.

This solution employs two files, *08-07FE.MDB* and *08-07BE.MDB*. You'll first need to link the data tables from *08-07BE.MDB* (the "backend" or data database) to *08-07FE.MDB* (the "frontend" or application database). Linking a data table allows you to use a table from one Access database within another Access database. Start Access and load *08-07FE.MDB*. Choose File → Get External Data Link Tables and select *08-07BE.MDB* as the Access link database. At the Link Tables dialog, select tblPeople and click OK. (To appreciate the extra demands made on a multiuser application, you may wish to move the *08-07BE.MDB* database to a file server on your local area network first.)

Splitting Multiuser Databases

This solution makes use of a common multiuser technique: splitting the application and data into separate databases. Multiuser application performance can be improved considerably if you place the data (or backend database) on the file server and a copy of the application (or frontend database) on each user's desktop. Access includes the Database Splitter Wizard, which makes it easy to split an existing database into data and application databases. Select Tools → Database Utilities → Database Splitter to run the wizard.

Once you've fixed up the link to tblPeople in the backend database, open the frmPeopleFindFirst form in form view and note how long it takes to load the form. Enter the value 60000 into the text box in the header of the form. Press the Goto Record button to move to the record with an ID of 60000. The time this operation takes is displayed to the right of the command button (see Figure 8-16).

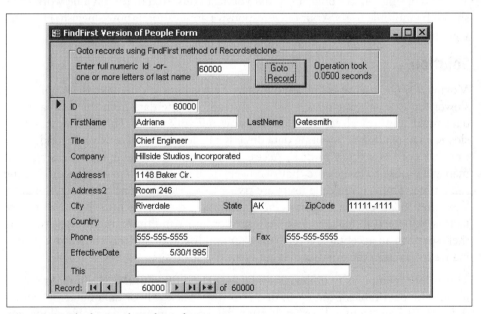

Figure 8-16. The frmPeopleFindFirst form

Now close the form and open the frmPeopleRSChange form in form view. This form is similar to frmPeopleFindFirst, except that it initially loads with only one record in its recordset. Because of this, load time should be faster than for frmPeopleFindFirst.

This form also differs in how it searches for records. Instead of using the potentially slow FindFirst method to navigate to a different record, it changes the record source of the form on the fly. Enter the value 60000 into the text box in the header of frmPeopleRSChange and press the Goto Record button. The time this operation takes should be faster than for frmPeopleFindFirst (see Figure 8-17).

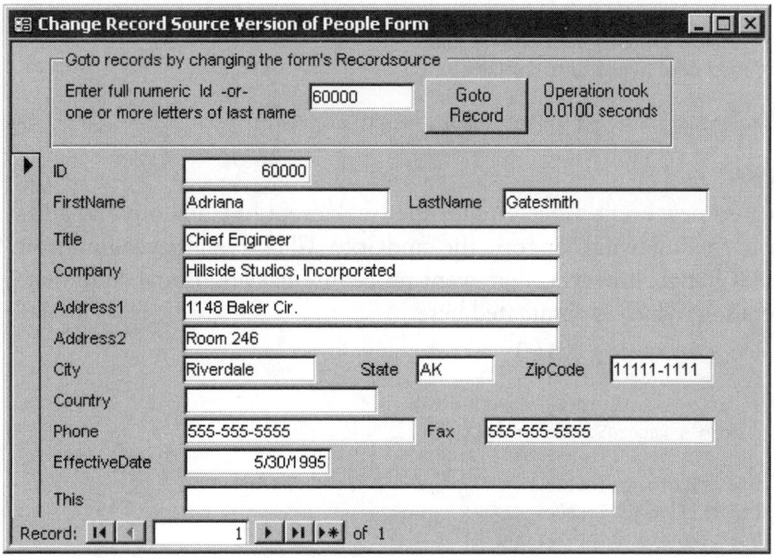

Figure 8-17. The more multiuser-friendly frmPeopleRSChange form

Although the performance difference between these two forms may be noticeable with 60,000 records in the sample database, it's not that great. With more records or across a busy network, however, the difference will be much more significant. Still, even without a noticeable performance improvement, this technique significantly reduces the load you are placing on the network.

Follow these steps to create a form that uses the record source changing technique of frmPeopleRSChange:

1. Create a new form or edit an existing form in design view. Change the Record-Source property of the form so that it initially loads no records. The most efficient way to do this is to use a Select statement that restricts the record source by its primary key field to a nonexistent record. For example, we used the following record source for frmPeopleRSChange:

```
SELECT * FROM tblPeople WHERE ID = 0
```

This will cause Access to place you on the new record that's normally at the end of a form's recordset. If you prefer, you can use a Select statement that returns some small subset of the records instead.

2. Add an unbound text box named txtGoto to the form's header. Add a command button control named cmdGoto to the right of the text box.

3. Create a new event procedure for the Change event of the txtGoto text box. (If you're unsure of how to do this, see "How Do I Create an Event Procedure?" in the Preface of this book.) Add the following code to the event procedure:

```
Private Sub txtGoto_Change( )

    ' Enable cmdGoto only when a character
    ' has been typed into txtGoto

    Me.cmdGoto.Enabled = (Not IsNull(Me.txtGoto.Text))

End Sub
```

4. Create a new event procedure for the Click event of cmdGoto and add code similar to the following (or copy the cmdGoto_Click event procedure from frmPeopleRSChange; however, that event procedure has additional code that times the operation, which is eliminated here):

```
Private Sub cmdGoto_Click( )

    ' Go to new record by changing the
    ' form's RecordSource property

    Dim ctlGoto As TextBox
    Dim ctlTime As TextBox
    Dim varCriteria As Variant
    Dim lngStart As Long
    Dim lngEnd As Long
    Dim dblTime As Double

    On Error GoTo HandleErr

    Const acbcQuote = """"

    ' Start the timer.
    lngStart = acb_apiGetTickCount( )

    Set ctlGoto = Me.txtGoto
    Set ctlTime = Me.txtTime

    ' Create criteria based on the type of data
    ' entered into txtGoto.
    If IsNumeric(ctlGoto.Value) Then
        varCriteria = "ID = " & CLng(ctlGoto.Value)
    Else
        ' A string, so search LastName.
        varCriteria = "LastName Like " & acbcQuote & _
        ctlGoto.Value & "*" & acbcQuote
    End If

    ' Change the form's recordset based on criteria.
```

```
        Me.RecordSource = "SELECT * FROM tblPeople WHERE " _
        & varCriteria

        lngEnd = acb_apiGetTickCount( )

        ' Now check the form's recordset to see if
        ' any records were found.

        With Me.Recordset
            If .EOF And .BOF Then
                MsgBox "No matching record found.", _
                vbOKOnly + vbCritical, "Goto Procedure"
            End If
        End With

        ' Post the time to txtTime.
        dblTime = (lngEnd - lngStart) / 1000
        ctlTime = "Operation took " & Format(dblTime, "##0.00") _
        & " seconds"

ExitHere:
    Exit Sub

HandleErr:
    Select Case Err.Number
    Case Else
        MsgBox "Error#" & Err.Number & ": " & Err.Description, _
        , "Goto Procedure"
        Resume ExitHere
    End Select
End Sub
```

See Section 8.7.3 for information on how to customize this code for your particular form.

5. Save the form and switch to form view to test it.

Discussion

In a multiuser environment, it's always important to limit the amount of data sent across the network to your desktop. By default, however, Access binds forms to all records in the table or query to which your form is bound. This is fine for smaller recordsets of perhaps less than 20,000 records (the exact cutoff figure will vary based on the speed of your PCs, the speed of your network cards and file server, and the average network load), but it can slow things considerably for moderately large recordsets. This solution improves the performance of the form and reduces network traffic by carefully limiting the records in the form's recordset.

By using a SQL statement that initially returns no records as the form's record source, you can quickly open the form in append mode. When the user enters a value in the txtGoto text box and presses the Goto Record button, code attached to the button's Click event changes the form's RecordSource to the correct record.

The event procedure behind the cmdGoto command button begins by setting up an error handler, declaring a few variables, and setting ctlGoto to point to the txtGoto text box control:

```
On Error GoTo cmdGotoClickErr

Dim ctlGoto As TextBox
Dim varCriteria As Variant

Const acbQuote = """"

Set ctlGoto = Me.txtGoto
```

Next, the criteria of the SQL Select statement is constructed using this code:

```
' Create criteria based on the type of data
' entered into txtGoto.
If IsNumeric(ctlGoto.Value) Then
    varCriteria = "ID = " & CLng(ctlGoto.Value)
Else
    ' A string, so search LastName
    varCriteria = "LastName Like " & acbQuote & _
    ctlGoto.Value & "*" & acbQuote
End If
```

In the case of the people form, we decided to be flexible and allow users to search on either last name or ID. You'll want to make sure the fields you allow the user to search are indexed. The code determines which field the user wishes to search by using the *IsNumeric* function to test if the entered value is a number. If so, the code constructs criteria using the ID field of tblPeople. If the entered value is non-numeric, then the code assumes the user wishes to search on LastName. Again, we add a bit of flexibility by allowing the user to enter partial matches—the criteria string is constructed using the Like operator. Because this is a Text field, we must surround the value with quotes, so we use the acbcQuote constant that we defined earlier in the procedure. Finally, we have added "*" (an asterisk) before the closing quote to perform a pattern match search.

If you wish, you can simplify this code on your own form to use a single field. Either way, you'll need to change the references to ID and LastName to match the names of the fields (*not* the control names) in your form's record source. If you decide to allow a search on a date/time field, make sure you surround the date/time value with # (pound signs) instead of quotes.

With the criteria built, the SQL statement is easily created:

```
' Change the form's recordset based on criteria.
Me.RecordSource = "SELECT * FROM tblPeople WHERE " & varCriteria
```

Of course, you'll need to replace tblPeople with the name of the table or query on which your form is based.

The remaining code determines if any records were found:

```
' Now check the form's recordset to see if
' any records were found.

With Me.Recordset
    If .EOF And .BOF Then
        MsgBox "No matching record found.", _
            vbOKOnly + vbCritical, "Goto Procedure"
    End If
End With
```

This portion of code is not absolutely required, because Access will pull up the "new" record if no matching records are found. However, you might prefer to notify the user when no records were found. You can do this by using the form's Recordset property to return a recordset object that you can inspect. If the recordset is empty, Access sets both the end of file (EOF) and beginning of file (BOF) flags to True, so you can use this fact to test for the absence of records in the form's recordset.

A simple error handler is included in this procedure. It's important to include error-handling code in all multiuser procedures to handle the cases where records are locked. See Chapter 10 for more information on developing multiuser applications.

The one negative side to using this technique is that users may find it restrictive if they are used to navigating freely among records using the navigation controls at the bottom of the form. The sample form allows users to grab a subset of records from tblPeople by entering a partial match on LastName. If you also need to return groups of records when using numeric primary key field searches, you can use two text boxes to allow users to search for a range of primary key values, perhaps including code that limits the range to some arbitrary number.

The techniques presented in this solution apply equally to client/server applications.

See Also

Additional optimization strategies for client/server applications are discussed in the Solution in Recipe 8.8 and in Chapter 14.

8.8   Accelerate Client/Server Applications

Problem

You are using Access as a front end to linked tables stored in a client/server database. You're not satisfied with the response time of your client/server application. What can you do to make it run faster?

Solution

You can apply a variety of optimization techniques when developing client/server applications. If you are attaching remote tables in databases such as SQL Server or

Oracle, you are accessing data through open database connectivity (ODBC) drivers. Typically, client/server applications using ODBC require more horsepower on the part of workstations and the network. By knowing how data is retrieved from the server, you can make your application run faster.

Another option is to create an Access Data Project (ADP). This is possible only if your data is stored in SQL Server. Instead of using ODBC, ADPs use a newer technology, OLE DB, to connect to the data. However, although OLE DB is newer, it isn't necessarily faster than linking to tables using ODBC. Chapter 14 includes several solutions related to the use of Access project applications.

There is no sample database for this solution. Here are some suggestions to consider when optimizing your linked-table client/server application:

1. Your forms should retrieve as few records as possible when loading (fetching data is a significant bottleneck in client/server applications). Design your form to retrieve few or no records by using the technique demonstrated in the Solution in Recipe 8.7.

2. Optimize the way your application connects to the server. When the user starts your application, log the user into the server using the OpenDatabase method. This establishes a connection and caches it in memory. Subsequent data access is faster because the connection has already been established. Use code similar to the following:

```
Sub PreConnectUser (strUser As String, strPass As String)
    Dim wrk As DAO.Workspace
    Dim db As DAO.Database
    Dim strConnect As Database

    strConnect = "ODBC;DSN=MyServer;DATABASE=dbCustomers;" _
      & "UID=" & strUser & ";" _
      "PWD="  & strPass & ";"
    Set wrk = DBEngine.Workspaces(0)
    Set db = wrk.OpenDatabase("", False, False, strConnect)
End Sub
```

3. Reduce connections by limiting recordsets to 100 records or fewer. Most servers (such as SQL Server) require two connections for recordsets of more than 100 records. By limiting the size of the recordset, you reduce the number of connections that need to be made, speeding up your application.

4. Offload as much query processing as possible to the server. Generally, your server will search and process data faster than the local Jet engine, especially if there are many concurrent users (this is probably the reason you moved to client/server in the first place). Design your queries to eliminate expressions or functionality not supported by the server. If the server does not support an expression or function used in your query, Access will process the query locally and performance will suffer. Read the documentation that comes with your

database server to determine which functionality is supported, and use profiling tools on the server (like the SQL Server Profiler) to see what is actually being processed on the server.

5. Add a timestamp field to a table to improve update and deletion performance. The server automatically updates Timestamp fields, also called Rowversion fields, when any data in a row is modified. If a table has a Timestamp field, Access can use it to determine quickly whether a record has changed. If the table doesn't have this field, Access needs to compare the contents of every field to see if the record has changed. Obviously, checking a single field is a lot faster. To add a Timestamp field to a table on the server, you can create and execute a SQL-specific query in Access using the ALTER TABLE statement with syntax similar to the following:

```
ALTER TABLE Customers ADD MyTimeStampCol TIMESTAMP
```

6. Avoid using server data to fill list box and combo box controls. The performance of these controls is generally poor when accessing server data. Instead, consider storing the data for the list box or combo box in a local database. This approach works if the data does not change frequently and can be easily copied from the server. See the Solution in Recipe 8.2 for more on list box and combo box performance issues and alternatives to their use.

7. For working with server data in code, ADO is more efficient than DAO. We can't discuss ADO coding techniques fully here, but take the time to learn ADO if you want to fill recordsets with server data or to execute server commands. (On the other hand, DAO recordsets tend to be more efficient, and simpler to use, when working with Jet-based data—data retrieved from *MDB* or *MDE* files.) Pay special attention to the CursorLocation property, which allows you to close a connection and still be able to work with the data in a client-side ADO recordset. Here is an example of opening a client-side recordset, disconnecting from the database, and then working with the data in the cached recordset:

```
Dim cnn As ADODB.Connection
Dim rst As ADODB.Recordset
Dim strEmployees As String

Set cnn = New ADODB.Connection
cnn.Open "Provider=SQLOLEDB.1;" _
  & "Data Source=(local);Initial Catalog=Northwind;" _
  & "User ID=username;Password=secretpwd"
Set rst = New ADODB.Recordset
rst.CursorLocation = adUseClient
rst.Open _
    Source:="SELECT EmployeeID," _
    & " LastName, FirstName" _
    & " FROM Employees" _
    & " WHERE EmployeeID = 5", _
    ActiveConnection:=cnn, _
    CursorType:=adOpenStatic, _
    Options:=adCmdText
```

```
Set rst.ActiveConnection = Nothing
cnn.Close
Set cnn = Nothing
Debug.Print rst("FirstName")
rst.Close
Set rst = Nothing
```

Discussion

Understanding how client/server applications differ from single-user and file-server applications is crucial to optimizing their performance. The key is in deciding when to let Access do the work and when to let the server do the work. With a few exceptions, you want the server to perform queries and Access to perform user-interface operations. Concentrate on minimizing the traffic across the network by reducing the data retrieved from and written to the server. To work with server data programmatically, use ADO rather than DAO.

Access includes a wizard called the Performance Analyzer. You should use this wizard to analyze the performance of all your forms (and other database objects). Although it is somewhat limited in the suggestions it can make, it's a nice way to check if you've missed any obvious problems. For example, when running the Analyzer against the queries in *08-04.MDB*, it will suggest adding several indexes.

CHAPTER 9

User Interface

No matter how much you do behind the scenes to create a solid and robust application, the users of your application see only your user interface. Certainly, perfecting the database and application design is crucial—but once that's done, it pays to devote considerable time to designing a user interface that is workable, aesthetically pleasing, and helps the users get their work done. By implementing the ideas and techniques in this chapter, you'll be on your way to creating an interface that has ease of use and productivity written all over it.

You'll learn how to take full advantage of special keystrokes to help users navigate through a complex application. You'll also learn how to create forms that have no menus or toolbars and how to create a map-based interface that lets users navigate by pointing to and clicking on various parts of a map.

Next, you'll learn how to ease data-entry pain with forms that let users mark their place while they peruse other records, and how to add shortcut menus to forms. You'll also see how you can create forms that carry data forward from record to record, how to hide complexity from your users with a dialog that expands on request to reveal complex options, and how to use a combo box not just to select from a list, but also to maintain that list with new entries as they are needed.

Finally, you'll learn how to create and use two generic, reusable components: a pop-up calendar form for entering dates that makes use of an ActiveX control, and a custom-built status meter form complete with an optional Cancel button.

 Several of the examples in this chapter take advantage of the DAO type library, rather than the default ADO library used by Access 2002 and Access 2003. Even though it's less "modern," DAO provides greater functionality, and generally better performance. In addition, using DAO makes it possible for these demonstrations to work in earlier versions of Access. If you want to try these techniques in your own applications, make sure you add the DAO reference to your project using the Tools → References menu item from within VBA—it won't be added by default.

9.1 Create Context-Sensitive Keyboard Shortcuts

Problem

You've used Access's AutoKeys macro to create keyboard shortcuts for your application, but you'd like the shortcut keys to change based on the currently active form. Is there an easy way to create context-sensitive keyboard shortcuts in Access?

Solution

The SetOption method of the Application object allows you to change global database options programmatically. This solution shows you how to combine this functionality with the Activate and Deactivate event properties of your forms to create custom key shortcut macros for each form of your application.

For an example of key assignments that depend on the active form, open *09-01. MDB*. This sample database contains information on units, assemblies that make up parts, and parts that make up assemblies. Open the frmUnit form in form view. At any time, you can press Ctrl-D to "drill down" to the next level of detail or Ctrl-R to revert to the previous level of detail. When you press Ctrl-D on frmUnit, frmAssembly is loaded; if you press Ctrl-D from frmAssembly, frmPart is loaded (see Figure 9-1). If you press Ctrl-D a third time while frmPart has the focus, nothing happens. Thus, the behavior of Ctrl-D changes based on its context. The Ctrl-R keyboard macro is similarly context-sensitive.

> To keep the example simple, we have not added the additional macro code necessary to keep the forms synchronized. You must manually use Ctrl-R to return to the previous level/form, then navigate to the desired record, and then use Ctrl-D to drill down if you wish to keep the forms synchronized.

To add context-sensitive AutoKeys macros to your own application, follow these steps:

1. Create a key assignment macro for each form in your application (you can use the same macro for more than one form if you like). Follow all the design rules for an AutoKeys macro, but give your macro a unique name when you are done. In the sample application, for instance, the three key assignment macros are called mcrUnitAutoKeys, mcrAssemblyAutoKeys, and mcrPartAutoKeys, so that the macro name reminds you of its function. Table 9-1 shows the settings for the mcrUnitAutoKeys macro.

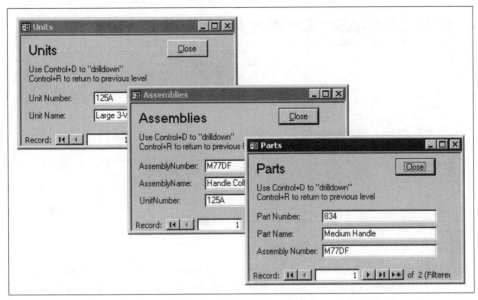

Figure 9-1. The sample database after pressing Ctrl-D twice

Table 9-1. Settings for the mcrUnitAutoKeys macro

Macro name	Action	Argument	Value
^D	OpenForm	Form Name	frmAssembly
		View	Form
		Where Condition	[UnitNumber]=[Forms]![frmUnit]![UnitNumber]
		Data Mode	Edit
		Window Mode	Normal
^R	Close	Object Type	Form
		Object Name	frmUnit

You'll probably want to add comments to your macro to make it easier to understand and maintain, as illustrated in Figure 9-2.

2. Import the basOptions module from 09-01.MDB into your own database.

3. Add a RunCode action to your AutoExec macro (or create a new macro named AutoExec containing this one action). Set the action's Function Name argument to:

```
=acbStoreOriginalAutoKeys( )
```

4. In the OnActivate event property of each of your forms, add a call to the *acbSetAutoKeys* function. This function takes a single argument, the name of the key assignment macro to use while that form is active. For example, on the frmUnit form in the sample application, this property is set to:

```
=acbSetAutokeys("mcrUnitAutokeys")
```

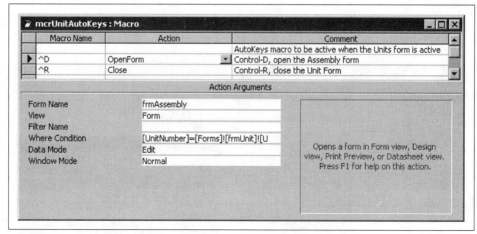

Figure 9-2. The mcrUnitAutoKeys macro

5. In the OnClose event of the *last* form to be closed in your application (typically, your main switchboard form), add a call to the *acbRestoreOriginalAutokeys* function. If there is more than one possible last form in your application, you'll need to add this function call to *every possible* last form. *acbRestoreOriginalAutokeys* takes no arguments. Figure 9-3 shows these calls in the sample application.

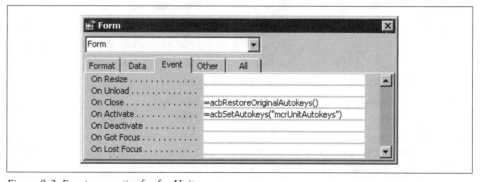

Figure 9-3. Event properties for frmUnit

Discussion

The special built-in Application object refers to your entire Access application. The GetOption method of this object lets you read the options stored under Tools Options, Tools Startup, and additional options that are available only programmatically. The Key Assignment Macro option, which was originally part of the View Options dialog in Access 2.0, is no longer available from the Access user interface, but fortunately it is still available programmatically.

Because the database options are stored in the user's registry, any changes you make to them will affect not only the current database but also any other database the user runs. It's best to store the original value of any option you change and restore it when your application is closed. The *acbStoreOriginalAutokeys* function uses the GetOption method to read the original key assignment macro name when your application is loaded and store it in the *mstrOriginalAutokeys* module-level variable. Like the rest of the functions in this solution, *acbStoreOriginalAutokeys* is very simple, consisting of one statement, a few comments, and an error handler:

```
Public Function acbStoreOriginalAutokeys( )

    ' Store the user's original Autokeys macro name
    ' so we can restore it when we're done.

    On Error GoTo HandleErr

    mstrOriginalAutokeys = Application.GetOption("Key Assignment Macro")

ExitHere:
    Exit Function

HandleErr:
    MsgBox "Error " & Err.Number & ": " & Err.Description, _
        , "acbStoreOriginalAutokeys( )"
    Resume ExitHere
End Function
```

The *acbRestoreOriginalAutokeys* function resets the option to its original value. This function should be called from the last open form. In the sample database, it is called from the Close event of frmUnit. Its source code is:

```
Public Function acbRestoreOriginalAutokeys( )

    ' Put the Autokeys macro setting back the way we found it.

    On Error GoTo HandleErr

    Application.SetOption "Key Assignment Macro", mstrOriginalAutokeys

ExitHere:
    Exit Function

HandleErr:
    MsgBox "Error " & Err.Number & ": " & Err.Description, _
        , "acbRestoreOriginalAutokeys( )"
    Resume ExitHere
End Function
```

Each form passes the name of its custom key assignment macro to the *acbSetAutokeys* function when the form is activated. The Activate event of the form calls this function. The function uses the SetOption method to take the passed macro and make it the key assignment macro. Its source code is:

```
Public Function acbSetAutokeys(strMacroName As String)

    ' Set a new Autokeys macro. Takes the name of the
    ' macro to use for keyboard reassignment.

    On Error GoTo HandleErr

    Application.SetOption "Key Assignment Macro", strMacroName

ExitHere:
    Exit Function

HandleErr:
    MsgBox "Error " & Err.Number & ": " & Err.Description, _
        , "acbSetAutokeys( )"
    Resume ExitHere
End Function
```

You can generalize this technique of using GetOption and SetOption to control many properties of your application at runtime—for example, to activate the status bar and toolbars or to allow the user to pick a new font for datasheets from a list you supply. You should always follow the same three basic steps:

1. Use GetOption to read the current option value and save it in a module-level variable.

2. Use SetOption to set your new value. Be sure to use the name of the option exactly as it appears in the Access online help.

3. Use SetOption to restore the original value when your application is closed.

Overlapping User Interface (UI) Methods

In a well-designed Windows application, keyboard shortcuts should not be the only method a user can employ to accomplish a task. Because they are hard for new users to discover or for infrequent users to remember, keyboard shortcuts should be used only as an alternative method of accomplishing a task. Make the task available from some other UI method, preferably one that is more easily discovered than a keyboard shortcut. Other UI methods include command buttons, toolbar buttons, standard menus, and shortcut menus.

To reduce the time delay in switching key assignment macros, we decided to reset the user's key assignment macro only when the last open form is closed. A safer but perhaps slower alternative would be to reset the key assignment macro in the Deactivate event of each form.

The individual calls to the *acbSetAutoKeys* function are attached to the forms' Activate events instead of their GotFocus events for a very good reason. Unless there are no controls on a form that can get the focus, the form itself will *never* receive the focus. Only forms consisting strictly of graphic objects and disabled controls will ever trigger a form-level GotFocus event.

It is interesting to note that AutoKeys functionality is just about the only thing left in Access that can be done only by using macros, not in VBA code.

9.2   Create a Form with No Menu or Toolbar

Problem

You'd like to completely disable menus for a form, and the toolbar too. Is there any way to remove menus and toolbars from a form?

Solution

If you set the MenuBar property of a form to point to a macro in Access that contains no macro actions, you can trick Access into not displaying any menus. This solution demonstrates this trick and also discusses how you can apply it to the global menus of an application. In addition, you'll learn how to use VBA code to remove a form's toolbar.

To create forms in your database without any menus, follow these steps:

1. Create a new macro sheet without any actions. The mcrNoMenus macro sheet in *09-02.MDB* has no macro actions.

2. Create a new form or open an existing form in design view. Select the menu macro from Step 1 as the MenuBar property for the form.

3. Add the following Activate and Deactivate event procedures to the form to remove the toolbar for this form only:

```
Private Sub Form_Activate( )
    DoCmd.ShowToolbar "Form View", acToolbarNo
End Sub

Private Sub Form_Deactivate( )
    DoCmd.ShowToolbar "Form View", acToolbarWhereApprop
End Sub
```

4. Optionally, you may wish to also eliminate right-click shortcut menus for your form. To do this, set the ShortcutMenuBar property of the form to No.

5. Save the form.

To see an example, load the *09-02.MDB* sample database. Open the frmCustomer-DefaultMenus form in form view and note that the default Access menu and toolbar are available at the top of the screen (see Figure 9-4). Close this form and open frm-CustomerNoMenus. Note the absence of any menu or toolbar for the form (see Figure 9-5).

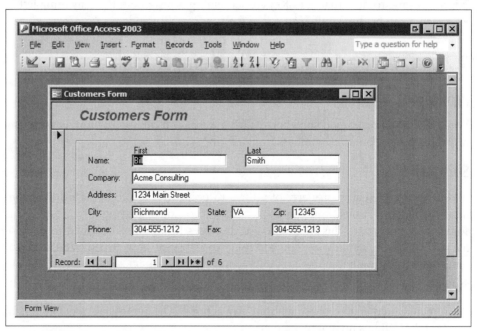

Figure 9-4. The frmCustomerDefaultMenus form with the default Access menu bar

Discussion

In early versions of Access, macros were the only method of creating custom menus. Despite the newer Command Bar menus and toolbars supported in recent versions of Access, you can still create custom menus in Access by creating menu macros. When you open a form with custom menus, Access reconstructs the custom menus from

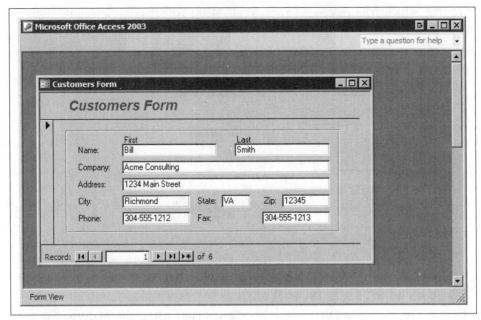

Figure 9-5. The frmCustomerNoMenus form with no menu bar

the hierarchy of macros attached to the form's MenuBar property. However, if you attach an empty macro to the MenuBar property, Access creates a blank menu for the form.

The ShowToolbar macro action, which you call in VBA using DoCmd.ShowToolbar, enables you to show or hide any toolbar. The code hides the default toolbar when the form becomes active. The Deactivate code is equally important—without it, that toolbar will remain hidden for all subsequent forms that you view. The Deactivate event procedure tells Access to show that toolbar again whenever it is appropriate.

You may want to eliminate menus for a form to reduce the complexity of your application or to remove potential chinks in your application's armor. Whenever you remove built-in functionality from forms, however, you must ensure that users of your forms can still perform essential activities. For example, you wouldn't want to remove menus and set the ControlBox and CloseButton properties of your form to No *unless* you have added either a toolbar button or a command button that could be used to close the form. Another alternative is to use the View Toolbars Customize dialog to create your own menus and toolbars containing only the commands you want to expose.

In addition to removing menus for a single form, you can set the application's default menu bar to point to an empty macro. Select Tools → Startup to set the default menu bar. In Figure 9-6, we set the default MenuBar property of the Startup dialog to mcrNoMenus, thus removing menus for all forms in the application for which custom menus were not created. Another option is to uncheck the AllowFullMenus property, which tells Access to remove all menu commands that allow users to switch to design view.

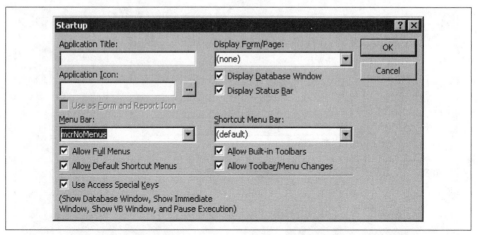

Figure 9-6. The Startup dialog allows you to customize various default properties

You can also customize the default shortcut menus using the Startup dialog by changing the AllowDefaultShortcutMenus and ShortcutMenuBar properties.

9.3   Create a Geographical Map Interface

Problem

You want to display a map and allow users to click on regions of the map. You want the form to react based on which region is clicked on. The regions aren't necessarily rectangular. How can you do this?

Solution

You can accomplish this task using a combination of bitmaps and transparent command buttons. Depending on how far from rectangular your shapes are, this task may be trivial or quite involved. By making the command buttons transparent, you make the application appear to react directly to mouse clicks on the map.

Open frmWesternUS in *09-03.MDB* (Figure 9-7). This form has been created with an imported bitmap file as the background. Above each state's image on the map there's at least one command button with its Transparent property set to Yes. Figure 9-8 shows the form named frmWesternUSDesign, in which the buttons are not transparent. Here you can see the actual layout of the command buttons.

To implement similar functionality in your own forms, follow these steps:

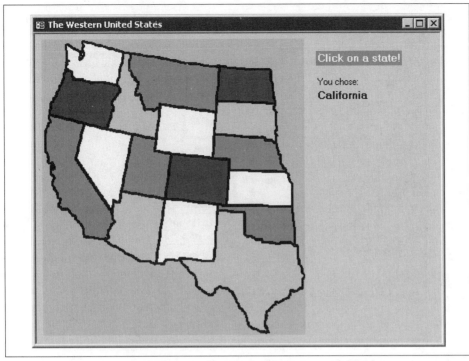

Figure 9-7. The finished map form, frmWesternUS, with transparent buttons

1. Create a new form. Click anywhere in the detail section of the form, and select Insert Object (or use the form design toolbox to place an unbound object frame control form on the form). Once you release the mouse button, Access displays a dialog requesting information about the object. At this point, you can create a new object by launching an application such as Microsoft Paint, or you can create an object from an existing file. If you choose the latter, a Browse button will appear. Click on the Browse button to select a file (see Figure 9-9). Choose the appropriate image for the background. For the example form, use *USWEST. BMP*.

2. Set the bitmap's SizeMode property to Clip. This disallows resizing of the bitmap, as you'll be overlaying the bitmap with command buttons.

 Using Shift and Ctrl plus the arrow keys is helpful in achieving exact placement of the command buttons. Use Shift-arrow to expand and contract the size of a control one pixel at a time; use Ctrl-arrow to move the control one pixel at a time.

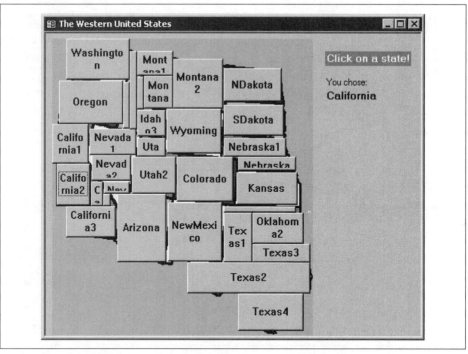

Figure 9-8. The same bitmap form with buttons showing

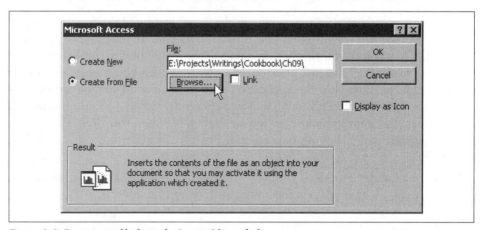

Figure 9-9. Browsing a file from the Insert Object dialog

3. Overlay each defined area of the bitmap with a command button, naming each as desired. Figure 9-8 shows the completed process for the sample form. You'll find that for odd-shaped regions, you'll need to use multiple buttons, as demonstrated for Idaho, Texas, and Nevada on the map.

4. Select all the command buttons (hold down the Shift key and click on each). On the properties sheet, set the Transparent property to Yes, making the selected controls invisible yet active. Figure 9-10 shows the sample form in design view; note that you can still see a faint outline of each button.

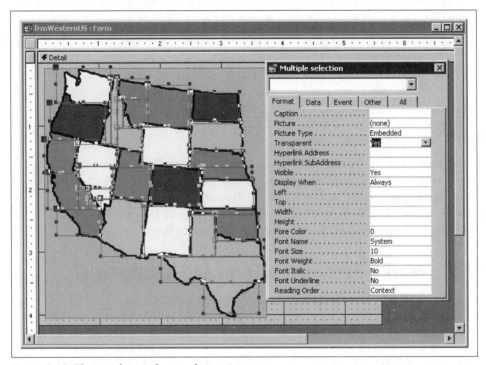

Figure 9-10. The sample map form in design view

5. For each transparent command button, call a function, passing it the name that describes the defined area (in this example, the name of the selected U.S. state) from the button's OnClick event property. For example, the OnClick event property for the command button overlaying the state of Wyoming calls the *HandleStateClick* function, passing it "Wyoming":

```
=HandleStateClick("Wyoming")
```

6. Create the function called in Step 5. This function can be either in the form's module (as we have created) or in a global module. It's up to you to decide what to do with the information passed to the function. In the sample form, the name of the state is passed to an unbound text box. The *HandleStateClick* function is shown here:

```
Private Function HandleStateClick(strState As String)
    Me.txtChosenState = strState
End Function
```

Discussion

Because each button has its Transparent property set to Yes (which is very different from having its Visible property set to No!), it's still active. You can click on transparent buttons and they can react to events. Each transparent button corresponds to some physical region on the bitmap, so you can have the buttons' Click event procedures react according to their location on the bitmap. If only Windows supported irregularly shaped command buttons!

The size of the bitmap is key to the effectiveness of this technique. If you lay out the buttons all over the bitmap and then decide to resize it, your buttons' locations will no longer be correct. Make sure that you've fixed the size of the bitmap before you start laying out buttons. Although you can select all the buttons and resize them as a group, this is not a perfect solution.

Don't spend too much time getting the transparent buttons placed exactly. On the example form, the buttons' placement is fairly precise, but that works only because most of the states in the west are generally rectangular (you'll notice that there's no eastern seaboard on the map). Users will typically click in the center of the region, so covering each pixel on the edge isn't a serious concern.

9.4 Mark a Record on a Form and Return to It Later

Problem

Sometimes you are interrupted when you're editing a record on a form and need to move quickly to some other record. You'd like a way to save your place and easily return to it later. Is there an easy way to do this in Access?

Solution

Access forms have a Bookmark property that is similar to the bookmark you use when you put a book down but want to be able to quickly return to where you left off. This solution shows how to use VBA code to store the bookmark value of a particular record and return to it, presenting this functionality to your users with a toggle button. The solution also shows you how to add a custom shortcut menu to a control.

Follow these steps to add the ability to return to a designated record in your own forms:

1. Create a new bound form or open an existing form in design view. Add a toggle button (*not* a command button) control to the form's header or footer section. In the frmCustomer sample form, we named our button tglMark and added it to the header section.

2. Create an event procedure attached to the Click event of the toggle button. (If you're unsure of how to do this, see Section P.5.5 in the preface of this book.) Add the following code to the event procedure:

```
Me.Private Sub tglMark_Click( )
    ' If toggle button is depressed, then
    ' mark this record; otherwise return
    ' to previously saved record.

    If Me.tglMark Then
        Call acbHandleMarkReturn(msMark)
    Else
        Call acbHandleMarkReturn(msReturn)
    End If
End Sub
```

3. Add the following code to the declarations area at the top of the code associated with your new form. This enumeration supplies all the possible values of the state of the marked row:

```
Public Enum MarkState
    msMark = 1
    msReturn = 2
    msDiscard = 3
End Enum
```

4. Add the following public function to the form's module:

```
Public Function acbHandleMarkReturn(msAction As MarkState)

    Static svarPlaceHolder As Variant

    Select Case msAction
        Case msMark
            ' Mark record position
            svarPlaceHolder = Me.Bookmark
            Me.tglMark.Caption = "Return to Saved Place"
        Case msReturn
            ' Return to marked position
            Me.Bookmark = svarPlaceHolder
            svarPlaceHolder = Empty
            Me.tglMark.Caption = "Save Place"
        Case msDiscard
            ' Reset marked position
            ' and unpress button
            svarPlaceHolder = Empty
            Me.tglMark.Caption = "Save Place"
            Me.tglMark.Value = False
        Case Else
            ' Shouldn't happen
            MsgBox "Unexpected value for intAction", _
                vbCritical + vbOKOnly, "acbHandleMarkReturn"
    End Select
End Function
```

5. To create a shortcut menu, select View → Toolbars Customize, make sure you are on the Toolbars tab in the dialog, and click the New button. Name your new pop-up menu popAbandon, as shown in Figure 9-11, and click OK. Note that this dialog is used for creating both toolbars and menus.

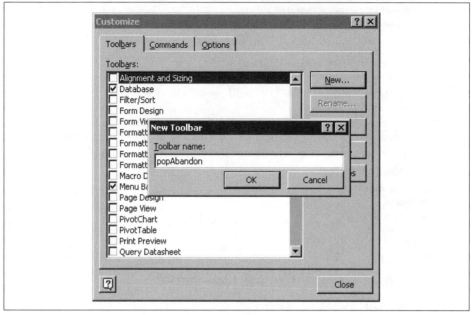

Figure 9-11. Creating a shortcut menu from the Toolbars tab of the Customize dialog

6. Click the Properties button in the Customize dialog, and select Popup for the type property. Click OK in the message box that appears, and click Close in the Toolbar Properties dialog.

7. Scroll down in the list of toolbars in the Customize dialog, and check Shortcut Menus. A special menu bar appears showing you all the shortcut menus. Click the down arrow next to Custom, the last menu item, and then click the right arrow next to popAbandon. This displays your blank shortcut menu as a small gray box.

8. In the Customize dialog, select the second tab, Commands. With the File category selected in the list on the left, click on Custom in the list of commands on the right, and drag a custom command over to your blank popAbandon menu, as shown in Figure 9-12.

9. Right-click on the new Custom item you created in your shortcut menu, and select Properties. In the Properties dialog, change the caption to &Abandon Saved Place. For the OnAction property, enter "=acbAbandonBookmark". Click the Close button in the Properties dialog, and click the Close button in the Customize dialog.

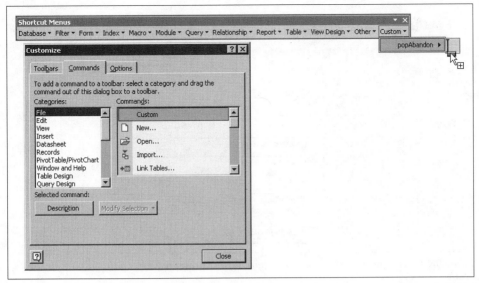

Figure 9-12. Adding a custom item to a shortcut menu

10. In the VBA editor, insert a new module and add this public function:

```
Public Function acbAbandonBookmark( )
    Call Form_frmCustomer.acbHandleMarkReturn(3)
End Function
```

11. In the form, set the ShortcutMenuBar property of the tblMark button to popAbandon.

12. Save the form and verify that it works correctly. Mark a record to return to, move to another record, right-click on the button, and your pop-up menu will enable you to abandon the place you had saved.

To see how this works, load the *09-04.MDB* database and open the frmCustomer form, which contains 500 customer records. Navigate to a record and begin to make a change to it. For example, in Figure 9-13, we made some edits to Margaret Woods's record before marking it. Click on the Save Place toggle button in the form's header to mark the current record and save your place in the recordset. The toggle button will remain depressed and its caption will change to Return to Saved Place (see Figure 9-14). Now navigate to some other record. Click on the toggle button again, and you will return instantly to the earlier "marked" record.

Mark the record again and navigate to yet another record. Perhaps this time you have changed your mind and wish to abandon the earlier marked record in favor of the current one. However, if you press the toggle button a second time, you will return to the previously marked record, losing your new place. You can remedy this situation by right-clicking while the mouse cursor is over the toggle button control. A shortcut menu giving you the option to abandon the previously marked record will

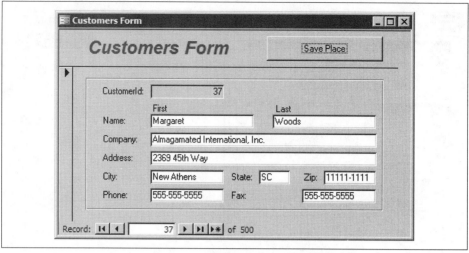

Figure 9-13. The frmCustomer form before marking the current record

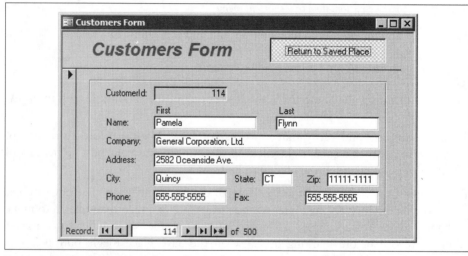

Figure 9-14. The frmCustomer form after marking the current record

appear (see Figure 9-15). Select this option, and you'll now be able to mark the current record instead.

Discussion

The mark-and-return facility built into the frmCustomer form has several interesting user interface aspects. First, the toggle button is the main user interface element. This control type is ideally suited for this situation because it is able to store binary state information that visually matches the two states you wish to represent (mark

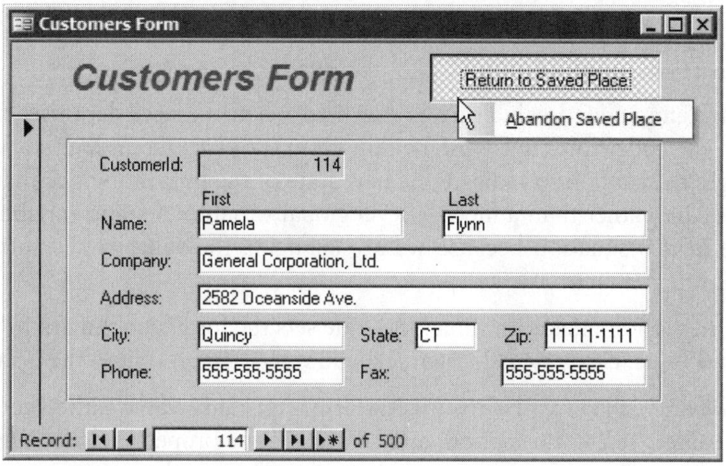

Figure 9-15. The toggle button's shortcut (right-click) menu

and return). Second, the shortcut menu, although a little less easily discovered than the toggle button, allows you to offer the extra "abandon" functionality without taking up a lot of screen space.

The actual code that implements the mark-and-return facility is small, and basically revolves around grabbing the form's Bookmark property and storing it between calls to the *acbHandleMarkReturn* function. This is handled by the Select Case statement in *acbHandleMarkReturn*:

```
Public Function acbHandleMarkReturn(msAction As MarkState)

    Static svarPlaceHolder As Variant

    Select Case msAction
        Case msMark
            ' Mark record position
            svarPlaceHolder = Me.Bookmark
            Me.tglMark.Caption = "Return to Saved Place"
        Case msReturn
            ' Return to marked position
            Me.Bookmark = svarPlaceHolder
            svarPlaceHolder = Empty
            Me.tglMark.Caption = "Save Place"
        Case msDiscard
            ' Reset marked position
            ' and unpress button
            svarPlaceHolder = Empty
            Me.tglMark.Caption = "Save Place"
            Me.tglMark.Value = False
        Case Else
            ' Shouldn't happen
```

```
                MsgBox "Unexpected value for intAction", _
                    vbCritical + vbOKOnly, "acbHandleMarkReturn"
        End Select
    End FunctionMe.
```

The `msMark` enumerated value case is executed when the user depresses the toggle button, so the code stores away the bookmark in the *svarPlaceHolder* static variable and changes the caption to indicate the new state of the button. Notice that we used a static variable rather than a module-level global variable. A static variable is a better choice in this situation because we are changing the value of the variable only within this one function.

When called with the `msReturn` value, the code sets the form's bookmark to the previously stored value, clears *svarPlaceHolder*, and resets the caption to the default.

Finally, when called with the `msDiscard` constant value, the code clears *svarPlaceHolder*, resets the caption, and sets the Value property of the toggle button control to `False`. This causes the toggle button to reset itself to the unpressed state, which is necessary because the function was called from the shortcut menu macro without toggling the button.

We made the *acbHandleMarkReturn* function public because we needed to call it from the shortcut menu. However, you can only call public functions that are in standard modules from toolbar buttons or menu items, which is why we needed the additional *acbAbandonBookmark* function to call the function that is in the form. Note the syntax that *acbAbandonBookmark* uses to call the public *acbHandleMarkReturn* function in the form, passing in the value `msDiscard` to specify that the bookmark should be abandoned:

```
    Public Function acbAbandonBookmark( )
        Call Form_frmCustomer.acbHandleMarkReturn(msDiscard)
    End Function
```

An alternate way to offer this functionality—the ability to browse other records and return to a previous record—is to create multiple instances of the same form. This method was demonstrated in the Solution in Recipe 2.11.

Bookmarks

A bookmark is an array of bytes that points to the current record of an open recordset (or in the case of the form's bookmark, the current record of a form's recordset). Bookmarks make sense only within the lifetime of the currently open recordset (or form). If you requery or close and rerun the query or form, the set of bookmarks will be different. A bookmark is not a record number; it's a dynamically created handle (or pointer) to the current record. To store bookmarks, you can use a variable of type Variant.

9.5   Carry Data Forward from Record to Record

Problem

You'd like to reduce the tedium of data entry by carrying forward selected values from one record to the next. Ideally, this feature will be user-selectable at runtime so that each user can indicate, on a control-by-control basis, whether the current value of a control should carry forward onto newly added records. Is there any way to implement this in Access?

Solution

There are two parts to this problem: the mechanics of carrying a value from one record to the next, and how best to let a user select which controls should carry forward values. The first part of the problem can be solved with a little VBA code to change the value of a control's DefaultValue property at runtime, squirreling away the original DefaultValue, if one exists, in the control's Tag property. The second part of the problem can be handled in a variety of ways; in this solution, we suggest using a small toggle button for each bound control that will offer the carry-forward feature.

To see an example, load the *09-05.MDB* database and open the frmCustomer form in form view. Note that many of the text box controls have a small, captionless toggle button located just to their right. Navigate to the record of your choice and depress one or more of the toggle buttons to indicate that you wish to carry forward that text box's value to newly added records (see Figure 9-16). Now jump to the end of the recordset and add a new record. (A quick way to accomplish this is to click on the rightmost navigation button at the bottom of the form.) The values for the "toggled" text boxes carry forward onto the new record (see Figure 9-17). To turn off this feature for a control, click again on its toggle button to reset it to the unselected state.

To add this functionality to your own forms, follow these steps:

1. Open your form in design view. Add a small toggle button control to the right of each bound control for which you wish to add a carry-forward feature. On the frmCustomer sample form, we added toggle controls to the right of the Company, Address, City, State, Zip, Phone, and Fax text boxes. Because you can't duplicate an AutoNumber field and you're unlikely to want to carry forward a customer's first or last name, we did not add toggle buttons for these controls.

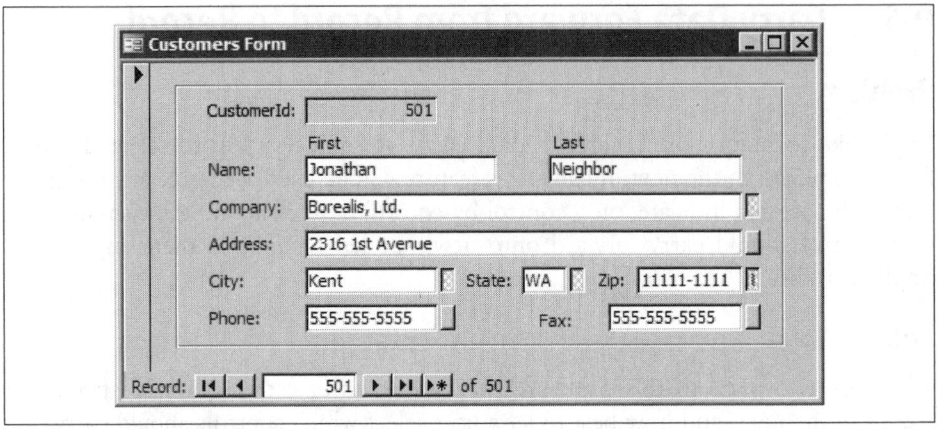

Figure 9-16. The toggle buttons to the right of several text boxes have been depressed

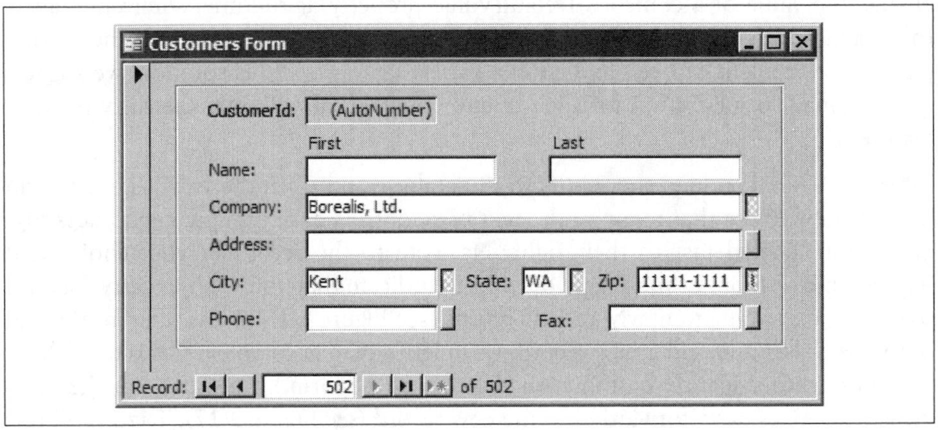

Figure 9-17. The values of the "toggled" text boxes have been carried forward

2. Adjust the toggle buttons' control properties to match those in Table 9-2.

Table 9-2. Property settings for tglPhone on frmCustomer

Property	Value
Width	0.1"
Height	0.1667"
ControlTip	Carry forward Phone value to new records
Tag	txtPhone
OnClick	=acbCarry([Form], [Screen].[ActiveControl])

Replace Phone with the label of the bound control to the left of the toggle button; replace txtPhone with the name of the bound control. Replace the Width and Height values with anything that works well on your form without unnecessarily cluttering it. We've found that a width of 0.1" works nicely with a height that matches the height of the bound control (on the sample form, the height of both the text box and the toggle button controls is 0.1667").

3. Add the following function to a global module (or import basCarryForward from *09-05.MDB*):

```
Public Function acbCarry(frm As Form, ctlToggle As Control)

    Dim ctlData As Control
    Const acbcQuote = """"

    ' The name of the data control this toggle control serves
    ' is stored in the toggle control's Tag property.
    Set ctlData = frm(ctlToggle.Tag)

    If ctlToggle.Value Then
        ' If the toggle button is depressed, place the current
        ' carry field control into the control's DefaultValue
        ' property. But first, store the existing DefaultValue,
        ' if any, in the control's Tag property.
        If Len(ctlData.DefaultValue) > 0 Then
            ctlData.Tag = ctlData.DefaultValue
        End If
        ctlData.DefaultValue = acbcQuote & ctlData.Value & acbcQuote
    Else
        ' The toggle button is unpressed, so restore the text box's
        ' DefaultValue if there is a nonempty Tag property.
        If Len(ctlData.Tag) > 0 Then
            ctlData.DefaultValue = ctlData.Tag
            ctlData.Tag = ""
        Else
            ctlData.DefaultValue = ""
        End If
    End If
End Function
```

Discussion

Although there are other ways to offer this functionality to users, the toggle button control works best because it stays depressed to indicate its special state. If we had instead used a menu item or code attached to the bound control's double-click event to indicate that a control should be carried forward, users might find it difficult to remember which fields they had selected to carry forward.

Because the toggle button controls are small and do not visually call out their purpose, we added control tips to each button to identify them. Control tips are nice because they don't take up any room on the form until a user leaves the mouse cursor positioned over the control for a few moments.

The Tag property—an extra property that Access allows us to use any way we want—is used in two ways in this solution. First, the Tag property of each toggle button indicates which bound control it serves: for example, tglState's Tag property is set to txtState. Second, the Tag property of each bound control stores the existing DefaultValue property so we do not overwrite it when we carry a value forward: for example, txtState contains an existing DefaultValue of WA.

All the work for this solution is done by the *acbCarry* function. This function is attached to each toggle button's Click event using the following syntax:

```
=acbCarry([Form], [Screen].[ActiveControl])
```

Rather than passing strings to the function, we pass a reference to the form object and a reference to the active control object. Passing object references instead of the name of the form or control is efficient because back in the function, we will have immediate access to all the object's methods and properties without having to create form and control object variables.

The *acbCarry* function does its magic in several steps. First, it extracts the name of the bound control served by the toggle button from the toggle button's Tag property:

```
Set ctlData = frm(ctlToggle.Tag)
```

Second, the function checks whether the toggle is up or down: if it's depressed, its value will be True. This executes the following section of code, which stores the bound control's DefaultValue property in its Tag property and then sets the Default-Value equal to the current value of the bound control, adding the necessary quotes along the way. Both DefaultValue and Tag contain string values:

```
If ctlToggle.Value Then
    ' If the toggle button is depressed, place the current
    ' carry field control into the control's DefaultValue
    ' property. But first, store the existing DefaultValue,
    ' if any, in the control's Tag property.
    If Len(ctlData.DefaultValue) > 0 Then
        ctlData.Tag = ctlData.DefaultValue
    End If
    ctlData.DefaultValue = acbcQuote & ctlData.Value & acbcQuote
```

When the toggle button is deselected, the function resets everything back to normal:

```
Else
    ' The toggle button is unpressed, so restore the text box's
    ' DefaultValue if there is a nonempty Tag property.
    If Len(ctlData.Tag) > 0 Then
        ctlData.DefaultValue = ctlData.Tag
        ctlData.Tag = ""
    Else
        ctlData.DefaultValue = ""
    End If
End If
```

Although the sample form uses only bound text boxes, this technique works equally well for all types of bound controls, with the exception of bound controls containing AutoNumber or OLE Object fields.

9.6 Create a Combo Box That Accepts New Entries

Problem

You're using combo boxes for data entry on your forms, and you want to allow users to add a new entry to the list of values in the combo box. Can you do this without forcing users to close the data entry form, add the record using a different form, and then return to the original form?

Solution

You can use the NotInList event to trap the error that occurs when a user types into a combo box a value that isn't in the underlying list. You can write an event procedure attached to this event that opens a pop-up form to gather any necessary data for the new entry, adds the new entry to the list, and then continues where the user started. This solution demonstrates how to create combo boxes that accept new entries by using the NotInList event and the OpenArgs property of forms.

Load the sample database *09-06.MDB* and open the frmDataEntry form in form view. This form allows you to select a U.S. state from the combo box, but the list is purposely incomplete for the example. To enter a new state, type its abbreviation in the form and answer Yes when Access asks whether you want to add a new record. A form will pop up, as shown in Figure 9-18, to collect the other details (in this case, the state name). When you close the form, you'll be returned to the original data entry form with your newly added state already selected in the combo box.

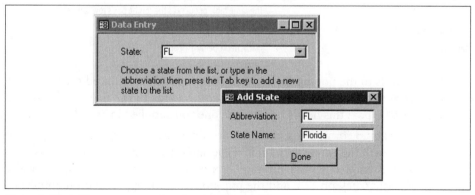

Figure 9-18. Adding a new record to the underlying table

To add this functionality to your own combo boxes, follow these steps:

1. Import the basNotInList module from *09-06.MDB* into your application.

2. Open your existing form in design view and create the combo box to which you wish to add records. Set the combo box properties as shown in Table 9-3.

Table 9-3. Property settings for combo box

Property	Setting
RowSourceType	Table/Query
RowSource	Any table or query
LimitToList	Yes

3. Create an event procedure attached to the NotInList event of the combo box control. (If you're unsure of how to do this, see Section P.5.5 in the the preface of this book.) Add the following code to the event procedure (shown here for a control named cboState):

```
Private Sub cboState_NotInList(NewData As String, Response As Integer)
    Response = acbAddViaForm("frmState", "txtAbbreviation", NewData)
End Sub
```

Replace the arguments to *acbAddViaForm* with the appropriate arguments for your own database: the name of the data entry form used to add new records to the combo box, and the name of the control on the data entry form that matches the first displayed column of the combo box.

4. Create the pop-up form that will be used to add new combo box values. Set the form properties as shown in Table 9-4.

Table 9-4. Property settings for the pop-up form

Property	Setting
RecordSource	The same table or query as the combo box's row source
DefaultEditing	Data Entry
OnLoad	=acbCheckOpenArgs([Form])

5. Add controls to the pop-up form for all table fields that you need the user to fill in. One of them should be the field that corresponds to the first visible column of the combo box; this field's name is the one you supplied in Step 3.

6. Save the pop-up form, using the name you supplied in Step 3. Now open the main form with the combo box on it. Type a new value into the combo box. You should be prompted with a message box asking if you want to add a record (Figure 9-19). Click on Yes, and the pop-up form will appear with the information you typed in the combo box control. Fill in the rest of the required information and close the pop-up form. The new information will be added to the combo box list and the new value will be selected in the combo box.

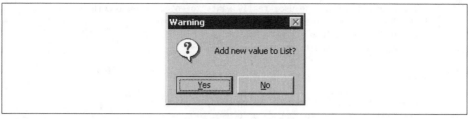

Figure 9-19. Prompt for new record

Discussion

When you have a combo box with its LimitToList property set to Yes, Access generates the NotInList event when the user types in a value that's not in the list. By default, this displays an error message. However, by creating a NotInList event procedure, you can intercept this message before it occurs and add the record to the list yourself.

When you're done processing the event, set the Response argument provided by Access to one of three possible constants:

- `acDataErrDisplay` tells Access to display the default error message.
- `acDataErrContinue` tells Access not to display the error message but to otherwise continue.
- `acDataErrAdded` tells Access not to display the error message but to requery the underlying list. This is the return value to use when you add the value yourself.

This solution uses a generic function, *acbAddViaForm*, to handle the record addition. To allow for the possibility that the user may not want to enter a new value (perhaps he or she mistyped the entry), the function displays a simple message box and quits if the user selects the No button. You also have to tell the original event procedure what to do with the data. The `acDataErrContinue` constant tells Access to suppress the default error message, but not to try to add the new value to the combo box. The code for *acbAddViaForm* is:

```
Public Function acbAddViaForm(strAddForm As String, _
   strControlName As String, strNewData As String) As Integer

   ' Add a new record to a table by calling a form, and then
   ' requery the calling form. Designed to be called from
   ' OnNotInList event procedures.
   '
   '    strAddForm - The form to be opened to add a record
   '    strControlName - The control on the add form that matches
   '        the displayed info in the calling combo box
   '    strNewData - The data as supplied by the calling combo box

   On Error GoTo HandleErr
```

```
    ' First, confirm that the user really wants to enter a new record.
    If MsgBox("Add new value to List?", vbQuestion + vbYesNo, _
      "Warning") = vbNo Then
        acbAddViaForm = acDataErrContinue
        Exit Function
    End If

    ' Open up the data add form in dialog mode, feeding it
    ' the name of the control and data to use.
    DoCmd.OpenForm FormName:=strAddForm, DataMode:=acAdd, _
      WindowMode:=acDialog, OpenArgs:=strControlName & ";" & strNewData

    ' Before control returns to the calling form,
    ' tell it we've added the value.
    acbAddViaForm = acDataErrAdded

ExitHere:
    Exit Function

HandleErr:
    MsgBox "Error " & Err.Number & ": " & Err.Description, _
      , "acbAddViaForm"
    Resume ExitHere
End Function
```

If the user wants to add the new record, the function opens the pop-up form in dialog mode. This pauses the function at this point (because a dialog-mode form won't
give up the focus until it is closed or hidden) and lets the user enter the required data
to complete the record:

```
    ' Open up the data add form in dialog mode, feeding it
    ' the name of the control and data to use.
    DoCmd.OpenForm FormName:=strAddForm, DataMode:=acAdd, _
      WindowMode:=acDialog, OpenArgs:=strControlName & ";" & strNewData
```

However, this leads to another issue. You can't fill in controls on the form before it's
opened, and you can't fill them in after because the form is open in dialog mode. The
acbAddViaForm function gets around this by using the OpenArgs property of the
form, which allows you to pass a text string to the form. You'll see later in this solution how this property is used by the form to fill in its key field.

After the pop-up form is closed, all you have to do is set the appropriate return value.
In this case, acDataErrAdded tells Access that you've added the value to the underlying table and that it can be used as the value for the combo box:

```
    ' Before control returns to the calling form,
    ' tell it we've added the value.
    acbAddViaForm = acDataErrAdded
```

When the pop-up form opens, the OnLoad event property calls the *acbCheckOpenArgs* function, which takes a form variable from the active form as its only parameter. This function is used to process the OpenArgs property of the form (which is

where the form places the parameter that was passed to it when it was opened). Its code is:

```
Public Function acbCheckOpenArgs(frm As Form)

    ' Designed to be called on loading a new form.
    ' Checks OpenArgs and, if it finds a string of
    ' the form "ControlName;Value", loads that
    ' value into that control.

    Dim strControlName As String
    Dim strControlValue As String
    Dim intSemi As Integer

    On Error GoTo HandleErr

    If IsNull(frm.OpenArgs) Then
        Exit Function
    Else
        intSemi = InStr(1, frm.OpenArgs, ";")
        If intSemi = 0 Then
            Exit Function
        End If
        strControlName = Left$(frm.OpenArgs, intSemi - 1)
        strControlValue = Mid$(frm.OpenArgs, intSemi + 1)
        ' This OpenArgs property may belong to someone else
        ' and just look like ours. Set the error handling
        ' to just ignore any errors on the next line.
        On Error Resume Next
        frm.Form(strControlName) = strControlValue
    End If

ExitHere:
    Exit Function

HandleErr:
    MsgBox "Error " & Err.Number & ": " & Err.Description, _
    , "acbCheckOpenArgs( )"
    Resume ExitHere
End Function
```

The *acbCheckOpenArgs* function has to be careful to avoid errors because it's called every time the form is opened. First, it's possible that no OpenArgs argument was passed in. Second, the OpenArgs argument might be there for another reason. Thus, if OpenArgs doesn't parse out as expected (in the format *ControlName;Value*), it's ignored.

If OpenArgs is in the correct format, the code parses out the value to be placed in the corresponding control on the form.

This solution is designed to be generic. You may find that you need a more specific function for a particular combo box. For example, you could allow users to cancel out of the pop-up form in case they decide against adding a new record, or you could use unbound text boxes on the data entry form to display pertinent information from the main form, adding context for data entry.

See Also

See "Programmatically Add Items to a List or Combo Box" in Chapter 7 for more information on working with list and combo boxes.

9.7   Create Animated Buttons

Problem

You'd like to add some pizzazz to your application. You've seen animated buttons in other applications; how do you create them on your forms?

Solution

Access command buttons have an under-documented property called PictureData that stores the bitmap displayed on the button face. This solution examines two ways to use this property. First, you will learn how to create "two-state" buttons with pictures that change when you click on them. Next, you will learn how to create continuously animated buttons that cycle through a set of pictures at all times, using the form's Timer event to display a smooth succession of bitmaps.

Load *09-07.MDB* and open frmAnimateDemo in form view (Figure 9-20). The top two buttons are two-state buttons whose pictures change when you click them. The Copy button (on the top left) shows a second document, and the Exit button (on the top right) shows the door closing just before it closes the form. The bottom two buttons are examples of animated button faces. (Only the Exit button on this form actually does anything when you press it.)

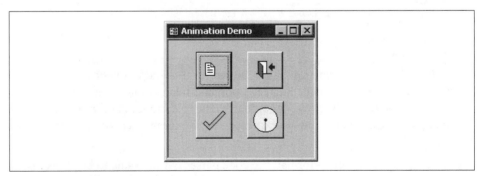

Figure 9-20. The frmAnimateDemo form

Two-state buttons

To add a two-state animated button to your form, follow these steps:

1. Open your form in design view. Place a pair of command buttons on the form. The first button should be sized correctly for your pictures and be located where you want the button to be displayed. The second button can be located anywhere and can be any size. For example, the two-state command button in the top left corner of frmAnimateDemo was created with cmdCopy and cmdCopy2. The cmdCopy button is shown selected in design view in Figure 9-21; cmdCopy2, which has been reduced in size to save space, is located just to the left of cmdCopy. Set the Visible property of the second command button to No.

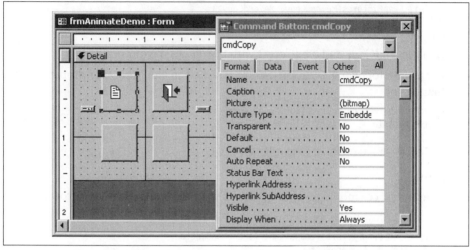

Figure 9-21. The frmAnimateDemo form in design view

2. Click on the first command button of the pair, select the Picture property on its properties sheet, and click the Build button (...) to the right of the property. When the Picture Builder Wizard appears, select the face you want your button to have in its unselected state (see Figure 9-22). You can use the Browse button to choose from bitmap files on your disk.

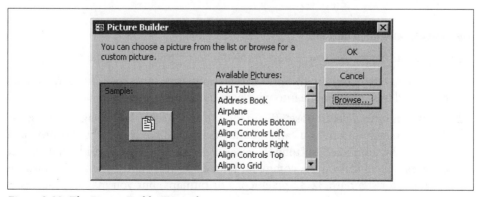

Figure 9-22. The Picture Builder Wizard

3. Click on the second command button of the pair, select the Picture property, and load the face you want your button to have when it is depressed, again using the Build button.

4. Create an event procedure attached to the MouseDown event of the first button. (If you're unsure of how to do this, see Section P.5.5 in the the preface of this book.) Add the following code to the event procedure:

```
Private Sub cmdCopy_MouseDown(Button As Integer, _
  Shift As Integer, X As Single, Y As Single)

    Call SwapPictures(Me.cmdCopy, Me.cmdCopy2)

End Sub
```

Replace cmdCopy and cmdCopy2 with the names of your buttons.

5. Create the following event procedure attached to the MouseUp property of the first button:

```
Private Sub cmdCopy_MouseUp(Button As Integer, _
  Shift As Integer, X As Single, Y As Single)

    Call SwapPictures(Me.cmdCopy, Me.cmdCopy2)

End Sub
```

Again, replace cmdCopy and cmdCopy2 with the names of your buttons.

6. Add the following subprocedure to the form's module:

```
Private Sub SwapPictures(cmdButton1 As CommandButton, _
  cmdButton2 As CommandButton)

    Dim varTemp As Variant

    varTemp = cmdButton1.PictureData
    cmdButton1.PictureData = cmdButton2.PictureData
    cmdButton2.PictureData = varTemp
    Me.Repaint

End Sub
```

Continuously animated buttons

To add a continuously animated button to your form, follow these steps:

1. From *09-07.MDB*, import tblButtonAnimation, frmButtonFaceChooser, basAnimate, and basCommonFile into your own database.

2. Open frmButtonFaceChooser (Figure 9-23) and select eight images for use on your animated button. You can type the filenames directly into the text boxes, or click on the numbered buttons to select files from the common file dialog. The pictures will appear on the command buttons as you choose them. The buttons are sized for standard 32 32-pixel icons or bitmaps, but you may use images of any size.

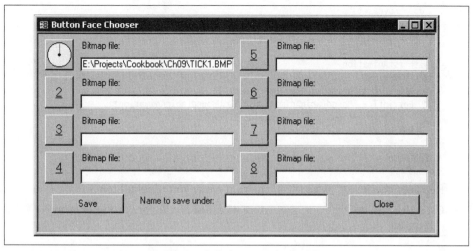

Figure 9-23. Choosing animation bitmaps with frmButtonFaceChooser

3. When you have selected eight bitmaps, enter an animation name to refer to this set of pictures (for example, "clock") and click on the Save button.

4. Create a new blank form and place a command button on it. Set the form's properties as shown in Table 9-5.

Table 9-5. Property settings for animated button form

Property	Value
OnLoad	Event Procedure
OnTimer	Event Procedure
TimerInterval	250

5. Enter the following code in the declarations section of the form's module:

```
Private Const acbcImageCount = 8

Private mintI As Integer
Private abinAnimation1(1 To acbcImageCount) As Variant
```

6. Create the following event procedure attached to the form's Load event:

```
Private Sub Form_Load()

    Dim db As DAO.Database
    Dim rstAnimation As DAO.Recordset
    Dim intI As Integer

    mintI = 0

    Set db = CurrentDb()
    Set rstAnimation = db.OpenRecordset("tblButtonAnimation", _
```

```
        dbOpenDynaset)

        ' Loop through the table, and load
        ' the animation images
        With rstAnimation
            .MoveFirst
            .FindFirst "AnimationName='checkmark'"
            For intI = LBound(abinAnimation1) To UBound(abinAnimation1)
                abinAnimation1(intI) = .Fields("Face" & intI)
            Next intI
            .Close
        End With
    End Sub
```

Replace 'checkmark' with the animation name you used in Step 3.

7. Create the following event procedure attached to the form's Timer event:

```
    Private Sub Form_Timer( )

        ' mintI is 0-based, but the arrays are 1-based, so add 1.
        Me.cmdCheck.PictureData = abinAnimation(mintI + 1)

        ' Bump to the next value, wrapping around at acbcImages
        ' (8, in this example).
        mintI = (mintI + 1) Mod acbcImages
    End Sub
```

Replace cmdCheck with the name of the command button you created in Step 4.

8. Save the form and open it in form view. You should see your animation running on the face of the button.

Discussion

Access stores the picture displayed on a command button in the PictureData property. This property is a binary representation of the bitmap displayed and is read/write in all views. To store the bitmap elsewhere, there are three choices: you can store it on another button, in a variable of the Variant data type, or in a table field of the OLE Object data type.

In this solution, you use all three of these techniques. The two-state buttons work by storing the normal image on the button you can see and parking the second image in a small, invisible button. You can still read and write the PictureData property of an invisible button. When you click the visible button, its MouseDown event procedure is called, which swaps the pictures on the visible and invisible buttons. The MouseUp event code swaps the pictures again to return the original picture to the button face.

For continuously animated buttons, the eight different button faces are stored in a table as Long Binary Data (this is what Access tells you if you open the table in datasheet view) in OLE Object fields. The form's Load event procedure reads these button faces into an array of variants, and its Timer event is used to fetch the next button face every 250 milliseconds in round-robin fashion.

In frmButtonFaceChooser, you'll find an easy way to load bitmaps into the tblButtonAnimation table. You can load a button's PictureData property by setting its Picture property to the name of any bitmap or icon file. The command buttons on this form use the Windows API common dialog functions to invoke the common file dialog. If you care to dig into these details, you'll find the common file dialog code in the basCommonFile module.

You can extend the animated button technique in several directions:

- By including multiple hidden buttons on your form, you can create a three-state button with a picture that changes when it is the currently selected button as well as when it is pushed.

- You can modify the event procedure to allow for animated buttons with more or less than eight frames of animation. To do this, break up the table of frames into two related tables, one holding the name of the animation and the number of frames, and the other holding the actual picture data.

- The sample form shows how to use two arrays and some additional code to have two continuously animated buttons on the same form. You might generalize this code as well, but watch out—forms with too many animated buttons look busy.

If you open the sample form and hold down any button, you'll see that the animations stop for as long as you keep the button depressed. This prevents the form's Timer events from firing.

 To see the effects of the MouseDown event, you must call the form's Repaint method, which tells Access to complete any pending screen updates. On the other hand, you don't need to do this in the MouseUp event (although it doesn't hurt if you do)—Access automatically repaints the screen after a MouseUp event.

9.8 Create an Expanding Dialog

Problem

You have a dialog with a lot of options, most of which are needed only in specific situations. You'd like to create this form as an expanding dialog, similar to forms that have an Advanced button revealing more options. How can you do this with your own form?

Technique

You can make a hidden section of the form become visible at runtime, and use the Window | Size to Fit Form command to force the form to expand to fit its new dimensions. This solution shows you how to create this type of form using an expanding form footer. You'll also learn how to minimize screen flashing while resizing the form by manipulating the form's Painting property.

Follow these steps to create your own expanding dialog form:

1. Create a new form. To make the form look like a dialog, set the properties of the form as shown in Table 9-6. Some of these property settings are optional, since the expanding technique will work with non-dialog forms too. The settings for the DefaultView and AutoResize properties are required.

Table 9-6. Property settings for a dialog form

Property	Value
DefaultView	Single Form
ScrollBars	Neither
RecordSelectors	No
NavigationButtons	No
AutoResize	Yes
AutoCenter	Yes
PopUp	Yes
Modal	Yes
BorderStyle	Dialog
MinMaxButtons	None

2. Select View → Form Header/Footer to add a footer section to the form. Set the Visible property of the footer section to No. Because you're interested in only the footer section, you may wish to grab the bar separating the detail and header sections and drag it up so the header section has a height of zero.

3. Partition the controls on your form into two groups: those you wish to display at all times, and those you wish to display only when the form is in the advanced (expanded) state. Place the first set of controls in the form's detail section; place the second set of controls in the footer section.

4. Add a button named cmdExpand with the caption "Advanced >>" to the detail section of the form. Create an event procedure attached to the Click event of the button. (If you're unsure of how to do this, see Section P.5.5 in the the preface of this book.) Add the following code to the event procedure (or copy the code from the frmExpandingDialog form's module in 09-08.MDB):

```
Private Sub cmdExpand_Click( )

    Dim sct As Section
    Dim blnExpanded As Boolean

    Const acbFirstBasicCtl = "txtFirstName"
```

```
    Const acbFirstAdvancedCtl = "txtOldPW"

    Set sct = Me.Section(acFooter)

    ' Keep track of the state of the form when first called.
    blnExpanded = sct.Visible

    ' If the form is in nonexpanded state, turn off
    ' form painting while expanding the form. This
    ' prevents the form from flashing.

    ' If the form is in expanded state, however, Access
    ' won't hide the expanded portion unless form
    ' painting is left on.
    If Not blnExpanded Then Me.Painting = False

    ' Expand the form if currently unexpanded, and vice versa.
    sct.Visible = Not blnExpanded

    ' Size to fit the form to expand or contract the form's
    ' borders to match the visibility of the section.
    DoCmd.RunCommand acCmdSizeToFitForm
    ' Change the button caption and repaint if necessary.
    If Not blnExpanded Then
        Me.cmdExpand.Caption = "Basic <<"
        Me.Painting = True
        Me(acbFirstAdvancedCtl).SetFocus
    Else
        Me.cmdExpand.Caption = "Advanced >>"
        Me(acbFirstBasicCtl).SetFocus
    End If

End Sub
```

Change the constant declarations so that acbcFirstBasicCtl is the name of the first control in the detail section of the form and acbcFirstAdvancedCtl is the name of the first control in the footer section of the form.

5. Save and close the form. The final form should look like the one shown in design view in Figure 9-24.

To demonstrate this new functionality, load the sample database *09-08.MDB* and open frmExpandingDialog in form view. The dialog form will display in its initial, contracted state (see Figure 9-25). Click on the Advanced button and the form will expand to reveal additional text boxes (see Figure 9-26). Click again on the button (now labeled Basic) to return to the contracted state. (This sample form is for demonstration purposes only; it doesn't do anything with the data you enter into it.)

Discussion

Because you set the Visible property of the form footer section to No, the footer does not appear when the form is first opened. In addition, because you set the

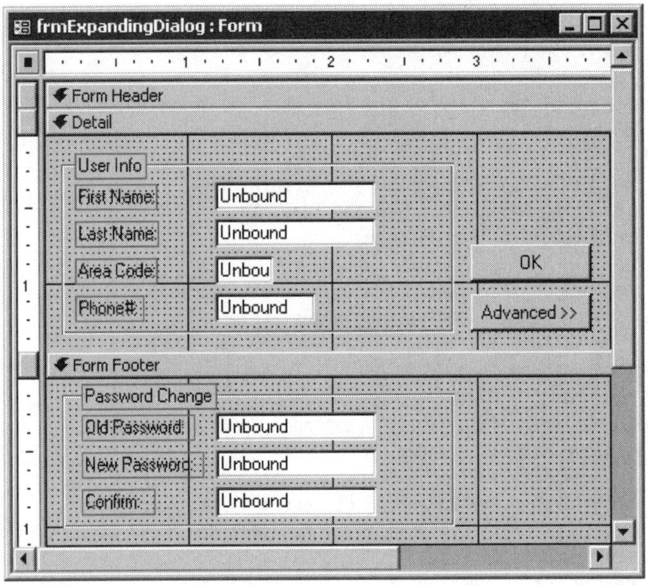

Figure 9-24. The frmExpandingDialog form in design view

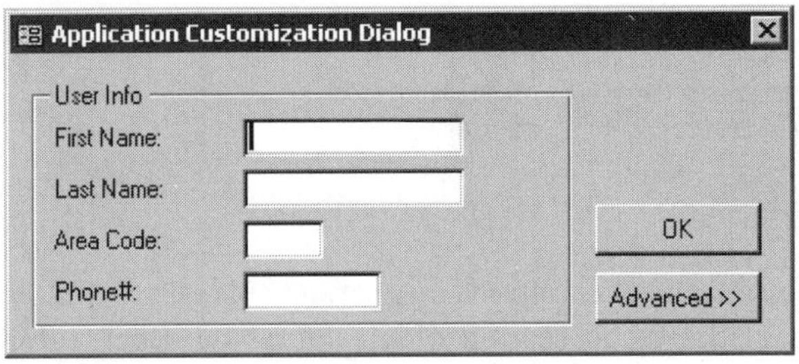

Figure 9-25. The frmExpandingDialog form in its contracted state

AutoResize property to Yes, Access resizes the form to show only the visible areas of the form.

Expansion of the form is handled by the code attached to the cmdExpand button's Click event. This event procedure begins by defining a few constants and variables. The two constants will be used later in the function to shift the focus to the first control of each section:

```
Dim sct As Section
Dim blnExpanded As Boolean

Const acbFirstBasicCtl = "txtFirstName"
Const acbFirstAdvancedCtl = "txtOldPW"
```

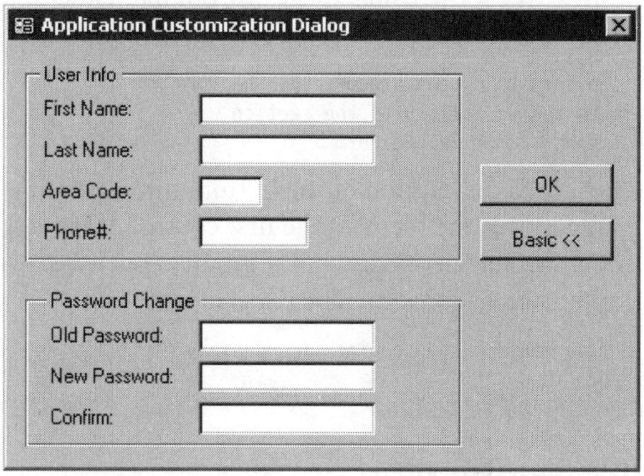

Figure 9-26. The frmExpandingDialog form in its expanded state

Next, the procedure sets the section variable to point to the form's footer section, using the built-in acFooter constant. In addition, it stores the current state of the Visible property of the section in the Boolean variable *blnExpanded*:

```
Set sct = Me.Section(acFooter)

' Keep track of the state of the form when first called.
blnExpanded = sct.Visible
```

If the form is currently contracted, it needs to be expanded, and vice versa. But before this is done, the code sets the form's Painting property to False if (and only if) the form is being expanded. The technique will work without performing this step, but the form will flash as it expands. On the other hand, if the form is being contracted, you shouldn't turn off Painting; if you do, the form will not properly repaint itself and the nonfunctional advanced section will remain painted on the screen. This step is accomplished with a single line of code and six lines of comments:

```
' If the form is in nonexpanded state, turn off
' form painting while expanding the form. This
' prevents the form from flashing.

' If the form is in expanded state, however, Access
' won't hide the expanded portion unless form
' painting is left on.
If Not blnExpanded Then Me.Painting = False
```

The form is then expanded or contracted by using Not to toggle the footer section's Visible property to the opposite of its current state:

```
' Expand form if currently unexpanded and vice versa.
sct.Visible = Not blnExpanded
```

The code then resizes the form using the RunCommand method of the DoCmd object to carry out the Window → Size to Fit Form menu command:

```
' Size to fit the form to expand or contract the form's
' borders to match the visibility of the section.
    DoCmd.RunCommand acCmdSizeToFitForm
```

The function then changes the caption of the button, turns painting back on if it was turned off, and finally moves the focus to the first control of the appropriate section. This last step is not absolutely necessary, but it's a nice touch because the normal tab sequence will not jump across sections. The relevant code is:

```
' Change the button caption and repaint if necessary.
If Not blnExpanded Then
    Me.cmdExpand.Caption = "Basic <<"
    Me.Painting = True
    Me(acbcFirstAdvancedCtl).SetFocus
Else
    Me.cmdExpand.Caption = "Advanced >>"
    Me(acbcFirstBasicCtl).SetFocus
End If
```

You can also apply this technique to non-dialog and bound forms. Although it's not commonly done, there's nothing to stop you from placing bound controls in the footer section of a form. On the other hand, it may be more appropriate to use a tabbed form for bound forms. See the Solution in Recipe 2.5 for more details.

9.9   Use an ActiveX Control

Problem

Access ships with the ActiveX Calendar control. How can you incorporate this and other custom controls into your Access applications?

Solution

ActiveX controls are not as commonly used in Access as they are in development environments such as Visual Basic, and some controls that work in other environments don't work well in Access. However, a number of controls have been created to work well in Access, and Microsoft ships one such control with the product: a very useful Calendar control. This solution shows you how to use the Calendar control in both bound and unbound modes. You'll also learn how to create a general-purpose reusable pop-up calendar form.

Load the *09-09.MDB* database and open frmAppointment1 in form view (see Figure 9-27). Create a new record, selecting a date by using the Calendar control's Month and Year combo box controls to navigate to the desired month and then clicking on the date on the calendar. Complete the rest of the record and close the form. Now open the tblAppointment table to verify that the date you selected was stored in the ApptDate field of that record.

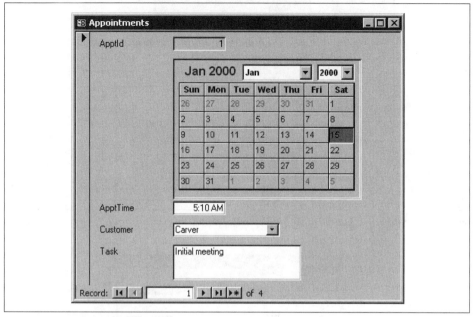

Figure 9-27. The frmAppointment1 form

Open frmAppointment2 in form view and select a date by clicking on the calendar button to the right of the ApptDate text box. A pop-up form will be displayed, where you can select a date again using the Calendar control (see Figure 9-28). Double-click on a date to select it and close the calendar pop-up form, or click once on a date and use the OK button. You may also wish to experiment with the Go to Today button, the Month and Year navigation buttons, and the Cancel button.

Add a bound Calendar control to your form

Follow these steps to add the Calendar control to an existing form to replace a text box for selecting dates:

1. Create a form (or edit an existing one) bound to a table that has a date/time field formatted as a date without time.

2. Select Insert → ActiveX Control. The Insert ActiveX Control dialog will appear, as shown in Figure 9-29. (The list of available controls that appear on your screen will likely differ from the list displayed here.)

   Select the Calendar control and click OK to close the dialog. Move and resize the control as needed. On the frmAppointment1 form, we resized the control to a width of 2.375" and a height of 1.8333".

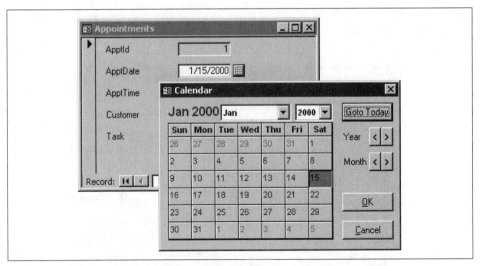

Figure 9-28. Selecting a date using the frmPopupCal form

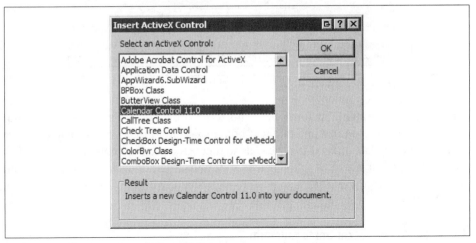

Figure 9-29. The Insert ActiveX Control dialog

3. Set the control's ControlSource property to point to the date field in the underlying record source for the form (see Figure 9-30).

4. Right-click anywhere on the embedded custom control to display its shortcut menu. Select Calendar Control Object → Properties from the shortcut menu, and the Calendar control properties sheet will appear (see Figure 9-31).

Use this to customize the various properties of the control. For example, we changed the properties shown in Table 9-7 to non-default values to make the calendar look better at a smaller size. Use the Apply button to preview the set-

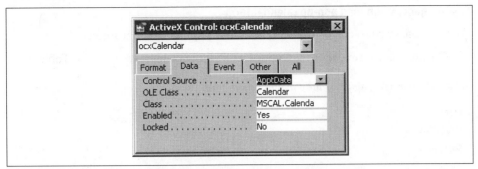

Figure 9-30. The calendar control can be directly bound to a field

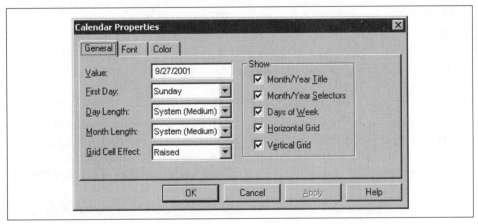

Figure 9-31. The custom properties sheet for the Calendar control

tings while keeping the properties sheet open. You may also wish to use the Help button to view the custom control's help file at this time. (Not all custom controls support the Apply and Help buttons.) When you're done, click on the OK button to close the custom properties sheet. These special custom control properties are also available from the Other tab of the control's regular properties sheet.

Table 9-7. Custom property settings for the Calendar control

Tab	Property	Value
General	DayLength	Short
	MonthLength	Short
Fonts	TitleFont	Font: MS Sans Serif; Font Style: Bold; Size: 9.65 points

5. Save the form and switch to form view to see it in action.

Create a generic unbound pop-up calendar form

Follow these steps to create a generic unbound pop-up calendar form:

1. Create a new form called frmPopupCal with the properties shown in Table 9-8.

Table 9-8. Property settings for the pop-up calendar form

Property	Value
DefaultView	Single Form
ScrollBars	Neither
RecordSelectors	No
NavigationButtons	No
AutoResize	Yes
PopUp	Yes
Modal	Yes
BorderStyle	Thin
MinMaxButtons	None

2. Select Insert → ActiveX Control. The Insert ActiveX Control dialog will appear, as shown in Figure 9-29. Select the Calendar control and click OK to close the dialog. Move and resize the control as needed. On the frmPopupCal form, we resized the control to a width of 2.4167" and a height of 1.9167". Name the control ocxCal.

3. Adjust the custom properties of the control as discussed in Step 4 of the previous section.

4. Add seven command button controls to the right of the control, as shown in Table 9-9.

Table 9-9. Command buttons for the pop-up calendar form

Control name	Caption
cmdToday	Goto Today
cmdPrevYear	<
cmdNextYear	>
cmdPrevMonth	<
cmdNextMonth	>
cmdOK	&OK
cmdCancel	&Cancel

5. Create an event procedure attached to the Click event of each button. (If you're unsure of how to do this, see Section P.5.5 in the the preface of this book.) Add the following event procedures to the appropriate buttons:

```
Private Sub cmdCancel_Click( )
    DoCmd.Close acForm, Me.Name
End Sub

Private Sub cmdNextMonth_Click( )
    Me.ocxCal.NextMonth
End Sub

Private Sub cmdNextYear_Click( )
    Me.ocxCal.NextYear
End Sub

Private Sub cmdOK_Click( )
    Me.Visible = False
End Sub

Private Sub cmdPrevMonth_Click( )
    Me.ocxCal.PreviousMonth
End Sub

Private Sub cmdPrevYear_Click( )
    Me.ocxCal.PreviousYear
End Sub

Private Sub cmdToday_Click( )
    Me.ocxCal.Today
End Sub
```

6. Add the following code to the event procedure attached to the form's Load event:

```
Private Sub Form_Load( )
    If Not IsNull(Me.OpenArgs) Then
        Me.CalDate = Me.OpenArgs
    End If
End Sub
```

7. Add the following code to the event procedure attached to the Calendar control's DblClick event:

```
Private Sub ocxCal_DblClick( )
    Call cmdOK_Click
End Sub
```

Note that this event will be found under the Other tab of the control's properties sheet, *not* under the Event tab.

8. Add the following two property procedures to the form's module:

```
Public Property Let CalDate(datDate As Date)
    Me.ocxCal = datDate
End Property

Public Property Get CalDate( ) As Date
    CalDate = Me.ocxCal
End Property
```

9. Save and close frmPopupCal.

10. Import the basCalendar module from *09-09.MDB* into your database.

11. Create a new form with a bound date text box control. This form will be used to test the pop-up calendar form created in Steps 1 through 10. Add a command button to the right of the text box control. Name it cmdPopupCal and add the following code to the event procedure attached to the command button's Click event:

```
Private Sub cmdPopupCal_Click( )

    Dim ctlDate As TextBox
    Dim varReturn As Variant

    Set ctlDate = Me.txtApptDate

    ' Request the date.
    varReturn = acbGetDate(ctlDate.Value)

    ' Change the value only if Null is not returned; otherwise
    ' the user cancelled, so preserve the existing value.
    If Not IsNull(varReturn) Then
        ctlDate = varReturn
    End If
End Sub
```

Change txtApptDate to the name of the text box created in this step.

12. Save the form, switch to form view, and test out the new pop-up form by clicking on the cmdPopupCal button.

Discussion

You insert a custom control into an Access form using the Insert → Custom Control command. The control can then be moved and resized as necessary. When you insert a custom control into an Access form, Access merges the properties of the control's container (a bound or unbound OLE frame control) with the properties of the custom control. The custom control's unique properties are placed on the Other tab of the control's regular properties sheet, but you can also manipulate these properties using the custom properties sheet created by the control's creator. You do this by right-clicking on the control and selecting Calendar Control Object → Properties from the shortcut menu.

In Step 3 of adding a bound Calendar control, you bound the Calendar control directly to a field in the form's underlying record source.

In the steps for creating a generic unbound pop-up calendar form, you created code that manipulated five different methods of the Calendar control: PreviousYear, Next-Year, PreviousMonth, NextMonth, and Today. For example, in the event procedure attached to cmdPreviousMonth, you added the following line of code:

```
Me.ocxCal.PreviousMonth
```

To find additional information on the methods, properties, and events of a particular custom control, you can use the Help button that appears on some (but not all) controls' custom properties sheets (see Figure 9-31). Alternately, you may have to load the control's help file separately or consult its printed documentation or electronic *README* file.

The frmPopupCal form contains two special procedures, called property procedures, that you may not have seen before. Using property procedures, you can create custom properties for a form that can be called from outside the form. This allows you to expose certain elements of the form to the outer world while keeping all of the form's controls and procedures—the form's inner workings—encapsulated within the form.

The Let property procedure creates a user-defined property for the form, controlling what happens when a calling routine sets the value of the form's property. The Get property procedure controls what happens when a calling routine requests the value of the property. The property procedure for frmPopupCal is simple, consisting of only an assignment statement, but you can do anything in a property procedure that you could do in a normal event procedure. For example, you can count the number of text box controls on a form in a Get property procedure, or you can set all the labels on a form to a certain color in a Let property procedure. The Solution in Recipe 9.10 contains examples of more complex property procedures.

 The data type of the parameter of the Let procedure (or of the last parameter, if the Let procedure contains multiple parameters) must match the data type of the return value of the Get property procedure.

The basCalendar module contains a wrapper function for the frmPopupCal pop-up calendar form. The *acbGetDate* wrapper function is shown here:

```
Function acbGetDate(varDate As Variant) As Variant

    Const acbcCalForm = "frmPopupCal"
```

```
' Open calendar form in dialog mode, passing it the current
' date using OpenArgs.
DoCmd.OpenForm acbcCalForm, WindowMode:=acDialog, OpenArgs:=Nz(varDate)

' Check if the form is open; if so, return the date selected
' in the Calendar control, close the pop-up calendar form,
' and pass the new date back to the control. Otherwise,
' just return Null.
If IsOpen(acbcCalForm) Then
    acbGetDate = Forms(acbcCalForm).CalDate
    DoCmd.Close acForm, acbcCalForm
Else
    acbGetDate = Null
End If

End Function
```

acbGetDate sends the calendar a date by using the OpenArgs property of the form (discussed in the Solution in Recipe 9.6) and requests a date from the form by using the CalDate user-defined property created using the Get property procedure. The Load event procedure of frmPopupCal sets the CalDate property to the OpenArgs property. In this case, it's necessary to use the OpenArgs property because you are opening the form in dialog mode, which makes it impossible to manipulate its properties directly.

Calling the *acbGetDate* wrapper function whenever you wish to use the pop-up calendar form to provide a date to your application ensures that you are always going through a single, consistent entry point. Thus, you never need to bother with opening or closing the form or worry about the names of the controls on frmPopupCal. Just use the following syntax to get a date using the pop-up form:

```
variable = acbGetDate(current value)
```

The pop-up calendar's AutoCenter property has been set to Yes so it will always appear in the center of the screen. You may wish to extend *acbGetDate* with optional left and top parameters so you can precisely position the pop-up calendar form on the screen when it is first opened.

The techniques presented in this solution can be applied to other Microsoft and third-party vendor custom controls, including controls that ship as part of the Visual Basic development environment.

9.10   Create a Generic, Reusable Status Meter

Problem

Access allows you to control the built-in status meter using the *SysCmd* function, but you have no control over the location or appearance of this status meter. How do you create a status meter that you can control?

Solution

You can create a status meter based on an Access form and control it using VBA routines. The status meter is composed of a Rectangle control and a Label control. By updating the Width property of the rectangle, you can control the meter's progress. Additionally, by updating the Caption property of the label, you can insert messages such as "50% complete." All the internal workings of the control can be encapsulated (hidden) inside the form.

For an example of a programmatically controlled status bar, open and run frmTest-StatusMeter from *09-10.MDB* (see Figure 9-32). To start the status meter, click the Start button and frmStatusMeter will pop up. If you want the status meter to include a Cancel button, check the Include Cancel button checkbox before clicking the Start button. The status meter will slowly advance to 100% and then close. If you've included a Cancel button, you can click on it at any time to immediately close the status meter and notify the calling form (frmTestStatusMeter) that the cancel has been requested.

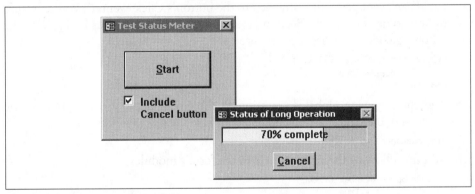

Figure 9-32. The frmStatusMeter form

Create a generic status meter

To create a generic status meter for your own application, follow these steps (or skip these steps entirely and import frmStatusMeter and basStatusMeter from *09-10.MDB* into your database):

1. Create a form and set its properties as shown in Table 9-10.

Table 9-10. Property settings for the status bar form

Property	Value
DefaultView	Single Form
ScrollBars	Neither
RecordSelectors	No

Table 9-10. Property settings for the status bar form (continued)

Property	Value
NavigationButtons	No
PopUp	Yes
BorderStyle	Thin
Control Box	No
MinMaxButtons	None
Close Button	No

2. Place a rectangle on the form, name it recStatus, and set its Width property to 0. Set its background color to the color of your choice.

3. Place a label on the form, name it lblStatus, and set its Width property to the total width you want the status bar to be. Set its Background to Clear. In the Label property, type in "0% Completed".

4. Add a command button control named cmdCancel with a caption of "Cancel". Create an event procedure attached to the button's Click event. (If you're unsure of how to do this, see the Section P.5.5 in the the preface of this book.) Add the following code to the event procedure:

```
Private Sub cmdCancel_Click( )
    mblnCancel = True
End Sub
```

5. Add the following global declaration to the global declarations section of the form's module:

```
Dim mblnCancel As Boolean
```

6. Add the following three procedures to the form's module:

```
Private Sub cmdCancel_Click()
    mblnCancel = True
End Sub

Public Sub InitMeter( _
  blnIncludeCancel As Boolean, strTitle As String)

    Me.recStatus.Width = 0
    Me.lblStatus.Caption = "0% complete"
    Me.Caption = strTitle
    Me.cmdCancel.Visible = blnIncludeCancel

    DoCmd.RepaintObject

    mblnCancel = False

End Sub

Public Property Let Value(intValue As Integer)
    Me.recStatus.Width = CInt(Me.lblStatus.Width * (intValue / 100))
```

```
        Me.lblStatus.Caption = Format$(intValue, "##") & "% complete"

        DoCmd.RepaintObject

    End Property

    Public Property Get Cancelled( ) As Boolean
        Cancelled = mblnCancel
    End Property
```

7. Save the form as frmStatusMeter and close it.

8. Create a new global module and add the following code (or import the module basStatusMeter from *09-10.MDB*).

```
    Private Const mconMeterForm = "frmStatusMeter"

    Private Function IsOpen(strForm As String)
        IsOpen = (SysCmd(acSysCmdGetObjectState, acForm, strForm) > 0)
    End Function

    Public Sub acbCloseMeter( )

        On Error GoTo HandleErr

        DoCmd.Close acForm, mconMeterForm

    ExitHere:
        Exit Sub

    HandleErr:
        Select Case Err.Number
            Case Else
                MsgBox "Error#" & Err.Number & ": " & Err.Description, , _
                    "acbCloseMeter"
        End Select
        Resume ExitHere
    End Sub

    Public Sub acbInitMeter(strTitle As String, fIncludeCancel As Boolean)

        On Error GoTo HandleErr

        DoCmd.OpenForm mconMeterForm
        Forms(mconMeterForm).InitMeter fIncludeCancel, strTitle

    ExitHere:
        Exit Sub

    HandleErr:
        Select Case Err.Number
            Case Else
                MsgBox "Error#" & Err.Number & ": " & Err.Description, , _
                    "acbInitMeter"
        End Select
```

```
        If IsOpen(mconMeterForm) Then
            Call acbCloseMeter
        End If
        Resume ExitHere
End Sub

Public Function acbUpdateMeter(intValue As Integer) As Boolean

    On Error GoTo HandleErr

    Forms(mconMeterForm).Value = intValue

    ' Return value is False if cancelled
    If Forms(mconMeterForm).Cancelled Then
        Call acbCloseMeter
        acbUpdateMeter = False
    Else
        acbUpdateMeter = True
    End If

ExitHere:
    Exit Function
HandleErr:
    Select Case Err.Number
        Case Else
            MsgBox "Error#" & Err.Number & ": " & Err.Description, , _
                "acbUpdateMeter"
    End Select
    If IsOpen(mconMeterForm) Then
        Call acbCloseMeter
    End If
    Resume ExitHere
End Function
```

9. Save and close the global module.

Use the generic status meter in your application

To use the generic status meter in your own applications, follow these steps:

1. When you wish to initialize the meter, use the following syntax:

   ```
   Call acbInitMeter(title, flag)
   ```

   where *title* is the title you want the status meter to assume, and *flag* is True (or -1) to display a Cancel button or False (or 0) to not display one. For example, this statement creates a status meter with the title Progress and a Cancel button:

   ```
   Call acbInitMeter("Progress", True)
   ```

2. To update the meter with a new progress value, use the following syntax:

   ```
   variable = acbUpdateMeter(value)
   ```

   where *value* is an integer between 0 and 100. *acbUpdateMeter* will place True or False in the return value. If the return value is False, the user has pressed the

Cancel button. (The return value will never be `False` if you choose not to include the Cancel button when initializing the status meter.) For example, to update the meter with a progress setting of 50%, you might call *acbUpdateMeter* like this:

```
blnOK = acbUpdateMeter(50)
```

3. To close the status meter form, use this syntax:

```
Call acbCloseMeter
```

Discussion

You can change the size of the rectangle by manipulating its Width property. The Rectangle control is placed behind a transparent Label control that defines the boundaries of the status meter and contains the status text. The status meter form is manipulated by three public wrapper functions contained in basStatusMeter: *acbInitMeter*, *acbUpdateMeter*, and *acbCloseMeter*. These functions, in turn, interact with frmStatusMeter through its exposed properties. The wrapper functions know the names of the properties and how to call them, but they know nothing of the inner workings of the form.

acbInitMeter initializes the status meter by opening the status meter form and calling the InitMeter method. At the same time, a parameter is passed that determines if the Cancel button is included on the status meter form:

```
DoCmd.OpenForm acbcMeterForm
Forms(acbcMeterForm).InitMeter blnIncludeCancel, strTitle
```

acbUpdateMeter sets the value of the status meter form's UpdateMeter property. It then checks the Cancelled property of the form to determine whether the user has clicked on the Cancel button. If so, it closes the status meter form and returns `False` to the calling procedure; otherwise it returns `True`:

```
Forms(acbcMeterForm).Value = intValue

' Return value is False if cancelled.
If Forms(acbcMeterForm).Cancelled Then
    Call acbCloseMeter
    acbUpdateMeter = False
Else
    acbUpdateMeter = True
End If
```

acbCloseMeter closes the status meter form using the DoCmd.Close method:

```
DoCmd.Close acForm, acbcMeterForm
```

When the InitMeter property is set by some external procedure, the InitMeter procedure runs the following code:

```
Me.recStatus.Width = 0
Me.lblStatus.Caption = "0% complete"
Me.Caption = strTitle
Me.cmdCancel.Visible = blnIncludeCancel
```

```
DoCmd.RepaintObject

mblnCancel = False
```

This code sets the Width property of the recStatus control to 0 and the Caption property of lblStatus to "0% complete", updates the form's Caption property with the *strTitle* parameter, and sets the cmdCancel button's Visible property to match the *blnIncludeCancel* parameter. The code then uses the RepaintObject method to force an update of the screen and resets the *mblnCancel* module-level global variable to False.

When the UpdateMeter property of the form is set to a value, the following code is executed by the UpdateMeter procedure:

```
Me.recStatus.Width = CInt(Me.lblStatus.Width * (intValue / 100))
Me.lblStatus.Caption = Format$(intValue, "##") & "% complete"

DoCmd.RepaintObject
```

This code updates the status meter by changing the width of the recStatus control relative to the width of the lblStatus control. This relative change ensures that the status meter rectangle never exceeds the limits as defined by the width of the lblStatus control. The routine then updates the Caption property of the lblStatus control to a formatted percentage value concatenated to the string "% complete". Once again, the code uses the RepaintObject method to force an update of the screen.

The Cancelled property of the status meter form is handled by the Cancelled Get property procedure. When called by an external procedure, this procedure returns the value of the module-level global *mblnCancel* variable. This variable, which was initialized to 0 by the IntitMeter Let property procedure, is set to False if the user clicks on the cmdCancel button in the cmdCancel_Click event procedure.

It's a good idea to encapsulate the inner workings of a generic utility form such as frmStatusMeter by keeping all the event procedures private and using procedures to expose a controlled user interface to calling procedures. Getting in the habit of thinking and coding in this object-oriented way will allow you to create generic components that you can reuse over and over again.

The pop-up status meter form's AutoCenter property has been set to Yes, so it will always appear in the center of the screen. You may wish to extend *acbInitMeter* with optional left and top parameters so you can precisely position the form on the screen when it is first opened.

CHAPTER 10

Multiuser Applications

Access offers native support, right out of the box, for multiuser applications. But this additional power brings with it some additional problems, chiefly those of coordinating multiple users who may be spread across a large network. This chapter explores some solutions to common problems in multiuser applications. You'll learn how to use a shared database table to help your users communicate with one another and see how to find out which users are logged in at any given time. You'll also learn how to implement basic transaction logging, how to determine who has a record locked, and how to prevent a user from locking a record for an excessive time period. Because multiuser applications often use Access security, we also explore the security system in detail. For instance, you'll learn how to properly secure your database, how to keep track of your users and groups, and how to check if they have blank passwords. You'll also see how you can maintain separate but synchronized copies of a database using Access replication.

 Several of the examples in this chapter take advantage of the DAO type library, rather than the default ADO library used by Access 2002 and Access 2003. Even though it's less "modern," DAO provides greater functionality, and generally better performance. In addition, using DAO makes it possible for these demonstrations to work in earlier versions of Access. If you want to try these techniques in your own applications, make sure you add the DAO reference to your project using the Tools → References menu item from within VBA—it won't be added by default.

10.1 Properly Secure Your Database

Problem

The database you've developed contains sensitive data to which you wish to limit access. You'd like to be able to create different classes of users so that some users have no access to this data, others can read the data but can't change it, and still others can modify the data. At the same time, you don't want to secure every object in the database this way; you'd like to apply security only to selected objects. Is this possible with Access?

Solution

Access supports two forms of security: workgroup-based security and database-password security. If you use the simpler database-password security system, you can assign only a single password to the entire database, which is inadequate for your purposes. Fortunately, your needs can be met by using the more sophisticated workgroup-based security system. However, securing a database this way can be tricky. This solution guides you through the process, starting with a completely unsecured database and finishing with a well-secured database that should meet your needs.

Before you can properly secure your database, you must have a security plan. Consider who will be using the database and what security permissions those users should have for each database object. With a plan in place, you can go about securing your database.

Make a security plan

The first step in creating a security plan is to make a list of the people who will be using the database. Write out the names of the users and put them into distinct groups. A user can be a member of more than one group, but you need to assign each user a unique name. Users will have to type in their usernames each time they log into Access, so you may wish to keep the names as short as possible (but still unique). In a small workgroup, you may be able to use an individual's first name; in larger settings, you may need to use the first name plus the first letter of the last name or some similar scheme to ensure uniqueness. For example, if you were charged with designing a secured database for the solution company, you might come up with the users and groups in Table 10-1.

Table 10-1. The plan of users and groups

Group	Members
Employees	Tom, Pat, Bill
Programmers	Paul, Peter
Managers	Joan, Thomas, Paul
Admins	Paul

There are several things to note in Table 10-1. First, Paul is both a manager and a programmer. Second, two individuals in this company are named Tom but, to ensure uniqueness, we've assigned one of the Toms the username Thomas. Third, we recommend using the following convention: make usernames singular and group names plural. Finally, you need to identify members of a special built-in group called

Admins. This group of users will have full access to all objects and will also be able to administer the security system.

Once you have come up with a plan of users and groups of users, you need to inventory your database objects and determine which groups of users can do what with which objects. While you *can* assign each user a separate set of permissions, it's better to assign permissions to groups of users; this makes adding or subtracting users later much easier. An object inventory for the solution company database (*10-01UNS.MDB*) is shown in Table 10-2.

Table 10-2. The object inventory

Object	Group	Access level
tblCustomer	Employees	Read, write access to data only
	Programmers	Read, write access to data and design
	Managers	Read, write access to data only
	Admins	Full access
tblEmployee	Employees	No access
	Programmers	Read, write access to data and design
	Managers	Read, write access to data only
	Admins	Full access
frmCustomer	Employees	Run access
	Programmers	Run, read, write access to design
	Managers	Run, read, write access to design
	Admins	Full access
frmEmployee	Employees	No access
	Programmers	Run, read, write access to design
	Managers	Run, read, write access to design
	Admins	Full access

Secure your database

Note that Access ships with a Security Wizard that will help you secure your database. With a plan in hand, you can now begin to secure your database, following these steps:

1. Choose Tools → Security → User-Level Security Wizard from the menu. The first dialog prompts you to create a new workgroup information file, and the second dialog (shown in Figure 10-1) prompts for the workgroup file information. The strings you enter here for the Workgroup ID (WID), name, and company will be encrypted to form a unique identifier. The default workgroup file, *system.mdw*, is the same across all installations of Access, and is thus not secure. At the bottom of the dialog you can choose either to make this workgroup file the default

or to create a shortcut to open the secured database. If you choose the first option, the workgroup file will be used with all databases. For most environments, the second option is a better choice. Click Next to continue the wizard.

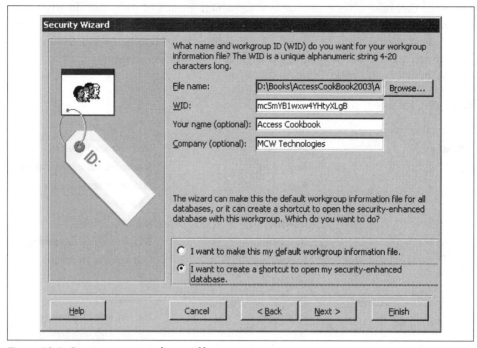

Figure 10-1. Creating a new workgroup file

2. You will see a tabbed dialog for selecting the database objects you want to secure. You'll probably want to secure all the objects in your database. Click the All Objects tab, then click the Select All button (see Figure 10-2). Click Next to continue.

3. The next dialog (see Figure 10-3) can create default groups for you. If you click on a group, you can see the permissions that will be granted to it. However, for this example, you'll create your own custom groups after the wizard has completed. Don't select any of these items, and click Next to continue.

4. The next dialog allows you to grant the Users group selected permissions on some objects. However, you probably don't want to do that, since permissions granted to the Users group are granted to everyone—all authorized users must be members of the Users group. The best policy here is to grant permissions only to your own custom groups, so don't select that option. Click Next to continue.

5. The next dialog allows you to create additional administrators and set a password on the administrator account that will be automatically created (see Figure 10-4). This name of this account comes from your Windows login. So if

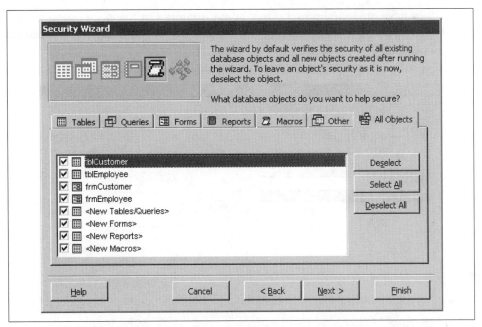

Figure 10-2. Selecting the objects to secure

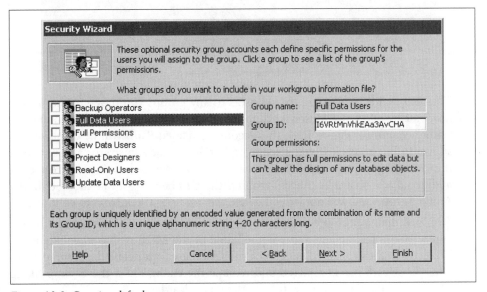

Figure 10-3. Creating default groups

you are logged in as Paul, as shown in Figure 10-4), then this account will be named Paul. Any additional administrators you create here will be added to the Admins built-in group, giving them irrevocable administrative powers in your secured database. You will therefore want to limit the number of administrators, as they have unlimited power. Only administrators can manage passwords and create and delete users and groups. Set a password for the administrator account and click the Next button.

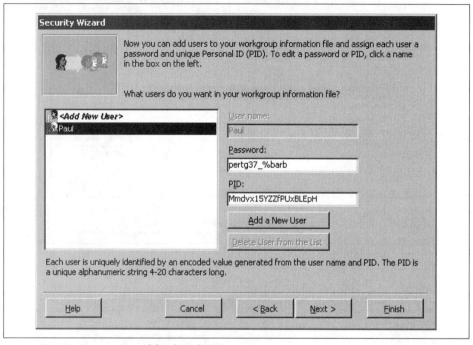

Figure 10-4. Setting a password for the Administrator account

6. The next dialog allows you to add users to any groups you have created. If you have not created any additional groups or administrative users, only the administrator account (in Figure 10-4, this account is named Paul) will be displayed, as shown in Figure 10-5. If you attempt to remove the administrator account from the Admins group, you will receive an error message unless you've created an additional administrator. Access requires there to be at least one member in the Admins group and will not let you delete the last user. Click Next to continue.

7. The final dialog prompts you for the name and location of the backup file (see Figure 10-6). The default value is the name of the MDB with a *.bak* extension. To revert to the unsecured version of your database, just delete the secured MDB after the wizard has completed and rename the extension of the backup file to MDB. Click the Finish button to complete the wizard.

The one-step Security Wizard report is then displayed. This report lists all the security options you've chosen, along with the settings for users, groups, and Personal IDs (PIDs). You should save this and lock it away in a safe place. Should you ever need to recreate your workgroup file, you can use the same settings. Be careful: if

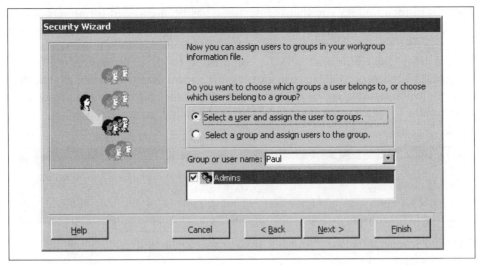

Figure 10-5. Adding users to groups

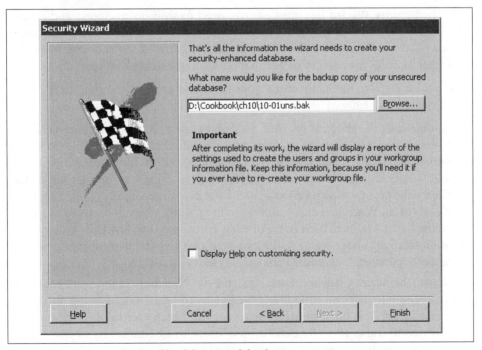

Figure 10-6. Creating a backup file of the secured database

your workgroup file is irretrievably lost and you can't restore it from a backup or recreate it, you could be locked out of your database forever. The wizard will save the report in snapshot format.

The wizard then notifies you that the database has been encoded (prior versions of Access refer to this as encrypted) and that you must log onto the secured database using the new workgroup file (see Figure 10-7). This means that the database can't be read by a text editor and can't be compressed by file-compression utilities. If being able to compress the database means more to you than the remote chance that someone will use a text editor to read strings out of the .*MDB* file, you can decode (decrypt) the database using Tools → Security → Encode/Decode Database....

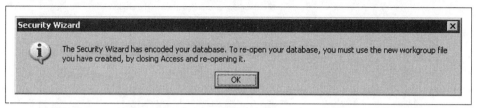

Figure 10-7. The wizard notifies you that the database has been encoded

Work with the secured database

Once the Security Wizard has finished, you need to shut down Access and restart. The Security Wizard creates a shortcut that automatically connects you to the newly secured database. Figure 10-8 shows the property settings of the shortcut. Note that the Target includes the /wrkgrp switch that points to the new workgroup file.

Follow these steps to manually create your users and groups according to the security model you've planned:

1. Double-click the shortcut on your desktop to open the newly secured database. Login as the administrator account you created when running the wizard (the one with the same name as your Windows login). Select Tools → Security → User and Group Accounts from the menu. This will load the User and Group dialog. Create the groups shown in Table 10-1 by clicking the Groups tab and then the New button. When you create a new group account, you will be asked to enter a Name and a Personal ID (PID). For each group account, enter the name of the group account under Name and a case-sensitive alphanumeric string between 4 and 20 characters long under Personal ID (see Figure 10-9).

2. Create the users. Click the Users tab and the New button to create each new user. The PID that you enter is not the password—you'll need to log on as each user to set an initial password for that user. Add each user to his or her groups, as listed in Table 10-1. By default, new users will be members of the built-in Users group; do not remove users from this group.

3. Assign permissions to the database objects. You will now take the object inventory in Table 10-2 and add permissions to the groups of your security plan. Select Tools → Security → User and Group Permissions. Select the Permissions tab and assign permissions to the groups according to your security plan.

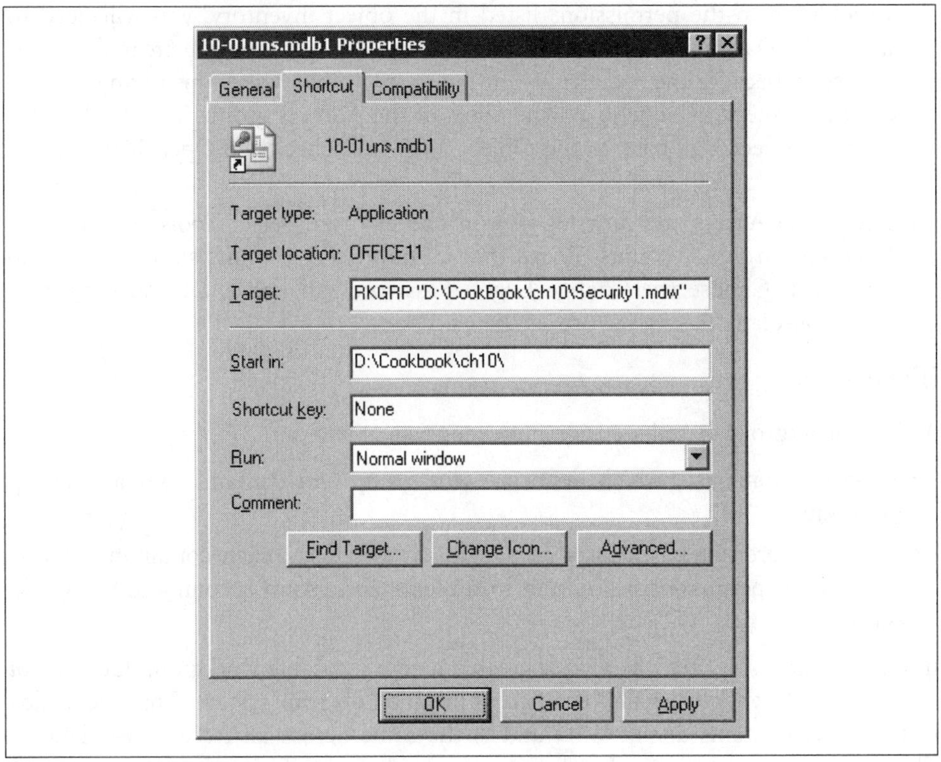

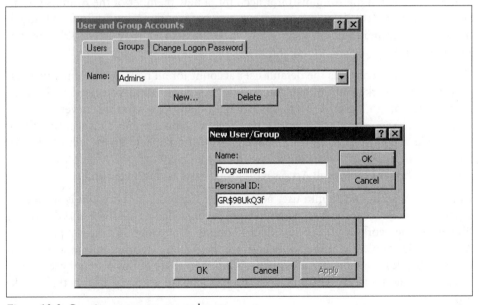

Figure 10-8. The property settings of the database shortcut

Figure 10-9. Creating custom groups and users

In addition to the permissions listed in the object inventory, you will need to assign the Database Open permission to each of the groups you created. This is necessary because the Security Wizard automatically revokes this permission for all users except those who are members of the Admins group. To add this permission, select Database as the Object Type and check the Open/Run permission.

4. Log out of Access and now log in as each new user. Select Tools → Security → User and Group Accounts. Recall that all new user accounts start out with no password. Choose the Change Logon Password tab and enter and confirm a new, non-blank password for each new account.

Discussion

Access's workgroup-based security model consists of two parts:

- A system database, which defines a workgroup and contains user and group accounts
- One or more databases associated with a workgroup, each containing objects (with their permissions) pointing to the user and group accounts in the workgroup

In Step 1 of this solution, the wizard created a new securable workgroup file. Do *not* use the default workgroup file that Access installed on your system. That file, called *system.mdw*, contains a null WID and is the same across all Access installations. Therefore, someone trying to break into your database can easily recreate it.

The wizard created the Administrator account, a new member of the Admins group, and then removed the default Admin user account from the Admins group. Although the Admin user and the Admins group have similar names, they are very different in Access security.

The *Admin user account* is the default user account for all new workgroups. Its presence in every workgroup allows you to ignore security until you need it, because Access attempts to log you on as Admin with a blank password whenever you start Access. By changing the password for this account, you are unhiding security. Once you assign a password to Admin, however, you must create a new administrator-level user account (in the example, we used the account Paul), since the Admin account is the same across all Access workgroups and is thus unsecurable.

Unlike the unsecurable Admin user account, the *Admins group account* is securable. In fact, this account is the key account in any secured Access database and derives its PID from the workgroup's WID. Each Admins group account is unique across Access workgroups. Therefore, you can't use the Admins account in one workgroup to try to break into another Access workgroup. Members of this account are able to modify and administer every object in every database associated with that workgroup.

The Security Wizard secures your database by removing all permissions to objects from all users other than the members of the Admins group and the person who ran the wizard. While it's certainly possible to secure your database without using the Security Wizard, it's easy to make a mistake and create a database with one or more security holes. Thus, using the wizard is a very good idea!

It's best not to assign object permissions explicitly to individual users; you'll find it easier to manage the security for a workgroup by considering the security of only groups. Occasionally, however, you may want to give a single user some special set of permissions. The actual level of permissions users get for a particular object is the sum of the permissions they have been assigned plus the permissions of each group in which they have membership.

Again, remember *not* to assign any permissions to either the Admin user account or the Users group account, as these accounts are the same in all workgroups and are thus unsecured.

10.2 Maintain Multiple Synchronized Copies of the Same Database

Problem

You have a database that you'd like to distribute to mobile salespeople. Multiple users update the central copy of the database on a daily basis, and the salespeople also need to make updates to their own copies of the database. Is there any way to let everyone make updates and synchronize these copies when a salesperson returns to the office and plugs into the network?

Solution

Access 95 introduced a powerful feature called *replication*, which allows you to keep multiple copies of the same database synchronized. Subsequent versions of Access have continued to improve on replication. In this solution, we discuss how to set up a database for replication, how to synchronize the replicas, and how to deal with synchronization conflicts.

Although it's easy to implement, it's difficult to undo the effects of replication. We recommend that you create a copy of your database and work with that copy while learning about replication. Do not experiment with a production database until you are ready to handle any problems that may arise.

Replicating a database

The steps for replicating a database using the Access menus are as follows:

1. Back up the database and safely store the backup.

2. Select Tools → Replication... → Create Replica. A dialog will appear informing you that the database must be closed before you can create a replica and that the database will increase in size. Choose Yes to proceed. A second dialog will ask you if you want to make a backup of the database before replicating it. Choose Yes if you didn't make a backup in Step 1, or No if you did. If you choose Yes, a backup of your database will be made with the *.BAK* extension. For example, the sample database *10-02.MDB* will be backed up to *10-02.BAK*.

3. You will then be prompted for the location of a replica. Access will create a *design master replica*, which takes the name of your original database, and a second replica of the design master, the name and location of which this dialog prompts for. You will end up with two identical databases. The dialog shown in Figure 10-10 is displayed on completion of the creation of the replicas, to inform you of the name and location of both the design master and the replica.

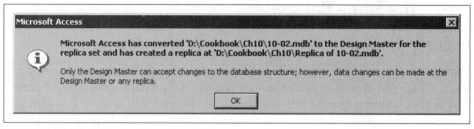

Figure 10-10. The create replica progress dialog

4. Once you click OK, the replication process is complete, and you will see the database container of the design master replica of the original database, as shown in Figure 10-11.

5. You can create additional replicas by opening an existing replica and selecting Tools → Replication... → Create Replica. Access allows you to create additional replicas from any member of the replica set. However, you can make design changes only in the design master replica.

6. Distribute the replicas to the salespeople's laptops. Do *not* copy replicas to multiple machines using DOS or the Windows Explorer. You must create an additional unique replica for each user who will be using the replicated database by choosing Tools → Replication... → Create Replica from the menu and specifying each laptop as the destination.

Synchronizing replicas

Replicas in a replica set remain independent of each other until you choose to synchronize them. You can synchronize only replicas that are members of the same

Figure 10-11. The database container of the replicated 10-02 database

replica set; that is, only copies derived from the same design master. You synchronize replicas a pair at a time. When you are ready to synchronize a pair of replicas—for example, when a salesperson returns to the office and plugs his laptop into the office network—follow these steps:

1. Start Access and open any of the replicas in the replica set.

2. Select Tools → Replication... → Synchronize Now.

3. Using the drop-down box, select the database with which you wish to synchronize (see Figure 10-12). If you don't see the replica you want to synchronize with, someone has probably moved it, so you'll need to navigate to it using the Browse button. Once you have located the replica, press OK to start the synchronization process.

4. A progress dialog will appear. If the synchronization process completed successfully, a dialog will appear confirming this fact and informing you that you need to close and reopen the database to see all changes. Select Yes to let Access close and reopen the database.

Resolving conflicts

If multiple users have made updates to the same record in different replicas, one or more users will be informed of conflicts when they close and reopen the database to complete synchronization. See Section 10.2.3 of this solution for more details on how Access determines which change "wins" a synchronization conflict.

If one or more of your edits "loses" in the exchange, you will see a dialog the next time you open the database, stating "This member of the replica set has conflicts

---

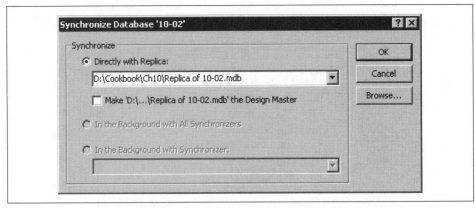

Figure 10-12. The Synchronize Database dialog

from synchronizing changes with other members. Do you want to resolve conflicts now?" To resolve the conflicts, follow these steps:

1. Choose Yes at the conflict dialog to start the resolution process.

2. A second dialog will appear, summarizing the conflicts that have occurred (see Figure 10-13). Select a table in the list box and press the View button to see the conflicts for that table.

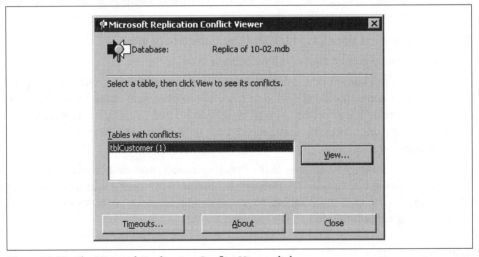

Figure 10-13. The Microsoft Replication Conflict Viewer dialog

3. After a brief delay, a conflict resolution form will appear for the table. A conflict resolution form for the tblCustomer table is shown in Figure 10-14.

4. For each conflict record, the conflict winner will appear on the lefthand side of the form and the conflict loser will appear on the right. Pick the version of the record that you feel is more "correct." If you'd like, you can edit one version,

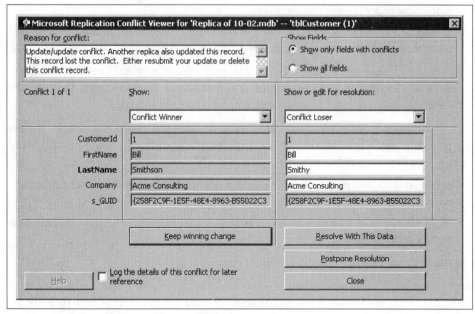

Figure 10-14. A conflict resolution form for tblCustomer

combining data from both versions or some third source of information. To resolve the conflicting record, press either the Keep Winning Change button, or the Resolve With This Data button. If you want to resolve the conflict later, choose the Postpone Resolution button. Repeat the process for each record in the conflict table.

5. Close the form and repeat Steps 2–4 for any remaining tables.

6. You will then need to propagate the changes to all the other replicas in the replica set by choosing Tools → Replication... → Synchronize Now.

Discussion

To summarize, when you replicate a database in Access, you change the database structure so that Access can track changes made to the database and later synchronize those changes with other copies of the database. Copies of a replicated database are called replicas; the original master copy is called the design master. You can make design changes only to the design master. The design master and its replicas make up a replica set. You can synchronize only members of a replica set.

When converting a nonreplicated database to a replicated one, Access makes the following changes:

- Adds additional tables to track changes

- Adds additional fields to each table to ensure uniqueness of records across replicas and to track changes

- Adds new properties to the database
- Changes any sequentially assigned AutoNumber fields to randomly assigned AutoNumber fields to reduce the possibility of AutoNumber conflicts

When you synchronize replicas, Access compares records in each replica using the hidden s_Generation field to determine if records have been updated. During synchronization, only changed rows are exchanged between replicas.

When conflicting edits are detected during a synchronization exchange, Access determines which edited version of a record "wins" an exchange using the following rules:

- If a record in one replica was changed more times than in the other replicas, it wins.
- If all copies of a record were changed an equal number of times, Access randomly picks a winner.

Only users with "losing" edits are notified of conflicts.

Replication works best when your replicas are only loosely coupled, and it isn't critical that all changes be synchronized as soon as they are made. It is best to replicate only tables, and not forms, reports, or other Access objects. Although Access supports replicating other database objects, it doesn't always work well. You may find that in attempting to synchronize design changes, only partial changes are propagated to the replicas, creating additional headaches. In addition, Access replication is suitable only when you anticipate a small or moderate number of updates to the same records in different replicas. If you need real-time synchronization or if you anticipate a high number of updates to the records across replicas (conflicts), you may wish to consider using the replication services built into server databases such as Microsoft SQL Server or some other system.

10.3 Create a Transaction Log

Problem

You want to keep a permanent record of activities in your database. With multiple users simultaneously changing data in your application, how can you keep track of who made which changes?

Solution

Client/server databases such as Microsoft SQL Server offer built-in transaction-logging facilities that provide both a permanent record and a way to recover from disasters by replaying the transaction log. This solution demonstrates a simpler transaction log using Access that tracks users and their edits without saving all the details that would be necessary to recreate the edits entirely.

Start Access and load *10-03.MDB*. Open frmBook and add a few records, update some existing records, and delete some records. Then review the information in tblLog; you'll find a record in this table for each change you made, as shown in Figure 10-15.

Figure 10-15. Examining changed records

To add this simple logging capability to your own database, follow these steps:

1. Create a new table, tblLog, with the fields shown in Table 10-3.

Table 10-3. Fields in tblLog

Field name	Data type
ActionDate	Date/Time
Action	Number (Byte)
UserName	Text
TableName	Text
RecordPK	Text

2. Import the module basLogging from *10-03.MDB* into your own database.

3. Add three event procedures to each form for which you wish to track changes. In the sample database, these event properties are attached to frmBook, and are shown in Table 10-4. Substitute the name of your own table for tblBook, and the primary key of the table for [BookID].

Table 10-4. Logging properties for frmBook

Property	Value
AfterInsert	=acbLogAdd("tblBook", [BookID])
AfterUpdate	=acbLogUpdate("tblBook", [BookID])
OnDelete	=acbLogDelete("tblBook", [BookID])

Discussion

Changing data through a form triggers a series of events. This technique assigns code to each event that indicates a change has been executed and uses that code to append a record to a logging table. You can use the *CurrentUser* function to keep track of who made the change and the *Now* function to record when it was made.

Since the three types of records in the logging table are similar, the functions are just wrappers for a single general-purpose function that actually adds the records. This function depends on enumerated values that are defined in the declarations section of the basLogging module:

```
Public Enum LogActions
    Add = 1
    Update = 2
    Delete = 3
End Enum
```

The *acbLog* function accepts as arguments all of the information that needs to be stored, opens a recordset on the log table, and then saves the information in a new record of that recordset:

```
Public Function acbLog( _
    strTableName As String, varPK As Variant, _
    Action As LogActions) As Integer

    ' Log a user action in the log table

    Dim db As DAO.Database
    Dim rstLog As DAO.Recordset

    On Error GoTo HandleErr

    Set db = CurrentDb( )
    Set rstLog = db.OpenRecordset( _
     "tblLog", dbOpenDynaset, dbAppendOnly)

    rstLog.AddNew
        rstLog("UserName") = CurrentUser( )
        rstLog("TableName") = strTableName
        rstLog("RecordPK") = varPK
        rstLog("ActionDate") = Now
        rstLog("Action") = Action
    rstLog.Update

    rstLog.Close

    acbLog = True

ExitHere:
    Exit Function

HandleErr:
```

```
        MsgBox "Error " & Err.Number & ": " & Err.Description, , "acbLog()"
        acbLog = False
        Resume ExitHere
    End Function
```

This technique demonstrates one reason why you should allow users to interact with your application only via Access forms: forms alone generate events you can trap. If you let users edit data directly via a table or query datasheet, you can't track the edits.

You could extend this technique to capture additional detail about the records being added, updated, or deleted. You might even add extra fields to the logging table to capture the actual data instead of just the primary key that identifies the changed record. This allows you to completely reconstruct the table at any point in time by inspecting the log file and making or removing changes. The drawback to enabling this capability is that it requires substantially more storage space, since you'll be storing a full copy of the data every time any part of it changes.

If you wish to log a table with a compound primary key, just replace the last parameter when calling the *acbLog* functions with a concatenation of each field that makes up the primary key. For example, to log an addition to the tblOrderDetail table with a primary key made up of OrderId and OrderItem, you would use the following function call in the AfterInsert event property:

```
    =acbLogAdd("tblOrderDetail", [OrderId] & "; " & [OrderItem])
```

acbLog opens a recordset on the logging table with the dbAppendOnly argument. This returns an initially blank recordset ready to receive new records instead of a full dynaset whose existing records can be edited. This gives you a performance boost when you are only adding new records and do not need to pull in existing records.

See Also

For more information on using DAO in Access databases, see "How Do I Use Data Access Objects (DAO) in New Databases?" in the Preface.

10.4   Send Messages to Other Users Without Using Email

Problem

When you have multiple users logged into your application, you want them to be able to communicate quickly and easily with one another. You need a simple interface for sending notes back and forth so users can check whether anyone else is editing a particular entry, compare notes on workflow, and so on. How can you implement this in Access?

Solution

You can keep your notes in a table in a shared database to which all users have access. Whenever someone writes a note to another user, that note is added as another record in this table. By using a form that makes use of the Timer event, you can monitor the status of this table from any Access application and notify users when new messages have arrived.

This solution employs two files, *10-04fe.MDB* and *10-04be.MDB*. Before you can try it, you'll need to link the data tables from *10-04be.MDB* (the "backend" or data database) to *10-04fe.MDB* (the "frontend" or application database). Linking a data table allows you to use a table from one Access database within another Access database. Start Access and load *10-04fe.MDB*. Choose File → Get External Data Link Tables, and select *10-04be.MDB* as the Access link database. At the Link Tables dialog, select tblMessage and click OK, as shown in Figure 10-16.

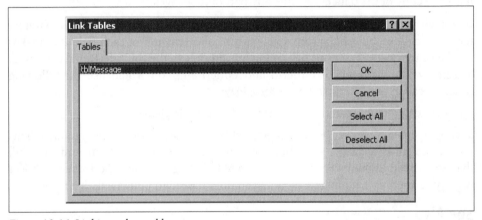

Figure 10-16. Linking a data table

Now you can test-drive this solution by sending a message to yourself. Open both frmSendMail and frmReceiveMail. Minimize the Receive Mail form. Select your username from the To combo box. If you haven't altered the default Access security settings, your username will be Admin, which should be confirmed in the From text box. Enter any message and click the Send Message button. In Figure 10-17, Peter has used frmSendMail to compose a message to Jean.

 In order to send messages between multiple users, you'll need to set up a workgroup that contains the users, and have each user log in as him or herself. See Section 10.1 for more information on setting up a workgroup.

Figure 10-17. Using frmSendMail to send a message

The Send Mail form will clear as soon as the message is sent. Within 10 seconds, the Receive Mail form will pop up with the message. Figure 10-18 shows how Jean would see the message from Peter. Click on the Mark as Read button to clear the Receive Mail form. If more than one message is waiting, you can navigate through them.

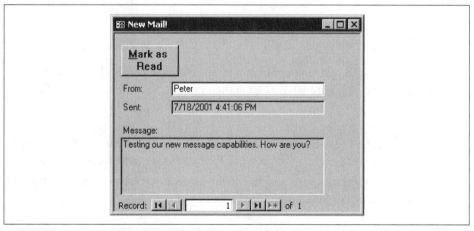

Figure 10-18. Using frmReceiveMail to receive a message

To use this technique in your own applications, follow these steps:

1. Identify the shared database you'll be using to hold the messages. This can be an existing shared database or a new one designed expressly for this purpose. Create a new table with the fields shown in Table 10-5. Make MessageID the primary key of this table, and save it as tblMessage.

Table 10-5. *Fields in tblMessage*

Field name	Data type
MessageID	AutoNumber
From	Text
To	Text
DateSent	Date/Time
DateReceived	Date/Time
Message	Memo

2. Close the shared database and open the database with which you want to send and receive messages. This is the database where you'll create the remaining objects. Import basMail and basFillUsers from *10-04fe.MDB* to this database.

3. Create a new form with the properties shown in Table 10-6.

Table 10-6. *Properties for frmSendMail*

Property	Value
Caption	Send Mail
DefaultView	Single Form
ScrollBars	Neither
RecordSelectors	No
NavigationButtons	No

4. Add two unbound text box controls and an unbound combo box control to the form, as shown in Figure 10-17. Name the first text box txtFrom. Set its Control-Source property to:

```
=CurrentUser( )
```

Name the second text box txtMessage and size it to hold the text of your message. Set the EnterKeyBehavior property for txtMessage to New Line in Field.

5. Name the combo box cboTo and size it the same as txtFrom. Set its combo box-specific properties to match those in Table 10-7.

Table 10-7. *Properties for the cboTo combo box*

Property	Value
RowSourceType	acbFillUserList
RowSource	
ColumnCount	1
ColumnHeads	No
ColumnWidths	
BoundColumn	1
ListRows	8
ListWidth	Auto

6. Add a command button to the form, with the properties shown in Table 10-8. The &Send Message caption makes the button respond to the Alt-S accelerator key shortcut.

Table 10-8. Properties for cmdSend

Property	Value
Name	cmdSend
Caption	&Send Message
OnClick	=acbSendMail( )

7. Save this form as frmSendMail.
8. Select File → Get External Data → Link Tables and link the tblMessage table you created in your shared database to this frontend database.
9. Create a new query based on tblMessage. Drag all the fields from the field list to the query grid. Set the query criteria as shown in Table 10-9. Save this query as qryNewMail.

Table 10-9. Criteria for qryNewMail

Field	Criteria
To	CurrentUser( )
DateReceived	Is Null

10. Create another new form, with the properties shown in Table 10-10.

Table 10-10. Properties for frmReceiveMail

Property	Value
RecordSource	qryNewMail
Caption	No mail
DefaultView	Single Form
AllowAdditions	No
ScrollBars	Neither
RecordSelectors	No
NavigationButtons	Yes
OnLoad	=acbCheckMail( )
OnTimer	=acbCheckMail( )
TimerInterval	10000

11. Add three bound text box controls to the form. Name the first one txtFrom, set the ControlSource to From, and size it to hold the sender's address. Name the second one txtSent, set the ControlSource to DateSent, and size it to hold the date and time the message was sent. Name the third one txtMessage, set the ControlSource to Message, and size it to hold the message text.

12. Add a watermark picture to the form using the additional form properties found in Table 10-11.

Table 10-11. Additional properties for frmReceiveMail

Property	Value
Picture	bitmap file
PictureType	Embedded
PictureSizeMode	Clip
PictureAlignment	Center
PictureTiling	No

In the sample database, we've used a simple bitmap created with the Windows Paint program to display a message in the center of the form. This bitmap, *NONEW.BMP*, is included on the CD-ROM. (CD content is available online at *http://examples.oreilly.com/accesscook*.) You can add this bitmap to your form or create your own.

13. Place a Rectangle control with the same background color as the form's detail section behind all of the controls on the form. After you have positioned it and sized it to take up the entire detail section, you can move it behind the other controls by selecting Format | Send to Back.

14. Add a command button to the form, with the properties shown in Table 10-12.

Table 10-12. Properties for cmdReceive

Property	Value
Name	cmdReceive
Caption	&Mark as Read
OnClick	=acbReceiveMail( )

15. Save this form as frmSendMail.

Discussion

This technique works by passing messages back and forth through tblMessage. The sending form is unbound, because when you send a message, you don't want to have to flip through all the previous messages. The *acbSendMail* function just takes whatever you type into the form and puts it into this table. It also uses the *CurrentUser* function to put your name into the From field of the table, and the *Now* function to time-stamp the message. The *acbSendMail* function is shown here:

```
Public Function acbSendMail() As Integer

    ' Take the message and user from the
    ' frmMailSend form and send it to the mail
    ' backend

    On Error GoTo HandleErr

    Dim db As DAO.Database
    Dim rstMail As DAO.Recordset
    Dim frmMail As Form

    Set db = CurrentDb()
    Set rstMail = db.OpenRecordset( _
      "tblMessage", dbOpenDynaset, dbAppendOnly)
    Set frmMail = Forms("frmSendMail")

    rstMail.AddNew
        rstMail("From") = CurrentUser()
        rstMail("To") = frmMail.cboTo
        rstMail("DateSent") = Now
        rstMail("Message") = frmMail.txtMessage
    rstMail.Update

    frmMail.cboTo = Null
    frmMail.txtMessage = Null

ExitHere:
    On Error Resume Next
    rstMail.Close
    Err.Clear
    Exit Function

HandleErr:
    MsgBox Err & ": " & Err.Description, , "acbSendMail()"
    Resume ExitHere
End Function
```

Opening the recordset with the `dbAppendOnly` flag accelerates the process of adding a new record because it avoids reading in the existing records that the send function doesn't care about.

The cboTo combo box uses a list-filling function to fill the combo box with a list of current users in the workgroup. List-filling functions were discussed in the Solution in Recipe 7.5. This particular function fills its list using security data access objects to iterate through the collection of users in the workgroup. We defer discussion of this topic to the Solution in Recipe 10.5.

The Receive Mail form is based on a query that finds all messages directed to the current user that have nothing in their DateReceived fields. By default, new records added from elsewhere on a network do not show up on an already-opened form; you must explicitly requery the form for this to happen. The *acbCheckMail* function automatically performs this requery at load time and once every 10 seconds to check for new mail. The *acbCheckMail* function is shown here:

```
Function acbCheckMail() As Integer

    ' Check for new mail, and if there is any,
    ' restore the received mail form

    On Error GoTo HandleErr

    Dim rstClone As DAO.Recordset
    Dim frmMail As Form

    Set frmMail = Forms("frmReceiveMail")
    frmMail.Requery

    Set rstClone = frmMail.RecordsetClone
    If Not rstClone.EOF Then
        rstClone.MoveFirst
        frmMail.Caption = "New Mail!"
        If IsIconic(frmMail.Hwnd) Then
            frmMail.SetFocus
            DoCmd.Restore
        End If
    Else
        frmMail.Caption = "No mail"
    End If

ExitHere:
    Exit Function

HandleErr:
    Select Case Err.Number
        Case 3021       ' no current record, do nothing
        Case Else
            MsgBox Err & ": " & Err.Description, , "acbCheckMail()"
    End Select
    Resume ExitHere
End Function
```

After the form is requeried, *acbCheckMail* checks for new mail by looking at the RecordsetClone property of the form. This property returns an exact duplicate of the form's underlying recordset. If there are any records to be shown, this Recordset-Clone will not be at its EOF, so the function changes the form's caption and, if it is currently minimized, restores the form to its full size. The function calls the Windows API function *IsIconic* (declared in the declarations section of basMail) to determine if the form is minimized.

We have used the form's Picture property, a rectangle, and the form's AllowAdditions property to add one more effect to the form: when the form's recordset is empty, all the controls on the form disappear and a bitmap reading "There are no new mail messages" appears on the form (see Figure 10-19).

Figure 10-19. frmReceiveMail displays a special message when there is no new mail

This trick is accomplished by setting the form's AllowAdditions property to No, adding a watermark picture to the form, and adding an opaque rectangle that hides the watermark when there are records in the form's recordset. When there are no records in a form's recordset and you have set AllowAdditions to No, Access hides all of the form's controls—including the unbound Rectangle control—and prominently displays the form's watermark, if there is one.

This method uses the Access username to track mail senders and recipients. To use it in production, you'll need to activate Access security (otherwise, everyone is signed on as the Admin user at all times). To activate security, simply use Security Change Password to assign a password to the Admin user. Then you can select Users from the Security menu and create as many new users as you like. Security was discussed in more detail in the Solution in Recipe 10.1.

To test this solution with multiple users, you'll need to have several machines available on a network. Make a copy of *10-04fe.MDB* for each computer, and use File → Get External Data Link Tables to link the same copy of tblMessage to each one. Log in as a different user at each computer, and you'll be able to send messages back and forth.

You can adjust the performance impact of this technique by changing the TimerInterval property of frmReceiveMail. This property measures the number of milliseconds between each execution of the OnTimer event. In the sample database, the TimerInterval property is set to 10000 milliseconds, or 10 seconds; its highest possible value is 65535, or just over a minute. If you want a longer delay, you can add a static integer variable to *acbCheckMail* and increment it more than once before you check for new mail.

See Also

For more on working with Outlook programmatically, see "Add a Contact and Send Email Through Outlook" in Chapter 12.

10.5   Programmatically Track Users and Groups

Problem

As the database administrator, you want to be able to track users and their groups within your workgroup. How can you gather the information you need?

Solution

Using Data Access Objects (DAO), you can retrieve all the information you need about users' names and groups. Once you have that information, you can use it in creating your applications.

The sample form frmUserGroups in *10-05.MDB* fills tables with the information you need and presents it to you in a list box. To test it, open and run frmUserGroups. Figure 10-20 shows the form in use for a sample workgroup.

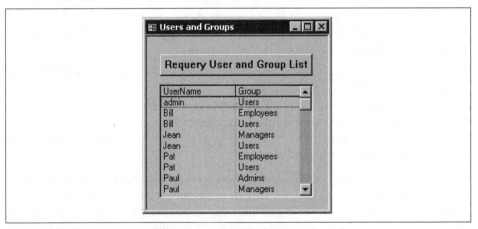

Figure 10-20. frmUserGroups shows users and groups for a sample workgroup

To gather this information in your own applications, follow these steps:

1. Create the tables you'll need to hold the information. Either import the three tables from *10-05.MDB*, or use the information in Table 10-13 to create your own.

Table 10-13. Table layouts for gathering user/group information

Table name	Field name	Field type	Primary key?
tblGroups	Group	Text	No
	GroupID	Counter	Yes
tblUserGroups	UserID	Number (Long Integer)	Yes
	GroupID	Number (Long Integer)	Yes
tblUsers	UserName	Text	No
	UserID	Counter	Yes

2. If you created your own tables in Step 1, you'll need to add an index to tbl-Groups. In the Indexes properties sheet (available by choosing View → Indexes when tblGroups is open in design mode), add a row as described in Table 10-14 for the index properties. Table 10-14 also shows the primary key row that should already exist in the Indexes properties sheet.

Table 10-14. Index settings for tblGroups

Index name	Field name	Sort order
Group	Group	Ascending
PrimaryKey	GroupID	Ascending

3. Either import the module basListUsers from *10-05.MDB*, or enter the following code into a global module. This is the code you'll use to fill the three tables you just created:

```
Public Sub acbListUsers( )
    ' Create tables containing all
    ' the users and groups in the current
    ' workgroup.
    '
    ' The results will be in:
    '    tblUsers, tblGroups and
    '    tblUserGroups.
    ' Run qryUserGroups to see sorted list.

    Dim db As DAO.Database
    Dim wrk As DAO.Workspace
    Dim rstUsers As DAO.Recordset
    Dim rstGroups As DAO.Recordset
    Dim rstUserGroups As DAO.Recordset
    Dim usr As User
    Dim intI As Integer
    Dim intJ As Integer


    ' Set up object variables.
    Set wrk = DBEngine.Workspaces(0)
    Set db = wrk.Databases(0)
```

```
            Set rstUsers = db.OpenRecordset("tblUsers")
            Set rstGroups = db.OpenRecordset("tblGroups")
            Set rstUserGroups = db.OpenRecordset("tblUserGroups")

            ' Refresh the Users and Groups collections
            ' so we see any recently added members
            wrk.Users.Refresh
            wrk.Groups.Refresh

            ' Clear out the old values
            db.Execute "DELETE * FROM tblUserGroups"
            db.Execute "DELETE * FROM tblUsers"
            db.Execute "DELETE * FROM tblGroups"

            ' Build up a list of all the groups in tblGroups
            For intI = 0 To wrk.Groups.Count - 1
                rstGroups.AddNew
                    rstGroups("Group") = wrk.Groups(intI).Name
                rstGroups.Update
            Next intI

            ' Loop through all the users, adding
            ' rows to tblUsers and tblUserGroups.
            For intI = 0 To wrk.Users.Count - 1
                ' Add a user to tblUsers.
                Set usr = wrk.Users(intI)
                rstUsers.AddNew
                rstUsers("UserName") = usr.Name
                rstUsers.Update
                rstUsers.Move 0, rstUsers.LastModified

                ' Now loop through all the groups
                ' that user belongs to, hooking up the rows
                ' in tblUserGroups.
                For intJ = 0 To usr.Groups.Count - 1
                    rstGroups.Index = "Group"
                    rstGroups.Seek "=", usr.Groups(intJ).Name
                    If Not rstUserGroups.NoMatch Then
                        rstUserGroups.AddNew
                            rstUserGroups("UserID") = rstUsers("UserID")
                            rstUserGroups("GroupID") = rstGroups("GroupID")
                        rstUserGroups.Update
                    End If
                Next intJ
            Next intI

            rstUsers.Close
            rstGroups.Close
            rstUserGroups.Close
    End Sub
```

4. Either import the query qryUserGroups from *10-05.MDB*, or create a new query, as follows. When Access asks you to add a table, just close the dialog. In design mode, click on the SQL button on the toolbar and enter the following expression:

```
SELECT tblUsers.UserName, tblGroups.Group
FROM tblUsers INNER JOIN (tblGroups INNER JOIN tblUserGroups
ON tblGroups.GroupID = tblUserGroups.GroupID)
ON tblUsers.UserID = tblUserGroups.UserID
ORDER BY tblUsers.UserName, tblGroups.Group;
```

Then save the query as qryUserGroups.

5. To produce the current list of users and groups, execute the code in *acbListUsers*. You can call it directly, use a button whose Click event calls the procedure, or call it from the debug window. (The sample form calls *acbListUsers* from the Click event of the cmdRequery button on the form.) Once you've executed that code, you'll have filled in the three tables. You can use qryUserGroups to retrieve the information you need, or create your own queries based on the three tables.

Discussion

This solution relies on the DAO object model to gather its information. The DBEngine object is at the root (the highest level) of the DAO object hierarchy, and it has a single collection, the Workspaces collection. Each workspace represents a session of the Access database engine (and unless you're writing sophisticated applications, you'll most likely never see more than a single concurrent workspace). The default workspace contains information about the collection of open databases (only one is open in the user interface—all others must be opened via VBA code) along with the available user and group collections. These are the collections you'll need for filling tables with the usernames and their groups. The code in the *acbListUsers* subroutine does all the work.

The *acbListUsers* function starts out by setting up object variables to refer to several recordset objects, and refreshes the Users and Groups collections of the workspace. This is necessary to make sure we see any recent changes to these collections made via the Access user interface or by another Access session. The relevant code is:

```
' Set up object variables.
Set wrk = DBEngine.Workspaces(0)
Set db = wrk.Databases(0)
Set rstUsers = db.OpenRecordset("tblUsers")
Set rstGroups = db.OpenRecordset("tblGroups")
Set rstUserGroups = db.OpenRecordset("tblUserGroups")

' Refresh the Users and Groups collections
' so we see any recently added members
wrk.Users.Refresh
wrk.Groups.Refresh
```

The next step entails deleting all the existing rows in the three tables, using the Execute method of the database object:

```
' Clear out the old values
db.Execute "DELETE * FROM tblUserGroups"
db.Execute "DELETE * FROM tblUsers"
db.Execute "DELETE * FROM tblGroups"
```

Once these lines of code have executed, the three tables will be empty.

The next step is to build up a list of all the groups. This is accomplished by looping through all the elements of the workspace's Groups collection. Just like all other collections in Access, the Groups collection provides a Count property indicating how many elements it contains. These items are numbered from 0 through Count-1, and we loop through them all, adding a row to tblGroups for each group in the collection:

```
' Build up a list of all the groups in tblGroups
For intI = 0 To wrk.Groups.Count - 1
    rstGroups.AddNew
        rstGroups("Group") = wrk.Groups(intI).Name
    rstGroups.Update
Next intI
```

Once tblGroups is filled in, we do the same for users. Just as the workspace contains a collection of groups, it also contains a collection of users. We can walk through the Users collection, adding a row at a time to tblUsers, as shown here:

```
' Loop through all the users, adding
' rows to tblUsers and tblUserGroups.
For intI = 0 To wrk.Users.Count - 1
    ' Add a user to tblUsers.
    Set usr = wrk.Users(intI)
    rstUsers.AddNew
    rstUsers("UserName") = usr.Name
    rstUsers.Update
    rstUsers.Move 0, rstUsers.LastModified

    ' See the next code example...

Next intI
```

Once a user is added, rows are added to tblUserGroups for each group that contains the current user. This is accomplished by enumerating through the Groups collection for the current user. (Note that there was a choice here. Each member of the workspace's Users collection has its own Groups collection, listing the groups to which it belongs, and each member of the workspace's Groups collection has its own Users collection, listing the members of the group. The code can either walk through the users, looking at the Groups collection in each, or walk through the groups, looking at the Users collection in each. This example walks through the workspace's Users collection, one at a time, studying the Groups collection in each one.) The following code loops through every item in the user's Groups collection, finding the matching name in tblGroups, and then adding a row to tblUserGroups containing both the user's UserID field (from tblUsers) and the GroupID field (from tbl-Groups). This way, tblUserGroups contains a single row for every user/group pair. The code is:

```
' Now loop through all the groups
' that user belongs to, hooking up the rows
' in tblUserGroups.
For intJ = 0 To usr.Groups.Count - 1
    rstGroups.Index = "Group"
    rstGroups.Seek "=", usr.Groups(intJ).Name
    If Not rstUserGroups.NoMatch Then
        rstUserGroups.AddNew
            rstUserGroups("UserID") = rstUsers("UserID")
            rstUserGroups("GroupID") = rstGroups("GroupID")
        rstUserGroups.Update
    End If
Next intJ
```

Once the code has looped through all the users and all the groups to which each user belongs, it closes all the objects:

```
rstUsers.Close
rstGroups.Close
rstUserGroups.Close
```

Now tblUsers, tblGroups, and tblUserGroups contain information about each user and the groups to which he or she belongs.

Once you've filled the three tables, you can easily perform lookups in your VBA code or create reports displaying security settings. You could also just lift pieces of the code from *acbListUsers* for use in your own applications. The next solution shows a simpler function, *acbAmMemberOfGroup*, which uses a similar technique to query on the fly if the current user is a member of a specific group.

The *acbListUsers* procedure is not production-quality code. To keep it simple, we left out the error-handling code, and any procedure of this nature that manipulates tables must include sufficient error-handling capabilities. Though it's not likely, some other user may have locked the output tables or, worse, deleted them, or you may not have permissions for the system tables you need in order to gather this information. In a production environment, it's best to trap errors and handle them.

In the list of users found in tblUsers, notice that there are two users that you might not have seen before: Creator and Engine. These two users are created by the Jet engine itself and cannot be used or manipulated by VBA code. As you'll see in the Solution in Recipe 10.7, you can create a Workspace object for any normal user, allowing that user to log into a new session of the Jet engine, but you can't use Creator or Engine to create new workspace objects. It's a good thing, too! Since neither can have a password (their passwords are always blank), this would otherwise provide a security breach. Because you can neither log on manually nor log on using the

CreateWorkspace method with either user, these two special users don't pose a security risk.

Once you know how to enumerate through collections, as shown in this solution, you should be able to apply the same techniques to other database collections and their objects. For more information, see Chapter 4.

10.6 Adjust an Application Based on Who's Logged In

Problem

You've secured your database so that certain classes of users can't edit data using a particular form or run a specific report, but this doesn't prevent them from trying to open the form or report and receiving a permission error. You'd like your application to adjust itself based on the current user's security level. Is there any way to accomplish this?

Solution

Using VBA code, you can create a function that determines if the current user is a member of a security group. Based on the value this function returns, you can change any runtime property of any form or control, thus adapting your application to the user's security level.

Because this solution makes use of Access Security, you'll need to join the workgroup you created when you secured the database before you can try the sample database.

Now start Access. You will be prompted for a username and password. Enter the name of a user from the Solution in Recipe 10.1's Table 10-1. With the exception of the Paul and Admin accounts, the passwords for these are blank. (The passwords for the built-in Admin account and the Paul account are both "password"; note that case is significant.)

Load *10-06.MDB* and open the frmSwitchboard form. Depending on which user you logged in as, you will see either a Manager-, Programmer-, or Default-level form. For example, Manager-level users will see two Manager buttons and a Close button. In addition, a Close menu item will be included in the File menu. In contrast, a member of the Programmers group will see two Programmer buttons, no Close button, and no File → Close menu item.

To implement this system in your own database, follow these steps:

1. Import the basGroupMember module into your database.

2. For each form you want to customize at runtime based on the user's group membership, attach an event procedure to the form's Open event that calls the acbAmMemberOfGroup function one or more times within an `If...Then` statement. Because users can be members of more than one group, you need to check for membership in the "highest"-level groups first, in decreasing order of security level.

3. Once you have determined the security level for the currently logged-in user, selectively hide and unhide controls on the form to suit your application's needs. You might also want to alter the caption of labels or other controls or customize other aspects of the form's look and feel. Finally, you can customize the menus for the form by changing the form's MenuBar property to point to different sets of menu macros. We have done all of this in the sample frmSwitchboard form. The runtime customizations to frmSwitchboard are summarized in Table 10-15.

Table 10-15. Customizations made to frmSwitchboard

Group	Visible buttons	lblMenu caption	File Close menu available?
Managers	Manager #1Manager #2Close	Manager Main Menu	Yes
Programmers	Programmer #1Programmer #2	Programmer Main Menu	No
(Default)	Default #1Default #2	Default Main Menu	No

The code that drives this customization process for frmSwitchboard is shown here:

```
Private Sub Form_Open(Cancel As Integer)
    ' Adapt switchboard to match level of logged in user.

    ' Because users can be members of more than one group,
    ' you need to check membership in decreasing order
    ' starting with the highest-level group.
    If acbAmMemberOfGroup("Managers") Then
        Me.cmdManager1.Visible = True
        Me.cmdManager2.Visible = True
        Me.cmdProgrammer1.Visible = False
        Me.cmdProgrammer2.Visible = False
        Me.cmdDefault1.Visible = False
        Me.cmdDefault2.Visible = False
        Me.cmdClose.Visible = True
        Me.lblMenu.Caption = "Manager Main Menu"
    ElseIf acbAmMemberOfGroup("Programmers") Then
        Me.cmdManager1.Visible = False
        Me.cmdManager2.Visible = False
        Me.cmdProgrammer1.Visible = True
        Me.cmdProgrammer2.Visible = True
        Me.cmdDefault1.Visible = False
        Me.cmdDefault2.Visible = False
```

```
            Me.cmdClose.Visible = False
            Me.lblMenu.Caption = "Programmer Main Menu"
        Else
            Me.cmdManager1.Visible = False
            Me.cmdManager2.Visible = False
            Me.cmdProgrammer1.Visible = False
            Me.cmdProgrammer2.Visible = False
            Me.cmdDefault1.Visible = True
            Me.cmdDefault2.Visible = True
            Me.cmdClose.Visible = False
            Me.lblMenu.Caption = "Default Main Menu"
        End If
    End Sub
```

Discussion

By default, the form is saved with the least-secure options set; if anything goes wrong, this provides a little extra assurance. When any user opens frmSwitchboard, the Load event procedure is called, and the form's look and feel is customized on the fly. Group membership is determined using the acbAmMemberOfGroup function found in basGroupMember:

```
Public Function acbAmMemberOfGroup(strGroup As String)

    Dim wrk As DAO.Workspace
    Dim usr As DAO.User
    Dim strTest As String

    Set wrk = DBEngine.Workspaces(0)

    ' Refresh collections to stay in synch with
    ' Access UI
    wrk.Users.Refresh
    wrk.Groups.Refresh

    ' Set up pointer to current user
    Set usr = wrk.Users(CurrentUser())

    ' Handle errors in line
    On Error Resume Next
    ' If any property of the Groups collection
    ' using the passed-in group works then we're
    ' a member. Otherwise an error will occur
    ' and we can assume we are not a member.
    strTest = usr.Groups(strGroup).Name
    acbAmMemberOfGroup = (Err.Number = 0)
    Err.Clear
End Function
```

This function is simple: it determines if a user is a member of a group by setting a pointer to the Users collection of the current user and then attempts to get the name of the group in the Groups collection of that user. If this fails, the user is not a member of the group in question. If it succeeds, the user must be a member of the group.

See the Solution in Recipe 10.5 for more details on the programmatic manipulation of user and group collections.

We could have based the form customizations on the name of the current user using the built-in CurrentUser function, but this requires us to consider each user individually, which should be avoided if possible. It's much easier to manage groups of users rather than individual users. Still, you can always add more tests to the If...Then statement in the Load event procedure.

 Versions of Access prior to Access 95 did not allow a user to check group membership unless the user was also a member of the Admins group, but the recent versions of Access allow this.

It's important that you include an Else clause in the If...Then statement of the Load event procedure to handle users who are not members of any of the groups for which you have tested. In the sample event procedure, we have tested for membership in only the Managers and Programmers groups. Any users who are not members of either group are handled by the Else clause.

You can use this technique to alter any runtime property in response to the user's group membership, including:

- Whether certain menu items appear.
- Whether certain controls are visible, and therefore active.
- What query a form is based on; some users can see more records than others.
- What data entry controls are visible; some users can enter more fields than others.
- What toolbars are shown.

10.7 List All Users with Blank Passwords

Problem

As database administrator, you need to ensure that every member of your workgroup has an Access password. You can use the NewPassword method to create a new password, and you understand why you can't retrieve the value of a user's password, but you need a way to find out whether a user has established a password yet. You'd like to create a list of all users, indicating which ones don't have passwords. How can you do this?

Solution

You can't retrieve users' passwords, but there's an easy way to find out if a user has a blank password: simply try to log onto the user's account using a blank password. If you succeed, you know the user has no password. With a lot of users this becomes a tiresome process, but fortunately, you can automate it using DAO and the Create-Workspace method.

The frmUserPasswords form fills a table with a list of users and whether their passwords are blank and then presents this information to you in a list box. To test it, open and run frmUserPasswords from *10-07.MDB*. Figure 10-21 shows the form in use for a sample workgroup.

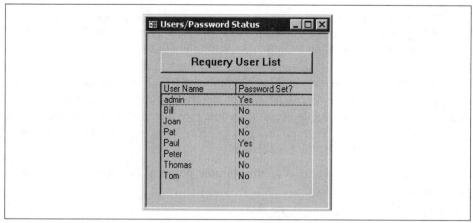

Figure 10-21. frmUserPasswords shows users and password status for a sample workgroup

To use this information in your own applications, follow these steps:

1. Create a table to hold the information. Either import the table tblUsers from *10-07.MDB*, or use the information in Table 10-16 to create your own table. Figure 10-22 shows the table in design mode.

Table 10-16. Table layouts for gathering user/group information

Field name	Field type	Primary key?
UserID	AutoNumber	Yes
UserName	Text	No
PasswordSet	Yes/No	No

2. Either import the module basFindBlank from *10-07.MDB*, or enter the following code into a global module. This is the code you'll use to fill the table you just created.

```
Public Sub acbFindBlankPasswords()
    ' Fill tblUsers with list of users, and
    ' whether or not their password is blank.

    Dim intI As Integer
    Dim usr As DAO.User
```

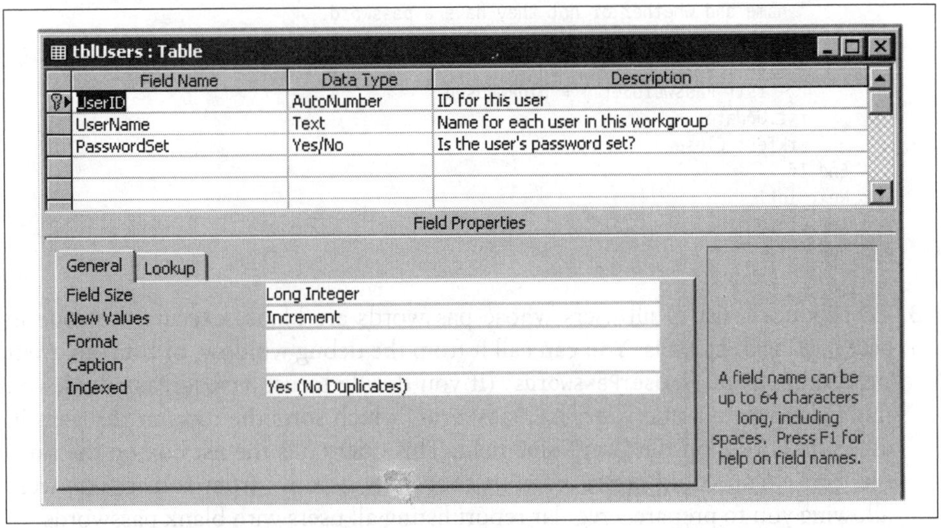

Figure 10-22. The tblUsers table in design mode

```
Dim db As DAO.Database
Dim wrk As DAO.Workspace
Dim wrkTest As DAO.Workspace
Dim rst As DAO.Recordset
Dim blnPwdUsed As Boolean
Dim strUser As String

Const acbcErrInvalidPassword = 3029

' Set up object variables.
Set wrk = DBEngine.Workspaces(0)
Set db = wrk.Databases(0)
Set rst = db.OpenRecordset("tblUsers")

db.Execute "DELETE * FROM tblUsers"

On Error Resume Next
' Loop through all the users.
For intI = 0 To wrk.Users.Count - 1
Set usr = wrk.Users(intI)
strUser = usr.Name

' Skip the two special users, since you can't log in
' as either of them via CreateWorkspace().
If strUser <> "Creator" And strUser <> "Engine" Then
    ' Try to log in with a blank password. If this
    ' doesn't fail, the user has a blank password.
    Set wrkTest = DBEngine. _
     CreateWorkspace("Test", strUser, "")
    blnPwdUsed = (Err = acbcErrInvalidPassword)

    ' Add a new row to tblUsers, storing the user's
```

```
              ' name and whether or not they have a password.
         rst.AddNew
             rst("UserName") = strUser
             rst("PasswordSet") = blnPwdUsed
         rst.Update
         wrkTest.Close
      End If
      Next intI
      rst.Close
   End Sub
```

3. To produce a list of all users whose passwords are blank, execute the code in
   acbFindBlankPasswords. You can call it from the debug window, or from an event
   procedure, as in frmUserPasswords. (If you decide to use frmUserPasswords, you
   must also create a query, qryUserPasswords, which sorts the rows in tblUsers in
   ascending order on the UserName field. This query fills the list box on the sample form.) You could create a report that pulls its rows from tblUsers as well,
   allowing you to prepare a regular report listing all users with blank passwords.

Discussion

acbFindBlankPasswords uses DAO to do most of its work. It starts by setting up the
object variables it needs to retrieve and store the password information. It uses the
Workspace object to loop through all the users (since the Workspace object provides the Users collection that you'll use), and the Recordset object refers to the table
into which you'll write the new data:

```
Set wrk = DBEngine.Workspaces(0)
Set db = wrk.Databases(0)
Set rst = db.OpenRecordset("tblUsers")
```

You then need to clear out the previous contents of tblUsers, so that later code can
fill in the table with the current list of users and their password status:

```
db.Execute "DELETE * FROM tblUsers"
```

The next step is to loop through the Users collection of the default Workspace
object. For each user, the code attempts to create a new workspace, as shown here:

```
For intI = 0 To wrk.Users.Count - 1
   Set usr = wrk.Users(intI)
   '
   ' See the next code sample.
   '
Next intI
```

The final step is the important one. For each user, the code calls the CreateWorkspace method of the DBEngine object. To call this method, you must supply three
parameters: the name for the new workspace (of course, since you only need the
result of attempting to create the workspace, the actual name doesn't matter), the
username, and the user's password. An empty string ("") is passed for the password.

An error indicates that the current user has a password, since the new workspace could not be created using the blank password. If there was no error, then that user does not have a password.

The code checks whether an error occurred, comparing the Access built-in Err value with the known error value that occurs when you attempt to create a workspace with an invalid password. Regardless of whether an error occurred, the code adds a new row to tblUsers and stores the username along with the password status in the table. Here is the code for these steps:

```
' Skip the two special users, since you can't log in
' as either of them via CreateWorkspace( ).
If strUser <> "Creator" And strUser <> "Engine" Then
    ' Try to log in with a blank password. If this
    ' doesn't fail, the user has a blank password.
    Set wrkTest = DBEngine. _
     CreateWorkspace("Test", strUser, "")
    blnPwdUsed = (Err = acbcErrInvalidPassword)

    ' Add a new row to tblUsers, storing the user's
    ' name and whether or not they have a password.
    rst.AddNew
        rst("UserName") = strUser
        rst("PasswordSet") = blnPwdUsed
    rst.Update
    wrkTest.Close
End If
```

As discussed in the Solution in Recipe 10.5, the Users collection contains two users that are not actually part of your workgroup: Creator and Engine. Access creates these two users but doesn't allow you to log on as either one, either from the command line or by creating a new workspace. Therefore, the code just skips these special users, since we don't really care whether their passwords are blank.

If you intend to use acbFindBlankPasswords in a production environment, you may wish to add some error-handling code to the procedure. Any time you write to tables, you should include some method of dealing with errors. At the least, the user (which could well be yourself) should be alerted that an error has occurred and given some information about the error.

10.8 Track Which Users Have a Shared Database Open

Problem

You need better control over a networked Access application. Is there any way you can track which users are logged in and which machines they are using?

Solution

Access tracks this information in the *.LDB* file, but that file sometimes lists users who have already logged out, so you can't just open it in Notepad and take a look. This solution opens a special ADO recordset that shows you exactly the information you need. The sample form lists user and machine names in a list box.

Import frmCurrentConnections (see Figure 10-23), which shows which users are logged into any shared database. Note that if you are using a split architecture, the shared database is the one that contains your tables. Open the VBA Editor and use the Tools → References dialog to ensure that you have a reference to Microsoft ActiveX Data Objects, Version 2.1 or later.

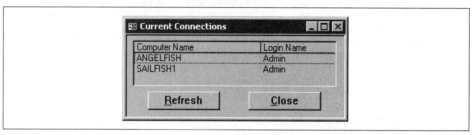

Figure 10-23. frmCurrentConnections shows which users are logged in

You can open the form at any time to see who's logged into the database. If you want to keep the form open, you can click the Refresh button to update the display. If you have not implemented security, all users will appear as Admin, but you will see their individual machine names, as in Figure 10-23.

Discussion

The key to this solution is the use of a very peculiar kind of ADO recordset that retrieves metadata from the Jet database engine. This metadata, also called *schema information*, is not data that you store in your tables, but data stored by the database engine—in this case, data about logged-in users, which is stored in the *.LDB* file. Here is the procedure that populates the list box:

```
Private Sub ListConnections()
    Dim cnn As ADODB.Connection
    Dim rst As ADODB.Recordset
    Dim strComputerName As String

    Set cnn = CurrentProject.Connection
    Set rst = cnn.OpenSchema(adSchemaProviderSpecific, , _
        "{947bb102-5d43-11d1-bdbf-00c04fb92675}")
    lboConnections.RowSource = vbNullString
    lboConnections.AddItem "Computer Name;Login Name"

    Do While Not rst.EOF
        If rst("Connected") Then
```

```
            strComputerName = rst("Computer_Name")
            lboConnections.AddItem _
             Left(strComputerName, _
             InStr(strComputerName, vbNullChar) - 1) & _
             ";" & rst("Login_Name")
        End If
        rst.MoveNext
    Loop
    rst.Close
    Set rst = Nothing
    Set cnn = Nothing
End Sub
```

After using that magic GUID value in curly braces to open the recordset, the code clears out the list box by setting its row source to an empty string. This allows the procedure to be called repeatedly to refresh the list as users come and go:

```
lboConnections.RowSource = vbNullString
```

The code then fills in the first row of data, which will become column headings because the list box ColumnHeads property is set to Yes. The ListConnections procedure uses a method of the list box that is new in Access 2002: AddItem. This method makes it a little easier to work with combo or list boxes that have a RowSourceType of Value List. You can populate such combo and list boxes by using a list of items delimited by semicolons or commas. Because this list box has two columns (the ColumnCount property is set to 2), the code must insert the data for both columns each time it calls AddItem. This is done by placing a semicolon between the columns:

```
lboConnections.AddItem "Computer Name;Login Name"
```

The fields of this recordset contain data terminated by a null character (i.e., a character with an ASCII value of 0). For the data to display correctly, you need to extract just the portion of the Computer_Name data that comes before the terminating null character. The following expression does this:

```
Left(strComputerName, InStr(strComputerName, vbNullChar) - 1)
```

The ADO code in this solution will work in Access 2000, but the AddItem method won't. You can use string concatenation to build up the value list in Access 2000, but be aware that value lists in Access 2000 are limited to 2,048 characters; this limit was increased to over 32,000 characters in Access 2002.

The *ListConnections* procedure is called from both the Load event of the form and the Click event of the Refresh button:

```
Private Sub Form_Load( )
    ListConnections
End Sub

Private Sub cmdRefresh_Click( )
    ListConnections
End Sub
```

In addition to the technique used in this solution, you can monitor the users in your application by using a utility that is available as a free download from Microsoft at *http://support.microsoft.com?kbid=1863*. This LDB viewer will work with Access 97, which used Version 3.51 of the Jet engine. The code in this solution is supported only by Jet Version 4.0 or later.

10.9   Determine if a Record Is Locked and by Whom

Problem

When you use pessimistic locking (discussed in the upcoming sidebar) in your applications, Access informs you if another user has locked a record by displaying an icon in the record selector of the form's detail section (shown in the upper-left corner of Figure 10-24). While this is nice, you may want to know who actually has the record locked. Is there any way to determine this?

Figure 10-24. A record has been locked, but by whom?

Solution

There is no built-in menu command or toolbar button that tells you who has a record locked, but you can create a VBA function that returns the username and the machine name of the user who has the current record locked. This solution shows you how to create such a function that you can call from any form.

Start Access and load the same copy of the *10-09.MDB* database on at least two machines on your network. (Alternately, you can use two instances of Access on a single machine.)

Customizing the Record-Locking Method

In Access 2000, Microsoft added an important new capability to the Jet database engine: record-level locking. In previous versions, if you locked the record being edited, you would also lock any other records that happened to be on the same data page as the edited one. A data page held 2,048 characters, so it was likely that locking would affect more than one record.

In Access 2000, Microsoft increased the size of data pages from 2,048 characters to 4,096 characters in order to support Unicode characters, which each consume 2 bytes. With such large pages, Microsoft decided that it needed to allow you to lock single records. In the Advanced page of the Tools → Options dialog, you can now choose to open the database using record-level locking. This avoids locking entire pages when locking the edited record. That dialog also allows you to select a default method of locking, which is applied to data sheets and to any new forms.

To change the method of locking for a form, open the form in design mode and modify the value of the form's RecordLocks property. If this property is set to EditedRecord, Access uses *pessimistic locking* for the form, which means that Access locks the page of records or the single record as soon as you change any data on the form (when the pencil icon appears in the form's record selector). If it's set to NoLocks, Access uses *optimistic locking* for this form, which means that Access locks the page of records or the single record only at the moment you save your changes.

For most forms, optimistic locking is the preferable setting, because it keeps records locked for a much shorter period of time. Sometimes, however, you'll need to employ pessimistic locking to ensure that no more than one user is editing a record at the same time. Record-level locking makes pessimistic locking much more practical, as it ensures that only the record being edited will be locked.

Open the frmEmployees form on the first machine (or instance), changing the data in any control of the form so that the pencil icon appears in the form's record selector. Don't release the lock by saving the record, and open the same form on the second machine. On the second machine, press the button with the image of a padlock. A message box should appear displaying the username and machine name of the user on the first machine who has locked the record (see Figure 10-25). (To get an accurate username, both machines should share the same system database file with security enabled. For more information on enabling security, see the Solution in Recipe 10.1.)

To add a lock identification button to your own forms, follow these steps:

1. Import the basRecordLock module from *10-09.MDB* into your database.

2. Add a command button to each form with the following in the command button's OnClick property:

```
=acbWhoHasLockedRecord([Form])
```

Figure 10-25. The username and machine name of the user who has locked the current record

Discussion

The acbWhoHasLockedRecord function's code is shown here:

```
Public Function acbWhoHasLockedRecord(frm As Form)
    ' Display a message box that says either:
    '   -No user has the current record locked, or
    '   -The user & machine name of the user who
    '    who has locked the current record.

    Dim rst As DAO.Recordset
    Dim blnMUError As Boolean
    Dim strUser As String
    Dim strMachine As String
    Dim strMsg As String

    On Error GoTo HandleErr

    ' Default message
    strMsg = "Record is not locked by another user."

    ' Clone the form's recordset and synch up to the
    ' form's current record
    Set rst = frm.RecordsetClone
    rst.Bookmark = frm.Bookmark

    ' If the current record is locked, then the next
    ' statement should produce an error that we will trap
    rst.Edit

ExitHere:
    ' Display either the default message or one specifying
    ' the user and machine who has locked the current record.
    MsgBox strMsg, , "Locking Status"
    Exit Function

HandleErr:
    ' Pass the error to acbGetUserAndMachine which will attempt
    ' to parse out the user and machine from the error message
    If Err.Number = 3188 Then
        ' Locked on this machine.
        strMsg = "Some other part of this application " _
        & "on this machine has locked this record."
```

```
        Else
            blnMUError = acbGetUserAndMachine(Err.Description, _
             strUser, strMachine)
            ' If the return value is True, then acbGetUserAndMachine
            ' was able to return the user and machine name of the user.
            ' Otherwise, assume the record was not locked.
            If blnMUError Then
                strMsg = "Record is locked by user: " & strUser & _
                 vbCrLf & "on machine: " & strMachine & "."
            End If
        End If
        Resume ExitHere
    End Function
```

This function accepts a single parameter: a pointer to a form. Using this form object, acbWhoHasLockedRecord clones the form's recordset, synchronizes the clone's current record with that of the form, and attempts to lock the current record. One of two things can happen as a result of this locking attempt:

- The attempt will succeed, meaning that the record was not locked by another user.

- The attempt will fail with an error message stating who has the record locked.

By parsing this error message, we can determine who has locked the record. Parsing the error message is accomplished by the *acbGetUserAndMachine* function, which is shown here:

```
Public Function acbGetUserAndMachine(ByVal strErrorMsg As String, _
 ByRef strUser As String, ByRef strMachine As String) As Boolean
    ' Parse out the passed error message, returning
    '  -True and the user and machine name
    '   if the record is locked, or
    '  -False if the record is not locked.

    Dim intUserPos As Integer
    Dim intMachinePos As Integer

    Const USER_STRING As String = " locked by user "
    Const MACHINE_STRING As String = " on machine "

    acbGetUserAndMachine = False

    On Error Resume Next
    intUserPos = InStr(strErrorMsg, USER_STRING)
    If intUserPos > 0 Then
        intMachinePos = InStr(strErrorMsg, MACHINE_STRING)
        If intMachinePos > 0 Then
            strUser = Mid$(strErrorMsg, _
             intUserPos + Len(USER_STRING), _
             intMachinePos - (intUserPos + Len(USER_STRING) - 1))
            strMachine = Mid$(strErrorMsg, _
             intMachinePos + Len(MACHINE_STRING), _
             (Len(strErrorMsg) - intMachinePos - _
```

```
                    Len(MACHINE_STRING)))
            End If
            acbGetUserAndMachine = True
        End If
    End Function
```

This function accepts as its argument the Description property of the Err object, which was generated by acbWhoHasLockedRecord. If it can successfully parse the error message and determine at least the username (and hopefully the machine name), it returns a True value to the calling routine with the names of the user and machine as the second and third parameters of the function call. There's nothing magic about this function—it uses the InStr function to locate certain landmarks in the passed error message.

Record-level locking makes the use of pessimistic locking much more practical than it has been in the past. However, you still run the danger of allowing a user to monopolize the record being edited. This solution shows how you can identify the guilty user, but it doesn't really solve the problem. The next solution enables you to prevent users from tying up records for longer than a set period of time.

10.10 Set a Maximum Locking Interval for a Record

Problem

You've employed pessimistic locking on your application's forms to prevent two users from making changes to the same record at the same time. Sometimes, a user will lock a record for an excessive period of time; for example, he might start to edit a record and then get a long phone call or leave for lunch without saving or canceling his edits. Is there any way to limit how long a user can lock a record and time out the user when the locking time limit has been exceeded?

Solution

There's no built-in database or form option for "maximum record lock interval," but you can create your own record lock timeout feature by making use of the form's Timer event. This solution shows you how to create such a facility using an event procedure attached to the form's Timer event.

To add a record lock timeout feature to your own application, follow these steps for each form for which you wish to enable this feature:

1. Open the form in design mode, and add to the form an unbound text box named txtMessage that will be used to display the countdown message. This control should be at least 3.45" wide and 0.1667" high. On the sample form, we

have placed txtMessage in the form's footer, but you can place it anywhere you'd like.

2. Change the form's TimerInterval property to 1000. This will cause any code attached to the form's Timer event to be executed every 1,000 ms (or 1 second).

3. Create an event procedure attached to the form's Timer event. Figure 10-26 shows how the properties sheet for the form should look after completing these steps.

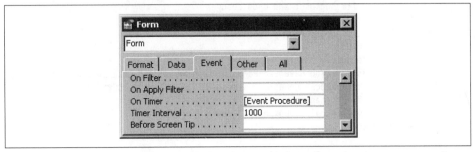

Figure 10-26. The event procedure attached to the Timer event will execute once every second

4. Add the following code to the form's event procedure:

```
Private Declare Function timeGetTime Lib "winmm.dll" () As Long

' Record lock timeout time in seconds
Private Const conMaxLockSeconds As Integer = 60

Sub cmdClose_Click()
    DoCmd.Close
End Sub

Private Sub Form_Timer()
    Dim intElapsed As Integer
    Dim strMsg As String
    Dim ctlmsg As Control

    Static slngTimerStart As Long
    Static sblnDirty As Boolean

    If Me.NewRecord Then
      Exit Sub
    End If

    Set ctlmsg = Me.txtMessage

    If Me.Dirty Then
        ' Record has been modified since last save
        If sblnDirty Then
            ' Elapsed time may be over one minute, so
            ' grab both the minutes and seconds portion
            ' of the elapsed time
```

```
            intElapsed = (timeGetTime - slngTimerStart) \ 1000
            If intElapsed < conMaxLockSeconds Then
                ' Update message control with remaining time
                strMsg = "Edit time remaining: " _
                 & (conMaxLockSeconds - intElapsed) & " seconds."
                ctlmsg = strMsg
                If intElapsed > (0.9 * conMaxLockSeconds) Then
                    ctlmsg.ForeColor = vbRed
                End If
            Else
                ' Timeout user and undo changes
                ctlmsg = ""
                ctlmsg.ForeColor = vbBlack
                Me.Undo
                sblnDirty = False
                MsgBox "You have exceeded the maximum record lock period (" & _
                 conMaxLockSeconds & " seconds). " & vbCrLf & vbCrLf & _
                 "Your changes have been discarded!", _
                 vbCritical + vbOKOnly, "Record Timeout"
            End If
        Else
            ' Start timing the edits
            slngTimerStart = timeGetTime
            sblnDirty = True
        End If

    ' Record has not been modified since last save
    Else
        If sblnDirty Then
            ' User has saved changes, so stop timer
            sblnDirty = False
            ctlmsg = ""
        End If
    End If
End Sub
```

Alternately, you can import the frmEmployees sample form from *10-10.MDB*, open frmEmployees in design mode, pull up the Timer event procedure code, and copy all the lines between `Private Sub Form_Timer( )` and `End Sub` to the clipboard. Close the sample form, open your own form's Timer event procedure, and paste the code from the sample form into your event procedure. Now delete frmEmployees from your database.

5. Save your form, and open and test it.

Now load the *10-10.MDB* database. Open the frmEmployees sample form to test out the record lock timeout feature. Make a change to an existing record and leave the record in an unsaved state. After a brief delay, a message appears in the form's footer informing you how many seconds of edit time remain (see Figure 10-27). The number counts down second by second; the message color changes to red when only a few seconds remain.

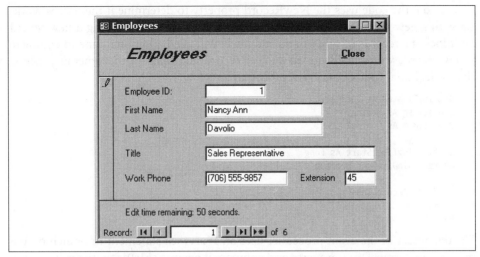

Figure 10-27. The changes to this record will be timed out unless they are saved

Finally, if you haven't either saved or undone your changes during the specified time interval, your edits will be undone and a confirming dialog will inform you of the event (see Figure 10-28).

Figure 10-28. The changes to the record have timed out

Discussion

The technique in this solution makes use of the form's Timer event, the form's Dirty property, and a couple of static variables to repeatedly check to see if the form has had unsaved changes for an extended period of time.

The timer procedure begins by declaring several variables, including the following static variables:

sblnDirty
> Saves a Boolean variable that notes if the form was dirty (i.e., has unsaved changes)

slngTimerStart
> Saves the date/time the record was first dirtied

In addition, the code uses the NewRecord property to determine if the user is working with a new record and exits if this is the case. Since a user adding a new record can't lock the records of other users and likely will need additional time to complete a new record, we decided not to subject record additions to the timeout process. Here's the initial code of the event procedure:

```
Dim intElapsed As Integer
Dim strMsg As String
Dim ctlmsg As Control

Static slngTimerStart As Long
Static sblnDirty As Boolean

If Me.NewRecord Then
   Exit Sub
End If
```

The remainder of the event procedure uses an If...Then statement to branch on the value of the form's Dirty property and compare it against *sblnDirty* (the value of the form's Dirty property the last time we checked). The process is summarized in Table 10-17.

Table 10-17. The state table for the Form_Timer event procedure

Current Dirty value	Value of sblnDirty	Action needed
True	True	Form remains dirty. Check if time limit has been exceeded and undo edits if so.
True	False	Form has just been dirtied, so set sblnDirty to True and slngTimerStart to the current number of milliseconds since Windows started, using the TimeGetTime API function.
False	True	User has saved changes, so set sblnDirty to False.
False	False	No action needed.

If the form is currently dirty (Me.Dirty = True) or was previously dirty (*sblnDirty* = True), and the elapsed time is less than conMaxLockSeconds, the following piece of code is executed:

```
intElapsed = (timeGetTime - slngTimerStart) \ 1000
If intElapsed < conMaxLockSeconds Then
    ' Update message control with remaining time
    strMsg = "Edit time remaining: " _
     & (conMaxLockSeconds - intElapsed) & " seconds."
    ctlmsg = strMsg
    If intElapsed > (0.9 * conMaxLockSeconds) Then
        ctlmsg.ForeColor = vbRed
    End If
Else
    ' ... See below ...
End If
```

The code updates the txtMessage control with the countdown message, changing the color of the text to red if the elapsed time is greater than 90% of conMaxLockSeconds to call extra attention to an impending timeout.

If the form is currently dirty (Me.Dirty = True) or was previously dirty (*sblnDirty* = True), and the elapsed time is greater than or equal to conMaxLockSeconds, the following piece of code is executed:

```
ctlmsg = ""
ctlmsg.ForeColor = vbBlack
Me.Undo
sblnDirty = False
MsgBox "You have exceeded the maximum record lock period (" & _
  conMaxLockSeconds & " seconds). " & vbCrLf & vbCrLf & _
  "Your changes have been discarded!", _
  vbCritical + vbOKOnly, "Record Timeout"
```

The edits to the record are undone by using the Undo method of the form. Next, the code puts up a message box to inform the user that the edits have been discarded.

If the form is currently dirty (Me.Dirty = True) but wasn't previously dirty (*sblnDirty* = False), *sblnDirty* is set to True and the starting time is stored away in *slngTimerStart*, as the following code shows:

```
' Start timing the edits.
slngTimerStart = timeGetTime
sblnDirty = True
```

If the form is not currently dirty (Me.Dirty = True) but was previously dirty (*sblnDirty* = True), the code stops the timer by setting *sblnDirty* to False and clearing txtMessage:

```
' User has saved changes, so stop timer.
sblnDirty = False
ctlmsg = ""
```

Finally, if the form is not currently dirty (Me.Dirty = True) and wasn't previously dirty (*sblnDirty* = False), nothing needs to be done.

Although the code for this solution could have been placed in a global module, we chose not to, since its two static variables must be maintained between calls to the event procedure. Because this code could be used in multiple forms within the application, we chose to encapsulate it within each form's event procedure. You may wish to split the code into two parts: one part that maintains the static variables in the form's Timer event procedure, and a second common component that lives in a global module. To accomplish this, you'd have to pass three variables (by reference) to the common function: a form variable referencing the form, and the two static variables, *sblnDirty* and *slngTimerStart*.

CHAPTER 11

Windows APIs

The Windows API has a bad rap among many Access programmers who think it's too hard to figure out, too hard to call, or just plain mysterious. We're here to prove that none of these is the case—even if you've never seen the Windows API programmer's reference, you can use the Windows API, given some help. In this chapter, we'll present some interesting uses of the Windows API from within Access, with example forms and modules for each solution. In most cases, using these in your own applications entails little more than simply importing a module or two and then calling the functions. We've divided the solutions in this chapter into three broad categories, as follows:

The Windows user interface
> You'll learn how to remove a form's system menu, how to maximize and minimize buttons at runtime, and how to draw attention to a specific form by flashing its titlebar or icon. We'll discuss language-independent classification of keypresses, so you can monitor exactly what keys have been pressed. We'll also show how to restrict mouse movement to a specific area on the screen.

The Windows shell
> You'll learn how to have asynchronous code run another program and pause until the other program is done before continuing. We'll demonstrate a method for shutting down Windows under program control and show you all the options of the associated API functions. You'll learn to find and run an application, given an associated data file, and how to determine if the application is already running. You'll see how to retrieve a list of all open top-level windows (generally, one per application) and how to close a window from your VBA code.

Files, drives, and hardware
> You'll learn how to set file date and time stamp information, which is useful if you're moving files around from within applications or making backups based on dates. You'll also learn how to retrieve information about your disk drives,

hardware, and the current Windows environment as well as how to connect and disconnect from remote network devices programmatically or using standard dialogs.

 Most of the solutions in this chapter instruct you to import one or more modules from the example databases. In each case, the module contains the Windows API user-defined types and function declarations you need for the example. If you've already imported a module with the specified name for a previous solution, you can skip it, since all modules with matching names contain the same code.

11.1 Remove a Form's System Menu and Maximize/Minimize Buttons

Problem

Access makes it easy to remove the control box (often called the system menu) and the minimize and maximize buttons when you design forms, but there doesn't seem to be a way to do this at runtime. You have an application for which you'd like to be able to remove these buttons to control how users interact with the application. Is there a way to remove these items and then replace them later?

Solution

Removing or replacing these window controls requires changing the style bits for the particular window. Every window maintains a 32-bit value that describes its physical characteristics: for example, its border type and the existence of scrollbars, a system menu, and the minimize and maximize buttons. The values are stored as bit flags, in which the state of a single bit in the 32-bit value indicates the value of some characteristic of the window. In general, you can't change the state of many of these flags without recreating the window; by setting or clearing the bits in the window's style value, however, you can force the system menu and the minimize/maximize buttons to appear or disappear.

Load and run frmSystemItems from *11-01.MDB*. This form, shown in Figure 11-1, allows you to add or remove the control menu, the minimize button, and the maximize button from the current form. Select items on the form to make the corresponding items visible, or deselect to remove them. Once you've made your choices, click on the Execute button, and the code will remove or replace the items you've chosen.

To include this functionality in your own applications, follow these steps:

1. Import the module basControl from *11-01.MDB*.
2. To remove or replace a form's system items, call the acbFormSystemItems subroutine, passing to it the four parameters shown in Table 11-1.

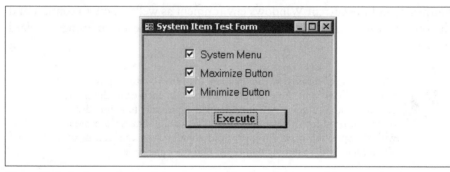

Figure 11-1. frmSystemItems allows you to remove or replace any of the system items

Table 11-1. Parameters for acbFormSystemItems

Parameter	Type	Value
frm	Form	Reference to the current form
blnShowSystemMenu	Integer	True = Show system menu; False = Hide
blnShowMaxButton	Integer	True = Show maximize button; False = Hide
blnShowMinButton	Integer	True = Show minimize button; False = Hide

For example, the following statement, called from a button's Click event in a form's module, will show the system menu but will hide the minimize and maximize buttons:

```
acbFormSystemItems Me, True, False, False
```

Though Access does provide the ControlBox, MaxButton, and MinButton properties for forms, they're read-only once the form is in use; if you need to alter these properties at runtime, you'll need to use acbFormSystemItems instead of changing the properties directly.

Old Versus New Use of Window Buttons

The behavior of the control box and minimize and maximize buttons has changed. If you're running Windows 95 or later, using acbFormSystemItems to remove one of the minimize or maximize buttons leaves them both visible but disables the one you've requested to hide. Removing them both with acbFormSystemItems makes them both invisible. Under Windows NT and earlier, these buttons are independent, and using the subroutine to remove one makes it invisible. Under Windows 95 or later, removing the control box also removes the minimize and maximize buttons. Under Windows NT or earlier, these items are independent.

Discussion

The bulk of the work in controlling these system items takes place in the private HandleStyles function in the basControl module. This function accepts a window handle (the hWnd property of a form) and three True/False values indicating which options you want to see and which you want removed. Like every window, the window you want to alter maintains a 32-bit value, its style value. Within that long integer, each of the 32 positions represents one of the possible styles for the window. If the bit is 1, the style is set on; if it's 0, the style is set off. HandleStyles builds up two long integers, each containing a series of 32 bits. The first, lngStylesOn, contains all 0s, except for the bits representing the styles you want turned on, which contain 1s. The other, lngStylesOff, contains all 1s, except for the bits representing the styles you want turned off, which contain 0s.

Using the AND operator to combine the current window style with lngStylesOff sets each style whose bit contains 0 in lngStylesOff to be 0. Using the OR operator to combine the current window style with lngStylesOn sets each style whose bit contains 1 in lngStylesOn to be 1. For example, suppose the current window style value is this:

```
10001000 10001010 10101011 01101101
```

The value in lngStylesOff contains 1s in all positions except the ones you want turned off, which contain 0s. If the value of lngStylesOff is this:

```
11111111 11111111 11111111 11111011
```

the result of using the AND operator with the original style and lngStylesOff will be this:

```
10001000 10001010 10101011 01101001
```

The value in lngStylesOn contains 0s in all positions except the ones you want turned on, which contain 1s. If the value of lngStylesOn is this:

```
00000000 00000000 00010000 10000000
```

the result of using the OR operator with lngStylesOn and the result of ANDing the original style with lngStylesOff will be this:

```
10001000 10001010 10111011 11101001
```

This final result will have three changed values: one bit that was 1 is now 0 due to the settings in lngStylesOff, and two bits that were are now 1 due to the settings in lnStylesOn.

To retrieve and replace the window's style information, the code uses the GetWindowLong and SetWindowLong API functions. Given a window handle and a flag (GWL_STYLE) indicating which 32-bit value to retrieve or set, these functions allow you to get the current value, do your work with it, and then set it back. This is the line of code that does all the work:

```
HandleStyles = SetWindowLong(hWnd, GWL_STYLE, _
    (GetWindowLong(hWnd, GWL_STYLE) And lngStylesOff) _
    Or lngStylesOn)
```

It sets the window style to be the value `GetWindowLong` retrieved, combined with the two style flags the code previously built up based on your choices.

The entire HandleStyles procedure looks like this:

```
Private Function HandleStyles(ByVal hWnd As Long, blnShowSystemMenu As Boolean, _
    blnShowMaxButton As Boolean, blnShowMinButton As Boolean) As Long

    Dim lngStylesOn As Long
    Dim lngStylesOff As Long

    On Error GoTo HandleStylesExit

    ' Set all bits off.
    lngStylesOn = 0

    ' Set all bits on.
    lngStylesOff = &HFFFFFFFF

    ' Turn ON bits to set attribute; turn OFF bits to turn attribute off.
    If blnShowSystemMenu Then
        lngStylesOn = lngStylesOn Or WS_SYSMENU
    Else
        lngStylesOff = lngStylesOff And Not WS_SYSMENU
    End If
    If blnShowMinButton Then
        lngStylesOn = lngStylesOn Or WS_MINIMIZEBOX
    Else
        lngStylesOff = lngStylesOff And Not WS_MINIMIZEBOX
    End If
    If blnShowMaxButton Then
        lngStylesOn = lngStylesOn Or WS_MAXIMIZEBOX
    Else
        lngStylesOff = lngStylesOff And Not WS_MAXIMIZEBOX
    End If

    ' Set the attributes as necessary.
    HandleStyles = SetWindowLong(hWnd, GWL_STYLE, _
        (acb_apiGetWindowLong(hWnd, GWL_STYLE) And lngStylesOff) _
        Or lngStylesOn)

        ' The 1 in the third parameter tells the window
        ' to repaint its entire border.
        Call SendMessage(hwnd, WM_NCPAINT, 1, 0)

HandleStylesExit:
    Exit Function
End Function
```

After the style bits are set, there's still one issue left: you must coerce the window into repainting itself so the changes become visible. Simply changing the styles isn't enough, because they don't become visible until the next time the window repaints its border.

If you resize the form, Access repaints the border, but there's no reasonable programmatic way to do this. To solve the problem, the procedure adds one more line. It calls the SendMessage API, which sends a specific message to any window (this time, it sends a message to the form itself). The message it sends, a constant named WM_NCPAINT, tells the form to repaint its non-client area (that is, its border):

```
' The 1 as the third parameter tells the window
' to repaint its entire border.
Call acb_SendMessage(hwnd, WM_NCPAINT, 1, 0)
```

11.2   Flash a Window's Titlebar or Icon

Problem

With so many windows open in your Access applications, it can be difficult to force your user's attention to a specific form. Is there a way to make the titlebar flash so that a form really stands out?

Solution

Windows supplies a simple API call, FlashWindow, that allows you to flash the titlebar of a form or its icon (if it's iconized) on and off. This solution will demonstrate how you can use the FlashWindow API call to draw attention to a specific form.

To include this functionality in your own applications, follow these steps:

1. Add this API declaration to your code in the declarations section of the form's module:

```
Private Declare Function FlashWindow Lib "User32" _
 (ByVal hWnd As Long, ByVal lngInvert As Long) As Long
```

In our example, the declaration is in the module for frmControlFlash.

2. Create a module-level variable (*mhWnd* in our example) to hold the flashed form's window handle:

```
Dim mhWnd As Long
```

3. Create a procedure attached to your controlling form's Timer event, causing the form to flash:

```
Private Sub Form_Timer( )
   FlashWindow mhWnd, True
End Sub
```

4. To turn the flashing on and off, add code like this to react to some event (on the sample form, you trigger the code in reaction to the Click event of the Flash button):

```
Private Sub cmdFlash_Click( )
    Dim strCaption As String
    Dim ctl As Control

    Set ctl = Me.cmdFlash
    strCaption = ctl.Caption
    If strCaption = "Flash" Then
        ' If the form's already open, this will just
        ' set the focus to that form.
        DoCmd.OpenForm "frmFlash"
        mhWnd = Forms("frmFlash").hWnd
        ' Change the button's caption to
        ' indicate its state.
        ctl.Caption = "Stop Flashing"
        Me.TimerInterval = 500
    Else
        ctl.Caption = "Flash"
        Me.TimerInterval = 0
        FlashWindow mhWnd, False
    End If
End Sub
```

To see an example of a flashing form, load and run frmControlFlash from *11-02.MDB*. That form loads a second form, frmFlash. By clicking the button on frmControlFlash, you can turn the flashing of frmFlash's titlebar on or off (see Figure 11-2). If you iconize frmFlash, it will continue to flash.

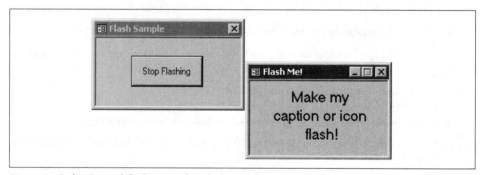

Figure 11-2. frmControlFlash causes frmFlash's titlebar to invert (flash)

Discussion

The FlashWindow API call takes two values as its parameters: the handle to a window and a logical value. When Windows creates a new window (as it does when you open a form in Access), it supplies the window with a unique 32-bit value, its handle, that any program can use to work directly with that window. Access gives you a form's handle in its hWnd property. Given that handle and a Boolean value (True or

False) indicating whether you want the window to invert or not, FlashWindow takes the requested action with the window you've indicated. For example:

```
FlashWindow Forms("frmFlash").hWnd, True
```

would make the titlebar of frmFlash look like it is selected, even if it isn't the currently active form. Sending False for the second parameter would revert to the form's original state (selected or deselected). Calling FlashWindow, passing True in the second parameter, is what makes the window look like it's flashing; this is where the Timer event comes in.

By reacting to a form's Timer event, you can have your code take effect at a set interval. In this case, you set the timer interval to be 500, or 1/2 of a second (the Timer-Interval property measures time in milliseconds, or 1/1,000 of a second):

```
Me.TimerInterval = 500
```

To make it so that the code attached to the Timer event never runs, set the Timer-Interval property to 0. That's how you control the flashing in this example: to turn flashing on, set the TimerInterval property to the rate at which you'd like the flashing to occur; to turn it off, just set the TimerInterval property to 0.

This example takes one extra step: when it turns off the flashing, it also makes sure that the caption bar of the flashed form is no longer inverted. That is, it calls FlashWindow one more time, forcing the flashing off:

```
Me.TimerInterval = 0
FlashWindow mhWnd, False
```

This ensures that no matter where in the cycle you turn off the flashing, the flashed form reverts to its normal appearance.

You can control the speed of the flashing by changing the TimerInterval property value. Currently, it's set at 500; you may want to speed that up. Be aware, though, that flashing is not a normal Windows mechanism; it goes against the Windows design standards, and should be used only for brief periods of time and in special circumstances.

Because FlashWindow accepts the handle to any window as its parameter, you could use this same technique to cause an application's main window to flash as well. For example, The Solution in Recipe 11.9 shows how to retrieve a list of all open top-level windows, and you could use the hWnd properties from that list with FlashWindow as well.

Note that even though the form's Timer event is set to do its work every 500 ms, it may take longer for your flashing form to start flashing. The code in the form's Timer event sends a message to Windows, telling it to flash the other form's titlebar, but that may take a few milliseconds on a slower machine. For the same reason, your form may not flash at exactly regular intervals. The form's timer handler is non-preemptive, meaning that it must wait for keyboard, mouse, and screen events to be handled first.

11.3 Classify Keypresses in a Language-Independent Manner

Problem

You need to be able to classify a keypress as a character, a digit, or neither. You also need to know if a character is uppercase or lowercase. You know you can write code to handle this, but if you do that, you're limiting yourself to a single national language, since languages classify their characters differently. Since Windows knows about various character sets, is there some way you can use Windows to do this work for you?

Solution

You could write VBA code to classify characters, but it wouldn't be language-independent. For example, the ANSI character 65 is an uppercase character in the standard multinational character set, but it may be different in another character set. If you want your applications to work in various languages, you must not assume specific character ranges. The Windows API includes a number of functions you can call to categorize characters based on their ANSI values. The isCharAlpha and isCharAlphaNumeric functions both are faster than the built-in VBA functions and are able to deal with international issues. Luckily, an ANSI value is exactly what the KeyPress event procedure in Access sends you, so you can use these functions from within KeyPress event procedures that you write.

In addition to the necessary function declarations, the sample database *11-03.MDB* includes a demonstration form showing all the ANSI characters and their classifications. Load and run `frmCharClasses` from *11-03.MDB*, and you'll see a display like that in Figure 11-3. By scrolling through the form, you'll be able to see all 255 ANSI characters and their classifications.

To use this functionality in your own applications, follow these steps:

1. Import the module basClassifyChars from *11-03.MDB* into your application.

2. To classify an ANSI value, call one or more of the functions in Table 11-2. Each of these functions takes as its parameter a value between 1 and 255. Each function returns a nonzero value if the character code you passed is a member of the function's tested group, or 0 if it's not. (As you can see from Table 11-2, some of the functions come directly from the Windows API and others return values based on those functions.) These functions will return correct values no matter which language version of Windows is running.

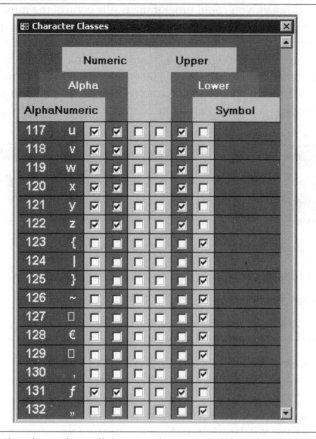

Figure 11-3. frmCharClasses shows all the ANSI characters and their classifications

Table 11-2. The character classification functions in basClassifyChars

Function	API?	Inclusion class
acb_apilsCharAlphaNumeric	Yes	Language-defined alphabetic or numeric characters
acb_apilsCharAlpha	Yes	Language-defined alphabetic characters
acblsCharNumeric	No	Alphanumeric, but not alphabetic
acblsSymbol	No	Not alphanumeric
acb_apilsCharUpper	Yes	Language-defined uppercase characters
acb_apilsCharLower	Yes	Language-defined lowercase characters

For example, imagine that you need to limit the number of characters typed into a text box, and the number of allowable characters isn't known until runtime. In addition, you want to allow only alphabetic or numeric values, but that isn't known until runtime either. Although you could programmatically control the input masks, creating a new one each time conditions change, it is simpler to handle this problem using the KeyPress event and some code that checks the state of the current keypress. The sample form, frmInputTest (Figure 11-4), shows a simple test form. The text box labeled "Enter some characters" allows you to enter up to as many characters as shown in the "Maximum number of characters" text box, and you can enter only characters whose type you've chosen in the character type option group.

Figure 11-4. frmInputTest uses character classifications to disallow keypresses

The code attached to txtCharTest's KeyPress event looks like this:

```
Sub txtCharTest_KeyPress (KeyAscii As Integer)

    ' Always allow a backspace.
    If KeyAscii = vbKeyBack Then Exit Sub

    ' If txtChars is non-null and greater than 0, and txtCharTest
    ' is non-null and has too many characters, set KeyAscii to 0.
    If Not IsNull(Me.txtChars) Then
        If Me.txtChars > 0 Then
            If Not IsNull(Me.txtCharTest.Text) Then
                If Len(Me.txtCharTest.Text) >= Me.txtChars Then
                    KeyAscii = 0
                End If
            End If
        End If
    End If
    ' In any case, if the keypress isn't the correct type,
    ' set KeyAscii to 0.
    If Me.grpCharType = 1 Then
        If (acb_apiIsCharAlpha(KeyAscii) = 0) Then KeyAscii = 0
    Else
        If (acbIsCharNumeric(KeyAscii) = 0) Then KeyAscii = 0
    End If
End Sub
```

In the KeyPress event, Access sends you the parameter *KeyAscii*, which contains the ANSI value of the key that was just pressed. To tell Access to disregard this key, modify its value to 0 during the event procedure. In this case, if there's no room left in the field (based on the number in Me.txtChars) or if the character is not the right type (based on calls to acb_apiIsCharAlpha and acbIsCharNumeric), the code sets the value of *KeyAscii* to 0, causing Access to disregard the keypress. Play with the sample form, changing the values, to see how the code works.

Discussion

Windows internally maintains information about the currently selected language and character set. For each language, certain characters are treated as uppercase and others aren't. Some characters in the character set represent alphabetic characters and others don't. It would be impractical to maintain this information for each language your application might use. Luckily, you don't have to manage this. The Access *UCase* and *LCase* functions handle case conversions for you, but Access doesn't include case-testing functions. That's the role of the functions introduced in this solution: they allow you to test the classification of characters, no matter what the language. Attempting to perform this task in VBA will cause you trouble if you plan on working internationally.

You may not need these routines often, but when you do, the API versions are both faster and more reliable than handwritten code would be. Don't count on specific ANSI values to be certain characters, uppercase or lowercase, because these values change from version to version of internationalized Windows.

11.4   Restrict Mouse Movement to a Specific Region

Problem

You'd like to be able to restrict mouse-cursor movement to certain areas of the current form. You think it would help users of your application if the mouse stays where it needs to be until they're done with it. How can you limit mouse movement in Access?

Solution

The Windows API's *ClipCursor* subroutine will limit the movement of the mouse to a single form or region on a form, as you'll see in this solution.

To try out this technique, load and run the frmClip form from *11-04.MDB*. This form, shown in Figure 11-5, limits the mouse movement to the area of the form once you click the large button. If you click the button again or close the form, code attached to either event frees the mouse cursor to move anywhere on the screen. If you move the form, Windows frees the mouse cursor for you.

To use this technique in your own applications, follow these steps:

1. Import the module basClipCursor from *11-04.MDB*. This module contains the function declarations and user-defined types that you'll need.

2. To limit the mouse to a single form, you'll need to get the form coordinates and tell Windows to use those coordinates as limits for the mouse. To do this, you'll

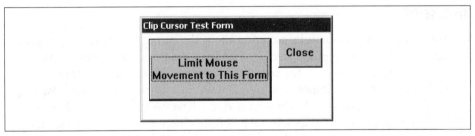

Figure 11-5. frmClip limits mouse movement to the area of the form

need code something like the following (because this code fragment uses Me, it must be in a form's module, not a global module):

```
Dim typRect as acb_tagRect

Call acb_apiGetWindowRect (Me.Hwnd, typRect)
Call acb_apiClipCursor(typRect)
```

3. To free the mouse cursor, use code like this:

```
Call acb_apiClipCursor(ByVal vbNullString)
```

See Section 11.4.3 for an example.

Discussion

The ClipCursor API routine (aliased as acb_apiClipCursor in the code) expects as its only parameter a user-defined data type consisting of four long integers representing coordinates of a rectangle. This data type has been declared for you in basClipCursor as acb_tagRect. This is a common data structure, used often with API routines that interact with the screen or printer. It is defined as follows:

```
Type acb_tagRect
    lngLeft As Long
    lngTop As Long
    lngRight As Long
    lngBottom As Long
End Type
```

When you want to restrict mouse movement, you'll need to retrieve the coordinates of the current form. You can accomplish this by calling the GetWindowRect API function (aliased as acb_apiGetWindowRect in the code), which will fill in an acb_tagRect structure with the left, top, right, and bottom coordinates of the window whose handle you pass it. Therefore, by calling acb_apiGetWindowRect with the handle of the current form, you'll retrieve the coordinates of that form in pixels:

```
Dim typRect as acb_tagRect
Call acb_apiGetWindowRect (Me.hWnd, typRect)
```

Once you've got a structure containing the coordinates of the current form, you can call ClipCursor and pass that filled-in structure to it. The sample form combines these API calls, as shown here:

```
Private Sub cmdClip_Click( )
    Dim typRect As acb_tagRect
    Static sstrCaption As String

    ' Static variable to keep track of clipping
    Static blnClip As Boolean

    If blnClip Then
        Me.cmdClip.Caption = sstrCaption
        Call acb_apiClipCursor(ByVal vbNullString)
    Else
        sstrCaption = Me.cmdClip.Caption
        Me.cmdClip.Caption = "Free the Mouse!"
        Call acb_apiGetWindowRect(Me.hWnd, typRect)
        Call acb_apiClipCursor(typRect)
    End If
    blnClip = Not blnClip
End Sub
```

In the sample routine, which is executed each time you click the large button on frm-Clip, blnClip alternates between True and False, keeping track of whether mouse clipping is currently in effect. If it is, the routine calls acb_apiClipCursor to disable clipping and resets the button's caption. If clipping is not in effect, the routine stores away the original caption, sets a new one ("Free the Mouse!"), retrieves the form's coordinates, and finally calls acb_apiClipCursor to restrict the cursor's movement.

To end the mouse-cursor restrictions, send a null value to acb_apiClipCursor. To do that, pass the vbNullString intrinsic constant by value. Because the acb_apiClipCursor procedure has been declared to accept any type of parameter, you can send it a structure in one call and a null value in another.

The method presented in this solution is not foolproof in Access. You're taking control of a feature that Access normally controls itself, and sometimes the interaction may be unpredictable. In this case, if you restrict the mouse movement to a single form, but then use the mouse to move or resize the form, Access will free the mouse for you. Therefore, if you want to *force* users to stay on a single form, you're better off using a modal form instead. If, on the other hand, you're just trying to ensure that the mouse remains in the area of the form where the users need it to be, the method described here is appropriate. Restricting the mouse movement is not meant for every application, but if you want to help your users out a little, try it.

11.5   Run Another Program and Pause Until It's Done

Problem

From within your application, you sometimes need to run another Windows application, or a DOS batch file or utility program that requires some time to do its job.

You'd like your Access application to pause until this other program has finished its work. Every time you try it, though, the code starts up the other application but then keeps on going. Is there a way to make Access wait until the other application has completed before moving on?

Solution

The Shell function in VBA (and the ShellExecute function we will mention in the Solution in Recipe 11.7) returns a unique long integer value representing the running task. You can use this value—the *instance handle* for the running application—to track the state of the application. Given an instance handle, you can use the Open-Process API function to retrieve the process handle for the process. Armed with that process handle, you can then call the GetExitCodeProcess function continually until it sees that the process has shut down. Because this happens automatically once a DOS application has finished running, you can use this technique to wait until a DOS window has closed before moving on in your application.

The sample form in *11-05.MDB*, frmTestWait, allows you to try starting both a DOS application and a Windows application, and wait for either to complete. There's also a button that allows you to start a DOS application but continue the attached code. In each of these cases, the sample code attempts to load the text file *C:\ACBTEST. TXT* (choosing either of the first two buttons sends the output of CHKDSK to *C:\ ACBTEST.TXT* for you) into a text box on the form once the application you've started finishes its work, as shown in Figure 11-6. (In the case where the code doesn't wait for the other application, of course, there's nothing to load.) Use frmTestWait, try each command button to test the functionality demonstrated in this solution. The first button runs CHKDSK, waits until it has written its output to *C:\ACBTEST.TXT*, and then loads the text file. The second button runs CHKDSK and immediately loads the text file. The final button, Run Notepad, loads a Windows application, Notepad, and waits until you've closed it before loading the text file.

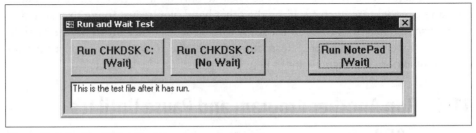

Figure 11-6. frmTestWait after it has run an application

To use this functionality in your own applications, follow these steps:

1. Import the module basRunApp from *11-05.MDB* into your application.

2. To run another application and wait for it to finish before going on with your code, call the acbRunAppWait subroutine, passing it two parameters: a command string telling it what to run, and an integer designating the window mode you'd like to use (see Table 11-3). These are essentially the same values you use when calling the ShellExecute Windows API function, as shown in the Solution in Recipe 11.7.

Table 11-3. Window display options using Shell

Value	VBA constant	Description
0	vbHide	Hidden
1	vbNormalFocus	Restored to its previous state (neither minimized nor maximized)
2	vbMinimizedFocus	Made visible and minimized
3	vbMaximizedFocus	Made visible and maximized
4	vbNormalNoFocus	Displayed, but doesn't gain the input focus
6	vbMinimizedNoFocus	Minimized (as an icon) when started

For example, to start the Windows calculator maximized, use a statement like this:

```
acbRunAppWait "CALC.EXE", vbMaximizedFocus
MsgBox "Done with the calculator."
```

You won't see the message box until you finish with the calculator.

Discussion

The secret to the acbRunAppWait subroutine is its use of the Windows API function GetExitCodeProcess. This function takes as a parameter the process handle of an application, which you can retrieve by calling the *OpenProcess* API function with the instance handle returned by the call to Shell. GetExitCodeProcess monitors a running process and retrieves that process's exit code. As long as the process continues to run, GetExitCodeProcess returns the value STILL_ACTIVE (defined in basRunApp).

Consider the following code, which checks for the existence of a running application:

```
Do
    ' Attempt to retrieve the exit code, which will
    ' not exist until the application has quit.
    lngRetval = GetExitCodeProcess(hProcess, lngExitCode)
Loop Until lngExitCode <> STILL_ACTIVE
```

Though this will almost do what you need, it won't quite succeed. You've left Access running a tight loop, waiting for the new application to finish. Unfortunately, this loop grabs all of Access's clock cycles, looping and waiting for the other application to be done. While this loop is active, Access is effectively dead. All the rest of Windows continues to work perfectly, but Access's only thread of execution is completely tied up. You'll see that Access simply can't update its screen, for example, while you're running Notepad.

The solution, then, is to be a good citizen, allowing Access its processing time. To do this, you must add a DoEvents statement inside the loop. This allows Access to continue working while this code loops, waiting for the application you started to finish. (See the Solution in Recipe 7.4 for more information on DoEvents.) Thus, the *acbRunAppWait* subroutine looks like this:

```
Public Sub acbRunAppWait(strCommand As String, intMode As Integer)
    ' Run an application, waiting for its completion
    ' before returning to the caller.

    Dim hInstance As Long
    Dim hProcess As Long
    Dim lngRetval As Long
    Dim lngExitCode As Long

    On Error GoTo acbRunAppWait_Err
    ' Start up the application.
    hInstance = Shell(strCommand, intMode)
    hProcess = OpenProcess(PROCESS_QUERY_INFORMATION Or SYNCHRONIZE, _
      True, hInstance)
    Do
        ' Attempt to retrieve the exit code, which will
        ' not exist until the application has quit.
        lngRetval = GetExitCodeProcess(hProcess, lngExitCode)
        DoEvents
    Loop Until lngExitCode <> STILL_ACTIVE

acbRunAppWait_Exit:
    Exit Sub

acbRunAppWait_Err:
    Select Case Err.Number
        Case acbcErrFileNotFound
            MsgBox "Unable to find '" & strCommand & "'"
        Case Else
            MsgBox Err.Description
    End Select
    Resume acbRunAppWait_Exit
End Sub
```

To use the Shell command, you must specify an executable file. If you need to run a DOS internal command or redirect the output from a program to a text file, you'll need to load a copy of *COMMAND.COM* to do your work. In addition, you'll need to use the /C switch, indicating to COMMAND.COM that you just want a temporary instance that should quit when the program you run finishes. For example, to run the CHKDSK.EXE program directly, you could use the following function call (all these examples assume that the necessary programs are available in the DOS PATH):

```
hInstance = Shell("CHKDSK.EXE", vbMinimizedNoFocus)
```

To run DIR, on the other hand, you'll need to start COMMAND.COM first:

```
hInstance = Shell("COMMAND.COM /C DIR C:\*.BAT", vbMinimizedNoFocus)
```

To redirect the output from a program to a text file, you'll also need to use COMMAND.COM:

```
hInstance = Shell("COMMAND.COM /C CHKDSK C: > C:\ACBTEST.TXT", _
  vbMinimizedNoFocus)
```

 You may also want to study the *FileRead* subroutine in the sample form's module, which demonstrates how to open a text file and read its contents directly into a control on a form.

11.6   Exit Windows Under Program Control

Problem

You'd like to be able to control what happens once you quit your applications: you may want to shut down Windows at the same time, or perhaps even reboot the machine. How can you do that from within Access?

Solution

The Windows API provides an ExitWindowsEx function that grants you control over exiting Windows, and you have a choice of three different things you can do: log off and await a new login; shut down to the point at which it's safe to turn off the computer's power; or reboot the computer. This solution demonstrates these simple functions.

To try closing Windows under program control, load and run frmExitWindows from *11-06.MDB*. This sample form, shown in Figure 11-7, allows you to choose from the three options. Make your choice and click on the Go button, which will execute the code necessary to quit in the manner you've specified.

To use this functionality within your own applications, follow these steps:

1. Import the module basExitWindows from *11-06.MDB*.
2. Call the function from Table 11-4 that best suits your needs. In each case, if the function returns at all, it indicates that some Windows process wasn't able to shut down and that your function call failed. This won't happen often.

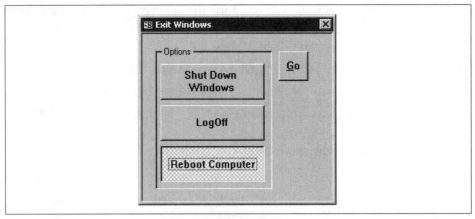

Figure 11-7. frmExitWindows presents three options

Table 11-4. Available functions for exiting Windows

Function	Description
acbLogOff	Shuts down all processes running in the security context of the process that called the function, then logs off the user. Depending on the operating system, you may find that all applications get the shutdown message except the one that called this function. Check the behavior of your target operating system.
acbReboot	Reboots the computer.
acbShutDown	Shuts down the system to a point at which it is safe to turn off the power. All file buffers are flushed to disk, and all running processes are stopped.

For example, to reboot your computer:

```
intRetval = acbReboot( )
```

Discussion

Normally, when you shut down Windows, it sends a message to check with every running application before shutting down. If other applications have any unsaved data files that require user intervention, you'll usually be asked if it's okay to save the files. Once all the applications have agreed to shut down, Windows shuts itself down.

Windows follows the same shutdown procedures when you use any of the functions listed in Table 11-4. The only difference is what happens after Windows shuts down.

The basExitWindows module is simple: it merely calls directly into the ExitWindowsEx API function. The entire module looks like this:

```
Declare Function acb_apiExitWindowsEx Lib "user32" Alias "ExitWindowsEx" _
 (ByVal uFlags As Long, ByVal dwReserved As Long) As Long

' EWX_FORCE
'    Forces processes to terminate. Instead of bringing up the
'    "application not responding" dialog for the user, this value
'    forces an application to terminate if it does not respond.
' EWX_LOGOFF
'   Shuts down all processes running in the security context
'    of the process that called the ExitWindowsEx function, then
'    logs off the user.
' EWX_REBOOT
'   Shuts down the system, then restarts the system.
' EWX_SHUTDOWN
'   Shuts down the system to a point at which it is safe to turn off
'    the power. All file buffers have been flushed to disk, and all
'    running processes have stopped.

Const EWX_LOGOFF = 0
Const EWX_SHUTDOWN = 1
Const EWX_REBOOT = 2
Const EWX_FORCE = 4

Public Function acbReboot( )
    acbReboot = acb_apiExitWindowsEx(EWX_REBOOT, 0)
End Function

Public Function acbShutDown( )
    acbShutDown = acb_apiExitWindowsEx(EWX_SHUTDOWN, 0)
End Function

Public Function acbLogOff( )
    acbLogOff = acb_apiExitWindowsEx(EWX_LOGOFF, 0)
    ' This is actually necessary only in some operating systems,
    ' but it can't hurt.
    Application.Quit acExit
End Function
```

Each function listed in Table 11-4 has its own role. You're most likely to use acbShutDown when your application is meant for users who use *only* Access. When they're done with your application, they're done with Windows. The other functions are more useful in utility applications other than Access; use your imagination! There may be reasons why you'd need to reboot; for example, perhaps you've changed a setting in the Windows registry for the user and you want it to take effect immediately.

Certainly, these are not functions that every application will need or that you will use every day. But if you need to control what happens once your application has done its work, they are valuable indeed.

11.7 Run the Application Associated with a Data File

Problem

You'd like to find a way to provide a list of existing files, allow users to select a file, and run the appropriate application for that file. Windows knows how to do this—for instance, when you double-click on a file with a *.TXT* extension in Explorer, Windows runs Notepad with that file. How can you provide this sort of functionality in your own applications?

Solution

Windows provides two API functions, FindExecutable and ShellExecute, that make running a related application possible from within Access. Both functions rely heavily on the Windows registry, which tracks the relationships between filename extensions and related executable programs. Figure 11-8 shows the results of running the *REGEDIT.EXE* program, which ships as part of Windows. REGEDIT allows you to add, edit, modify, or delete file associations. (The registry editor is named *REGEDT32.EXE* under Windows NT and, though it looks different, it functions in a similar manner.)

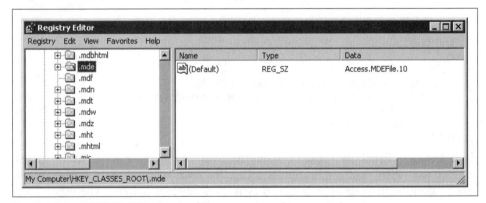

Figure 11-8. REGEDIT.EXE, showing file types registered on a typical system

 Be sure not to change any of the entries in the registry when looking through REGEDIT.

In this solution, you use the FindExecutable function to get the name of the executable file associated with a selected data file. You also use the ShellExecute function to run the executable file, with the selected data file opened and ready to edit.

Load and run `frmTestExecute`, shown in Figure 11-9. To use this form, select a path (it defaults to your Windows directory when it first loads). Once the list box fills with all the files in the specified directory, click on one with the mouse. If there's an active file association for the selected file, the form will display that executable file-name in a text box. If there's an associated executable file, you can run it and load your chosen file by double-clicking on the list box or clicking on the checkmark button.

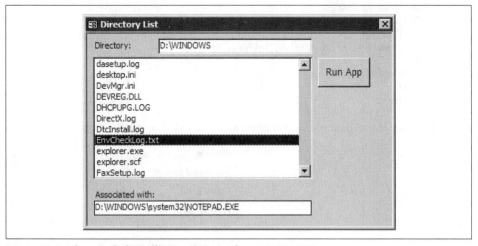

Figure 11-9. The sample form, frmTestExecute, from 11-07.MDB

To use this functionality in your own applications, follow these steps:

1. Import the module basShellAPI from *11-07.MDB* into your application.

2. To find the executable file associated with a given document, use the FindExecutable API function (aliased as `acb_apiFindExecutable` in the code). Call it with the three parameters described in Table 11-5.

Table 11-5. Parameters for the FindExecutable API function

Parameter	Type	Description
strFile	String	The filename that has an association in the registration database
strDir	String	The drive letter and path for the default directory (you can use "." to indicate the current directory)
strResult	String	A buffer to contain the returned executable name

The FindExecutable function returns an integer error code. If the value is greater than 32, the function has succeeded. Otherwise, it returns one of the error codes in Table 11-6 (note that these error codes are shared by several functions). If the function succeeded, *strResult* will be a null-terminated string containing the associated executable file. You'll need to trim off that trailing null character. One easy way to do this is by using the TrimNull function in basShellAPI, as follows:

```
Private Function TrimNull(strValue As String)

    ' Trim strValue at the first
    ' null character you find.

    Dim intPos As Integer
    intPos = InStr(strValue, vbNullChar)
    If intPos > 0 Then
        TrimNull = Left$(strValue, intPos - 1)
    Else
        TrimNull = strValue
    End If
End Function
```

Table 11-6. Some shared error codes for FindExecutable and ShellExecute

Value	Meaning
0	System error occurred
2	File not found
3	Path not found
5	Sharing violation occurred
8	Not enough memory to start the task
27	Association incomplete
31	No association in the Registration Database for the file extension
32	DLL not found

For example, the following code will find the executable file associated with *MyFile. OOG*:

```
Dim strBuffer As String
Dim strResult As String

strBuffer = Space(128)
strResult = ""

intRetval = acb_apiFindExecutable("MyFile.OOG", ".", strBuffer)
If intRetval > acbcHinstanceErr Then
    ' Use the TrimNull function in basShellAPI
    ' to remove the trailing null character.
    strResult = TrimNull(strBuffer)
End If
' Now, strResult holds either "" or the name
' of the executable you need.
```

To make this simpler, basShellAPI includes the acbFindExecutable function. This function requires the same parameters and returns the same values as acb_apiFindExecutable, but it handles the details of initializing the string buffer and trimming off the trailing null character for you. You'll want to use this function instead of calling the Windows API directly, as it will ensure that you use the correct methods for sending and receiving strings.

Once you know the name of the executable file associated with the selected document, you'll want to execute it with the ShellExecute API function. You could, of course, use the Shell command, but ShellExecute gives you a bit more flexibility, as a comparison of the two shows:

- ShellExecute returns an error code if something goes wrong, but Shell requires that you write error-handling code to trap and deal with errors. In the long run, using ShellExecute is simpler.

- ShellExecute allows you to specify the default drive/directory for your application. Shell does not.

- ShellExecute provides a few more options than Shell; see Table 11-8 for details.

- Not that you'll use it often, but ShellExecute allows you to specify the action to take on opening a file. If you want to print the file rather than open it, specify the "print" operation for the second parameter.

 If your only intent is to run the executable associated with a file, you don't need to call FindExecutable explicitly. Instead, you can pass the file name to ShellExecute, and it will find the executable for you. In this example, we wanted to display the associated executable, so we divided the task into two API function calls.

To use the ShellExecute function, call it with the six parameters shown in Table 11-7.

Table 11-7. Parameters for the ShellExecute API function

Parameter	Type	Description
hWnd	Integer	The handle of the window to be used as the parent for message boxes that may appear.
strOp	String	The operation to perform. Normally, can only be "open" or "print".
strFile	String	The name of the program to start.
strParams	String	Command-line arguments for the executable program. Normally, the name of the file to load into the application.
strDir	String	The default drive/directory for the application when it starts up.

Table 11-7. Parameters for the ShellExecute API function (continued)

Parameter	Type	Description
intShowCmd	Integer	Specification of how to show the new window when the application starts up. For a list of values, see Table 11-8.

Table 11-8 lists all the possible values for the *intShowCmd* parameter. These values control how the new application's window appears on the Windows desktop.

Table 11-8. Window display options for the intShowCmd parameter to ShellExecute

Constant	Value	Meaning
acbSW_HIDE	0	The window is hidden when started.
acbSW_SHOWNORMAL	1	The window is restored to its previous state (neither minimized nor maximized).
acbSW_SHOWMINIMIZED	2	The window is made visible and minimized.
acbSW_SHOWMAXIMIZED	3	The window is made visible and maximized.
acbSW_SHOWNOACTIVATE	4	The window is displayed, but doesn't gain the input focus.
acbSW_MINIMIZE	6	The window is minimized (as an icon) when started.
acbSW_SHOWMINNOACTIVE	7	The window is made visible and minimized, but doesn't receive the input focus.
acbSW_SHOWNA	8	The window is displayed without any change to the window's state (remains minimized, normal, or maximized).
acbSW_RESTORE	9	The window is restored to its previous state (neither minimized nor maximized). (Same as acbSW_SHOWNORMAL.)

For example, to run the program C:\OOGLY\MKOOGLE.EXE (which created MyFile.OOG) maximized on the screen, you could run code like this from a form's module:

```
intRetval = acb_apiShellExecute(Me.hWnd, "open", "C:\OOGLY\MKOOGLE.EXE", _
    "MyFile.OOG", "C:\OOGLY", acbSW_SHOWMAXIMIZED)
```

Discussion

You can call the FindExecutable function to retrieve an associated executable file for a given document, and then pass both the executable name and the document name to ShellExecute to load them. For example, you might use code like this in your application:

```
Dim intRetval As Integer
Dim strBuffer As String

intRetval = acbFindExecutable("MyFile.XXX", ".", strBuffer)
If intRetval <= acbHInstanceErr Then
    MsgBox "Unable to find executable. Error " & intRetval & "."
Else
    ' You're only here if you found the executable.
    intRetval = acb_apiShellExecute(Me.hWnd, "open", strBuffer, _
        "MyFile.XXX", "C:\NewDocs", acbSW_SHOWMAXIMIZED)
    If intRetval <= acbHInstanceErr Then
        MsgBox "Unable to load application. Error " & intRetval & "."
    End If
End If
```

You may find it interesting to work your way through the sample form frmTestExecute. It uses the AddItem method of the ListBox control (added in Access 2002) to add file names retrieved from a Collection object. The code fills the collection by calling the FillDirlist method, in the basFillList module.

The methods presented in this solution rely heavily on the Windows registry. It may be useful to dig through the file associations in the registry (as discussed in the earlier sidebar) and see how Windows finds applications itself when you double-click on data files.

 If you're using Windows 98 or Windows Me, you'll need to take into consideration file and path names that include embedded spaces. Windows 2000, Windows XP, and later operating systems handle spaces in file names without any trouble. For earlier operating systems, make sure you surround file and path names that include spaces with quote marks (Chr$(34)) in order to ensure proper handling when you call the ShellExecute API function.

11.8   Check to See if an Application Is Already Running

Problem

You need to start up other Windows programs from within your Access application—for instance, to send data to Excel or to format a report in Word. If you just use the Shell command to start these programs, you may end up with multiple instances of the application. How can you tell if an application is already running before you attempt to start it?

Solution

There are a number of solutions to this problem, and none, unfortunately, are as easy as you might like. To ask Windows whether Excel is currently running and receive an answer, you must know the Windows class name for the main window of the application. This solution explains the format of the question and how to ask it. In addition, it demonstrates how to switch to a running application from your Access application.

If you have code that interacts with applications external to Access, it is often useful to be able to determine whether the application is running. The sample form, frmAppsRunning (Figure 11-10), asks Windows the question, "Is this app running?" for each of six predefined window classes, and you can add one more of your own. For each application that frmAppsRunning finds, it fills in the window handle (hWnd) column and the window caption column on the form. The AppActivate command in Access requires that you know the exact title of the window, so this form uses code from Chapter 4 (in basAccessCaption) to retrieve the caption for each running application. Finally, you can click on any of the enabled buttons in the right-hand column to switch to the running application.

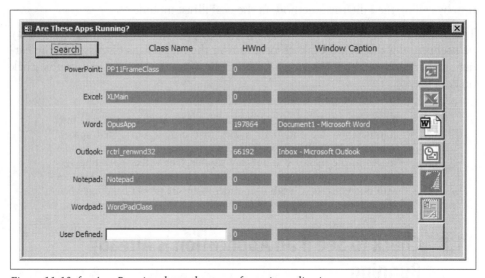

Figure 11-10. frmAppsRunning shows the state of certain applications

Try the sample form with Microsoft applications you have installed. Press F1 to bring up Help, and then switch back to Access and click on the Search button on the sample form. This will reinitiate the search for active applications, and it will find *WINHELP.EXE* running. Click on the question-mark icon to switch back to Win-Help.

Follow these steps to include this functionality in your own applications:

1. Import the modules listed in Table 11-9 from *11-08.MDB* into your application.

Table 11-9. Modules to import from 11-08.MDB

Module	Contains
basCaption	*acbGetAccessCaption, acbGetWindowCaption, acbSetAccessCaption*
basUsage	*acbIsAppLoaded*

2. To be able to ask Windows the question, "Is some application running?", you'll need to know the Windows class name for the main window of the application. Table 11-10 lists the names for several Windows applications.

Table 11-10. Windows application class names

Application	Class name
Access (all versions)	OMain
Excel (all versions)	XLMain
Explorer	ExploreWClass
Outlook (all versions)	rrctrl_renwnd32
Notepad	Notepad
PowerPoint 2003	PP11FrameClass
WordPad	WordPadClass
Microsoft Word (all versions)	OpusApp

3. The class names are somewhat arbitrary. Because they're assigned by the development staff, not by the marketing or documentation departments, class names often reflect the project's code name or the state of mind of the developer.

Finding Class Names

There are many ways to find the class names for applications' main windows. The simplest is to use the sample form for the Solution in Recipe 11.9, which displays a list of open windows and their class names. If you want to know the class name for a specific application, open it and run the sample form. The second column will list the class name for you.

---

4. To check whether a given application is currently running, use the acbIsAppLoaded function in basUsage. Pass a class name to this function as a parameter, and it returns the window handle of the application if it's running, or 0 if it's not. For example, this will return a nonzero value if Microsoft Word is currently running (note that the class names are not case-sensitive):

```
hWnd = acbIsAppRunning("opusapp")
```

5. Once you know the window handle for the application, you can use the AppActivate command in Access to make that application active. To do this, you'll need to know the exact window caption. To make that easier, you can call the acbGetWindowCaption function in basCaption before attempting to activate the application. For example, this code will switch to Excel, if it's running:

```
Dim hWnd as Integer

hWnd = acbIsAppLoaded("XLMain")
If hWnd <> 0 Then
   AppActivate acbGetWindowCaption(hWnd)
End If
```

6. If the application you want to activate isn't currently running (acbIsAppLoaded returned 0), use the *Shell* command to start it. In this case, you'll need to know the DOS executable filename for the given application (*EXCEL.EXE*, for example). The example form doesn't attempt to load the applications if they aren't already loaded, but your own application can load the program as needed.

Discussion

The acbIsAppLoaded function couldn't be simpler: It calls a single Windows API function. The entire routine looks like this:

```
Function acbIsAppLoaded (ByVal varClassName As Variant) As Long
    If IsNull(varClassName) Then
        acbIsAppLoaded = 0
    Else
        acbIsAppLoaded = acb_apiFindWindow(CStr(varClassName), 0&)
    End If
End Function
```

This routine allows you to pass in a class name. If the class name isn't null, the function calls the FindWindow API function (aliased as acb_apiFindWindow), which takes a class name and returns the window handle of the first instance of that class it finds. acbIsAppLoaded returns that handle to its caller.

This example uses the following code from basCaption to determine the caption of a window, given its window handle. Although this code isn't the focus of this section, you'll need to include it if you want to find a window's caption.

```
Declare Function acb_apiSetWindowText Lib "user32" _
 Alias "SetWindowTextA" (ByVal hwnd As Long, _
 ByVal lpString As String) As Long
Declare Function acb_apiGetWindowText _
 Lib "user32" Alias "GetWindowTextA" (ByVal hwnd As Long, _
 ByVal lpString As String, ByVal aint As Long) As Long

Public Function acbGetWindowCaption(ByVal hwnd As Long) As Variant

    ' Get any window's caption, given its hWnd.
```

```
    Dim strBuffer As String
    Dim intLen As Integer

    Const acbcMaxLen = 128

    If hwnd <> 0 Then
        strBuffer = Space(acbcMaxLen)
        intLen = acb_apiGetWindowText(hwnd, strBuffer, acbcMaxLen)
        acbGetWindowCaption = Left$(strBuffer, intLen)
    End If
End Function
```

Don't expect `acbIsAppLoaded` to distinguish between multiple copies of the same application. That is, if you have two copies of Notepad running, you can't count on `acbIsAppLoaded` to return the handle to a specific instance of Notepad: it will return the handle of the first instance it comes across. But that shouldn't bother you, as you're simply trying to find out if *any* copy of the application is currently running.

11.9   Retrieve a List of All Top-Level Windows

Problem

You know you can determine if specific applications are currently running (as shown in the Solution in Recipe 11.8), but now you'd like to obtain a list of all the running applications. That way, you could decide, as part of your application, what to present to your users. Is there a way to walk through all the open main windows and build up a list?

Solution

Windows includes API functions that allow you to walk down and around the tree of open windows, starting with the main desktop window. This solution provides a function that will do that for you, filling an array with information on each top-level window. You can then use that array to list applications, switch to them, or close them (see the Solution in Recipe 11.10 for information on closing other windows).

Load and run frmListWindows from *11-09.MDB*. This sample form fills a list box with all the top-level windows and provides a button that uses the VBA AppActivate command to display the selected window. In addition, the "Show visible windows only" checkbox allows you to add invisible windows to the list. Of course, attempting to use AppActivate to switch to an invisible window will fail. Figure 11-11 shows the sample form in action.

To include this functionality in your own applications, follow these steps:

1. Import the module basWindowList from *11-09.MDB*. This module includes the API declarations, constants, and wrapper functions that you'll need to list and select top-level windows.

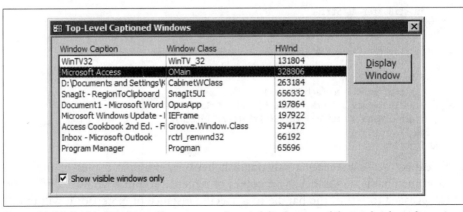

Figure 11-11. *frmListWindows allows you to select and display any of the top-level windows*

2. In your code, declare an array of type acb_tagWindowInfo to hold the list of open windows, like this:

```
Dim atypWindowList( ) As acb_tagWindowInfo
```

3. Call acbWindowList, passing the array to be filled in and a Boolean value indicating whether to show visible windows only. The function returns the number of windows it finds. After the function call, your array will have *intCount* rows, with each row containing information about a specific top-level window. For example, this call will fill the array with information about all the visible top-level windows:

```
intCount = acbWindowList(atypWindowList( ), True)
```

4. In your application, decide which (if any) window you'd like to display, perhaps by looping through all the elements of the array. Use the *AppActivate* command, along with the window name, to activate the selected window:

```
AppActivate atypWindowList(intI).strCaption
```

Discussion

This example uses several functions for navigating through the hierarchy of windows. Table 11-11 describes the functions.

Table 11-11. *Windows API navigation functions*

Function	Purpose
GetDesktopHWnd	Retrieve the window handle for the main desktop window. All applications are children of this window.
GetWindow	Find a window in a specified relation to a specified window. In this case, you'll be looking for the first child window of the desktop window.
GetWindowLong	Retrieve one of the 32-bit pieces of information stored with a window's structure in memory. You'll need to retrieve the style information (using the GWL_STYLE constant) so you can tell whether a window is visible.

Table 11-11. Windows API navigation functions (continued)

Function	Purpose
GetClassName	Retrieve the window class name for the specified window.

The acbWindowList function first retrieves a handle to the main desktop window, using GetDesktopHWnd. Once it knows that, it can find the handle for the desktop's first child window, using GetWindow. From then on, as long as the handle for the current window isn't 0, the code loops, filling in the array with information about the current window and then moving on to the next window with the *GetWindow* function. You'll note that the loop skips windows without captions (of which there are quite a few). Windows maintains a number of top-level hidden windows without captions for its own use. In addition, by specifying the *blnVisibleOnly* parameter for acbWindowList, you can include or exclude invisible windows. Windows sets up a number of invisible windows, and you probably won't want them to show up in your list. If you're interested, however, pass in False for this parameter to add all the hidden windows to your list. The code for the acbWindowList function is as follows:

```
Type acb_tagWindowInfo
    strCaption As String
    hWnd As Long
    strClass As String
End Type

Public Function acbWindowList(aWI( ) As acb_tagWindowInfo, _
    ByVal blnVisibleOnly As Boolean) As Integer

    ' Fill an array with a list of all the currently
    ' open top-level windows.

    Dim hWnd As Long
    Dim strCaption As String
    Dim intCount As Integer
    Dim lngStyle As Long

    ' Get the desktop window and, from there, the first
    ' top-level window.
    hWnd = acb_apiGetDesktopWindow( )
    hWnd = acb_apiGetWindow(hWnd, GW_CHILD)

    ' Loop through all the top-level windows.
    Do While hWnd <> 0
        strCaption = acbGetCaption(hWnd)
        If Len(strCaption) > 0 Then
            ' If you got a caption, add one element to the output
            ' array, and fill in the information (name and hWnd).
            lngStyle = acb_apiGetWindowLong(hWnd, GWL_STYLE)
            ' The Imp operator (Implies) returns True unless
            ' the first condition is True and the second is False,
            ' so this condition will be true unless you're
            ' showing visible only and the window is not visible.
```

```
            If blnVisibleOnly Imp (WS_VISIBLE And lngStyle) Then
                ReDim Preserve aWI(0 To intCount)
                aWI(intCount).strCaption = strCaption
                aWI(intCount).hWnd = hWnd
                aWI(intCount).strClass = CalcClassName(hWnd)
                intCount = intCount + 1
            End If
        End If
        ' Move to the next top-level window.
        hWnd = acb_apiGetWindow(hWnd, GW_HWNDNEXT)
    Loop

    ' Return the number of windows.
    acbWindowList = intCount
End Function
```

You may find it instructive to study the code in the sample form's module. It calls acbWindowList and then uses a list-filling callback function to fill the list box on the form with window captions, classes, and handles. This is a perfect example of when you'd use such a function: you need to fill a control with data from an array that can't be gathered until the application is running, and the array might be too large to fit within the character limit imposed when you call the control's AddItem method.

Some of the windows on the list exist at the time the form is filling its list, but are not available (the Access Immediate window, for example). You can attempt to switch to them, but the attempt will fail. The code attached to the checkmark button's Click event disregards errors, so it just keeps going if an error occurs when it tries to switch the active window. See the Solution in Recipe 11.10 for information on deleting windows in this list.

11.10 Close a Running Windows Application

Problem

As part of some of your large Access applications, you often allow users to start other Windows tools (Notepad, Calculator, Calendar, etc.); once those tools are open, your application doesn't touch them. Some users have complained about all the "junk" left over once your application closes. Is there some way you can close another window from your Access application? That way, on the way out you can close any tools your application has opened.

Solution

The Solution in Recipe 11.9 demonstrated the retrieval of a list of all the running Windows applications' captions, class names, and window handles. Once you know that information, it's easy to close an application: given a window handle, simply tell it to close. Using the Windows API PostMessage function, you can close any window at any time. Of course, some applications (those that support Automation; see

Chapter 12 for more information) allow themselves to be closed programmatically without using the Windows API. Other applications that don't support Automation will require either the API method described here, or SendKeys, which is unreliable at best.

Load and run frmListWindows from *11-10.MDB*. This form, shown in Figure 11-12, is similar to the sample form in the Solution in Recipe 11.9 with the addition of the Stop App button, which lets you close the selected window. Try a few; you can even close Access this way, if you want.

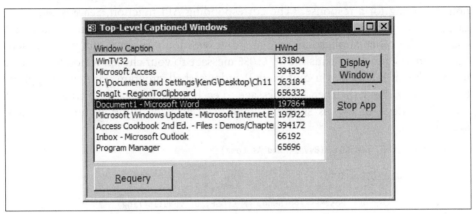

Figure 11-12. frmListWindows includes a Stop App button

 Some top-level windows shouldn't be closed—you should never include a form like this as part of an end-user application. On the other hand, given an array of window captions and handles, you could programmatically decide which window to close and close it yourself from within your application. This form is a demonstration of the power of the method, not a tool you'd actually use.

To use this functionality in your own applications, follow these steps:

1. Import the modules basWindowList (if you haven't already for the Solution in Recipe 11.9) and basCloseWindows.

2. Follow the steps listed in the Solution in Recipe 11.9 to create and fill in the array of top-level windows.

3. Decide which window you want to close. Windows sometimes appends document names to the application name (e.g., "Microsoft Word—11-10.DOC"), so check against just the first portion of the window name in your array. For example:

```
For intI = 0 To intCount - 1
    If Left$(atypWindowList(0).strCaption, 14) = "Microsoft Word" Then
        ' You found a match. Do something.
    End If
Next intI
```

4. When you've found the item you want to close, use the acbCloseWindow function, passing to it the handle of the window you care about:

```
If acbCloseWindow(atypWindowList(intI).hWnd) = 0 Then
    ' If you got 0 back, it got the message!
End If
```

Discussion

The acbCloseWindow function calls the PostMessage API function. By posting a message to a particular window, you are telling it to do something, but you don't bother waiting for a response. (The corresponding API function, SendMessage, *does* cause you to wait for a response. You can use SendMessage if you want to stop and wait for the other application to close, but we don't recommend it.) The acbCloseWindow function sends the WM_CLOSE message to your chosen window, telling it to shut down. It's as if you quit your Windows shell program with some applications running. Your shell sends a message to each main application window to shut down because Windows is shutting down. The acbCloseWindow function, then, looks like this:

```
Function acbCloseWindow (ByVal hWnd As Long)

    Const WM_CLOSE = &H10

    acbCloseWindow = PostMessage(hWnd, WM_CLOSE, 0, vbNullString)
End Function
```

The purpose of this wrapper function that calls PostMessage is to prevent you from having to remember how to post a message to a window. It's a lot simpler to call acbCloseWindow than to call PostMessage directly.

Sending a WM_CLOSE message to a window doesn't necessarily close it. If that application has an unsaved document, it will pop up its own dialog asking what you want to do with that unsaved document. In the sample form, if this happens, the list box won't be updated correctly. Once you return from your duties with the foreign application, press the Requery button on the form to force it to search again for all open applications.

11.11 Set File Date and Time Stamps

Problem

Access makes it easy to retrieve the modification date and time for files on disk, using the FileDateTime function. In one application, though, you need to be able to reset the last-modification date of files manually; the Access FileCopy function doesn't reset file date and time stamps, and you'd like copied files to have the current time. Is there a Windows API call that allows you to set file date and time stamps?

Solution

Windows provides the GetFileTime and SetFileTime API functions. Both work with three different date/time values: date of creation, date of last access, and date of last write. You want to preserve the date of creation and update the dates of last access and update. The code shown in this example will allow you to do this.

The sample form, frmTimeStamp, allows you to select a filename. The function then displays the date and time of last modification for the file, as shown in Figure 11-13. In addition, you can set a new file date, time, or both (the function retains whichever setting you don't change, if you just change one).

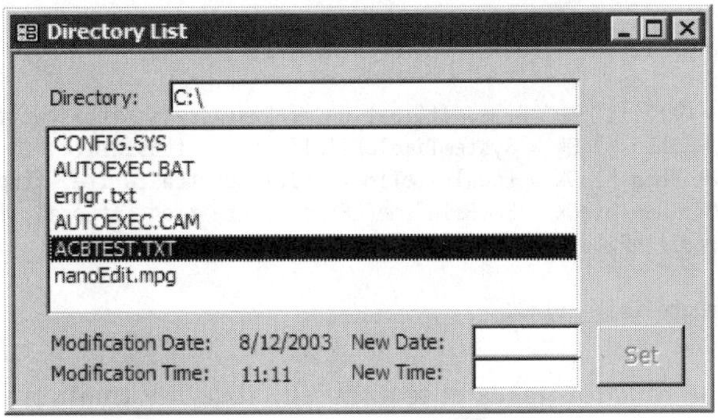

Figure 11-13. frmTimeStamp shows a selected file's modification date and time

To set file date and time information in your own applications, follow these steps:

1. Import the module basTimeStamp from *11-11.MDB*. This module includes the type definitions and Windows API declarations you'll need, as well as a VBA function to convert dates and times as retrieved from the API call into date/time values that Access can understand. If you want to use this sample form in your own applications, you'll also need to import basFillList, which includes functions to retrieve the list of files.

2. To set the modification-date information for a specific file, call the acbSetFileDateTime function, passing it a filename and a date/time value as parameters. For example, the following code will change the last-modification time and date for *C:\AUTOEXEC.BAT* to the current date and time:

```
blnOK = acbSetFileDateTime("C:\AUTOEXEC.BAT", Now)
```

Discussion

The *acbSetFileDateTime* function consists of three basic steps. Its source code is:

```
Public Function acbSetFileDateTime( _
 strFileName As String, varDate As Date) As Boolean
   Dim hFile As Long
```

```
    Dim of As OFSTRUCT
    Dim st As SYSTEMTIME
    Dim ftCreation As FILETIME
    Dim ftLastAccess As FILETIME
    Dim ftLastWrite As FILETIME
    Dim ftLocal As FILETIME
    Dim blnOK As Boolean

    st.wYear = Year(varDate)
    st.wMonth = Month(varDate)
    st.wDay = Day(varDate)
    st.wHour = Hour(varDate)
    st.wMinute = Minute(varDate)
    st.wSecond = Second(varDate)

    hFile = OpenFile(strFileName, of, OF_READWRITE)
    If hFile > 0 Then
        blnOK = GetFileTime(hFile, ftCreation, ftLastAccess, ftLastWrite)
        If blnOK Then blnOK = SystemTimeToFileTime(st, ftLastWrite)
        If blnOK Then blnOK = LocalFileTimeToFileTime(ftLastWrite, ftLocal)
        If blnOK Then blnOK = SetFileTime(hFile, ftCreation, ftLocal, ftLocal)
        CloseHandle hFile
    End If
    acbSetFileDateTime = blnOK
End Function
```

The first step the function takes is to copy the date information from the Access Date-type variable into a structure that the API can use:

```
' In the declarations section:
Private Type SYSTEMTIME
    wYear As Integer
    wMonth As Integer
    wDayOfWeek As Integer
    wDay As Integer
    wHour As Integer
    wMinute As Integer
    wSecond As Integer
    wMilliseconds As Integer
End Type

' In the function:
Dim st As SYSTEMTIME

st.wYear = Year(varDate)
st.wMonth = Month(varDate)
st.wDay = Day(varDate)
st.wHour = Hour(varDate)
st.wMinute = Minute(varDate)
st.wSecond = Second(varDate)
```

Next, the function must open the requested file with read/write access so that it can write to the file's time stamp:

```
hFile = OpenFile(strFileName, of, OF_READWRITE)
```

If this succeeds, the function then retrieves the current time stamps, converts the system time structure to a file time structure, converts that time from local time to the internal generalized time that Windows uses, and finally sets the file time:

```
blnOK = GetFileTime(hFile, ftCreation, ftLastAccess, ftLastWrite)
If blnOK Then blnOK = SystemTimeToFileTime(st, ftLastWrite)
If blnOK Then blnOK = LocalFileTimeToFileTime(ftLastWrite, ftLocal)
If blnOK Then blnOK = SetFileTime(hFile, ftCreation, ftLocal, ftLocal)
CloseFileHandle hFile
```

The function sets both the time of last access and the time of last write to be the date and time you've specified.

When you select the Set button on the sample form, Access executes the following procedure:

```
Private Sub cmdSetTime_Click( )
    Dim varDate As Date
    Dim strDate As String
    Dim strTime As String

    strDate = IIf(IsNull(Me.txtNewDate), Me.txtDate, Me.txtNewDate)
    strTime = IIf(IsNull(Me.txtNewTime), Me.txtTime, Me.txtNewTime)
    varDate = CVDate(strDate & " " & strTime)
    If Not acbSetFileDateTime(GetPath( ), varDate) Then
        MsgBox "Unable to set the file date!"
    Else
        Me.txtDate = Format(varDate, "Short Date")
        Me.txtTime = Format(varDate, "Short Time")
    End If
End Sub
```

This procedure retrieves the dates you've typed on the form, converts them to an Access date/time value, and then sets the date for the file you've selected. Note that the example uses the existing date or time for any value you didn't enter. Because the Set button isn't enabled unless you enter at least the date or the time, there's no need to worry about when they're both null.

Unless you take the extra step of converting the passed-in date/time value from local time to the internal time Windows uses (Greenwich Mean Time), the time you set will be off by the difference in time zones between your time and the standardized time. The call to LocalTimeToFileTime takes care of this for you. Of course, this counts on the local time having been set correctly on the local system.

11.12 Retrieve Information About Available Drives

Problem

You'd like to be able to gather specific information about the disk drives in your computer: for example, how large they are, how much space is free, whether they're local or remote, and whether they're removable or not. Access does not provide this information. Is it available using a Windows API function?

Solution

The Windows API provides three functions that you can use to extract information about the drives in your computer: `GetLogicalDriveStrings`, which returns a string containing a list of all the logical drives; `GetDriveType`, which returns information about the specified drive; and `GetDiskFreeSpace`, which returns information about the total and free disk space for a specified drive.

Load and run `frmDiskSpace` from *11-12.MDB*. This form, shown in Figure 11-14, contains a list box with information about all the logical drives in your system. To fill the list box, the example code walks through all the drives returned from a call to `GetLogicalDriveStrings`, calling the other two functions for each drive.

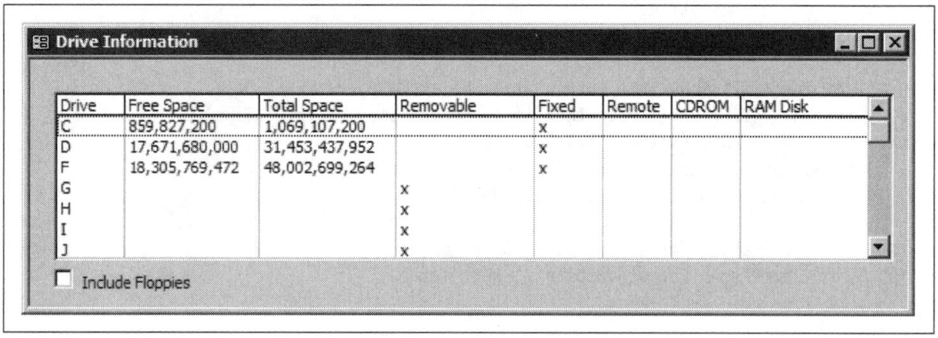

Figure 11-14. frmDiskSpace shows information about all the installed drives

To use these functions in your own applications, follow these steps:

1. Import the modules `basDiskInfo` and `basToken` from *11-12.MDB*.

2. To call the functions, use the information in Table 11-12. Each function takes only a single parameter, the drive to be interrogated.

Table 11-12. The functions in basDiskInfo

Function	Purpose	Return value	Example
acbGetFreeSpace	Retrieve the amount of free space on the specified drive.	Variant (the amount of free disk space, in bytes), or Null if the function failed	lngFree = acbGet-FreeSpace("C")
acbGetTotalSpace	Retrieve the total amount of space on the specified drive.	Variant (the amount of total disk space, in bytes), or Null if the function failed	lngTotal = acbGetTotal-Space("C")
acbIsDriveCDROM	Verify that a drive is a CD-ROM.	True if CD-ROM, False otherwise	fCD = acbIsDriv-eCDROM("D")

Table 11-12. The functions in basDiskInfo (continued)

Function	Purpose	Return value	Example
acbIsDriveFixed	Verify that a drive is a hard disk.	True if a hard disk, False otherwise	fFixed = acbIsDrive-Fixed("C")
acbIsDriveLocal	Verify that the specified drive is local.	True if local, False if remote	fLocal = acbIsDriveLo-cal("C")
acbIsDriveRAMDisk	Verify that a drive is a RAM disk.	True if RAM disk, False otherwise	fRAM = acbIsDriveRAM-Disk("F")
acbIsDriveRemote	Verify that the specified drive is a network drive.	True if remote, False if local	fNetwork = acbIsDriveR-emote("E")
acbIsDriveRemovable	Verify that the specified drive is for removable media.	True if removable, False otherwise	fRemovable = acbIsDriveR-emovable("A")

Discussion

The sample form doesn't actually use any of the acbIs functions listed in Table 11-12; these functions are supplied only for your own applications. Instead, it calls the acbGetDrives function in basDiskInfo, which fills an array of acb_tagDriveInfo structures directly with information about each of the installed drives, physical or logical.

The structure looks like this:

```
Type acb_tagDriveInfo
    strDrive As String
    varFreeSpace As Variant
    varTotalSpace As Variant
    fRemovable As Boolean
    fFixed As Boolean
    fRemote As Boolean
    fCDROM As Boolean
    fRamDisk As Boolean
End Type
```

It stores all the information that the sample form displays. The sample form then uses a list-filling callback function to display the information in a list box. (For more information on list-filling callback functions, see Chapter 7.)

The acbGetDrives function starts out by calling the Windows API function GetLogicalDriveStrings. This function returns a string containing all the logical drives on your machine, in this format:

```
C:0D:0G:0H:0
```

where the 0s indicate null characters, Chr$(0). (VBA provides the vbNullChar constant that's equivalent to Chr$(0).) The acbGetDrives function loops through this string, using the acbGetToken function in basTokens to pull out the drive names, one at a time, and then gathering information about each. The source code for acbGetDrives is:

```
Public Function acbGetDrives(astrDrives( ) As acb_tagDriveInfo, _
    fIncludeFloppies As Boolean)
    ' Fill astrDrives( ) with all the available logical drive letters.

    Dim strBuffer As String
    Dim intCount As Integer
    Dim intI As Integer
    Dim varTemp As Variant
    Dim lngType As Long

    Const conMaxSpace = 1024

    strBuffer = Space(conMaxSpace)

    intCount = GetLogicalDriveStrings(conMaxSpace - 1, strBuffer)
    strBuffer = Left(strBuffer, intCount)
    intI = 1
    intCount = 0
    Do
        varTemp = acbGetToken(strBuffer, vbNullChar, intI)
        If Len(varTemp & "") > 0 Then
            ' The next statement will be true except in the
            ' case where the drive < C and you DON'T want
            ' to include floppies. Then it'll skip the drive.
            If (UCase(Left(varTemp, 1) < "C")) Imp fIncludeFloppies Then
                intCount = intCount + 1
                ' Get the drive name.
                astrDrives(intCount).strDrive = varTemp

                ' Get the drive type, and set the flags accordingly.
                lngType = GetDriveType(varTemp)
                Select Case lngType
                    Case DRIVE_REMOVABLE
                        astrDrives(intCount).fRemovable = True
                    Case DRIVE_FIXED
                        astrDrives(intCount).fFixed = True
                    Case DRIVE_REMOTE
                        astrDrives(intCount).fRemote = True
                    Case DRIVE_CDROM
                        astrDrives(intCount).fCDROM = True
                    Case DRIVE_RAMDISK
                        astrDrives(intCount).fRamDisk = True
                End Select

                ' Get the drive space information.
                astrDrives(intCount).varTotalSpace = acbGetTotalSpace(varTemp)
                astrDrives(intCount).varFreeSpace = acbGetFreeSpace(varTemp)
            End If
            intI = intI + 1
        End If
```

```
      Loop Until Len(varTemp & "") = 0
      acbGetDrives = intCount
   End Function
```

The acbGetTotalSpace and acbGetFreeSpace functions both call the private Get-DiskSpace function, which in turn calls the GetDiskFreeSpace API function. GetDiskSpace takes the four pieces of information returned from GetDiskFreeSpace—sectors per cluster, bytes per sector, free clusters, and total clusters—and returns the calculated value that you've requested:

```
Private Function GetDiskSpace(ByVal strDrive As String, _
 fTotal As Boolean) As Variant

   ' Input:
   '     strDrive: String representing drive letter
   '     fTotal: True for total space on drive, False for free space on drive
   ' Output:
   '     Free or Total space, if no error. Null, otherwise.

   Dim lngSectorsPerCluster As Long
   Dim lngBytesPerSector As Long
   Dim lngFreeClusters As Long
   Dim lngTotalClusters As Long

   ' Force the string into the correct format.
   strDrive = Left(strDrive, 1) & ":\"
   If GetDiskFreeSpace(strDrive, lngSectorsPerCluster, lngBytesPerSector, _
    lngFreeClusters, lngTotalClusters) Then
      GetDiskSpace = lngSectorsPerCluster * lngBytesPerSector * IIf(fTotal, _
       lngTotalClusters, lngFreeClusters)
   Else
      GetDiskSpace = Null
   End If
End Function
```

If you want to dig a bit further, investigate the GetVolumeInformation API function. This function retrieves even more information about the specified drive, including its volume name, serial number, whether or not compression is enabled, the filesystem type (FAT, HPFS, NTFS), and other information about how data is stored on that drive. This information is of less importance to Access developers than to system application developers, so we don't discuss it here.

11.13 Collect and Display Information on the System and the Access Installation

Problem

Your application really needs to know some information about the computer on which it's running. In addition, you'd like to add some professional polish and an

---

About… box that shows information about the computer, the resources, and the user. Access doesn't provide any way to find this information. How can you gather it?

Solution

You can use the Windows API to retrieve information about the system on which your program is running. By using these various functions as the control sources for unbound controls, you can present a selection of system information to your user.

Load *11-13.MDB* and open frmSystemInfo in regular form view (see Figure 11-15). This form includes five "pages" of information about the current computer and its resources. If you like the look of this form, use it as-is in your own applications. (You'll need to import the form, frmSystemInfo, its subform, fsubInfo, and the module, basSystemInfo, into your application, as directed in Step 1.)

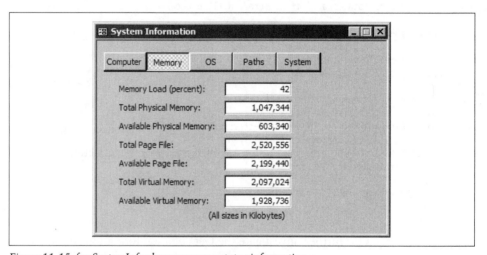

Figure 11-15. frmSystemInfo shows memory status information

To create a similar form in your own application, follow these steps:

1. Import the module basSystemInfo from *11-13.MDB* into your own application. This module contains all the constants, API declarations, and wrapper functions that you'll need.

2. Create a new form. Place an unbound text box (or checkbox, or option group; see fsubInfo for hints) on the form for each piece of information you wish to display. Set the control sources as shown in Table 11-13. The sample form, frmSystemInfo, uses an option group that lets you choose which page of the subform, fsubInfo, you'd like to see. This has nothing to do with the functionality of the sample beyond cosmetics; it just makes it easier to group the information.

Table 11-13. Control sources for text boxes on frmSystemInfo

Item	Control source
Screen resolution	=acbGetScreenX( ) & " x " & acbGetScreenY( )
Mouse installed	=acbMouseInstalled( )
Keyboard type	=acbKeyboardType( )
Memory load	=acbGetMemoryStatus(0)
Total physical memory	=acbGetMemoryStatus(1)
Available physical memory	=acbGetMemoryStatus(2)
Total page file	=acbGetMemoryStatus(3)
Available page file	=acbGetMemoryStatus(4)
Total virtual memory	=acbGetMemoryStatus(5)
Available virtual memory	=acbGetMemoryStatus(6)
Operating system version	=acbGetOSInfo(0) & "." & acbGetOSInfo(1)
Build number	=acbGetOSInfo(2)
Platform	=acbGetOSInfo(3)
Windows directory	=acbWindowsDirectory( )
System directory	=acbSystemDirectory( )
Temp path	=acbTempPath( )
Access directory	=acbAccessDirectory( )
OEM ID	=acbGetSystemStatus(0)
Page size	=acbGetSystemStatus(1)
Lowest memory address	=acbGetSystemStatus(2)
Highest memory address	=acbGetSystemStatus(3)
Active processor mask	=acbGetSystemStatus(4)
Number of processors	=acbGetSystemStatus(5)
Processor type	=acbGetSystemStatus(6)

Discussion

The functions used here employ a variety of techniques to return the requested information. In general, they query the low-level Windows API to retrieve hardware and Windows environment information. We've wrapped each low-level function in an Access function to handle data type conversions from the dynamic link libraries (DLLs) used by Windows into the format that Access can understand.

frmSystemInfo uses several functions to return information about the current computer:

Screen resolution

The acbGetScreenX and acbGetScreenY functions use the GetSystemMetrics API function to return the size of the screen in pixels. This API function can return many other details about your system, including the width of the window borders, the size of the icons, and whether a mouse is installed. To call it, just pass it one of the constants shown later, in Table 11-14; it will return the requested value to you. For example:

```
Public Function acbGetScreenX( )
    ' Retrieve the screen width in pixels.
    acbGetScreenX = GetSystemMetrics(SM_CXSCREEN)
End Function
```

Mouse installed

Again, the *GetSystemMetrics* function does the work:

```
Public Function acbMouseInstalled( ) As Boolean
    ' Is a mouse installed?
    acbMouseInstalled = CBool(GetSystemMetrics(SM_MOUSEPRESENT))
End Function
```

Keyboard type

The *GetKeyboardType* function provides the answers:

```
Public Function acbKeyboardType( )
    ' Retrieve information about the keyboard.
    ' Call GetKeyboardType with
    '    0   Keyboard Type
    '    1   Keyboard SubType (depends on the manufacturer)
    '    2   Number of function keys
    acbKeyboardType = GetKeyboardType(0)
End Function
```

Memory information

The GlobalMemoryStatusEx function fills in a user-defined data structure with information about the current memory load, available and total real and virtual memory, and paging space. We've wrapped all this information up in the acbGetMemoryStatus function:

```
Public Function acbGetMemoryStatus(intItem As Integer) As Variant

    ' Retrieve system memory information
    ' In:
    '    intItem: Which piece of information to retrieve
    '        0: Memory load (0 to 100)
    '        1: Total physical memory in bytes
    '        2: Available physical memory in bytes
    '        3: Total size in page file in bytes
    '        4: Available page file in bytes
    '        5: Total virtual memory in bytes
    '        6: Available virtual memory in bytes
    ' Out:
    '    Return Value: The requested information

    Dim MS As MEMORYSTATUSEX

    ' Set the length member before you call GlobalMemoryStatus.
    MS.dwLength = Len(MS)
```

```
    GlobalMemoryStatusEx MS
    Select Case intItem
        Case 0
            acbGetMemoryStatus = MS.dwMemoryLoad * 10000 / 1024
        Case 1
            acbGetMemoryStatus = MS.dwTotalPhys * 10000 / 1024
        Case 2
            acbGetMemoryStatus = MS.dwAvailPhys * 10000 / 1024
        Case 3
            acbGetMemoryStatus = MS.dwTotalPageFile * 10000 / 1024
        Case 4
            acbGetMemoryStatus = MS.dwAvailPageFile * 10000 / 1024
        Case 5
            acbGetMemoryStatus = MS.dwTotalVirtual * 10000 / 1024
        Case 6
            acbGetMemoryStatus = MS.dwAvailVirtual * 10000 / 1024
        Case Else
            acbGetMemoryStatus = 0
    End Select
End Function
```

Although it seems odd, the code in acbGetMemoryStatus is performing an important conversion. Because the values filled in by the GlobalMemoryStatusEx method are so large, you must use Currency values to contain the results. In order to store large values, VBA scales the contents of Currency variables by a factor of 10,000. Therefore, when you want to use the values here, you must multiply them by 10,000. In addition, to convert from bytes to KB, the code divides the totals by the number of bytes in a kilobyte, 1024.

Operating system information

The GetVersionEx API function does the work here. To simplify its use, we've provided the acbGetOSInfo function, as follows. Note that the Platform ID value simply indicates whether you're running a Windows 95-based operating system (such as Windows 98 or Windows ME) or a Windows NT-based operating system, such as Windows 2000, Windows XP, or Windows Server 2003. You can definitely retrieve more detailed results than this—see the documentation at *http://msdn.microsoft.com* for more information.

```
Public Function acbGetOSInfo(intItem As Integer) As Variant

    ' Retrieve operating system information
    ' In:
    '     intItem: Which piece of information to retrieve
    '         0: Major Version
    '         1: Minor version
    '         2: Build Number
    '         3: Platform ID
    '             0 = Win32s (not going to happen!)
    '             1 = Win95
    '             2 = WinNT
```

```
' Out:
'     Return Value: The requested information

Dim OSInfo As OSVERSIONINFO

' Set the length member before you call GetVersionEx.
OSInfo.dwOSVersionInfoSize = Len(OSInfo)
If GetVersionEx(OSInfo) Then
    Select Case intItem
        Case 0
            acbGetOSInfo = OSInfo.dwMajorVersion
        Case 1
            acbGetOSInfo = OSInfo.dwMinorVersion
        Case 2
            ' Get just the low word of the result.
            acbGetOSInfo = OSInfo.dwBuildNumber And &HFFFF&
        Case 3
            acbGetOSInfo = OSInfo.dwPlatformId
    End Select
Else
    acbGetOSInfo = 0
End If
End Function
```

Directories

To retrieve the Windows directory, call `acbWindowsDirectory`, shown in the following code. For the Windows System directory, call `acbSystemDirectory`; for the temporary storage path, call `acbTempPath`; and to find out which directory Access is running from, call `acbAccessDirectory`. (Note that `acbAccessDirectory` doesn't actually use the Windows API to find the location of Access; the SysCmd function in Access makes that information available.)

```
Public Function acbWindowsDirectory( )
    ' Retrieve the Windows directory.
    Dim strBuffer As String
    Dim intCount As Integer

    strBuffer = Space(MAX_PATH)
    intCount = GetWindowsDirectory(strBuffer, MAX_PATH)
    acbWindowsDirectory = CleanPath(Left(strBuffer, intCount))
End Function
```

System information

The GetSystemInfo API function provides all the information. To make this easier for you, we've provided the acbGetSystemStatus function, shown in the following code. Call this function with a number representing the piece of information you want.

```
Public Function acbGetSystemStatus(intItem As Integer) As Variant

    ' Retrieve system status information
    ' In:
    '     intItem: Which piece of information to retrieve
    '         0: Computer identifier, specific to OEM
```

```
'          1: Returns page size and specifies the granularity of page
'             protection and commitment
'          2: Lowest memory address accessible to applications and
'             dynamic link libraries (DLLs)
'          3: Highest memory address accessible to applications and DLLs
'          4: Mask representing the set of processors configured into
'             the system
'             Bit 0 is processor 0; bit 31 is processor 31
'          5: Returns the number of processors in the system
'          6: Type of the current processors in the system
'          7: Allocation granularity in which memory will be allocated
'             on (usually 64K)
' Out:
'    Return Value: The requested information

Dim SI As SYSTEM_INFO

GetSystemInfo SI
Select Case intItem
   Case 0
      acbGetSystemStatus = SI.dwOemID
   Case 1
      acbGetSystemStatus = SI.dwPageSize
   Case 2
      acbGetSystemStatus = SI.lpMinimumApplicationAddress
   Case 3
      acbGetSystemStatus = SI.lpMaximumApplicationAddress
   Case 4
      acbGetSystemStatus = SI.dwActiveProcessorMask
   Case 5
      acbGetSystemStatus = SI.dwNumberOrfProcessors
   Case 6
      acbGetSystemStatus = SI.dwProcessorType
   Case 7
      acbGetSystemStatus = SI.dwAllocationGranularity
   Case Else
      acbGetSystemStatus = 0
   End Select
End Function
```

Table 11-14. Subset of the options for GetSystemMetrics

Constant name	Value	Meaning
SM_CXSCREEN	0	Width of screen.
SM_CYSCREEN	1	Height of screen.
SM_CXVSCROLL	2	Width of arrow bitmap on a vertical scrollbar.
SM_CYHSCROLL	3	Height of arrow bitmap on a horizontal scrollbar.
SM_CYCAPTION	4	Height of window title. This is the title height plus the height of the window frame that cannot be sized (SM_CYBORDER).
SM_CXBORDER	5	Width of window border.
SM_CYBORDER	6	Height of window border or dimensions of a single border, in pixels.

Table 11-14. Subset of the options for GetSystemMetrics (continued)

Constant name	Value	Meaning
SM_CXFIXEDFRAME	7	Width of frame when window has the WS_DLGFRAME style.
SM_CYFIXEDFRAME	8	Height of frame when window has the WS_DLGFRAME style.
SM_CYVTHUMB	9	Height of scroll box on vertical scrollbar.
SM_CXHTHUMB	10	Width of scroll box (thumb) on horizontal scrollbar.
SM_CXICON	11	Width of icon.
SM_CYICON	12	Height of icon.
SM_CXCURSOR	13	Width of cursor.
SM_CYCURSOR	14	Height of cursor.
SM_CYMENU	15	Height of single-line menu bar.
SM_CXFULLSCREEN	16	Width of window client area for a full-screen window.
SM_CYFULLSCREEN	17	Height of window client area for a full-screen window (equivalent to the height of the screen minus the height of the window title).
SM_CYKANJIWINDOW	18	Height of Kanji window.
SM_MOUSEPRESENT	19	Nonzero if the mouse hardware is installed.
SM_CYVSCROLL	20	Height of arrow bitmap on a vertical scrollbar.
SM_CXHSCROLL	21	Width of arrow bitmap on a horizontal scrollbar.
SM_DEBUG	22	Nonzero if the Windows version is a debugging version.
SM_SWAPBUTTON	23	Nonzero if the left and right mouse buttons are swapped.
SM_CXMIN	28	Minimum width of window.
SM_CYMIN	29	Minimum height of window.
SM_CXSIZE	30	Width of bitmaps contained in the titlebar.
SM_CYSIZE	31	Height of bitmaps contained in the titlebar.
SM_CXFRAME	32	Width of window frame for a window that can be resized. (Obsolete; use SM_CXFIXEDFRAME instead.)
SM_CYFRAME	33	See SM_CXFRAME (height, instead). (Obsolete; use SM_CYFIXEDFRAME instead.)
SM_CXMINTRACK	34	Minimum tracking width of window.
SM_CYMINTRACK	35	Minimum tracking height of window.
SM_CXDOUBLECLK	36	Width of the rectangle around the location of the first click in a double-click sequence. The second click must occur within this rectangle for the system to consider the two clicks a double-click.
SM_CYDOUBLECLK	37	See SM_CXDOUBLECLK (height, instead).
SM_CXICONSPACING	38	Width of rectangles the system uses to position tiled icons.
SM_CYICONSPACING	39	Height of rectangles the system uses to position tiled icons.
SM_MENUDROPALIGNMENT	40	Alignment of pop-up menus. If this value is zero, the left side of a pop-up menu is aligned with the left side of the corresponding menu-bar item. If this value is nonzero, the left side of a pop-up menu is aligned with the right side of the corresponding menu-bar item.
SM_PENWINDOWS	41	Handle of the Pen Windows DLL if Pen Windows is installed.

Table 11-14. Subset of the options for GetSystemMetrics (continued)

Constant name	Value	Meaning
SM_DBCSENABLED	42	Nonzero if current version of Windows uses double-byte characters; zero otherwise.
SM_CMOUSEBUTTONS	43	Number of buttons on the mouse, or zero if no mouse is present.
SM_SECURE	44	Nonzero if security is present; zero otherwise.
SM_CXMINSPACING	47	With SM_CYMINSPACING, dimensions of a grid cell for minimized windows, in pixels. Each minimized window fits into a rectangle this size when arranged. These values are always greater than or equal to SM_CXMINIMIZED and SM_CYMINIMIZED.
SM_CYMINSPACING	48	See SM_CXMINSPACING.
SM_CXSMICON	49	With SM_CYSMICON, recommended dimensions of a small icon, in pixels. Small icons typically appear in window captions and in small icon view.
SM_CYSMICON	50	See SM_CXSMICON.
SM_CXSMSIZE	52	With SM_CYSMSIZE, dimensions of small caption buttons, in pixels.
SM_CYSMSIZE	53	See SM_CXSMSIZE.
SM_CXMENUSIZE	54	Width of menu bar buttons (such as multiple document (MDI) child Close), in pixels.
SM_CYMENUSIZE	55	Height of menu bar buttons (such as multiple document (MDI) child Close), in pixels.
SM_ARRANGE	56	Flags specifying how the system arranges minimized windows.
SM_CXMINIMIZED	57	Width of a normal minimized window, in pixels.
SM_CYMINIMIZED	58	Height of a normal minimized window, in pixels.
SM_CXMAXTRACK	59	Default maximum width of a window that has a caption and sizing borders. The user cannot drag the window frame to a size larger than these dimensions.
SM_CYMAXTRACK	60	See SM_CXMAXTRACK (height, instead).
SM_CXMAXIMIZED	61	Default width of a maximized top-level window, in pixels.
SM_CYMAXIMIZED	62	Default height of a maximized top-level window, in pixels.
SM_NETWORK	63	The least significant bit is set if a network is present; otherwise, it is cleared. The other bits are reserved for future use.
SM_CLEANBOOT	67	Value that specifies how the system was started: 0 (Normal boot), 1 (Fail-safe boot), 2 (Fail-safe with network boot). Fail-safe boot (also called SafeBoot) bypasses the user's startup files.
SM_SHOWSOUNDS	70	Nonzero if the user requires an application to present information visually in situations where it would otherwise present the information only in audible form; zero otherwise.
SM_CXMENUCHECK	71	Width of the default menu checkmark bitmap, in pixels.
SM_CYMENUCHECK	72	Height of the default menu checkmark bitmap, in pixels.
SM_SLOWMACHINE	73	Nonzero if the computer has a low-end (slow) processor, zero otherwise.
SM_CMETRICS	75	Number of system metrics and flags.

Some of the flags supported by GetSystemMetrics behave differently under different operating systems. Make sure you check the documentation (online at *http://msdn. microsoft.com*) for operating-system dependencies. You'll also find other options that you can add to this form; we didn't include every available option here.

In addition to the functions listed here, you may find the SystemParametersInfo API function useful. It allows you to set and retrieve many system parameters, but calling it is a bit more difficult than calling GetSystemMetrics. If you have access to a Windows API reference, you may want to dig into this useful function.

11.14 Create and Cancel Network Connections Programmatically

Problem

You'd like to be able to connect to remote network devices from within your own Access applications. You know that you could do this manually, using Explorer or File Manager, but there must be some internal API for controlling these connections. Is there some way you can manage connections from within Access?

Solution

Windows provides a rich interface to its networking subsystem through its API. Many of the function calls are difficult, if not impossible, to call from VBA because of the language's lack of pointer variable types. Some important calls, however, are quite simple to use, as you'll see in this solution. The example form will demonstrate connecting to and disconnecting from remote devices (printers and drives) using common dialogs or using code with no user interface.

Load and run frmNetworkSample from *11-14.MDB*. Figure 11-16 shows the form in use on a small Windows 2000 network. This sample form, demonstrating all the capabilities covered in this solution, does the following:

- Retrieves the current username and computer name.
- Walks through all 26 possible drive letters and displays any drive mappings connected to those drives.
- Allows you to delete any of the displayed drive connections.
- Provides a method for adding new connections, where you supply the four necessary parameters.
- Uses the common dialogs for adding and canceling drive and printer connections.

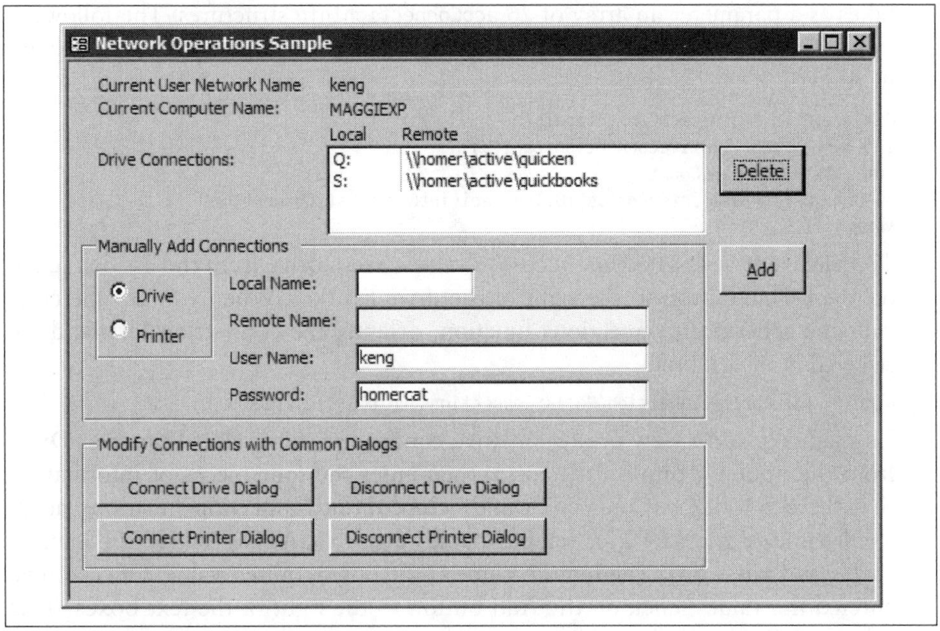

Figure 11-16. frmNetworkSample allows you to add and cancel connections manually or by using the common dialogs

Though you would never use this exact form in an application, it allows you to experiment with all the functionality covered in this solution. To use these API calls in your own applications, follow these steps:

1. Import the module basNetwork from *11-14.MDB*. This module contains all the API function declarations, wrapper functions, data type declarations, and error constants you'll need.

2. The sample form, frmNetworkSample, displays the current username. To retrieve this information in your own code, call the acbGetUser function from basNetwork. Its return value is the name of the currently logged-in user. For example:

   ```
   Debug.Print acbGetUser( )
   ```

3. The sample form also displays the current computer name. To retrieve this information yourself, call the acbGetComputerName function from basNetwork. Its return value is the name of the current computer. For example:

   ```
   Debug.Print acbGetComputerName( )
   ```

4. The list box on the form displays all the current connections. You can choose one and delete it (see Step 5). To retrieve a list of all 26 possible drives and their connections in your own application, call acbListConnections, a function that

takes as a parameter an array of 26 acbConnectionInfo structures. The following example fills the list with drive information, then prints it out to the Immediate window:

```
Dim aci(0 To 25) As acbConnectionInfo
intCount = acbListDriveConnections(aci( ))
For intI = 0 To intCount
    Debug.Print aci(intCount).strDrive, aci(intCount).strConnection
Next intI
```

5. To delete a drive connection once you've selected a drive from the list box, click on the Delete button to the right of the drive list box. When you do, the code calls the acbCancelConnections function, deleting the connection for the drive selected in the list box:

```
blnOK = (acbCancelConnection(Me.lstConnections.Column(0), True) = 0)
```

6. To manually add a new printer or drive connection, first select Printer or Drive from the option group on the form, then enter the four pieces of information that the acbAddDriveConnection and acbAddPrintConnection functions need: local name (e.g., "LPT1:"), remote name (e.g., "\\GATEWAY\HPLJ4"), username, and password. The remote name is the only required value. Once you've entered the values, click on the Add button to the right of the text boxes. This calls the following code:

```
If Me.grpDeviceType = 1 Then
    ' The '& ""' below converts from null values to strings.
    '
    ' Drive
    blnOK = (acbAddDriveConnection(Me.txtLocalName & "", _
        Me.txtRemoteName & "", Me.txtUserName & "", Me.txtPassword & "") = 0)
    Else
    ' Printer
    blnOK = (acbAddPrinterConnection(Me.txtLocalName & "", _
        Me.txtRemoteName & "", Me.txtUserName & "", Me.txtPassword & "") = 0)
    End If
End If
```

7. To use the common dialogs for adding or canceling connections, click on any of the four buttons at the bottom of the form. Each calls a single line of Windows API code that pops up the appropriate dialog. The next section describes these function calls in detail.

Discussion

The following sections describe all you need to know to use the networking functionality demonstrated on the sample form. Though you could call the API functions directly, in each case we've provided a wrapper function to shield you from as much detail as possible. For each of the various wrapper functions, we provide information on how to call them, what parameters to send, and what values to expect back.

Most of the functions either return or set an error value, indicating the outcome of the function call. Though there are too many possible errors to list them all here, Table 11-15 lists most of the common ones that you'll receive when making these function calls.

Table 11-15. Common networking errors

Value	Constant	Description
0	NO_ERROR	No error occurred.
5	ERROR_ACCESS_DENIED	Access is denied.
66	ERROR_BAD_DEV_TYPE	The network resource type is not correct.
67	ERROR_BAD_NET_NAME	The network name cannot be found.
85	ERROR_ALREADY_ASSIGNED	The local device name is already in use.
86	ERROR_INVALID_PASSWORD	The specified network password is not correct.
170	ERROR_BUSY	The requested resource is in use.
234	ERROR_MORE_DATA	More data is available.
1200	ERROR_BAD_DEVICE	The specified device name is invalid.
1201	ERROR_CONNECTION_UNAVAIL	The device is not currently connected, but it is a remembered connection.
1202	ERROR_DEVICE_ALREADY_REMEMBERED	An attempt was made to remember a device that had previously been remembered.
1203	ERROR_NO_NET_OR_BAD_PATH	No network provider accepted the given network path.
1204	ERROR_BAD_PROVIDER	The specified network provider name is invalid.
1205	ERROR_CANNOT_OPEN_PROFILE	Unable to open the network connection profile.
1206	ERROR_BAD_PROFILE	The network connection profile is corrupt.
1208	ERROR_EXTENDED_ERROR	An extended error has occurred.
1222	ERROR_NO_NETWORK	The network is not present or not started.
1223	ERROR_CANCELED	The user canceled a dialog.
2250	ERROR_NOT_CONNECTED	This network connection does not exist.

Retrieving information

To retrieve the current user's name, call the acbGetUser function:

```
Public Function acbGetUser(Optional varErr As Variant) As String
```

```
    Dim strBuffer As String
    Dim lngRetval As Long
    Dim lngSize As Long

    lngSize = conMaxPath
    Do
        strBuffer = Space(lngSize)
        lngRetval = WNetGetUser(0&, strBuffer, lngSize)
    Loop Until lngRetval <> ERROR_MORE_DATA
    If lngRetval <> NO_ERROR Then
        acbGetUser = ""
    Else
        acbGetUser = TrimNull(strBuffer)
    End If
    varErr = lngRetval
End Function
```

The acbGetUser function calls the Windows API to retrieve the currently logged-in user's name. Note that there are several ways for the Windows API and Access to communicate the length of data to be returned. In this case, the code sets up a buffer of arbitrary length and calls the Windows API. If the buffer was large enough, it fills it in with the requested name. If not, it returns the value ERROR_MORE_DATA, indicating that it needs more space. It then passes back in the *lngSize* variable the actual number of characters it does need, and the code loops around, trying again with the specified size.

If you want to know the exact error that occurred in the attempt to retrieve the current user's name, you can pass a variant variable in as a parameter to acbGetUser. It's optional, but if you supply the value, the function will pass back the error code to you in that variable. For example:

```
Dim varErr as Variant
' If you care about the error:
Debug.Print acbGetUser(varErr)
Debug.Print "The error was: "; varError
' If you don't care about any errors:
Debug.Print acbGetUser( )
```

To retrieve the current computer's name, call the acbGetComputerName wrapper function. Windows stores the current computer's name in the registry database and reads it from there when necessary. To shield your code from having to know exactly where that piece of information is stored, Windows provides the GetComputer-Name API function.

The following function, acbGetComputerName, handles the passing of data between Access and Windows for you:

```
Public Function acbGetComputerName( ) As String

    ' Retrieve the network name of the current computer.
```

```
    Dim strBuffer As String
    Dim lngSize As Long
    Dim blnOK As Integer

    lngSize = conMaxComputerNameLength+ 1
    strBuffer = Space(lngSize)

    blnOK = GetComputerName(strBuffer, lngSize)
    acbGetComputerName = Left$(strBuffer, lngSize)
End Function
```

Note that in this case, the API function gives you no second chance. If the buffer wasn't large enough, it just returns as much as it could fit into the buffer you passed.

To retrieve the name of the remote device connected to a named local device, call the acbGetConnection function. Pass to it the local device name and an optional variable in which to receive the error code. It will return to you the remote device name connected to the requested local name. For example:

```
    Debug.Print acbGetConnection("LPT1:")
```

might return a value like this (a *server**share* name):

```
    \\WOMBAT\HPLJ4
```

The function works the same way for drive connections.

The acbGetConnection function works the same way as the acbGetUser function: it calls the API function once with an arbitrarily sized buffer. If that isn't enough room, it'll try again with the buffer resized to fit. Its source code is:

```
    Public Function acbGetConnection( _
     strLocalName As String, Optional varErr As Variant) As String

        Dim strBuffer As String
        Dim lngRetval As Long
        Dim lngSize As Long

        lngSize = acbcMaxPath

        Do
            strBuffer = Space(lngSize)
            lngRetval = WNetGetConnection(strLocalName, strBuffer, lngSize)
        Loop Until lngRetval <> ERROR_MORE_DATA

        If lngRetval <> NO_ERROR Then
            acbGetConnection = ""
        Else
            acbGetConnection = TrimNull(strBuffer)
        End If
        varErr = lngRetval
    End Function
```

Adding and canceling connections using common dialogs

Adding or canceling a connection with a common dialog in Windows is easy: just make a single function call, as shown in Table 11-16. Each wrapper function expects a single parameter: a window handle for the parent of the dialog window. Most of the time, this will just be Me.hWnd or Screen.ActiveForm.hWnd.

Table 11-16. Wrapper functions for common dialog connections

Function name	Action
acbConnectDriveDialog	Add a drive connection.
acbDisconnectDriveDialog	Cancel a drive connection.
acbConnectPrintDialog	Add a printer connection.
acbDisconnectPrintDialog	Cancel a printer connection.

For example, to pop up the common drive connection dialog, you'd call:

```
blnOK = acbConnectDriveDialog(Me.hWnd)
```

The code in each of the wrapper functions is similar and quite trivial. In each case, the code just calls a single Windows API function. We've provided the wrappers only to provide a consistent interface for all the API functions; there's no real reason not to call the API functions directly, except for a tiny bit of convenience. For example, the acbConnectPrintDialog function looks like this:

```
Public Function acbConnectPrintDialog(hWnd As Long) As Long
    ' Use the common print connection dialog to create a new connection.
    acbConnectPrintDialog = WNetConnectionDialog(hWnd, RESOURCETYPE_PRINT)
End Function
```

Adding and canceling connections with no user intervention

Adding or canceling a connection "silently" requires a bit more work, but it's not a problem. Table 11-17 lists the available wrapper functions, and the information they require.

Table 11-17. Functions to manually add and cancel connections

Function name	Action	Parameters	Description
acbAddDriveConnection	Add a drive connection.	*strLocalName* As String	Local name, like "LPT1:" or "G:".
		strRemoteName As String	Remote name, like "\\SERVER\SHARE".
		strUserName As String	Username to be used. If empty, uses default user's name.
		strPassword As String	Password for the user specified. If empty, uses the default user's password.

Table 11-17. Functions to manually add and cancel connections (continued)

acbAddPrintConnection	Add a printer connection.	*strLocalName* As String, *strRemoteName* As String, *strUserName* As String, *strPassword* As String	See parameters for *acbAddDriveConnection*.
acbCancelConnection	Cancel any connection.	*strLocalName* As String	Local name of resource to disconnect.
		blnForce As Boolean	If True, forces disconnection even if the device is in use. If False, the function returns an error if it tries to disconnect an active device.

For example, the following code fragment adds a new printer connection for LPT2: to the CanonColor printer on server Bart, set up for the current user and password:

```
blnOK = acbAddPrintConnection("LPT2:", "\\BART\CanonColor", "", "")
```

Each of these functions will return an error value (NO_ERROR (0)) if there was no error, or return some other error from Table 11-15 if an error occurs. Functions that add connections call the private function AddConnection, which in turn calls the Windows API to create that connection, as shown here:

```
Public Function acbAddDriveConnection( _
 strLocalName As String, strRemoteName As String, _
 strUserName As String, strPassword As String)

    acbAddDriveConnection = AddConnection( _
     RESOURCETYPE_DISK, strLocalName, _
     strRemoteName, strUserName, strPassword)
End Function

Private Function AddConnection(intType As Integer, _
 strLocalName As String, strRemoteName As String, _
 strUserName As String, strPassword As String)

    ' Internal function, provided for adding new connections.
    ' Call acbAddPrinterConnection or acbAddDriveConnection instead.

    Dim nr As NETRESOURCE
    Dim lngRetval As Long

    nr.lpLocalName = strLocalName
    nr.lpRemoteName = strRemoteName
    nr.dwType = intType
    lngRetval = WNetAddConnection2(nr, strPassword, _
     strUserName, CONNECT_UPDATE_PROFILE)
    AddConnection = lngRetval
End Function
```

The acbCancelConnection function is simple. It calls directly to the Windows API, canceling the connection for the named local device:

```
Public Function acbCancelConnection( _
  strName As String, blnForce As Boolean) As Long
    acbCancelConnection = WNetCancelConnection2( _
      strName, CONNECT_UPDATE_PROFILE, blnForce)
End Function
```

You may find it interesting to work through all the code in basNetwork. There are some interesting twists involved in transferring information between Access and the Windows API, especially since it seems that every API function that involves strings uses a different mechanism for indicating how much space it needs.

It would be useful to have a function that could enumerate all network resources, and of course Windows itself provides functions to do this. Unfortunately, calling these functions from Access requires a great deal of effort, because VBA just doesn't support the necessary mechanisms (specifically, pointers) to make it possible. It's possible, but it's beyond the scope of this book.

Automation

No Access application exists in isolation. Because Windows is a multitasking operating system, you will often want to be able to link Access with other Windows applications. Windows provides two mechanisms for communicating between applications: Object Linking and Embedding (OLE), which has been renamed ActiveX, and Dynamic Data Exchange (DDE), an older technology that is supported primarily for backward compatibility. ActiveX is easy for users and application programmers to work with and allows for the creation of custom controls. It also accommodates Automation, making it possible for Access to control various applications using VBA.

This chapter presents examples of using Automation with several Microsoft Office products. You'll also find an example of using DDE to perform a task with the Windows shell. You'll learn to activate an embedded ActiveX object (a sound file), and you'll learn how to control Access itself via Automation. You'll see how to use the statistical, analytical, and financial prowess of the Excel function libraries directly from Access, as well as how to retrieve Word Summary Info for any selected document. Then you'll dig into Automation, creating a form that allows you to alter properties of Microsoft Graph objects on the form. Finally, you'll delve into PowerPoint, which in previous incarnations didn't support Automation, and you'll see an example of automating tasks in Outlook. These examples will show how you can manipulate and create objects in these applications directly from Access.

 Almost all of the examples in this chapter ask you to set a reference within VBA, using the Tools → References menu item. Because this book supports multiple versions of Office, we've selected the Office 11 type libraries in each example. You'll need to modify the instructions to set a reference to the correct type library in each case, based on the version of Office you have installed. Besides these version numbering differences, all the examples should behave the same, no matter which version of Office you're using.

12.1 Play an Embedded Sound File from Within an Application

Problem

Your application stores WAV files as OLE objects within a table, and you'd like to be able to play them on demand. You know that users can double-click on the icon in a form to play the sounds, but you'd like some control over this. Is there a way to play one of these embedded sounds when you need to?

Solution

Access gives you substantial control over the use of OLE objects. Using the Action property of the control that's displaying the OLE object, you can tell the object to activate itself, copy itself to or paste itself from the Windows clipboard, update its data, and close or delete itself. The Action property can be used for bound or unbound OLE objects and graphs, too. You can also call up the Insert Object or Paste Special dialog to place data into the control. This solution uses a bound OLE field, but it works just as well with an unbound object on a form.

Load and run frmOLE (shown in Figure 12-1) from 12-01.MDB. This is a continuous form, pulling the data from the table tblOLE. If you click on an Activate button, the form activates that OLE object, which is stored in the OLEObject field of the table. The sample table includes a few WAV files, one Microsoft Graph object, and a MIDI file. Clicking on the Activate button will either play the sound or activate Microsoft Graph so you can edit the tiny graph object. Click on the Insert button to call up the Insert Object dialog, which allows you to insert any OLE object you like into the table. Click on the Open button to open the object in its own editing window rather than activating it in place.

Follow these simple steps to create such a form:

1. Create a new table or modify an existing table, adding a column (named OLE-Object in the sample) with its Data Type set to OLE object. Note that you cannot index on an OLE field, and therefore it can't be your primary key for the table.

2. Create a new form. To emulate the sample form, the only property you need to set is the DefaultView property. Set it to Continuous Forms so that you'll see multiple rows at the same time. This isn't necessary, but it will make your form look like the sample.

3. Create a bound OLE object (the cactus picture with the XYZ across the top on the toolbar) on the form. The code in this example is based on a control named objOLE; adjust the code appropriately if you name your control something else.

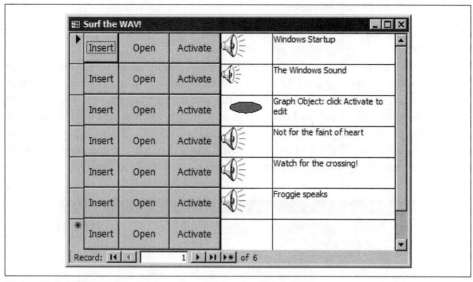

Figure 12-1. frmOLE allows you to play or insert OLE objects

The sample form includes the description field from tblOLE as a text box, but this isn't used in the sample code.

4. Add three buttons: cmdOpen, cmdActivate, and cmdInsert, with captions Open, Activate, and Insert, respectively. Attach the following code to the Activate button's Click event (see the Preface for more information on creating event procedures):

```
Private Sub cmdActivate_Click( )
    Dim ctl As Control

    On Error Resume Next
    Set ctl = Me.objOLE
    ctl.Verb = acOLEVerbPrimary
    ctl.Action = acOLEActivate
    Err.Clear
End Sub
```

Attach the following code to the Insert button's Click event:

```
Private Sub cmdInsert_Click( )
    On Error Resume Next
    Me.objOLE.Action = acOLEInsertObjDlg
    Err.Clear
End Sub
```

Attach the following code to the Open button's Click event:

```
Private Sub cmdOpen_Click( )
    Dim ctl As Control

    On Error Resume Next
    Set ctl = Me.objOLE
    ' Open, rather than just activate in place.
```

```
      ctl.Verb = acOLEVerbOpen
      ctl.Action = acOLEActivate
      Err.Clear
   End Sub
```

5. Save your form and run it. When you click on the Insert button, you'll see the Insert Object dialog (Figure 12-2). This dialog allows you to create a new object or to insert one from an existing file. Once you make your choice, Access places the object into the table and displays it on the form. When you want to activate the object, click on the Activate button. For a WAV or MIDI file, this causes your sound to play; for a Microsoft Graph object, it activates Microsoft Graph. To open an editing window for the object, click on the Open button.

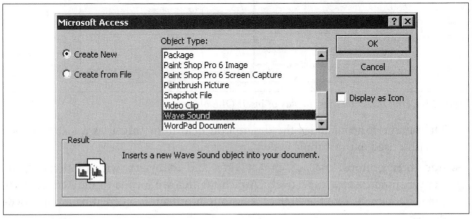

Figure 12-2. The Insert Object dialog

Discussion

The Action property for OLE objects in Access is different from almost any other property, in that setting its value causes an action to take place. Normally, properties describe characteristics of an object, and methods cause actions to take place. In this case, however, when you set the Action property to the constant acOLEActivate, Access activates the control at the time you set the property. If you set the Action property to the constant acOLEInsertObjDlg, Access displays the modal Insert Object dialog at the time you change the property. By changing the OLE control's Action property, the code tells Access what action to take at that point. By changing the Verb property from acOleVerbPrimary (to activate the object) to acOleVerbOpen, you control how the object is opened: in place, or in its own window.

Table 12-1 lists the values that you're likely to use for the Action property. Others are available, but this list will get you started. For more information, see the online help topics on the Action and Verb properties.

Table 12-1. Possible values of the Action property

Constant	Value	Description
acOLECopy	4	Same as choosing the Edit Copy menu item. Copies the OLE object onto the Windows clipboard.
acOLEPaste	5	Same as choosing the Edit Paste menu item. Pastes the OLE object from the Windows clipboard into your control.
acOLEUpdate	6	Retrieves the most current data for the OLE object from the application that created it and displays it as a graphic.
acOLEActivate	7	Same as double-clicking the control. You must set the control's Verb property before you can use this Action.
acOLEClose	9	Closes the OLE object and ends the active connection with the application that provided the object.
acOLEInsertObjDlg	14	Displays the Insert Object modal dialog, allowing the user to insert an object.

This technique works just as well for unbound objects on forms. For example, if you have an embedded Word document, you could use code to activate the OLE object (named Embedded0 in the following example), set its first paragraph to bold, and then close the object:

```
Dim objWord As Object
' Activate the OLE object, using the primary verb.
Me.Embedded0.Verb = acOLEVerbPrimary
Me.Embedded0.Action = acOLEActivate
Set objWord = Me.Embedded0.Object.Application.WordBasic

objWord.StartOfDocument
objWord.ParaDown 1, 1
objWord.Bold 1
Set objWord = Nothing
' Close the OLE object.
Me.Embedded0.Action = acOLEClose
```

By the way, if you need to play a WAV file but don't want to embed an OLE object or use OLE at all, you can use the Windows API sndPlaySound function to do your work. (This function is aliased as acb_apiSndPlaySound in *12-01.MDB*.) Just insert the following declarations and constants in a form's module:

```
Private Declare Function sndPlaySound Lib "winmm.dll" _
 Alias "sndPlaySoundA" (ByVal lpszSoundName As String, _
 ByVal uFlags As Long) As Long
Private Const SND_SYNC = &H0
Private Const SND_ASYNC = &H1
Private Const SND_NODEFAULT = &H2
Private Const SND_LOOP = &H8
Private Const SND_NOSTOP = &H10
```

Table 12-2 describes the possible flag values for the sndPlaySound function call.

Table 12-2. Possible values for the intFlags parameter to sndPlaySound

Constant	Value	Description
SND_SYNC	0	Plays the sound synchronously and does not return from the function until the sound ends.
SND_ASYNC	1	Plays the sound asynchronously and returns from the function immediately after beginning the sound. To terminate a sound once it's started, call *acb_ apiSndPlaySound*, passing vbNullChar as the first parameter.
SND_NODEFAULT	2	Doesn't play the default sound if the requested sound can't be found.
SND_LOOP	8	The sound continues to play repeatedly until you call *acb_ apiSndPlaySound* with the first parameter set to vbNullChar. You must also specify the SND_ ASYNC flag to loop sounds.
SND_NOSTOP	16	Returns immediately with a value of FALSE without playing the requested sound if a sound is currently playing.

Normally, you'll call the sndPlaySound function to play the WAV file. If you use the SND_ASYNC or SND_LOOP flags, you'll need to call the sndPlaySound function again, passing the vbNullChar constant as the first parameter. The following code example is the simplest way to play a WAV file using the Windows API. You can try this out by loading the form frmSndPlaySound from *12-01.MDB* and pressing the button on the form, which executes the following code:

```
Private Sub Button0_Click()
    Dim varSound As Variant
    Dim intFlags As Integer
    Dim intResult As Integer
    Dim strWinDir As String
    Dim intCount As Integer

    Const conMaxLen = 255

    ' Find the Windows directory.
    strWinDir = Space(conMaxLen)
    intCount = GetWindowsDirectory(strWinDir, conMaxLen)
    strWinDir = Left(strWinDir, intCount)

    ' Get the file name, using the common file open dialog.
    varSound = acbCommonFileOpenSave(InitialDir:=strWinDir, _
      Filter:=acbAddFilterItem("", "WAV Files", "*.WAV"), _
      DialogTitle:="Choose a WAV File")
    If Not IsNull(varSound) Then
        intFlags = SND_ASYNC Or SND_NODEFAULT
        intResult = sndPlaySound(varSound, intFlags)
        If intResult = 0 Then
            MsgBox "Unable to play sound."
        End If
    End If
End Sub
```

This example is complicated by the fact that it uses the Windows File Open dialog to request the name of the WAV file that you'd like to play (the folder named Media is a good place to look), but the heart of the routine is quite simple.

See Also

For more information on working with the Windows API, see Chapter 11.

12.2   Print an Access Report from Excel

Problem

You keep and work with your data in Excel, but you'd like to print reports using Access. You know you can use the Access Report Wizard directly from Excel, but you'd like more control over the process. Can you do this using VBA?

Solution

Access allows you to control its actions using Automation. Anything you can do directly from Access, you can also do from Excel. This solution uses Automation to link your Excel worksheet to an Access database, use that data as the data source for a report, and then remove the linked table. Because you can directly link to an Excel worksheet from Access, this process doesn't need to involve importing the data—you can use it as-is, live, in your Excel environment.

To try out the sample database, first load *12-02.XLS* into Excel. This workbook includes the data (shown in Figure 12-3) and the VBA code that controls the sample. Next, click the Open Access Report button, which causes Excel to load a copy of Access and then load *12-02.MDB*, link the current data to that database, and display the report in print preview mode.

To use this technique in your own applications, follow these steps:

1. Create a database, including a report that you'd like to print. You may want to link the Excel data that's going to be the data source now, so that it's easier to create the report. You can leave it linked (in which case you'll want to modify the example code in your spreadsheet to not relink the table) or you can delete the link once you've created the report.

2. In Excel, create a new workbook or use an existing one. Add a new module (choose Tools Macro Visual Basic Editor, and then Insert Module) and enter the following code (or copy it from *12-02.XLS*):

```
Option Explicit

Const conXLS = "12-02.xls"
Const conMDB = "12-02.mdb"
Const conTableName = "CustomersXLS"
Const conReportName = "Customers"
```

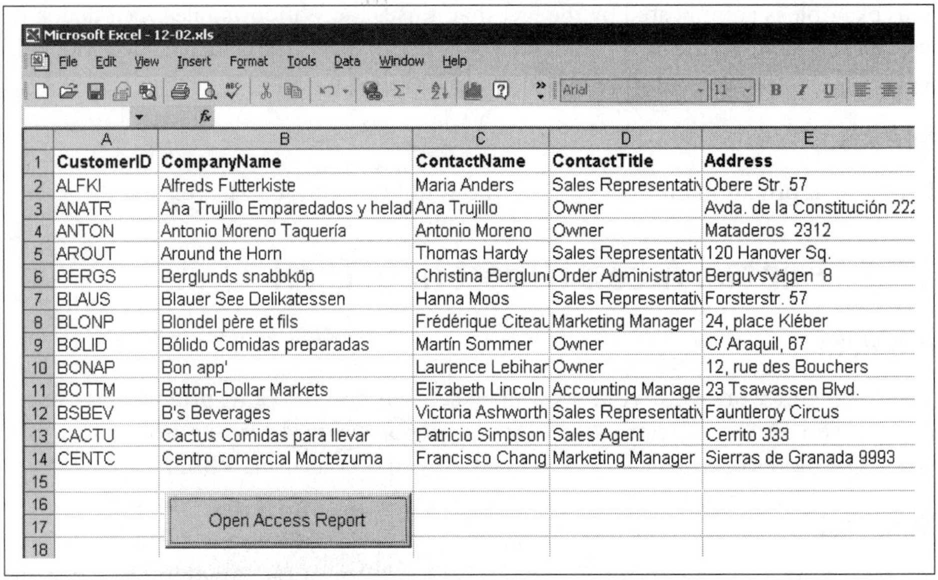

Figure 12-3. Use data in Excel to print a report in Access

```
Private Sub HandleAccessReport( )
    ' This sample assumes that the database and
    ' the spreadsheet are in the same directory.
    ' It doesn't HAVE to be that way, of course,
    ' but it makes this simple example much simpler.
    Dim accApp As Access.Application

    Dim strPath As String
    Dim strDatabase As String
    Dim strXLS As String

    On Error GoTo HandleErr

    ' Get the location of the files.
    strPath = FixPath(ActiveWorkbook.Path)
    strDatabase = strPath & conMDB
    strXLS = strPath & conXLS

    ' Launch a new instance of Access.
    Set accApp = New Access.Application

    ' Open the database.
    With accApp
        .OpenCurrentDatabase filepath:=strDatabase, Exclusive:=True

        ' Link the spreadsheet to Access.
        With .DoCmd
            .TransferSpreadsheet _
                TransferType:=acLink, _
```

```
                    SpreadsheetType:=acSpreadsheetTypeExcel9, _
                    TableName:=conTableName, _
                    Filename:=strXLS, _
                    HasFieldNames:=True

                ' Open the report in preview mode.
                .OpenReport conReportName, acViewPreview
                ' Delete the attached table.
                .DeleteObject acTable, conTableName
            End With
        End With

ExitHere:
        Set accApp = Nothing
        Exit Sub

HandleErr:
        MsgBox Err & ": " & Err.Description, , _
         "Error in HandleAccessReport"
        Resume ExitHere
End Sub

    Private Function FixPath(strPath As String) As String
        If Right(strPath, 1) = "\" Then
            FixPath = strPath
        Else
            FixPath = strPath & "\"
        End If
    End Function
```

3. Choose the Tools → References... menu item and, from the list of references, check the Microsoft Access 11.0 Object Library item, as shown in Figure 12-4. (Select the object library corresponding to the version of Access that you're using—if you're using Office 2002, for example, select Access 10.0 Object Library in this dialog box.) This will add an explicit reference to the Access type library to your project, making Access's object model and constants available to your code.

4. In the code you've just entered, modify the constants conXLS and conMDB to match the names of your spreadsheet and database, respectively. Also modify the conTableName and conReportName constants to match the data source for your report (its RecordSource property) and the name of the report itself.

5. The example code expects three conditions to be true:
   - The spreadsheet and the database are in the same directory.
   - The spreadsheet data includes the field names in the first row.
   - The path that contains the files is not the drive's root directory.

Make sure that all these assumptions are met. You could code around all three of these, but these reflect the way the example was set up.

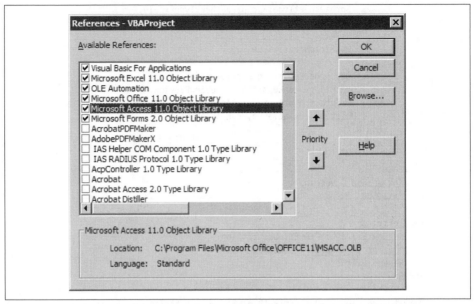

Figure 12-4. Use the References dialog to set a reference to Access in Excel

6. Add a command button to your worksheet. Place the following code in its OnClick event:

```
Private Sub cmdAccess_Click( )
    Call HandleAccessReport
End Sub
```

7. Save your spreadsheet. When you click the button you've created, it will start Access, link the table, print the report, delete the link, close the database, and quit Access.

Discussion

This example uses Automation to control Access directly from Excel. The process of printing the report can be broken down into four steps:

- Get the reference to Access and open the database.
- Link the Excel worksheet to the database.
- Print the report.
- Clean up.

The next few paragraphs discuss these items. The HandleAccessReport procedure in Step 2 includes all the code for this process.

To retrieve a reference to Access, you can use the Access Application object. The line of code that does the work looks like this:

```
Dim accApp As Access.Application
Set accApp = New Access.Application
```

To open the database, use the OpenCurrentDatabase method of the Application object:

```
With AccApp
    .OpenCurrentDatabase filepath:=strDatabase, Exclusive:=True
```

Access provides three methods that work with the current database from Automation:

- OpenCurrentDatabase (not to be confused with the DAO method, OpenDatabase) opens a database in the Access user interface. If a database is already open, you'll get a runtime error.

- CloseCurrentDatabase closes the current database. This method will generate a runtime error if there's no current database.

- NewCurrentDatabase creates a new database altogether. Once you've done this, you can use OLE Automation to create all the objects you need in that database as well.

In addition to these three methods, the Access Application object provides two useful properties: UserControl and Visible. The UserControl property returns True if you opened Access under your own power, or False if Automation started Access. The property is read-only and lets your code work differently depending on how the database was loaded. The Visible property allows you to control whether an instance of Access started via Automation is visible or not. If UserControl is True, you cannot change the Visible property. If UserControl is False, the default value for Visible is False, but you can set it to be True with code like this:

```
' Set the Application's Visible property to True
' if OLE Automation initiated the session.
With accApp
    If Not .UserControl Then
        .Visible = True
    End If
End With
```

To link the Excel spreadsheet to the Access database, use the TransferSpreadsheet method of the DoCmd object. This method allows you to import or link a spreadsheet to the database, depending on the parameters you set. In this example, the code specifies that the spreadsheet is of type acSpreadsheetTypeExcel9 (this applies to Excel 2000 and later), includes field names in the top row, and is to be linked, not imported:

```
With .DoCmd
    .TransferSpreadsheet _
        TransferType:=acLink, _
        SpreadsheetType:=acSpreadsheetTypeExcel9, _
        TableName:=conTableName, _
        Filename:=strXLS, _
        HasFieldNames:=True
```

Once you've executed the TransferSpreadsheet method, your database will include an attached table, with the name stored in `strTableName`, that retrieves data from the spreadsheet whose name is in `strXLS`.

To print the report, use the OpenReport method of the DoCmd object, as shown in the following code fragment, which opens the report in print preview mode using the `acViewPreview` constant:

```
.OpenReport conReportName, acViewPreview
```

If you want the report to be sent directly to the printer, use the `acViewNormal` constant.

To clean up once your report has finished printing, the code first deletes the linked table, then closes the database, and finally shuts down the instance of Access that it initiated. To delete the table, it uses the DeleteObject method of the DoCmd object. To close the current database, it uses the CloseCurrentDatabase method of the Application object. Finally, to shut down Access, it uses the Quit method of the Application object. The cleanup code is:

```
With DoCmd
    ' Do all the work here...
    .DeleteObject acTable, strTableName
End With
' This isn't necessary, but it's neat.
.CloseCurrentDatabase
' Quit Access now.
.Quit
End With
Set obj = Nothing
```

You aren't limited to running Access from Excel—you can have any Automation client (including Access itself) start up a new copy of Access to accomplish Access tasks from that host.

12.3   Use Excel's Functions from Within Access

Problem

Excel offers an amazing array of statistical, analytical, and financial functions that you'd like to be able to use in Access. You know you can control embedded Excel worksheets, but is there some way to call Excel functions from within Access?

Solution

Access users often ask how they can use Excel functions directly from Access. Using OLE Automation, you can actually request Excel to use its built-in functions to perform calculations and return a value back to your Access application. This requires starting Excel, however, and that can take time, so you wouldn't normally do this for a single calculation. But for a number of calculated values or a single calculation that would be too difficult or time-consuming in Access, it's worth tapping into the connections between Access and Excel.

There are many ways to use Automation to link Excel and Access. You can embed an Excel spreadsheet or chart object into an Access form and control the Excel objects programmatically, as in the example shown in the Solution in Recipe 12.6. You can also use OLE Automation from Access to create and manipulate Excel objects *without* using an embedded spreadsheet or chart. These methods are detailed in both the Access and Excel manuals. This solution uses the Excel application engine without creating any other specific Excel objects.

To test the OLE communication between Access and Excel, load frmTestExcel from *12-03.MDB* and click the button on the form to start the test. The code attached to the button will start up Excel and run a series of tests, calling Excel to retrieve the results for a number of function calls. After all the tests, the sample form will look like Figure 12-5. You can run the tests either by writing directly to spreadsheet cells to test the multiple-value functions or by using arrays. The checkbox on the form lets you try both methods.

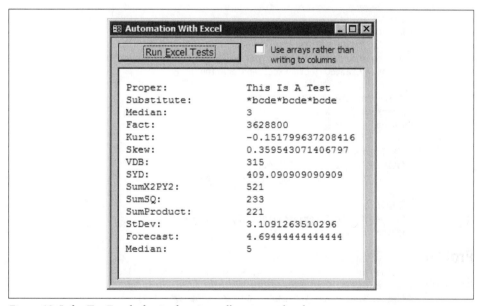

Figure 12-5. frmTestExcel after its function calls are completed

The sample form tests two different types of function calls you can make to Excel from Access: functions that accept simple parameters, and functions that require multiple values (ranges) as parameters.

The following steps describe how set up the example form:

1. Create a new form containing a single text box (named txtResults on the sample form) and a command button to run the Excel tests (as in Figure 12-5).

2. Import the module basExcel from *12-03.MDB*. This module contains a function that copies data from a column in Access to a spreadsheet column in Excel. The module also includes a function that copies data from a column in Access to an array, which OLE Automation can use in place of a range.

3. Enter the following code into the form's module (click on the Build button on the toolbar or choose View → Code):

```
Private Sub AddLine(strLabel As String, varValue As Variant)
    Me.txtResults = Me.txtResults & vbCrLf & _
    " " & Left(strLabel & Space(20), 20) & varValue
    DoEvents
End Sub

Private Function TestExcel()
    Dim obj As Excel.Application
    Dim intCount As Integer
    Dim blnUseArrays As Boolean

    Me.txtResults = Null
    blnUseArrays = Nz(Me.chkUseArrays)

    DoEvents
    AddLine "Starting Excel:", "Please wait..."

    ' If you know Excel is open, you could use GetObject()
    Set obj = CreateObject("Excel.Application")

    ' Clear out the results text box.
    Me.txtResults = Null
    DoEvents

    ' String functions
    AddLine "Proper:", obj.Proper("this is a test")
    AddLine "Substitute:", obj.Substitute("abcdeabcdeabcde", "a", "*")

    ' Simple math functions
    AddLine "Median:", obj.Median(1, 2, 3, 4, 5)
    AddLine "Fact:", obj.Fact(10)

    ' Analytical functions
    AddLine "Kurt:", obj.Kurt(3, 4, 5, 2, 3, 4, 5, 6, 4, 7)
    AddLine "Skew:", obj.Skew(3, 4, 5, 2, 3, 4, 5, 6, 4, 7)
    AddLine "VDB:", obj.VDB(2400, 300, 10, 0, 0.875, 1.5)
    AddLine "SYD:", obj.SYD(30000, 7500, 10, 10)

    If blnUseArrays Then
        ' Using arrays
        Dim varCol1 As Variant
        Dim varCol2 As Variant
        ' Copy two fields to columns
        Call acbCopyColumnToArray(varCol1, "tblNumbers", "Number1")
        Call acbCopyColumnToArray(varCol2, "tblNumbers", "Number2")
```

```
                ' Print out calculations based on those ranges
                AddLine "SumX2PY2:", obj.SumX2PY2(varCol1, varCol2)
                AddLine "SumSQ:", obj.SumSQ(varCol1)
                AddLine "SumProduct:", obj.SumProduct(varCol1, varCol2)
                AddLine "StDev:", obj.STDEV(varCol1)
                AddLine "Forecast:", obj.ForeCast(5, varCol1, varCol2)
                AddLine "Median:", obj.Median(varCol1)
            Else
                ' Using ranges
                Dim objBook As Workbook
                Dim objSheet As Worksheet

                Dim objRange1 As Range
                Dim objRange2 As Range

                ' Create the workbook.
                Set objBook = obj.Workbooks.Add
                Set objSheet = objBook.WorkSheets(1)

                ' Copy two fields to columns
                intCount = acbCopyColumnToSheet(objSheet, "tblNumbers", "Number1", 1)
                intCount = acbCopyColumnToSheet(objSheet, "tblNumbers", "Number2", 2)

                ' Create ranges
                Set objRange1 = objSheet.Range("A1:A" & intCount)
                Set objRange2 = objSheet.Range("B1:B" & intCount)

                ' Print out calculations based on those ranges
                AddLine "SumX2PY2:", obj.SumX2PY2(objRange1, objRange2)
                AddLine "SumSQ:", obj.SumSQ(objRange1)
                AddLine "SumProduct:", obj.SumProduct(objRange1, objRange2)
                AddLine "StDev:", obj.STDEV(objRange1)
                AddLine "Forecast:", obj.ForeCast(5, objRange1, objRange2)
                AddLine "Median:", obj.Median(objRange1)
                ' Convince Excel that it needn't save that
                ' workbook you created.
                obj.ActiveWorkbook.Saved = True
                Set objRange1 = Nothing
                Set objRange2 = Nothing
                Set objSheet = Nothing
            End If

    ExitHere:
        ' Quit and clean up.
        obj.Quit
        Set obj = Nothing
    End Function
```

4. In the properties sheet for the command button, enter the value:

```
=TestExcel( )
```

in the OnClick event property.

5. With a module open in design mode, choose the Tools → References... menu item. Choose Microsoft Excel 11.0 Object Library from the list of choices (this item will be on the list if you installed Excel correctly—select the version that you have installed, which may be something besides Excel 11.0). This provides your VBA code with information about the Excel object library, properties, methods, and constants.

6. Open the form in run mode and click the command button. This will call the TestExcel function and fill the text box with the results.

Discussion

Excel obligingly exposes all of its internal functions to external callers via the Application object. The following sections describe the necessary steps to call Excel functions directly from Access.

 No matter which Excel function you call, the return value will be a variant. Declare a variable as a variant if it will contain the return value from an Excel function. In the examples, the return values went directly to a text box, so you didn't need to select a data type.

Setting up communication with Excel

Before you can call any Excel function, you must start Excel and create an object variable in Access to link the two applications. You'll always use code like this to create this linkage:

```
Dim objExcel As Excel.Application
Set objExcel = CreateObject("Excel.Application")
```

By linking with Excel's Application object, you can request Excel to evaluate any of its internal functions for you. Creating the object will take a few seconds, as Excel needs to be started. Calling CreateObject will start a new hidden instance of Excel, even if Excel is already running.

You have two other choices. If you know Excel is already running, you can use GetObject to retrieve a reference to an object within Excel or to the Excel Application object. The following code will retrieve a reference to the Application object if Excel is already running:

```
Set objExcel = GetObject(, "Excel.Application")
```

If you've set up a reference to Excel using the Tools References... menu item (this is necessary for this example to run), you should be able to use the following code to retrieve a reference to the Excel Application object:

```
Set objExcel = New Excel.Application
```

Calling simple Excel functions

Once you've created your Access object that refers to the Excel Application object, you can ask Excel to perform simple calculations for you. For example, to use the Excel Product function, use code like this:

```
Dim varProd As Variant
varProd = obj.Product(5, 6)
```

After this call, the variable *varProd* will contain the value 30.

For example, TestExcel, in frmTestExcel's module, uses the following code fragment to call four Excel functions: Proper, Substitute, Median, and Fact. Each of these functions requires one or more simple parameters and returns a single value. (The AddLine function calls just add the value returned by the function call to the text box on the sample form. These four functions are the first four in the output text box.) The relevant code fragment is:

```
' String functions
AddLine "Proper:", obj.Proper("this is a test")
AddLine "Substitute:", obj.Substitute("abcdeabcdeabcde", "a", "*")

' Simple math functions
AddLine "Median:", obj.Median(1, 2, 3, 4, 5)
AddLine "Fact:", obj.Fact(10)
```

Excel supplies many simple functions like these that Access doesn't have. Some of these functions (Proper, for example) are easy enough to replicate in VBA (the StrConv function will convert strings to proper case), but if you already have a connection to Excel, it makes sense to use Excel to retrieve these sorts of values rather than writing the code yourself.

To call analytical or statistical functions in Excel, use the same technique. With the reference to the Excel Application object, call any function that takes simple parameters and returns a single value. The next four examples on the sample form call the Kurt, Skew, VDB, and SYD functions:

```
' Analytical functions
AddLine "Kurt:", obj.Kurt(3, 4, 5, 2, 3, 4, 5, 6, 4, 7)
AddLine "Skew:", obj.Skew(3, 4, 5, 2, 3, 4, 5, 6, 4, 7)
AddLine "VDB:", obj.VDB(2400, 300, 10, 0, 0.875, 1.5)
AddLine "SYD:", obj.SYD(30000, 7500, 10, 10)
```

Sometimes you'll need to call Excel functions that require a variable number of values, or you'll want to use the data in a table as the input to an Excel function. In these cases, you have two choices: you can either call the Excel function using a spreadsheet range as the input, or you can pass a VBA array directly to the function, which will convert the array and treat it as a built-in range of values. In either case, you'll need a method of getting the Access data into the spreadsheet or into an array so you can use that data as input to the function.

Calling Excel functions using ranges

To copy a column of data from an Access table or query into an Excel spreadsheet column, call the acbCopyColumnToSheet function, found in the basExcel module in *12-03.MDB*:

```
Public Function acbCopyColumnToSheet( _
  objSheet As Excel.Worksheet, strTable As String, _
  strField As String, intColumn As Integer)

    ' Copy a column from a table to a spreadsheet.
    ' Place the data from the given field (strField) in
    ' the given table/query (strField) in the specified
    ' column (intColumn) in the specified worksheet object
    ' (objSheet).
    ' Return the number of items in the column.

    Dim rst As DAO.Recordset
    Dim db As DAO.Database
    Dim intRows As Integer
    Dim varData As Variant

    Set db = CurrentDb( )
    Set rst = db.OpenRecordset(strTable)
    Do While Not rst.EOF
        intRows = intRows + 1
        objSheet.Cells(intRows, intColumn).Value = rst(strField).Value
        rst.MoveNext
    Loop
    rst.Close
    acbCopyColumnToSheet = intRows
End Function
```

Given a reference to an Excel sheet, a table or query name, a field name, and a column number for the Excel sheet, acbCopyColumnToSheet walks down all the rows of Access data, copying them to the Excel sheet. The function returns the number of rows that it copied over to Excel. For example, to copy the Unit Price field values from the tblProducts table to the first column of the open spreadsheet in Excel, use:

```
intCount = acbCopyColumnToSheet(objSheet, "tblProducts", "Unit Price", 1)
```

 To keep it simple, this version of the acbCopyColumnToSheet function doesn't include error checking, but any code used in real applications should check for errors that might occur as you move data from Access to Excel.

Once you've copied the data to Excel, you can create an object that refers to that range of data as a single entity. Most Excel functions will accept a range as a parameter if they accept a group of values as input. For example, the Median function used previously accepts either a list of numbers or a range.

To create a range object in Access, use the Range method, passing a string that represents the range you want. The following example, used after the form copies the data from a table over to Excel, calculates the median of all the items in the column:

```
Dim objRange1 As Excel.Range

Set objRange1 = objSheet.Range("A1:A" & intCount)
AddLine "Median:", obj.Median(objRange1)
```

Some Excel functions require two or more ranges as input. For example, the SumX2PY2 function, which returns the sum of the squares of all the values in two columns (that is, $x^2 + y^2$), takes two ranges as its parameters. The following code fragment, also from the sample form, copies two columns from tblNumbers to the open sheet in Excel and then performs a number of calculations based on those columns:

```
' Copy two fields to columns.
intCount = acbCopyColumnToSheet(objSheet, "tblNumbers", "Number1", 1)
intCount = acbCopyColumnToSheet(objSheet, "tblNumbers", "Number2", 2)

' Create ranges.
Set objRange1 = objSheet.Range("A1:A" & intCount)
Set objRange2 = objSheet.Range("B1:B" & intCount)

' Print out calculations based on those ranges.
AddLine "SumX2PY2:", obj.SumX2PY2(objRange1, objRange2)
AddLine "SumSQ:", obj.SumSQ(objRange1)
AddLine "SumProduct:", obj.SumProduct(objRange1, objRange2)
AddLine "StDev:", obj.STDEV(objRange1)
AddLine "Forecast:", obj.ForeCast(5, objRange1, objRange2)
AddLine "Median:", obj.Median(objRange1)
```

Calling Excel functions using arrays

Rather than writing to a spreadsheet directly, you might find your work faster if you load a column of data into an array and send it to Excel that way. This avoids multiple Automation calls to Excel (each time you place a value into a cell in Excel, you're going through a *lot* of internal Automation code). The drawback, of course, is that you're loading all your data into memory. On the other hand, if you're working with so much data that it won't fit into memory, Automation will be too slow to be of much use, anyway!

To copy a column of data to an array, call the acbCopyColumnToArray function (from basExcel in *12-03.MDB*), shown in the following code. Pass a variant variable (variants can hold entire arrays in VBA), a table name, and a field name to the function, and it will return the number of rows it placed into the array. This function walks through all the rows in your recordset, copying the values from the specified column into the array:

```
Public Function acbCopyColumnToArray( _
  varArray As Variant, strTable As String, strField As String)
```

```
' Copy the data from the given field (strField) of the
' given table/query (strTable) into a dynamic array (varArray)

' Return the number of rows.

Dim db As DAO.Database
Dim rst As DAO.Recordset
Dim intRows As Integer

Set db = CurrentDb( )
Set rst = db.OpenRecordset(strTable)
rst.MoveLast
ReDim varArray(1 To rst.RecordCount)
rst.MoveFirst
Do While Not rst.EOF
    intRows = intRows + 1
    varArray(intRows) = rst(strField).Value
    rst.MoveNext
Loop
rst.Close
acbCopyColumnToArray = intRows
End Function
```

Once you've copied the data into arrays, you can call functions in Excel, passing those arrays as if they were ranges. Excel understands that it's receiving multiple values and returns the same results as the tests involving ranges:

```
' Copy two fields to columns.
Call acbCopyColumnToArray(varCol1, "tblNumbers", "Number1")
Call acbCopyColumnToArray(varCol2, "tblNumbers", "Number2")

' Print out calculations based on those ranges.
AddLine "SumX2PY2:", obj.SumX2PY2(varCol1, varCol2)
AddLine "SumSQ:", obj.SumSQ(varCol1)
AddLine "SumProduct:", obj.SumProduct(varCol1, varCol2)
AddLine "StDev:", obj.STDEV(varCol1)
AddLine "Forecast:", obj.ForeCast(5, varCol1, varCol2)
AddLine "Median:", obj.Median(varCol1)
```

This method is both simpler and faster than writing to a spreadsheet. However, if you're working with large volumes of data, you'll want to copy the data to a spreadsheet for Excel to process instead of copying it all into an array.

Closing Excel

Once you're done with your Access/Excel session, you must close the Excel application. If you don't, OLE will continue to start new instances of Excel every time you attempt to connect with Excel.Application (using CreateObject), eating up system resources each time.

To close Excel, use its Quit method:

```
obj.Quit
```

Finally, release any memory used by Access in maintaining the link between itself and Excel. The following code releases any memory that the reference to Excel might have been using:

```
Set obj = Nothing
```

Comments

Because it takes time to start Excel once you call the CreateObject function, build your applications so that all work with Excel is isolated to as few locations in your code as possible. Another alternative is to make your object variables global; then, you can have your application start Excel if it needs to and leave it open until it's done. Don't forget to close Excel, however, to avoid using up your system memory and resources.

When you're done with the Automation application, you'll need some way of closing down. As with the CreateObject function, each application reacts differently to your attempts to shut it down. You'll need to know how each application you use expects to be closed. Excel won't quit unless you explicitly order it to, using the Quit method. If you just set the object variable that refers to Excel.Application to the value Nothing without executing the Quit action, the hidden copy of Excel will continue running, chewing up memory and resources.

Excel exposes rich and varied inner workings via Automation, but taking advantage of those capabilities is nearly impossible without reference materials. This solution barely scratches the surface of what's available to you in Access from Excel. If you need to use the two products together, use the Object Browser in the Visual Basic Editor to explore the objects in the Excel object model. You can bring up the help topic for each object from within the Object Browser.

See Also

A good reference book for Excel programming is *Writing Excel Macros* by Steven Roman (O'Reilly). The Solution in Recipe 12.6 will give you a chance to explore a few of the more interesting corners of the Excel object model. For more information on sorting, using VBA, see "Sort an Array in VBA" in Chapter 7.

12.4 Perform a Mail Merge from Access to Word

Problem

You'd like to be able to do a mail merge to Word using Access data, without having to launch the mail merge from Word using its mail merge features.

Solution

Access allows you to output data directly to any format using the DoCmd.OutputTo functionality. You can then run a mail merge from Word to a predefined Word template that contains the merge codes.

First you must create the Word template that holds your merge codes; then you can write the code in Access that performs the merge. The sample application *12-04. MDB* contains a table and a query that retrieves the data to be sent to Word.

To perform a mail merge from Access to Word, follow these steps:

1. In Access, create the query that you will use for your data. Copy the rows from the datasheet view of the query and paste them into a Word document.

2. Save the Word document in the same folder as the Access database. The sample application uses the name *qryCustomers.doc*.

3. In Word, create a template by choosing File New Template from the menu. Fill in the plain text for your main merge document.

4. Choose Tools → Mail Merge from the menu to add the merge fields to the template. Use the Active Document option and select the Word document you created in Step 2. This will add the merge toolbar to your application.

5. Insert the merge codes for the fields in your template, then save the template in the same folder as *qryCustomers.doc* and the Access database.

6. In Access, write the code to perform the mail merge. Declare two module-level constants for the name of the template and the name of the query:

```
Private Const conTemplate As String = "acbMailMerge.dot"
Private Const conQuery As String = "qryCustomers"
```

7. Set a reference to the Word library by choosing Tools → References... and selecting the Word library from the list of objects, as shown in Figure 12-6.

8. Create a procedure to perform the mail merge. Here's the complete listing:

```
Public Sub MailMerge( )
    Dim strPath As String
    Dim strDataSource As String

    Dim doc As Word.Document
    Dim wrdApp As Word.Application

    On Error GoTo HandleErrors
    ' Delete the rtf file, if it already exists.
    strPath = FixPath(CurrentProject.Path)
    strDataSource = strPath & conQuery & ".doc"
    Kill strDataSource

    ' Export the data to rtf format.
    DoCmd.OutputTo acOutputQuery, conQuery, _
     acFormatRTF, strDataSource, False
```

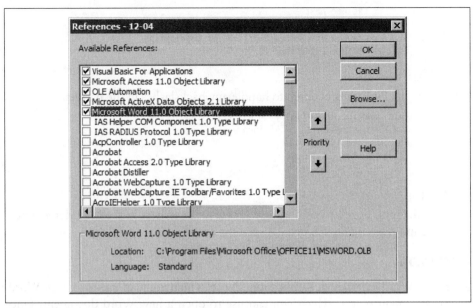

Figure 12-6. Set a reference to the Word library

```
    ' Start Word using the mail merge template.
    Set wrdApp = New Word.Application
    Set doc = wrdApp.Documents.Add(strPath & conTemplate)

    ' Do the mail merge to a new document.
    With doc.MailMerge
        .OpenDataSource Name:=strDataSource
        .Destination = wdSendToNewDocument
        .SuppressBlankLines = True
        With .DataSource
            .FirstRecord = wdDefaultFirstRecord
            .LastRecord = wdDefaultLastRecord
        End With
        If .State = wdMainAndDataSource Then
            .Execute
        End If
    End With

    ' Display the mail merge document.
    wrdApp.Visible = True

ExitHere:
    Set doc = Nothing
    Set wrdApp = Nothing
    Exit Sub

HandleErrors:
    Select Case Err.Number
        Case 53          ' File not found.
```

```
            Resume Next
        Case Else
            MsgBox Err.Number & ": " & Err.Description
            Resume ExitHere
    End Select
End Sub
```

9. Create the FixPath procedure to handle any backslashes in the pathname:

```
Private Function FixPath(strPath As String) As String
    If Right(strPath, 1) = "\" Then
        FixPath = strPath
    Else
        FixPath = strPath & "\"
    End If
End Function
```

10. Test the procedure by positioning your cursor anywhere in the MailMerge proce-
    dure and pressing the F5 key.

Discussion

Microsoft Word exposes an Application object, which you can use to launch Word,
and a Document object, which you can use to open a new Word document. Once
you've launched Word, you can use all its capabilities from your Access application.
The following sections outline the steps involved in communicating with Word via
Automation.

Starting the connection with Word for Windows

To be able to work with Word from Access, you must create an object variable to
refer to the Word Application object. You also need a Document variable to work
with a specific Word document. The following code fragment defines these variables:

```
Dim doc As Word.Document
Dim wrdApp As Word.Application
```

The next step is to delete any previously existing data source documents:

```
strPath = FixPath(CurrentProject.Path)
Kill strPath & conQuery & ".doc"
```

If the document doesn't exist, the error handler will simply resume on the next statement and create a new document containing the data from the query using the OutputTo method of the DoCmd object:

```
DoCmd.OutputTo acOutputQuery, conQuery, _
  acFormatRTF, strPath & conQuery & ".doc", False
```

Performing the mail merge

To launch Word and create a new document based on the mail merge template, set
the Application object to a new instance of Word.Application. Set the Document

object to create a new document using the Application's Add method, basing it on your template:

```
Set wrdApp = New Word.Application
Set doc = wrdApp.Documents.Add(strPath & conTemplate)
```

Once the document is open, use the Document object's MailMerge method to merge the data to a new document:

```
With doc.MailMerge
    .OpenDataSource Name:=strDataSource
    .Destination = wdSendToNewDocument
    .SuppressBlankLines = True
    With .DataSource
        .FirstRecord = wdDefaultFirstRecord
        .LastRecord = wdDefaultLastRecord
    End With
    If .State = wdMainAndDataSource Then
        .Execute
    End If
End With
```

In Access 2002 and later you must use the .OpenDataSource method in your code, but this isn't required in Access 2000.

Finishing the mail merge

To display the Word documents, set the Application object's Visible property to True:

```
wrdApp.Visible = True
```

Once the Word document is displayed, clean up by setting the Word object variables to Nothing. This frees up the memory and system resources:

```
Set doc = Nothing
Set wrdApp = Nothing
```

You'll see both the new document, named Document1 (based on the template), and the actual merge documents. You can save the merge documents or print them from Word.

12.5 Add an Item to the Startup Group

Problem

As part of your application, you would like to be able to allow users to add an application to the Startup menu so that your application will start up when Windows does. You just can't figure out how to put the information into the Startup group. Is there a way to communicate between Access and the Windows shell so you can do this?

Solution

This is a case where the old technology called DDE comes in handy. The Windows shell accepts commands using DDE that allow you to create and delete groups and items. You can also retrieve lists of existing groups and items within those groups. This solution explains most of the Windows shell's DDE interface.

To test out the DDE interface, load and run the form frmShell from *12-05.MDB*. This form, shown in Figure 12-7, allows you to view groups and their items, create and delete groups and items, and display a particular group. It will decide whether to use the group/item or the folder/shortcut terminology after determining whether you are using the Windows 9x shell or the Windows NT/Windows 2000 Program Manager, respectively.

 You'll find several references to Program Manager and PROGMAN throughout this solution, as well as the use of the group/item notation rather than folder/shortcut, but the effect is the same either way: you can create groups and items in the Program Manager or in the Windows shell, depending on your environment.

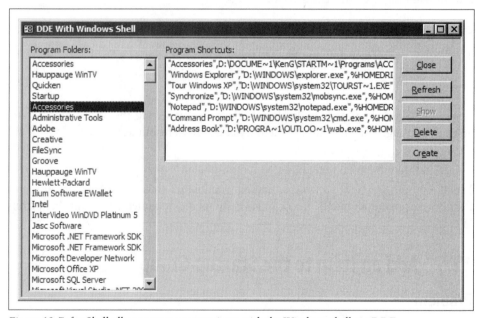

Figure 12-7. frmShell allows you to communicate with the Windows shell via DDE

Once you select a group from the list on the left in Figure 12-7, the form will display the group's items in the list on the right. If you select the first item in the righthand list—the group itself—the form will display the information Windows stored about that group. Once you've selected a group in the righthand list box, you can click the Show button to have Windows display that group. The code attached to the Show button requests Windows to open the group window using style 3 (see Table 12-8 for a list of window styles). As described later, in the sidebar Switching Focus," Windows may grab the focus, depending on the previous state of the group window you've selected.

> The shell DDE interface does not support long filenames, and attempts to enter long filenames will fail with an error. The example form displays long filenames using the 8.3 short version of the name—usually six characters, followed by a "~1" (or a higher digit).

Select an item in the group (any row except the first in the righthand list box), and the form will display all the information that Windows stores about that item. Figure 12-8 shows frmShell with an item selected.

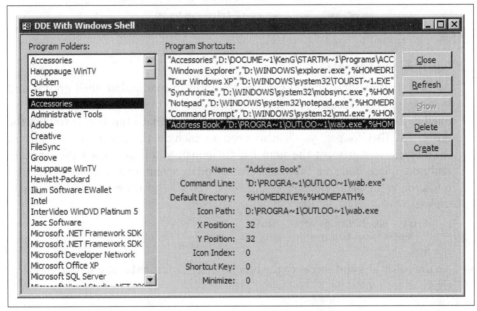

Figure 12-8. frmShell with a group selected and its information displayed

With either a group or an item selected, you can create or delete a group or an item. If you've selected a group, pressing the Delete button will instruct Windows to delete that group; if you've selected an item, Windows will delete that item. Regardless of what's selected, pressing the Create button will pop up a dialog asking whether you want to create a new item or a new group. Either choice will pop up the appropriate dialog requesting the necessary information.

The following sections describe how to use the sample forms in your own applications, and then explain most of the DDE interface to the Windows shell. Although more DDE options are available, the most useful tasks can be accomplished with the tools provided here.

Using the sample forms

To include the sample forms from *12-05.MDB* in your own applications, follow these steps:

1. Import the objects shown in Table 12-3 into your application.

Table 12-3. Objects to import from 12-05.MDB

Object	Name	Purpose
Form	frmNew	Choose new group or new item.
Form	frmNewGroup	Enter new group information.
Form	frmNewItem	Enter new item information.
Form	frmShell	Main form.
Module	basShell	Perform DDE conversations with Windows shell.
Module	basSortArray	Sort arrays (list of program groups).
Module	basToken	Pull apart strings (item and group information on frmShell).

2. Load and run frmShell.

   As described previously, you can use the form to manipulate shell groups and items from your Access application. If you want to use only some parts of frmShell in your application instead of the whole thing, that's fine too. If you use the group list (lstGroups), you'll also need to include the function that fills it, FillGroups. If you want the item list (lstItems), you'll also need FillItems. In addition, place code in lstGroup's AfterUpdate event that requeries lstItems once you've made a selection in lstGroups. You'll end up with an event procedure like this:

   ```
   Private Sub lstGroups_AfterUpdate ( )
       Me.lstItems.Requery
   End Sub
   ```

   To use other bits and pieces of the functionality of frmShell, you'll need to investigate its form module.

Using DDE with the Windows shell

If your main interest is simply to use DDE to control the Windows shell, follow these steps:

1. Import the module basShell from *12-05.MDB* into your own application. This module is completely self-contained and includes a number of functions that will set up the DDE conversation, do the work or retrieve the information you need, and then terminate the conversation. Because we've hidden all the details of the DDE, you needn't worry about getting all the syntax and parameters correct.

2. Depending on your needs, call one or more of the wrapper procedures described in Table 12-4. All of these functions are covered in detail in Section 12.4.3 (see Table 12-9).

Table 12-4. Procedures in basShell to aid in using DDE between Access and Windows shell

Procedure	Purpose
acbPMCreateGroup	Create a group, given a group name and a pathname for the group file.
acbPMCreateItem	Create a new item, given the group name, the item name, the command line, the default directory, and whether or not to run the application minimized.
acbPMDeleteGroup	Delete a group, given the name of the group to delete.
acbPMDeleteItem	Delete an item from a group, given the name of the group and the name of the item.
acbPMGetGroups	Fill a dynamic array with all the groups.
acbPMGetItems	Fill a dynamic array with all the items for a particular group.
acbPMShowGroup	Show a particular group, given the name of the group and the window mode to use.
acbPMShowMessages	Allow callers outside this module to show or hide messages. Pass in True to show messages, False to hide them (no DDE involved).

Discussion

The Windows shell supports two operations: you can either request information using the DDERequest function (Table 12-5 lists the DDERequest items) or execute actions using the DDEExecute subroutine (Table 12-6 lists the most useful subset of the shell's DDEExecute command-string interface). DDE conversations between Access and the shell involve three steps:

1. Initiate the conversation.
2. Perform the necessary tasks.
3. Terminate the conversation.

Retrieving information from the Windows shell

Table 12-5 describes the two groups of information you can request from Windows. The sample form, frmShell, uses both to fill its two list boxes.

Table 12-5. DDERequest topics for the Windows shell

To retrieve	Program	Topic	Item	Returns
List of groups	PROGMAN, or Folders	PROGMAN, or App-Properties	PROGMAN	List of existing groups, separated with CR/LF pair
List of items in a group	PROGMAN, or Folders	PROGMAN, or App-Properties	<Group Name>	List of items in the specified group, separated with CR/LF pair

To retrieve a list of groups from Windows using the Access DDERequest function, you must first initiate a conversation with the PROGMAN program on the PROGMAN topic, requesting information on the PROGMAN item; even if you use the undocumented "Folders" program name and "AppProperties" topic, it still expects you to request information on the PROGMAN item. The DDERequest call returns a carriage-return/line-feed (CR/LF) delimited string of group names. It's up to your code to pull apart the list of groups and place them into whatever data structure is most convenient for you. To simplify this task, you can use the acbPMGetGroups function in basShell. It accepts, as a parameter, a dynamic array to fill in with the list of groups. This function performs the DDERequest for you and calls the private CopyToArray function to break apart the returned stream of groups and fill the array you've sent it. It returns the number of items in the array. Its source code is:

```
Public Function acbPMGetGroups(avarGroups( ) As Variant)

    ' Fill a dynamic array with all the Program Manager groups.

    Dim lngChannel As Long
    Dim strGroups As String
    Dim intCount As Integer

    On Error GoTo HandleErr
    ' Most replacement shells will start PROGMAN for you if you attempt
    ' to start up a DDE conversation with it. That is, you won't need
    ' to Shell( ) PROGMAN if you're using a replacement shell.
    lngChannel = DDEInitiate("PROGMAN", "PROGMAN")
    strGroups = DDERequest(lngChannel, "PROGMAN")
    intCount = CopyToArray(strGroups, avarGroups( ))

ExitHere:
    acbPMGetGroups = intCount
    On Error Resume Next
    DDETerminate lngChannel
    Err.Clear
    Exit Function

HandleErr:
    MsgBox Err.Number & ": " & Err.Description, , "acbGetProgmanItems"
    Resume ExitHere
End Function
```

To call this function from your own code, use code like this:

```
Dim avarGroups( ) as Variant
Dim intCount as Integer

intCount = acbPMGetGroups(avarGroups( ))
' If you want the list sorted, call acbSortArray, in basSortArray.
acbSortArray avarGroups( )
```

To retrieve a list of items within a selected group, use the acbPMGetItems function, which works almost exactly as acbPMGetGroups does. This time, however, pass in a group name along with the dynamic array to be filled in; the function uses the group name as the topic, instead of PROGMAN (see Table 12-5). It calls the CopyToArray function to move the items into the dynamic array. You generally won't sort the array, however, unless you store the first item; this first item returns information about the group window itself. The rest of the rows contain information about the individual items. To use acbPMGetItems, you might use code like this:

```
Dim avarGroups( ) as Variant
Dim avarItems( ) as Variant
Dim intCount as Integer

intCount = acbPMGetGroups(avarGroups( ))
intCount = acbPMGetItems(avarGroups(0), avarItems( ))
' List all the item information for the specified group.
For intI = 0 To intCount - 1
    Debug.Print avarItems(intI)
Next intI
```

Executing tasks

The Windows shell includes a command-string interface, which you can access via DDE, that allows you to execute tasks involving groups and items within those groups. Table 12-6 lists the functions addressed in this solution. Other commands are available (they're documented in the Windows SDK documentation), but they're not as useful for Access programmers.

Table 12-6. DDEExecute commands for the Windows shell

Function	Parameters	Comments
AddItem	See Table 12-7	Uses *CreateGroup* first to select the group.
CreateGroup	GroupName[, GroupPath]	Selects the group if it exists; otherwise, creates it.
DeleteGroup	GroupName	
DeleteItem	ItemName	Uses *CreateGroup* first to select the group.
ShowGroup	GroupName, ShowCommand	See Table 12-8 for *ShowCommand* values.

In each case, you use the Access DDEExecute procedure to communicate with the shell. You must construct a string containing the function name, parentheses, and any arguments for the function. For example, to create a group from within Access, you can use code like this:

```
Dim intChannel as Integer
intChannel = DDEInitiate("PROGMAN", "PROGMAN")
DDEExecute intChannel, "[CreateGroup(My Group, MYGROUP.GRP)]"
```

The command string must be surrounded by square bracket delimiters ([]). Luckily, the Windows shell is far more relaxed about the use of embedded quotes than almost any other DDE-enabled application. For example, WinFax Pro's implementation of DDE requires quotes embedded in command strings you send to it; the Windows shell accepts embedded quotes but doesn't require them.

Some functions, such as AddItem, allow quite a few parameters, almost all of which can be left blank (see Table 12-7). To use the AddItem command to add a new item, you must first select a group in which to add the item. To do this, use the Create-Group command, which creates a group if necessary or selects it if it already exists. The only required AddItem parameter is the command line. Note that both X- and Y-coordinates are necessary if you choose to specify coordinates for the icon. For example, to create a new icon to run *C:\EDIT\MYEDIT.EXE* with the description My Editor minimized in the My New Group group, use code like this (you'd normally include error-handling code, too):

```
Dim intChan As Integer
intChan = DDEInitiate("PROGMAN", "PROGMAN")
' First select the group (or create it).
DDEExecute intChan, "[CreateGroup(My New Group)]"
' Use commas to delimit parameters (even missing ones).
DDEExecute intChan, "[AddItem(C:\EDIT\MYEDIT,My Editor,,,,,,1)]"
```

Table 12-7. Parameters for the AddItem function

Parameter	Required?	Used in sample?	Description
CmdLine	Yes	Yes	Command line to run the application. Must be at least the executable filename, but can also include parameters as necessary.
Name	No	Yes	Name that appears below the icon in the group.
IconPath	No	No	Name and path of the icon file to use. If an executable file is specified, use the first icon in that file. If left blank, use the first icon in the executable file specified in the CmdLine parameter.
IconIndex	No	No	Index of the icon in the specified IconPath file (or the specified executable). Otherwise, if missing, use the first icon specified.
Xpos	No	No	X-position of the icon within the group, as an integer. Both this and Ypos are required to set the specific position. If left blank, use the next available position.
Ypos	No	No	Y-position of the icon within the group, as an integer.
DefDir	No	Yes	Default (or working) directory for the application.
HotKey	No	No	Hot key for this application, stored as an integer.
fMinimize	No	Yes	Run Minimized (1 = True, 0 = False).
fSeparateMemSpace	No	No	In Windows NT only, run the application in a separate memory space (applies to 16-bit applications only).

Switching Focus

Using the ShowGroup command sometimes moves the focus to the shell but usually does not. Whether the focus switches depends on the state you request for the program group and on its current state. Though you could make a matrix of options, comparing current states (minimized, normal, or maximized) against the new window state (1-8, as in Table 12-8), the rules are quite simple. If you change the state of a group that's currently minimized, the focus will switch to the shell. That means that if you choose actions 1, 3, or 4 for a group that is currently minimized, the shell will grab the focus. You can try this yourself, calling the acbPMShowGroup function and passing it the name of a group and a new window style.

Table 12-8. Window style command values for the ShowGroup function

Window style value	Action
1	Activate and display the group window. If it was minimized or maximized, restore it to its original position (normalized).
2	Activate the group window and display it as an icon.
3	Activate the group window and display it maximized.
4	Display the group window normalized and leave the current group selected.
5	Activate the group window and display it in its current placement.
6	Minimize the group window.
7	Minimize the group window and leave the current group selected.
8	Display the group window in its current placement and leave the current group selected.

Using the wrapper procedures

To make your DDE programming simpler, the module basShell includes wrapper procedures that handle all the details for you. (Table 12-4 provides a description of each of the wrapper procedures; Table 12-9 lists the parameters.) The module also provides functions that handle each of the commands described in Table 12-6. In some cases (AddItem, for example), the wrapper functions don't allow you to specify all the possible parameters for the command string. If you find these wrapper functions too limiting, you can modify them so they allow you to pass in whatever parameters you like.

All the wrapper procedures (except acbPMShowMessages) in Table 12-9 perform the same set of steps to communicate with the Windows shell. To simplify the code and centralize error handling, those steps have been pulled into a single private procedure in basShell, DDEExecutePM, which is shown in the following code example:

```
Private Function DDEExecutePM(strCommand As String) As Boolean
```

```
' DDEExecute with the passed-in command. If it succeeds,
' return True. If it fails, return False.

' At this point, this function handles error messages itself.
' You could move this out of here to a higher level, if you
' want, by setting the SHOW_MESSAGES constant to False.

Dim lngChannel As Long

On Error GoTo HandleErr

lngChannel = DDEInitiate("PROGMAN", "PROGMAN")
DDEExecute lngChannel, strCommand
DDEExecutePM = True

ExitHere:
    On Error Resume Next
    DDETerminate lngChannel
    Err.Clear
    Exit Function

HandleErr:
    If Not mfHideMessages Then
        MsgBox Err.Number & ": " & Err.Description, , "DDEExecutePM"
    End If
    DDEExecutePM = False
    Resume ExitHere
End Function
```

Given a string to execute, this code initiates the DDE channel, uses DDEExecute to execute the command, and then terminates the connection. If all goes according to plan, the procedure returns a True value. If an error occurs, it displays a message box (unless you've used the acbPMShowMessages procedure to disable warning messages) and then returns False.

Table 12-9 lists the parameters for the wrapper procedures in basShell. Each of these procedures (except acbPMShowMessages) returns True if the function succeeded, or False if it failed. Unless you've called the acbPMShowMessages subroutine to disable messages, a message will appear before deleting a group or item or if any error occurs.

Table 12-9. Parameters for the wrapper procedures in basShell

Procedure	Parameter	Data type	Parameter description
acbPMCreateGroup	varName	Variant	Name of the new group.
	varGroupPath	Variant	Name of the group file (can be Null, in which case Windows uses a name of its own choosing).
acbPMCreateItem	varGroup	Variant	Name of the group in which to create the new item.

Table 12-9. Parameters for the wrapper procedures in basShell (continued)

Procedure	Parameter	Data type	Parameter description
	`varName`	Variant	Descriptive name for the new item; appears under the icon.
	`varCommandLine`	Variant	Command line to execute when this icon is chosen. Cannot be Null.
	`varDirectory`	Variant	Default (working) directory when the application starts up.
	`varMinimized`	Variant	Logical value: run the app minimized?
acbPMDeleteGroup	`varName`	Variant	Group to delete.
acbPMDeleteItem	`varGroup`	Variant	Group from which to delete the item.
	`varName`	Variant	Name of the item to delete.
acbPMShowGroup	`varName`	Variant	Name of the group to show.
	`intMode`	Integer	Window mode, as listed in Table 12-8.
acbPMShowMessages	`fShow`	Integer	Logical value: display messages during DDE wrapper functions? If True, functions use message box if errors occur and when deleting items. This subroutine sets a module global variable, so you need to call it only once per session.

For example, to use the wrapper functions to add an icon to the My Group group that will run *C:\EDIT\MYEDIT.EXE* minimized with the description My Editor (as in the example that called `AddItem` directly), you could use code like this:

```
Dim fSuccess As Boolean

' Disable error messages.
acbPMShowMessages False
fSuccess = acbPMCreateItem("My Group", "My Editor", _
  "C:\EDIT\MYEDIT.EXE", Null, True)
If Not fSuccess Then MsgBox "Unable to create new item!"
```

This example also calls `acbPMShowMessages` to disable error messages from within `acbCreateItem`, so the code fragment itself can handle them.

For examples of each of the wrapper functions, check out the code in frmShell's module.

Comments

Though this solution covers a great deal more than the original question required, all the information here will be useful to Access programmers working with the DDE interface to the Windows shell.

The sample form, frmShell, is not only a good example of using DDE to converse with Windows, it's also a useful tool on its own. Because it allows you to see what's in each group without having to open and close each group's window, it's a quick and easy way to clean out your groups. Of course, some extra work would be required for it to be a really useful tool, but it's a good start.

In 16-bit applications, DDEInitiate returns a short integer (16-bit) handle. In Access 95 and later (and other 32-bit applications), this function returns a long integer (32-bit) handle. If you have existing code that uses DDE, you'll want to convert the variables containing the return values into long integers.

The Windows shell has an undocumented DDE application → topic pair that is not supported by the original Program Manager or any of the major third-party shell substitutes: Folders → AppProperties. This syntax seems to be just an alias for the regularly documented DDE interface, because the item name syntax and all the operations are identical in both cases.

This undocumented syntax can be of some benefit. If you are going to add the functionality to interact with the shell, you can use code like the following to determine if your user is running the Windows 9x shell:

```
Public Function acbNewShell ( ) as Boolean
    Dim lngChannel as Long
    On Error Resume Next
    lngChannel = DDEInitiate("Folders","AppProperties")
    acbNewShell = (lngChannel <> 0)
    DDETerminate lngChannel
End Function
```

You'll notice that the example uses this function (as well as a public flag) to decide whether to call the various shell objects "groups" and "items" (as in the Windows NT Program Manager) or "folders" and "shortcuts" (as in the Windows 9x shell).

To shield you from the details of the DDE conversation and to isolate the DDE code in one routine, each of the command-string replacement functions calls the DDEExecutePM function. This makes the code neat and easy to understand, but it does have a potential disadvantage: calling DDEInitiate and DDETerminate every time you call a wrapper function adds substantial time and overhead to your application. If you make many calls to Window via DDE, you'll want to reconsider this design. For most applications, though, this shouldn't be a problem.

12.6   Send Access Data to Excel and Create an Excel Chart

Problem

You want to export data from Access to Excel and create a chart programmatically.

Solution

You can use an ADO Recordset object to export data to Excel programmatically, then use Automation with Excel to create a chart based on the exported data.

Load and run frmExcel from *12-06.MDB*. This form calls out to Excel, passing in the values from a recordset to create an Excel spreadsheet and chart based on sales data from the Northwind sample database (see Figure 12-9).

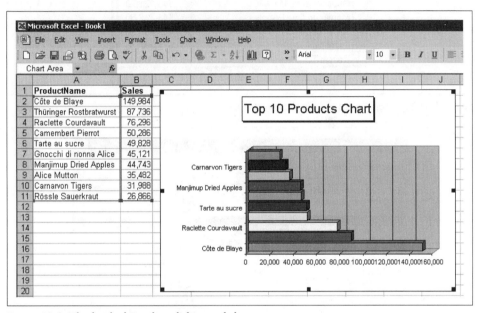

Figure 12-9. The finished Excel worksheet and chart

Here's how you can create Excel charts in your own Access applications:

1. Create the query that will hold your data. In the sample database, you'll find qryTopTenProducts, which calculates the top 10 products by dollar amount sold. There are two columns: the product name and the total dollar amount. The datasheet view of the query is shown in Figure 12-10.

2. Set a reference in your project to the Microsoft Excel object library and the ADO library, as shown in Figure 12-11.

3. Create the procedure that exports the data to Excel and creates a sample chart. Here's the complete listing:

```
Private Const conQuery = "qryTopTenProducts"
Private Const conSheetName = "Top 10 Products"

Public Sub CreateExcelChart( )

    Dim rst As ADODB.Recordset
```

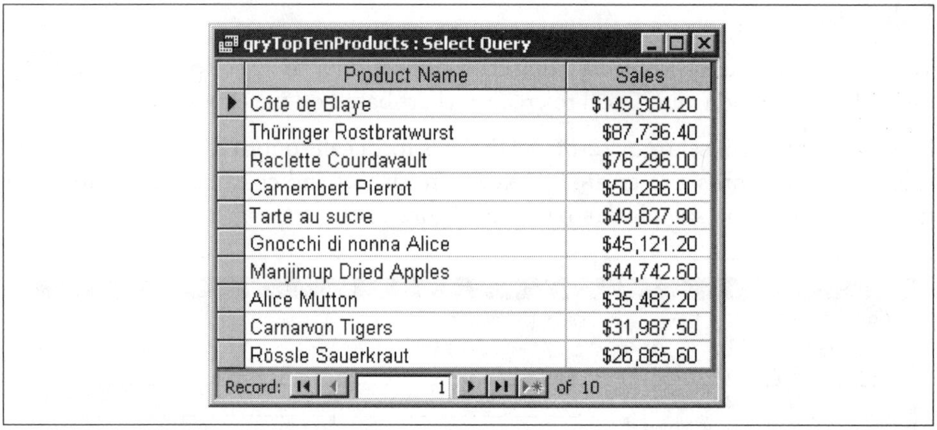

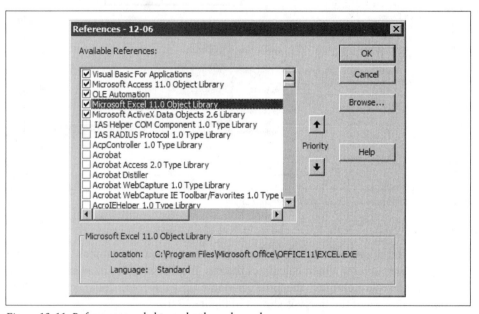

Figure 12-10. qryTopTenProducts in datasheet view

Figure 12-11. References needed to make the code work

```
' Excel object variables
Dim xlApp As Excel.Application
Dim xlBook As Excel.Workbook
Dim xlSheet As Excel.Worksheet
Dim xlChart As Excel.Chart

Dim i As Integer

On Error GoTo HandleErr

' Create Excel Application object.
```

```
Set xlApp = New Excel.Application

' Create a new workbook.
Set xlBook = xlApp.Workbooks.Add

' Get rid of all but one worksheet.
xlApp.DisplayAlerts = False
For i = xlBook.Worksheets.Count To 2 Step -1
    xlBook.Worksheets(i).Delete
Next i
xlApp.DisplayAlerts = True

' Capture reference to first worksheet.
Set xlSheet = xlBook.ActiveSheet

' Change the worksheet name.
xlSheet.Name = conSheetName

' Create recordset.
Set rst = New ADODB.Recordset
rst.Open _
 Source:=conQuery, _
 ActiveConnection:=CurrentProject.Connection

With xlSheet
    ' Copy field names to Excel.
    ' Bold the column headings.
    With .Cells(1, 1)
        .Value = rst.Fields(0).Name
        .Font.Bold = True
    End With
    With .Cells(1, 2)
        .Value = rst.Fields(1).Name
        .Font.Bold = True
    End With

    ' Copy all the data from the recordset
    ' into the spreadsheet.
    .Range("A2").CopyFromRecordset rst

    ' Format the data.
    .Columns(1).AutoFit
    With .Columns(2)
        .NumberFormat = "#,##0"
        .AutoFit
    End With
End With

' Create the chart.
Set xlChart = xlApp.Charts.Add
With xlChart
    .ChartType = xl3DBarClustered
    .SetSourceData xlSheet.Cells(1, 1).CurrentRegion
    .PlotBy = xlColumns
```

```
            .Location _
                Where:=xlLocationAsObject, _
                Name:=conSheetName
        End With

        ' Setting the location loses the reference, so you
        ' must retrieve a new reference to the chart.
        With xlBook.ActiveChart
            .HasTitle = True
            .HasLegend = False
            With .ChartTitle
                .Characters.Text = conSheetName & " Chart"
                .Font.Size = 16
                .Shadow = True
                .Border.LineStyle = xlSolid
            End With
            With .ChartGroups(1)
                .GapWidth = 20
                .VaryByCategories = True
            End With
            .Axes(xlCategory).TickLabels.Font.Size = 8
            .Axes(xlCategoryScale).TickLabels.Font.Size = 8
        End With

        ' Display the Excel chart.
        xlApp.Visible = True

ExitHere:
        On Error Resume Next
        ' Clean up.
        rst.Close
        Set rst = Nothing
        Set xlSheet = Nothing
        Set xlBook = Nothing
        Set xlApp = Nothing
        Exit Sub

HandleErr:
        MsgBox Err & ": " & Err.Description, , "Error in CreateExcelChart"
        Resume ExitHere
End Sub
```

Discussion

Two constants are declared in this procedure—one for the name of the query used to export data, and one for the name of the worksheet in Excel:

```
Private Const conQuery = "qryTopTenProducts"
Private Const conSheetName = "Top 10 Products"
```

You need to declare an ADO Recordset variable as well as Excel Application, Workbook, Worksheet, and Chart object variables:

```
Dim rst As ADODB.Recordset
```

```
' Excel object variables
Dim xlApp As Excel.Application
Dim xlBook As Excel.Workbook
Dim xlSheet As Excel.Worksheet
Dim xlChart As Excel.Chart

Dim i As Integer
```

The Application object variable is needed to launch Excel; the Workbook variable is needed to create a new workbook; the Worksheet variable is needed to work with the worksheet when exporting the data; and the Chart variable is needed for creating and manipulating the chart.

The first section of code launches Excel, creates a new workbook, removes all but one worksheet, and renames the worksheet:

```
Set xlApp = New Excel.Application
Set xlBook = xlApp.Workbooks.Add
xlApp.DisplayAlerts = False
For i = xlBook.Worksheets.Count To 2 Step -1
    xlBook.Worksheets(i).Delete
Next i
xlApp.DisplayAlerts = True
Set xlSheet = xlBook.ActiveSheet
xlSheet.Name = conSheetName
```

Next, the ADO recordset is created based on the saved query:

```
Set rst = New ADODB.Recordset
rst.Open _
 Source:=conQuery, _
 ActiveConnection:=CurrentProject.Connection
```

Once the recordset is opened, the field names are copied into the Excel worksheet and formatted:

```
With xlSheet
    With .Cells(1, 1)
        .Value = rst.Fields(0).Name
        .Font.Bold = True
    End With
    With .Cells(1, 2)
        .Value = rst.Fields(1).Name
        .Font.Bold = True
    End With
```

Only a single line of code is needed to copy the data from the ADO recordset to the Excel worksheet:

```
.Range("A2").CopyFromRecordset rst
```

Next, the columns are formatted one at a time, using Autofit to size the rows to the widest entry, and assigning a number format to the second column:

```
    .Columns(1).AutoFit
    With .Columns(2)
```

```
        .NumberFormat = "#,##0"
        .AutoFit
    End With
End With
```

The chart is then created and formatted using the Chart object:

```
Set xlChart = xlApp.Charts.Add
With xlChart
    .ChartType = xl3DBarClustered
    .SetSourceData xlSheet.Cells(1, 1).CurrentRegion
    .PlotBy = xlColumns
    .Location _
    Where:=xlLocationAsObject, _
    Name:=conSheetName
End With
```

Setting the location loses the references, so you must retrieve a new reference to the Chart object. The chart is then formatted using the methods and properties of the Chart object:

```
With xlBook.ActiveChart
    .HasTitle = True
    .HasLegend = False
    With .ChartTitle
        .Characters.Text = conSheetName & " Chart"
        .Font.Size = 16
        .Shadow = True
        .Border.LineStyle = xlSolid
    End With
    With .ChartGroups(1)
        .GapWidth = 20
        .VaryByCategories = True
    End With
    .Axes(xlCategory).TickLabels.Font.Size = 8
    .Axes(xlCategoryScale).TickLabels.Font.Size = 8
End With
```

The worksheet and chart are then displayed by setting the Application object's Visible property to True:

```
xlApp.Visible = True
```

Finally, the cleanup code runs, shutting down all the objects that have been used and reclaiming memory:

```
rst.Close
Set rst = Nothing
Set xlSheet = Nothing
Set xlBook = Nothing
Set xlApp = Nothing
```

The examples shown here barely scratch the surface of the capabilities of Excel Automation. Excel has a complex object model that is very easy to get lost in!

If you can't figure out the proper syntax for working with an Excel Automation object, launch Excel and choose Tools → Macro → Record new macro from the menu, then record the actions that you are having problems with. Once you stop the macro recorder, you can examine the code that was created by pressing Alt-F11 and expanding the Modules node. You may then be able to figure out how to plug the code into your Access code.

12.7 Create a PowerPoint Presentation from Access Data

Problem

You need to create similar Microsoft PowerPoint presentations over and over. You currently take an existing presentation, copy it to a new location, and modify it as necessary, resulting in a number of copies of the same text littering your hard disk. It seems that you could just store all the text and its formatting information in an Access table and then create the presentation programmatically when necessary. Then, you could choose just the slides you need, make modifications as necessary, and have only one place where you store the data. Is this possible?

Solution

Microsoft PowerPoint (part of Microsoft Office) offers an amazingly rich set of objects, methods, and properties. Even though it's not a developer's tool, its object model is spectacularly deep, especially in comparison to Access's. It appears that you can do anything programmatically from an Automation client (such as Access) that you can do manually, using PowerPoint as an Automation server—so the answer to the original question is "Yes!" You can definitely create presentations programmatically from Access using tables to store all the information about your presentation.

This solution involves two major activities: setting up the data in tables and using the interface to create your presentation. This section demonstrates both activities.

To try out the sample application, load and run frmPowerPoint from *12-07.MDB*. First choose a template from the combo box's list of templates; then enter a filename to which to save your presentation (click on the "..." button to use the common File Open/Save dialog). Click the Create Presentation button to start PowerPoint and create the presentation. Figure 12-12 shows the sample form in action.

To use this technique to create your own presentations, follow these steps:

1. Import from *12-07.MDB* the tblParagraphs, tblSlides, tlkpLayouts, and tlkpOptions tables.

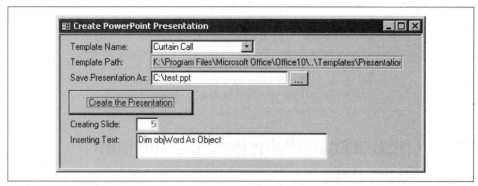

Figure 12-12. Use frmPowerPoint to create PowerPoint presentations from within Access

2. Import the frmPowerPoint, zfrmParagraphs, and zsfrmSlides forms (the last two are for setting up your slides only and are not part of the sample's user interface).

3. Import the basCommonFile, basGetTemplate, basPowerPoint, and basRegistry modules.

4. Open one of the modules in design mode and choose the Tools → References... menu item. For the code to work, your database must include an explicit reference to the DAO and PowerPoint type libraries. Find the options labeled Microsoft DAO Type Library and PowerPoint Object Library (select the most current version of each product), and make sure they're both checked. Figure 12-13 shows the References dialog as it might appear on your machine once you've found and selected the references.

5. Open the basGetTemplate module. Modify the first constant (conTemplates) so that it reflects the version of PowerPoint you have installed. The sample is configured for Office 2003; if you're using Office XP, change the "11.0" in the string to "10.0"; if using Office 2000, change it to "9.0".

 You can skip Steps 1 through 5 if you want to use *12-07.MDB* as it is.

6. Plan your presentation carefully. You may want to play around in PowerPoint for a while, browsing the slide layouts, before you begin adding data to tables. Or you may want to take an existing presentation and enter it into Access (this is how we originally created this example set of data).

7. Delete all the rows from tblSlides and tblParagraphs, the two tables containing the presentation information (you may want to make copies of the originals first, in case you need to refer back to them). Leave the two tables whose names start

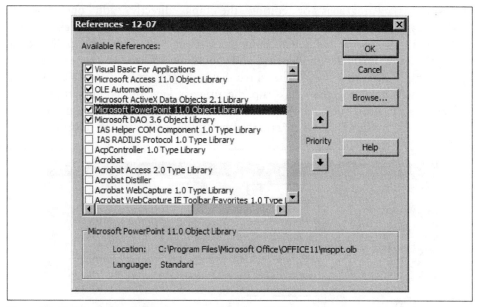

Figure 12-13. Use the Tools > References... dialog to add library references

with "tlkp" alone: these tables are necessary for the application to run and contain information about enumerations provided by the PowerPoint object model.

8. Using zsfrmSlides or editing the table directly, add one row to tblSlides for each slide in your presentation. The SlideNumber field is used for sorting the slides in the presentation (you can enter them in the table in any order you like, but make sure the SlideNumber field reflects the desired output order). The SlideLayout field tells PowerPoint which of its layouts you want to use for the slide: choose its value from the combo box, which pulls its values from tlkpLayouts. It may take some experimentation to find the layout you want. The Include field tells the application whether or not to create a slide in PowerPoint; this way, you can create all your slides in Access but export only selected slides to PowerPoint. Figure 12-14 shows zsfrmSlides gathering slide information.

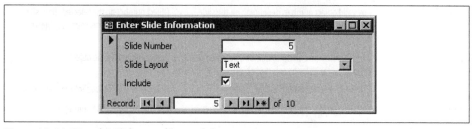

Figure 12-14. Use zfrmSlides to add new slides to your presentation

9. Using `zsfrmParagraphs` or editing the table directly, add one row to `tblParagraphs` for each paragraph on each slide in your presentation. Table 12-10 lists the fields with comments about each. This table is linked to `tblSlides` on the SlideNumber field and should include one row for each output paragraph that you need. The three fields, `SlideNumber`, `ObjectNumber`, and `ParagraphNumber`, together make up the primary key; the combination of the three must be unique (none of these fields can be left blank for a given paragraph). Figure 12-15 shows `zsfrmParagraphs` gathering paragraph information.

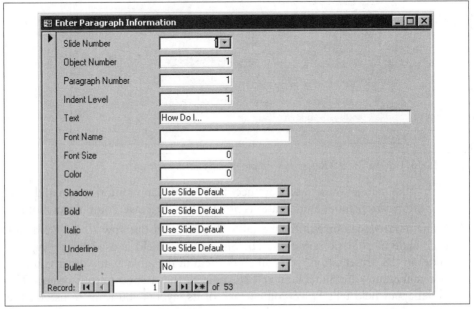

Figure 12-15. Use zsfrmParagraphs to add or edit paragraph text and properties

Table 12-10. Field values allowed in tblParagraphs

Field	Values	Description
SlideNumber	Any valid slide number.	Slide number for this paragraph.
ObjectNumber	Any valid object number, depending on the slide layout. This example app does not support adding new objects.	Object number on the selected slide. All text boxes and other items count as objects.
ParagraphNumber	A contiguous, incrementing number, based on previous paragraphs in the selected object.	Paragraph within the object.
IndentLevel	An integer between 1 (no indent) and 5.	Number of levels to indent this paragraph.
Text	Any text, up to a reasonable length (six or seven words).	Text for the selected paragraph.
FontName	Any valid installed font. Leave blank to use the default font for the style you've selected.	Name of the font for this paragraph.

Table 12-10. Field values allowed in tblParagraphs (continued)

Field	Values	Description
FontSize	Any valid font size (1 to 127). 0 indicates that you want to use the default font size for the style you've selected	Font size for this paragraph.
Color	Numeric value representing the color you want to use for your paragraph. 0 indicates that you want to use the default color for the style you've selected.	Color for this paragraph.
Shadow	Select from Yes (-1), No (0), or Use Slide Default (1).	Shadow for this paragraph?
Bold	Select from Yes (-1), No (0), or Use Slide Default (1).	Make this paragraph bold?
Italic	Select from Yes (-1), No (0), or Use Slide Default (1).	Make this paragraph italicized?
Underline	Select from Yes (-1), No (0), or Use Slide Default (1).	Underline this paragraph?
Bullet	Select from the values provided in the lookup table, tlkpBulletTypes.	Type of bullet to use.

10. Before creating your presentation, peruse the data in tblSlides, making sure that the Include field is set the way you want it (i.e., to include or exclude each slide).

11. Using frmPowerPoint as previously described, create your presentation in PowerPoint.

Discussion

Creating the presentation boils down to four basic steps:

- Start PowerPoint (and shut it down once you're finished).
- Create the presentation.
- Loop through tblSlides, creating the slides one at a time.
- For each slide, loop through the appropriate rows of tblParagraphs, placing and formatting text.

You'll find all the necessary code in basPowerPoint in *12-07.MDB*. The following sections describe in detail how these steps work.

Starting and stopping PowerPoint

To create the presentation, you must first retrieve a reference to the PowerPoint Application object. If PowerPoint is already running, the GetObject function will be able to retrieve the object reference. If not, the code will jump to an error handler, which will try the CreateObject method. Once the procedure has created and saved the slide presentation, if the code started PowerPoint, it will try to close PowerPoint; if not, it will leave the application running. The following skeleton version of the CreatePresentation function (shown later in its entirety) handles the application startup and shutdown:

```
Public Function CreatePresentation(blnShowIt As Boolean, _
 ByVal varTemplate As Variant, varFileName As Variant)

    Dim app As PowerPoint.Application
    Dim blnAlreadyRunning As Boolean

    On Error GoTo HandleErrors

    ' Assume that PowerPoint was already running.
    blnAlreadyRunning = True

    Set app = GetObject(, "PowerPoint.Application")

    ' Do the work, creating the presentation.
    If Not blnAlreadyRunning Then
        app.Quit
    End If
    Set app = Nothing

ExitHere:
    Exit Function

HandleErrors:
    Select Case Err.Number
        Case conErrCantStart
            Set app = New PowerPoint.Application
            blnAlreadyRunning = False
            Resume Next

        ' Handle other errors...
    End Select
    Resume ExitHere
End Function
```

Creating the presentation

To create the presentation, you must add a new presentation to the application's collection of open presentations. To add a new item to the collection, use the Add method of the Presentations collection of the Application object:

```
' Get a reference to that new presentation.
Set pptPresentation = app.Presentations.Add(WithWindow:=False)
```

The Add method of the Presentations collection allows you to create the new presentation with or without a window. If you want Power-Point to be visible while it's creating the presentation, you can set this parameter to True instead of False. However, if it's set to True, the code that creates the slides runs noticeably slower, and you'll have to contend with other user-interface issues (PowerPoint will request confirmation on overwriting existing presentations when you save this one, for example). We suggest leaving this parameter set to False unless you have some overriding reason to change it.

Once you've created the presentation, the code uses the ApplyTemplate method of the new Presentation object, given the name of the template you've chosen from frmPowerPoint:

```
If Len(varTemplate & "") > 0 Then
    pptPresentation.ApplyTemplate varTemplate
End If
```

The code then calls the user-defined CreateSlides function, passing to it the new Presentation object, to create all the slides for the presentation.

This section and the previous one draw their code from the CreatePresentation function in basPowerPoint. Here's the function in its entirety:

```
Public Function CreatePresentation(blnShowIt As Boolean, _
  ByVal varTemplate As Variant, varFileName As Variant)

    ' Highest-level routine. Actually create the
    ' presentation, and set up the slides.

    Dim pptPresentation As PowerPoint.Presentation
    Dim lngResult As Long
    Dim app As PowerPoint.Application
    Dim blnAlreadyRunning As Boolean

    On Error GoTo HandleErrors

    ' Assume that PowerPoint was already running.
    blnAlreadyRunning = True

    Set app = GetObject(, "PowerPoint.Application")

    ' If the caller wants to see this happening, make the
    ' application window visible and set the focus there.
    If blnShowIt Then
        app.Visible = True
        AppActivate "Microsoft PowerPoint"
    End If

    ' Get a reference to that new presentation.
    Set pptPresentation = app.Presentations.Add(WithWindow:=False)
    If Len(varTemplate & "") > 0 Then
        pptPresentation.ApplyTemplate varTemplate
    End If

    lngResult = CreateSlides(pptPresentation)
    pptPresentation.SaveAs FileName:=varFileName
    If Not blnAlreadyRunning Then
        app.Quit
    End If
    Set app = Nothing
```

```
ExitHere:
    Exit Function

HandleErrors:
    Select Case Err.Number
        Case conErrCantStart
            Set app = New PowerPoint.Application
            blnAlreadyRunning = False
            Resume Next

        Case conErrFileInUse
            MsgBox "The output file name is in use." & vbCrLf & _
                "Switch to PowerPoint and save the file manually.", _
                vbExclamation, "Create Presentation"

        Case Else
            MsgBox "Error: " & Err.Description & " (" & Err.Number & ")", _
                vbExclamation, "Create Presentation"
    End Select
    Resume ExitHere
End Function
```

Creating each slide

Once you've created the presentation, the next step is to loop through all the rows in tblSlides, creating the slide described by each row. The code in CreateSlides, shown next, does the work. It boils down to a single line of code: you must call the Add method of the Slides collection for the current presentation to add each slide:

```
Set objSlide = obj.Slides.Add(intCount, rstSlides("SlideLayout"))
```

As you can see, you must provide the Add method with the index of the slide you're creating and the layout type for the slide. (See the table tlkpLayouts for all the possible layouts and the associated enumerated value for each.) The CreateSlides function walks through tblSlides one row at a time, creating the slide and calling the user-defined CreateSlideText function for each slide whose Include flag is set to True.

The complete source code for the CreateSlides function is:

```
Private Function CreateSlides(obj As Presentation)
    ' obj is the PowerPoint presentation object.
    ' It contains slide objects.

    Const acbcDataSource = "qrySlideInfo"

    Dim rstSlides As DAO.Recordset
    Dim db As DAO.Database
    Dim objSlide As PowerPoint.Slide

    Dim intSlide As Integer
    Dim intObject As Integer
```

```
Dim intParagraph As Integer
Dim intCount As Integer
Dim strText As String
Dim blnDone As Boolean

On Error GoTo HandleErrors

Set db = CurrentDb( )
Set rstSlides = db.OpenRecordset( _
  "Select * from tblSlides Where Include Order By SlideNumber")
blnDone = False
Do While Not rstSlides.EOF And Not blnDone
    If rstSlides("Include") Then
        intCount = intCount + 1
        ' Add the next slide.
        Set objSlide = obj.Slides. _
         Add(intCount, rstSlides("SlideLayout"))
        If Not CreateSlideText( _
         objSlide, rstSlides("SlideNumber")) Then
            blnDone = True
        End If
    End If
    rstSlides.MoveNext
Loop

ExitHere:
    If Not rstSlides Is Nothing Then
        rstSlides.Close
    End If
    Exit Function

HandleErrors:
    Select Case Err.Number
        Case Else
            MsgBox "Error: " & Err.Description & " (" & Err.Number & ")", _
            vbExclamation, "Create Slides"

    End Select
    Resume ExitHere
End Function
```

Creating the text

Creating the slide text can be broken down into these small steps:

1. Retrieve the list of pertinent paragraphs from tblParagraphs.

2. Loop through all the rows, adding a paragraph to the specified object for each.

3. Loop through the rows again, setting the formatting for each paragraph.

Why loop through the rows for each slide twice? Because of the way PowerPoint handles inserted text, you must first insert the rows, and then go back and format those rows. Otherwise, each new paragraph will "inherit" the formatting of the previous paragraph. To work around this in the simplest manner possible, the code inserts each of the paragraphs and sets the indent and bullet, then makes a second pass through the paragraphs and sets the necessary formatting. Although this may take a bit longer, it simplifies the code.

The following paragraphs describe each step from the CreateSlideText function, which is shown in its entirety later in this section.

To retrieve the list of paragraphs that apply to the current slide, CreateSlides passes the slide object and its index as arguments to CreateSlideText. Given that index, CreateSlideText can request just the paragraphs associated with that slide from tblParagraphs:

```
Set db = CurrentDb( )

' Go get the text that applies to this slide.
Set rst = db.OpenRecordset("SELECT * FROM tblParagraphs " & _
 "WHERE SlideNumber = " & intSlideNumber & _
 " ORDER BY ObjectNumber, ParagraphNumber")

Call InsertText(rst, objSlide)
```

The next step is to insert the slides, text, indents, and bullets into the presentation. The InsertText procedure takes care of this task, given a reference to the recordset and to the slide. This code retrieves various fields from the recordset (which contains information for this one slide only), inserts the text it finds in the table into the shape, and then sets the indent level and bullet type based on information from the recordset:

```
Private Sub InsertText(rst As DAO.Recordset, sld As PowerPoint.Slide)
    Dim pptShape As PowerPoint.Shape
    Dim intParagraph As Integer

    Do Until rst.EOF
    ' Insert all the paragraphs and indents, to get them right first.
    ' Then we'll go back and insert the formatting. This is required
    ' because of the way PowerPoint carries fonts forward from one
    ' paragraph to the next when inserting paragraphs.

        Set pptShape = sld.Shapes(rst("ObjectNumber"))
        pptShape.TextFrame.TextRange.InsertAfter rst("Text") & vbCrLf
        With pptShape.TextFrame.TextRange. _
         Paragraphs(rst("ParagraphNumber"))
            If Not IsNull(rst("IndentLevel")) Then
                .IndentLevel = rst("IndentLevel")
            End If
```

```
            .ParagraphFormat.Bullet.Type = rst("Bullet")
        End With
        rst.MoveNext
    Loop
End Sub
```

Next, the code in CreateSlideText moves back to the beginning of the recordset and begins a loop that updates the formatting for each paragraph on the slide. For each row in the recordset, CreateSlideText retrieves a reference to the necessary slide object. Each object on the slide that can contain text is numbered, and the recordset contains an index (intObject) indicating which object you want to place your text into. If the value of the index in the recordset does not equal the current object index on the slide, the code retrieves a reference to the correct shape on the slide:

```
If intObject <> rst("ObjectNumber") Then
    intObject = rst("ObjectNumber")
    Set pptShape = objSlide.Shapes(intObject)
End If
```

The code then retrieves a reference to the correct paragraph so that it can work with the various properties of that paragraph:

```
Set pptTextRange = pptShape.TextFrame.TextRange. _
 Paragraphs(rst("ParagraphNumber"))
```

Next, CreateSlideText sets the formatting properties corresponding to each field in tblParagraphs:

```
With pptTextRange.Font
    If Not IsNull(rst("FontName")) Then
        .Name = rst("FontName")
    End If
    If rst("FontSize") > 0 Then
        .Size = rst("FontSize")
    End If
    If rst("Color") > 0 Then
        .Color = rst("Color")
    End If

    ' Set Yes/No/Use Default properties.
    If rst("Shadow") <> conUseDefault Then
        .Shadow = rst("Shadow")
    End If
    If rst("Bold") <> conUseDefault Then
        .Bold = rst("Bold")
    End If
    If rst("Italic") <> conUseDefault Then
        .Italic = rst("Italic")
    End If
    If rst("Underline") <> conUseDefault Then
        .Underline = rst("Underline")
    End If
End With
```

Once CreateSlideText has set all the necessary properties, it moves on to the next row. If at any point it encounters an error setting the properties of a given paragraph, it moves on to the next paragraph. (You might consider beefing up this error handling, but for the most part, it works fine.) Here, then, is the complete source for CreateSlideText:

```
Private Function CreateSlideText( _
 objSlide As PowerPoint.Slide, intSlideNumber As Integer)
    Dim db As DAO.Database
    Dim rst As DAO.Recordset
    Dim pptShape As PowerPoint.Shape
    Dim intObject As Integer
    Dim intParagraph As Integer
    Dim pptTextRange As PowerPoint.TextRange
    Dim objFormat As PowerPoint.TextEffectFormat
    Dim strFontName As String
    Dim fnt As PowerPoint.Font

    On Error GoTo HandleErrors

    Set db = CurrentDb( )

    ' Go get the text that applies to this slide.
    Set rst = db.OpenRecordset("SELECT * FROM tblParagraphs " & _
     "WHERE SlideNumber = " & intSlideNumber & _
     " ORDER BY ObjectNumber, ParagraphNumber")

    ' Now walk through the list of text items, sticking
    ' them into the objects and applying properties.

    Call InsertText(rst, objSlide)

    rst.MoveFirst
    Do Until rst.EOF
        ' Update the status information on the form.
        With Forms("frmPowerPoint")
            .UpdateDisplay rst("SlideNumber"), rst("Text")
            .Repaint
        End With

        ' No need to grab a reference to the shape each
        ' time through. Cache this value for later use.
        If intObject <> rst("ObjectNumber") Then
            intObject = rst("ObjectNumber")
            Set pptShape = objSlide.Shapes(intObject)
        End If

        ' Get a reference to the paragraph in question,
        ' then set its paragraph properties.
        Set pptTextRange = pptShape.TextFrame.TextRange. _
         Paragraphs(rst("ParagraphNumber"))

        With pptTextRange.Font
```

```
                If Not IsNull(rst("FontName")) Then
                    .Name = rst("FontName")
                End If
                If rst("FontSize") > 0 Then
                    .Size = rst("FontSize")
                End If
                If rst("Color") > 0 Then
                    .Color = rst("Color")
                End If

                ' Set Yes/No/Use Default properties.
                If rst("Shadow") <> conUseDefault Then
                    .Shadow = rst("Shadow")
                End If
                If rst("Bold") <> conUseDefault Then
                    .Bold = rst("Bold")
                End If
                If rst("Italic") <> conUseDefault Then
                    .Italic = rst("Italic")
                End If
                If rst("Underline") <> conUseDefault Then
                    .Underline = rst("Underline")
                End If
            End With

CreateSlideTextNext:
            rst.MoveNext
        Loop
        CreateSlideText = True

ExitHere:
        On Error Resume Next
        rst.Close
        Set rst = Nothing

        Set db = Nothing
        Exit Function

HandleErrors:
        CreateSlideText = False
        Select Case Err.Number
            Case conErrInvalidObjectIndex
                Resume CreateSlideTextNext

            Case Else
                MsgBox "Error: " & Err.Description & " (" & Err.Number & ")",_
                vbExclamation, "Create Slides Text"

        End Select
        Resume ExitHere
End Function
```

Comments

This solution uses only a small subset of the PowerPoint Automation interface. A great deal more functionality is available to you if you dig deep enough to find it. For example, you might want to support more of the text or bullet attributes than we've chosen, or dig into slide transitions, builds, and animation. Use the Object Browser (press F2 in a module window), shown in Figure 12-16, to help dig through the PowerPoint object model. You can work your way down through the hierarchy in an orderly fashion. For example, find the Application object in the left window, then browse through the right window until you find the Presentations collection. On the left, find the Presentations collection, and on the right, find the Add method. That's how we wrote this solution: by digging through the various objects, collections, methods, and properties that the Object Browser displays.

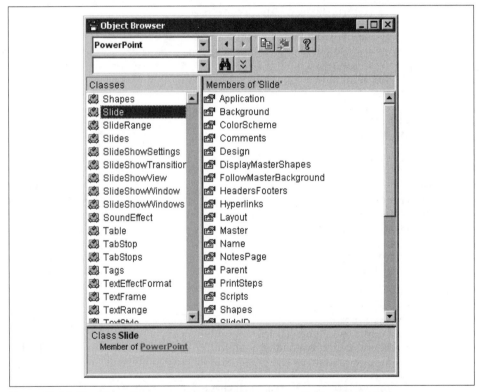

Figure 12-16. The Object Browser makes it possible to dig around in object models

You may also want to look at basGetTemplate, which includes a substantial amount of code dedicated to retrieving a list of all of PowerPoint's design templates. As it's installed, PowerPoint places the location of these templates in your registry. Two interesting issues are involved here: finding the name of the directory where the templates have been installed, and creating an array containing the names of the templates. Once the code creates the array, it uses the standard list-filling callback function mechanism, described in Chapter 7, to populate the combo box on the sample form. Though these topics are beyond the scope of this solution, you may find it useful to dig into the code, which has comments to help you through it.

12.8 Add a Contact and Send Email Through Outlook

Problem

You maintain an Access database full of contact information. You'd like to be able both to add contact information to your Outlook address book and to send email messages easily, using the email address stored in a particular row. How can you add these features to your form without forcing your users to load Outlook and work there?

Solution

Outlook provides a rich programming model, and it's easy for you to programmatically create contacts and send email. You'll find that solving these problems requires little more than creating an object in memory, setting some properties, and calling the correct methods. This sample provides a form that demonstrates code you can use.

 Because of the serious threat of email viruses, the Outlook team has "locked down" the programmability features of Microsoft Outlook. The level of the virus support may be different depending on which version of Outlook you have installed and what service release you've added. In testing this demonstration, you may see an alert warning you that someone is attempting to modify your address book. You can safely dismiss that dialog for this demonstration, but you should never take it lightly in real use.

Load and run frmContacts from *12-08.MDB*. This form, shown in Figure 12-17, allows you to edit contact information within Access. You can click on Send Email to create a new email message to the address you've provided in the contact record. Click on Add Contact to copy the contact information to a new contact item within Outlook. Note that the Send Email button isn't available unless you've specified an email address, and the Add Contact button isn't available unless you've specified a LastName value.

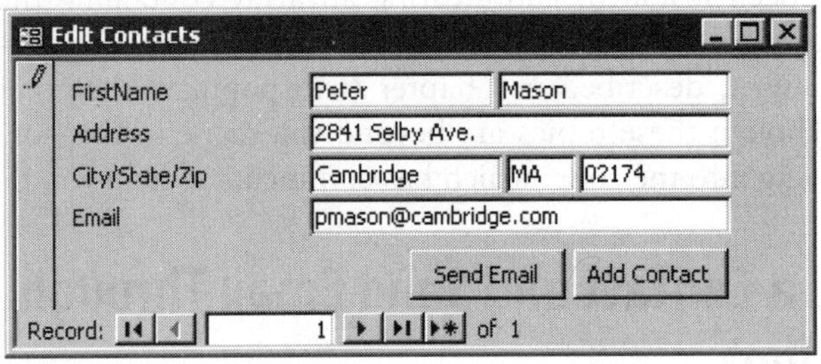

Figure 12-17. frmContacts allows you to work with Outlook contacts and send email

Follow these steps to create a form like frmContacts:

1. Import the module basAutomateOutlook from *12-08.MDB*.

2. Open basAutomateOutlook and use the Tools → References... menu item to add a reference to the Microsoft Outlook Type Library. (Select the most current version of the library, or the version you're intending to target.)

3. Import tblContacts from *12-08.MDB*.

4. Either import frmContacts from *12-08.MDB*, or create your own form. (If you import the existing form, you can skip to Step 8.) You can create a new form based on your tblContacts. You can add fields and modify field names as necessary in the underlying table (tblContacts), but you'll need to modify the code that follows to match, if you do.

5. Add the following procedure to the form's module to handle enabling and disabling the two command buttons:

```
Private Sub HandleEnabling(varEmail As Variant, _
  varFirstName As Variant)
    Me.cmdEmail.Enabled = Len(varEmail & "") > 0
    Me.cmdContact.Enabled = Len(varFirstName & "") > 0
End Sub
```

6. Add event procedures to call HandleEnabling from the form's Current event and from the two important text boxes' Change events:

```
Private Sub Email_Change( )
    Call HandleEnabling(Me.Email.Text, Me.FirstName)
End Sub

Private Sub FirstName_Change( )
    Call HandleEnabling(Me.Email, Me.FirstName.Text)
End Sub

Private Sub Form_Current( )
    Call HandleEnabling(Me.Email, Me.FirstName)
End Sub
```

Note that in the Email text box's Change event, you must use the Text property (not the default Value property) if you want to refer to the current value in the control. This is a confusing area in Access forms: while in the middle of editing a control on an Access form, the Text property contains the actual, current text. The Value property (which is the default property, so you needn't explicitly specify it) contains the original text in the control, before you began editing it. In this example, the Change event procedures must refer to the Text property of the current control (the one being changed) but the Value property of the other control.

7. In the Click event procedures for the two command buttons, add code to call the appropriate procedures in basAutomateOutlook:

```
Private Sub cmdContact_Click( )
    Call AddContact(Me.FirstName, Me.LastName, Me.Address, _
    Me.City, Me.State, Me.PostalCode, Me.Email)
End Sub

Private Sub cmdEmail_Click( )
    Call SendEmail(Me.Email)
End Sub
```

8. Run your form, add some data, and try out the two buttons on the form. Clicking Send Email should bring up the Outlook email editor. Clicking Add Contact should copy data to the contact editor in Outlook and leave the editor available for you to continue editing.

Discussion

All the power of this example is buried in basAutomateOutlook's code. This section will work through each of the procedures you'll find in that module.

Although this section gives you a good start working with Outlook programmatically, you'll find that Outlook has an extremely rich and powerful object model, allowing you to work with contacts, mail items, and schedule items, as well as the entire Outlook user interface.

The first block of code in basAutomateOutlook looks like this:

```
Private ola As Outlook.Application
Private nsp As Outlook.NameSpace

Public Sub InitOutlook( )
    ' Initialize a session in Outlook.
    Set ola = New Outlook.Application

    ' Return a reference to the MAPI layer.
```

```
    Set nsp = ola.GetNamespace("MAPI")

    ' Let the user log into Outlook with the Outlook
    ' Profile dialog, then create a new session.
    nsp.Logon , , True, False
End Sub

Public Sub CleanUp( )
    ' Clean up public object references.
    Set nsp = Nothing
    Set ola = Nothing
End Sub
```

This code block includes module-level variables that refer to the Outlook Application and Namespace objects. Each example (and any code you write that works with Outlook) will probably need these variables as well, so it made sense to simply make them module-level, available to all procedures in the module.

Each procedure in this example calls the InitOutlook procedure, which instantiates a new copy of Outlook if it's not already running, or grabs onto the existing instance if it is already running. (Outlook does not allow itself to start up multiple times, so you'll never have multiple copies concurrently running in memory.) After this code runs, you can use the variable ola to refer to the running instance of Outlook:

```
    Set ola = New Outlook.Application
```

Next, the code creates a new Workspace object. You're required to log in whenever you work with data within the Outlook data store, and the Namespace object provides this capability. Since you pass in the parameter MAPI to the GetNameSpace method, it might appear that there are other namespaces you might want to use, but that's not the case; Outlook uses only the MAPI namespace, and you'll always pass that parameter to the GetNameSpace method:

```
    ' Return a reference to the MAPI layer.
    Set nsp = ola.GetNamespace("MAPI")
```

Finally, the InitOutlook procedure calls the Logon method of the Namespace object, allowing you to log into Outlook. If Outlook is already running, you won't see a dialog. If not, you'll see the standard dialog shown in Figure 12-18.

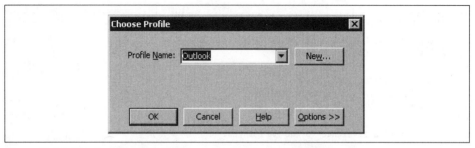

Figure 12-18. This familiar dialog appears when you log into Outlook

The portion of the code that handles logon is:

```
' Let the user log into Outlook with the Outlook
' Profile dialog, then create a new session.
nsp.Logon , , True, False
```

 You might want to investigate the Namespace object's Logon method in Outlook's online help—it has several options that allow you to pass authentication information within the method call. You can control whether to show the dialog, as well.

Next in the sample module, the CleanUp procedure releases the module-level variables. If your code started up Outlook (that is, it wasn't already running), releasing those variables should allow Outlook to shut down.

The AddContact method, shown here, simply creates a new Outlook contact, given the information you pass to it:

```
Public Sub AddContact(varFirstName As Variant, varLastName As Variant, _
  varAddress As Variant, varCity As Variant, varState As Variant, _
  varPostalCode As Variant, varEmail As Variant)
    Dim cti As Outlook.ContactItem

    InitOutlook
    Set cti = ola.CreateItem(olContactItem)
    cti.FirstName = varFirstName & ""
    cti.LastName = varLastName & ""
    cti.HomeAddressStreet = varAddress & ""
    cti.HomeAddressCity = varCity & ""
    cti.HomeAddressState = varState & ""
    cti.HomeAddressPostalCode = varPostalCode & ""
    cti.Email1Address = varEmail & ""
    cti.Display

    Set cti = Nothing
    CleanUp
End Sub
```

This procedure accepts parameters containing all the fields you gathered on your Access form. (Look back at the call to the AddContact method to see that you're passing in all the values from the original form.) It starts by initializing Outlook, calling the InitOutlook procedure you've already seen. It then calls the CreateItem method, creating a new Outlook ContactItem object, and sets properties of the contact:

```
Set cti = ola.CreateItem(olContactItem)
cti.FirstName = varFirstName & ""
cti.LastName = varLastName & ""
cti.HomeAddressStreet = varAddress & ""
cti.HomeAddressCity = varCity & ""
cti.HomeAddressState = varState & ""
cti.HomeAddressPostalCode = varPostalCode & ""
cti.Email1Address = varEmail & ""
```

Finally, the procedure calls the Display method of the ContactItem object to display the unsaved item. (If you want to save the item before displaying it, call the Save method before calling the Display method.) The Display method isn't synchronous—that is, the code continues running, releases the ContactItem object from memory, and cleans up the module-level variables created earlier.

You may wonder why releasing the cti, ola, and nsp variables doesn't close the contact editor and shut down Outlook. That would happen only if you never displayed the contact within an editor for the user to see. Once you do that, though, Outlook is effectively "owned" by the user, and unless you explicitly call the Quit method of the Outlook Application object, it's now up the user to close the contact editor. When that happens, Outlook will shut down because no other references to it exist. Of course, if Outlook had been running before you ran the code, it would continue to run afterwards, since the variables used within the procedures here are simply additional references to the running copy of Outlook.

The SendEmail procedure shown here works much like the AddContact procedure:

```
Public Sub SendEmail(varTo As Variant)
    Dim mli As Outlook.MailItem

    InitOutlook
    Set mli = ola.CreateItem(olMailItem)
    mli.To = varTo & ""
    mli.Subject = "Message for Access Contact"
    mli.Display

    Set mli = Nothing
    CleanUp
End Sub
```

SendEmail receives the email address of the recipient and creates a new email message addressed to that recipient in Outlook. (You could, of course, gather and pass more information for the email message, such as the subject, in this procedure call. The sample merely sends the recipient.) SendEmail sets the To field of the new email message, creates a subject for you, and then displays the new, unsent email message in Outlook. It's up to the user to complete and send the email message.

If you wanted to actually send a message programmatically, you could supply the Subject and Body fields (and any others you'd like to supply) in your code, and then call the Send method of the MailItem object. For this example, we've simply created the message and dumped you into the email editor in Outlook.

Of course, there's much more to the Outlook object model than we've been able to show here. Start by exploring the data provided by the VBA Object Browser (press F2 from within a VBA module, select Outlook from the list of libraries in the upper-left corner of the window, and start digging). You can find several good books on programming the Outlook object model, and don't forget to check out the online help.

Make sure to try out various versions of Outlook if you're shipping an application to end users. The Outlook security patch and the various versions of security models are sure to hamper your applications if you intend to work with contacts or send email to contacts in the address book programmatically.

See Also

If you want to "fake" sending email, using Access only, see "Send Messages to Other Users Without Using Email" in Chapter 10.

CHAPTER 13

Data Access Pages

When data access pages (DAPs) were introduced in Access 2000, they drew a lot of attention from Access developers who were looking for easy ways to move their data to the Web. DAPs promised to provide an Access-based designer that would allow developers to create web pages based on data, just as forms and reports were. Unfortunately, because of the limitations of the DAP design tools, the often-crippled functionality of the resulting pages (such as the inability to update data), and the requirement that users of the pages must have Office 2000 licenses, DAPs were not widely used.

In Access 2002, DAPs were greatly enhanced. The designer is now on par with Access's form and report designers. Data on pages can be updated under most circumstances, and users without Office XP licenses can legally work with DAPs in the browser, albeit with a limited feature set. However, you'll still need to use Microsoft Internet Explorer 5 and later to view and work with DAPs, and users will still need to have the Office Web Components installed locally.

Perhaps the biggest limitation to DAPs is the way they connect to data. DAPs use ADO recordsets behind the scenes to retrieve and update data. These ADO recordsets are opened on your users' machines, which means that your users must have direct access to the data. The only workaround—using recordsets that are opened on a web server—requires that you set up a complicated technology called Remote Data Services (RDS), which goes beyond the scope of this book. Without RDS, you can't use DAPs to work with data over the Internet, even though you can view the data in a browser.

Still, the Access 2002 implementation has made DAPs a feasible and welcome choice for displaying and editing data, particularly on an intranet (because of the IE and local processing requirements). Database developers may also find that DAPs provide a good starting point in acquiring web database skills.

DAPs are quite different from Access forms and reports. In this chapter, we'll address issues that you are likely to encounter as you begin to use DAPs. Many of these issues involve getting the page to look the way you want it to look. We'll also talk about how you can keep your pages and data properly linked together, and we'll show you how you can use VBScript to add new functionality to your pages.

In order to use any of the existing samples in your own environment, you will need to update the ConnectionString property for each page. Within Access, when you attempt to open the existing pages in the page designer, you'll receive a warning indicating that the connection is invalid. Right-click on the page within the designer, select the Page Properties item from the context menu, and select the Data tab in the Properties window. Select the ConnectionString property, and click the build button (...) to the right of the property. On the Connection page of the Data Link Properties dialog box, browse to the appropriate location of the sample database. The Solutions in Recipe 13-5 and Recipe 13-6 show techniques to avoid this extra step.

 DAPs in Access 2002 and Access 2003 are very different from DAPs in Access 2000. Not only did Microsoft greatly enhance the functionality of pages designed in Access, but the designer itself also includes many more features. Therefore, we have not addressed the Access 2000 version of DAPs in this chapter.

13.1 Replace Navigation Button Images with Your Own Images

Problem

The navigation section in a DAP uses button images that are different from the rest of the pages on your intranet. How can you use your own images on the navigation buttons of a DAP?

Solution

The image on a navigation button is named in the button's Src property. By default, the Src property for each navigation button is set to an image stored within the Office Web Component library. You can change the property's value to name an image of your own choosing. You can (and should) also provide an "inactive" version of the image that can be displayed when the button is not relevant to the current context. For example, the First and Previous navigation buttons should be disabled when the user is viewing the first record. The code to change the image based on context has already been written for you; you need only supply an image in the same location and with the same name as the active version of the button, but with the string "Inactive" appended to the name. That is, you might have one image named *MyFirstButton.gif* and another named *MyFirstButtonInactive.gif*.

In order to try out the sample provided for this section, please see the introduction to this chapter, which describes how you can update the connection information and connect the DAP to the sample database.

To add your own images to the navigation buttons on a DAP, follow these steps (or open 13-01.mdb to see the completed sample):

1. Create the images you want to use for the navigation buttons. The Previous and Next buttons for our sample page are shown in Figure 13-1.

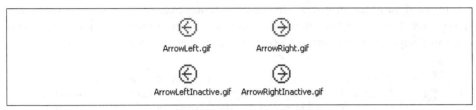

Figure 13-1. Active and inactive versions of the Previous and Next buttons

2. Create a DAP and add whatever controls you'd like. Once you've added fields from tables or queries, you'll see a default navigation section like the one shown in Figure 13-2.

Figure 13-2. The default navigation section includes several buttons

3. Eliminate any buttons you don't want. For our simple example, we eliminated all buttons except the Previous and Next buttons. To get rid of a button, either select it and press the Delete key, or right-click the navigation control, select Navigation Buttons from the context menu, and toggle off the buttons you don't want.

4. Select a navigation button and display its properties sheet.

5. Find the Src property (in the Other page of the properties sheet). Change the property's value to the name of the image you want displayed, as shown in Figure 13-3. Note that the properties sheet seems to insist on storing the full path to the image, even when it is entered as a relative path.

6. Repeat Step 5 for each button you need to change.

7. Test the resulting page. Our sample page looks like Figure 13-4.

Discussion

All the functionality for a navigation button is contained within the DataSourceControl Office Web Component. The name of the image to use, though, is stored in the

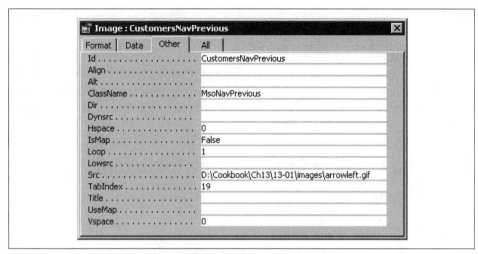

Figure 13-3. Specify the image you want displayed in the Src property

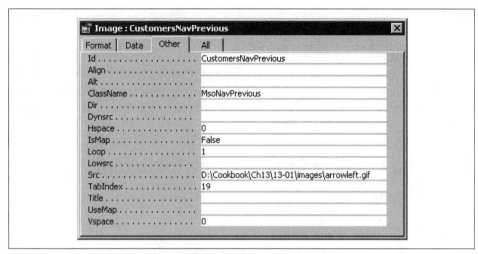

Figure 13-4. The look of our page is now consistent with the rest of our intranet

HTML source of the page. The component itself checks for the name with the "Inactive" string to adjust the appearance of the button relative to the context.

The properties sheet appears to store a full path to the image. That is, you might type in the following text:

```
Images\ArrowLeft.tif
```

But when you leave the property, the value will be adjusted to show a full path and filename:

```
c:\MyPages\Images\ArrowLeft.tif
```

Internally, however, the HTML source is storing a relative path. If the path to the page changes but it retains an *Images* subfolder, the page will not break; the image in the relative path will still be found. (The same can't necessarily be said of your data, of course.)

13.2 Use Labels or Other Controls for Record Navigation

Problem

You don't want to use images for the navigation buttons on your pages; you'd prefer to simply use labels that say "Previous", "Next", and so forth.

Solution

The default navigation images function as they do because each is a member of a particular class. You can use another type of control for navigation by adding the correct class name to the control's ClassName property.

Our solution, found in the Custom Nav Text DAP in the sample database, uses labels to create the look shown in Figure 13-5.

 In order to try out the sample provided for this section, please see the introduction to this chapter, which describes how you can update the connection information and connect the DAP to the sample database.

To use labels as navigation controls, follow these steps (or open *13-02.MDB* to see the completed sample):

1. Create a new page and add whatever data you'd like.
2. Delete all navigation control buttons from the navigation section.
3. Place labels in the navigation control section for each navigation function (First, Previous, Next, Last).
4. Select the "First" label and view its properties sheet. The ClassName property should read:

    ```
    MSTheme-Label
    ```

5. Change the ClassName property so that it includes the appropriate class for the first navigation button, msoNavFirst. The ClassName property should now read:

    ```
    MSTheme-Label msoNavFirst
    ```

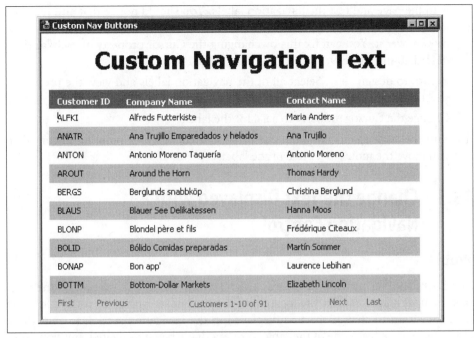

Figure 13-5. This page uses navigation labels instead of images

6. Change the ClassName properties for each navigation control to include the class name for its function. Table 13-1 lists all the classes for navigation controls.

Table 13-1. Navigation functions and their class names

Function	Class name
First	msoNavFirst
Previous	msoNavPrevious
Next	msoNavNext
Last	msoNavLast
New	msoNavAddNew
Delete	msoNavDelete
Save	msoNavSave
Undo	msoNavUndo
Sort Ascending	msoNavSortAsc
Sort Descending	msoNavSortDesc
Filter by Selection	msoNavFilter
Filter Toggle	msoNavToggleFilter
Help	msoNavHelp
Recordset Label	msoNavRecordsetLabel

7. Run the page and test the navigation labels. You should notice that although the labels function properly, the cursor turns into an I-beam when you move the mouse over it. You can fix this by changing the Cursor property of each label, as described in Steps 8-9.

8. Return to design view. Select all of the navigation labels and view the properties sheet.

9. Change the Cursor property to hand for the labels.

10. Run the page again. Now the cursor should change to a pointing finger when you move the mouse over one of the labels.

13.3   Change the Text Displayed with a Navigation Control

Problem

The DAP designer provides a recordset label in the navigation section of the page that includes record counts, the location of the current set within the total, and some text. You want to change the text displayed in the navigation section to something else. You can see the name of the table or query that's being navigated, but you don't know how to change the way the record counts are displayed.

Solution

Don't let the InnerText property fool you. The recordset label control also includes a RecordsetLabel property that controls how the record count is displayed. You'll need to use its special syntax, though, to get the exact display you want.

We've started with a simple page, shown in Figure 13-6 with its default recordset label. By default, a tabular page's recordset label shows the table name, number of records, and range of records currently displayed.

We'd like to change the page so that the recordset label looks like the one shown in Figure 13-7.

To change the default recordset label, follow these steps (or open 13-03.mdb to see the completed sample):

1. Open the page you want to change in design view.

2. Select the recordset label. If you're using the mouse to select the control, you'll need to click twice: the first click selects the navigation control and the second click selects the recordset label.

3. Display the properties sheet for the recordset label. Select the Data page to see the RecordsetLabel property.

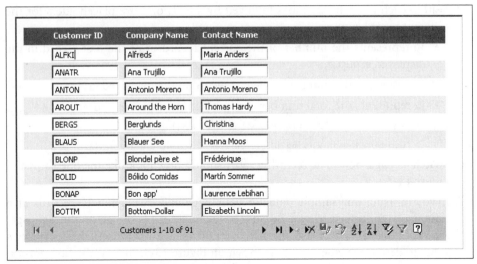

Figure 13-6. A page with its default recordset label

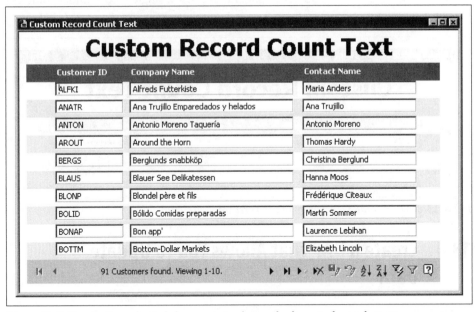

Figure 13-7. Use the RecordsetLabel property to change the format of record counts

4. Notice the default value for the property. In our example, it looks like this:

```
Customers |0 of |2;Customers |0-|1 of |2
```

The format has two portions, separated by a semicolon. The first portion determines what the label will look like when only one record is displayed on the page; the second portion determines what the label will look like if more than one record is displayed on the page.

Within each portion, the pipes followed by a 0, 1, or 2 are placeholders for the different record counts:

- |0 represents the number of the current record or of the first record in the displayed group.
- |1 represents the number of the last record in the displayed group.
- |2 represents the total number of records in the entire recordset.

5. Change the RecordsetLabel property to look like this:

    |2 Customers found. Viewing |0.;|2 Customers found. Viewing |0-|1.

6. Switch to page view. The recordset label should now look like the one shown in Figure 13-7.

7. If you're using our sample data for your page and displaying 10 records at a time, move to the last record. Because only one record is shown on the last page, the recordset label will use the first portion of the RecordsetLabel property's value to define the label's text, as shown in Figure 13-8. In fact, the first portion of the RecordsetLabel property is used both for pages where the DataPageSize property is 1 and for multirecord pages that show a single record under some circumstances.

Figure 13-8. The recordset label when only one record is displayed

13.4   Create a DAP that Allows You to Update Data

Problem

Most of the time, the pages you create are updateable; that is, the user can change the underlying data. Occasionally, though, the data can't be changed, and it isn't clear to you why not.

Solution

DAPs in Access 2000 were almost never updateable. Since Access 2002, however, most of the limitations have gone away, and you can nearly always edit the underlying data. If each group on your page is based on a single table or table query, the data is always updateable. If you base a group on a multitable, one-to-many query, the table on the "many" side of the join (or "most-many," if there are several tables) is editable only if the key field of that table is placed on the page and the UniqueTable property for the group is set to that table.

There are two ways to create an updateable page based on a multitable query. The careful way requires that the key field of the table you want to update be the first field placed in the group. Follow these steps (exactly) to create an updateable page the careful way:

1. Create a new page and find the query you want to use in the field list window. We'll use qryProductCategory in the sample database.
2. Add the key field of the table you want to edit to the page. In our example, the table is Products and its key field is ProductID.
3. Add whatever other fields you'd like and switch to page view. You should be able to edit fields from the Products table (except ProductID, which is an AutoNumber field).

The second way to create an updateable page is to place fields in whatever order you like, but include the key field and remember to set the UniqueTable property. To experiment with this technique, first follow these steps to create a page that isn't updateable:

1. Create a new page and find the query you want in the field list.
2. Add fields from the query to the page, but leave off the key field, ProductID.
3. Add the ProductID field to the page.
4. Switch to page view. You won't be able to edit any fields on the page.

At this point, the page is not updateable because the DataSource control doesn't support the ability to update both sides of a one-to-many query, and it needs more information to figure out which table is on the "many" side of the join. To make this page updateable, follow these steps (or open *13-04.MDB* to see the completed sample):

1. Return to design view.
2. Display the properties sheet for the header section, and find the UniqueTable property (in the Data page of the properties sheet). The UniqueTable property tells the DataSource control which of the tables is on the "many" side of the relationship.
3. Select Products from the drop-down list, as shown in Figure 13-9.
4. Switch to page view. You will now be able to edit fields from the Products table.

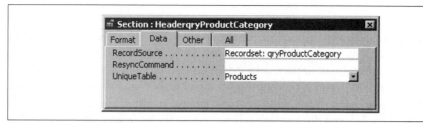

Figure 13-9. Selecting the "many" table in a relationship

To make the page read-only again, just delete the ProductID from the page. The key field of the "many" table must be displayed on the form, although you can hide it by changing the Visibility property of the control.

Sometimes you may want to restrict the user from updating data on a page. To do so, look for the AllowAdditions, AllowDeletions, and AllowEdits properties on the Group Level properties sheet. If you want to keep the user from editing only certain controls, keep the AllowEdits property set to True, but change the ReadOnly property of the individual controls to True as necessary.

13.5 Create One File to Store Connection Information for All DAPs in an Application

Problem

You have many DAPs that all use the same data source. The data source's name and location are subject to change; for example, the pages point to a sample data source when you're working on their design and to a production data source when you deploy them. But if you move the data source to a different folder or change the name of the data source, the links your DAPs use will probably break. You'd like to be able to change the data source in one place, rather than making the change on every page.

Solution

Starting with Access 2002, you can use a connection file, rather than a hardcoded string, to define the source of the data for each page. Microsoft provides two types of files for storing data connection information: Microsoft Data Link (also called Universal Data Link, or *.udl*) files, and Office Data Connection (*.odc*) files. You can create a data connection file that points to the test data, create and test your pages, and then switch to live data by editing the data connection file.

Essentially, both *.udl* and *.odc* files store an ADO connection string. We'll walk you through the steps to create and edit each type of file, and then talk about how to reference a connection file in your DAPs.

The *.udl* format has been around longer, so we'll discuss it first. A *.udl* file is a text file that stores the same provider and data source information you would use to set up an ADO connection. To create a *.udl* file, follow these steps:

1. Open Windows Explorer and browse to the folder where you'd like to create the file.

2. Right-click in the file list and select New from the context menu.

3. If you don't see the Microsoft Data Link option, skip to Step 4. You'll see the dialog shown in Figure 13-10. Move on to Step 6.

4. Select New Text Document. Give the text document any name you like, but be sure to use the *.udl* extension instead of *.txt*. (Disregard the warning from Windows Explorer about changing the file extension.)

5. Double-click the *.udl* file. You'll see the dialog box shown in Figure 13-10.

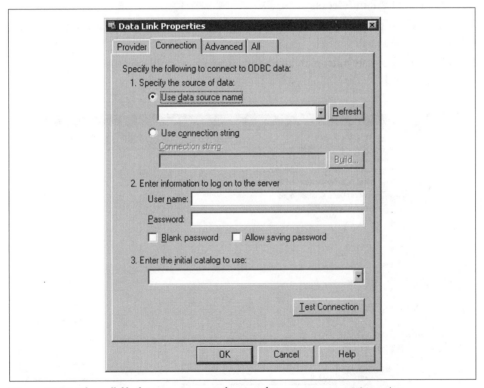

Figure 13-10. The .udl file format uses a simple wizard to create a connection string

6. Use the dialog to set up the connection you want. The instructions given here describe how to set up a connection to an Access database.

7. Select the Provider page and choose Microsoft Jet 4.0 OLE DB Provider.

8. Select the Connection page and enter the database name in the first text box. Click the Test Connection button to verify your settings.

9. Click OK to save the *.udl* file.

> If you need to change a *.udl* file and modify its connection settings, just right-click on it in Windows Explorer and choose Open from the context menu. You'll see the same dialog as before, and you can use it to change any aspect of the connection.

The *.odc* format was new with Office XP. It stores information about the connection in an HTML format and uses the Office Web Components to display information about the database when you view the *.odc* file in Internet Explorer. To create an *.odc* file, follow these steps:

1. Open any DAP in Access.

2. Display the properties sheet for the page and find the ConnectionFile property (on the Data page).

3. Click the Browse button next to the property. You'll see the dialog shown in Figure 13-11.

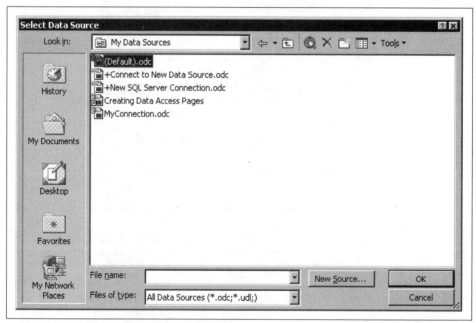

Figure 13-11. By default, .odc files are stored in My Data Sources, a subfolder of My Documents

4. Click the New Source button next to the "File name" drop-down list. You'll see the dialog shown in Figure 13-12.

Figure 13-12. The Jet provider falls into the Other/Advanced category

5. To create an .odc file that points to an Access database, select Other/Advanced from the list box and click the Next button. You'll see a dialog like the one used for Microsoft Data Links, as shown in Figure 13-13.

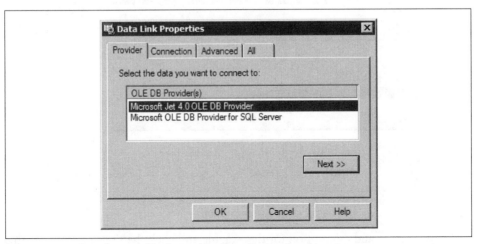

Figure 13-13. The .odc wizard looks just like the .udl wizard at this point

6. Select Microsoft Jet 4.0 OLE DB Provider and click the Next button.

7. Type in the name of the database you want to point to and click the OK button. You'll see the dialog shown in Figure 13-14. The dialog shows you the tables in the database, but you can't actually make a selection here. You're defining a file to point to the database, not a particular table or query.

8. Click the Next button. You'll see the final wizard page shown in Figure 13-15.

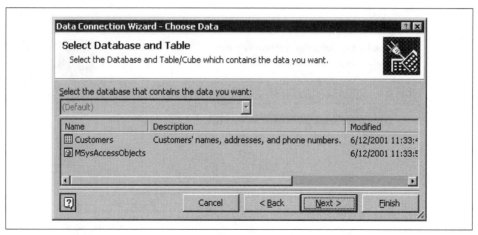

Figure 13-14. *You can't select a table at this point*

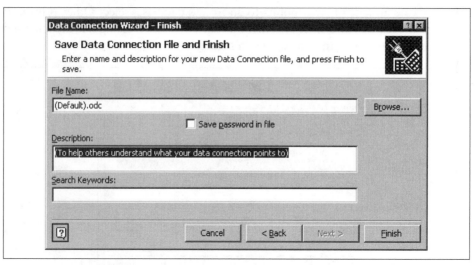

Figure 13-15. *Provide a meaningful name and description*

9. Type a name and description for the *.odc* file and click the Finish button. At this point, you can choose your new connection file as the connection file for the DAP with which you're working.

> Although Access' user interface is extremely confusing on this point, if you modify the ConnectionFile property and select a connection file that isn't in the My Data Connections folder, you must supply a full path. The dialog box you'll use in order to select the file doesn't allow you to supply the full path, however. Therefore, if you want to specify a *.udl* or *.odc* file that isn't in the My Data Connections folder, you must type the full path and file name by hand, in the ConnectionFile property.

If you want to change an *.odc* file to point to a different location, you'll need to open it in a text editor. Follow these steps to make the change quickly:

1. The easiest way to open the file in Notepad is to right-click on the *.odc* file in Windows Explorer and choose Edit in Notepad from the context menu. The text file will look something like Figure 13-16.

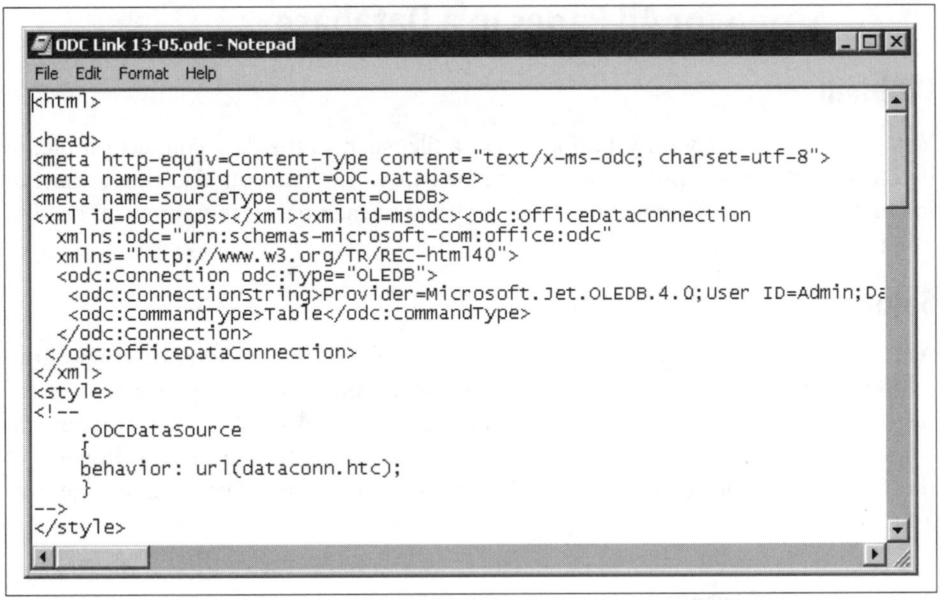

```
ODC Link 13-05.odc - Notepad                                    _ □ X
File  Edit  Format  Help
<html>

<head>
<meta http-equiv=Content-Type content="text/x-ms-odc; charset=utf-8">
<meta name=ProgId content=ODC.Database>
<meta name=SourceType content=OLEDB>
<xml id=docprops></xml><xml id=msodc><odc:OfficeDataConnection
  xmlns:odc="urn:schemas-microsoft-com:office:odc"
  xmlns="http://www.w3.org/TR/REC-html40">
  <odc:Connection odc:Type="OLEDB">
   <odc:ConnectionString>Provider=Microsoft.Jet.OLEDB.4.0;User ID=Admin;Da
   <odc:CommandType>Table</odc:CommandType>
  </odc:Connection>
 </odc:OfficeDataConnection>
</xml>
<style>
<!--
   .ODCDataSource
   {
   behavior: url(dataconn.htc);
   }
-->
</style>
```

Figure 13-16. A portion of the text file in Notepad

2. Select Edit → Find from the Notepad menu and type:

   source=

   into the text box. Click the Find Next button.

3. The cursor should be on the "Source=" string that precedes the path and filename of the *.mdb* file. You can modify the path directly, then select File → Save from the menu.

4. Close Notepad.

To use either type of data connection file to supply the data source for your page, simply set the ConnectionFile property of each page to the name of the connection file. When you set the ConnectionFile property, Access automatically adds the ConnectionString property as well, but the ConnectionFile takes precedence. That is, if the ConnectionFile's information changes, the ConnectionString property will be updated automatically the next time the page is opened.

You can use the Pages page of the Tools → Options dialog to set a default ConnectionFile property. Then, all new pages will use your connection file as the ConnectionFile property value.

13.6   Programmatically Change the Connection String for All Pages in a Database

Problem

You don't want to rely on yet another extra file, such as the data connection file, to determine how your application is supposed to work. But you also don't want to manually change the ConnectionString property of each page every time you need to point to a different data source.

Solution

As long as you can count on having Access available every time you need to point to a different data source, it's easy to change the ConnectionString property of every page programmatically. You'll need to iterate through the collection of pages and change the ConnectionString property. Note that ConnectionString is a property of the DataSource control for the page; you can refer to the DataSource object as MSODSC.

We've supplied sample code in the database for this item. Take a look at the *ChangeConnectString* function in basResetConnectionString.

To see how the code works, follow these steps:

1. Close the database and open Windows Explorer. Change the name of the sample database, *13-06.MDB*, to *13-06-test.MDB*.

2. Open *Customers.htm* in Internet Explorer. You'll receive two messages: one informs you that the data provider could not be initialized, and the other tells you that the database could not be found. After you close the message boxes, the browser window will look like Figure 13-17. The #Name? syntax will be familiar to most Access developers; it means the data source couldn't be found.

3. Close the browser window.

4. Open *13-06-test.MDB*. Open the basResetConnectionString module.

5. If the Immediate window is not displayed, press Ctrl-G to open it. Type ?ChangeConnectString( ), as shown in Figure 13-18. Press Enter.

6. As the code runs, you'll see two alerts that look like Figure 13-19 (one for each DAP in the database). There's no apparent way to get around these alerts; even the SetWarnings method has no effect on them. Close each dialog to move on.

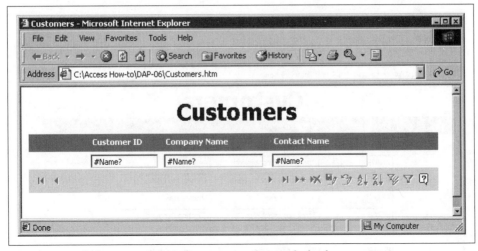

Figure 13-17. The browser window after renaming the sample database

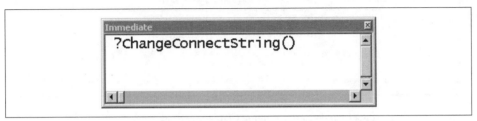

Figure 13-18. Running the ChangeConnectString function from the Immediate window

Figure 13-19. Alerts like this will appear as the code runs

7. Return to Windows Explorer and double-click *Customers.htm* to open it in the browser. The page will be displayed with no error messages, as shown in Figure 13-20. The code "fixed" the connection string so that it points to the database in which the data access page object is located.

Discussion

The complete ChangeConnectString function looks like this:

```
Public Function ChangeConnectString( ) As Boolean

' Code sets the connection string for all pages so that the data source
' is the database in which the data access page object is stored.
```

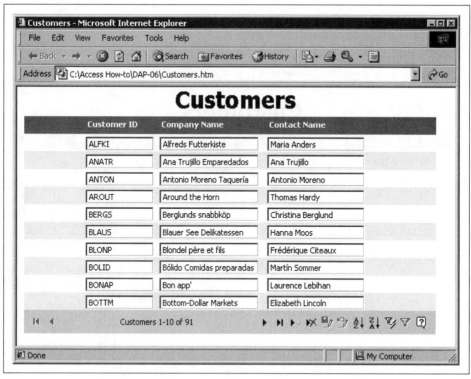

Figure 13-20. The browser window after running ChangeConnectString

```
' Run this function whenever there is a chance that the database name
' has changed.

On Error GoTo HandleErr

    Dim objDAP As AccessObject
    Dim dapPage As DataAccessPage
    Dim strConnectionDB As String

    ' This code assumes that the connection string should point to the
    ' current database. You could make the solution more generic by
    ' making strConnectionDB an input parameter, perhaps set with a
    ' custom form that includes a Browse button.

    ' It would be great if you could simply supply the
    ' relative path to the database, but that doesn't work.
    ' You must supply the full name, including the path.
    strConnectionDB = CurrentProject.FullName

    ' Turn off warnings and screen painting.
    DoCmd.Hourglass True
    Application.Echo False, "Updating pages"
    DoCmd.SetWarnings False
```

```
' AllDataAccessPages contains AccessObjects, not DataAccessPage objects.
' You must open the data access page in design view to change the
' connection string. Note that you will get a message notifying you
' that the connection is broken. SetWarnings False should probably
' suppress this, but it doesn't.
For Each objDAP In CurrentProject.AllDataAccessPages
    DoCmd.OpenDataAccessPage objDAP.Name, acDataAccessPageDesign
    Set dapPage = DataAccessPages(objDAP.Name)
    dapPage.MSODSC.ConnectionString = _
      "Provider=Microsoft.Jet.OLEDB.4.0;" & _
      "Data Source=" & strConnectionDB
    DoCmd.Close acDataAccessPage, dapPage.Name, acSaveYes
Next objDAP

ChangeConnectString = True

ExitHere:
    ' Turn on warnings and screen painting.
    DoCmd.Hourglass False
    DoCmd.SetWarnings True
    Application.Echo True
    Exit Function

HandleErr:
    MsgBox Err.Number & ": " & Err.Description, "ChangeConnectString"
    Resume ExitHere
End Function
```

The code begins by setting up three variables:

```
Dim objDAP As AccessObject
Dim dapPage As DataAccessPage
Dim strConnectionDB As String
```

We need both *objDAP* and *dapPage* because the collection of all pages in a project returns a collection of AccessObject objects, but only DataAccessPage objects support a property to get at the DataSource control object, which in turn supports the ConnectionString property.

The code sets the value of the string variable to the name of the current project:

```
strConnectionDB = CurrentProject.FullName
```

It then turns on the hourglass and turns off warnings and screen updates:

```
DoCmd.Hourglass True
Application.Echo False, "Updating pages"
DoCmd.SetWarnings False
```

If you ran the test we described, you have seen that SetWarnings has no effect on the message box that notifies you that the data link is broken.

The code uses the AllDataAccessPages collection of the CurrentProject object to iterate through the pages:

```
For Each objDAP In CurrentProject.AllDataAccessPages
```

.

```
    .
    .
    .
    Next objDAP
```

The ConnectionString property can't be changed unless the page is in design view, so the code opens each page in turn and sets a DataAccessPage object variable to the open page:

```
DoCmd.OpenDataAccessPage objDAP.Name, acDataAccessPageDesign
Set dapPage = DataAccessPages(objDAP.Name)
```

It's the OpenDataAccessPage method that triggers the message box regarding the broken link.

The next line of code does the work:

```
dapPage.MSODSC.ConnectionString = _
  "Provider=Microsoft.Jet.OLEDB.4.0;" & _
   "Data Source=" & strConnectionDB
```

ConnectionString is a property of the DataSource control that is automatically included on every bound DAP. In code, the DataSource control is called MSODSC.

Once the string has been changed, the code saves and closes the DAP and moves on to the next page object:

```
DoCmd.Close acDataAccessPage, dapPage.Name, acSaveYes
```

Finally, after the code has iterated through all the pages, the cleanup work is done. The code turns the hourglass off, sets warnings on, and turns screen painting on:

```
' Turn on warnings and screen painting.
DoCmd.Hourglass False
DoCmd.SetWarnings True
Application.Echo True
```

If any part of the code fails, the function returns a False value.

 It would seem that you could simply use the name of the database (without its path) if it was in the same folder as the page file (the *.htm* file). Unfortunately, this doesn't work. Therefore, you'll need to update the connection string information any time you move your database and page files to a new location.

13.7   Change the Default Settings for New DAPs

Problem

You don't like the default colors for the background of the caption and footer section, or for the alternate row in a tabular page. You also wish you didn't have to change the ConnectionFile property for every page you create to point to the same *.udl* file.

Solution

Access's Tools → Options dialog now includes a Pages page where you can set defaults for any new pages you create. Changing the defaults will have no effect on existing pages.

To see how the color options affect the look of your new pages, follow these steps:

1. Create a new DAP. Add a table to the page and request a Tabular layout.

2. Switch to page view. Unless your defaults have already been changed, you'll see a caption with a steelblue background, and every other row will have a white-smoke background.

3. Close the page.

4. Select Tools Options from the main Access menu. Click the Pages tab. You'll see the dialog shown in Figure 13-21.

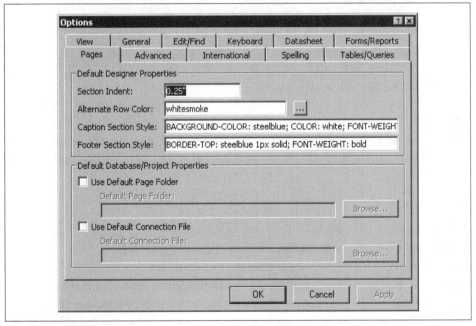

Figure 13-21. The default Pages options

5. Change the alternate row color to thistle.

6. Edit the Caption Section Style text box to use plum instead of whitesmoke as the background color. The dialog will now look like Figure 13-22.

7. Click the OK button to accept the changes and close the dialog.

8. Create a new page. Add a table to the page and request a Tabular layout.

9. Switch to page view. You'll now see a caption with a thistle background, and every other row will have a plum background.

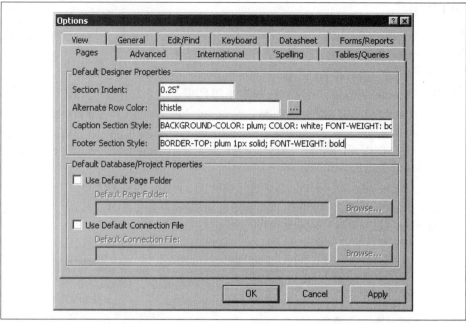

Figure 13-22. The Pages options after editing

Discussion

We used the Options dialog to change the look of two sections. All the options for pages are listed in Table 13-2. You can play around with these until you find the look you want.

Table 13-2. Page options

Option	Description
Section Indent	Defines the distance between the section and the page margin.
Alternate Row Color	Defines the color for every other row in a tabular page.
Caption Section Style	Uses standard HTML syntax to define the style for the caption section, where it exists.
Footer Section Style	Uses standard HTML syntax to define the style for the footer section, where it exists.
Use Default Page Folder	Specifies whether to store all pages (the actual *.htm* files) in a folder other than the folder of the current database.
Default Page Folder	If Use Default Page Folder is checked, specifies the folder where *.htm* files should be stored.
Use Default Connection File	Specifies whether to use a connection file (*.udl* or *.odc*) for all new pages.
Default Connection File	If Use Default Connection File is checked, specifies the connection file to be used.

13.8 Use Parameters Set in One DAP to Open Another

Problem

In Access, every report your users run starts with a dialog prompting them for input parameters, such as the requested timeframe for the report. How can you do the same thing with DAPs? You'd like the user to fill in start and end dates in the browser, and then open the page using those dates as a "where condition."

Solution

There are several ways to handle this issue; we'll show you two. Both solutions discussed here require that you base your DAP on a query that uses input parameters in the criteria. The first solution allows the DataSource control to do the work for you, much like allowing Access to display the Input Parameter dialog when you run a query that requires parameters. The second solution requires you to create another page that asks the user to enter the criteria, much like using a form to feed the query on which a report is based. This solution provides more flexibility but requires you to write some code in VBScript. The VBScript code uses cookies to pass information between the two pages.

The first solution requires no extra work on your part—it simply takes advantage of the DataSource component's built-in functionality. To test it out with our sample database, follow these steps:

1. Open our sample query from *13-08.MDB*, qryOrdersByDate, in design view. The query is shown in Figure 13-23. Note the input parameters, [*Start Date*] and [*End Date*], used as criteria.

2. Run the sample query. You'll be prompted for start and end dates with the built-in Input Parameter dialog shown in Figure 13-24. Enter any dates between July 1996 and May 1998 to see the query result.

3. Close the query.

4. Create a DAP based on the query. Add whatever fields you'd like. You can also use our sample page, Sample with No Code, if you'd prefer.

5. Run the page. Before the page is displayed, you'll see the Enter Parameters dialog shown in Figure 13-25.

6. Enter start and end dates and click the OK button. You'll see the page, filtered to show only orders between those dates.

The second solution allows you to show the user your own parameter request dialog as an HTML page. To do this, you'll need to create a page to collect the parameters and then add code to both that page and the data page to use the values entered in the parameter page as the parameters of the query.

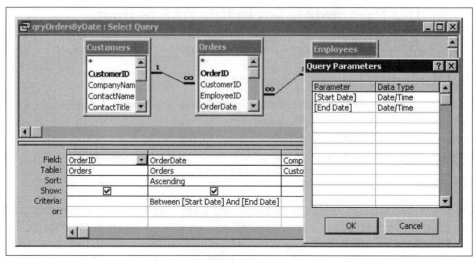

Figure 13-23. *The data source for our pages uses parameters in the criteria*

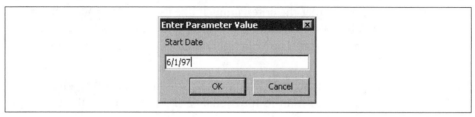

Figure 13-24. *The Input Parameter dialog*

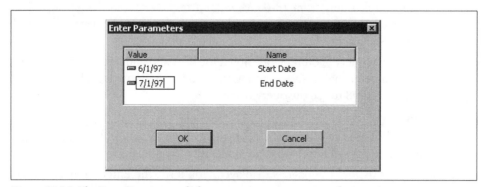

Figure 13-25. *The Enter Parameters dialog*

First, try out our sample by following these steps:

1. The sample won't work if you run it from within Access. Switch to Internet Explorer.

2. Open *Param OrdersByDate.htm* in the sample folder. The page is shown in Figure 13-26. It simply prompts for the criteria to be used in another DAP.

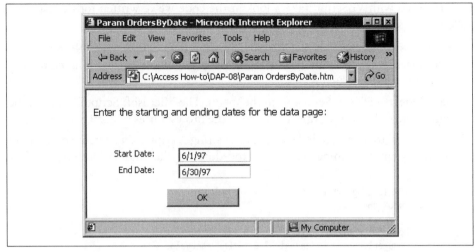

Figure 13-26. Param OrdersByDate.htm in a browser window

3. Enter start and end dates and click the OK command button. The *OrdersBy-Date.htm* DAP will open in the browser. You'll see only orders between the dates you specified.

Discussion

Param OrdersByDate.htm and *OrdersByDate.htm* work by using VBScript code to read and write information to a cookie that stays available for only one browser session.

Cookies, as you probably know, are bits of text that store information about what you are doing during a browser session. They are sometimes written out to disk so that the code used on a web site "remembers" what you were doing from one browser session to the next. In our case, the cookie will be available only in memory; it won't be written out to disk, and it will be deleted once the data page is displayed.

If your background is in database development, VBScript may be new to you. You can use scripts written in VBScript to enhance your DAPs, just as you can use VBA to enhance your forms and reports. If you already know VBA, you won't find VBScript particularly difficult to write. We won't attempt to teach you about VBScript or the document object model you'll use to control your page; we'll just touch on the key concepts for this sample. There are two key differences between VBA and VBScript that you should be aware of before we review the code:

- You won't be working in the VB Editor when you write VBScript. You'll probably use the Microsoft Script Editor, but you can use any text or HTML editor, including Notepad.

- Variables cannot be typed in VBScript. All variables are variants.

To get started with VBScript, take a look at the code we've written for this sample. Follow these steps to look at the code:

1. In Access, open the *Param OrdersByDate.htm* data access page. Note that the two text box controls are named txtStartDate and txtEndDate. The command button is named cmdOK.

2. Select View → HTML Source from the menu. The Microsoft Script Editor will be launched, and you'll see the HTML code the browser uses to display the page.

3. Press Ctrl-F to do a search. Search for the string "script". The cursor should land on the script containing the event procedure for the cmdOK button's onclick event:

```
<SCRIPT language=vbscript>
Sub cmdOK_onclick( )

    Document.cookie = "startdate=" & txtStartDate.value
    Document.cookie = "enddate=" & txtEndDate.value

    window.navigate("OrdersByDate.htm")

End Sub
</SCRIPT>
```

The first two lines of code use the document's Cookie property to record the parameters entered in the text boxes. Each time the code sets the cookie to a new *variable = value*, that string is appended to whatever the string already contains, with a semicolon separating the *variable = value* pairs. That is, if the start date is 6/1/97 and the end date is 6/30/97, the cookie will look like this:

```
startdate=6/1/97;enddate=6/30/97
```

The third line of code causes the browser to open *OrdersByDate.htm*.

4. Close the Microsoft Script Editor and the *Param OrdersByDate.htm* data access page.

5. Open the *OrdersByDate.htm* data access page in design view.

6. Select View → HTML Source to launch the Microsoft Script Editor. Search for the word "script".

7. There are two custom scripts in this data access page. The first contains a general-use function named ReadVarInCookie. The code looks like this:

```
<SCRIPT language=vbscript>

    Function ReadVarInCookie(strVariable)

    Dim varSplit
    Dim intCount
    Dim intFind
```

```
varSplit = split(document.cookie,"; ")
for intCount = lbound(varSplit) to ubound(varSplit)
    if left(varSplit(intCount),len(strVariable)) = strVariable then
        ' Figure out what's on the other side of the equals sign.

        intFind = instr(varSplit(intCount),"=")
        ReadVarInCookie = mid(varSplit(intCount),intFind + 1)
        exit function
    end if
next

ReadVarInCookie = "NOT_FOUND"

End Function
```

```
</SCRIPT>
```

The function takes an argument of the variable names for which we're searching (startdate and enddate, in our case). It returns the value associated with that variable name. Remember, it's the cookie that is being searched for the variable and value, and the cookie looks like this:

```
startdate=6/1/97;enddate=6/30/97
```

The first line following the variable declarations uses the built-in Split function to parse the document's cookie into an array of *variable = value* pairs. That is, it looks for semicolons and creates an array element for each string between the semicolons:

```
varSplit = split(document.cookie,"; ")
```

The for loop iterates through each element in the resulting array and checks the first part of the element to see if the string matches the name of the variable sent:

```
for intCount = lbound(varSplit) to ubound(varSplit)
    if left(varSplit(intCount),len(strVariable)) = strVariable then
```

If the if statement evaluates to True, the code looks for the value on the other side of the equals sign and returns that value:

```
intFind = instr(varSplit(intCount),"=")
ReadVarInCookie = mid(varSplit(intCount),intFind + 1)
```

If the variable name is not found, the function returns the value NOT_FOUND.

8. Scroll down to the second script. This script is not tied to an event, nor is it even contained in a procedure. Rather, the script runs when the page loads:

```
<SCRIPT language=vbscript>

dim strStart
dim strEnd

strStart = ReadVarInCookie("startdate")

strEnd = ReadVarInCookie("enddate")
```

```
MSODSC.RecordsetDefs("qryOrdersByDate").parametervalues.Add "[Start Date]",
strStart
MSODSC.RecordsetDefs("qryOrdersByDate").parametervalues.Add "[End Date]", strEnd

    document.cookie = "startdate=NULL;expires=Monday, 01-Jan-95 12:00:00 GMT"
    document.cookie = "enddate=NULL;expires=Monday, 01-Jan-95 12:00:00 GMT"
</SCRIPT>
```

The script calls the ReadVarInCookie function to find the values of startdate and enddate:

```
strStart = ReadVarInCookie("startdate")
strEnd = ReadVa1fp found, the code uses the DataSource component's object model
to set parameter values for the query on which the page is based:
MSODSC.RecordsetDefs("qryOrdersByDate").parametervalues.Add "[Start Date]",
strStart
MSODSC.RecordsetDefs("qryOrdersByDate").parametervalues.Add "[End Date]", strEnd
```

Finally, the code clears the cookie by setting the variable values to Null and providing an expiration date in the past:

```
document.cookie = "startdate=NULL;expires=Monday, 01-Jan-95 12:00:00 GMT"
document.cookie = "enddate=NULL;expires=Monday, 01-Jan-95 12:00:00 GMT"
```

We've only just touched the surface of coding DAPs. To go farther, you'll need to learn more about the document object model that Internet Explorer supports, and also about the Microsoft Office Data Source Control (MSODSC), the object model used in DAPs for retrieving and updating data.

CHAPTER 14

SQL Server

Microsoft has always made it easy to connect to SQL Server data from Access by allowing you to create linked tables using Open Database Connectivity (ODBC). You have also been able to create pass-through queries in Access that use ODBC to send commands to SQL Server for processing.

In Access 2000, Microsoft introduced a new way of using Access to work with SQL Server. Instead of creating regular MDB databases and using ODBC, you could create a new kind of application called an Access Data Project (ADP). ADPs don't use the Jet database engine and ODBC; instead, they use an OLE DB connection to a SQL Server database. In ADPs, you have the ability to view and modify SQL Server objects, and you can create forms, reports, and data access pages based on your SQL Server data.

In this chapter, we present a range of tips for using both traditional MDBs and the new ADPs to create Access applications that read and manipulate data stored in a SQL Server database. Several of the examples make use of the Northwind and Pubs sample databases that ship with SQL Server.

14.1 Dynamically Link SQL Server Tables at Runtime

Problem

Your Access SQL Server database uses linked tables and views in SQL Server. You have set up security and permissions in SQL Server and want to make sure that each user's linked tables are attached under their own permissions, not another user's permissions. In addition, you don't want the users to be prompted for an additional login ID and password each time they use a table.

Solution

If you link SQL Server tables from an Access database using the File Get External Data menu commands, you will be prompted to use or create a Data Source Name (DSN). The main drawback to DSNs is that they need to be installed on every user's machine. A better solution is to use VBA code to link or relink tables. You can supply connection information in the Connection string without having to create a DSN.

This technique uses DAO to create new TableDef objects in each database when the application starts up. The startup form for the application has a dialog where the user can supply a login and password to be used to connect to SQL Server. The list of table names is stored in a local Access (Jet) database.

To add this technique to your application, follow these steps:

1. Create a table to hold the names and properties of the SQL Server tables to which your application will link. In the *14-01.MDB* sample database, the local table is named tblSQLTables. The column definitions are listed in Table 14-1.

Table 14-1. Column definitions for tblSQLTables

Column name	Data type	Primary key?	Required?
SQLTable	Text 50	Yes	Yes
SQLDatabase	Text 50	No	Yes
SQLServer	Text 50	No	Yes

2. Enter data in the table. Figure 14-1 shows the datasheet view of the table used to store data about the tables that are linked from the Northwind database on the local SQL Server.

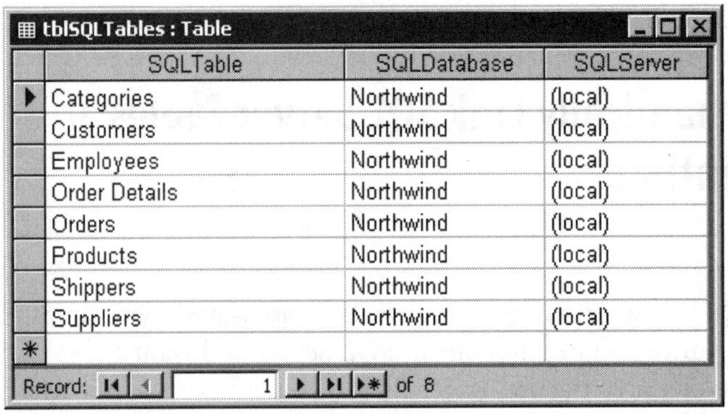

Figure 14-1. tblSQLTables has entries to link to the tables in the Northwind database

3. Create the startup form. The example shown in Figure 14-2 uses an option group to determine whether integrated security (Windows XP, Windows 2000,

or Windows NT authentication) or a SQL Server login and password is being used. If a SQL Server login is selected, users can enter their logins and passwords in the text boxes.

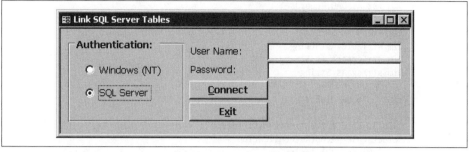

Figure 14-2. The startup form allows users to supply login information for the linked tables

4. Once you've created the form and the necessary controls, you'll need to write the code to set up the links. In design view, select the OnClick event of the Connect command button and choose Event Procedure. This will open the VBA code window.

5. You'll need to set a reference to the DAO 3.6 Object Library by choosing Tools → References... and checking the Microsoft DAO 3.6 Object Library, as shown in Figure 14-3.

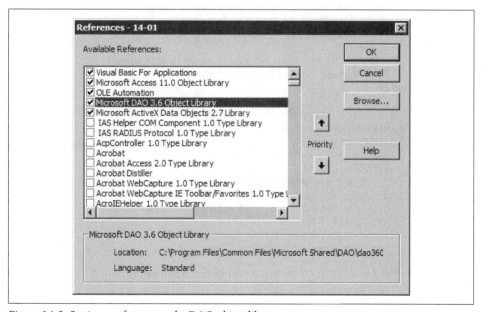

Figure 14-3. Setting a reference to the DAO object library

6. Here's the complete code listing for the cmdConnect_Click event procedure:

```
Private Sub cmdConnect_Click( )
    Dim db As DAO.Database
    Dim tdf As DAO.TableDef
    Dim rst As DAO.Recordset
    Dim strServer As String
    Dim strDB As String
    Dim strTable As String
    Dim strConnect As String
    Dim strMsg As String

On Error GoTo HandleErr

    ' Build base authentication strings.
    Select Case Me.optAuthentication
        ' Windows/NT login
        Case 1
            strConnect = "ODBC;Driver={SQL Server};Trusted_Connection=Yes;"
        ' SQL Server login
        Case 2
            strConnect = "ODBC;Driver={SQL Server};UID=" _
            & Me.txtUser & ";PWD=" & Me.txtPwd & ";"
    End Select

    ' Get rid of any old links.
    Call DeleteLinks

    ' Create a recordset to obtain server object names.
    Set db = CurrentDb
    Set rst = db.OpenRecordset("tblSQLTables", dbOpenSnapshot)
    If rst.EOF Then
        strMsg = "There are no tables listed in tblSQLTables."
        GoTo ExitHere
    End If

    ' Walk through the recordset and create the links.
    Do Until rst.EOF
        strServer = rst!SQLServer
        strDB = rst!SQLDatabase
        strTable = rst!SQLTable
        ' Create a new TableDef object.
        Set tdf = db.CreateTableDef(strTable)
        ' Set the Connect property to establish the link.
        tdf.Connect = strConnect & _
            "Server=" & strServer & _
            ";Database=" & strDB & ";"
        tdf.SourceTableName = strTable
        ' Append to the database's TableDefs collection.
        db.TableDefs.Append tdf
        rst.MoveNext
    Loop
```

```
            strMsg = "Tables linked successfully."

            rst.Close
            Set rst = Nothing
            Set tdf = Nothing
            Set db = Nothing

    ExitHere:
            MsgBox strMsg, , "Link SQL Tables"
            Exit Sub

    HandleErr:
        Select Case Err
            Case Else
                strMsg = Err & ": " & Err.Description
                Resume ExitHere
        End Select
    End Sub
```

The completed application is shown in *14-01.MDB*, which contains the local table used to store data about the tables that are linked from the Northwind SQL Server database. A startup form contains the relinking code.

Discussion

The first step in linking SQL Server tables is to build the ODBC Connection string that will be used to link the tables. You could use a DSN, but you'd have to create the DSN if it didn't exist. We find it easier to simply build a dynamic string with all the required information. The first part of the string contains connection information that will be the same for every table:

```
Select Case Me.optAuthentication
    ' Windows/NT login
    Case 1
        strConnect = "ODBC;Driver={SQL Server};Trusted_Connection=Yes;"
    ' SQL Server login
    Case 2
        strConnect = "ODBC;Driver={SQL Server};UID=" _
        & Me.txtUser & ";PWD=" & Me.txtPwd & ";"
End Select
```

The next step is to delete any old linked SQL Server tables by calling the DeleteLinks procedure:

```
Call DeleteLinks
```

The DeleteLinks procedure walks through the current database's TableDefs collection, deleting only linked ODBC tables. Here's the complete listing:

```
Private Sub DeleteLinks( )
    ' Delete any leftover linked tables from a previous session.

    Dim tdf As DAO.TableDef
```

```
On Error GoTo HandleErr
For Each tdf In CurrentDb.TableDefs
    With tdf
    ' Delete only SQL Server tables.
        If (.Attributes And dbAttachedODBC)  = dbAttachedODBC Then
            CurrentDb.Execute "DROP TABLE [" & tdf.Name & "]"
        End If
    End With
    Next tdf

ExitHere:
    Set tdf = Nothing
    Exit Sub

HandleErr:
    MsgBox Err & ": " & Err.Description, , "Error in DeleteLinks( )"
    Resume ExitHere
    Resume
End Sub
```

The next step is to create a recordset that lists the table names, the SQL Server database name, and the SQL Server itself. If no tables are listed, the procedure terminates. This portion of code is as follows:

```
Set db = CurrentDb
Set rst = db.OpenRecordset("tblSQLTables", dbOpenSnapshot)
If rst.EOF Then
    strMsg = "There are no tables listed in tblSQLTables."
    GoTo ExitHere
End If
```

Next, walk through the recordset, creating a new TableDef object for each table listed. The Connect property is set to the base connection string, with the server and database name concatenated. The TableDef object's SourceTableName is set to the table name in the database, and the TableDef object is appended to the TableDefs collection. This portion of code resides in the following Do Until loop:

```
Do Until rst.EOF
    strServer = rst!SQLServer
    strDB = rst!SQLDatabase
    strTable = rst!SQLTable
    ' Create a new TableDef object.
    Set tdf = db.CreateTableDef(strTable)
    ' Set the Connect property to establish the link.
    tdf.Connect = strConnect & _
        "Server=" & strServer & _
        ";Database=" & strDB & ";"
    tdf.SourceTableName = strTable
    ' Append to the database's TableDefs collection.
    db.TableDefs.Append tdf
    rst.MoveNext
Loop
```

Once the TableDefs are appended, the cleanup code runs and the user is notified that the tables have been successfully linked:

```
        strMsg = "Tables linked successfully."

        rst.Close
        Set rst = Nothing
        Set tdf = Nothing
        Set db = Nothing

    ExitHere:
        MsgBox strMsg, , "Link SQL Tables"
        Exit Sub
```

The technique discussed here for relinking tables works well in any version of SQL Server and is not specific to any version of Access. Any time you use DAO in your code, you need to open the Tools → References... dialog in the Visual Basic editor and make sure that a reference is set for the Microsoft DAO library: the version of DAO used in Access 2000 or later is 3.6.

 Although you can link SQL Server tables using ADOX, the SQL Server tables are then read-only in Access.

14.2 Dynamically Connect to SQL Server from an ADP

Problem

When you create a new ADP, you are prompted for connection information that is saved with the ADP. If you want to change it later, you need to choose File → Connection from the menu and manually input new connection information in the Data Link dialog. Since the users of your ADP may not know how to do that, they would be connecting to SQL Server using your security credentials, not their own. You'd like to create a project that automatically opens the Data Link dialog and prompts the users for their own connection information instead of displaying your connection information.

Solution

This solution involves creating an unbound ADP (an ADP that is not yet connected to a SQL Server database) and prompting the user to fill in the connection information by displaying the Data Link dialog.

Since connection information is saved with the ADP, you need to create a new ADP with no connection information.

Follow these steps to implement this functionality in your ADPs:

1. Create a new ADP by choosing File → New and clicking on Project (Existing Data), as shown in Figure 14-4.

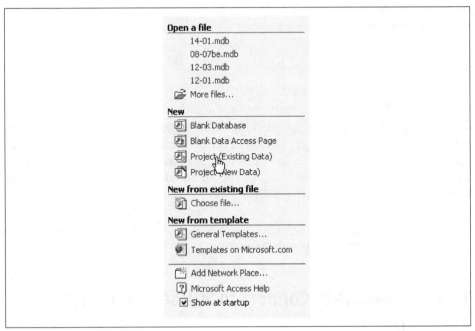

Figure 14-4. Creating a new ADP

2. Designate a location for the new project when prompted. When the Connection dialog opens, press Cancel. Do not fill in any connection information.

3. You will now have an empty project. You want to create a startup form like the one shown in Figure 14-5.

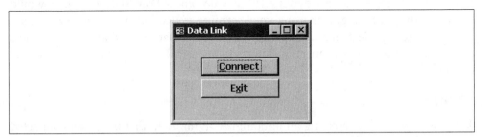

Figure 14-5. The startup form for the ADP

4. This form has a button that allows users to change their connection information. However, you want to prompt them to connect to the SQL Server database the first time they connect, so place the following code in the Form_Load event:

```
Private Sub Form_Load( )
    If Not CurrentProject.IsConnected Then
        DoCmd.RunCommand acCmdConnection
    End If
End Sub
```

5. The code for the Connect button simply executes the same line of code a second time:

```
Private Sub cmdConnect_Click( )
    DoCmd.RunCommand acCmdConnection
End Sub
```

Discussion

The DoCmd.RunCommand statement allows you to execute almost any item that appears in the built-in Access menus, as shown in the Object Browser in Figure 14-6. In this case, you are invoking the Data Link dialog by using the acCmdConnection constant.

When the form loads, the CurrentProject's IsConnected property is checked. The first time the form loads, you want to prompt for connection information before proceeding. Once users type in their credentials, this information will be saved. Should the users ever want to change their connection information, the Connect button on the form will allow them to do so.

If you need to dynamically connect at runtime and don't want to save connection information, you can connect and disconnect in code by taking advantage of the CurrentProject.OpenConnection and CurrentProject.CloseConnection methods. To open a project, use OpenConnection, passing in your connection information as a string:

```
CurrentProject.OpenConnection strConnect
```

The connection string, strConnect, looks like this for integrated security against the Northwind database on the local server:

```
PROVIDER=SQLOLEDB.1;INTEGRATED SECURITY=SSPI;PERSIST SECURITY INFO=FALSE;INITIAL
CATALOG=Northwind;DATA SOURCE=(local)
```

The following connection string works for a SQL Server user named Dudley with a password of "password":

```
PROVIDER=SQLOLEDB.1;PERSIST SECURITY INFO=TRUE;USER
ID=Dudley;PASSWORD=password;INITIAL CATALOG=Northwind;DATA SOURCE=(local)
```

The sample project, *14-02code.adp*, demonstrates this technique.

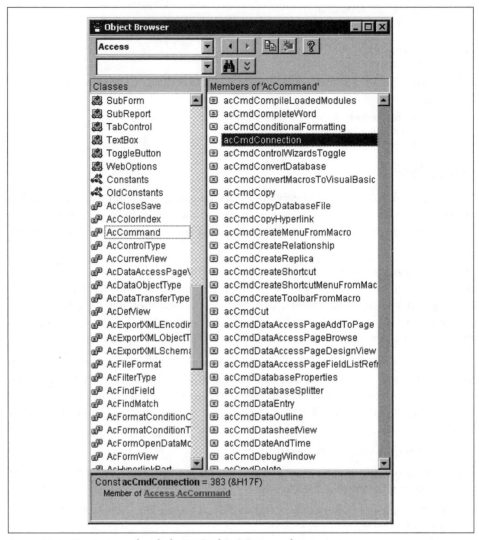

Figure 14-6. Constants used with the DoCmd.RunCommand statement

14.3 Share an ADP from a Shared Network Folder

Problem

You want to share an ADP on a network. However, the second user who attempts to open the ADP gets an error message.

Solution

This solution involves opening the ADP using the `/runtime` switch.

Follow these steps to create a shared ADP:

1. Create a shortcut on each user's desktop. In the Properties dialog, enter information using the format shown in Figure 14-7.

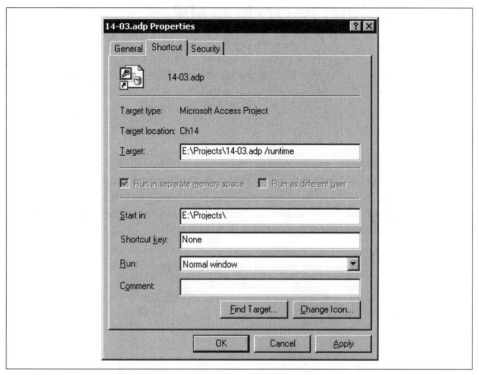

Figure 14-7. Properties for creating a shortcut for a shared ADP

2. Copy the shortcut to each user's machine.

Discussion

ADPs are intended for single-user activity. Using the `/runtime` switch allows you to get around this limitation by opening the ADP as read-only.

In Access MDB databases, the Jet database engine allows multiple users to share a frontend database containing forms, reports, queries, and code, just as they can share backend databases that contain data. If necessary, the Jet engine can lock resources in the database to prevent multiple users from interfering with each other.

ADPs don't have the benefit of the Jet database engine, so Access has no way to handle multiple users of a single project file. Users can share SQL Server data, but usually each user needs her own ADP. You can get around this by using the /runtime command-line option to force the ADP to be read-only. In this case, Access detects that there is no danger of users interfering with each other because they can't change anything, so it allows multiple users to work with the same ADP.

14.4   Fill the Drop-Down Lists When Using ServerFilterByForm in an ADP

Problem

You have turned on the ServerFilterByForm property. However, when users open the form and select from the combo boxes, the only choices are Is Null and Is Not Null. How do you get the combo boxes to show a list of valid values for that field?

Solution

If you turn on the ServerFilterByForm property, your form will open in a special view that turns text boxes into combo boxes. This allows users to define their own server filters at runtime, which are then processed by SQL Server before the record source data is returned to the form. However, you'll often see only the values shown in Figure 14-8 when you expand one of the combo boxes.

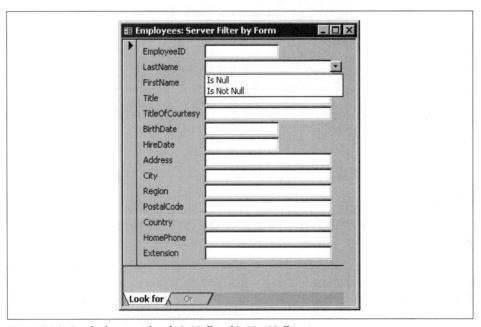

Figure 14-8. Combo boxes with only Is Null and Is Not Null options

Each text box on the form has a FilterLookup property that has three settings:

Never
> A combo box list will contain only two items: Is Null and Is Not Null.

Always
> A combo box with a full list of values will be created for that text box.

Database Default
> Access will populate the list either with all the values or with only Is Null/Is Not Null, depending on the settings in the Edit/Find tab of the Tools → Options dialog shown in Figure 14-9.

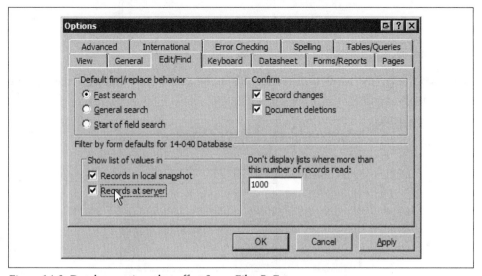

Figure 14-9. Database options that affect ServerFilterByForm

Follow these steps to change the database defaults to always show a list of available items when using ServerFilterByForm:

1. Open the database whose options you want to change.

2. Choose Tools → Options from the menu.

3. Check the "Records at server" option shown in Figure 14-9.

If you don't want to change this option globally, follow these steps to set the list of values on a form-by-form basis:

1. In design view, open the form in which you want to enable a full list of values for ServerFilterByForm. Select all the text boxes you want to enable.

2. Set the FilterLookup property on the Data tab in the properties sheet to Always, as shown in Figure 14-10.

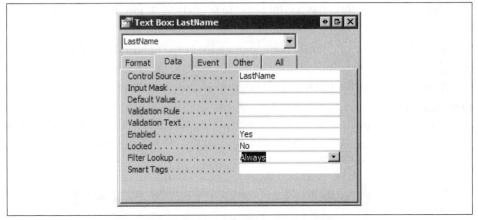

Figure 14-10. Set the FilterLookup property for the control on a form

When you open the form to filter records now, you'll see some real data in the combo boxes, as shown in Figure 14-11.

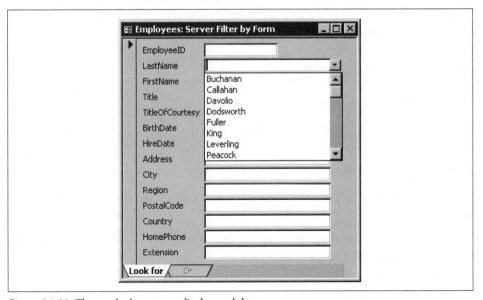

Figure 14-11. The combo boxes now display real data

Discussion

The data to populate the combo boxes must, of course, come from the server. Setting the FilterLookup property for the controls or setting the "Records at server" option for the entire project runs additional queries that populate each combo box with a domain of real values from which the user can choose.

When you set the ServerFilter property on a form, regular filtering with the form's Filter property is unavailable.

Because populating combo boxes with real values entails extra round trips to the server to retrieve the data for the lists, it defeats the purpose of using the ServerFilter property in the first place, so don't overuse this feature. The benefit is that the interface is more user-friendly when the user can select from actual values instead of guessing.

You'll have to evaluate your own applications to determine whether or not the extra data filtering is worth the extra load on the server. If the form would otherwise load a lot of records, and if the lists you are loading aren't too big, you would probably improve performance by using ServerFilterByForm. To be safe, adjust the ServerFilterByForm setting at the control level rather than by setting the database default for the entire project.

14.5   Pass Parameters to Stored Procedures from Pass-Through Queries in an MDB

Problem

You are calling stored procedures that require parameters by using pass-through queries. How can you pass parameters to the pass-through query from your form? If you include a reference to the form in the pass-through query, you get an error message from SQL Server.

Solution

Pass-through queries are not processed in the same way as regular Access queries against linked tables. The SQL syntax you type in a pass-through query is passed directly to SQL Server. Any references to forms or controls on forms in a pass-through query are meaningless to SQL Server, so you must pass the actual values for your parameters.

A pass-through query has three important properties:

SQL
> The SQL property contains the textual content of the pass-through query. This must be a valid Transact-SQL statement.

ODBCConnectStr
> The connection string contains information that the query uses to connect to SQL Server. You can specify a DSN, or use a string containing all the requisite connection information, as shown in the Solution in Recipe 14.1.

ReturnsRecords

> The ReturnsRecords property specifies whether or not the query returns records. An action query that just modifies data without retrieving anything would have this property set to No or False.

Figure 14-12 shows the properties sheet for a pass-through query to the pubs sample database in SQL Server.

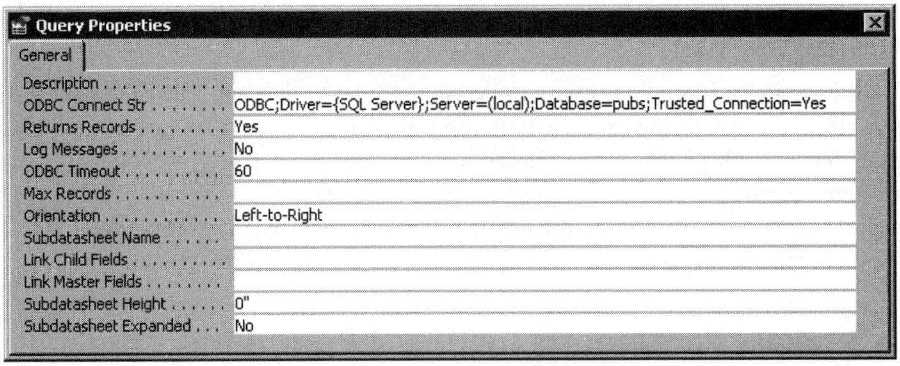

Figure 14-12. Pass-through query properties

The most versatile way to set these properties is to write a procedure that sets them at runtime by using a DAO QueryDef object. You'll then need to set parameter values to the procedure for connection information, the SQL string that comprises the pass-through query, and whether or not the query returns records.

To modify a pass-through query at runtime, follow these general steps:

1. Open a new module and set a reference to the DAO object library.

2. Create a new public procedure. Here is the complete code listing:

```
Public Sub acbPassThrough( _
  ByVal QueryName As String, _
  ByVal SQLStatement As String, _
  Optional ConnectStr As Variant, _
  Optional ReturnsRecords As Boolean = True)

    Dim qdf As DAO.QueryDef
    Dim strConnect As String

    Set qdf = CurrentDb.QueryDefs(QueryName)

    ' If no connection information is supplied,
    ' connection information from the query is used.
    If IsMissing(ConnectStr) Then
        strConnect = qdf.Connect
    Else
        strConnect = CStr(ConnectStr)
```

```
          End If

            ' Set query properties to parameter values.
            qdf.Connect = strConnect
            qdf.ReturnsRecords = ReturnsRecords
            qdf.SQL = SQLStatement

    ExitHere:
            Set qdf = Nothing
            Exit Sub

    HandleErr:
            MsgBox Err & ": " & Err.Description, , "Error in acbPassThrough"
            Resume ExitHere
    End Sub
```

3. To test the procedure, create a new query and choose Query SQL-Specific Pass-through from the menu.

4. Save the query, naming it qryPassThrough.

5. Create a form with text boxes and optionally a combo box to test the procedure. The sample form in *14-05.MDB* uses the byroyalty stored procedure from the pubs sample database. It takes an input parameter for the royalty percentage. You can change the values on the form shown in Figure 14-13 to adjust any of the arguments needed to call the acbPassThrough procedure.

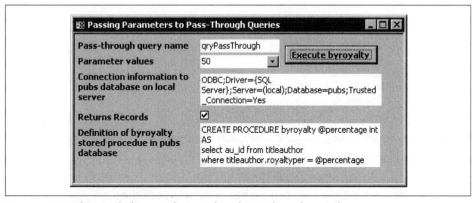

Figure 14-13. The sample form used to test the acbPassThrough procedure

6. Write the following code in the Click event of the command button to pass the parameters to acbPassThrough:

```
    Private Sub cmdExecute_Click( )
        Dim strQuery As String
        Dim strSQL As String
        Dim strConnect As String
        Dim fReturnsRecs As Boolean

        strQuery = Me.lblQuery.Caption
```

```
        strConnect = Me.lblConnection.Caption
        fReturnsRecs = CBool(Me.ckReturnsRecords)
        strSQL = "EXEC byroyalty " & Me.cboParameter

        Call acbPassThrough(strQuery, strSQL, strConnect, fReturnsRecs)
        Me.RecordSource = strQuery
        Me.txtAuID.Visible = True
    End Sub
```

7. Test the procedure by clicking the "Execute byroyalty" command button on the form.

Discussion

The acbPassThrough procedure can modify any saved pass-through query by using the DAO QueryDef object:

```
Dim qdf As DAO.QueryDef
Dim strConnect As String

Set qdf = CurrentDb.QueryDefs(QueryName)
```

There is an optional parameter for the ConnectStr argument. If a connection string is not supplied, the one saved with the QueryDef object is used:

```
If IsMissing(ConnectStr) Then
    strConnect = qdf.Connect
Else
    strConnect = CStr(ConnectStr)
End If
```

The properties for the query are then set to the values passed into the procedure:

```
qdf.Connect = strConnect
qdf.ReturnsRecords = ReturnsRecords
qdf.SQL = SQLStatement
```

This actually permanently saves changes to the query—if you open the query in design view after executing the procedure, you'll see the last properties that were set.

The values on the form are simply collected from the relevant text boxes and combo boxes, and passed to the procedure. Then the form is requeried and the new results of the pass-through query are loaded as the record source of the form.

Access lets you create ad hoc queries by using the CreateQueryDef syntax and specifying an empty string for the parameter name. However, using a previously saved query eliminates the overhead of creating a new object from scratch and then discarding it.

 The result set returned from a pass-through query is always read-only.

14.6   Pass Parameters to Stored Procedures from an ADP

Problem

You have a form that is based on a stored procedure. How do you pass parameter values from a combo box to the stored procedure?

Solution

The InputParameters property allows you to pass parameters to the form's record source. The InputParameters property can be used with stored procedures or with direct Transact-SQL statements. If you use the InputParameters property with a SQL statement, you must formulate the SQL statement with a question mark as the parameter placeholder:

```
SELECT * FROM MyTable WHERE Price > ?
```

You then need to set the InputParameters property of the form, specifying the parameter name and data type, and where the value can be obtained. In the case of a SQL statement using question marks, the name you choose for the parameter is not important:

```
Price money = Forms!frmOrderInputParameter!txtSearch
```

Here's how to set up your forms to supply input parameters to stored procedures:

1. The example form in *14-06.adp* has a combo box for the user to select a royalty percentage. Set the form's RecordSource property to the byroyalty stored procedure, as shown in Figure 14-14.

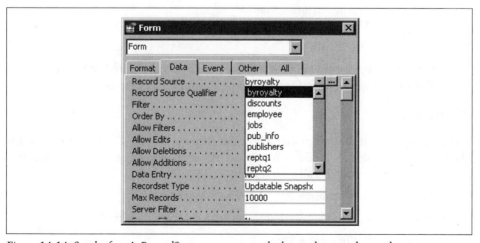

Figure 14-14. Set the form's RecordSource property to the byroyalty stored procedure

2. Set the InputParameters property to the following expression:

```
@percentage int=Forms!frmParameters!cboParameter
```

3. Type the following code in the combo box's AfterUpdate event:

```
Me.Requery
```

4. Run the form. The form opens, but no data is displayed because no value has been specified for the @percentage parameter and there are no records with a blank percentage. Select an item from the combo box and the form will be requeried, picking up the value from the combo box and reexecuting the stored procedure.

Although this technique eventually works, it's not an ideal solution because it involves a wasted round trip to the server the first time the form opens. The stored procedure executes with a null value in the place of a valid parameter value that would return records. No error is returned—there simply weren't any matching records.

A more efficient solution is to write code that sets the record source only when a royalty percentage has been selected:

1. Open the form in design view and delete the form's RecordSource property setting (byroyalty) and the InputParameters property setting.

2. Delete the existing code in the AfterUpdate event of the combo box and replace it with the following:

```
Private Sub cboParameter_AfterUpdate( )
    Me.RecordSource = "EXEC byroyalty " & Me.cboParameter.Value

    ' Run this code only the first time the combo box
    ' is requeried.
    If Me.txtAuID.Visible = False Then
        Me.txtAuID.Visible = True
        DoCmd.RunCommand acCmdSizeToFitForm
    End If
End Sub
```

3. Test the form by opening it in form view. The byroyalty stored procedure will be executed only when the user selects an item from the combo box.

Discussion

The form opens in unbound mode, with no record source set. The text box that displays the au_id value is hidden. When the AfterUpdate event of the combo box occurs, the form is automatically requeried:

```
Me.RecordSource = "EXEC byroyalty " & Me.cboParameter.Value
```

Then the text box is unhidden so that the result set can be displayed:

```
If Me.txtAuID.Visible = False Then
    Me.txtAuID.Visible = True
    DoCmd.RunCommand acCmdSizeToFitForm
End If
```

Figure 14-15 shows the form with all of the records displayed.

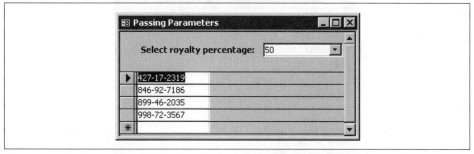

Figure 14-15. A form that passes a value to a stored procedure

Although you could leave the form with the original property settings specifying the stored procedure name in the RecordSource property and the parameter value in the InputParameters property on the properties sheet, it wastes a round trip across the network in a request for records that will always fail.

Whenever you are creating applications against server data, it is a good idea to minimize your use of network and server resources as much as possible. You will then be able to support a larger number of users and provide better performance.

14.7 Use Controls as Parameters for the Row Source of Combo and List Boxes in an ADP

Problem

Cascading combo boxes—where the list in the second combo box changes based on the selection in the first—can provide an effective way to limit the number of records returned from SQL Server. You have a series of cascading combo boxes that are based on stored procedures that have parameters. The value that the user selects in the first combo box should determine the contents of the list in the second combo box. How do you pass the parameter values from one combo box to another?

Solution

You can easily use a stored procedure as the row source for a combo box in Access 2002 or later, as long as the stored procedure doesn't have a parameter. Figure 14-16 shows the properties sheet for the Country combo box on frmCustomer in *14-07.adp* that lets a user select from a list of countries.

The stored procedure definition simply selects a distinct list of countries from the Customers table in the Northwind database:

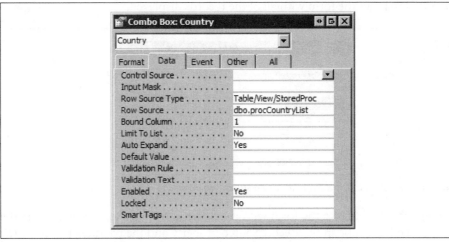

Figure 14-16. A combo box based on a stored procedure with no parameter

```
CREATE PROC procCountryList
AS
SELECT DISTINCT Country
FROM Customers
ORDER BY Country
```

However, the Select Customer combo box is based on the procCustomersByCountry stored procedure, which has an input parameter called *@Country*. It's designed to filter customers by country, so that a user can pick a country before selecting a single customer to edit. The code for the procCustomersByCountry stored procedure is:

```
CREATE PROC procCustomersByCountry
   @Country nvarchar(15)
AS
SELECT CustomerID, CompanyName
FROM Customers
WHERE Country = @Country
ORDER BY CompanyName
```

The Select Customer combo box does not get its RowSource property assigned unless a user selects a country first. In the AfterUpdate event of the Country combo box, a SQL string is constructed that executes the stored procedure with the selected parameter:

```
Private Sub Country_AfterUpdate( )
    Dim strCountry As String
    Dim strSQL As String

    strCountry = Me.Country & ""
    strSQL = "EXEC procCustomersByCountry " & strCountry
    If Len(strCountry) > 0 Then
        Me.cboCustomer.RowSource = strSQL
    End If
End Sub
```

In the AfterUpdate event of the Customer combo box, the form's RecordSource property is then set:

```
Private Sub cboCustomer_AfterUpdate( )
    Dim strSQL As String
    strSQL = "EXEC procCustomerSelect " & Me.cboCustomer
    Me.RecordSource = strSQL
    If Not Me.Detail.Visible Then
        Me.Detail.Visible = True
        DoCmd.RunCommand acCmdSizeToFitForm
    End If
End Sub
```

Here is the stored procedure being used for the record source:

```
CREATE PROC procCustomerSelect
  @CustomerID nchar(5)
AS
SELECT *
FROM Customers
WHERE CustomerID = @CustomerID
ORDER BY CompanyName
```

Here's how you can implement this functionality in your forms:

1. Create the necessary stored procedures for your combo boxes and forms.

2. For the first combo box based on a stored procedure that is not parameterized, simply assign the name of the stored procedure to the row source.

3. In the OnEnter or the OnGotFocus event of the second combo box, pick up the value from the first combo box and concatenate it to execute the stored procedure on which the second combo box is based:

   ```
   Me.cboCustomer.RowSource = "EXEC MyProc " & Me.FirstComboBox
   ```

Discussion

Not assigning a row source at design time allows you to dynamically execute a parameterized stored procedure by concatenating the parameter value to an EXECUTE statement. Every time the parameter value changes, you create a new row source for the dependent combo box.

If this seems like a lot of work, there is an easier way that isn't documented in the Access help file. This technique is illustrated in frmSimple in *14-07.adp*. You can name the first combo box with the same name as the parameter (without the @ sign). Base the second combo box on the first combo box by using a query with a parameter that has the same name as the first combo box, and requery the second combo box in the AfterUpdate event of the first combo box. Figure 14-17 shows the properties in the second combo box.

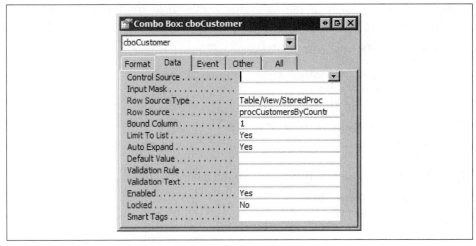

Figure 14-17. Setting the properties of the second combo box

The code in the AfterUpdate event of the first combo box is simply to requery the second combo box:

```
Me.SecondCombo.Requery
```

In the example shown in *14-07.adp*, the form itself is not a bound form. In other words, its record source is assigned at runtime in the AfterUpdate event of the combo box, which selects an individual customer. If you were using this example on a bound form to filter records, you would need to call the code in the AfterUpdate event in the OnCurrent event as well.

14.8   Reference Data from More than One SQL Server Database in an ADP

Problem

You'd like to have your ADP connect to multiple SQL Server databases at one time. However, the Data Link dialog allows room for only one SQL Server database.

Solution

Although at first glance this seems to be a problem, the solution is readily at hand with SQL Server's three-part naming convention. You are probably already familiar with the OwnerName.ObjectName syntax for referring to SQL Server objects, which is needed when users other than the owner (or creator) of that object wish to use the object. The three-part naming syntax is:

```
DatabaseName.OwnerName.ObjectName
```

To refer to another SQL Server database in your ADP, follow these steps:

1. Create a new project and link it to the Northwind database. You can look at the list of tables and see only the tables from Northwind.

2. Create a new form. Type the following statement into the RecordSource property of the form:

   ```
   SELECT * FROM pubs.dbo.authors
   ```

3. You will then see the Field List for the authors table in the pubs database. Figure 14-18 displays the Field List from the sample form, frmPubsAuthorsSQL, and shows that the form is now bound to data in the pubs database, not the Northwind database.

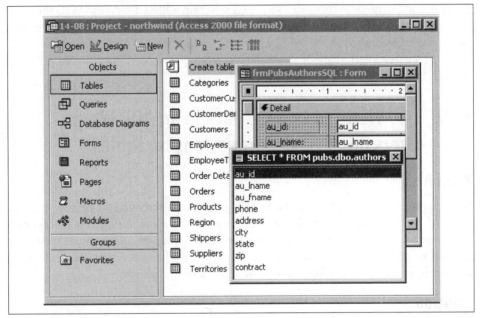

Figure 14-18. The Field List from frmPubsAuthorsSQL

4. Alternately, you can create a view in the Northwind database that selects data from the pubs.authors table:

   ```
   CREATE VIEW vwPubsAuthors
   AS
   SELECT au_id, au_lname, au_fname, phone,
     address, city, state, zip, contract
   FROM pubs.dbo.authors
   ```

You can then base forms and reports in your Northwind project on the view.

Discussion

SQL Server allows users to access other databases residing on the same server when the three-part naming syntax is used. However, users must have been granted permissions in the source database if data is to be accessed with a direct SQL statement. SQL Server will return a permissions error message if those permissions have not been granted.

Working with data from multiple databases is easy in ADPs, even though you see the objects from only one database listed in the database window. Just remember to use the three-part naming syntax.

If the data you need is not just in another database but on another server, it gets a little more complicated. In this case, you need to set up a linked server in SQL Server to access the data. Linked servers in SQL Server use OLE DB providers, which means you are not limited to only SQL Server data. Linked servers allow you to use SQL Server as a gateway to many different data sources, just as you may use Access databases to link to multiple data sources.

14.9   Use Views to Update Data in an ADP When Users Don't Have Permissions on Tables

Problem

You have secured your SQL Server 2000 database and removed all permissions for users to directly interact with tables. You have created views and granted users permissions to update data through the views instead. However, users normally are not allowed to update data through views when they don't have access to the underlying tables. How can you allow them to update tables through views?

Solution

Whenever you secure your database in SQL Server, you have the option of denying permissions on tables and granting permissions for users to work with the data only through secondary objects such as views, stored procedures, or user-defined inline functions. As long as both the underlying table and the secondary object have the same owner, SQL Server does not check permissions on the underlying table, and simply executes the action based on user permissions granted on the secondary object. For example, you can deny permissions for users to select data from a table, and then create a view that selects data from the table. Then grant users permissions to use the view, as shown in Figure 14-19.

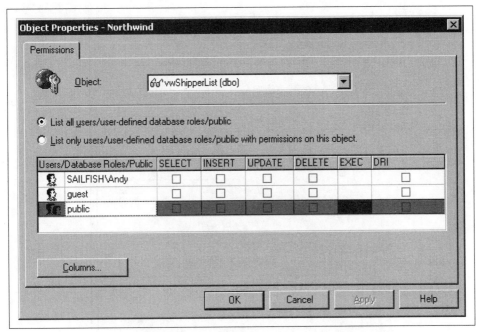

Figure 14-19. Using SQL Server Enterprise Manager to grant permissions for views

You can then update data through the view instead of the table, as long as you have permissions granted on the view. This allows you to control which rows and columns in the table your users can access.

However, in an ADP, Access doesn't use the view to update the data even if the view is the record source of a form. A peek at a Profiler session in SQL Server shows that when you update the form, Access creates an update statement directly against the base tables.

You can solve this problem by adding an option to the view that will force Access to run its updates against the view rather than against the base tables. If you use the WITH VIEW_METADATA option when you create (or alter) your view, SQL Server will send Access metadata (column names and data types) from the view rather than from the underlying tables, and Access will use the view to update data. If you use Access to create the view, you can set this option by setting the "Update using view rules" property, as shown in Figure 14-20.

If you are using Access 2000, you need to type in the WITH VIEW_ METADATA option manually, since it doesn't show up in the Properties dialog. This option wasn't supported in SQL Server 7.0.

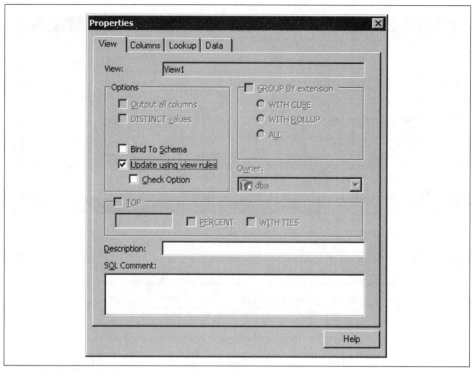

Figure 14-20. The "Update using view rules" property

Use the following steps to allow your users to update data through views when they don't have permissions on the underlying tables:

1. Revoke or deny all permissions to the public role for the table (or tables) on which the view will be based.

2. Create a view that selects data from the table by using the VIEW_METADATA option or selecting the "Update using view rules" checkbox. This example selects data from the Shippers table:

```
CREATE VIEW vwShipperList
WITH VIEW_METADATA
AS
SELECT ShipperID, CompanyName, Phone
FROM Shippers
```

3. Grant INSERT and UPDATE permissions on the view.

4. To test the view, use it as the record source of a form. Make sure to fully qualify your references with the ownername.objectname syntax.

5. Log on as another user who does not have permission on the underlying tables. You should now be able to update data or insert data, but not delete an existing shipper.

Discussion

When Access requests data for a view in browse mode, it also retrieves metadata that it uses to construct update, insert, and delete statements. The VIEW_METADATA option specifies that SQL Server returns enough metadata information about the view for Access to implement updateable client-side cursors that work with the view instead of the base tables.

This technique is not available in SQL Server 7.0 or earlier because the VIEW_METADATA option did not exist prior to the release of SQL Server 2000. This new feature makes it possible to take advantage of bound Access forms without having to sacrifice security. Few SQL Server database administrators are willing to give users unrestricted permissions to update tables. Views offer more control, but the most control comes from using stored procedures, and, unfortunately, there is nothing like the VIEW_METADATA option for stored procedures.

CHAPTER 15

Office Web and SharePoint

Data Access Pages represent just one of several options for creating web pages connected to Access databases. You can also use FrontPage 2003, with or without Windows SharePoint Services, to create Access-connected web pages.

Windows SharePoint Services, a server component that is part of Windows 2003 Server, is a great system for easily creating collaborative, team-based web sites consisting of various lists and documents. Access 2003 can work with SharePoint in two ways. First, you can use Access as a frontend to your SharePoint list and documents. That is, you can create a SharePoint management interface using Access forms and reports to help manage your SharePoint sites. In addition, you can use SharePoint to create data-driven web sites that draw their data from Access databases and display the data using the Data View Web Part.

FrontPage 2002 and 2003 also allow you to connect web sites to Access databases without using Windows SharePoint Services. You can use FrontPage to create an HTML form that sends its results to an Access database. You can also use the FrontPage Database Interface Wizard to quickly create a frontend to an Access table.

15.1 Work with SharePoint Data from Access

Problem

Windows SharePoint Services makes it easy to create collaborative, team-based web sites consisting of various lists and documents. Is it possible to use Access as a frontend to SharePoint data?

Solution

 This solution requires Access 2003 and a web server running Windows SharePoint Services.

Access 2003 supports the linking to (and importing of) SharePoint lists and document libraries. To link to a SharePoint data source, follow these steps:

1. Select File → Get External Data → Link Tables... to open the Link dialog box. Under the Files of Type dropdown control, select Windows SharePoint Services (WSS). Access starts the Link to Windows SharePoint Services wizard as shown in Figure 15-1.

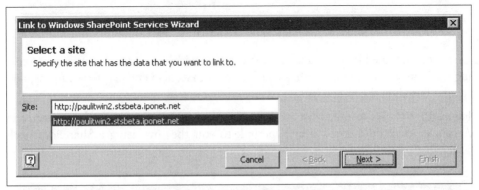

Figure 15-1. Selecting the SharePoint site to which you wish to connect on the first page of the Link to Windows SharePoint Services wizard

2. Enter the URL of a Windows SharePoint Services (WSS) site into the site textbox and click Next. At this point you may be prompted to login to the site.

3. At the second page of the wizard you will be prompted to select a list as shown in Figure 15-2. Some SharePoint lists, such as the Events and Tasks lists, provide multiple views of the list. If you wish to link to each of these views, then select "Link to one or more views of a list" and select the list from the Lists listbox. Otherwise, if you wish to link to several lists, select "Link to one or more lists" and hold down the SHIFT or CTRL key to select multiple lists in the Lists listbox.

4. If you checked "Retrieve IDs for lookup columns," then the next page of the wizard will present a set of related lists that you will need to include in order to update the lists. You can deselect the related lists at this point, but if you do you will be unable to update data in the linked lists.

5. Click Finish to complete the link process and create the linked tables.

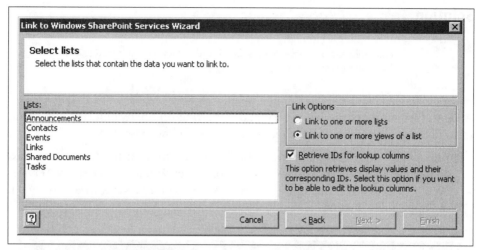

Figure 15-2. Selecting the SharePoint lists on the second page of the wizard

Once you've linked to a list you can open the list within Access to view or edit existing list items or create new items. You can, of course, also create queries, forms, and reports based on the linked lists.

Figure 15-3 shows a linked list in datasheet view. You can modify data directly in Access or click on a row's Edit hyperlink to edit the row using a SharePoint web page.

ID	Edit	Title	Modified	Created	Created By	Modified By
3 [....]		20% Discount for Members at	10/15/2003 3:15:24 AM	10/15/2003 3:15:24 AM	Paul E. Litwin	Paul E. Litwin
2 [....]		New Employee --	9/17/2003 8:49:02 AM	9/16/2003 10:43:50 AM	Paul E. Litwin	Paul E. Litwin
1 [....]		Welcome to your new team	3/24/2003 1:09:01 PM	3/24/2003 1:09:01 PM	STSBETA\st sadminacct	STSBETA\st sadminacct
(AutoNumber)						

Record: |◄| ◄ | 4 | ► |►|| ►* | of 4

Figure 15-3. The Announcements list in datasheet view

Discussion

You can use Access to create various reports on usage of your SharePoint site. Link to each of the SharePoint lists and create reports based on the linked lists. This way there is no need to master some other reporting package; use the reporting tool with which you are most comfortable: Access.

You can also import SharePoint list data into an Access database by selecting File → Get External Data → Import...

Versions of Access prior to Access 2003 cannot be used to link to SharePoint lists. In addition, you can only link to sites using Windows SharePoint Services 2.0 or later.

15.2 Create a SharePoint Data View Web Part Based on Access Data

Problem

FrontPage 2003 makes it easy to extend SharePoint sites to include data from databases, web services, XML documents, and other sources and display that data using the Data View Web Part. You can easily link to SQL Server data and display that within a Data View Web Part but it's not clear how you link to data in an Access database. Is this possible?

Solution

 This solution requires FrontPage 2003 and a web server running Windows SharePoint Services.

It's not totally obvious, but by hand-coding an OLEDB connection string you can create a Data View Web Part based on an Access database connection.

To create an Access database connection, follow these steps:

1. Startup FrontPage 2003 and either open an existing SharePoint site or create a new SharePoint site.

 A SharePoint site can only be created on a Windows 2003 Server machine running Windows SharePoint Services.

2. Select Data → Insert Data View... to display the FrontPage Data Source Catalog task pane.

3. Under the Database Connections section of the Data Source Catalog, click the Add to Catalog... hyperlink. FrontPage displays the Data Source Properties dialog box.

4. From the Data Source Properties dialog box, click the Configure Database Connection... button.

5. At the Configure Database Connection dialog box, select "Use custom connection string" option, and click on the Edit... button as shown in Figure 15-4.

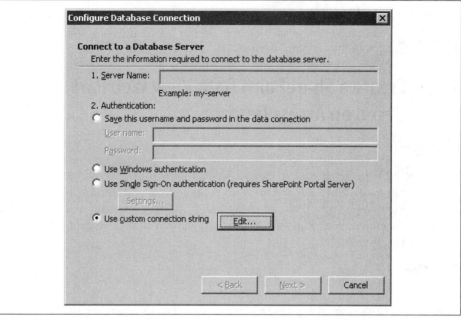

Figure 15-4. In order to connect to an Access database, you must select the "Use custom connection string" option and click on the Edit button

6. FrontPage presents the Edit Connection String dialog box. At this point you are on your own—FrontPage offers absolutely no help in building the OLEDB connection string. Fortunately, it's not that difficult to create a connection string.

7. At the Edit Connection String dialog box, enter a connection string that points to the *15-02.MDB* sample database as shown in Figure 15-5 and click Next.

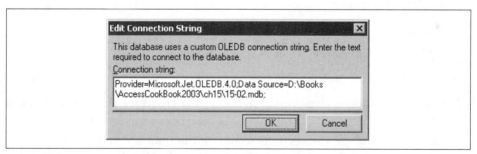

Figure 15-5. Enter a Jet connection string into the Edit Connection String dialog box

More than likely, you will need to modify the path to the database shown in Figure 15-5 to reflect the location of the sample database on your computer.

The connection string needs to follow this basic syntax:

```
Provider=Microsoft.Jet.OLEDB.4.0;
Data Source=path_to_database;
User Id=user_name;Password=password;
```

If you are not using a secured database, as in this example, you can leave the User Id and Password portions of the connection string out.

8. At the next page of the dialog, select the name of a table—for this example, select the tblRunners table—and click Finish.

9. FrontPage 2003 returns you to the Data Source Properties dialog box. Click on General tab of the dialog box and enter the following name into the Name text-box:

```
RunnersTable
```

10. Click OK to dismiss the dialog box and create the connection.

To place a Data View Web Part on a web page that connects to an Access database connection, follow these steps:

1. Add a new page to the site by selecting File → New... On the New task pane, click on "More page templates..." under New page.

2. Click on the Web Part Pages tab of the Page Templates dialog box, select one of the Web Part page templates, and click OK.

3. FrontPage adds a new page to the site containing one or more Web Part zones. Click one of the Web Part zones, and select Data → Insert Data View... to open the Data Source Catalog.

4. Click on the RunnersTable database connection and select Insert Data View from the popup menu.

5. FrontPage adds a Data View Web Part to the page.

6. Select File → Save to save the new page and select File → Preview in Browser to display the page in your browser. The page should look similar to the one shown in Figure 15-6.

Discussion

If you look at the HTML behind the Data View Web Part you will see that the Data View performs its magic using XML and XSLT. In fact, if you look closely, you will see that the Data View doesn't copy the data into the page. Instead, it sets up a link back to the original Access database. This way, the web page is never out of sync with the data in the database.

While Access works well in small workgroup scenarios, it is not a good choice if you expect a moderate number (over a dozen or so) of simultaneous users. In these cases, you'd be better off moving the data into SQL Server or MSDE.

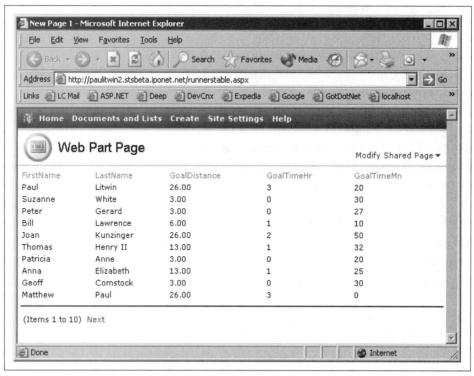

FirstName	LastName	GoalDistance	GoalTimeHr	GoalTimeMn
Paul	Litwin	26.00	3	20
Suzanne	White	3.00	0	30
Peter	Gerard	3.00	0	27
Bill	Lawrence	6.00	1	10
Joan	Kunzinger	26.00	2	50
Thomas	Henry II	13.00	1	32
Patricia	Anne	3.00	0	20
Anna	Elizabeth	13.00	1	25
Geoff	Comstock	3.00	0	30
Matthew	Paul	26.00	3	0

(Items 1 to 10) Next

Figure 15-6. This page displays data from an Access database using a Data View Web Part

See Also

See Building XML Data-Driven Web Sites with FrontPage 2003. *http://msdn. microsoft.com/library/default.asp?url=/library/en-us/odc_fp2003_ta/html/odc_ fpbldgxmlwebs.asp*

15.3   Conditionally Format a Data View Web Part

Problem

You'd like to be able to highlight certain values or rows within a table of data. Is this possible if you are displaying the data on a web page using a Data View Web Part?

Solution

Not only is it possible to conditionally format the data in a Data View Web Part, but you can do it without any programming. For example, let's say you wished to highlight the runners listed in the Data View Web Part from the Solution in Recipe 15-2 that were running races of 10 or more miles. Follow these steps to highlight the rows where distance is greater than or equal to 10 miles:

1. Startup FrontPage 2003 with the existing Data View Web Part you created in the Solution in Recipe 15-2.

2. Click anywhere on the Data View Web Part. FrontPage will display the Data View Options icon as shown in Figure 15-7. Click on the icon, and select Conditional Formatting... from the dropdown menu. FrontPage opens the Conditional Formatting task pane.

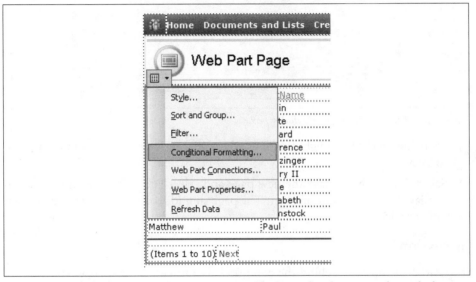

Figure 15-7. Clicking on the Data View Options icon displays a dropdown menu from which you can select Conditional Formatting

3. Back on the Data View, select a row in the grid by clicking in the left-hand margin of the row.

4. Click on the Create button in the Conditional Formatting task pane and select Apply Formatting from the dropdown menu. FrontPage displays the Condition Criteria dialog box.

5. In the Condition Criteria dialog box, click on the top row to create a new condition. Under Field Name select GoalDistance. Select Greater Than Or Equal under Comparison and enter "10" under Value. The completed condition should look similar to the one shown in Figure 15-8. Click OK to finalize the condition.

6. FrontPage displays the Modify Style dialog box. Click the Format button and select Border... from the dropdown menu.

7. At the Borders and Shading dialog box, click the Shading tab and select a yellow background color and click OK twice to dismiss the dialog box.

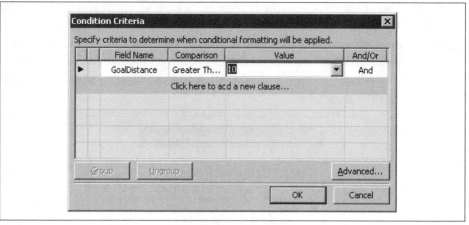

Figure 15-8. The Condition Criteria dialog box

8. FrontPage should highlight the rows where goal distance is greater than or equal to 10 miles.

9. Select File → Save to save the new page and select File → Preview in Browser to display the page in your browser. The page should look similar to the one shown in Figure 15-9.

Discussion

If you look at the code behind the conditionally formatted Data View, you will see that the conditional formatting is applied using the following XSLT transformation:

```
<xsl:if test="@GoalDistance &gt;= '10'">background-color: #FFFF00;</xsl:if></xsl:
attribute>
```

If you are savvy in XSLT you can tweak the XSLT code directly.

See Also

See Building XML Data-Driven Web Sites with FrontPage 2003. *http://msdn.microsoft.com/library/default.asp?url=/library/en-us/odc_fp2003_ta/html/odc_fpbldgxmlwebs.asp*

15.4 Create a Master/Detail Page using Data View Web Parts

Problem

You'd like to create a page that displays two Data Views based on an Access database, with the Data Views linked to each other so that if you select a row in the

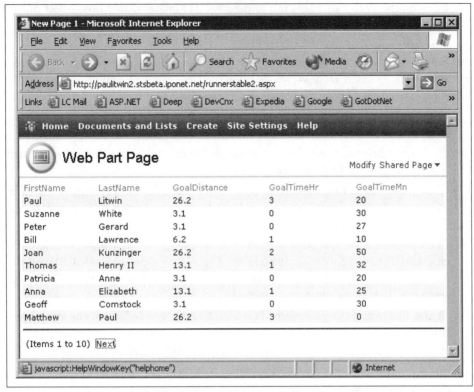

Figure 15-9. The completed page highlights all runners with goal distances of 10 or more miles

master Data View, it will filter the rows in the detail Data View so that only related rows are displayed. Is this possible to set up using FrontPage?

Solution

You can link two Data View Web Parts together by creating a Web Part connection. For example, you might create one Data View that retrieves rows from the tblRunners table located in the *15-04.MDB* database and another Data View that displays the related rows from the tblRaces table. Follow these steps to create a web page that displays this master/detail relationship between the two tables:

1. Following the steps from the Solution in Recipe 15.2, add an additional database connection to the FrontPage Data Source Catalog task pane that retrieves rows from the tblRaces table located in the *15-04.MDB* sample database. Name the database connection "RacesTable".

2. Add a new page to the site by selecting File → New... On the New task pane, click on "More page templates..." under New page.

3. Click on the Web Part Pages tab of the Page Templates dialog box, select one of the Web Part page templates that contains at least two Web Part zones, and click OK.

4. FrontPage adds a new page to the site. Click on one of the Web Part zones, and select Data → Insert Data View... to open the Data Source Catalog.

5. Click on the RunnersTable database connection and select Insert Data View from the popup menu. FrontPage adds a Data View Web Part based on the RunnersTable database connection to the page.

6. Click on a second Web Part zone on the page and select Data‡Insert Data View... to open the Data Source Catalog.

7. Click on the RaceTable database connection and select Insert Data View from the popup menu. FrontPage adds a Data View Web Part based on the RacesTable database connection to the page.

8. Click anywhere on the Data View Web Part based on the RunnersTable database connection. FrontPage displays the Data View Options icon. Click on the icon and select Web Part Connections... from the dropdown menu. FrontPage starts the Web Part Connections wizard.

9. At the first wizard page, select "Provide Data Values To" from the dropdown control.

10. On the second wizard page, select "Connect to a Web Part on this page".

11. On the third wizard page, shown in Figure 15-10, select "RacesTable" for the target Web Part and "Provide Data Values To" for the target action.

12. On the fourth wizard page you need to specify the relationship used to link the two Data Views together. Select the MemberId column in both tables as shown in Figure 15-11.

13. On the fifth page of the wizard you must choose which column in the master Web Part (the RunnersTable Data View) on which FrontPage should create a hyperlink to the detail part (the RacesTable Data View). You can also indicate which column FrontPage should render in boldface to indicate the currently selected master Web Part row. Select LastName for both of these fields as shown in Figure 15-12.

14. On the sixth page of the wizard, click Finish to create the connection.

15. Select File → Save to save the new page and select File → Preview in Browser to display the page in your browser. The page should look similar to the one shown in Figure 15-13.

Figure 15-10. On this page of the Web Part Connections wizard you indicate what action to take on the target Web Part

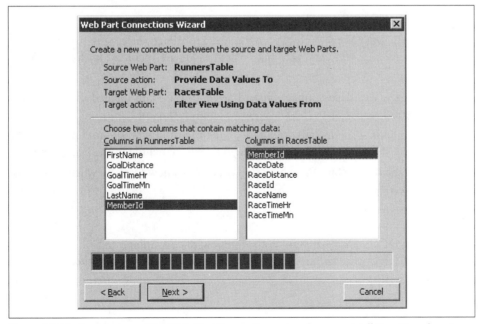

Figure 15-11. On this page of the Web Part Connections wizard you must tell FrontPage how to relate the data behind the two Web Parts

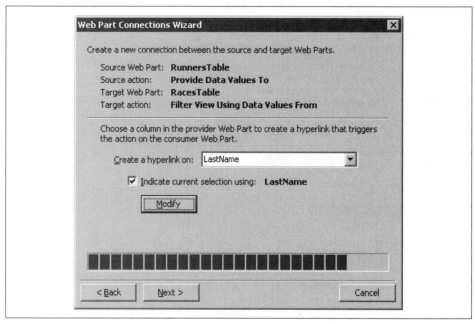

Figure 15-12. On this page of the Web Part Connections wizard you indicate how to link the two Web Parts

Discussion

When adding a Data View Web Part to a page, FrontPage selects the first five fields to display. However, you can customize which fields are included in the Data View by following these steps:

1. Click on the database connection and select Show Data instead of Insert Data View. FrontPage displays the Data View Details task pane.

2. From the Data View Details task pane, click the mouse while holding down the SHIFT or CTRL key to select the fields you wish to include in the Data View.

3. Click on the Insert Data View hyperlink to create a new Data View using the custom set of fields.

See Also

See Building XML Data-Driven Web Sites with FrontPage 2003. *http://msdn. microsoft.com/library/default.asp?url=/library/en-us/odc_fp2003_ta/html/odc_ fpbldgxmlwebs.asp*

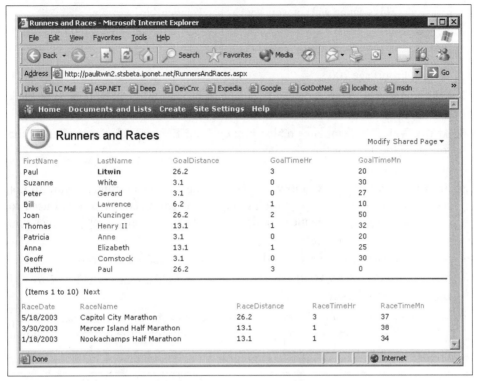

Figure 15-13. When the LastName field in the upper Data View is selected, the lower Data View is filtered to only show matching rows

15.5 Post Web Form Data to an Access Database

Problem

You want to be able to collect data from a user of your web site and post the data to an Access database. You are not using a SharePoint server and you'd prefer to accomplish this task with little or no programming. Is there a way to use FrontPage to collect form data and send it to an Access database?

Solution

You can use Form Page Wizard to help you create a web page that collects information from a user using an HTML form and posts it to one of a number of different choices. A database, however, is not one of the choices. Fortunately, with a little post-wizard wizardry, you can change the form so it points its data to an Access database. Follow these steps to create a form that posts to an Access database:

This solution will not work with a SharePoint-enabled web site.

1. Startup FrontPage 2003.

2. Select Select File → New... to create a new web site. On the New task pane, click on "One page Web site..." under New Web site.

3. At the Web Site Templates dialog box click on Empty Web Site and enter the following location for the web site:

   http://localhost/15-05

   FrontPage creates a new empty web site on the current machine. If you do not have a Microsoft web server running on the current machine, you will need to change localhost to the name or address of a Microsoft web server for which you have site creation privileges.

4. Select File → Import. Click on Add File... from the Import dialog box.

5. Navigate to the *15-05.MDB* sample database and click Open. Click OK to add the database to the site.

6. When you click OK, FrontPage recognizes that you are importing a database and asks you if you wish to create a database connection for the database as shown in Figure 15-14.

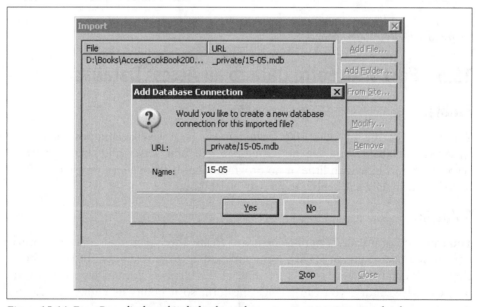

Figure 15-14. FrontPage displays this dialog box when you attempt to import a database

7. Enter "15-05" for the database connection name and click Yes to import the database and create the database connection.

8. FrontPage displays an additional dialog box suggesting that the database be moved to the fpdb folder. This is a good practice, so you should click Yes.

9. Select File → New... to create a new page. On the New task pane, click on "More page templates..." under New page.

10. Click on the General tab of the Page Templates dialog box, select the Form Page Wizard template, and click OK.

11. FrontPage starts the Form Page wizard. Click Next at the first page of the wizard which merely tells you about the wizard.

12. At the second page of the wizard, click Add to add a new question to the form. The questions you will add to the form are listed in Table 15-1.

Table 15-1. Adding questions to the form

Type	Prompt	Variable name	Additional information
String	First Name:	txtFirstName	Maximum length = 20
String	Last Name:	txtLastName	Maximum length = 20
Number	Age	txtAge	Maximum length = 3
One of several options	Sex:	txtSex	Radio buttons = Male, Female

After adding the four fields, the wizard should look like Figure 15-15.

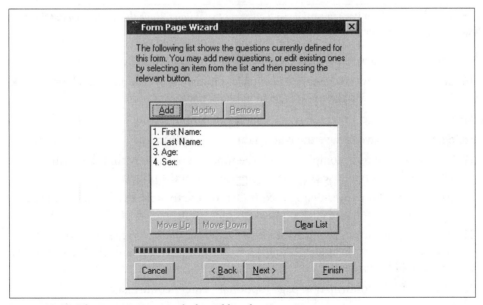

Figure 15-15. The Form Page wizard after adding four questions

13. Click Next. FrontPage displays the Presentation Options page of the wizard. The default responses should be fine, so click Next.

14. FrontPage displays the Output Options page as shown in Figure 15-16. Notice that there isn't any option to save the results to a database. This is an obvious oversight on the part of the FrontPage team, but you will be able to remedy this problem later. For now, select "save results to a text file" and click Finish.

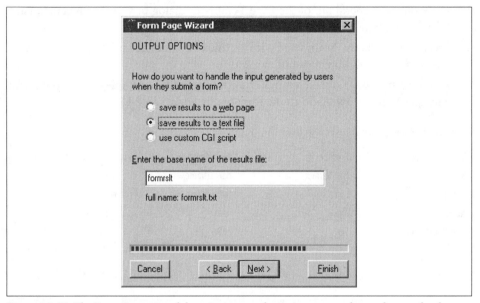

Figure 15-16. The Form Page wizard doesn't give you the option to save the results to a database, but this can be fixed later

15. Select File → Save to save the page, naming it "register.asp".

16. Select File → New... to create a new page. On the New task pane, click on "Blank Page" under New page to create a new blank page.

17. On the new page, enter the text "Thank you for registering".

18. Select File → Save to save the page, naming it "confirm.asp".

19. When the wizard is complete, click the mouse anywhere within the form. Right-click on the form and select Form Properties from the popup menu.

20. At the Form Properties dialog box, under Where to store results, select the Send to database option and click on the Options... button.

21. At the Options for Saving Results to Database dialog box, select the "15-05" database connection under Database Connection to Use and tblRegister under Table to hold form results.

22. Under URL of confirmation page (optional), enter "confirm.asp".

23. Click the Saved Results tab and modify each field so that it maps to the fields in tblRegister according to Table 15-2:

Table 15-2. Mapping the form fields to tblRegister fields

Form field	Database column
txtAge	Age
txtFirstName	FirstName
txtLastName	LastName
txtSex	Sex

24. Click OK to dismiss the Options for Saving Results to Database dialog box and OK to dismiss the Form Properties dialog box.
25. Change the heading of the page to "Registration Form" and replace the introductory text on the form with "Please register by completing the following form."
26. Select File → Save to save the changes you have made to the register.asp page.
27. Select File → Preview in Browser to display the page in your browser. The page should look similar to the one shown in Figure 15-17. Enter data into each of the fields and click Submit Form.
28. Open the *15-05.MDB* database to verify that the data was added to the tblRegister table.

Discussion

You don't need to use the Form Page wizard to connect a form to an Access database. If you'd prefer to setup the form yourself, go ahead and create the form, skipping steps 9-15 of the solution. The remainder of the solution, however, should still apply.

If you don't have an existing Access database to work with, you can have FrontPage create a new one for you. From the Options for Saving Results to Database dialog box (see Step 21), click on the Create Database... button to create a new database. FrontPage creates a new database and hooks the form up to a table in the database named Results.

The steps in this solution apply when using FrontPage 2003. However, except for some trivial differences, the steps are virtually identical when using FrontPage 2002.

See Also

See Database Power with Microsoft FrontPage version 2002. *http://msdn.microsoft. com/library/default.asp?url=/library/en-us/odc_fp2003_ta/html/odc_fpbldgxmlwebs.asp*

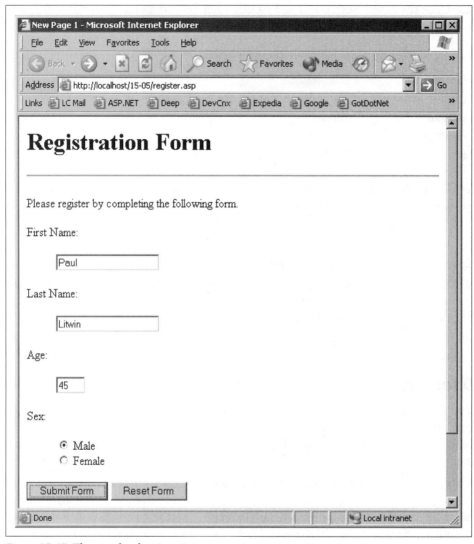

Figure 15-17. The completed registration page

15.6 Create a Web Frontend to an Access Table Using FrontPage

Problem

While SharePoint is amazing, it has several limitations. First, it requires a server running Windows 2003 server and Windows SharePoint Services. In addition, the Data View Web Part is read-only and provides no mechanism for updating the data. Is there a way to use FrontPage to create a web frontend to your Access data without employing SharePoint?

Solution

You can use the FrontPage Database Interface Wizard to create a complete web site that lets you view and edit data from a database table. The trick in this solution is to create the database connection *before* running the wizard. Follow these steps to create a web site based on the tblAlbums table from the *15-06.MDB* database:

 This solution will not work with a SharePoint-enabled web site.

1. Startup FrontPage 2003.
2. Select Select File → New... to create a new web site. On the New task pane, click on "One page Web site..." under New Web site.
3. At the Web Site Templates dialog box click on Empty Web Site and enter the following location for the Web site:

   `http://localhost/15-06`

   FrontPage creates a new empty Web site on the current machine. If you do not have a Microsoft web server running on the current machine, you will need to change localhost to the name or address of a Microsoft web server for which you have site creation privileges.
4. Select File → Import. Click on Add File... from the Import dialog box.
5. Navigate to the *15-06.MDB* sample database and click Open. Click OK to add the database to the site.
6. When you click OK, FrontPage recognizes that you are importing a database and asks you if you wish to create a database connection for the database.
7. Enter "15-06" for the database connection name and click Yes to import the database and create the database connection.
8. FrontPage displays an additional dialog box suggesting that the database be moved to the fpdb folder. This is a good practice so you should click Yes.
9. Select File → New... to create a new web site. On the New task pane, click on "One page Web site..." under New Web site.
10. At the Web Site Templates dialog box, select Database Interface Wizard, making sure to check the "Add to current Web site" checkbox before clicking on the OK button.
11. FrontPage starts the Database Interface Wizard, the first page which is shown in Figure 15-18.

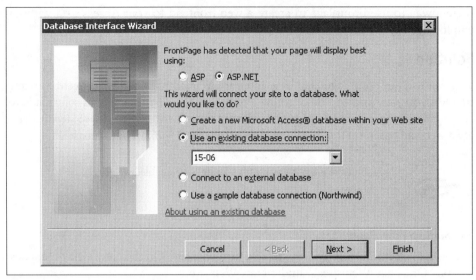

Figure 15-18. The first page of the FrontPage Database Interface Wizard

12. On the first page of the wizard, under "FrontPage has detected that your page will display best using:", select "ASP.NET" unless you'd prefer to use the older ASP technology.

 You will need to choose ASP instead of ASP.NET if your web server is not configured to support ASP.NET.

13. Under "This wizard will connect your site to a database. What would you like to do?", select "Use an existing database connection", select "15-06" from the dropdown control, and click Next.

14. On the second page of the wizard, under "Select the table or view you would like to use for this database connection", select the "tblAlbums" table. Accept the default location for the new files and click Next.

15. On the third page of the wizard you are given the opportunity to modify the columns to be displayed. There's no need to modify the columns, so click Next.

16. On the fourth page of the wizard, you are asked which pages you wish to include. For this example, check all three checkboxes as shown in Figure 15-19.

17. On the fifth wizard page, you are asked to supply a user name and password to protect the database editor. Enter a user name and password or check the "Don't protect my submission page or my database editor with a username and password" checkbox.

18. Click Finish to complete the wizard.

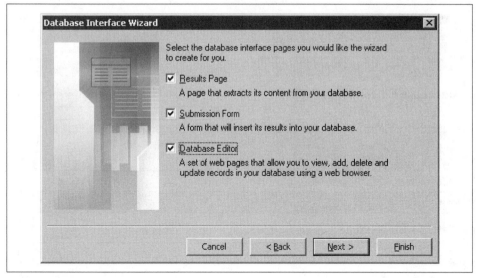

Figure 15-19. On the fourth page of the Database Interface Wizard you can select which pages you wish for the wizard to create

19. The wizard creates a number of pages. Under the 15-06_interface\tblAlbums folder you should find the results_page.aspx page. Select File‡Preview in Browser to display this page in your browser.

20. Click on the Database Editor hyperlink to bring up the database editor, which should look similar to the page shown in Figure 15-20.

Discussion

You aren't limited to one database interface per web site. You can rerun the FrontPage Database Interface Wizard as many times as you like, creating set of pages for either different tables within the same Access database or different databases. Just remember to check the "Add to current Web site" checkbox before clicking on the OK button when selecting the Database Interface Wizard template.

The steps in this solution apply when using FrontPage 2003. However, except for a few differences, the steps are virtually identical when using FrontPage 2002. (One big difference: FrontPage 2002 doesn't give you the choice of creating the site using ASP or ASP.NET; it always uses the older ASP technology.)

Alternatives to FrontPage

There are a number of technologies you can use to create a web frontend to an Access database, including: Data Access Pages, SharePoint, ASP.NET, Active Server Pages (ASP), Cold Fusion, PHP, and Java Server Pages (JSP). Data Access Pages are discussed in detail in Chapter 13. In addition, an ASP.NET example is included in Chapter 17.

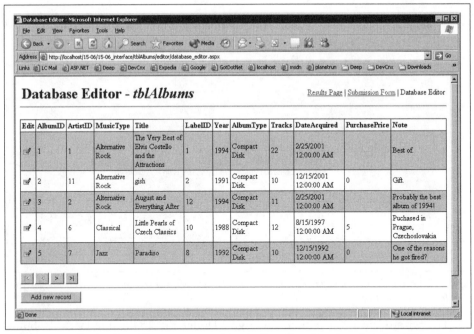

Figure 15-20. The database editor page created by the FrontPage Database Interface Wizard

With a wealth of options, you may be wondering which solution will work best for you. Ultimately, a number of factors will help you arrive at a decision. Do you want a solution that you can create quickly with little or no programming? If so, then you probably will want to use the FrontPage Database Interface Wizard (as demonstrated in this solution), Data Access Pages, or SharePoint. Use SharePoint (along with FrontPage) if you need to create a workgroup-based portal. One disadvantage of the SharePoint approach is that you cannot modify the Access data. You can use the FrontPage Database Interface Wizard, as demonstrated in this solution, to quickly create an ASP- or ASP.NET-based frontend to Access that you can then modify and extend using Visual InterDev (if you are using ASP), or Visual Studio .NET (if you are using ASP.NET). Finally, you can also use Data Access Pages, but only for smaller intranet-based sites.

If you're not averse to programming, you may want to use Visual Studio .NET to create an ASP.NET-based web site, or Visual InterDev to create an ASP-based site. In most cases, ASP.NET is the better choice because it provides a programming object model that is more similar to Access than ASP. Other, non-Microsoft options include Cold Fusion, PHP, and Java Server Pages (JSP). You can also use Macromedia's Dreamweaver MX to create Cold Fusion, PHP, and JSP web sites (as well as ASP- and ASP.NET-based sites).

When Access won't do the job

Keep in mind that Access might not be the most appropriate database to use in many Internet-based scenarios. As mentioned in the Solution in Recipe 15.2, Access works well in small workgroup settings, but if you expect a moderate number (over a dozen or so) of simultaneous users, you'd be better served with a server-based database such as SQL Server.

See Also

See Database Power with Microsoft FrontPage Version 2002.
*http://msdn.microsoft.com/library/default.asp?url=/library/en-us/dnfp2k2/html/fp_
dbpower.asp*

CHAPTER 16

Smart Tags

Have you noticed that in recent versions of Excel some cells have little purple triangles in the lower left corner? When you move the mouse over these cells a symbol appears that you can click to reveal a menu of actions related to the contents of that cell. Similar behavior is available in Word for words with a special purple dotted underline. These special features are *smart tags*.

Smart tags are a way for applications to provide users with context-sensitive actions related to the data appearing on screen. These actions can be available across multiple applications for the same pieces of data. Smart tags were introduced in Office XP, where you could use them in Word, Excel, and Outlook (with Word as the Outlook email editor or when reading HTML mail). In Office 2003 smart tag capabilities have been extended and now Access developers can also incorporate smart tags into their applications.

If you're already familiar with smart tags from working in Word or Excel, you'll find that the implementation of smart tags in Access is a little different. Unlike the implementation of smart tags found in Word and Excel, Access does not support recognizers. In Word or Excel, special code components called recognizers must be created to distinguish which words provide smart tag actions. Access 2003 allows you to attach smart tags to database fields or form controls. The smart tags appear for any text appearing in datasheet views or forms containing those fields, or in the designated controls.

For added control, the View Forms/Reports tab in the Tools → Options dialog box allows you to toggle on or off a setting to Show Smart Tags on Forms.

There are three built-in smart tags that ship with Access 2003:

- Person Name, which enables users to send email to a contact, schedule a meeting, or edit contact information stored in Microsoft Outlook.
- Financial Symbol, which enables users to look up information about a company on MSN MoneyCentral based on the company's stock symbol.

- Date, which enables users to schedule a meeting or display the Outlook calendar based on a particular date.

You can attach one or more of these smart tags to a field or control via the Properties windows in the table designer or the forms designer.

In addition to working with the smart tags that ship with Access 2003, you can also create your own custom smart tags by using a specially formatted XML list or by writing your own smart tag DLL. Smart tag DLLs can be written in Visual Basic 6.0 or in managed code (Visual Basic .NET or C#). By using code to create custom smart tags, you can also take advantage of new features that were added in Office 2003, like dynamic captions, temporary smart tags, and smart tags that expire.

In this chapter you'll learn how to use the smart tags that ship with Access to look up financial data and to access Outlook contacts and scheduling. You'll also learn how to create your own custom smart tags and how to deploy them with your application.

16.1   Use the Built-in Smart Tags

Problem

How can I enable a user to scroll through a list of names on a form and launch Outlook's Contacts dialog box, so that the user can add the selected person as a contact?

Solution

You can use the built-in Person smart tag to add or change contact information stored in Microsoft Outlook. The Person smart tag allows you to take the following actions:

- Send an email message to a contact.
- Schedule a meeting with a contact.
- Open and edit a contact's information.
- Add the name in the control to your list of contacts.

It's very easy to add the Person smart tag to a label, text box, or combo box control on a form by following these steps:

1. Open frmEmployees in 16-01.mdb in design view, select the FullName text box, and press F4 to bring up the Properties window. Click the Data tab and click to the right of the Smart Tags option to load the Smart Tags dialog box.
2. Select the Person Name checkbox, as shown in Figure 16-1, and click OK. This will add the following text to the SmartTags option in the dialog box:

   `"urn:schemas-microsoft-com:office:smarttags#PersonName"`

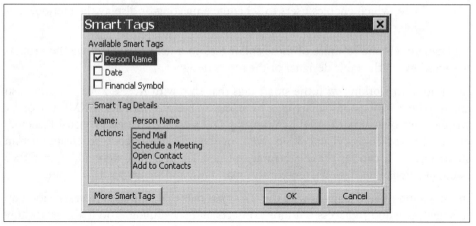

Figure 16-1. Adding the Person smart tag to a control on a form

3. Display the form in form view and click the control where you added the smart tag. The sample application contains a form, frmEmployees, with a smart tag on the Name text box. When you click in the text box, the smart tag icon is displayed, as shown in Figure 16-2.

Figure 16-2. The Person smart tag displayed in form view

4. Selecting the Add to Contacts option will launch Outlook's new contact window, as shown in Figure 16-3. You can then enter the new contact information for that person.

Discussion

When you use a smart tag to enter a new contact in Outlook, the entire contents of the control are automatically copied to Outlook. If the form control that has the

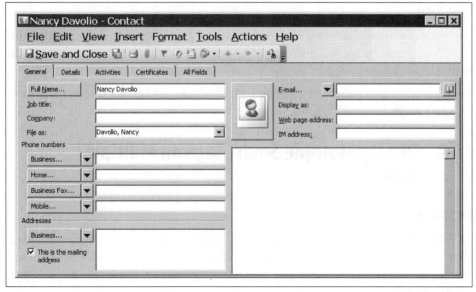

Figure 16-3. The name displayed in Access is automatically entered for the new contact

associated smart tag contains only the last name, then that is what will be copied to Outlook. If you want both the last name and first name copied, then create an expression for the Control Source property:

```
=[FirstName] & " " & [LastName]
```

 If you are attaching a smart tag to a combo box control, then the data displayed in the combo box will be used, not the data in the bound column.

You can add smart tags to label, text box, and combo box form controls. Smart tags are not supported for reports. In addition, you can add smart tags to the following controls on a Data Access Page:

- Label
- Bound Span
- Text Box
- Scrolling Text
- Drop-down List
- Hyperlink

See Also

For more coverage of working with smart tags in Access 2003, see this MSDN article: *http://msdn.microsoft.com/library/default.asp?url=/library/en-us/odc_wd2003_ta/html/odc_wdov.asp*

To learn other techniques for working with Outlook, see "Add a Contact and Send Email Through Outlook" in Chapter 12.

16.2 Display Multiple Smart Tags on Multiple Forms

Problem

I have a table in my database that is used for many forms. I'd like to use the Person Name smart tag as well as the Date smart tag on the LastName field. I have already created the forms. How can I create multiple smart tags on LastName without having to create them separately on each form?

Solution

It's understandable that you might want to use the Date smart tag in conjunction with the Person smart tag. Fortunately, Access easily supports assigning multiple smart tags to a control on a form or a field in a table.

You can take two actions with the built-in Date smart tag:

- Schedule a meeting.
- Display your calendar.

If you create a smart tag on a field in a table, then any forms you create subsequently will inherit the smart tag. The documentation states that previously existing forms will not inherit a smart tag created on a table field if the smart tag is created after the forms. However, the help file was apparently written before additional functionality was added that does allow for forms to inherit smart tags, as you'll see in this recipe.

Follow these steps to add the Person and Date smart tags to the LastName field in the Employees table:

1. Open the Employees table in the sample application in design view.
2. Select the LastName Field and click the builder button to the right of the Smart Tags property at the bottom of the General tab.
3. Select the Person Name and Date checkboxes in the Smart Tags dialog box and click OK. This will create the following entry in the Smart Tags property, where the smart tags are listed in a semicolon-delimited string:

```
"urn:schemas-microsoft-com:office:smarttags#date";
"urn:schemas-microsoft-com:office:smarttags#PersonName"
```

4. Click to the left of the Smart Tags property, and you will see another smart tag, which when expanded includes the option Update Smart Tags everywhere Last-Name is used. Select this option, and select any existing forms you wish to inherit the new smart tags. In this example, frmEmployees can inherit the smart tags.

5. Save the table and view it in datasheet view. Figure 16-4 shows the Date smart tag menu displayed for the Last Name field.

Figure 16-4. Multiple smart tags are displayed with flyout menus

6. Open frmEmployees. You should see both smart tags displayed when you click in the LastName control.

7. Click the New Object: AutoForm button on the toolbar to create a new form based on the table. Note that the Last Name TextBox has inherited the smart tag. Open the existing form and note that the smart tag property is also displayed.

Discussion

When you create a smart tag on a table, Access gives you the ability to propagate the smart tag to any new forms that you may create. You can also propagate the smart tag to any forms that you may have created prior to creating the smart tag.

If you delete the smart tag from the table and do not select the "Update Smart Tags everywhere" option, then form smart tags that were inherited from table smart tags will not be deleted. Make sure that you select the "Update Smart Tags everywhere" option if you want inherited smart tags to be removed from the forms as well as the table.

16.3   Display Smart Tags when Application Starts

Problem

My application makes extensive use of smart tags. Since this is a global setting, some users may have turned off the display of smart tags. How can I ensure that smart tags are displayed when my application starts up?

Solution

The display of smart tags is controlled by a checkbox in the Tools → Options dialog box under the Forms/Reports tab. These settings apply to Access as a whole, and once changed, take effect for all running applications. Figure 16-5 shows the dialog box with the display of smart tags turned on.

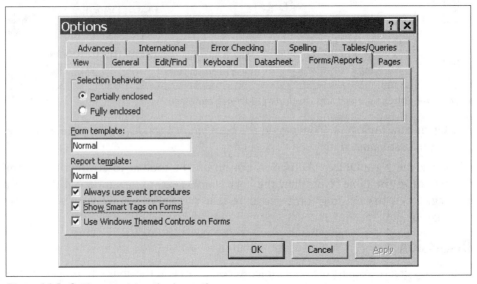

Figure 16-5. Setting smart tag viewing options

The best place to set options for your application is in a startup form, which can run code to ensure that settings are the way you need them to be. The sample application is configured to use a form named frmStartup, by setting the Display/Form Start Page property in the Tools → Startup dialog box, as shown in Figure 16-6.

Follow these steps in your startup form to ensure that smart tags are displayed for your application:

1. Create a variable in the declarations section of the form that you will use to retrieve and store the user's current settings. Options controlled by checkboxes return either True or False. However, retrieving and setting options in code requires the Variant data type, not a Boolean, as you might expect.

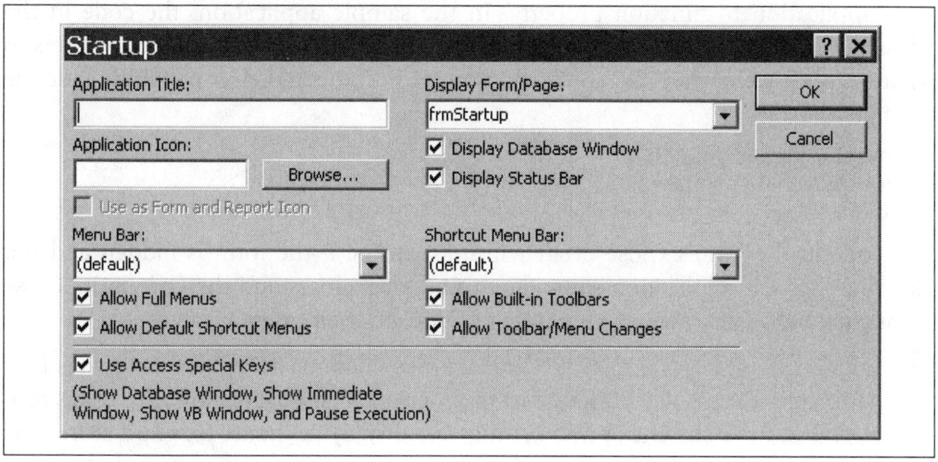

Figure 16-6. Configuring a startup form

```
Option Explicit

Private varSmartTagOn As Variant
```

2. In the form's Open event, retrieve the user's current settings using the GetOption method. If smart tags are not turned on, then use SetOption to turn them on. The sample application collects the user's name using the InputBox function and displays it in a label control that has the Person Name smart tag attached:

```
Private Sub Form_Open(Cancel As Integer)
    ' Retrieve user's SmartTag settings
    varSmartTagOn = Application.GetOption( _
      "Show Smart Tags on Forms")

    ' Display smart tags if needed
    If Not varSmartTagOn Then
        SetOption "Show Smart Tags on Forms", True
    End If

    lblName.Caption = InputBox( _
      "Type your name:", "Welcome Message", "")
End Sub
```

3. In the form's Close event, reset the user's smart tag options to their original values:

```
Private Sub Form_Close( )
    ' Restore user's smart tag option setting
    Application.SetOption "Show Smart Tags on Forms", varSmartTagOn
End Sub
```

Discussion

By saving the smart tag settings in a variable, you can ensure that your application behaves in a polite way, only changing the user's global settings that are needed for your application to function properly. In the sample application, the code in the Close button event handler closes the form and resets the user's smart tag options to whatever they were when the application opened. You could elect to simply hide the form instead:

```
Private Sub cmdClose_Click( )
    Me.Visible = False
End Sub
```

The code in the form's Close event will not execute if the form is hidden and not closed. When the application shuts down, the form closes and the code in its Close event runs and resets the user's smart tag options to their original values.

The frmStartup form in the sample database also contains a Toggle Smart Tags button that toggles the display of the smart tags option. The ToggleShowSmartTags procedure reverses the current option settings for displaying smart tags and stores the new setting in the varSmartTagOn variable:

```
Private Sub ToggleShowSmartTags( )
    ' Toggle smart tag settings
    varSmartTagOn = Not varSmartTagOn
    Application.SetOption "Show Smart Tags on Forms", varSmartTagOn
    MsgBox "Application Settings = " & varSmartTagOn, , "Show Smart Tags"
End Sub
```

You can test the code by opening frmStartup and frmTest side by side. You can see the smart tags on both forms enabled or disabled as you click the Toggle Smart Tags button on frmStartup.

16.4 Execute a Smart Tag Action Without Displaying the Smart Tag

Problem

In my application I would like to use the Financial Symbol smart tag so that users will be directed to the Stock Quote on MSN MoneyCentral. I don't want to display the smart tag, which also presents two additional actions—this might confuse the user. How can I configure a combo box control so that when the user selects a symbol, the Stock Quote on MSN MoneyCentral is automatically displayed in a browser window?

Solution

The built-in smart tags that ship with Access are somewhat limited in that they do not allow you to configure them by adding or removing actions. The Financial Symbol smart tag looks up information about a financial symbol on MSN MoneyCentral, allowing you to take the following actions:

- Obtain a stock quote on MSN MoneyCentral.
- Obtain a report about the company on MSN MoneyCentral.
- Obtain recent news about the company on MSN MoneyCentral.

In Access, you enable the Financial Symbol smart tag on a field or control that contains a financial symbol—the familiar abbreviations seen on stock tickers.

To execute only a single action—obtaining a stock quote—you need to enable smart tags in code by setting a control's SmartTags property. Once you've enabled the smart tag in your code, you can then execute a smart tag action. Once the action executes, you can then disable the smart tag so that it is never displayed to the user.

Follow these steps to configure a combo box to use the Financial Symbol smart tag to display a stock quote when the user selects an item:

1. Create a combo box control on a form. In the sample application, the Row Source property is set to a query that selects the ticker symbol and company name from the Companies table. The Bound Column is set to the ticker symbol since that is the value that will be used for the Financial Symbol smart tag.

2. Create an event procedure for the AfterUpdate event. This event runs after the user selects an item in the combo box. The code turns off screen painting so that setting the smart tag property will not cause screen flashing:

```
Private Sub cboTickers_AfterUpdate()
    On Error GoTo HandleErr

    Me.Painting = False
```

3. The code then sets the financial symbol smart tag for the control:

```
Me.cboTickers.Properties("SmartTags").Value = _
    "urn:schemas-microsoft-com:office:smarttags#stockticker"
```

4. The code then executes the first action of the smart tag. The SmartTags collection represents the smart tags assigned to the control, and SmartTagActions is the collection of available actions. You refer to them by their ordinal position in the list:

```
Me.cboTickers.SmartTags(0).SmartTagActions(0).Execute
```

5. Once the action has executed, remove the smart tag control so that it will never be displayed to the user:

```
Me.cboTickers.Properties("SmartTags").Value = ""
```

6. Whenever you turn off painting on the form, you should implement an error handler and exit label to ensure that painting gets turned back on again, even if an error occurs:

```
ExitHere:
    Me.Painting = True
    Exit Sub
```

```
HandleErr:
    MsgBox Err.Number & " " & Err.Description
    Resume ExitHere
End Sub
```

Here is the complete code listing:

```
Private Sub cboTickers_AfterUpdate()
    On Error GoTo HandleErr

    Me.Painting = False

    ' Set the financial symbol smart tag
    Me.cboTickers.Properties("SmartTags").Value = _
     "urn:schemas-microsoft-com:office:smarttags#stockticker"

    ' Execute the first action listed
    Me.cboTickers.SmartTags(0).SmartTagActions(0).Execute

    ' Remove the financial symbol smart tag
    Me.cboTickers.Properties("SmartTags").Value = ""

ExitHere:
    Me.Painting = True
    Exit Sub

HandleErr:
    MsgBox Err.Number & " " & Err.Description
    Resume ExitHere
End Sub
```

Discussion

The SmartTags collection contains one or more SmartTag objects. You can refer to a
single SmartTag object in the collection by using the Item method or the index. The
collection is zero-based, so the following code fragment refers to the first SmartTag
for the ctl control:

```
ctl.SmartTags(0)
```

 Unlike in Access, the SmartTags collections in Microsoft Excel and
Microsoft Word are one-based.

The SmartTag object has several properties, such as Application, IsMissing, Name
and Property. The SmartTagActions property represents a collection of actions for an
individual smart tag. These actions are processes that are programmed into a smart
tag as individual SmartTagAction objects. The SmartTagAction object has several
properties and a single method, Execute. In this example, the first SmartTagAction
in the SmartTagActions collection is executed:

```
SmartTagActions(0).Execute
```

By dynamically assigning a smart tag in code, executing an action, and then removing the smart tag, you can take advantage of built-in smart tag functionality without presenting unnecessary options to the user.

16.5 Create a Smart Tag on a Table in an Access Project

Problem

I would like to create a smart tag on a table in my Access Project (.adp). When I open the SQL Server table in the table designer in my Access project, I do not see the smart tag property, although it is listed for controls in the Forms designer.

Solution

In SQL Server, the smart tag property has to be set as an extended property since it is not one of the standard SQL Server table properties. This requires that you run SQL Server's built-in sp_addextendedproperty system stored procedure to add it as an extended property. The syntax shown in SQL Server Books Online for sp_addextendedproperty is not that easy to figure out, as you can see from this listing:

```
sp_addextendedproperty
    [ @name = ] { 'property_name' }
    [ , [ @value = ] { 'value' }
        [ , [ @level0type = ] { 'level0_object_type' }
        , [ @level0name = ] { 'level0_object_name' }
            [ , [ @level1type = ] { 'level1_object_type' }
            , [ @level1name = ] { 'level1_object_name' }
                [ , [ @level2type = ] { 'level2_object_type' }
                , [ @level2name = ] { 'level2_object_name' }
                ]
            ]
        ]
    ]
```

Follow these steps to add the PersonName smart tag to the LastName column in the Employees table in the NorthwindCS SQL Server database:

1. Launch the SQL Server Query Analyzer and connect to your SQL Server as a system administrator.

2. Type the following code in the query window or load it from *16-05.SQL* in the sample directory:

```
USE NorthwindCS
GO
EXEC sp_addextendedproperty 'MS_SmartTags',
 'urn:schemas-microsoft-com:office:smarttags#PersonName',
 'user', dbo, 'table', Employees, 'column', LastName
GO
```

3. Click the Execute Query button on the toolbar or press F5 to run the query.

4. Open the 16.05.adp sample project and open the Employees table in datasheet view. You will see the PersonName smart tag displayed for every entry in the LastName column in the Employees table.

Discussion

In order to execute sp_addextendedproperty, the minimum permissions required are membership in the db_owner and db_ddladmin fixed database roles. The code listing here assumes that you are running it as a system administrator (the dbo user).

Unlike creating a smart tag in an Access/Jet database, there is no way to propagate the new extended property to any previously existing forms automatically. However, new forms that you create on the Employees table will inherit the new Person Name smart tag set on the LastName column. You can test to see if the code executed correctly by creating a new AutoForm on the Employees table, as shown in Figure 16-7.

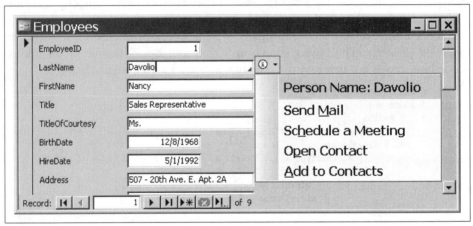

Figure 16-7. A new form created after running sp_addextendedproperty inherits the smart tag extended property

 Access does not itself have a full-featured development environment for creating SQL Server applications. There are many features missing, such as the ability to administer SQL Server security. It is highly recommended that you purchase the Developers Edition of SQL Server, which Microsoft has made available for a nominal price. Even if you are using MSDE, you can install the client tools, which include the SQL Server Enterprise Manager, Query Analyzer, and Profiler. You can find more information about the Developers Edition version of SQL Server at *http://www.microsoft.com/sql/howtobuy/development.asp*.

See Also

For more information on working with extended properties in SQL Server, see the SQL Server help topic, "Using Extended Properties on Database Objects."

16.6 Create a Custom Smart Tag to Get a Weather Report

Problem

I have a call list of customer names. I'd like to use a smart tag on the postal code field to retrieve a weather report for that postal code so that when I make the call, I can talk about the weather. How can I create a custom smart tag that retrieves the weather forecast from the Internet for a given postal code?

Solution

There are two different approaches to creating your own smart tags: you can create an XML file or you can create a dynamic-link library (DLL). Using an XML file is the best solution when you want to create a smart tag that simply navigates to a location on the Internet (or an intranet). Creating a DLL is the preferred approach when your smart tag is more complex and you need more flexibility or conditional logic. In this example you'll learn how to create an XML-based smart tag.

The first step is to create the XML file. This example will navigate to the weather forecasting section of the MSNBC Web site at *http://www.msnbc.com*. It takes multiple mouse clicks and typing in a zip code to find local weather conditions if you obtain the weather forecast for a given zip code manually. Once you get there, if you look at the URL of the local weather page after typing in the zip code 96708, you'll see that the URL looks like the following:

```
http://www.msnbc.com/news/wea_front.asp?tab=oth&czstr=96708&ta=y&accid=96708
```

You can create your own XML smart tag (this example is called Weather.XML) by creating an XML file using the following format. Note that the FL:url tag contains the revised URL with the literal zip code replaced by {TEXT} placeholders:

```
<FL:smarttaglist xmlns:FL="urn:schemas-microsoft-com:smarttags:list">
    <FL:name>Local Weather</FL:name>
    <FL:description>Your local weather report on MSNBC.</FL:description>
    <FL:moreinfourl>http://msdn.microsoft.com/office</FL:moreinfourl>
    <FL:smarttag type="urn:schemas-microsoft-com:office:smarttags#weather">
        <FL:caption>Local Weather Report</FL:caption>
        <FL:terms>
        </FL:terms>
        <FL:actions>
            <FL:action id="LocalWeather">
                <FL:caption> -- Get Weather</FL:caption>
```

```
<FL:url>http://www.msnbc.com/news/wea_front.asp?tab=oth&amp;
    czstr={TEXT}&amp;ta=y&amp;accid={TEXT}</FL:url>
      </FL:action>
    </FL:actions>
  </FL:smarttag>
</FL:smarttaglist>
```

Once you've created the Weather.XML smart tag, deploy it by copying or saving it to the following location:

```
\Program Files\Common Files\Microsoft Shared\Smart Tag\LISTS\
```

Follow these steps to use the Weather.XML smart tag in Access:

1. Shut down any running copies of Access that may have been active when you saved Weather.XML to the \Smart Tag\LISTS\ folder. This is necessary to restart the smart tag engine.

2. Open the Access application (*16-06.MDB*).

3. Open the frmCustomers form in design view. Select the PostalCode text box and press F4 to bring up the Properties window.

4. Click the builder button (…) to bring up the Smart Tag dialog box and select the Local Weather Report option, as shown in Figure 16-8. Click OK.

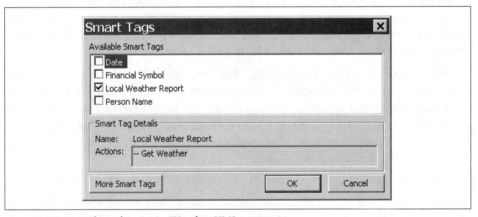

Figure 16-8. Attaching the custom Weather.XML smart tag

5. Display the form in form view, scroll through the records, and select the smart tag as shown in Figure 16-9. Select the Get Weather option and you will be redirected to the msnbc.com weather forecast for that zip code.

Discussion

Here's how the Weather.XML smart tag file works:

The first line of the XML file defines a smart tag and the smart tag list namespace. In this example, the urn:schemas-microsoft-com namespace is used, but this is not

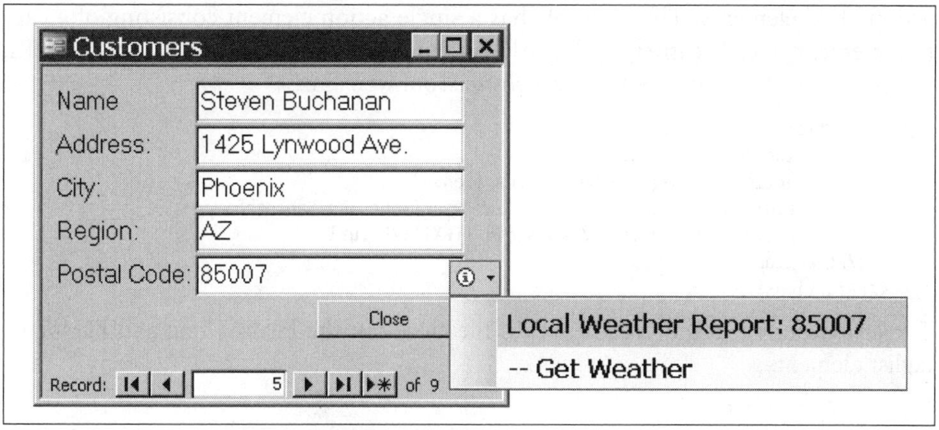

Figure 16-9. The deployed Weather.XML smart tag

required. You can provide any unique namespace name that you want. You must enclose the entire smart tag within the FL:smarttaglist element:

```
<FL:smarttaglist xmlns:FL="urn:schemas-microsoft-com:smarttags:list">
```

The next three lines define the name, description, and a URL to get more information about the smart tag by using the <FL:name>, <FL:description>, and <FL:moreinfourl> elements:

```
<FL:name>Local Weather</FL:name>
<FL:description>Your local weather report on MSNBC.</FL:description>
<FL:moreinfourl>http://msdn.microsoft.com/office</FL:moreinfourl>
```

The FL:smarttag element's type attribute defines a smart tag type, which is a unique, arbitrary identifier for a smart tag on a user's computer. The smart tag type has two parts: the namespace URI and a tag name:

```
<FL:smarttag type="urn:schemas-microsoft-com:office:smarttags#weather">
```

The URI is conventionally some derivation of your company's name (microsoft-com is used here), and the tag name must consist of the "#" symbol and some unique string (#weather). You could have the same URI with a different tag, say #directions, the combination of which would create a second smart tag type.

The following lines consist of the caption and terms. The caption shows up on the smart tag (see Figure 16-9), and the terms are not needed for Access since it does not require or support the recognizers that are needed when working with smart tags in Word or Excel:

```
<FL:caption>Local Weather Report</FL:caption>
<FL:terms>
</FL:terms>
```

The next text block defines the set of actions, or verbs, for the smart tag, which is fully enclosed with an actions element. The actions element contains one or more action child elements. This example has a single action element consisting of a caption element (Get Weather) and a url element, which provides the associated URL for the action, navigating to the *www.msnbc.com* web site:

```
<FL:actions>
  <FL:action id="LocalWeather">
    <FL:caption> -- Get Weather</FL:caption>
      <FL:url>http://www.msnbc.com/news/wea_front.asp?tab=oth&amp;
      czstr={TEXT}&amp;ta=y&amp;accid={TEXT}</FL:url>
  </FL:action>
</FL:actions>
```

The last two lines in the Weather.XML file close out the FL:smarttag and FL:smarttaglist elements:

```
  </FL:smarttag>
</FL:smarttaglist>
```

Although easy to create, the XML file approach can't do much other than open a web site. One advantage of this technique is that you can update the XML file on the user's computer without having to rewrite your application or reinstall any components.

16.7   Create a Custom Smart Tag DLL

Problem

Users of my application prefer to use datasheet view for browsing data. I'd like to provide a smart tag that will enable them to open forms and reports. How can I create a custom smart tag that will allow users to open a form that shows all orders for a customer as well as open a report that shows total sales for a customer?

Solution

If you want to provide conditional processing for smart tag actions then you must create a smart tag DLL, using Visual Basic 6.0 or Visual Basic .NET. In this solution, you'll see how you can use Visual Basic 6.0 to accomplish this.

If you prefer, you can use Visual Basic .NET to create the smart tag DLL. In Chapter 17 you'll learn how to create .NET programs that can be called by Access. For smart tags, there is no particular advantage to using Visual Basic .NET and Visual Basic 6.0 will be more familiar to Access programmers who have worked with VBA, so we have chosen to use Visual Basic 6.0 for this example.

Setting up the DLL project

Follow these steps to create the DLL project using Visual Basic 6.0:

1. Launch Visual Basic 6.0 and create a new DLL project. The sample application is named AccessSmartTag, and it includes one class, stActions. The stActions class provides the Actions interface that defines the smart tag actions you want to take.

2. Add the references shown in Figure 16-10. The reference to the Microsoft Smart Tags 2.0 Type Library is required. This example also has a reference to the Microsoft Access 11.0 Object Library so that you can work with Access objects from your smart tag code and the Microsoft DAO 3.6 Object Library so that you can work with data objects.

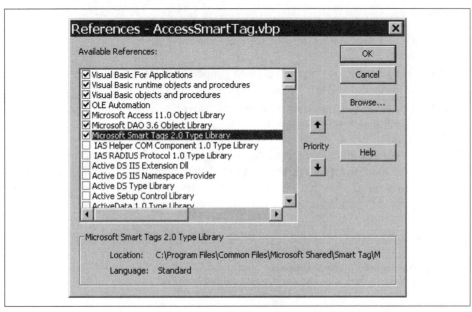

Figure 16-10. Setting references to the Microsoft Smart Tags 2.0 Type Library, the Access 11.0 Object Library, and the Microsoft DAO 3.6 Object Library

3. Place the following statements in the Declarations of the stActions class. You do not need a Recognizer interface for a smart tag that is designed to work exclusively with Access:

```
Option Explicit

Implements ISmartTagAction
Implements ISmartTagAction2
```

4. The next step is to implement the smart tag action interface by creating properties and methods that describe the smart tag action DLL. Most of these properties are fairly straightforward and just return a requested string. The ISmartTagAction_ProgId() is the language-independent unique identifier that

corresponds to the ProgID of the DLL class. In this example, the name of the project is AccessSmartTag, and the class name is stActions:

```
Private Property Get ISmartTagAction_ProgId( ) As String
    ISmartTagAction_ProgId = "AccessSmartTag.stActions"
End Property
```

5. The ISmartTagAction_Name property is a short phrase that describes the DLL:

```
Private Property Get ISmartTagAction_Name(ByVal lcid As Long) As String
    ISmartTagAction_Name = "Demo Smart Tag Actions"
End Property
```

6. The ISmartTagAction_Desc property is a longer description of the DLL:

```
Private Property Get ISmartTagAction_Desc(ByVal lcid As Long) As String
  ISmartTagAction_Desc = _
    "This is a Sample SmartTag used to open Forms and Reports."
End Property
```

7. The ISmartTagAction_SmartTagCount property reflects the number of smart tag types. This example contains one smart tag, so the count is 1:

```
Private Property Get ISmartTagAction_SmartTagCount( ) As Long
    ISmartTagAction_SmartTagCount = 1
End Property
```

8. Each smart tag type is defined by a namespace to keep it unique, which is defined in the ISmartTagAction_SmartTagName property. SmartTag type names are always in the format of namespaceURI#tagname. In this example, the (ismarttag = 1) condition isn't strictly necessary since there is only one smart tag type defined, but this shows a pattern you could use for handling multiple types:

```
Private Property Get ISmartTagAction_SmartTagName(ByVal ismarttag As Long) As String
  If (ismarttag = 1) Then
    ISmartTagAction_SmartTagName = _
      "schemas-microsoft-com/smarttag/northwind#openform"
  End If
End Property
```

9. The ISmartTagAction_SmartTagCaption property allows you to specify the caption that will be used:

```
Private Property Get ISmartTagAction_SmartTagCaption( _
    ByVal ismarttag As Long, ByVal lcid As Long) As String
    ISmartTagAction_SmartTagCaption = "Access Smart Tag Demo"
End Property
```

10. The ISmartTagAction_VerbCount is where you specify the number of verbs in the smart tag. In this example, there are two actions that the smart tag can take: opening a form or opening a report:

```
Private Property Get ISmartTagAction_VerbCount(ByVal bstrName As String) As Long
    If (bstrName = "schemas-microsoft-com/smarttag/northwind#openform") Then
        ISmartTagAction_VerbCount = 2
    End If
End Property
```

11. Smart tag action clients will first ask action DLLs for a unique ID integer for each of the verbs it wants to support, passing in the name and ordinal number for each one. Generating the unique ID is totally up to the action DLL, which gives the action DLL more flexibility. For example, a smart tag action DLL can specify the same VerbID value for the same action across smart tag types, or it can use the same VerbID for similar variants of an action. In this example, the ISmartTagAction_VerbID property returns iVerb (the same ordinal number passed in) back to the action client as the unique ID:

```
Private Property Get ISmartTagAction_VerbID( _
 ByVal bstrName As String, ByVal iVerb As Long) As Long
    ISmartTagAction_VerbID = iVerb
End Property
```

12. The ISmartTagAction_VerbNameFromID property is used internally to represent the verb ID:

```
Private Property Get ISmartTagAction_VerbNameFromID(ByVal idVerb As Long) _
  As String
    Select Case idVerb
        Case 1
            ISmartTagAction_VerbNameFromID = "openCustomers"
        Case 2
            ISmartTagAction_VerbNameFromID = "openReport"
        Case Else
            ISmartTagAction_VerbNameFromID = ""
    End Select
End Property
```

13. The code in the ISmartTagAction2_VerbCaptionFromID2 property checks the VerbID and then uses the "///" syntax to get cascading menus in the smart tag. Figure 16-11 shows the results when the smart tag is accessed in the client application:

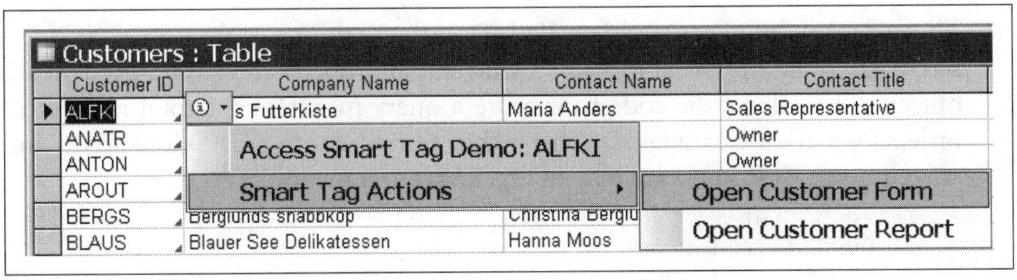

Figure 16-11. Displaying a fly-out smart tag

```
Private Property Get ISmartTagAction2_VerbCaptionFromID2( _
 ByVal VerbID As Long, ByVal ApplicationName As String, _
 ByVal LocaleID As Long, ByVal Properties As SmartTagLib.ISmartTagProperties, _
 ByVal Text As String, ByVal Xml As String, ByVal Target As Object) As String
    If (VerbID = 1) Then
        ISmartTagAction2_VerbCaptionFromID2 = _
        "Smart Tag Actions///Open Customer Form"
```

```
    ElseIf (VerbID = 2) Then
        ISmartTagAction2_VerbCaptionFromID2 = _
        "Smart Tag Actions///Open Customer Report"
    End If
End Property
```

14. The ISmartTagAction2_InvokeVerb2 method provides code to perform the actions that the smart tag takes. The first section of the code sets a variable to point to the Target, which is the Access control object passed in. If the smart tag is defined on a Table object instead of a form control, then Access creates a control under the covers that gets passed to the smart tag DLL:

```
Private Sub ISmartTagAction2_InvokeVerb2( _
ByVal VerbID As Long, ByVal ApplicationName As String, _
ByVal Target As Object, ByVal Properties As SmartTagLib.ISmartTagProperties, _
ByVal Text As String, ByVal Xml As String, ByVal LocaleID As Long)

On Error GoTo HandleErr:
    Dim cb As Access.Control
    Set cb = Target
```

15. The next block of code validates that the control source is CustomerID. If not, a MsgBox statement provides feedback to the user that the smart tag only works when attached to the CustomerID. If the smart tag is attached to CustomerID, the code gets a reference to the Access.Application object from the Target's Application property:

```
If cb.ControlSource <> "CustomerID" Then
    MsgBox "This action only works if you run it on the Customer ID field.", _
    vbOKOnly, "Smart Tag Error"
    GoTo ExitHere
Else
    Dim app As Access.Application
    Set app = cb.Application
End If
```

16. The code then branches based on VerbID. If the VerbID is 1, then the code sets a reference to the Application object's CurrentDb property to gain access to DAO objects. This allows the code to execute a query to obtain the total number of orders for a given CustomerID. This is then retrieved into a DAO Recordset, and passed to the Customers form as an OpenArgs argument:

```
If VerbID = 1 Then
    Dim db As DAO.Database
    Dim rs As DAO.Recordset
    Set db = app.CurrentDb

    Dim strQry As String
    Dim strOrders As String
    strQry = "SELECT Count(*) AS NumOrders FROM Orders WHERE CustomerID='" _
    & cb.Value & "';"
    Set rs = db.OpenRecordset(strQry)
    If Not rs.EOF Then
        strOrders = "Total number of orders: " & rs!NumOrders
```

```
Else
    strOrders = "No orders for this customer"
End If
rs.Close

app.DoCmd.OpenForm "Customers", _
    WhereCondition:="[CustomerID] = '" & cb.Value & "'", _
    OpenArgs:=strOrders
```

17. If the second action is chosen, then the code opens rptCustomers report, pass-
    ing the CustomerID as the WhereCondition argument (without this WhereCon-
    dition, the report would open displaying all the customers):

```
ElseIf VerbID = 2 Then
    app.DoCmd.OpenReport "rptCustomers", _
    View:=acViewPreview, _
    WhereCondition:="[CustomerID] = '" & cb.Value & "'"
End If
```

18. The error handling code is mainly useful for debugging. It displays any error
    information in a MsgBox statement:

```
ExitHere:
    Exit Sub

HandleErr:
    MsgBox Err.Number & " " & Err.Description, _
    vbCritical, "Error in AccessSmartTag.ISmartTagAction2_InvokeVerb2"
    Resume ExitHere
End Sub
```

Compiling and registering the DLL project

Once you've written the code, build the DLL project by choosing File → Make
AccessSmartTag DLL from the menu. This will create the correct registry entries.
Launch regedit from the Windows Start → Run menu. To obtain the CLSID for the
action handler, navigate to the following node in the Registry:

```
HKEY_CLASSES_ROOT\AccessSmartTag.stActions\Clsid
```

Double-click the Clsid node to obtain the value, as shown in Figure 16-12. Copy it to
the clipboard and close the regedit window without saving.

You can then edit the registry directly or create a reg file to update the registry
entries. Use Notepad to create a new file and name it Reg_AccessSmartTag.reg. The
file should contain the following text. However, you will need to replace the value
shown in the curly braces with the value that you copied to the Clipboard from the
Registry in the previous step:

```
Windows Registry Editor Version 5.00

[HKEY_CURRENT_USER\Software\Microsoft\Office\Common\Smart Tag\Actions\
{9F7503BB-4BBA-4A4A-B1A5-A0DF0A0187F5}]
```

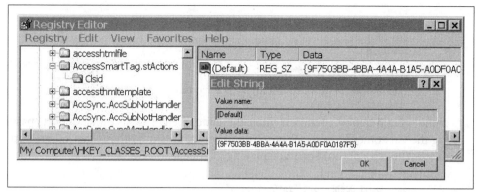

Figure 16-12. Obtaining the Clsid from the AccessSmartTag.stActions

In case you ever need to unregister the smart tag, create a second file named Unreg_ AccessSmartTag.reg. The file should contain the following text. Again, replace the value shown here in the curly braces with the value copied to the Clipboard:

```
Windows Registry Editor Version 5.00

[-HKEY_CURRENT_USER\Software\Microsoft\Office\Common\Smart Tag\Actions\
{9F7503BB-4BBA-4A4A-B1A5-A0DF0A0187F5}]
```

Save both files and double-click Reg_AccessSmartTag.reg. This will create the entries in the registry so that Access can recognize the smart tag actions.

Open the *16-07.MDB* sample database and open the Customers form in design view. View the code in the form's Open event, which displays anything passed in the OpenArgs event in the form's Caption property:

```
Private Sub Form_Open(Cancel As Integer)
' Display any OpenArgs in the Caption
    Dim str As String
    str = Me.OpenArgs & ""
    If Len(str) > 0 Then
        Me.Caption = str
    End If
End Sub
```

Close the form and open the Customers table in design view. Assign the smart tag to the CustomerID field, as shown in Figure 16-13.

Save the table and view it in datasheet view. When you choose the first smart tag action, the Customers form will open with the total number of orders for the selected customer displayed in the form's Caption. If you choose the second smart tag action, then the rptCustomers report will open displaying sales data for the selected customer.

Discussion

You can write a smart tag DLL in any language that supports writing COM add-ins. You can also write a smart tag DLL in managed (.NET) code.

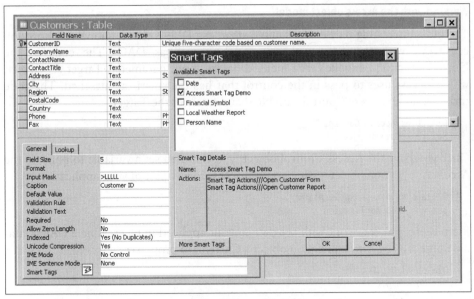

Figure 16-13. Assigning the smart tag to the CustomerID field in the Customers table

There are two interfaces involved in implementing smart tag actions: the ISmartTagAction interface and the ISmartTagAction2 interface. These interfaces provide the client application with the information needed to support smart tag actions. The ISmartTagAction interface is compatible with Office XP, and the ISmartTagAction2 interface is specific to Office 2003, and allows you to tap into new functionality.

> You do not need to implement the ISmartTagRecognizer and ISmartTagRecognizer2 interfaces in a smart tag DLL targeted specifically for Access because Access does not use recognizers.

The role of an ISmartTagAction interface is to provide actions for individual smart tag types. Each smart tag type is defined by a namespace URI plus its tag name to keep it unique. A "#" character is appended to the namespace URI and is used to separate the namespace URI from its tag name, as shown in this example, where "schemas-microsoft-com/smarttag/northwind" is the namespace URI and "openform" is the tag name. The combination results in the fully qualified name of the smart tag type. The URI portion of the property name ensures that it is globally unique and unambiguous, so that two tags with the same tag name (openform) can be differentiated:

```
Private Property Get ISmartTagAction_SmartTagName( _
  ByVal ismarttag As Long) As String
    ISmartTagAction_SmartTagName = _
      "schemas-microsoft-com/smarttag/northwind#openform"
End Property
```

Working with the Access object model

The most interesting part of the sample smart tag DLL is that it shows you how you can work with the Access object model as well as DAO. The code in the ISmartTagAction2_InvokeVerb2 method has an input parameter, Target As Object, which Access uses to pass in the control that has the smart tag attached. The code then creates an Access.Control variable that references the Target:

```
Dim cb As Access.Control
Set cb = Target
```

Once you have the Access Control object, you can then set a variable to point to the Access Application object, giving you full access to any part of your application:

```
Dim app As Access.Application
Set app = cb.Application
```

From there, you can work with the data in your application by creating a DAO Database object using the Application object's CurrentDb property:

```
Dim db As DAO.Database
Set db = app.CurrentDb
```

The code goes on to open a Recordset based on a query that counts the total number of orders for the selected customer, writing it to a String variable. It then opens the form to display the selected customer and passes that count value in the OpenArgs argument of the Application object's DoCmd.OpenForm method:

```
app.DoCmd.OpenForm "Customers", _
  WhereCondition:="[CustomerID] = '" & cb.Value & "'", _
  OpenArgs:=strOrders
```

When the Customers form opens, the code in the Open event evaluates whether any data has been passed in the OpenArgs argument, and then displays that information in the form's Caption property. If the form is opened normally without any OpenArgs data being passed to it, then the default caption is displayed:

```
Private Sub Form_Open(Cancel As Integer)
    Dim str As String
    str = Me.OpenArgs & ""
    If Len(str) > 0 Then
        Me.Caption = str
    End If
End Sub
```

The code for opening a report uses similar techniques. Creating a smart tag DLL allows you full access to the entire Access object model, and allows you to create conditional logic for your smart tag. Smart tags can be a good way to provide extra functionality for users who prefer working in datasheet view.

See Also

See the Preface for more information on working with DAO to access data.

CHAPTER 17

.NET

In the beginning of 2002, Microsoft introduced a new initiative called *.NET* that radically changed the Microsoft programming world. Microsoft .NET programs run on top of a runtime environment called the Common Language Runtime. Microsoft .NET provides a consistent programming model across desktop and web applications and across development languages. In this new development world, many of the old ways of programming have been thrown out the window. Microsoft .NET minimizes "DLL hell" and no longer uses the registry to install programs. All languages that run under .NET share common systems for data types, accessing data, security, garbage collection, and exception handling.

Access 2003 and earlier versions of Access, however, do not live in the world of .NET. Instead, they live in the world of the Component Object Model, or COM. By default, a COM-based program does not know how to talk to a .NET-based program. Fortunately, Microsoft created a mechanism for .NET to interoperate with the older COM-based world.

In this chapter you will find various examples that demonstrate how .NET and Access can coexist. You'll learn how to call a .NET component from Access, even when there are potentially incompatible features present in the component. You'll explore how to connect to an Access database to retrieve and update data. You'll see how to call .NET web services from Access. You'll learn how to call .NET web services that return both simple data types and complex data types. Finally, you'll learn how to automate Access from a .NET application in order to print an Access report.

The topics in this chapter all require the presence of the .NET Framework 1.1 and Visual Studio .NET 2003. If you do not have Visual Studio .NET 2003 (or a later version of Visual Studio .NET) installed on your system you will be unable to work through the topics in this chapter. See the Preface for advice on where to find free or evaluation editions of both tools.

17.1 Call a .NET Component from Access

Problem

Access makes it easy to call code inside a component built using Visual Basic 6.0 or another COM-based programming language (see Chapter 12). By default, however, Access can't normally call code in a .NET component. Is there some way that Access can call a .NET component created using Visual Basic .NET, Visual C# .NET, or another .NET language?

Solution

By default, .NET components can't be called by Access and other COM programs for at least two reasons. First, .NET components are not installed into the registry. In order to automate a component, however, certain registry entries must be present. Second, .NET components aren't COM components; they aren't structured to look and behave like a COM component and they have separate and distinct type systems.

Fortunately, the Microsoft .NET SDK includes a utility, *RegAsm.exe*, that you can use to create a COM-callable wrapper for a .NET component. *RegAsm.exe* also registers the .NET component so that it can be called from a COM program such as Access.

One nice feature of .NET is that it only takes a single line of code to determine the current Windows user name. Trying to do this from Access requires at the very least a cumbersome Windows API call.

Follow these steps to create a simple .NET component, UserNameVB, that contains a single class named UserName with a single method, GetUserName, which returns the current user name:

1. Start Visual Studio .NET.
2. Create a new VB .NET Class Library project named UserNameVB.
3. Delete the initial *Class1.vb* file from the project.
4. Select Project → Add Class... to add a new class file to the project named *UserName.cls*.
5. Add a method named GetUserName to the class that returns the Environment. UserName property. The complete code for the UserName class should look like the following:

```
Public Class UserName
    Public Function GetUserName( ) As String
        Return Environment.UserName
    End Function
End Class
```

6. Compile the project by selecting Build → Build Solution. If all goes well, the status bar will display "Build succeeded."

At this point you could easily create a .NET Windows Form or Web Form application that calls the .NET component. To make it callable from Access, however, you need to use the RegAsm utility to create a COM-callable wrapper component that will call UserNameVB on your behalf. RegAsm also takes care of making the necessary registry entries as well so that Access and other COM programs can see your component.

Follow these steps to make the UserNameVB component callable from Access:

1. From the Microsoft Visual Studio .NET 2003 Start menu, select Visual Studio .NET Tools → Visual Studio .NET Command Prompt to create a Visual Studio .NET command prompt.

 Do not use the Command Prompt menu entry found under Accessories. This command prompt will not have the needed path settings that allow you to run the .NET command line tools.

2. Navigate to the folder containing the compiled assembly by using the CD command. By default, the assembly should be found in the following location:

```
C:\Documents and Settings\<yourusername>\My Documents\Visual Studio Projects\
UserNameVB\bin
```

3. Use the .NET registration assembly utility (*RegAsm.exe*) to register the *UserNameVB.dll* by entering the following into the command prompt window:

```
regasm UserNameVB.dll /tlb:UserNameVB.tlb /codebase
```

RegAsm will display a warning about this being an unsigned assembly but you can safely ignore the warning.

Now you are ready to create the Access application that will call the UserNameVB component. Follow these steps to create an Access form that calls the .NET component:

1. Create a new Access form named frmGetUserName.

2. Add a command button to the form named cmdGetUserName and a label named lblUserName.

3. From the VBA IDE, select Tools → References. At the References dialog, select the UserNameVB component (see Figure 17-1).

4. Attach the following code to the Click event of the cmdGetUserName command button to instantiate the UserNameVB.UserName class and call its GetUserName method:

```
Private Sub cmdGetUserName_Click( )
    Dim objUN As UserNameVB.UserName
```

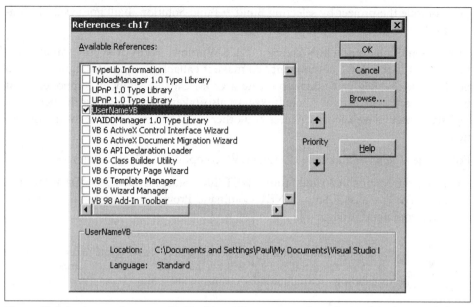

Figure 17-1. Setting a reference to the UserNameVB component from the Tools References dialog

```
Set objUN = New UserNameVB.UserName

lblUserName.Caption = objUN.GetUserName( )
End Sub
```

5. Load and run the form, clicking on the cmdGetUserName command button to return the current user name as show in Figure 17-2.

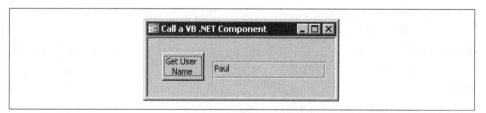

Figure 17-2. This form calls a .NET component to determine the current Windows user name

Note: The steps for the solution are virtually identical if using another .NET programming language such as C#. The only differences would be in the type of project (you would choose to create a Visual C# .NET class library) and the source code of the component. In addition to the VB version of the component, you can find a C# version of the component, named UserNameCS, in this chapter's sample code.

Discussion

An alternate solution

There is an alternate technique for creating a .NET component that can be called from Access and other COM programs that requires a bit less work than the solution presented here. This solution, however, only works with Visual Basic .NET.

The basic difference with this version of the solution is to create a special type of class library, called a COM Class, that automatically enables it to be called from a COM application. Here are the steps:

1. Follow Steps 1–3 of the solution.
2. Select Project → Add → Add New Item.... At the Add New Item dialog box, select the COM Class template and name the file *UserName.cls*.
3. Follow Steps 5–6 of the solution.
4. Skip Steps 7–9 of the solution. They are no longer necessary.
5. Follow the remaining steps of the solution.

Note: this version of the solution will only work with a Visual Basic . NET project.

Not all .NET components are callable

Not all .NET components can be called from Access and other COM programs. The main limitation is that you can't instantiate any objects for classes containing parameterized constructors. A *constructor* is code that executes when an instance of a class is created. Constructors are similar in concept to the Class_Initialize event handler within a Visual Basic 6 class. .NET, however, allows you to create constructors that can accept parameters, so-called *parameterized constructors*. COM, however, has no way to call a class containing a parameterized constructor. If you attempt to create an object from a .NET class that contains a parameterized constructor, you will get a runtime error. A workaround for this issue is presented in topic 17.2.

Another limitation of calling .NET components from Access is that you won't be able to access any properties, methods, or events marked as static (also know as shared). A static member of a .NET class is a member that applies across all instances of a class. Static members cannot be called from Access or other COM programs.

See Also

Microsoft Office and .NET Interoperability (*http://msdn.microsoft.com/library/default.asp?url=/library/en-us/dnofftalk/html/office11012001.asp*).

17.2 Call a .NET Component Containing a Parameterized Constructor

Problem

Attempting to call a .NET class containing a parameterized constructor generates the compile error "Invalid use of New keyword". Is there some sort of workaround so that I can call a .NET class containing a parameterized constructor?

Solution

To see the problem, you will need to follow these steps:

1. Start a Visual Studio .NET command prompt and run the RegAsm utility program on the Geometry.dll file found in the Geometry\bin folder of this chapter's sample files using the following syntax (see topic 17.1 for more details on the Visual Studio .NET command prompt and running the RegAsm utility):

   ```
   regasm Geometry.dll /tlb: Geometry.tlb /codebase
   ```

   RegAsm will display a warning about this being an unsigned assembly but you can safely ignore the warning.

2. Load the *17-02.MDB* database and open the frmCircleDirect form in Design view.

3. From the VBA IDE, select Tools → References. At the References dialog, select the Geometry component.

4. Close and save the form.

5. Open frmCircleDirect in form view. Enter a numeric value into the Radius textbox and click the Calculate button. Access should respond with the error shown in Figure 17-3.

6. Click OK. Select Run → Reset and close the form.

The Circle class is shown here:

```
Public Class Circle
    ' NOTE: This class contains a
    ' parameterized constructor which
    ' prevents it from being called
    ' by a COM program.

    Private RadiusVal As Double

    Public Sub New(ByVal Radius As Double)
        ' This constructor takes a parameter
        RadiusVal = Radius
    End Sub

    Public Property Radius() As Double
```

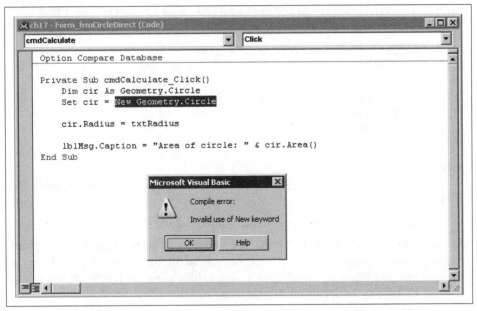

Figure 17-3. This compile error is triggered when you attempt to instantiate a .NET class containing a parameterized constructor

```
            Get
                Return RadiusVal
            End Get
            Set(ByVal Value As Double)
                RadiusVal = Value
            End Set
        End Property

        Public Function Area() As Double
            Return Radius ^ 2 * System.Math.PI
        End Function

        Public Function Circumference() As Double
            Return 2 * Radius * System.Math.PI
        End Function
    End Class
```

This class is inaccessible from Access because its constructor (the New subroutine) contains a parameter. The trick to being able to call the inaccessible class from Access is to create a helper class that you can use to call the unavailable class. To create a helper class that you can use to call the Circle class, follow these steps:

1. Exit Access completely. This is necessary because otherwise Access may place a lock on the existing Geometry.tlb type library.

2. Start Visual Studio .NET and load the Geometry project.

3. Open *Geometry.vb* and add the following class after the Circle class's End Class statement:

```
Public Class CircleCOM
    Inherits Circle

    Sub New( )
        ' Call base class' constructor
        ' with dummy radius value.
        MyBase.New(1)
    End Sub

End Class
```

Notice that the new class, CircleCOM, inherits from the original inaccessible Circle class.

4. Compile the project by selecting Build → Build Solution.

5. Start a Visual Studio .NET command prompt and run the RegAsm utility program on the updated Geometry.dll file found in the Visual Studio Projects\Geometry\bin folder of this chapter's sample files using the following syntax (see topic 17.1 for more details on running the RegAsm utility):

```
regasm Geometry.dll /tlb: Geometry.tlb /codebase
```

RegAsm will display a warning about this being an unsigned assembly but you can safely ignore the warning.

6. Restart Access and load the *17-02.MDB* database. Open the frmCircleUsing-Helper form in design view.

7. From the VBA IDE, select Tools → References. Verify that the Geometry component is selected.

8. Note the source code behind the Calculate command button:

```
Private Sub cmdCalculate_Click( )
    Dim cirCOM As Geometry.CircleCOM
    Set cirCOM = New Geometry.CircleCOM

    cirCOM.Radius = txtRadius

    lblMsg.Caption = "Area of circle: " & cirCOM.Area( )
End Sub
```

9. Close and save the form.

10. Open frmCircleUsingHelper in form view. Enter a numeric value into the Radius textbox and click the Calculate button. Access should display the result as shown in Figure 17-4.

Discussion

The helper class could have been constructed in a number of ways. Although we chose to use a derived class, the helper class could also have been independent of the

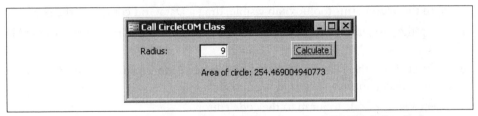

Figure 17-4. frmCircleUsingHelper instantiates a helper class, CircleCOM, which calls the inaccessible class, Circle

original class. The helper class could live within the same component or in a separate component. In this example, we chose to make the helper class a derived class that lives in the same component as the inaccessible class.

In this example, you were able to use the CircleCOM class to call the Circle class. In instantiating the Circle class, CircleCOM passed a dummy radius value to the constructor. Because Circle also included a Radius property, you were able to specify the radius value prior to calling the Area method. There may be some classes where properties that duplicate the constructor parameters are not available. In these cases, it may be difficult if not impossible to create a helper class that is able to instantiate the inaccessible class for you.

Many of the built-in classes of the .NET Framework contain parameterized constructors. This means that you will need to create a lot of helper classes in order to work with these classes.

17.3   Retrieve Access Data from an ASP.NET Application

Problem

Your ASP.NET web site needs to access data from one of your Access databases. How do you retrieve Access data using ADO.NET?

Solution

Follow these steps to create an ASP.NET page, AltRock.aspx, which displays a list of alternative rock albums from the *17-03.MDB* database using a DataGrid control:

1. Start Visual Studio .NET.

2. Create a new Visual Basic .NET ASP.NET Web Application project.

3. Under location, enter "http://localhost/Music" and click OK.

4. Delete the initial WebForm1.aspx file from the project.

5. Select Project → Add Web Form... to add a new web form page to the project named AltRock.aspx.

6. With the Web Forms toolbox tab visible, drag a DataGrid control to the page.

7. Using the Property sheet, change the ID of the new DataGrid control to dgrAltRock.

8. Right-click on the DataGrid control and select Auto Format... from the popup menu. Select a format of your liking and click OK.

9. Select View → Code to jump to the code editor.

10. Add the following code to the very top of the page (above the Class statement) to import the System.Data.OleDb namespace:

```
Imports System.Data.OleDb
```

11. Add the following code to the Page_Load event handler to establish a connection to the *17-03.MDB* database:

```
' You will need to edit the Data Source value to correspond
' to the location of the 17-03.mdb database on your system.
Dim cnx As OleDbConnection = _
 New OleDbConnection("Provider=Microsoft.Jet.OLEDB.4.0;" & _
 "Data Source=D:\Books\AccessCookBook2003\ch17\17-03.mdb")
cnx.Open()
```

As noted by the comment in the code you will need to edit the path to the *17-03. MDB* database to match where the database is located on your system.

12. Add the following code to retrieve the rows returned by the database's qryAlternativeAlbums query as a OleDbDataReader:

```
' Constuct a OleDbCommand to execute the query
Dim cmdAltRock As OleDbCommand = _
 New OleDbCommand("qryAlternativeAlbums", cnx)

' Odd as it may seem, you need to set the CommandType
' to CommandType.StoredProcedure.
cmdAltRock.CommandType = CommandType.StoredProcedure

' Run the query and place the rows in an OleDbDataReader.
Dim drAltRock As OleDbDataReader
drAltRock = cmdAltRock.ExecuteReader()
```

13. Add the following code to bind the drAltRock OleDbDataReader to the dgrAltRock DataGrid control on the page:

```
' Bind the OleDbDataReader to the DataGrid
dgrAltRock.DataSource = drAltRock
dgrAltRock.DataBind()
```

14. Save the page and preview it in your browser by right-clicking on the file name (*AltRock.aspx*) in the Solution Explorer window and selecting View in Browser from the popup menu. The resulting page should look similar to the one shown in Figure 17-5.

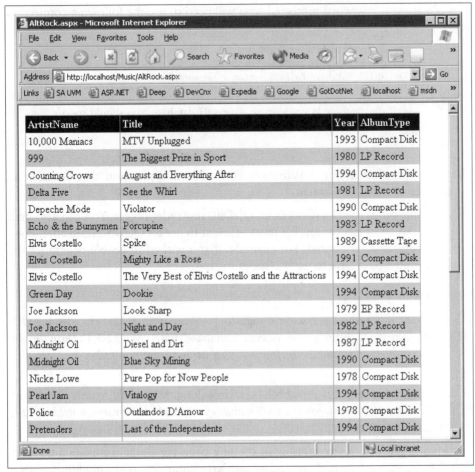

Figure 17-5. The data behind this DataGrid was retrieved from the 17-03.MDB database using the .NET OleDb provider

Discussion

Probably the trickiest part of retrieving data from an Access database using ADO. NET is in creating the connection string. The basic syntax of the connection string is as follows:

```
"Provider=Microsoft.Jet.OLEDB.4.0;" & _
"Data Source=path_to_database"
```

If you are using a workgroup-secured database, you will need to add User Id and Password items to the connection string:

```
"Provider=Microsoft.Jet.OLEDB.4.0;" & _
"Data Source=path_to_database;" & _
"User Id=user_name;Password=password;"
```

If the database is password-protected, you will need to use the following connection string:

```
"Provider=Microsoft.Jet.OLEDB.4.0;" & _
"Data Source=path_to_database;" & _
"Jet OLEDB:Database Password=database_password;"
```

 If the database is stored in an Access 97 database, you should specify the Jet 3.51 provider (Microsoft.Jet.OLEDB.3.51) instead of the Jet 4.0 provider.

The steps for constructing a Windows Forms-based application that accesses an Access database are fairly similar.

This example binds the DataGrid to an OleDbDataReader object. You can also bind a DataGrid to a DataSet object. It's more efficient to use an OleDbDataReader; however, its usage is more limited. For example, if you wished to enable paging for the DataGrid, you would have to use a DataSet instead.

See Also

The following link provides a walkthrough for working with Access data from ADO. NET: Walkthrough: Editing an Access Database with ADO.NET (*http://msdn. microsoft.com/library/default.asp?url=/library/en-us/dnadonet/html/adon_wtaccessdb. asp*).

Another helpful article on ADO.NET is Unlocking Microsoft Access Data with ADO.NET (*http://msdn.microsoft.com/library/default.asp?url=/library/en-us/dnofftalk/ html/office12062001.asp*).

The following article discusses how to create a pageable DataGrid using a DataSet: (*http://msdn.microsoft.com/library/default.asp?url=/library/en-us/dnaspp/html/aspnet-pageablesortable.asp*).

If you're having trouble creating ADO.NET connection strings, check out Able Consulting's Connection Strings page (*http://www.able-consulting.com/ADO_Conn.htm*).

17.4   Call a Web Service from Access

Problem

A web service is a specially constructed component that you can access over standard web protocols. To call a web service, however, you must pass it messages encoded using Simple Object Access Protocol (SOAP). Access does not directly support the SOAP protocol. Is there any way to call a web service from Access?

Solution

Microsoft has released several toolkits that can be used by Microsoft Office programmers to call web services. This solution assumes you are using Access 2003 with Microsoft Office 2003 Web Services Toolkit. See the discussion section of this topic on calling web services from earlier versions of Access.

The RunnerCalculator web service contains a number of methods that provide pacing calculations for long distance running. This web service can be found at *www.deeptraining.com/webservices*. One of the RunnerCalculator methods, GetPaceDouble, can be used to calculate the pace in minutes per mile for a given distance and total time. Follow these steps to create an Access 2003 form that uses this web service to calculate pace for a user-entered distance and time:

1. If you haven't yet done so, download and install the Microsoft Office 2003 Web Services Toolkit.

2. Start Access 2003 and create an unbound form named frmPaceCalculator.

3. Add the controls to the form listed in Table 17-1:

Table 17-1. Controls for frmPaceCalculator

Control	Name
TextBox	txtDistance
TextBox	txtHours
TextBox	txtMinutes
TextBox	txtSeconds
CommandButton	cmdCalculatePace
Label	lblPace

4. From the VBA editor, select Tools → Web Service → References.... This menu item is added to the VBA editor by the Microsoft Office 2003 Web Services Toolkit.

5. At the Microsoft Office 2003 Web Services Toolkit dialog box, select the Web Service URL radio button and enter the following address into the URL textbox:

    www.deeptraining.com/webservices/runnercalculator.asmx

6. The RunnerCalculator service and its methods should be displayed in the SearchResults box. Check the checkbox to the left of RunnerCalculator and click the Add button at the bottom of the dialog box to add a reference to the RunnerCalculator service. The Microsoft Office 2003 Web Services Toolkit dialog box is shown in Figure 17-6.

7. The toolkit adds a new class module to the Access project with the name clsws_RunnerCalculator. This class serves as a proxy for making calls to the

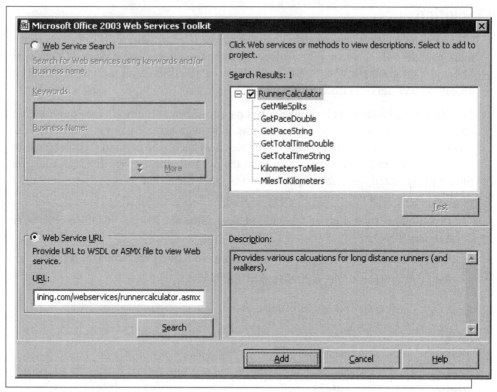

Figure 17-6. You use the Microsoft Office 2003 Web Services Toolkit dialog box to locate a web service and set a reference to it

web service. The code in this class will take care of speaking to the web service using the SOAP protocol.

8. Attach the following code to the cmdCalculatePace button's Click event to use the proxy class to call the RunnerCalculator web service:

```
Private Sub cmdCalculatePace_Click()
    Dim prxRunnerCalc As clsws_RunnerCalculator
    Dim strResult As String

    On Error GoTo HandleErr
    DoCmd.Hourglass True

    ' Instantiate proxy class
    Set prxRunnerCalc = New clsws_RunnerCalculator

    If Len(txtDistance) > 0 And Len(txtHours) > 0 And _
    Len(txtMinutes) > 0 And Len(txtSeconds) > 0 Then
        ' Call GetPaceString method via proxy class
        strResult = prxRunnerCalc.wsm_GetPaceString(txtDistance, _
        txtHours, txtMinutes, txtSeconds)
        lblPace.Caption = "Average Mile Pace: " & strResult
```

```
        Else
            MsgBox "You must enter values for each text box.", _
                vbOKOnly + vbCritical, "Pace Calculator"
        End If

ExitHere:
        On Error GoTo 0
        DoCmd.Hourglass False
        Exit Sub

HandleErr:
        MsgBox "Error " & Err.Number & ": " & Err.Description, _
            vbOKOnly + vbCritical, "Pace Calculator"
        Resume ExitHere
End Sub
```

9. Save the form and open it in form view. Enter values into each of the textboxes and click on the Calculate Pace button. The form should look like the one shown in Figure 17-7.

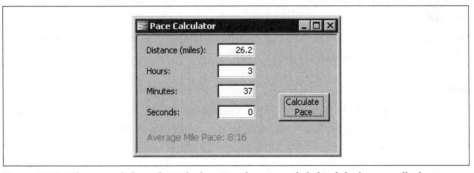

Figure 17-7. When you click on the Calculate Pace button, code behind the button calls the proxy class, which calls the RunnerCalculator web service

Discussion

When you set a reference to a web service using the Microsoft Office 2003 Web Services Toolkit, the toolkit creates a proxy class with the name clsws_*webservice*, where *webservice* is the name of the web service. The proxy class takes care of calling the web service using SOAP and processing the response, again using the SOAP protocol.

For every method of a web service, the Microsoft Office 2003 Web Services Toolkit creates a corresponding method of the proxy class with the name wsm_*method*, where *method* is the name of the web service method. Thus, calling the web service is as simple as instantiating the proxy class and calling the proxy method corresponding to the method in the web service.

Calling web services from earlier versions of Access

If you wish to call a web service from Access XP or an earlier version of Access the solution steps will differ from those shown here. If you're using Access 2002, you need to download and install the Microsoft Office XP Web Services Toolkit 2.0. The steps to use the Office XP toolkit are fairly similar to using the Office 2003 toolkit. If you need to call a web service from Access 2000 or an earlier version of Access, you'll need to use the Microsoft SOAP Toolkit 3.0. This toolkit is geared more towards Visual Studio 6.0 developers, but can also be used from VBA code.

Locating the toolkits

The Microsoft Office 2003 Web Services Toolkit can be found at *http://www. microsoft.com/downloads/details.aspx?FamilyID=fa36018a-e1cf-48a3-9b35-169d819ecf18&DisplayLang=en.*

The Microsoft Office XP Web Services Toolkit 2.0 can be found at *http://msdn. microsoft.com/library/default.asp?url=/library/en-us/dnxpwst2/html/odc_offxpwstoolkit2.asp.*

The Microsoft SOAP Toolkit 3.0 can be found at *http://msdn.microsoft.com/library/default.asp?URL=/downloads/list/websrv.asp.*

See Also

Integrating XML Web Services Into Microsoft Office Solutions (*http://msdn. microsoft.com/library/default.asp?url=/library/en-us/dnofftalk/html/office09062001. asp*).

17.5   Work with a Web Service that Returns a DataSet

Problem

Some web services return complex objects that are not readily understood by Access. For example, you might wish to call a web service that returns a .NET DataSet. Is it possible to call such a web service from Access?

Solution

Web services communicate using the text-based protocols HTTP and SOAP. Thus, any complex objects must be converted from the normal binary format into text. This process is known as serialization. .NET automatically serializes many of its built-in objects, including the DataSet, into XML. Thus, a .NET-based web service that returns a DataSet, in reality returns an XML document that represents the DataSet.

When possible, the Microsoft Office 2003 Web Services Toolkit maps complex object return values into compatible types. The serialized XML representation of a DataSet returned by a web service is mapped by the toolkit into an MSXML2.IXMLDOMNodeList object. This object is part of the MSXML component that you can use to navigate through XML documents from Access.

The RunningCalculator web service introduced in the Solution in Recipe 17.4 contains the GetMileSplits method which returns a DataSet filled with mile splits for a given distance and total time. Follow these steps to create an Access form that calls the GetMileSplits method, navigates through the XML returned by the web service, and populates an unbound listbox control on the form with the mile splits:

1. If you haven't yet done so, download and install the Microsoft Office 2003 Web Services Toolkit.

2. Start Access 2003 and create an unbound form named frmSplitCalculator.

3. Add the controls listed in Table 17-2 to the form. Size the controls to your liking.

Table 17-2. Controls for frmSplitCalculator

Control	Name
TextBox	txtDistance
TextBox	txtHours
TextBox	txtMinutes
TextBox	txtSeconds
CommandButton	cmdCalculateSplits
ListBox	lstSplits

4. From the VBA editor, select Tools → Web Service → References…. This menu item is added to the VBA editor by the Microsoft Office 2003 Web Services Toolkit.

 If you've already completed the Solution in Recipe 17.4 and are working within the same database, you can skip Steps 4–7.

5. At the Microsoft Office 2003 Web Services Toolkit dialog box, select the Web Service URL radio button and enter the following URL into the URL textbox:

www.deeptraining.com/webservices/runnercalculator.asmx

6. The RunnerCalculator service and its methods should be displayed in the SearchResults box. Check the checkbox to the left of RunnerCalculator and click the Add button at the bottom of the dialog box to add a reference to the RunnerCalculator service.

7. The toolkit adds a new class module to the project with the name clsws_Runner-Calculator. This class serves as a proxy for making calls to the web service. The code in this class will take care of speaking to the web service using the SOAP protocol.

8. Attach the following code to the cmdCalculateSplits button's Click event to use the clsws_RunnerCalculator proxy class to call the GetMileSplits method:

```
Private Sub cmdCalculateSplits_Click()
    Dim prxRunnerCalc As clsws_RunnerCalculator
    Dim nlDS As MSXML2.IXMLDOMNodeList
    Dim i As Integer

    ' Clear any existing items from the listbox
    For i = lstSplits.ListCount - 1 To 0 Step -1
        lstSplits.RemoveItem (i)
    Next

    ' Add the headings to the list
    lstSplits.ColumnWidths = "0.35"";1"""
    lstSplits.ColumnHeads = True
    lstSplits.AddItem ("Mile;Split")

    On Error GoTo HandleErr
    DoCmd.Hourglass True

    ' Instantiate proxy class
    Set prxRunnerCalc = New clsws_RunnerCalculator

    If Len(txtDistance) > 0 And Len(txtHours) > 0 And _
      Len(txtMinutes) > 0 And Len(txtSeconds) > 0 Then
        ' Call GetMileSpilts method via proxy class
        ' This method returns a .NET DataSet which gets
        ' serializedd into XML.
        ' XML is returned by the proxy as the type
        ' MSXML2.IXMLDOMNodeList.
        Set nlDS = prxRunnerCalc.wsm_GetMileSplits(txtDistance, _
          txtHours, txtMinutes, txtSeconds)

        Call ProcessSplits(nlDS)
    Else
        MsgBox "You must enter values for each text box.", _
          vbOKOnly + vbCritical, "Splits Calculator"
    End If

ExitHere:
        On Error GoTo 0
        DoCmd.Hourglass False
        Exit Sub

HandleErr:
    MsgBox "Error " & Err.Number & ": " & Err.Description, _
        vbOKOnly + vbCritical, "Splits Calculator"
    Resume ExitHere
End Sub
```

9. Add the following code to the module to use the MSXML component to process the returned XML data and add the split values to the lstSplits listbox:

```
Private Sub ProcessSplits(nlDS As MSXML2.IXMLDOMNodeList)
    Dim nlPace As MSXML2.IXMLDOMNodeList
    Dim nodData As MSXML2.IXMLDOMNode
    Dim nodRow As MSXML2.IXMLDOMNode
    Dim nodField As MSXML2.IXMLDOMNode
    Dim strItem As String

    On Error GoTo HandleErr

    ' Grab the second node -- the data -- from the
    ' returned node list
    Set nodData = nlDS.Item(1)

    ' Get the Pace nodes (rows)
    Set nlPace = nodData.selectNodes("//MileSplits/Pace")
    ' For each Pace node
    For Each nodRow In nlPace
        ' Get the child nodes of Pace, i.e., the fields
        For Each nodField In nodRow.childNodes
            Select Case nodField.nodeName
                Case "Mile"
                    ' Grab the Mile value
                    strItem = nodField.nodeTypedValue
                Case "SplitString"
                    ' Grab the SplitString value
                    strItem = strItem & ";" & nodField.nodeTypedValue
                    ' Add the strItem value to the listbox
                    lstSplits.AddItem strItem
            End Select
        Next
    Next

ExitHere:
        On Error GoTo 0
        DoCmd.Hourglass False
        Exit Sub

HandleErr:
    MsgBox "Error " & Err.Number & ": " & Err.Description, _
        vbOKOnly + vbCritical, "Process Splits"
    Resume ExitHere
End Sub
```

10. Save and open the form to test it out. Enter values into each of the textboxes and click on the Calculate Splits button. The form should look similar to the one shown in Figure 17-8.

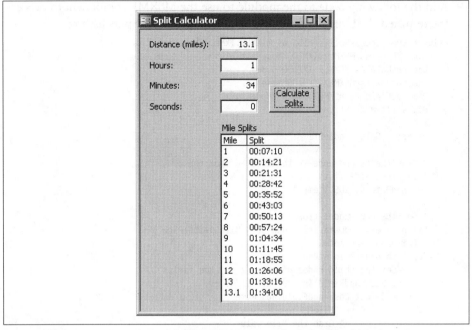

Figure 17-8. The code behind the Calculate Splits button calls the RunningCalculator service's GetMileSplits method, processes the returned serialized DataSet, and adds the splits to the listbox

Discussion

When you establish a reference to a web service using the Microsoft Office 2003 Web Services Toolkit, the toolkit, among other things, sets a reference to the Microsoft XML v 5.0 type library, which allows you to use MSXML without having to manually set a reference to the type library.

Processing the returned XML

The MSXML component contains a number of objects, properties, and methods for working with XML documents. You can find online documentation for MSXML at the following URL:

```
http://msdn.microsoft.com/library/default.asp?url=/library/en-us/xmlsdk/htm/xml_obj_
ixmldomnodelist_4kvo.asp
```

In order to create the code that processes a serialized DataSet using MSXML you need to understand the layout of the XML returned by the web service method. For . NET web services, you can obtain basic documentation about the web service and its methods by directly navigating to the web service (the asmx file) using Internet Explorer. Thus, for the RunnerCalculator service, you could obtain information about the web service at this address:

```
www.deeptraining.com/webservices/runnercalculator.asmx
```

When you do this you should see a screen that looks similar to the one shown in Figure 17-9.

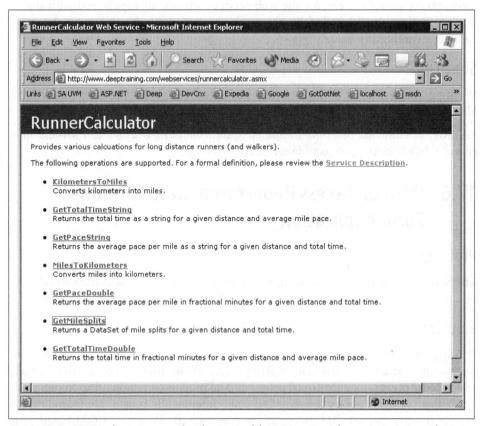

Figure 17-9. .NET web services supply a basic set of documentation when you navigate to them

You may find it helpful to take a look at the web services' Web Services Description Language (WSDL) document, which you can get to by clicking on the Service Description link (see Figure 17-9). You can think of the WSDL as the equivalent of a type library for a web service.

If the web service was created with Microsoft .NET 1.0 you can also use a special automatically-generated test form to call a web service method interactively from Internet Explorer. This test form is available by clicking on the name of a method you wish to test (see Figure 17-9). In Microsoft .NET 1.1 (Visual Studio .NET 2003), by default, you no longer get the test form when calling the web service remotely. If you're using a .NET 1.1 web service, the test form is disabled when used from a remote client (anything other than localhost), so you can't depend on the test form for help.

Of course, neither the .NET 1.0 test form nor the WSDL for a web service takes the place of good documentation. If you are using a web service in a production environment, you're going to need for the web service's creator to supply you with documentation that should include a thorough discussion of the web services input parameters and return value.

See Also

Working with ADO.NET Datasets in Microsoft Office (*http://msdn.microsoft.com/library/default.asp?url=/library/en-us/dnofftalk/html/office08012002.asp*).

MSXML documentation (*http://msdn.microsoft.com/library/default.asp?url=/library/en-us/xmlsdk/htm/xml_obj_ixmldomnodelist_4kvo.asp*).

17.6 Print an Access Report from .NET Windows Form Application

Problem

The Solution in Recipe 12.2 illustrates how to print an Access report from Excel. Is it also possible to print an Access report from a .NET Windows Form application?

Solution

Printing an Access report from another application requires you to automate the Access application. The Solution in Recipe 12.2 shows how to do this from Excel, which like Access is a COM-based program. The process for automating Access from a .NET application is very similar. The only difference is that a .NET application cannot directly call a COM program (or component). To call a COM-based program from .NET, you must obtain a runtime callable wrapper that calls the COM-based program on your behalf. (This process is the reverse of calling a .NET component from a COM-based program as discussed in the Solution in Recipe 17.1.) Runtime callable wrappers are also known as *interop assemblies*.

Using the Office 2003 setup program, you can install the interop assemblies for various Office applications, including Access. Depending on the path you take through the Office 2003 setup program, you may or may not have installed the interop assemblies. Fortunately, you can modify an existing Office 2003 installation to add one or more interop assemblies. The interop assemblies are listed under each product in the Office 2003 setup program under the heading ". NET Programmability Support."

If you have installed the interop assemblies, when you set a reference to Access 2003 or another Office application from Visual Studio .NET, your code will automatically use the installed interop assembly.

Follow these steps to create a Windows Form application named AccessReporter that automates Access 2003, opens the *17-06.MDB* database, and runs the rptArtistAlbum report:

1. Start Visual Studio .NET.
2. Create a new VB .NET Windows Application project named AccessReporter.
3. Delete the initial Form1.vb file from the project.
4. Select Project → Add Windows Form... to add a Windows Form file to the project named PrintArtistReport.vb.
5. Add the controls listed in Table 17-3 to the form. Size the controls to your liking.

Table 17-3. Controls for the Windows Form file for the project PrintArtistReport.vb

Control	Name	Text
Label	lblArtist	Artist:
ComboBox	cboArtist	n/a
Button	cmdRunReport	Run Report
Checkbox	chkPreview	Preview report before printing

6. Double-click the cmdRunReport button control to jump to the code editor window.
7. Select Project → Add Reference... to display the Visual Studio .NET Add Reference dialog box.
8. Click the COM tab, select "Microsoft Access 11.0 Object Library" from the upper listbox, and click the Select button as shown in Figure 17-10. Click OK to dismiss the dialog box.

 If you do not see Microsoft Access 11.0 Object Library listed in the upper listbox of the COM tab of the Visual Studio .NET Add Reference dialog box, then you have not installed the Access 2003 interop assembly. To install the interop assembly, start the Add or Remove Programs Control Panel applet. Choose to change the Microsoft Office 2003 installation. From the setup program, choose Add or Remove Features. On the next page of the setup wizard, ensure that the Access and "Choose advanced customization of applications" checkboxes are selected and click Next. Under the Microsoft Office Access node, make sure the ".NET Programmability Support" entry is enabled and click Update.

9. Add the following line of code at the top of the code window before the Class statement to import the Microsoft.Office.Interop namespace:

```
Imports Access = Microsoft.Office.Interop.Access
```

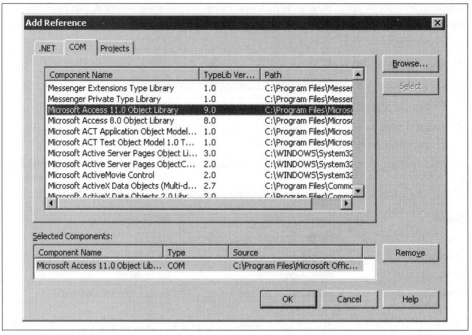

Figure 17-10. The Visual Studio .NET Add Reference dialog box

10. You also need to add the following Imports statement (below the other Imports statement) to import the System.Data.OleDb namespace:

```
Imports System.Data.OleDb
```

11. Add the following code to the PrintArtistReport class module, just beneath the Inherits statement to define two module-level constants:

```
Private Const strDb As String = "D:\Books\AccessCookBook2003\ch17\17-06.mdb"
Private Const strRpt As String = "rptArtistAlbums"
```

You will need to edit the path to the *17-06.MDB* database to match the location of the database on your system.

12. Add the following code to the form's load event handler to populate the cboArtists combobox control with a list of Artists from the tblArtists table in the *17-06.MDB* database:

```
Private Sub PrintArtistReport_Load(ByVal sender As System.Object, _
  ByVal e As System.EventArgs) Handles MyBase.Load
    ' This code populates the cboArtists control
    ' with the list of artists from the 17-06.mdb database.

    Dim cnx As OleDbConnection = New OleDbConnection( _
      "Provider=Microsoft.Jet.OLEDB.4.0;Data Source=" & strDb)

    Dim strSql As String = "SELECT ArtistId, ArtistName " & _
      "FROM tblArtists ORDER BY ArtistName"
```

```
            Dim daArtists As OleDbDataAdapter = New OleDbDataAdapter(strSql, cnx)

            Dim dsArtists As DataSet = New DataSet
            daArtists.Fill(dsArtists, "Artists")

            cboArtist.DataSource = dsArtists.Tables("Artists").DefaultView
            cboArtist.DisplayMember = "ArtistName"
            cboArtist.ValueMember = "ArtistId"
        End Sub
```

13. Add the following code to the cmdRunReport's Click event handler to open the report:

```
    Private Sub cmdRunReport_Click(ByVal sender As System.Object, _
     ByVal e As System.EventArgs) Handles cmdRunReport.Click
        Dim accApp As Access.Application
        Dim strWhere As String

        ' Construct where clause
        strWhere = "ArtistId = " & cboArtist.SelectedValue

        ' Instantiate the Access application
        accApp = New Access.Application

        'Open database
        accApp.OpenCurrentDatabase(strDb)

        If chkPreview.Checked Then
            ' Make Access visible and open report
            ' in print preview.

            ' Display report in Print Preview.
            accApp.DoCmd.OpenReport(strRpt, Access.AcView.acViewPreview, , _
             strWhere)

            ' Make Access visible so you can see the report.
            ' It will be up to the user to shut down Access.
            ' However, Access will not be released from memory until
            ' this application shuts down.
            accApp.Visible = True
        Else
            ' Go ahead and print directly. No need
            ' to make Access visible or to leave open.

            ' Print report to printer and quit Access.
            accApp.DoCmd.OpenReport(strRpt, Access.AcView.acViewNormal, , _
             strWhere)
            accApp.DoCmd.Quit()

            ' Force Access to shutdown now.Unless you include this code,
            ' Access won't be removed from memory until this app shuts down.
            System.Runtime.InteropServices.Marshal.ReleaseComObject(accApp)
        End If
    End Sub
```

14. Select Project → AccessReporter Properties to display the Project Properties Pages dialog box. On the Common Properties, General page of the dialog box, select the PrintAccessReport form as the startup object and click OK to close the dialog box.

15. Select File → Save All to save the open files.

16. Select Debug → Start to run the application. Select an artist from the combobox control, ensure that the "Preview report before printing" checkbox is selected, and click on Run Report to open the rptArtistAlbums report in Print Preview view. The AccessReporter application is shown in Figure 17-11.

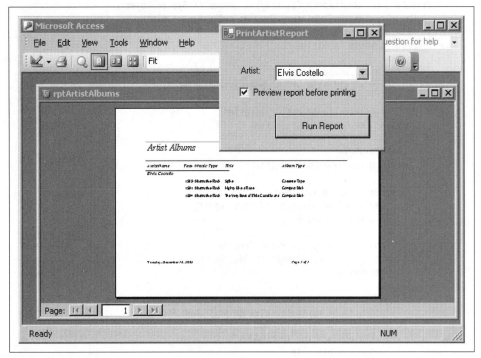

Figure 17-11. The AccessReporter Windows Form application is shown in front of the Access report it has previewed

17. Close Access and quit the AccessReporter application.

Discussion

Here's the basic process followed by the AccessReporter application to run the Access report:

- When AccessReporter starts it calls the startup form, PrintArtistReport.

- As the PrintArtistReport form is loaded it executes the form's Load event handler, which populates the cboArtists combobox with data from the *17-06.MDB* database using ADO.NET.

- When the cmdRunReport button is clicked by the user, the code attached to the cmdRunReport_Click event handler automates Access, and uses the OpenReport method to open the rptArtistAlbum report, passing it the selected Artist as a parameter.

Shutting down Access

The PrintArtistReport form includes a checkbox control to determine if the report is to be previewed or printed. If the report is to be previewed, then it is necessary to make Access visible to allow the user to view the report. In this case, it will be up to the user to close down Access:

```
accApp.DoCmd.OpenReport(strRpt, Access.AcView.acViewPreview, , _
    strWhere)
accApp.Visible = True
```

If the report is to be sent to a printer, the code takes a different path. There's no need to make Access visible. In fact, Access is shut down after the printing is complete:

```
accApp.DoCmd.OpenReport(strRpt, Access.AcView.acViewNormal, , _
    strWhere)
accApp.DoCmd.Quit( )
```

This code alone, however, will not remove Access from memory. That feat is accomplished with this additional line of code:

```
System.Runtime.InteropServices.Marshal.ReleaseComObject(accApp)
```

If you do not call the ReleaseComObject method, Access will not be removed from Memory until the AccessReporter application is closed.

Communicating parameters to Access

When automating Access 2003, you have no way to supply parameters to a parameter query, thus you must devise some other technique to pass parameters from your .NET application to Access. In many situations, you can construct a WHERE clause and pass it to the report using the fourth parameter of the call to the OpenReport method. This is the technique that was used in this solution.

There may be some situations where constructing a WHERE clause is too cumbersome. For example, if you used a listbox control that allowed for multiple rows to be selected, the WHERE clause could be inordinately long. In this case, another option would be to use a "parameters" table to which you would add the selected rows. You could then create a query that joined to this parameters table and base the report on this query. Before running the report your code would need to iterate through the rows in the listbox and, using ADO.NET, insert a row into the "parameters" table for each row of the selected listbox rows.

Interop assemblies

There are two types of interop assemblies: primary interop assemblies and alternate interop assemblies. Anyone can generate an *alternate interop assembly* (AIA) for any component by setting a reference to a COM component from Visual Studio .NET (which generates the AIA by calling the tlbimp utility that ships with the .NET Framework). A *primary interop assembly* (PIA) is the official interop assembly that has been produced and signed by the component's author. While the tlbimp utility usually does a good job in generating the AIA for a component, there may be situations where the types are not mapped properly. PIAs, on the other hand, are usually hand-optimized beyond the code automatically generated by tlbimp. Whenever it is available it's preferable to use the PIA rather than an AIA.

 When setting a reference to a COM component or program from Visual Studio .NET, it will always use the PIA if one has been installed on the system. Otherwise, it will create an AIA and use that instead.

As mentioned in the solution, Office 2003 ships with PIAs for each of its applications. You can download the PIAs for Access 2002 and the other Office XP applications from the following URL:

    http://msdn.microsoft.com/library/default.asp?url=/downloads/list/office.asp

Microsoft has no plans to supply PIAs for Office 2000 or Office 97, so you will have to generate and use AIAs for these applications.

See Also

See A Primer to the Office XP Primary Interop Assemblies (*http://msdn.microsoft.com/library/default.asp?url=/library/en-us/dnofftalk/html/office10032002.asp*).

CHAPTER 18

XML

Support for *Extensible Markup Language* (XML) in Access 2003 has been greatly expanded from the XML support available in Access 2002. As you may be aware, Microsoft has chosen XML as the backbone for all of their .NET technologies. Access 2002 included XML support for importing and exporting data as well as for presenting data, but there was little support for transforming data by using XSLT stylesheets or for describing the structure if data using XML schemas. These capabilities were added in Access 2003, which provides very full-featured support for working with XML documents and technologies when importing or exporting data.

XML Overview

If you're not already familiar with working with XML, you may find all of the acronyms a bit confusing at first. However, XML syntax itself is fairly easy to understand.

The XML file

The first line of an XML file is the XML declaration, which specifies that the file is an XML document, that it conforms to the XML version 1.0 specification, and that it uses the UTF-8 character set. Most XML documents have this declaration, but Access is also capable of importing XML documents that do not:

```
<?xml version="1.0" encoding="UTF-8" ?>
```

The body of the XML file consists of tags similar to the tags used in HTML. Start tags begin with open angle brackets and end with closing angle brackets:

```
<Car>
```

End tags begin with an open angle bracket and a slash, and end with a closing angle bracket:

```
</Car>
```

The Car tag is also the name of the *element*. While HTML works with a limited set of elements, XML allows you to create your own, as long as you conform to some basic rules:

- Names can contain only alphanumeric characters, the underscore character (_), hyphens (-), or a period (.).
- Element names cannot contain white space and must start with a letter or the underscore character.

The values in XML elements are found between the start tag and end tag, similarly to the way that text is represented in HTML. In this example, the Car element has a value of Mini Cooper:

```
<Car>Mini Cooper</Car>
```

XML elements can be nested, but they can't overlap. The Car element can have sub-elements, such as Make, Model and Price:

```
<Car>
  <Make> Mini Cooper</Make>
  <Model>S</Model>
  <Price>$20,000</Price>
</Car>
```

 Note that spaces, tabs and line feeds are ignored by the XML parser. They are used to make XML documents more readable.

You can also have multiple nested sets of elements in the same XML file, and elements can be repeated:

```
<Car>
  <Make> Mini Cooper</Make>
  <Model>S</Model>
  <Price>$20,000</Price>
</Car>
<Car>
  <Make> Lexus</Make>
  <Model>LS430</Model>
  <Price>$60,000</Price>
</Car>
```

Root elements and namespaces

The above sample alone would not comprise a valid XML file. Each valid XML document must have a single root, or top-level, element. This allows the XML file to be represented as a tree, with all of the elements as branches off of the main root element. In this example, the starting tag is named dataroot, and has a *namespace declaration*:

```
<?xml version="1.0" encoding="UTF-8" ?>
<dataroot xmlns:od="urn:schemas-microsoft-com:officedata">
  <Car>
    <Make> Mini Cooper</Make>
    <Model>S</Model>
    <Price>$20,000</Price>
  </Car>
  <Car>
    <Make> Lexus</Make>
    <Model>LS430</Model>
    <Price>$60,000</Price>
  </Car>
</dataroot>
```

There are three parts to the namespace declaration:

- xmlns: identifies the dataroot element as containing an XML namespace.
- od: identifies the prefix assigned to the namespace.
- "urn:schemas-microsoft-com:officedata" is the Uniform Resource Identifier, or URI, which uniquely identifies the namespace. This particular namespace is generated whenever you save Access data in XML format.

In this example, all of the elements in the document are part of one namespace, but multiple namespaces can be used in a single XML document. In that case, the prefix assigned to each namespace is used with the element names to identify which namespace they belong to. This allows differentiation between identically named elements from different namespaces.

When you view an XML file in a browser, you can see the hierarchy of data, as shown in Figure 18-1.

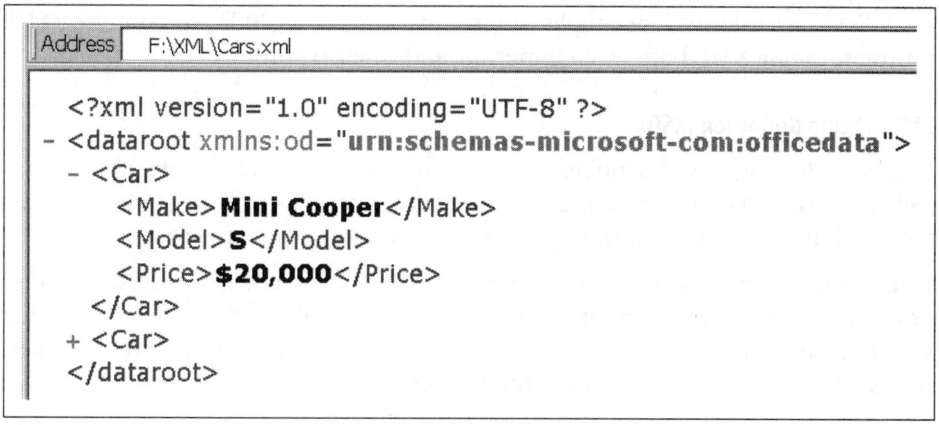

Figure 18-1. Viewing the XML file in a browser window

Clicking the plus sign (+) expands the tree view so that you can view the data in the nested elements.

Attributes

Another option is to represent the data using *attributes* in addition to elements. Each attribute has a name and a value, as shown in this example where each Car element has a Make, Model, and Price attribute:

```
<?xml version="1.0" encoding="UTF-8" ?>
<dataroot xmlns:od="urn:schemas-microsoft-com:officedata">
  <Car Make="Mini Cooper" Model="S" Price="$20,000" />
  <Car Make="Lexus" Model="LS430" Price="$60,000" />
</dataroot>
```

You can represent the data as either elements or attributes. However, when you import or export XML data with Access, you have no choice—you must use elements, not attributes, for Access to be able to correctly parse the XML file. One major problem is that if your XML input is not structured using elements, then you may not like the way that Access imports the data. To get around this problem, you need to convert your XML to the element-based format that Access expects. To get around this limitation, you can use an XML technology named Extensible Stylesheet Language Transformations, or XSLT.

Extensible Stylesheet Language Transformations (XSLT)

XSLT is an XML-based language for transforming an XML document into another form. The result can be another XML document or any type of text document. XSLT combines some procedural language features along with rule-based language features. XSLT stylesheets are XML documents that define templates and how to apply them. The templates in XSLT documents contain rules for matching XML elements and attributes in the document that is being transformed and instructions for reformatting those elements and attributes. You will often hear XSLT stylesheets referred to as "XSLT transforms," or simply "transforms." In Access 2003, you can use XSLT for transforming XML both when importing and when exporting data.

XML Schema Definition (XSD)

XSD provides a way of describing the structure of data contained in an XML file, as well as constraints applied to the data, including data types. This is similar to the table definitions and relationships you use to define data structure in Access.

When you export data, you can have Access generate a schema, or XSD, file that describes the data. When importing XML, you can import an XSD file to define the structure and data types of the data being imported. When you import XSD files, Access creates tables based on the definitions in the files.

18.1 Import XML Structured as Elements

Problem

You need to import simple XML data into a new table.

Solution

You can import XML into a new table from the File menu when the Tables category is selected in the Objects pane by following these steps:

1. Open *18-01.MDB*.
2. Choose File → Get External Data → Import to bring up the Import dialog box.
3. In the Files of type drop-down list at the bottom of the dialog box, select XML (*.xml, *.xsd).
4. In the File name dialog box, navigate to the XML file you want to import, and click Import, which will load the XML Import dialog box. The samples include an XML file named 18-01.XML that you can use.
5. Expand the plus sign (+) to show the structure of the XML file and click the Options button to expand the dialog box, as shown in Figure 18-2.

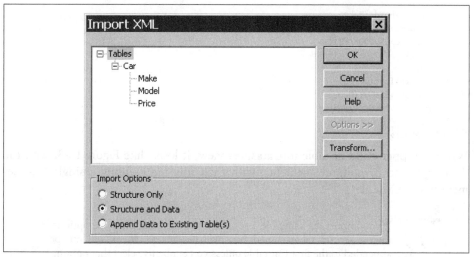

Figure 18-2. Viewing the structure of an XML file when importing into Access

6. The Options button shown in Figure 18-2 enables you to specify how you'd like the XML imported. If you choose Structure and Data as shown here, a new table will be created. Click OK twice to confirm the import.

A new table named Car has been created.

Discussion

When importing an XML file that has the structure Access expects, containing a hierarchical set of nested elements, the table name is derived from the first element after the root, in this case Car. The Make, Model and Price elements become columns in the table. The source XML file looks like this:

```
<?xml version="1.0" encoding="UTF-8" ?>
<dataroot xmlns:od="urn:schemas-microsoft-com:officedata">
  <Car>
    <Make>Mini Cooper</Make>
    <Model>S</Model>
    <Price>20,000</Price>
  </Car>
  <Car>
    <Make>Lexus</Make>
    <Model>LS430</Model>
    <Price>60,000</Price>
  </Car>
  <Car>
    <Make>Porsche</Make>
    <Model>Boxter</Model>
    <Price>43,000</Price>
  </Car>
  <Car>
    <Make>Ford</Make>
    <Model>Mustang</Model>
    <Price>25,000</Price>
  </Car>
  <Car>
    <Make>Toyota</Make>
    <Model>Camry</Model>
    <Price>20,000</Price>
  </Car>
</dataroot>
```

When you open the Car table in Datasheet view, it looks like Figure 18-3, with the data organized by column (element), with each row representing a single Car element in the XML file.

 If you import the same file a second time, choosing the same options, then a second table named Car1 will be created. Rows will not be appended to the first Car table unless you explicitly select that option.

See Also

The following MSDN article gives a good explanation of XML namespaces: *http://msdn.microsoft.com/library/default.asp?url=/library/en-us/dnexxml/html/xml05202002.asp?frame=true*

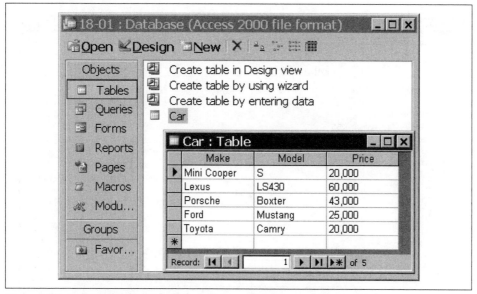

Figure 18-3. The Car table in Datasheet view

18.2   Import XML into Existing Tables

Problem

When you import XML into a new table, the data is read as Text, regardless of whether some elements contain numeric values. You need the XML data to conform to certain data types for each element.

Solution

The simplest way to solve the problem is to create a table structure prior to importing the data. In Recipe 18.1, all of the columns in the new table are created as Text with a maximum size of 255, as shown in Figure 18-4 where the Price column is selected.

Follow these steps to create a table structure that better matches your XML data:

1. Open the *18-02.MDB* database.

2. Create a new table named Car (to match the name of the first element that follows the root element in the XML file). It's important that the name of the table match this element.

3. Create the columns and data type shown in Table 18-1.

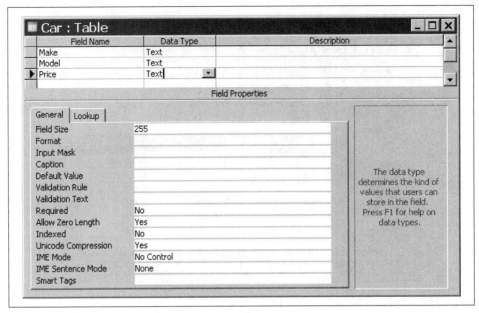

Figure 18-4. The numeric data for Price is imported as Text

Table 18-1. Columns and data types for Car

Column name	Data type
Make	Text 20
Model	Text 20
Price	Currency

4. Save the table and close the Table Designer.

5. Choose File → Get External Data → Import to display the Import dialog box.

6. In the Files of type drop-down list at the bottom of the dialog box, select XML (*.xml, *.xsd).

7. In the File name dialog box, navigate to the XML file you want to import, and click Import, which will load the XML Import dialog box. Select the 18-02.xml file and click Import.

8. Click Options and choose Append Data to Existing Table(s) as shown in Figure 18-5. Click OK and then OK again.

9. Open the Car table in datasheet view. You will see that the XML data has been appended to the table correctly.

Discussion

This example works because there is an exact mapping between the element names in the XML file and the table and field names in the Access Car table, so Access can

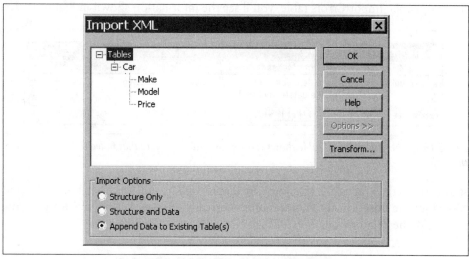

Figure 18-5. Appending XML data to an existing table

figure out where the data is supposed to go. As long as the data in the XML file does not have any anomalies, then this solution will work nicely.

Access will be unable to import the data in certain rows if there is a data type mismatch. Consider the following XML file, *18-02-bad.xml*:

```
<?xml version="1.0" encoding="UTF-8" ?>
<dataroot xmlns:od="urn:schemas-microsoft-com:officedata">
  <Car>
    <Make>Mini Cooper</Make>
    <Model>S</Model>
    <Price>20,000</Price>
  </Car>
  <Car>
    <Make>Ford</Make>
    <Model>Edsel</Model>
    <Price>unknown</Price>
  </Car>
</dataroot>
```

The Price element for the second car, the Edsel, is unknown. The Price column in the Car table is expecting a currency value. When you perform the insert, appending to the existing table, you'll see the error message shown in Figure 18-6.

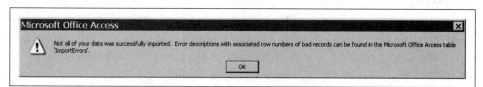

Figure 18-6. Error message appending bad XML to an existing table

If you open the ImportErrors table, you'll see the information shown in Figure 18-7.

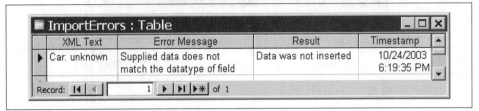

Figure 18-7. The ImportErrors table shows error information for data that failed to be appended to the table

If you open the Car table as shown in Figure 18-8, you'll see that the Make and Model for the Edsel row of data imported correctly. However, the Price for that row is set to 0, the default value.

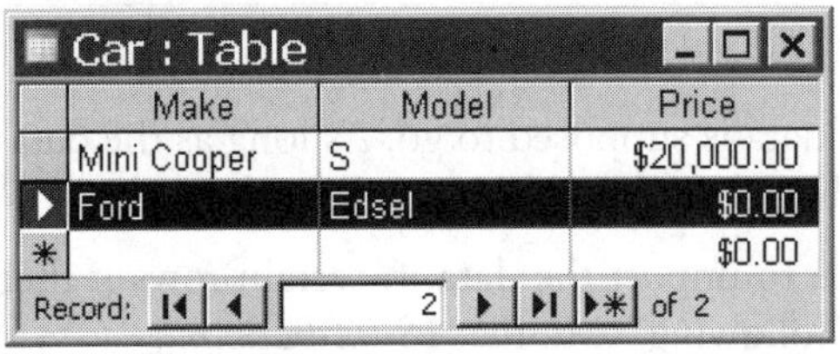

Figure 18-8. Access fails to import data from an XML file where it can't convert the data to the correct data type

If there is no default value specified for the Price column, then no value will be entered for Price, but Make and Model will be imported successfully. If the Required property for Price is set to Yes, then the entire row will be skipped, and you'll have an additional row in the ImportErrors table with the following data in the Error Message column:

> Microsoft JET Database Engine: The field 'Car.Price' cannot contain a Null value because the Required property for this field is set to True. Enter a value in this field.

18.3 Import XML Using a Schema (XSD)

Problem

You need to import an XML file that has a certain schema. but don't know ahead of time what the schema will be. You need to create a table that has the correct data types, and then generate a new AutoNumber primary key for each row appended to the table.

Solution

If you want to apply a particular schema when you import an XML file, you need to import the schema file, or XSD, before importing the data. If you have already created a table with the desired structure, you can have Access save the schema for you by exporting the table and saving the schema as a separate file. This is an easy way to use Access to create schema files. You can also manually create a schema file by using a text editor, and save it with an XSD file extension. You also can use a schema file that has been provided to you by your company or by a partner. Follow these steps to import a schema file and then an XML file:

1. Open the *18-03.MDB* sample database.

2. Choose File → Get External Data → Import from the menu to load the Import dialog box.

3. In the Files of type drop-down list at the bottom of the dialog box, select XML (*.xml, *.xsd).

4. In the File name dialog box, navigate to 18-03.xsd, and click Import, which will load the XML Import dialog box shown in Figure 18-9. Note that the Options button is disabled. When you import a schema, there is no data involved. Click OK and then OK again.

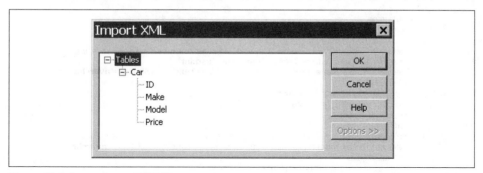

Figure 18-9. Importing an XSD file

5. Open the Car table in design view. Note that the table includes a column named ID for a primary key as well as the columns for the data contained in the XML source file. Close the table.

6. To import the XML data, Choose File → Get External Data → Import from the menu to load the Import dialog box.

7. In the Files of type drop-down list at the bottom of the dialog box, select XML (*.xml, *.xsd).

8. In the File name dialog box, navigate to 18-03.xml, and click Import, which will load the XML Import dialog box. Expand the plus sign and note that the same

three columns, Make, Model and Price are displayed. Click the Options button and select Append Data to Existing Table(s). Click OK and OK again.

9. Open the Car table in datasheet view. Note that an Autonumber value has been inserted for each row. Close the table.

Discussion

Once you have a schema file, you can view its structure using Internet Explorer, which indents all of the schema information for you, as shown in Figure 18-10.

```
<?xml version="1.0" encoding="UTF-8" ?>
- <xsd:schema xmlns:xsd="http://www.w3.org/2001/XMLSchema" xmlns:od="urn:schemas-microsoft-
   com:officedata">
- <xsd:element name="dataroot">
  - <xsd:complexType>
    - <xsd:sequence>
        <xsd:element ref="Car" minOccurs="0" maxOccurs="unbounded" />
      </xsd:sequence>
      <xsd:attribute name="generated" type="xsd:dateTime" />
    </xsd:complexType>
  </xsd:element>
- <xsd:element name="Car">
  - <xsd:annotation>
    - <xsd:appinfo>
        <od:index index-name="PrimaryKey" index-key="ID" primary="yes" unique="yes" clustered="no" />
        <od:index index-name="ID" index-key="ID" primary="no" unique="no" clustered="no" />
      </xsd:appinfo>
    </xsd:annotation>
  - <xsd:complexType>
    - <xsd:sequence>
        <xsd:element name="ID" minOccurs="1" od:jetType="autonumber" od:sqlSType="int"
          od:autoUnique="yes" od:nonNullable="yes" type="xsd:int" />
      - <xsd:element name="Make" minOccurs="0" od:jetType="text" od:sqlSType="nvarchar">
        - <xsd:simpleType>
          - <xsd:restriction base="xsd:string">
              <xsd:maxLength value="20" />
            </xsd:restriction>
          </xsd:simpleType>
        </xsd:element>
      - <xsd:element name="Model" minOccurs="0" od:jetType="text" od:sqlSType="nvarchar">
        - <xsd:simpleType>
          - <xsd:restriction base="xsd:string">
              <xsd:maxLength value="20" />
            </xsd:restriction>
          </xsd:simpleType>
        </xsd:element>
        <xsd:element name="Price" minOccurs="1" od:jetType="currency" od:sqlSType="money"
          od:nonNullable="yes" type="xsd:double" />
      </xsd:sequence>
    </xsd:complexType>
  </xsd:element>
</xsd:schema>
```

Figure 18-10. The XSD file used to create the Car table

Visual Studio .NET provides an excellent tool for viewing and modifying XSD schema files. When you open a schema file in Visual Studio .NET, you get a graphical designer very similar to the Access Relationships window.

The file references two schemas. The xsd namespace references the XML Schema standard at the W3C's web site. The od namespace references the Office data schema developed by Microsoft for Office data types:

```
- <xsd:schema xmlns:xsd="http://www.w3.org/2001/XMLSchema"
    xmlns:od="urn:schemas-microsoft-com:officedata">
```

The dataroot element is defined using a complexType XML Schema element, which enables it to contain other elements—in this case, Car elements. The maxOccurs="unbounded" attribute value means that the contents of the dataroot element, in this case Car, can occur an unlimited number of times. The xsd:element ref attribute indicates that Car is defined elsewhere in this XSD file:

```
<xsd:element name="dataroot">
  <xsd:complexType>
   <xsd:sequence>
    <xsd:element ref="Car" minOccurs="0" maxOccurs="unbounded" />
   </xsd:sequence>
   <xsd:attribute name="generated" type="xsd:dateTime" />
  </xsd:complexType>
</xsd:element>
```

The Car element is defined next, which comprises the table definition. Application-specific information is stored in the <xsd:annotation> and <xsd:appinfo> tags, which Access uses to describe indexes defined on the table. This allows Access to define characteristics that aren't part of the W3C schema definition vocabulary. These Access-specific items defined by the Office data schema are referenced by the od namespace. The <xsd:complexType> tag means that the Car data type itself is a complex type that contains other types:

```
<xsd:element name="Car">
<xsd:annotation>
  <xsd:appinfo>
   <od:index index-name="PrimaryKey" index-key="ID" primary="yes"
    unique="yes" clustered="no" />
   <od:index index-name="ID" index-key="ID" primary="no"
    unique="no" clustered="no" />
  </xsd:appinfo>
</xsd:annotation>
<xsd:complexType>
```

The next section of the XSD file defines the columns of the table, their data types, sizes, and properties. Note that the ID element is tagged with both the od:jetType="autonumber" and the od:sqlSType="int" attributes:

```
<xsd:sequence>
  <xsd:element name="ID" minOccurs="1" od:jetType="autonumber"
  od:sqlSType="int" od:autoUnique="yes" od:nonNullable="yes" type="xsd:int" />
  <xsd:element name="Make" minOccurs="0" od:jetType="text"
  od:sqlSType="nvarchar">
  <xsd:simpleType>
    <xsd:restriction base="xsd:string">
    <xsd:maxLength value="20" />
  </xsd:restriction>
  </xsd:simpleType>
  </xsd:element>
    <xsd:element name="Model" minOccurs="0" od:jetType="text"
    od:sqlSType="nvarchar">
    <xsd:simpleType>
    <xsd:restriction base="xsd:string">
    <xsd:maxLength value="20" />
  </xsd:restriction>
  </xsd:simpleType>
  </xsd:element>
  <xsd:element name="Price" minOccurs="1" od:jetType="currency"
    od:sqlSType="money" od:nonNullable="yes" type="xsd:double" />
  </xsd:sequence>
  </xsd:complexType>
</xsd:element>
```

All of the columns are defined with both Jet and equivalent SQL Server data types. This allows you to import the XSD file into an Access Project (.adp). One step you would have to perform manually for SQL Server is setting the Identity property of the SQL Server table after you have imported the XSD file and prior to importing the XML file.

See Also

The World Wide Web Consortium (W3C) site contains the following primer on XML Schema:

http://www.w3.org/TR/xmlschema-0/

The following MSDN article gives a good overview of XML Schema:

http://msdn.microsoft.com/library/default.asp?url=/library/en-us/dnxml/html/understandxsd.asp?frame=true

18.4   Export XML

Problem

You need to export Access data to an XML file so that it can be used in another application.

Solution

There are several different approaches to exporting XML data from Access, depending on the results that you want. The *18-04.MDB* sample database has three tables, Car, Customer, and Preferences. The Car and Customer tables contain information about cars and customers, and the Preferences table contains information about which cars a customer prefers. The Preferences table is related to both the Car and Customer tables.

Exporting all of the data in related tables

If you wish to export all of the data in related tables, you can do so easily from the File menu. Follow these steps to export data as XML from the Preferences table:

1. Select the Preferences table in the database window. Right-click and select Export, and choose XML in the Save as type drop-down list at the bottom of the dialog box. Type a name for the XML file and click the Export button.

2. Leave the default options selected, and click the More Options button to expand the Lookup Data node. Check the two check boxes for Car and Customer, as shown in Figure 18-11. Since Car and Customer are both related to Preferences, Access allows you to select them here.

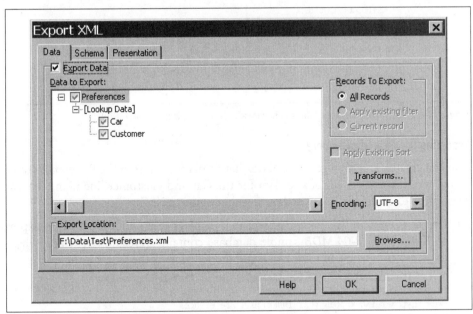

Figure 18-11. The Export XML dialog box allows you to select related tables

3. Click the OK button. Figure 18-12 shows the XML that is generated, with one element each of Preferences, Car, and Customer data displayed.

```
<?xml version="1.0" encoding="UTF-8" ?>
- <dataroot xmlns:od="urn:schemas-microsoft-com:officedata"
    xmlns:xsi="http://www.w3.org/2001/XMLSchema-instance"
    xsi:noNamespaceSchemaLocation="Preferences.xsd" generated="2003-
    11-16T18:08:44">
  - <Preferences>
      <CustID>1</CustID>
      <CarID>2</CarID>
      <Ranking>1</Ranking>
    </Preferences>
  + <Preferences>
  + <Preferences>
  + <Preferences>
  + <Preferences>
  - <Car>
      <CarID>1</CarID>
      <Make>Mini Cooper</Make>
      <Model>S</Model>
      <Price>20000</Price>
    </Car>
  + <Car>
  + <Car>
  + <Car>
  + <Car>
  - <Customer>
      <CustID>1</CustID>
      <CustLname>Smathers</CustLname>
      <CustFname>Millicent</CustFname>
    </Customer>
  + <Customer>
  + <Customer>
  </dataroot>
```

Figure 18-12. Exporting related tables generates XML for the data in each table

Exporting the data from a query

You can create a query to generate XML that displays data from the Preferences table along with the associated lookup data for the Car and Customer line items. Follow these steps to create the query and output the results to XML:

1. Create a query in the query designer that displays the results you wish to export to XML. The *18-04.MDB* sample database contains qryCustomer, which selects the Customer name and Car make and model. Here is the SQL for the query:

   ```
   SELECT [CustLname] & ", " & [CustFname] AS Name, Preferences.Ranking,
   Car.Make, Car.Model
   FROM Customer INNER JOIN (Car INNER JOIN Preferences
   ON Car.CarID = Preferences.CarID) ON Customer.CustID = Preferences.CustID
   ORDER BY [CustLname] & ", " & [CustFname], Preferences.Ranking;
   ```

2. Save the query and close the query designer. Right-click on the query in the database window and choose Export. Then select XML in the Save as type drop-

down list at the bottom of the dialog box. Type a name for the XML file and click the Export button.

3. Click the Export button and then click the More Options button. Select the Schema tab and note that the default options include exporting schema information in a separate schema document, as shown in Figure 18-13. Click OK.

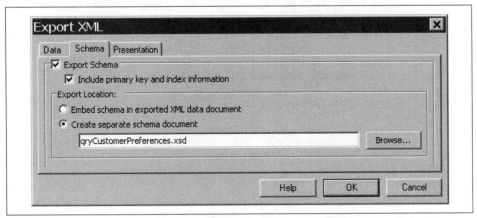

Figure 18-13. You can create a separate XSD schema document or embed the schema along with data in one XML document

This time the generated XML document contains an element for each row that the query returns, as shown in Figure 18-14.

Discussion

When you use the Access Export menu to export XML data, Access reads the table relationships and allows you to select related tables. The Schema tab on the Export dialog box allows you to select whether to create a separate schema file or to embed the schema information along with the data in one XML file. If you want to export data showing lookup data from related tables, you can export a query to XML—this also allows you to select the rows and columns to include or to export data based on expressions.

18.5 Exporting Selected Columns to an HTML Table

Problem

You'd like to export data from a table as XML and display it in an HTML table. However, you only want to display selected columns from the table, not the entire table.

```
        <?xml version="1.0" encoding="UTF-8" ?>
      - <dataroot xmlns:od="urn:schemas-microsoft-com:officedata"
        xmlns:xsi="http://www.w3.org/2001/XMLSchema-instance"
        xsi:noNamespaceSchemaLocation="qryCustomerPreferences.xsd"
        generated="2003-11-16T18:29:33">
      - <qryCustomerPreferences>
          <Name>Fouquet, George</Name>
          <Ranking>1</Ranking>
          <Make>Porsche</Make>
          <Model>Boxter</Model>
        </qryCustomerPreferences>
      - <qryCustomerPreferences>
          <Name>Meister, Frederika</Name>
          <Ranking>1</Ranking>
          <Make>Mini Cooper</Make>
          <Model>S</Model>
        </qryCustomerPreferences>
      - <qryCustomerPreferences>
          <Name>Meister, Frederika</Name>
          <Ranking>2</Ranking>
          <Make>Lexus</Make>
          <Model>LS430</Model>
        </qryCustomerPreferences>
      - <qryCustomerPreferences>
          <Name>Smathers, Millicent</Name>
          <Ranking>1</Ranking>
          <Make>Lexus</Make>
          <Model>LS430</Model>
        </qryCustomerPreferences>
```

Figure 18-14. Exporting a query to XML produces an element for each row of data returned by the query

Solution

If you wish to export data using only selected columns, you can do so with a query, but you can also accomplish this by using an XSLT transform. Using a transform has the added benefit of allowing you to format the data as HTML. Follow these steps to export only the Make and Model data from the Car table and to format the data as an HTML table:

1. Select the Car table in the database window, right-click and select Export, and choose XML in the Save as type drop-down list at the bottom of the dialog box.

2. Type a name for the XML file ending with an htm suffix and click the Export button. This example assumes that the output file is named Cars.htm.

3. Click the More Options button to load the Export XML dialog box shown in Figure 18-15. You can change the output file name here if you didn't change it in the previous dialog box.

4. Click the Transforms button. If the transform doesn't show up in the list, click the Add button to browse to it. This example uses a transform named 18-05.xsl.

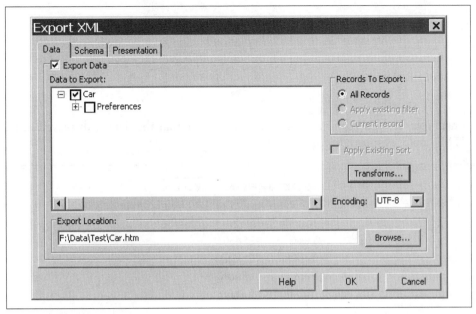

Figure 18-15. Selecting the output location and filename

Click OK and OK again. Access will create a Car.htm and a Car.xsd file in the destination directory.

Discussion

The 18-05.xsl file used to transform the data contains two templates. The dataroot template contains code for creating an HTML document with an HTML table. The Car template creates the rows in the HTML table and cells containing only the Make and Model data. This transform works against a hidden XML document that is created from all the data in the table:

```
<?xml version="1.0" encoding="UTF-8"?>
<xsl:stylesheet
 xmlns:xsl="http://www.w3.org/1999/XSL/Transform" version="1.0" >
<xsl:output method="html" version="4.0" indent="yes" />

<xsl:template match="dataroot">
   <html>
      <body>
        <table>
            <xsl:apply-templates select="Car" />
        </table>
      </body>
   </html>
</xsl:template>

<xsl:template match="Car">
```

```
    <tr>
      <td><xsl:value-of select="Make" /></td>
        <td><xsl:value-of select="Model" /></td>
    </tr>

  </xsl:template>

</xsl:stylesheet>
```

When you view *Car.htm* in a browser, you can see that the data is displayed in an HTML table, as shown in Figure 18-16.

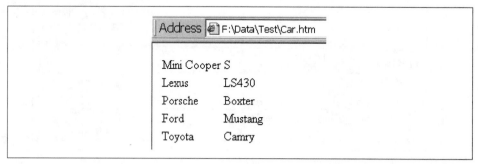

Address   F:\Data\Test\Car.htm

Mini Cooper S	
Lexus	LS430
Porsche	Boxter
Ford	Mustang
Toyota	Camry

Figure 18-16. The output generated by the XSL transform when viewed in a browser

Choose View > Source from the menu and you'll see the following HTML:

```
<html>
    <body>
        <table>
            <tr>
                <td>Mini Cooper</td>
                <td>S</td>
            </tr>
            <tr>
                <td>Lexus</td>
                <td>LS430</td>
            </tr>
            <tr>
                <td>Porsche</td>
                <td>Boxter</td>
            </tr>
            <tr>
                <td>Ford</td>
                <td>Mustang</td>
            </tr>
            <tr>
                <td>Toyota</td>
                <td>Camry</td>
            </tr>
        </table>
    </body>
</html>
```

This example is very simple and creates just a bare-bones table. You can modify the HTML sections of the XSLT to specify colors, borders, fonts, and so on to create whatever custom formatting you need.

See Also

The following W3C page contains links to many resources on XSLT:

http://www.w3.org/Style/XSL/

18.6   Export Unrelated Tables

Problem

You want to export Access data to a single XML file, but the tables you wish to export are not related to each other. How do you select tables and create a single XML output file?

Solution

You must write VBA code to export multiple unrelated tables to a single XML file. The Access object model provides the ExportXML method, which has an Additional-Data parameter that takes an object of type AdditionalData.

The *18-06.MDB* sample database contains three unrelated tables: Car, Customer, and Dealer. There is a single module, basExport, which contains the function ExportUn-related. The code creates an AdditionalData object, and adds the Customer and Dealer tables to it. The ExportXML method uses the Car table as the DataSource, and uses the AdditionalData object to add the Customer and Dealer data to the output:

```
Dim adTables As AdditionalData
Set adTables = Application.CreateAdditionalData
adTables.Add "Customer"
adTables.Add "Dealer"
Application.ExportXML _
  ObjectType:=acExportTable, _
  DataSource:="Car", _
  DataTarget:="c:\test\Unrelated.xml", _
  AdditionalData:=adTables
```

Figure 18-17 shows the XML file in a browser, with only one element from each table expanded. All of the data from all of the tables has been exported.

Discussion

A number of enhancements were added to the Access object model to facilitate importing and exporting XML data programmatically. The full syntax and all of the optional arguments for the ExportXML method are shown here:

```xml
<?xml version="1.0" encoding="UTF-8" ?>
- <dataroot xmlns:od="urn:schemas-microsoft-com:officedata" generated="2003-11-16T21:51:29">
  - <Car>
      <CarID>1</CarID>
      <Make>Mini Cooper</Make>
      <Model>S</Model>
      <Price>20000</Price>
    </Car>
  + <Car>
  + <Car>
  + <Car>
  + <Car>
  - <Customer>
      <CustID>1</CustID>
      <CustLname>Smathers</CustLname>
      <CustFname>Millicent</CustFname>
    </Customer>
  + <Customer>
  + <Customer>
  - <Dealer>
      <DealerID>1</DealerID>
      <DealerName>Floom Ford</DealerName>
    </Dealer>
  + <Dealer>
  + <Dealer>
  + <Dealer>
  </dataroot>
```

Figure 18-17. The XML output for unrelated tables

```
ExportXML (ObjectType As AcExportXMLObjectType, Datasource As String,
    [DataTarget As String], [SchemaTarget As String], [PresentationTarget as String],
    [ImageTarget As String], [Encoding As AcExportXMLEncoding], [OtherFlags As Long],
    [WhereCondition As String], [AdditionalData as AdditionalData])
```

The OtherFlags optional argument, which was not used in the example, allows you to specify the following self-descriptive options, which are exposed as AcExportXMLOtherFlags enumerations:

- acEmbedSchema
- acExcludePrimaryKeyAndIndexes
- acRunFromServer
- acLiveReportSource
- acPersistReportML

> When you need to apply a transform programmatically for either importing or exporting XML, use the TransformXML method. The ImportXML and ExportXML methods do not have DataTransform parameters.

18.7 Export Using a Where Clause

Problem

You want to export a subset of rows in a table that match cartain search criteria instead of exporting the entire table.

Solution

There are two different approaches you can take, depending on how you want the output to look. The first approach is to design a query, and export the query to XML, as shown in the Solution in Recipe 18.4. The second is to use the ExportXML method. (You also could use an XSLT transform, but that would be inefficient unless you also need to format the data.)

The *18-07.MDB* sample application has a saved query named qryCarsLessThan40. The SQL Select statement looks like this:

```
SELECT Car.CarID, Car.Make, Car.Model, Car.Price
FROM Car
WHERE (((Car.Price)<40000));
```

When you export the query to an XML file by following the steps in the Solution in Recipe 18.4, the XML generated looks like that shown in Figure 18-18.

```
    <?xml version="1.0" encoding="UTF-8" ?>
  - <dataroot xmlns:od="urn:schemas-microsoft-com:officedata"
      xmlns:xsi="http://www.w3.org/2001/XMLSchema-instance"
      xsi:noNamespaceSchemaLocation="WhereQuery.xsd" generated="2003-
      11-17T17:57:09">
    - <qryCarsLessThan40>
        <CarID>1</CarID>
        <Make>Mini Cooper</Make>
        <Model>S</Model>
        <Price>20000</Price>
      </qryCarsLessThan40>
    - <qryCarsLessThan40>
        <CarID>4</CarID>
        <Make>Ford</Make>
        <Model>Mustang</Model>
        <Price>25000</Price>
      </qryCarsLessThan40>
    - <qryCarsLessThan40>
        <CarID>5</CarID>
        <Make>Toyota</Make>
        <Model>Camry</Model>
        <Price>20000</Price>
      </qryCarsLessThan40>
    </dataroot>
```

Figure 18-18. XML generated by a query with a WHERE clause

The *18-07.MDB* sample application also has a function named `ExportWhere` located in basExportXML. Instead of using a query, this code exports the Car table and programmatically applies a WhereCondition of "Price < 40000":

```
Application.ExportXML _
   ObjectType:=acExportTable, _
   DataSource:="Car", _
   DataTarget:="c:\test\Where.xml", _
   WhereCondition:="Price < 40000"
```

Figure 18-19 shows the output that is generated.

```
          <?xml version="1.0" encoding="UTF-8" ?>
      - <dataroot xmlns:od="urn:schemas-microsoft-com:officedata"
          generated="2003-11-17T17:54:13">
        - <Car>
            <CarID>1</CarID>
            <Make>Mini Cooper</Make>
            <Model>S</Model>
            <Price>20000</Price>
          </Car>
        - <Car>
            <CarID>4</CarID>
            <Make>Ford</Make>
            <Model>Mustang</Model>
            <Price>25000</Price>
          </Car>
        - <Car>
            <CarID>5</CarID>
            <Make>Toyota</Make>
            <Model>Camry</Model>
            <Price>20000</Price>
          </Car>
        </dataroot>
```

Figure 18-19. XML generated using ExportXML with a WhereCondition

Discussion

When you create a saved query with a Where clause and export it, each element is named with the query name, qryCarsLessThan40, as shown in Figure 18-18. When you use the ExportXML method and supply the optional WhereCondition argument, then the name of the table, Car, is used. Although you could rename the query to something less cumbersome than qryCarsLessThan40, you cannot name it Car since there already is a table by that name in the database.

Using the WhereCondition parameter rather than relying on a query also provides extra flexibility. You can use code to construct whatever criteria are needed for the WhereCondition at runtime, rather than having to hard-code the criteria into a query.

18.8   Export a Report

Problem

You want to export a report that can be displayed on your web site. You'd like to preserve the formatting of the original report.

Solution

One of the new features in Access 2003 is the ability to export reports to XML, preserving formatting and displaying aggregates (totals, counts, averages, and so on). You can export formatted reports to ASP or to HTML.

The *18-8.MDB* sample database contains a report named rptCustomer that displays customer preferences, as shown in Figure 18-20. The report has an aggregate function that counts the number of cars ranked, and displays the make and model for each. The following sections show you how you can export the report to HTML and to ASP.

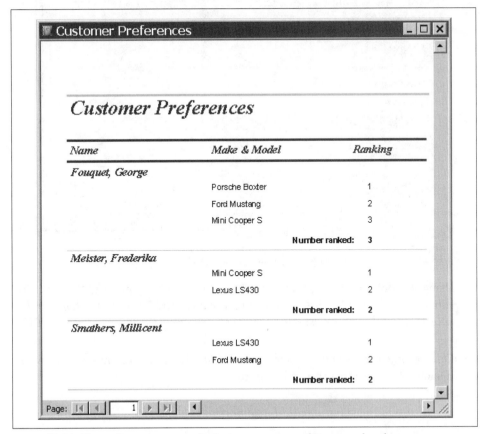

Figure 18-20. The rptCustomer report displaying customer preferences and rankings

Exporting to HTML

Follow these steps to export the report to HTML:

1. Right-click on the rptCustomer report in the *18-8.MDB* database window and choose Export from the menu.

2. Select XML from the Save as type drop-down at the bottom of the dialog box.

3. Name the output file CustomerPreferencesHTM and click OK.

4. Select all three checkboxes on the Export XML dialog box, and click the More Options button.

5. Specify the output folder where the output files will be located and click the Presentation tab. Make sure that HTML is selected, as shown in Figure 18-21. Click OK.

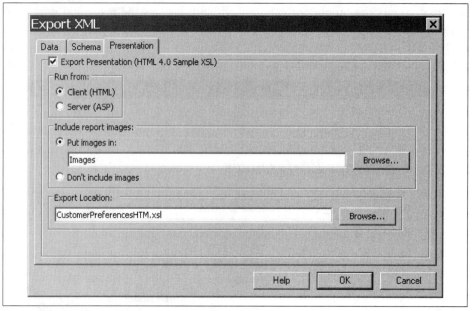

Figure 18-21. Choosing the presentation format for the report

6. Using Windows Explorer, browse to the location where you saved the files. You should see four files listed: *CustomerPreferencesHTM.htm*, *CustomerPreferencesHTM.xml*, *CustomerPreferencesHTM.xsd*, and *CustomerPreferencesHTM.xsl*.

7. Double-click the *CustomerPreferencesHTM.htm* file to load it into your browser. It should look like that shown in Figure 18-22.

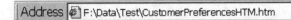

Customer Preferences

Name	Make & Model	Ranking
Fouquet, George		
	Porsche Boxter	1
	Ford Mustang	2
	Mini Cooper S	3
	Number ranked:	**3**
Meister, Frederika		
	Mini Cooper S	1
	Lexus LS430	2
	Number ranked:	**2**
Smathers, Millicent		
	Lexus LS430	1
	Ford Mustang	2
	Number ranked:	**2**

Monday, November 17, 2003   *Page 1 of 1*

Figure 18-22. The results of saving a report to HTML

Exporting to ASP

Follow these steps to export the report to ASP:

1. Right-click on the rptCustomer report in the *18-8.MDB* database window and choose Export from the menu.

2. Select XML from the Save as type drop-down at the bottom of the dialog box.

3. Name the output file CustomerPreferencesASP and click OK.

4. Select all three checkboxes on the Export XML dialog box, and click the More Options button.

5. Specify the output folder where the output files will be located (this can be an IIS application folder) and click the Presentation tab. Select the ASP option and click OK (see Figure 18-23).

6. In order to display the report, you will need to copy the four files created—*Cus-tomerPreferencesASP.asp*, *CustomerPreferencesASP.asp*, *CustomerPreference-sASP.asp*, and *CustomerPreferencesASP.asp*—to your web server, unless you had the wizard place them there.

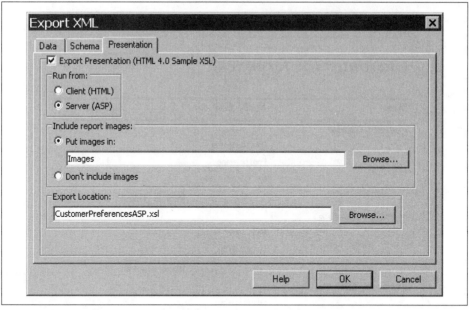

Figure 18-23. Specifying ASP output for the report

7. Launch *CustomerPreferencesASP.asp* using the HTTP protocol. The report should look like that shown in Figure 18-24:

```
http://localhost/TestApps/CustomerPreferencesASP.asp
```

Discussion

Dissecting the HTML

When you export a report to HTML, Access does a lot of work under the covers to ensure that the output looks almost identical to the output of the report when rendered in Access. Access generates quite a bit of VBScript code to achieve these results.

Open the *CustomerPreferencesHTM.htm* file in Notepad or another text editor to see how the code applies a transform on the *CustomerPreferencesHTM.xml* file by invoking the *CustomerPreferencesHTM.xsl*:

```
<HTML xmlns:signature="urn:schemas-microsoft-com:office:access">
<HEAD>
<META HTTP-EQUIV="Content-Type" CONTENT="text/html;charset=UTF-8"/>
</HEAD>
<BODY ONLOAD="ApplyTransform( )">
</BODY>
<SCRIPT LANGUAGE="VBScript">
  Option Explicit

  Function ApplyTransform( )
```

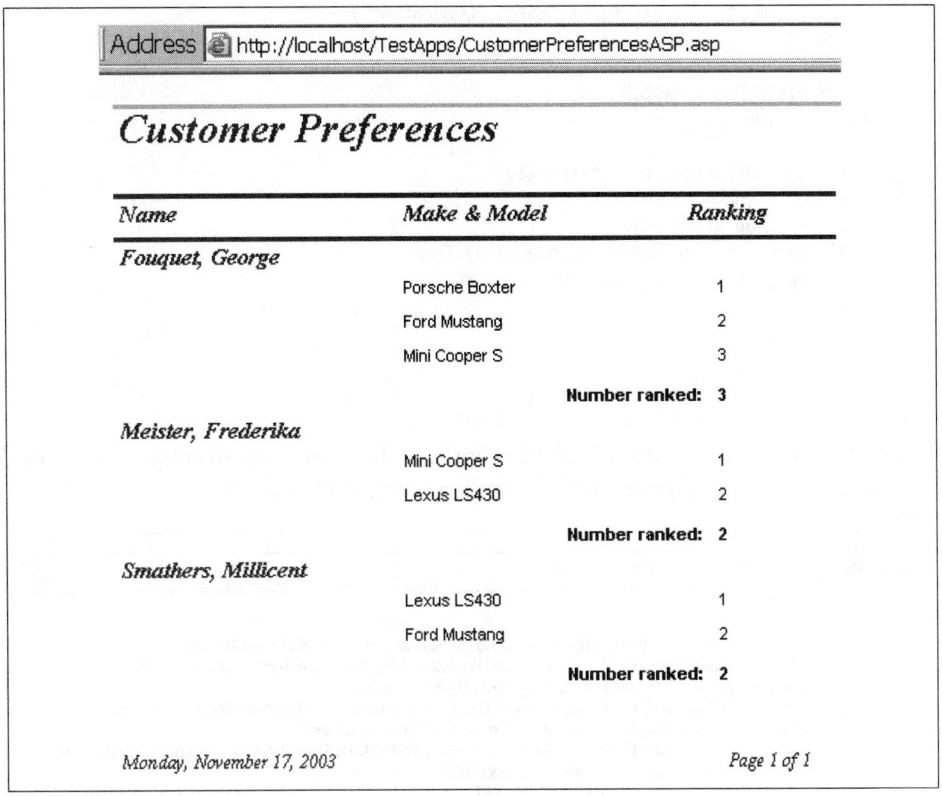
Address http://localhost/TestApps/CustomerPreferencesASP.asp
Customer Preferences
Name
Make & Model
Ranking
Fouquet, George
Porsche Boxter
1
Ford Mustang
2
Mini Cooper S
3
Number ranked: 3
Meister, Frederika
Mini Cooper S
1
Lexus LS430
2
Number ranked: 2
Smathers, Millicent
Lexus LS430
1
Ford Mustang
2
Number ranked: 2
Monday, November 17, 2003
Page 1 of 1

Figure 18-24. Loading the report as ASP

```
  Dim objData, objStyle

  Set objData = CreateDOM
  LoadDOM objData, "CustomerPreferencesHTM.xml"

  Set objStyle = CreateDOM
  LoadDOM objStyle, "CustomerPreferencesHTM.xsl"

  Document.Open "text/html","replace"
  Document.Write objData.TransformNode(objStyle)
End Function

Function CreateDOM( )
  On Error Resume Next
  Dim tmpDOM

  Set tmpDOM = Nothing
  Set tmpDOM = CreateObject("MSXML2.DOMDocument.5.0")
  If tmpDOM Is Nothing Then
    Set tmpDOM = CreateObject("MSXML2.DOMDocument.4.0")
  End If
  If tmpDOM Is Nothing Then
```

```
    Set tmpDOM = CreateObject("MSXML.DOMDocument")
  End If

  Set CreateDOM = tmpDOM
End Function

Function LoadDOM(objDOM, strXMLFile)
  objDOM.Async = False
  objDOM.Load strXMLFile
  If (objDOM.ParseError.ErrorCode <> 0) Then
    MsgBox objDOM.ParseError.Reason
  End If
End Function

</SCRIPT>
</HTML>
```

The CustomerPreferencesHTM.xsl file contains all of the formatting for the report, and is quite complex. Figure 18-25 shows just a fragment of the file.

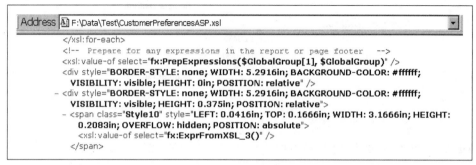

Figure 18-25. The xsl contains the formatting instructions for rendering the XML

After the formatting instructions, the file contains more VBScript code that has been generated to handle reporting engine features such as evaluating expressions, running sums, sorting and grouping and so on. The code is commented, so you can examine it and see what it's doing.

Dissecting the ASP

When you choose to output the XML to ASP, the page is intended to run on the server, and different code is generated. If you attempt to load the ASP page from the file system, you will get an error.

If you open *CustomerPreferencesASP.asp* in Notepad or another text editor, you will see the following code which invokes the *.xml* and *.xsl* files:

```
<%
Set objData = CreateDOM
objData.async = false
```

```
if (false) then
  Set objDataXMLHTTP = Server.CreateObject("Microsoft.XMLHTTP")
  objDataXMLHTTP.open "GET", "", false
  objDataXMLHTTP.setRequestHeader "Content-Type", "text/xml"
  objDataXMLHTTP.send
  objData.load(objDataXMLHTTP.responseBody)
else
  objData.load(Server.MapPath("CustomerPreferencesASP.xml"))
end if

Set objStyle = CreateDOM
objStyle.async = false
objStyle.load(Server.MapPath("CustomerPreferencesASP.xsl"))
Session.CodePage = 65001

Response.ContentType = "text/html"
Response.Write objData.transformNode(objStyle)

Function CreateDOM( )
  On Error Resume Next
  Dim tmpDOM

  Set tmpDOM = Nothing
  Set tmpDOM = Server.CreateObject("MSXML2.DOMDocument.5.0")
  If tmpDOM Is Nothing Then
    Set tmpDOM = Server.CreateObject("MSXML2.DOMDocument.4.0")
  End If
  If tmpDOM Is Nothing Then
    Set tmpDOM = Server.CreateObject("MSXML.DOMDocument")
  End If

  Set CreateDOM = tmpDOM
End Function
%>
```

The *CustomerPreferencesASP.xsl* file is structured similarly to the *CustomerPrefer-encesHTM.xsl* file, with formatting instructions for how the report is to be rendered at the bottom of the page.

These built-in export capabilities for Access reports show that outputting the data as XML and formatting it using XSLT is a powerful approach. With the proper XSLT transformations, your Access reports can be exported to any text-based document format.

See Also

The \Program Files\Microsoft Office\OFFICE11\AccessWeb directory, which is created when you install Access, contains additional transforms to assist you in creating your own XSL stylesheet. See *Rpt2HTM4.xsl*, used to transform Access reports into ReportML, which describes the presentation-specific attributes of a report. The *Rpt2DAP.xsl* transform also found in the folder can be used to transform ReportML into a data access page (DAP).

Index

We'd like to hear your suggestions for improving our indexes. Send email to *index@oreilly.com*.

Orientation property (Printer object), 229, 238
outer join, 45
Outlook, xvi, 609
    adding or editing contact information using smart tags, 699–702
Outlook 2002, 521
output devices, 237
    choosing at runtime, 246
    retrieving list of installed, 228
    setting default, 231
OutputTo method (DoCmd object), 574, 576

P

page breaks, 156
Page property (reports), 141, 143
page ranges, 125
page totals, 131
PageHeader property (reports), 127, 133
pages
    different headers/footers, 140
    displaying multiple, 76
Painting property (forms), 192, 421, 425
paper sources, controlling, 241
PaperBin property (Printer object), 238, 241, 243
PaperSize property (Printer object), 229, 238
ParamArray keyword, 326, 329
parameter queries, 749
    creating recordsets based on, 57
    printing values, 112
    specifying criteria at runtime, 2
    using form-based prompts, 4
parameterized constructors, 727
    calling .NET components containing, 728–731
parameters
    controls as, 665
    named parameters, 212
    passed to procedures, 659
    passing arrays as, 334
    passing variable number of, 325
    printing values, 112
    square brackets and, 2
    using across multiple DAPs, 639
    using optional, 97
Parent property (labels), 69
parentheses (), 327
Partition function, 29, 31, 32
pass-through queries, 659, 660

passwords
    for new accounts, 450
    retrieving all blank, 477–481
    security model and, 221
Paste Special dialog, 554
pattern matching, 382
Performance Analyzer (Access), 386
performance considerations
    accelerating load time, 349
    caching algorithms and, 376
    calculating median and, 270
    comparing techniques, 375
    forms execution, 357
    linked tables and, 384
    supplying input parameters, 664, 665
    TimeInterval property and, 467
    tracking user changes, 459
    VBA code, 372
permissions
    assigning, 448
    attaching linked tables and, 645
    granted to Users group, 444
    inheriting through groups, 223
    recommendations for assigning, 224, 225, 443
    Security Wizard and, 451
    updating data with views, 670
persistence, user-defined properties and, 344
Person Name smart tag, 698
Person smart tag
    adding or editing contact information in Outlook, 699–702
    allowable actions, 699
    using with Date smart tag, 702–703
Personal Identifier (PID), 222, 446, 448, 450
pessimistic locking, 484–488
    setting maximum locking interval for record, 488–493
PgDn key, 69
PgUp key, 69
PHP, 695
Picture Builder Wizard (Access), 417
Picture property (buttons)
    animated buttons, 417, 421
    Build button and, 80
Picture property (forms)
    communicating without email, 464, 467
    removing form watermarks, 359
PictureAlignment property (forms), 464
PictureData property (buttons), 416, 420
PictureData property (controls), 260
PictureSizeMode property (forms), 464

About the Authors

Ken Getz is a developer, writer, and trainer, working as a senior consultant with MCW Technologies, LLC (*http://www.mcwtech.com*), a Microsoft Solution Provider. Ken divides his time evenly between developing applications; writing books, articles, and courseware; and training, both in training classes and at industry conferences He has been selected by Microsoft as a Microsoft Regional Director for Southern California. He has written several technical books for developers, including the best-selling *Access Developer's Handbook* series (Sybex) and *VBA Developer's Handbook* series (Sybex) and is coauthor of *ASP.NET Developer's Jumpstart* (Addison-Wesley). With coauthors Andy Baron and Mary Chipman, Ken wrote AppDev's C#, ASP.NET, VB.NET, and ADO.NET courseware (*http://www.appdev.com*), and he appears in the video training for these courses as well. You'll find Ken's articles published regularly in several industry journals, including *MSDN* magazine, and he is a technical editor for Advisor Publications' *VB.NET Technical Journal* and *Access/VB/SQL Advisor* magazine. Ken also speaks regularly at a large number of industry events. You can reach Ken at *keng@mcwtech.com*, *http://www.mcwtech.com*, or *http://www.developershandbook.com*.

Paul Litwin is one of the founders of Deep Training, a developer-owned training company providing exceptional training on Microsoft .NET (*http://www.deep-training.com*). Paul is the editor-in-chief of *asp.netPRO*, a magazine for the professional ASP.NET developer (*http://www.aspnetpro.com*). He is also the president of Litwin Consulting, providing development and mentoring services in ASP, ASP.NET, Visual Basic, SQL Server, XML, Microsoft Access, and related technologies. Paul is the Conference Chair of Microsoft ASP.NET Connections and speaks regularly at industry events, including Microsoft Tech Ed, Microsoft Office Development and Deployment Conference, ASP Connections, and VB Connections. He is the author of several books, including *ASP.NET for Developers* (Sams), *Access 2002 Desktop Developer's Handbook* (Sybex), and *Access 2002 Enterprise Developer's Handbook* (Sybex). He has written numerous articles for *asp.netPRO* magazine, *Visual Basic Programmer's Journal*, *Microsoft Office Pro*, *PC World*, *Smart Access*, and other publications. You can reach him at *paul@litwinconsulting.com*.

Andy Baron is a senior consultant at MCW Technologies, a Microsoft MVP (Most Valuable Professional) since 1995, and a contributing editor for Advisor Media and Pinnacle Publications. Andy is coauthor of the *Microsoft Access Developer's Guide to SQL Server* (Sams), and he writes and presents courseware for Application Developers Training Company (*http://www.appdev.com*).

Colophon

Our look is the result of reader comments, our own experimentation, and feedback from distribution channels. Distinctive covers complement our distinctive approach to technical topics, breathing personality and life into potentially dry subjects.

The animal on the cover of *Access Cookbook*, Second Edition is a northern tamandua. The tamandua is also known as the collared, or lesser, anteater. There are two species of tamandua: the northern tamandua (*Tamandua mexicana*), found in Central America and the northwestern part of South America; and the southern tamandua (*Tamandua tetradactyla*), which can be found further south. Tamanduas have coarse, yellowish, or brownish fur with black markings and are about half the size of their rarer relatives, the giant anteaters (*Myrmecophaga tridactyla*). They can grow to be about 60 centimeters long, with a prehensile tail of approximately the same length, and reach weights of 6 to 13 pounds.

Tamanduas are occasionally found on the ground, but they prefer living in the trees, where they hunt for ant and termite nests. Like all anteaters, tamanduas have long snouts and extremely long tongues that they use to collect and eat their prey. Since no teeth are necessary for this kind of meal, anteaters' teeth have been reduced during their evolution. However, unlike the completely toothless giant anteaters, tamanduas still have some small teeth remaining (which are useful for consuming the fruits that supplement their diets). They use the sharp claws on their front paws to open ant and termite nests, but they are careful to not destroy the nests completely and take just a small portion of the colony before they go for the next nest. This strategy preserves the colonies for future feedings. Tamanduas are primarily active during the night and sleep through the day in hollow trees or the forks of trees, securing themselves by wrapping their tails around branches.

Reg Aubry was the production editor and copyeditor for *Access Cookbook*, Second Edition. Darren Kelly, Genevieve d'Entremont, and Claire Cloutier provided quality control. Julie Hawks wrote the index.

Ellie Volckhausen designed the cover of this book, based on a series design by Edie Freedman. The cover image is a 19th-century engraving from *Cuvier's Animals*. Emma Colby produced the cover layout with QuarkXPress 4.1 using Adobe's ITC Garamond font. David Futato designed the CD-ROM label.

David Futato designed the interior layout. Julie Hawks converted the files from Microsoft Word to FrameMaker 5.5.6 using tools created by Mike Sierra. The text font is Linotype Birka; the heading font is Adobe Myriad Condensed; and the code font is LucasFont's TheSans Mono Condensed. The illustrations that appear in the book were produced by Robert Romano and Jessamyn Read using Macromedia Free-Hand 9 and Adobe Photoshop 6. The tip and warning icons were drawn by Christopher Bing. This colophon was written by Rachel Wheeler.